STUDIES IN ANCIENT
ISRAELITE WISDOM

THE LIBRARY
OF
BIBLICAL STUDIES

Edited by

Harry M. Orlinsky

STUDIES IN ANCIENT ISRAELITE WISDOM

Selected, with a
Prolegomenon, by

JAMES L. CRENSHAW

KTAV PUBLISHING HOUSE, INC.
NEW YORK, NEW YORK
1976

Library of Congress Cataloging in Publication Data
Main entry under title:

Studies in ancient Israelite wisdom.

   (Library of Biblical studies)
   Includes bibliographical references.
   1. Wisdom literature—Criticism, interpretation, etc.—
Addresses, essays, lectures. 2. Wisdom—Biblical teaching
—Addresses, essays, lectures. I. Crenshaw, James L.
II. Series.
BS1455.S83   223'.06'6   75-31986
ISBN O-87068-255-5

TABLE OF CONTENTS

JAMES L. CRENSHAW

I. THE ANCIENT NEAR EASTERN SETTING AND ISRAELITE WISDOM

II. THE ESSENTIAL STRUCTURE OF WISDOM THOUGHT

To my mother,
whose children call her blessed,
and to the memory of my father

PREFACE

As editor of an anthology, I cannot presume to speak in behalf of all those authors whose essays appear in the present volume. The impact of their voices, individually and collectively, in shaping my own thought has been so far reaching that one could say, in a real sense, we speak in unison even when differing with one another. I wish, however, to proclaim my own gratitude to these scholars who have assisted me in the endless quest for wisdom and understanding. My debt to them is huge, my gratitude, greater. My desire is that the reader will also be caught up in this dialogue, and will, like the editor, spend many profitable hours testing the "traditions" of scholarship in the light of personal experience.

The complete anthology is, of course, as elusive as Dame Wisdom herself. The reader may think that better essays exist on one topic or another, and that other subjects should have been covered. I ask only one consideration of the person so inclined: keep in mind the purpose of the volume and the difficulty of obtaining permission to print some essays. I have sought to provide a comprehensive volume on wisdom literature, with emphasis upon seminal studies in English covering major areas of research.

I am conscious that many excellent articles do not appear in these pages. Some were too costly, others not available for reproduction, and still others were excluded after much careful study. The Prolegomenon seeks to make amends insofar as possible for any major omission. In it I have tried to pay honor to many whose works do not appear here: Walter Baumgartner, J. Coert Rylaarsdam, Hans Heinrich Schmid, Hartmut Gese, Kurt Galling, J. P. Audet, William McKane, Walter Brueggemann, and a host of others.

Anyone who has edited a comparable volume knows how much labor has gone into the preparation of this book. In that endeavor my assistant, Ray Newell, rendered valuable service both in securing hundreds of articles from obscure journals and Festschriften, and in reading and

criticizing the manuscript. The reader will join me in gratitude to Douglas A. Knight and Brian W. Kovacs for translating the German articles
into English. Those appearing in English for the first time are I, 3 and
4; II, 1; and V, 1.

As I bring to a close this project that has occupied so many months
of my time, I wish to thank Harry M. Orlinsky, the editor of this series,
for choosing me to assume responsibility for the volume on Israelite wisdom, and for providing judicious council at every stage of its implemen-
tation. My gratitude goes, also, to Bernard Scharfstein, the editor of
KTAV, for the care with which he has undertaken the production of
this volume.

JAMES L. CRENSHAW
Professor of Old Testament
Vanderbilt Divinity School

Oct. 20, 1975

ACKNOWLEDGMENTS

Georg Fohrer, "Sophia," reprinted with permission from *Kittel's Theological Dictionary of the New Testament,* VII (Grand Rapids: Wm. B. Eerdman's Publishing Co., 1971), 476-496.

R. B. Y. Scott, "Solomon and the Beginnings of Wisdom in Israel," reprinted with permission from *Vetus Testamentum Supplement,* 3 (1955), 262-279.

Albrecht Alt, "Die Weisheit Salomos," reprinted with permission from *Theologische Literaturzeitung,* 76 (1951), 139-144.

Ernst Würthwein, "Die Weisheit Ägyptens und das Alte Testament," reprinted with permission from *Wort und Existenz, Studien zum Alten Testament* by Ernst Würthwein (Vandenhoeck & Reprecht, 1970), 197-216.

Berend Gemser, "The Instructions of 'Onchsheshonqy and Biblical Wisdom Literature," reprinted with permission from *Vetus Testamentum Supplement,* 7 (1960), 102-128.

F. Charles Fensham, "Widow, Orphan, and the Poor in Ancient Near Eastern Legal and Wisdom Literature," reprinted with permission from *Journal of Near Eastern Studies,* 21 (1962), 129-139.

Walther Zimmerli, "Zur Struktur der alttestamentlichen Weisheit," reprinted with permission from *Zeitschrift für die alttestamentlichen Wissenschaft,* 51 (1933), 177-204.

Berend Gemser, "The Spiritual Structure of Biblical Aphoristic Wisdom," reprinted with permission from *Adhuc Loquitur: Collected Essays of Dr. B. Gemser,* ed. A. Van Selms & A. S. Van der Woude (Leiden: E. J. Brill, 1968), 138-149.

Robert Gordis, "Quotations in Wisdom Literature," reprinted with permission from *Jewish Quarterly Review,* 30 (1939/40), 123-147.

Addison D. G. Wright, "The Riddle of the Sphinx: The Structure of the Book of Qoheleth," reprinted with permission from *The Catholic Biblical Quarterly,* 30 (1968), 313-334.

Gerhard von Rad, "Job XXXVIII and Ancient Egyptian Wisdom," reprinted with permission from *The Problem of the Hexateuch and Other Essays* (Edinburgh & London: Oliver & Boyd, 1965), 281-291.

John F. Priest, "Where is Wisdom to Be Placed?," reprinted with the permission of the *Journal of the American Academy of Religion*, successor to the *Journal of Bible and Religion* from vol. 31 (1963), 275-282.

James L. Crenshaw, "Popular Questioning of the Justice of God in Ancient Israel," reprinted with permission from *Zeitschrift für die alttestamentlichen Wissenschaft*, 82 (1970), 380-395.

Walther Zimmerli, "The Place and Limit of the Wisdom in the Framework of the Old Testament Theology," reprinted with permission from *Scottish Journal of Theology*, 17 (1964), 146-158.

Patrick W. Skehan, "A Single Editor for the Whole Book of Proverbs," reprinted with the permission of The Catholic Biblical Association of America from *Studies in Israelite Poetry and Wisdom, CBQ Monograph Series* 1 (1971), 15-26.

Matitiahu Tsevat, "The Meaning of the Book of Job," reprinted with permission from *Hebrew Union College Annual*, 37 (1966), 73-106.

James G. Williams, "What Does It Profit a Man?: The Wisdom of Koheleth," reprinted with permission from vol. 20 (1971), 179-193 of *Judaism*, 15 East 84th Street, New York, N.Y. 10028; Editor, Robert Gordis. Copyright 1971 by The American Jewish Congress.

R. N. Whybray, "Proverbs VIII 22-31 and Its Supposed Prototypes," reprinted with permission from *Vetus Testamentum*, 15 (1965), 504-514.

Alexander A. Di Lella, "Conservative and Progressive Theology: Sirach and Wisdom," reprinted with permission from *The Catholic Biblical Quarterly*, 38 (1966), 139-154.

R. B. Y. Scott, "Folk Proverbs of the Ancient Near East," reprinted from the *Transactions of the Royal Society of Canada*, Vol. 15 (1961), 47-56, with permission of the Editor.

Johannes Fichtner, "Jesaja unter den Weisen," reprinted with permission from *Theologische Literaturzeitung*, 74 (1949), 75-80 and *Gottes Weisheit* (Stuttgart: Calwer Verlag, 1965), 18-26.

Gerhard von Rad, "The Joseph Narrative and Ancient Wisdom," reprinted with permission from *TheProblem of the Hexateuch and Other Essays*, 292-300.

Samuel Terrien, "Amos and Wisdom," from *Israel's Prophetic Heritage*, edited by Bernhard W. Anderson and Walter Harrelson, 108-115. Copyright 1962 by Bernhard W. Anderson and Walter Harrelson. By permission of Harper & Row, Publishers, Inc.

Roland E. Murphy, "A Consideration of the Classification "Wisdom Psalms'," reprinted with permission from *Vetus Testamentum Supplement*, 9 (1962), 156-167.

Luis Alonso-Schökel, "Sapiential and Covenant Themes in Genesis 2-3," *Theology Digest*, 13 (1965), 3-10 (*Modern Biblical Studies*, 49-61). Permission granted by Editors of *Theology Digest*, St. Louis, Mo.

James L. Crenshaw, "Method in Determining Wisdom Influence upon 'Historical' Literature," originally published in *Journal of Biblical Literature*, 88 (1969), 129-142. Used by permission.

I wish to thank the authors, editors, and publishers for permission to reproduce the essays in this volume. The quality of the articles justified resetting the whole book, but costs of doing so rendered such procedure prohibitive. Hopefully the convenience of having such a treasury of articles on wisdom literature in a single volume will enable the reader to overlook the photo-mechanical process by which they are reproduced and the unfortunate absence of italics in transliterations of Hebrew in articles translated into English.

ABBREVIATIONS

AA—Alttestamentliche Abhandlungen
AB—Anchor Bible
AcOr—Acta Orientalia
AJSL—American Journal of Semitic Languages and Literatures
AnB—Analecta Biblica
ANQ—Andover Newton Quarterly
AO—Der Alte Orient
ATD—Das Alte Testament Deutsch
Bib—Biblica
BAT—Die Botschaft des Alten Testaments
BBB—Bonner Biblische Beiträge
BhTh—Beiträge historische Theologie
BO—Bibbia e Oriente
BS—Biblotheca Sacra
Bib Theol Bulletin—Biblical Theology Bulletin
BWANT—Beiträge zur Wissenschaft vom Alten und Neuen Testament
BZAW—Beihefte zur Zeitschrift für die altestamentliche Wissenschaft
BZ—Biblische Zeitschrift
CB—Century Bible
CBQ—Catholic Biblical Quarterly
CBQMS—Catholic Biblical Quarterly Monograph Series
CBSC—Cambridge Bible for Schools and Colleges
CJTh—Canadian Journal of Theology
Con Jud—Conservative Judaism
EB—Echter Bibel
EThl—Ephemerides Theologicae Lovanienses
EvTh—Evangelische Theologie
JAOS—Journal of the American Oriental Society
JBR—Journal of Bible and Religion
JSOR—Journal of the Society of Oriental Research
HAT—Handbuch zum Alten Testament

HKAT—Handkommentar zum Alten Testament
HSAT—Die heilige Schrift des Alten Testaments
HUCA—Hebrew Union College Annual
Inter—Interpretation
IB—The Interpreter's Bible
IDB—The Interpreter's Dictionary of the Bible
ICC—The International Critical Commentary
IThQ—Irish Theological Quarterly
JAAR—Journal of the American Academy of Religion
JAOS—Journal of the American Oriental Society
JBL—Journal of Biblical Literature
JCS—Journal of Cuneiform Studies
JEA—Journal of Egyptian Archeology
JEOL—Jaarbericht ex Oriente Lux
JNES—Journal of Near Eastern Studies
JQR—Jewish Quarterly Review
JSS—Journal of Semitic Studies
Jud—Judaism
KAT—Kommentar zum Alten Testament
KHAT—Kurzer Hand-Commentar zum Alten Testament
KKANT—Kritischer Commentar Altes und Neues Testament
LD—Lectio divina
LUA—Lunds Universitets Arsskrift
MVÄG—Mitteilungen der Vorderasiatisch—Ägyptischen Gessellschaft
NCB—New Century Bible
NTT—Norsk Theologisk Tidsskrift
OLZ—Orientalistische Literaturzeitung
OTL—The Old Testament Library
PAAJR—Proceedings of the American Academy for Jewish Research
RB—Revue Biblique
RGG—Die Religion in Geschichte und Gegenwart
RHPR—Revue d'Histoire et de Philosophie Religieuses
RHR—Revue de l'Historie des Religions
SBL—The Society of Biblical Literature
SB—Sources bibliques
SBT—Studies in Biblical Theology
ScE—Sciences ecclésiastiques
SGV—Sammlung gemeinverständliche Vorträge
SJTh—Scottish Journal of Theology

SNVAO—Skrifter utgitt av Det Norske Videnskaps-Akademi i Oslo
SOTSMS—Society of Old Testament Study Monograph Series
SPOA—Les sagesses du Proché-Orient ancien
SQAW—Schriften und Quellen der alten Welt
STU—Schweizerische Theologische Umschau
SVT—Supplements to Vetus Testamentum
ThA—Theologische Abhandlungen
ThGl—Theologie und Glaube
ThLZ—Theologische Literaturzeitung
ThR—Theologische Rundschau
ThSt—Theologische Studiën
ThWB—Theologische Wörterbuch, ed. R. Kittel
TUMSR—Trinity University Monograph Series in Religion
VS—Verbum Salutis
VT—Vetus Testamentum
VuF—Verkündigung und Forschung
WMANT—Wissenschaftliche Monographien zum Alten und Neuen
    Testament
WZ—Wissenschaftliche Zeitschrift
ZÄS—Zeitschrift für Ägyptische Sprache und Altertumskunde
ZAW—Zeitschrift für die alttestamentliche Wissenschaft
ZDMG—Zeitschrift der Deutschen Morgenländischen Gesellschaft
ZNW—Zeitschrift für die neutestamentliche Wissenschaft
ZSystTh—Zeitschrift für Systematische Theologie
ZThK—Zeitschrift für Theologie und Kirche

STUDIES IN ANCIENT ISRAELITE WISDOM:
PROLEGOMENON

In a sense, wisdom literature can be labeled an orphan in the biblical household. Virtually ignored as an entity until the beginning of this century, "wisdom" suffered the indignity of judgment by alien standards and the embarrassment of physical similarities to non-Israelite parents. In addition, she had a twin (Sirach and Wisdom of Solomon) who was in some circles even excluded from the privileged status of canonical authority, although none could deny her likeness to the more favored sister. Orphans, however, have a champion whose intentions none can frustrate. Perhaps it was inevitable, then, that this special orphan would become queen for a day, and possibly even Queen Mother.

The negative assessment of wisdom arose because it was difficult if not impossible to fit her thought into the reigning theological system. The verdict of G. Ernest Wright represents the dominant position for several decades: "The difficulty of the wisdom movement was that its theological base and interest were too narrowly fixed; and in this respect Proverbs remains near the pagan source of wisdom in which society and the Divine work in history played no real role." [1] In short, wisdom does not accord with the preconceived notion of theology as a recital of God's action in history. As a consequence of the inability to integrate wisdom into salvation history, Gerhard von Rad places wisdom at the end of the first volume of his *Old Testament Theology* [2] and gives it the title "Israel's Response." The inappropriateness of such a procedure has often been noted, [3] for wisdom cannot be viewed as an answer to the dominant theme of saving history. Walther Eichrodt's treatment of wisdom, [4] although less bound to a Procrustean bed constructed out of salvation history, offers little improvement, for there is little if any attempt to accept wisdom on her own ground. Rather, later developments in the realm of speculation about Dame Wisdom and the identification of wisdom and spirit are given the lion's share of attention. In one area, however, Eichrodt makes significant

1

strides forward. I refer to his recognition of the importance of creation to the thought of the sages. Still, he views creation largely in terms of divine activity in history.

Even when conscious attention is diverted from the exclusively historical concern of so much Old Testament scholarship, wisdom still gives the impression of a foreign body. Thus Hartmut Gese writes: "It is well known that the wisdom literature constitutes an alien body in the world of the Old Testament." [5] This verdict is substantiated by reference to an absence of (1) a covenant relationship with God, (2) any account of the revelation at Sinai, and (3) a concept of Israel's special election and consequently of Yahweh's saving deeds for his people. Instead, wisdom is said to be directed toward the individual, and consequently to break down all national limits. Gese concludes that "from the point of view of Yahwism wisdom can only appear as wholly secular." [6] Horst D. Preuss moves a step farther afield. [7] The similarities between Israelite wisdom and that of her pagan environment lead him to view wisdom literature as devoid of revelatory content. For him wisdom is Israel's attempt to shape herself in the image of her neighbors, and the resulting creature is paganism pure and simple. The international character of wisdom, its universalistic appeal, is here understood as an inherent deficiency. Wisdom thus suffers the fate of one who is insufficiently Hebraic at a time when a premium is placed on Hebrew thought.

Still another factor contributed to wisdom's minor role in the drama of biblical interpretation. Fully half of her representatives (Sirach and Wisdom of Solomon) enjoy only deutero-canonical status. Inevitably Protestant and Jewish scholars were affected by the fact that there were substantial areas in which canonical and deutero-canonical texts agreed in form, vocabulary, and subject matter. Difficulty in making sharp distinctions between the two bodies of literature resulted in a leveling of the authority granted canonical wisdom.

Theological trends are born, and sooner or later are borne away. Today all three factors that deprived wisdom of her rightful dignity appear to be suffering an eclipse. [8] History as the key to an understanding of the theological distinctiveness of ancient Israel has been found lacking, [9] and with this recognition comes renewed appreciation for those texts which offer a universalistic alternative. [10] The crisis brought on by an exclusive emphasis upon mighty acts of God in history has sent many scholars in search of another refuge. Wisdom's shade tree has suddenly become a haven for many, and the excitement of new discovery fills the air. So, too, do the excesses of exuberant converts. Roland Murphy sums up the situation well: "However, the trend to disregard the wisdom literature has reversed itself. Now the question would rather be, where has Old Testament wisdom failed to appear?"[11] The shrinking planet has renewed our appreciation for the understanding of reality expressed in traditions other than our own, so that wisdom's affinities with Egyptian and Mesopotamian texts has now become an asset rather than a liability. Furthermore, the ecumenical spirit and the sudden explosion of Roman Catholic scholarship in the wake of Vatican II have done much to offset the stigma of deutero-canonicity from which wisdom suffered.

But wisdom remembers yet another day when the discovery of an Egyptian text[12] and the proclamation of its originality at the expense of its Israelite manifestation led to a dozen years when all eyes were focused on her, without any substantial improvement of her status. The orphan, it follows, wears the royal crown, newly bestowed upon her, with supreme modesty. She knows the fickleness of scholarship.

Defining the Term Wisdom

Thus far I have spoken of wisdom as if her identity, if not her status, were a matter of common knowledge. But that is far from the case. Since the year 1908 when Hans Meinhold first recognized her separate existence,[13] she has stood largely as a mirror image of the scholar painting her portrait. At first almost ubiquitous in the Old Testament, she later settled down in five literary complexes (Proverbs, Job, Qoheleth, Sirach, Wisdom of Solomon), only in recent years taking up residence once again throughout the canonical literature.

The many attempts to define wisdom in ancient Israel have not been altogether successful. Von Rad, for instance, defines wisdom as broadly as possible. For him wisdom is "practical knowledge of the laws of life and of the world, based on experience."[14] At the other extreme is my own definition in terms of four kinds of wisdom: juridical, nature, practical, and theological. "Accordingly, one must distinguish between family/clan wisdom, the goal of which is the mastering of life, the stance hortatory and style proverbial; court wisdom, with the goal of education for a select group, the stance secular, and method didactic; and scribal wisdom, the goal being education for all, the stance dogmatico-religious, and the method dialogico-admonitory." Or again, wisdom is "the quest for self-understanding in terms of relationships with things people and the Creator . . . on three levels: (1) nature wisdom which is an attempt to master things for human survival and well-being, and which includes the drawing up of onomastica and study of natural phenomena as they relate to man and the universe; (2) juridical and *Erfahrungsweisheit* (practical wisdom) with the focus upon human relationships in an ordered society or state; and (3) theological wisdom, which moves in the realm of theodicy, and in so doing affirms God as ultimate meaning" even when denying a purpose to life.[15]

Other definitions fall somewhere between these two in their degree of specificity. Henri Cazelles focuses upon the anthropocentricity of wisdom. He writes: "Wisdom is the art of succeeding in human life, both private and collective. It is grounded in humanism, in reflexion on and observation of the course of things and the conduct of man."[16] Guy P. Couturier emphasizes the origins of wisdom as the significant factor, for in this initial stage of development wisdom is "the totality of life experiences transmitted by a father to his son, as a spiritual testament."[17] By far the briefest definition with which I am acquainted is that of Alexander W. Kenworthy, for whom wisdom is "the ability to cope."[18]

Recognizing on the one hand the danger of being so general that the result is a tautology, and on the other so specific that the definition is useless or inaccurate, some authorities refuse to offer a definition. But a definite pre-understanding is operative, whether verbalized or not. The boldest step thus far has recently been taken by R. N. Whybray, who avoids the term "wisdom" in favor of "the intellectual tradition."[19] Whybray has discerned better than most the fact that all of these definitions founder at one point or another, for wisdom is an attitude, a body of literature, and a living tradition.

Even when it was deemed impossible to define wisdom, certain pejorative adjectives were used all too frequently. It is little credit to biblical scholars that the corrective came from Egyptologists, who readily discerned the inadequacy of such descriptions as eudaemonistic and humanistic.[20] Still it was left to an Old Testament interpreter, Hans Heinrich Schmid, to break through the additional fallacy of the adjective "non-historical."[21] With the discovery that every aphorism or didactic poem has its own history and participates in the historical features of the period in which it arose, the concept of internationalistic wisdom lost something of its cogency. The consequent search for the distinctive characteristics of wisdom literature that reflect particular histories is still in its infancy, but contains much promise. In any event, it is no longer possible to describe wisdom as eudaemonistic, non-historical, humanistic or international.

But the rejection of these terms must not conceal the fact that they have functioned usefully in the past. In truth, wisdom does ask what is good for man, and envisions the good as health, honor, wealth, and length of days. But this pragmatism which sought to secure the good life must be understood in terms of the concept of order ordained by God and entrusted to man's discovery and safe-keeping. Thus one may rightfully claim that the emphasis upon man as the center of all values constitutes humanism. But the peculiar religious context within which such humanism flourished demands that one use some qualifying phrase like theological humanism.[22] Similarly, none can deny the universality of wisdom's language and concerns, the timeless problems of human existence and general observations about life. But one must go further to acknowledge the fact that these maxims and reflections are inevitably expressed in the nuances of the particular culture giving birth to the comprehensions of reality falling under the rubric "wisdom."

Both the correction of previous misunderstandings and the working definitions above suggest that significant progress has been made. The matter is further complicated, however, by the *sui generis* character of the book of Job, which has prompted some scholars to exclude it from the category "wisdom literature."[23] One can appreciate the objections to this masterful enigma, for it does have elements of the lament.[24] Furthermore, it has imbibed the revelatory spirit to a far greater degree than any of the other literary complexes representative of wisdom thought. On the other hand, the book so closely resembles wisdom texts in Mesopotamian literature that one hesitates to exclude it from a discussion of Israelite wisdom. In addition, the subject matter is largely that which claimed the attention of the sages, so one cannot go astray, it seems, by including Job in wisdom literature. Hence I shall work from the assumption that wisdom literature consists of Proverbs, Job, Qoheleth, Sirach, Wisdom of Solomon, and a few Psalms. I am fully aware of the subjective nature of my decision; but this limited view of wisdom literature is more defensible than the equally subjective umbrella approach. The consequence of this minimal stance on my part is obvious: I shall not base any conclusions on such texts as Gen. 1-3, the Joseph narrative, the succession narrative, Amos, Isaiah, Habakkuk, Jeremiah, Esther, or the like, whatever the merit of the claim that these reflect wisdom thinking.

Queen for a Day: Posing the Problems

Earlier I alluded to the brief period when wisdom had maximum exposure, namely, the years between 1924 and 1936.[25] This unprecedented burst of activity, generated by the discovery of a definite literary relationship between the Egyptian Instruction of Amen-em-opet and Pr. 22:17-24:22, set the stage for most subsequent research. The crucial issue, of course, was the question of affinities between a biblical text and an Egyptian Instruction. But still another issue came to the fore during this flurry of scholarship, namely, the structure of wisdom thought.[26] Now and then, too, some acknowledgment of a third set of problems surfaced. I have in mind the question of forms, which means not only the actual delineation of types of literature but also the setting in which they arose, took shape, and acted out their unique histories.[27] This period, then, set the questions occupying the minds of most scholars who labor in the area of wisdom today. The snail's pace we have followed can be discerned by working through Hugo Gressmann's pioneer study of 1925, Walter Baumgartner's two survey articles of 1933 and 1951, and R. B. Y. Scott's assessment of the current state of research in 1970.[28] Significant strides have been taken, nonetheless, and much recent work promises to open new paths leading to fruitful results. In discussing this fifty years of research I shall focus upon the three vital issues already mentioned: (1) affinities, (2) forms, and (3) structure.

I. AFFINITIES

The Bible itself recognizes Israel's kinship with her neighbors in the area of wisdom. Solomon's wisdom, it is claimed, surpassed that of all the peoples of the east and of Egypt (I Kgs. 4:30 M.T. 5:10). The study of the relationship between Israelite wisdom and that of other peoples of the ancient Near East is but a continuation of an ancient endeavor. The question of affinities, however, is greater than mere comparison of Israelite literature with similar texts from Egypt, Ugarit, and Mesopotamia. There is a significant amount of canonical literature outside the above-mentioned wisdom corpus that resembles certain elements of wisdom thought. This literature, too, raises the question of affinity. In short, the problem is both external to the canon and internal.

External Similarities

Israelite wisdom compares herself to that of Edom and Egypt. In the case of Edom little if anything has survived. Robert H. Pfeiffer has attempted to recover Edomitic wisdom in the Bible (Gen. 1-11, Job, Qoheleth, Ps. 88-89, Pr. 30-31:1-9),[29] but the argument cannot compel assent inasmuch as it is purely hypothetical. Even if Job and his friends were non-Israelites, which in itself is debatable, that remarkable fact would not constitute proof that the author of the Book of Job was an Edomite. The patriarchal setting of the story may explain the choice of names and locality. It seems preferable, therefore, to maintain scepticism about the extent of Edomite wisdom within the Bible. Egyptian influence upon the Bible is yet another matter; the shadow of Egypt extends beyond Proverbs as far as Qoheleth and possibly Sirach.

Egyptian presence in the wisdom literature of Israel was acknowledged as early as 1909 by Hermann Gunkel.[30] The extent of this foreign impact was not perceived, however, until the epoch-making analysis of Paul Humbert.[31] There is general agreement that the Israelite author of Pr. 22:17-24:22 borrowed from an Egyptian source eleven sayings of the original thirty, although the hypothesis of the opposite dependency has been revived relatively recently.[32] Egyptian influence upon Israelite wisdom extends beyond the actual appropriation of sayings from Amen-em-opet. It surfaces in such metaphors as that of God weighing the heart, righteousness as the foundation of the throne,[33] and possibly the garland of honor in Proverbs. Perhaps, too, Egyptian influence rests behind the satire on the professions in Sir. 38:24-39:11, which echoes remarkably the Instruction of Duauf,[34] and the idea of a royal *Bekenntnis* that inspired the form of the early chapters of Qoheleth. Even more important, however, is the role of *ma'at* (order, justice),[35] which appears to have influenced the total thought of Israel's wisdom as well as the concept of a personified Wisdom. While many scholars argue for an Egyptian origin of the metaphor of the righteous man as a flourishing tree and the concept of *to'eba* (abomination) of Yahweh, it is probable that these fall into the category of universal language.

Some would argue that the Israelite practice of addressing the pupil as *beni* (my son) derives from Egyptian Instructions, in which the father teaches his son all he has learned about life.[36] Recent research into the early period of Israelite wisdom in which the leader of the clan instructed his sons in the means of getting the most out of life offers yet another explanation for this form of address, and renders the hypothesis of Egyptian origin both unnecessary and improbable.[37] Others have called attention to the contrast between wise man and hot tempered fool, which finds its parallel in the Egyptian opposite types of men (the silent one and the passionate man).[38] It is noteworthy, however, that "the silent one" or its equivalent does not become a technical term in Israel as it did in Egypt.

The Mesopotamian relationship with Israelite literature differs in kind if not in degree. The literary prototypes of Proverbs, Job, and Qoheleth point more to a commonality of ideas than to direct literary relationship. The problem of innocent suffering prompted literary treatment in early Sumerian times, and representatives of subsequent cultures

tried their hand at it as well. The dialogue form prevails in the so-called
"Babylonian Theodicy," while the theophany provides the solution in "I
Will Praise the Lord of Wisdom." Furthermore, the scepticism surfacing
in Qoheleth is even more extreme in "The Pessimistic Dialogue between a
Master and his Slave." The impact of Mesopotamian thought upon
Qoheleth may extend beyond this text to the Gilgamesh Epic, if the arguments of Oswald Loretz are trustworthy.[39] The case remains open, however; for the advice of Siduri to Gilgamesh, which reappears as a theme in
Qoheleth, is probably a universal response to the reality of finitude. In
essence, then, the influence of Mesopotamian wisdom thought upon that
of Israel consists of literary form and content; in both, the Israelite authors
surpassed the prototypes in excellence.

In what way did Israelites come into contact with Egyptian and
Mesopotamian wisdom literature? Scholars have assumed the points of
contact were the royal courts of Solomon and Hezekiah, where both foreign
scribes and Israelite counselors would have worked, the latter of whom
may have received their training in foreign courts. The evidence for an
institution of wise men at the court is by no means conclusive, however.
Those advocating such a function of the wise men must concede that the
literary heritage of the sages is scarcely "courtly in subject matter or viewpoint."[40] Perhaps the Canaanites mediated the wisdom tradition to ancient
Israel.[41] Unfortunately literary remains from Ras Shamra have yielded
minimal support for this theory,[42] for the epithet about El as wise and the
lone wisdom text of Babylonian origin offer little encouragement to the
notion that Canaanites mediated wisdom to Israel.

I have neglected to mention Greek influence until now; this fact alone
points to progress made in wisdom research. Earlier scholars sought to
demonstrate Greek influence upon Qoheleth and even saw Job as a Greek
drama. But the much-discussed Graecisms in Qoheleth have dwindled to
virtual non-existence,[43] and the cyclic view of nature is now seen against
a Near Eastern mythological background. Consequently, Greek presence
in Qoheleth no longer functions as the decisive key to understanding its contents. A similar discrediting of Greek influence upon Job has taken place,
for any dramatic theory founders since events in the book do not progress
toward a climax. Stated differently, the only drama in Job is psychological. Of course Hellenism made a powerful impact upon Sirach and
Wisdom of Solomon, both in literary form and in subject matter; yet even
here restraint must be exercised. The Greek ideas are by no means taken
over without much ado, as Johann Marböck[44] made abundantly clear for
Sirach and Patrick Skehan and James Reese[45] demonstrated for Wisdom

of Solomon. Greek impact is definitely discernible in, among other things, hymnic praise of the sun, the section in praise of great men, the epithet "He is the All," and belief in immortality (in Sirach), rhetorical devices such as *sorites,* the description of wisdom (in Wisdom of Solomon). In each case, Israelite authors have chosen what could be integrated into Hebraic thought with minimal distortion of the latter. Scholars are becoming much more appreciative today of the care with which foreign matter has been incorporated into Israel's own traditions.

Internal Influence

Ironically at the very moment that caution is the watchword in the area of extra-Biblical influence scholars have thrown caution to the wind in assessing wisdom influence within the Bible itself. Various types of argument have been used to prove that sages left their mark outside the literary corpus usually attributed to them. These arguments consist of vocabulary, subject matter, and world view. Unfortunately they labor under two distinct disadvantages: (1) they cannot escape circular reasoning, and (2) they neglect to take with sufficient seriousness the existence of a common linguistic stock and the universality of many concerns dealing with the human situation. In light of these two facts, wisdom scholarship is in dire need of methodological precision.

The futility of using vocabulary as the clue to wisdom's presence outside the wisdom corpus has been demonstrated recently by R. N. Whybray.[16] More cautious than most interpreters who adopt this method of discerning wisdom's impact upon the non-sapiential corpus, Whybray finally concedes the circularity of his approach. The problem can be stated quite simply: the wisdom corpus alone (itself the result of a subjective decision on the part of each interpreter) defines what is in the last resort "wisdom." The corollary of this minimal assertion is that nothing outside this corpus can be taken as specifically wisdom unless present also in wisdom texts. In short, a word or theme that occurs outside the wisdom corpus cannot be shown to be "wisdom" thought unless used in a purely technical sense. Rather, similarities may be examples of a common linguistic stock. In effect, the recent spate of books and articles arguing the presence of wisdom throughout the biblical canon fail to make their case precisely because of operative presuppositions as to what constitutes wisdom. If, then, the succession narrative is by definition wisdom, a study of thematic considerations in wisdom literature and in the "historical" account turns up nothing that contradicts the hypothesis and proves nothing unassumed from the outset.

Johannes Fichtner's arguments about Isaiah, lately revived and examined in much greater detail by J. William Whedbee and Joseph Jensen,[47] illustrate well the problem of working with vocabulary in common use throughout Israel. For Fichtner the only legitimate explanation for the shared vocabulary (parables, puns, wisdom terminology) was schooling on Isaiah's part at the feet of sages. Two things immediately come to mind. First, Isaiah may have borrowed the language of the wise men (if such it be) for his own purposes, so the hypothesis that the prophet had once been a sage is superfluous. Second, it is by no means certain that Isaiah used distinctive wisdom language. Mere usage of a few words referring to the intellectual life of man or the mockery of Egyptian wise men, together with analogies taken from nature, cannot sustain the weight of the theory. Whedbee alters the situation little. The addition of the *hoi* oracles, the use of *'esah,* and the highly dubious concept of a divine plan prove next to nothing about Isaiah and wisdom.

A much stronger case has been made by Jensen, whose painstaking analysis of the use of *torah* in Isaiah is in many ways an admirable exercise in caution. Yet even Jensen frequently falls prey to the circularity of reasoning that haunts wisdom research.

For example, Jensen's thesis is considerably weakened where wisdom influence is supported by an appeal to conjectured wisdom texts (Gen. 2-3, Deuteronomy, and the like), dubious wisdom themes (possession of the land, way of the people) or everyday linguistic usage (father/son, *šmr,* abomination, listen). The procedure of labeling as wisdom any passage that presents special difficulty to the hypothesis of wisdom influence seems highly questionable (Mic. 3:1), as does an appeal to such commonly shared virtues as concern for the *déclassé* or the idea of authority figures as teachers. Of course God (El) is wise, and together with the king and father, instructs man; but this didactic role of El, the king, and the father does not make them sages. Nor is it legitimate to claim that Isaiah called the wise men back to their genuine theology (wisdom comes from God rather than human investigation) and taught them that man possesses wisdom only as a charismatic gift. Literary dependency like this is no easy matter to document; one must be considerably more cautious in assessing Isaiah's impact upon the thought of the sages.

The situation differs little in regard to the claim that Amos was a product of the spiritual *Heimat* of the sages. First advanced by Samuel Terrien, this thesis was submitted to closer scrutiny by Hans Walter Wolff, who argued that Amos be understood against the background of ancient clan wisdom.[48] I have pointed out the weaknesses of this hypothesis elsewhere, and have sought to demonstrate yet another tradition, the theophanic, behind Amos' words.[49] Wolff's form critical analysis of certain rhetorical features of Amos requires further clarification of the nature of clan wisdom. To lend cogency to his thesis, Wolff needs to distinguish the wisdom of the clan from that of the Israelite court and to demonstrate Amos' similarities with the former. No such demonstration has yet appeared.

A different kind of argument has been advanced to prove the influence of wisdom upon the Joseph story and the Succession Narrative.[50] This line of reasoning falls into categories of thematic interest or world view. Gerhard von Rad thinks the view of history underlying the Joseph narrative is distinct from the usual understanding of divine action in history. In Gen. 37, 39-50 God is depicted as the one who guides history to its destination by working in and through human beings. Such a sophisticated view of providence belongs, according to von Rad, to the world view of the sages. Thus Joseph is understood as a model of instruction, and the story is said to function as an example of the wise man who overcomes all obstacles and rises to a position of prestige and power. Much in the story detracts from von Rad's theory, as I have attempted to show.[51]

Another example of thematic considerations as the determining factor in attempting to discern wisdom influence is R. N. Whybray's work on the Succession Narrative. Here, too, the manner of viewing God's control of human affairs is decisive. Whybray thus extends von Rad's own procedure one step farther, for the same concept of providence pervades the Joseph story and the account of the collapse of David's family. This view of direct wisdom influence upon the Succession Narrative suffers grievous difficulty, not the least of which is the role played by representatives of wisdom in the story. Whybray's refutation of my objections to his theory hinges upon what appears as subjective assessment of the climactic point in the story and the hypothesis of irony in key passages.[52] For these and other reasons I remain unconvinced.

Similar objections can be raised against H. J. Hermisson's discussion of wisdom and history.[53] While a plausible case can be made for an interest in history by the sages, one must remain alert to areas in which wise men merely share the perspectives of their day. Hence the parallels between the Succession Narrative and wisdom literature prove nothing more than that sages did not isolate themselves from humanity and create their own distinctive vocabulary in every instance. The interpreter must be careful not to assume that only a wise man could cultivate an interest in affairs of the court, the principle of retribution, human psychology, the danger of pride, and the power of the spoken word at the right time. Ample evidence that prophets and priests responsible for instruction were not oblivious to these matters exists.

The attempt to understand Gen. 1-11 or portions thereof as a product of wise men labors under the same difficulty.[54] While none can deny the presence of vocabulary describing human intelligence, or even of themes focusing upon the consequences of folly, all must admit that these so-called wisdom influences are not the exclusive domain of sages. The similarities between the view of history represented in Gen. 1-11 and that of the Deuteronomistic history are too pronounced to be ignored. One could conceivably take note of this similarity and still maintain a wisdom background. No scholar has argued more persuasively for sapiential influence upon Deuteronomy than Moshe Weinfeld,[55] who maintains that a positive relationship between Deuteronomy and wisdom can be discerned in the type of humanism reflected in both and in the didactic characteristics of each literary complex.

Most extreme in his position regarding wisdom's influence is Shemaryahu Talmon,[56] who views Esther as a literary work of the sages. Talmon's thesis rests upon a perceptive analysis of the text of Esther, together with appeal to the role of Nadin in the Story of Ahiqar. Unfortunately Talmon neglected to take seriously numerous points of dissimilarity between Esther and wisdom literature. The result cannot persuade anyone who does not concede Talmon's assumptions, often unexpressed. Those who would see Daniel as a wisdom book are at one with Talmon in ignoring the weight of evidence tipping the scales precariously in a direction other than wisdom. In my view, Daniel's literary category is undoubtedly apocalyptic.

However, if von Rad were correct in his thesis that apocalyptic is the child of wisdom,[57] even this objection would be muted. Evidence does not appear to support von Rad in his endeavor to relate wisdom and apocalyptic. In my judgment, the emphasis upon the "times and seasons" in Daniel has little in common with the earlier wisdom concept of the appropriate time. The same must be said of Hans Peter Müller's hypothesis that mantic wisdom finds expression in Ugarit and in Daniel.[58] Such skill in the magical art of incantation has nothing in common with Israelite literature. While the wise man in Egypt and in Mesopotamia was skilled in magical arts, the Israelite sage is never associated with ritual procedure prior to Sirach, and in fact seems antagonistic to the cult.[59]

I have not mentioned every attempt to discover wisdom influence outside the wisdom corpus. But similar objections could be raised to these forays into Exodus, Deuteronomy, Habakkuk, Jonah, Jeremiah, Ezekiel, and so forth.[60] They have not yet succeeded in breaking out of the circular reasoning or in giving sufficient weight to common linguistic stock. Even in rare instances when an author gave some attention to the methodological problems, little progress has been made in demonstrating direct influence. On the other hand, most of these scholars have taken huge strides toward the elucidation of the biblical text. Insights into the rhetorical devices, thematic considerations, and vocabulary of these so-called wisdom texts has been remarkable. The side effect of these strides is less fortunate; wisdom has ceased to have any distinctive meaning. Like Sheol in proverbial lore, its definition is constantly expanding.

In summation, there is at present both a trend toward caution in claiming extra-canonical dependency or positive relationships, and a readiness to find wisdom influence throughout the Bible. The latter reflects the exuberance of new discovery comparable to the period immediately following the identification of the positive relationship between Amen-em-opet and Proverbs. The excesses of such excitement must not blind scholars to the fact that many of their arguments presuppose what they attempt to demonstrate.

II. FORMS

In contrast to research in the area of prophetic literature, very little work has been done on the literary forms characteristic of wisdom.[61] A problem confronts us at the outset: what is the simplest literary unit? It has generally been assumed that the basic unit is the one-line verse, consisting of two stichs in parallelism. Others, however, have argued for a two-line unit as original, often viewing the shorter unit as an inclusio or an abbreviated saying. Customarily various collections have been dated on the basis of the simplicity of the form, among other factors. Since Pr. 1-9 contains several longer units, this seemed to confirm a later date than was thought to be the case in other collections of Proverbs. This dating procedure could then appeal to Sirach, which makes use of frequent paragraph units. Egyptian evidence seemed to confirm such a reading of the facts, until the discovery of the Instruction of 'Onchsheshonqy. Unfortunately for the simple evolutionistic theory, the literary form of the very late 'Onchsheshonqy is that of the simplest unit, presumably quite early.[62] In any event, one can no longer date a text simply on the basis of the complexity or simplicity of literary form.

Earlier critics also assumed the existence of popular proverbs prior to the literary stage of development. Appeal was made to such proverbs outside the wisdom corpus, particularly by Otto Eissfeldt in his fundamental study of the *mashal*.[63] Eissfeldt's thesis has been submitted to a devastating critique recently by Hermisson,[64] who denies the virtual existence of folk proverbs. Even the so-called folk proverbs give evidence of stylistic composition that is best explained as literary, Hermisson argues. Therefore, the proverbs are products of the schools and reflect the didactic interests and skills of wise men. R. B. Y. Scott has turned to this question in a recent study.[65] Scott rejects Hermisson's conclusions and argues once again for the existence of folk proverbs. While the final word has not yet been written, it seems Scott has the better argument. Consequently, I think one can move beyond the literary stage of proverbial composition to an oral period when the astute observer of human behavior and natural events coined brief maxims that represented the distillate of his knowledge.

If one assumes that the ground form of the proverb was a sentence composed of two members in parallelism, and that some of these proverbs are popular in origin, can he trace the development from one line to longer series within Proverbs? Johannes Hempel has addressed himself to this problem, with considerable success.[66] He writes of expansions by the use of the particle *kî*, the formulation of series, and of thematic and aesthetic units. Various means of linking several proverbs occur: a common letter (Pr. 11:9-12b; 20:7-9, 24-26); the same introductory word (Pr. 15:13-14, 16-17); the same idea (Pr. 16); the use of an acrostic (Pr. 31:10-31); paradoxical unity (Pr. 26:4-5); and numbers (Pr. 30:24-28). Thematic units characterize later proverbs (Pr. 1-9) and Sirach, and poems aimed at aesthetics occur with relative frequency in Job, Qoheleth, and Wisdom of Solomon. While much progress has been made in tracing the emergence of larger units, little is known about the perplexing issue of intentional or accidental arrangement of the total sayings in Proverbs or Qoheleth. Zimmerli has recently taken up this problem, concluding that Qoheleth is neither a tractate with a discernible scope and single theme, nor a loose collection of sentences. In short, a decision cannot be made on the basis of the present state of knowledge, for evidence points in both directions.[67] In any case, the final semblance of unity has come a long way from the initial admonition that stood alone. The first undergirding of the authority of admonition by means of motive clauses, reasons, results, or threats has borne rich fruits.

Any investigation into the nature of the forms of wisdom literature must distinguish between constants and variables, or to use the language of Rudolph Bultmann, the constitutive and ornamental features of various forms.[68] I would designate as ornamental such features as paranomasia, rhetorical devices, antithesis, personification, and the like. Each of these enhances the literary character of the sentence, instruction, disputation, or whatever form is being embellished. These ornamental features have a dual purpose, the one aesthetic, and the other practical. Actually the two goals are intrinsically related: the more pleasing to eye or ear, the more persuasive the content. The constitutive features give to the literary piece its wisdom character, hence they cannot be dispensed with if the saying is to retain its integrity.

The basic constitutive form is the proverb, which finds expression either as a sentence or as an instruction. As William McKane has emphasized so convincingly, these two types of proverbs are characteristic of the wisdom literature of Egypt and Mesopotamia as well as of Israel.[69] While it is common knowledge that the instruction strives to teach a moral, even the former of these two, the sentence, may be didactic. I refer to admonition and prohibition, both of which rest on the cumulative authority of tradition. Furthermore, even when the sentence appears to have no didactic intent, one must recognize the effect of the didactic context into which it has ultimately been placed. Hence the sentence is seldom morally neutral. The instruction is consciously pedagogic, and utilizes both motive clause and warning to enhance its persuasive power.

Other constitutive forms, which I have discussed elsewhere,[70] consist of riddle, fable and allegory, hymn and prayer, disputation, autobiographical narrative, lists, and didactic poetry and narrative. The riddle, now in disintegrated form within wisdom literature, may lurk behind certain numerical proverbs and perhaps some of the erotic proverbs where a *double entendre* is evident. Strictly speaking, the fable is missing from Israelite wisdom, although it abounds in Mesopotamian texts. But the allegory occurs in two places, the first, in germ only, in the description of a wife as a cistern (Pr. 5:15-23); the other, fully developed, links up with the one in Pr. 5 by referring to a woman as a well (Qoh. 12:1-6). The central theme of this text, however, is the debilitating effect of old age. The wisdom hymn praises Yahweh as creator, and introduces the figure of wisdom personified. This hymn eventually sings the praises of wisdom alone, and identifies wisdom and torah. A few Psalms (1; 49; 19; 33; 39; 104; 127) closely parallel such hymnic texts and are, therefore, designated Wisdom Psalms. Prayers within wisdom literature contain a strong didactic element; but this didacticism does not distinguish them as a wisdom form, for the doxology of judgment outside wisdom literature makes frequent use of didactic prayers. The disputation consists of a mythological introduction, a debate between friends, and a divine resolution. This is precisely the form of Job, although other elements are present (legal terminology, cultic laments). A variant of the disputation, specifically the "imagined speech," occurs in a number of wisdom texts. The autobiographical narrative (reflexion? confession?) is found in the early chapters of Qoheleth and in Proverbs (4:3-9; 24:30-34). I would suggest that the autobiographical narrative functioned as a certificate of credentials for the head of a school. The presence of onomastica or lists in Israelite wisdom is not certain. There is some evidence, nevertheless, that certain passages in Job and Sirach rest upon onomastica, and Wisd. of Sol. 7:17-20 can be understood as a brief list of curricular subjects in Israelite schools. Finally, didactic narrative (Pr. 7:21-23), problem poetry (Ps. 49), and historical retrospect (Sir. 44-50; Wisd. of Sol. 10-19), although resembling literature outside the wisdom corpus, have been used with great power by the sages.

So far it has not been possible to ascertain the sociological setting of different literary types. Much recent discussion has centered on wisdom's existence in the period of the Israelite clan. Erhard Gerstenberger has sought to show a close connection between apodictic law and the wisdom of the clan.[71] He places emphasis upon the admonitory style of the father, which resembles absolute prohibition. Against this explanation for the origin of wisdom, Wolfgang Richter has sought to demonstrate the existence of a group ethic rather than a clan ethic.[72] According to Richter, there is a fundamental difference between negatives with *lo'* and those with *'al*. Each, therefore, reflects a different ethos. Yet a third emphasis comes from Hermisson, who argues for the existence of a school in ancient Israel.[73] Wisdom literature would then be viewed as compositions by professional sages for use in the instruction of other wise men. The evidence for each of these positions is meager; as a result it seems impossible to speak in more than probabilities. Still the balance of probability inclines toward the theory of clan wisdom literature. The argument for a temple school has little to commend it, in my view, and rests upon questionable analogy with Egypt and Mesopotamia. Whybray's recent examination of the evidence places a huge question mark over the theory of an Israelite school during the period of the monarchy, and with it, the idea of court wisdom.[74] If he is correct, it will be necessary to reformulate the customary description of wisdom's development during Solomon's reign.

The Solomonic "Aufklärung"

Gerhard von Rad argued that the era of Solomon was revolutionary in character, representing a sharp break with the past. For him, as for Martin Buber, earlier Yahwism was wholly sacral; the Solomonic period abandons all cultic associations in favor of a radically secular understanding of reality. Previously God's action was thought to take place as a mighty intervention and was restricted to a sacred place, charismatic figure, or covenanted people. Now, however, a breath of fresh air flows through Solomon's court. For the first time man becomes aware of himself as man. The discovery of his rational powers and new dimensions of experience effects "a concentration upon the phenomenon of man in the broadest sense, his potentialities and limitations, his psychological complexity and profundity."[75] Providence is now revealed to the eyes of faith in every sphere of life, private or public, and God is thought to work behind the scenes, guiding the course of human events toward the goal which he alone perceives. The impetus for this revolution, so von Rad thinks, was David.

Walter Brueggemann has attempted to develop more fully this understanding of David as the catalyst of the Solomonic enlightenment.[76] He interprets various incidents in the story of David as indicative of spiritual maturity rather than shrewd conduct. The audacity of eating sacred bread is said to reflect David's new idea of the holy; his strange behavior 'after the death of his infant son is an act of profound faith; the pouring out of the water acquired at such great peril is a sacral act expressing a bond with those who risked their lives to satisfy his thirst; the blank check handed David's family is God's way of assuring him that he is free by virtue of God's trust in him.[77]

Both von Rad and Brueggemann think of the Solomonic era as a literary revolution. Scribes, foreign and domestic, grace the court of Solomon, and literature flourishes. Brueggemann even views the Yahwist as David's theologian,[78] and interprets much of the Yahwistic narrative against the background of the Davidic era. Von Rad, on the other hand, insists that the Succession Document was composed prior to the Yahwistic narrative. The latter, he contends, must be understood in terms of (1) the hidden activity of God and (2) the near-fulfillment in David of the ancient tribal territorial claims about the extent of Israel's dominion in the land of promise. Von Rad also sees the Solomonic era as a blossoming of economic and cultural life, leading to an international culture. As an expression of this openness to the world of the ancient Near East, a strong institution of wise men emerges at Solomon's court. In this environment the king becomes proficient—and even creative—in the art of composing proverbs and songs, according to von Rad. Here he appeals to Albrecht

Alt's interpretation of the tradition about Solomon's wisdom as encyclopedic knowledge (onomastica) expressed for the first time in poetic form.[79]

This radically altered way of looking at divine activity was not without its hidden dangers, however. Von Rad hints at the chilling blast of scepticism that brought in its wake, though belatedly, the pessimism of Qoheleth. This crisis in the intellectual spirit, and its relationship to the Solomonic era of enlightenment, received its classic expression in an essay by Kurt Galling.[80] Once the action of God is left to the eyes of faith, it soon becomes easy to deny altogether any divine concern for the welfare of mankind. The result is the discovery of life *in tormentis*.

It stands to reason, von Rad argues, that the wise men at the court of Solomon would need an educational model by which to communicate their ideal to potential courtiers. Such a model exists, von Rad claims, in the Joseph story. Here is manifested the educational ideal of early wisdom (Pr. 10-22:16; 22:17-24:22; 25-29). Von Rad thinks that a court setting for this wisdom is beyond question: "None would dispute the fact that this early wisdom literature belongs within the context of the royal court, and that its principal aim was to build up a competent body of future administrators."[81] Joseph, then, maifests this wisdom ideal of self-control, modesty, intelligence, restraint, godly fear. He demonstrates, among other things, the ability to speak well at the decisive moment, give sound advice, and function effectively at the king's court. Von Rad finds confirmation of this interpretation in the theological prespective of the Joseph story, which tolerates the cult and is sparing in mentioning God. Twice the narrator brings God into the picture, each time at crucial junctures (Gen. 45:8 and 50:20). In each of these, good wisdom-theology surfaces, he claims. In short, man proposes but God disposes[82]; the opposition between divine economy and human intention is a central issue in wisdom theology. The chill factor is present, however, according to von Rad; in this regard he points to the element of resignation that undercuts the importance of human activity. In support of his hypothesis, von Rad also claims certain characteristics of normal Israelite thought are absent (historico-political interests, a cultic etiological motive, and salvation history), thus indirectly confirming a wisdom background for the Joseph story. He concludes: the "Joseph story, with its strong didactic motive, belongs to the category of early wisdom writing."[83]

This view of the Joseph narrative overlooks a number of essential facts which I have enumerated in the course of a study on methodology in determining wisdom influence upon "historical" literature.[84] The cogency of the argument prompted George Coats to attempt a compromise between the two positions.[85] He proposes to break down the Joseph story into at least two versions, the earlier kernel consisting of Gen. 39-41. This story within a story, Coats thinks, does reflect wisdom concerns: "At each stage the focus is on Joseph's skill as a responsible administrator."[86] The emphasis, according to Coats, is upon proper use of power by an administrator already in office, not the means of rising to it. While Coats hesitates to assert wisdom as the sole background for this kernel, he thinks the hypothesis highly probable. Less certain about the existence of a school, however, Coats prefaces his remarks about the Solomonic enlightenment with the adjective "so-called." In the end he minimizes the importance of wisdom, and describes the purpose of the narrative in much broader terms. This threefold purpose includes the tracing of the life of a family through tragic division to reconciliation, the characterizing of political officials who hold the power of life and death, and the positing of hope for one who was believed to be beyond hope.

The ramifications of this theory about a Solomonic enlightenment are manifold. They affect radically the reconstruction of a history of wisdom literature and tradition. Since first advanced as an hypothesis—and without any compelling proof—this theory has become an operative datum for most discussions of wisdom. The time has come, it seems, to ask what evidence exists for the theory of a Solomonic enlightenment. Anticipating the results of this inquiry, there is scant evidence indeed.

The first thing that must be said is that traditions about Solomon's vast wisdom are legendary in character, as R. B. Y. Scott has made clear.[87] Furthermore, references to Solomon in the headings of various collections in Proverbs do not take us back prior to the time of Hezekiah. In essence, then, the only support for a Solomonic enlightenment is inferential; it is based on an analogy with Egyptian court life. While such a view of the facts may be historically probable, one must recognize that nothing demands the existence of an institution of wise men at Solomon's court. Nor is Alt's interpretation of the Solomonic legend, which Anton Causse has called "le mirage salomonien,"[88] the only possible one. The legend may have preceded the actual selection of proverbial collections to be canonized. We simply do not know whether other collections existed or not; Israel at one time may have had proverbs dealing with birds, trees, snakes, and the like, just as she apparently had riddles, now lost to posterity.

Second, there is serious doubt that Israel's literature prior to Solomon can be characterized as pan-sacral. Von Rad overworks this facet of his theory. It is puzzling that the largely secular Samson narrative is overlooked in his argument.[89] These legends are, of course, difficult to date; but the traditions must surely antedate the period of Solomon. In effect they suggest that alongside sacral narratives like the story of King Saul, of which von Rad makes so much, there were also stories of a different sort that breathed a free, secular spirit. There is absolutely no compelling evidence that the Joseph story, the Succession Narrative, and the Yahwist come from the time of David and Solomon. This, too, is an inference, albeit a plausible one. D. B. Redford's analysis points to some of the difficulties in dating the Joseph story at this time[90]; and if Martin Noth is correct that the essentials of the Yahwistic narrative existed much earlier than Solomon, then strong doubt is cast upon von Rad's claim that this narrative demonstrates an enlightenment during Solomon's reign. In short, von Rad's theory about literary development from sacral to secular and the sequence of Joseph story, Succession Document, to Yahwist is a doubtful hypothesis. It deserves to be treated as such.

It is highly interesting that von Rad himself insists on making a sharp distinction between the Yahwistic narrative and wisdom. In essence, his student, H. J. Hermisson, was merely carrying von Rad's line of reasoning to its ultimate conclusion.[91] Still von Rad recoils from such a positive relationship between wisdom and history, and insists that the differences are significant.

Class Ethic

A corollary of belief in the existence of an active wisdom movement under Solomon's sponsorship is the emergence of a class ethic. Whoever opts for the existence of class ethics within wisdom literature must face up to certain difficulties.[92] In the first place, a folk origin of aphorisms would suggest that the proverbs reflect the ethos of the total society rather than that of a distinct group within it. Second, Scott's claim that the maxims do not participate in a single world view or setting, if true, would mean that the assumption of a class ethic is ill conceived. Again, the experiential base of wisdom sayings argues against a class ethic, for the saying can only be valid if it takes into account the totality of experience insofar as it is possible to do so.

One way to skirt these problems is to define class ethic rather broadly as the ethos of a specific social group. As Brian Kovacs has discerned, the tacit assumption of the form criticism enterprise amounts to precisely this sort of thing.[93] A number of scholars have attempted to view the wise men as landed gentry.[94] This presumption of an upper leisure class is based on analogy with the scribal tradition in later Judaism, which has recently been clarified at many points by Ephraim Urbach.[95] The view is also supported by the fact that the wise men seem not to have possessed either the power or the inclination to correct injustice. Such is surely the case in Qoheleth. While this hypothesis of the gentleman farmer as the author and transmittor of wisdom literature is plausible, there is no great emphasis in "the intellectual tradition" on the special concerns of the wealthy farmer.

This leads to a second possible definition of class ethic, that of a restricted in-group morality. The wise men make a sharp distinction between the sage and the fool; the latter has rejected wisdom and is consequently wicked, an agent of chaos. Two different standards apply, then, to the in-group and to outsiders. But this does not necessarily imply closure; Kovacs points out that there are demonstrations of openness in the concern for the *déclassé* (the widow, the fatherless, the poor, the oppressed, the powerless).[96] Furthermore, the inner disposition was deemed most significant. This concern for intentionality gave the sage a stance from which to attack popular religion in which the deed alone was thought important. Herein lies an element of protest against the status quo. But the wise man was not revolutionary; indeed, there are indications of discrete silence in the face of wrong. I refer to the ambivalent attitude of the sage toward bribery.

What, then, of the professional code of the wise? This brings us to a restrictive definition of class ethic. Clearly there evolves from the literature of the wise a pattern of behavior that is calculated to assure the good life. But can one argue that this code of conduct is intended solely for members of a wisdom establishment? In favor of this narrow view of the code of conduct is the internationalism of wisdom, the high level of continuity among Egyptian, Israelite, and Mesopotamian wisdom texts. Such a shared world view would seem to argue for a special class with undeniable self-consciousness. On the other hand, there is nothing that demands such an exclusive view of the ethical code in wisdom literature, while much points to a concern for the instruction of young people in general. In this regard it is worth noting that Job uses a cultic text as the standard by which his life is measured (Job 31).[97] Can one really imagine a sage doing that if he thought his own group possessed an exclusive code of ethics?

In short, there is evidence of class ethic in wisdom literature, but not in the narrow sense of the term. Consequently, Kovacs' conclusion merits close attention: "Court and king sayings, instruction and discipline, an ethic of restraint, observance of proprieties, and a system of authority suggest a professional ethic of administrators or officials." [98] My own inclination is to play down the administrative role of wise men, and in its place to put major emphasis upon family ethics. But even the latter type of wisdom had its own view of order, its authoritative spokesman, and its sense of propriety. Perhaps it is even possible to discern three different "class ethics," those of the family, the court, and the "teacher." But, of course, the broader definitions are operative here.

Who, then, were the transmittors of the wisdom tradition? If there may not have been an established court wisdom, and if even the existence of an institution "the wise men" is dubious, who is responsible for the compilation and preservation of wisdom literature? Must we resort to the scepticism of R. N. Whybray for whom there is only an intellectual tradition? Perhaps, but Whybray's answer takes us no further than previous theories: it merely recognizes our inability to say precisely who the wise men were.

Can we even speak of a wisdom *movement,* as if there were representatives with common goals and aspirations? Does wisdom represent a fundamentally different phenomenon from prophecy, for example? Such questions indicate how little we really know about wisdom. Much literature has been written about the alleged upper class bias of the wise men, but the evidence for this interpretation of the sages was largely inferential. Robert Gordis' fundamental study of this problem, now supplemented by Urbach's research into the social status of the wise men during the Pharisaic period, is suggestive, but our knowledge of sociological conditions in ancient Israel is still in its infancy.

In short, it is at present neither possible to write a chronological history of the development of wisdom literature nor to place each of the forms within its proper setting. Besides this inability to discern absolute dates and functions of the literature, it is impossible to write a history of the institution or persons responsible for compiling and transmitting the literature. Their origins are obscure, as is the overall development of the tradition. We do not even know whether wise men functioned in each generation as royal advisors, or if they ran a school for the elite members of Israelite society. In actual fact, we do not know who either could have, or would have, read the literature of the sages, or for what purposes.

III. STRUCTURE

The fundamental exploration of the structure of Israelite wisdom took place more than forty years ago. In it Walther Zimmerli[99] underlined the anthropocentric character of wisdom thought, together with its non-authoritative tone. The wise man, he argued, began with the question: "What is good for man?" In contrast to the powerful prophetic word, which carries the authority of its divine source, the advice (*'esah*) of the wise man aimed at compelling assent rather than obedience. Zimmerli noted that the wise man refused to appeal to the decrees of creation, but depended solely on the power of persuasion.

Subsequent research has called the non-authoritative nature of the wisdom saying into question.[100] Instrumental in this eroding of the ground upon which Zimmerli stood has been the examination of the spiritual structure of biblical aphoristic literature, the study of the meaning of the root *'esah,* and the sociological setting within which the wise man uttered his word. Perhaps a useful distinction can be made between the saying addressed to a potential member of the wise men and a word spoken to an outsider. The former saying would, of course, carry the heavy weight of tradition and personal authority. On the other hand, when a wise man confronted those who did not subscribe to the world view of the sages he had to depend upon his intellectual powers of rational argumentation. One could almost say that clan wisdom would be highly authoritative in that the patriarch speaks to the members of his family, whereas court wisdom depends completely upon the power of logical and psychological persuasion.

In Zimmerli's pioneer study of the structure of wisdom the concept of order does not assume the significance it has in later works. Many scholars today have taken over the Egyptian concept of *ma'at*[101] and define Israelite wisdom in terms of an attempt to discover and maintain order in the personal and social arenas of life. The wise man, according to this understanding, is one who both *creates* order and brings his life into harmony with the *established* order of the universe.

Now the belief in order implies design or purpose, from which man can profit. Much has recently been made of the concept of timeliness or propriety as the goal of all wisdom. The wise man is one who knows the right time and place, the person who exercises propriety. Thus one finds outright contradictions in proverbial sayings, once even juxtaposed (Pr. 26:4-5). They are preserved because of a desire to consider all variables in a given situation. Both statements are true, and one must choose which of the two is called for by the situation itself.

The willingness to face up to contradictions arises out of the fact that wisdom is an open system, although a tendency toward frozen dogma in the area of retribution certainly developed. But the sage knew that there were limitations to the comprehension of reality, both in terms of intellectual capacity and divine inscrutability. Ultimately the wise man or woman had to concede the poverty of intellect, for "man proposes but God disposes" (Pr. 16:9; 19:21; 21:30-31). The ever present incalculable ingredient to every experience promoted an openness to various possibilities and a recognition of one's limits.

Undergirding the wise person's view of reality was a profound theological conviction. Because reality was created to reward virtue and punish vice, the sage was remarkably at home in the world—so long as the conviction of justice prevailed. In Israel this religious orientation found expression in the recurring theme, "The fear of the Lord is the essence of wisdom." Even outside Israel, both in Egypt and in Mesopotamia, there was a tendency toward monotheism within wisdom thought. Furthermore, this religious sentiment extended beyond the external cultic ritual, reaching as far as the inner motivation. The absence in Israelite wisdom of a concept of divine grace was felt most keenly by Qoheleth, whose religious perspective is devoid of any positive relationship. The cleft between practical maxims based on experience and knowledge acquired through revelation was eased gradually in a process of theologization that is described by J. Coert Rylaarsdam in a profound little book.[102]

This process of theologization is by no means a simple one. In all likelihood it came about in three stages. The first of these is the introduction of the notion of the fear of the Lord as the first principle of wisdom. Much early wisdom appears to have been remarkably "secular" in mood and content; its fundamental purpose was to encapsulate precious observations about reality for the benefit of posterity. The subject matter is largely domestic; agrarian interests and natural phenomena abound. Still those who accumulated this valuable insight into the way things hold together belonged to the people of the Lord, and thus saw themselves as a covenanted people. Small wonder that they came to express their faith in God and in the course of daily happenings in one and the same breath. Indeed the admonitions, motivations, and threats were soon strengthened by appeal to a common faith. Such appeal is no radically new departure, for it links up with the ancient concept of order bestowed upon the universe by a deity who rewards virtue and punishes vice.

The second stage of religionization is the attempt to deal with the difficult problem of divine presence in the world of human discourse. How can it be that truth emerges from an observation of nature and culture? Is it possible that revelation occurs within ordinary human decisions apart from the prophetic oracle, priestly ritual, or poetic vision? The representatives of the wisdom tradition were convinced their observations about reality touched base with the ultimate truth possessed only by God. They expressed this conviction in terms of divine presence, hypostasis. This heavenly figure, Wisdom, enlightens the sages by dwelling in their midst. By this means the sages of Israel managed to salvage something of the ancient Near Eastern fertility concept, namely the highly desirable bride who is more at home in the divine than in the human sphere.

A third kind of theologization came to be employed by Jesus ben Sira. I have in mind the identification of torah with wisdom. Once this equation has been made, it is possible to incorporate the sacred history of Israel into the wisdom tradition. Accordingly, ben Sira goes one step beyond identifying torah and wisdom; he sings a hymn in praise of the great men in Israel's sacred past. Furthermore, in him one sees the sage at worship: prayers and psalms abound in his collected sayings.[103]

The speculation about Dame Wisdom in Proverbs 8, Job 28, Sirach 24, and Wisdom of Solomon 7 may possibly be integrally related to the struggle over divine injustice. In my opinion, however, hypostasis responds to *two* factors: the problem of theodicy and the need to relate wisdom thought to Yahwistic faith. Whybray puts the matter this way: hypostasis was not intended to bridge a gulf between God and man, but between wisdom and Yahwism.[104] Into this void came Dame Wisdom, who seems to be modeled upon the figure of Ma'at in Egyptian speculation. The personification of wisdom functions to bestow authority upon wisdom, and to demonstrate divine concern for mankind. The latter was a particularly vexing problem throughout much of the period during which wisdom literature flourished. This claim of a personification of God in wisdom, although not fully developed until Wisdom of Solomon, affirms that God has placed in the human mind a point of contact between heaven and earth, and that this rational principle dwells among the people of Israel in a special manner.

Such a process of religionization exacerbated old problems while softening still others. The assumption of divine control over human affairs to assure the triumph of virtue became more and more difficult to maintain. While some sages closed their eyes to the grim reality of innocent suffering, others wrestled with the problem mightily. Indeed "the Lord of the Old Testament was not one to be painted into a corner by the persistent formulations of the sages."[105] Thus the authors of Job and Qoheleth champion the freedom of God to act contrary to human definitions of justice. The crisis that emerged was the threat of a return to the chaos prior to the creative word; in other words, the mythical *regressus ad initium* takes up residence in the thought of the sages. The close association of creation and retribution has not as yet been formulated satisfactorily, in my opinion. In what follows I shall attempt to break new ground in this difficult area of research.

The Function of Creation Theology

The function of creation theology within the thought of the sages remains something of a mystery to this day. To be sure, scholars have not been completely silent about this fundamental problem. Perhaps the most comprehensive statement is that of Walther Zimmerli: "Wisdom thinks resolutely within a framework of a theology of creation. Its theology is creation theology." [106] While making less claim as to the place of creation theology in wisdom, Johannes Fichtner goes farther in describing the nature of the belief in creation. He writes: "Belief in the creator God is connected with faith in the God of retribution in a twofold manner."[107] Fichtner goes on to demonstrate these points of contact between creation and retribution in the areas of divine sovereignty and order, both cosmic and social. Yet neither Zimmerli nor Fichtner gave sufficient attention to the role of creation in wisdom thought to justify their remarks about the centrality of creation theology to the wise men. Astonishingly, to this day no one has devoted a full scale essay to this problem despite the constant refrain in scholarly works that wisdom thought and creation theology are inseparably bound together. Any attempt to provide such an analysis of creation theology within the framework of wisdom needs to clarify the role of creation in the total thought of Israel before going on to demonstrate the distinctiveness of the function of creation theology in wisdom literature. Two points merit consideration.

The first observation takes up the valuable insight associated with Hermann Gunkel.[108] Creation cannot be divorced from the concept of chaos. The implications of this recognition of the absolute necessity for maintaining tension between creation and chaos have not always been felt; the result has been a terminological confusion that distorts most discussions of creation. This semantic lack of clarity has prompted Dennis J. McCarthy to suggest that we should speak in terms of "ordering" rather than "creating".[109] By this means the tension between chaos and creation is given prominence, although without the unnecessary and unproven assumption of *annual* threats of chaos that Israel had to guard against by correct ritual.

A second observation has to do with the role of creation thought in ancient Israel as currently understood. This consensus of scholarship can be described as follows. Creation is not a primary datum of Israel's faith, but plays a subservient role to redemption. The placing of creation narratives at the beginning of the Hebrew Bible notwithstanding, creation functions to support saving history. Furthermore, the antiquity of a belief in creation is conceded; but its centrality to Canaanite thought posed a threat to Yahwism until Deutero-Isaiah conceived of a brilliant response to that problem. It follows that creation occupies a place on the periphery of Israelite thought, rather than at the center. Hence an Old Testament theology that does justice to the thought of Israel must relegate creation to the sidelines. While this interpretation of the theological importance of belief in creation is associated with Gerhard von Rad,[110] it has been widely accepted.

This widespread understanding of creation's minimal place in the theological enterprise has recently been contested by a specialist in wisdom literature. Hans Heinrich Schmid's[111] investigations in the area of order in the ancient Near East led him to conclude that creation is the framework within which historical views move, that the dominant background of all Old Testament thinking and faith is the idea of the comprehensive world order and with it creation faith in the wider sense of the word, and that creation faith is not a peripheral idea in biblical theology but its essence. From yet another perspective, Theodore M. Ludwig[112] joins forces with Schmid in contesting the secondary role of creation. Ludwig examines the traditions of establishing the earth in Deutero-Isaiah; his results suggest to him "that creation faith in Deutero-Isaiah is not merely subsumed under election or redemption faith." My own challenge to the prevailing view of creation was formulated independently of Schmid or Ludwig, and seeks to move a step further by recognizing the tension within the biblical texts themselves. I shall argue that in one sense both von Rad and Schmid are right. The clue to my understanding is the attempt to take seriously the concept of chaos within a discussion of creation. Three points stand out: (1) the threat of chaos in the cosmic, political, and social realms evokes a response in terms of creation theology; (2) in wisdom thought, creation functions primarily as defense of divine justice; and (3) the centrality of the question of God's integrity in Israelite literature places creation theology at the center of the theological enterprise.

The Threat of Chaos

It is no longer necessary to justify the claim that the concept of order lies at the heart of wisdom thinking. This conclusion rests on an exhaustive analysis of Israel's wisdom within the context of ancient Near

Eastern sapiential literature. Now the order established in the beginning by the creator is ever subject to the threatening forces of chaos, both human and divine. The eruption of disorder came at the very point where the retribution scheme gave way; this crisis of confidence in divine power or goodness surfaced early in Mesopotamia, Egypt, and Israel. The literary deposit of this heroic struggle is living testimony to the awesome power of the forces of chaos that placed a question mark over the belief in a correspondence between virtue and reward. We can recognize the threat of chaos in three fundamental areas. The first realm in which the forces of disorder spill over into the marketplace is that of human perversion.

This intrusion of chaos can be illustrated with reference to Qoheleth, about whom Hans Wilhelm Hertzberg has written: "There is no doubt: the book of Qoheleth was composed with Genesis 1-4 before the eyes of the author; the life view of Qoheleth is formed out of the creation stories." [113] In light of this assessment of the significance for Qoheleth of creation narratives, I turn to Qoh. 7:29 ("Lo, only this have I found: God has made man upright [yašar], but they have sought out many contrivances"). I need not tarry to consider the vast implication of the rare word ḥiššᵉbonôt or the feminine subject of the perversion. It suffices to observe that the former derives largely from a desire to link this verse to 7:25 and 7:27 where a similar word occurs (ḥešbôn), while the latter may be understood generically. In any case, man is only one/one thousandths better than woman. The meaning of the verse is clear in spite of these difficulties. It asserts that mankind alone is responsible for the corruption of the order of the created world.

A similar point pervades Sir. 15:14, where Ben Sira responds to a vocal group bent on indicting God for causing human iniquity. Rejecting the assertion that God led man astray, Sirach contends that "It was he who created man in the beginning, and he left him in the power of his own inclination" (cf. 10:18). It has hitherto gone unnoticed that the brief formula of debate, lo' to'mar, occurs in contexts the overwhelming majority of which wrestle with the problem of divine justice. This propensity of formula and theme is not limited to biblical sources, but also occurs in the Instructions of Ani, Amen-em-opet, and 'Onchsheshonqy. [114]

Another manifestation of chaos appears in the area of human ignorance. A prominent answer to the problem of evil in Mesopotamia, this stress upon the limits of human comprehension is set within the discussion of creation in Qoheleth as well. This is true both of 3:11[115] and of 7:13-14. In the former, Qoheleth writes: "He has made *everything* beautiful in its own time; he has also placed a sense of the remote past and future in their minds, but without man being able to discover the work God does from beginning to end." The avoidance of the Priestly and Yahwistic terminology of creation renders somewhat tenuous Hertzberg's claim that Qoheleth wrote with Genesis 1-4 before him. Still one could claim that the alteration is intentional. More importantly, Qoh. 3:11 asserts the orderliness of creation (this must be the meaning of *yapeh be'itô*). At the same time, however, the broken sentence introduces grave qualification to such beauty.[116] God has created man so that he simply cannot know the proper time for anything despite his boasts to the contrary (cf. 8:17). Qoheleth offers further clarification of this ambiguous gift of *ha'olam* in 3:14 ("I know that whatever God does will remain into the ages; there is no adding to or subtracting from it, for God has made it so that men would fear him"). Here the *yir'at YHWH* approaches numinous dread rather than the fear of God that is the essence of all knowledge. Coupled with the *ha'olam* of 3:11, *yir'at YHWH* gives voice to Qoheleth's existence *in tormentis*. The reason for this torment lies in Qoheleth's recognition that the fundamental premise of wisdom, namely that there is a positive correlation between one's being and one's outward condition, has collapsed under the forces of chaos.

A similar agony rests behind Qoh. 7:13-14. Here Qoheleth takes up a proverb that otherwise appears in 1:15 ("The crooked cannot be straightened, nor the missing tallied"), but varies the form considerably ("Consider the work of God; for who can straighten that which he has bent?"). While the use of the rare word *taqen*, which elsewhere means to bring disparate voices into harmony (Sir. 47:9) or to arrange proverbs (Qoh. 12:9), is interesting, it does not seem nearly as significant as *'iwwetô*. Used of scales *'iwwah* alludes to their falsification (Am. 8:5), but the term can also refer to misleading someone (Ps. 119:78; Job 19:6). Especially informative is Lam. 3:34-36, in which it is claimed that the Lord does not delight in (look upon!) the misleading of a man during litigation. It is this sense of perversion that stands out in Job 8:3; 34:12 and Ps. 146:9. The twofold question in Job 8:3 is poignant indeed: "Will God pervert (*ye'awwet*) justice, or Shaddai pervert right?" Here one notes the repetition of the *ye'awwet*, together with the parallelism of *mispat* and *sedeq*. Similarly, Elihu contends that "Surely God will not act wickedly, nor will Shaddai pervert justice" (34:12). On the other hand, the champion of the prisoner, the righteous, the orphan, and the stranger also perverts the way of the wicked (Ps. 146:9).

The claim that Zeus can "easily make the crooked straight" which

Harry Ranston[117] cites from Hesiod, *Works,* 7 is entirely beside the point, since Qoheleth complains about *man's* inability to correct what is bent. The practical conclusion to this incapacity to alter the divine decrees is provided in Qoh. 7:14 ("On the good day be happy and on the evil day consider; this as well as that, God has made so that man is unable to find out anything that will follow him"). Robert Gordis aptly sums up the sense of these two verses: "(they) are an admirable epitome of Koheleth's thought—God is all-powerful, man must resign himself to ignorance regarding the meaning and purpose of life." [118] Of course the verse recalls Job 2:10, with its recognition that both good and evil derive from God and must be accepted as a gift in each instance, that is, with gratitude.

The human inability to penetrate the shield erected by God to prevent the creature from discovering the divine mystery leads on to thought about the work of God in yet another verse (Qoh. 11:5). In this instance presumably Qoheleth has reference to the divine creative deed rather than to subsequent redemptive acts, or even to *whatever* God does. The verse argues from the lesser to the greater: "Just as you do not know what the direction of the wind is, or how bones (come) in the womb of a pregnant woman, so you do not know the work of God who does everything." In short, human beings know less about God's work and the future than about the mysterious origin of the wind or of a foetus. However, this ignorance of the ultimate mystery of life does not lead to an ignoring of the divine command to replenish the earth. Nor does the recognition that God has placed a limit upon humanity while reserving the truth for himself impel Qoheleth into suicide, in spite of his spiritual kinship with the Babylonian Qoheleth in the matter of limits imposed upon man from without.

Qoheleth is not the only sage who struggled with a conviction about the bankruptcy of human wisdom, whether owing to divine caprice or human fallibility. The sceptical author of Pr. 30:1-4 parodies traditional assertions by turning them into rhetorical questions.[119] It occasions little surprise that someone rebukes this sceptic for adding to the words of God (30:5-6), for there is here certainly a new dimension to the affirmation that God has gathered the wind in his fists and wrapped up the waters in a garment. How vastly different is the agonized query: "Who has established (*heqim*) all the ends of the earth? What is his name, and what is his son's name? Surely you know!" Here one confronts the outer limits of such emphasis on divine inscrutability as is found in Sir. 11:4 and 16:21, which describe God's work as wonderful and hidden like a tempest which no one can see.

While elements of divine caprice have surfaced to some degree in the discussions of responsibility for evil and of human limitations, the arbitrary actions of the creator come to prominence when sin and punishment are addressed. The connection of sickness and guilt survives even the challenge presented by Job, and tempers Sirach's remarks about the place of physicians and medicines (Sir. 38:1-15). The evidence of tension within Sirach's mind provides testimony to the force of the argument that sickness is punishment for sin. While he can speak in the spirit of the old view ("He who sins before his Maker, may he fall into the care of a physician," 38:15), Sirach is also convinced that the divine physician created medicines and doctors. Precisely in this area of disparity between inner state and external condition the forces of chaos made their strongest impact.

A third domain in which chaos erupted for the sage concerns the consciousness of divine presence. From the beginning the sage held in creative tension the idea of the presence of the creator who sustains his universe and the recognition of the hiddenness of the distant ruler. Conscious of the ethical dimensions stemming from the fact that rich and poor alike owe their origin to one maker (Pr. 14:31; 17:5; cf. 20:12 and 29:13), the sage also knew the silence of eternity that gave rise to despair and ethical nihilism. The result was the inevitable fear of God-forsakenness to the destructive forces. In response to this terror over divine abandonment of the order established at the beginning and now threatened, the sages introduced the idea of Dame Wisdom (Pr. 3:19-20; 8:22-31; Sir. 1:4, 9, 14; 23:20; 24:3, 8-9) within the context of creation thought. There is some evidence, it seems, in support of the position advocated by Burton Mack,[120] namely that hypostasis responds in part to the question of theodicy. The traditions about Wisdom (ḥokmah) fulfill a desire to make God both accessible and active at a time when serious doubt is cast on his justice.

Creation as Defense of Divine Justice

The question of theodicy lies at the heart of the book of Job; so does creation theology. The juxtaposition of these two themes is even verbalized in several places. When Eliphaz draws to a close the marvelous description of the numinous moment of revelation, he preserves the divine word vouchsafed to him ("Can man be more just than God ['elôah], or a mortal purer than his maker [me'osehû]?", Job 4:17). This, indeed, comes to be the crucial issue in Job's confrontation with God, and for his Titanism Job is soundly rebuked by the creator ("Will you even frustrate my own justice; will you condemn me as guilty in order that you may be innocent?", 40:8).

The converse of Job's behavior is voiced by Elihu in 36:3, where we read "I will carry ['essa'] my knowledge from afar, and ascribe justice to my maker [lepo'ali]. In 32:22 Elihu assures us that his word can be trusted, for he does not know how to flatter since "my maker will quickly bear me away" (yissa'eni). Still another sharp attack upon divine justice occurs in Job's speech recorded in 10:4. Here the victim of divine abuse cries out: "Do you have eyes of flesh, or do you see as man sees?" Job then argues at length that God's hands fashioned and made him like clay, that he poured him out like milk and curdled him like cheese, clothing him with skin and flesh and knitting him together with bones and sinews. Indeed, God granted Job life, covenant love, and happiness of spirit. Why then, Job asks, do you destroy the works that your hands so lovingly fashioned? (10:8-12). In response to Job's query, Elihu avers that God is untouched by human conduct since his greatness does not depend upon man's behavior. Nevertheless, this defendant of God agrees with Job that his creator ('osai) [!] gives songs in the night (zemirôt) and teaches man more than birds and beasts, that is, more than the experiential knowledge of the sages (35:10). Elihu moves on to emphasize the absurdity of Job's Titanism: "Can you, like him, spread out the skies, hard as molten metal?" (37:18).

The divine speeches force Job to recognize his absence when the creative deed was conceived and brought to fruition. By excluding Job from the original creation God impresses upon him the sheer absurdity of Job's attempt to be an equal of God.[121] The puny creature who has boldly faced God and demanded justice now discovers the folly of struggling with one stronger than he. Even the mighty Behemoth, before whom all other creatures cringe in terror, found his strength no match for the creator, but submitted to him docilely. This conqueror of the powers of chaos is equally adept in areas requiring finesse rather than sheer power. His majestic touch scatters snow, hoar frost, or dew upon the whole earth. In short, the divine speeches divest Job of his Titanic defiance by calling attention to the grandeur of creation. The remaining allusions to creation (9:9; 26:1-14; 31:15) are intended to strengthen the case for divine justice, or to highlight the agony of Job deriving from God's failure to use his obvious power in a way that assures universal justice. In a word, creation theology functions in Job to undergird the cogency of the argument for divine justice despite strong and convincing evidence to the contrary.

This same use of creation theology to answer the attacks upon divine justice pervades the thought of Sirach, who moves considerably beyond Job in providing answers for the apparent prosperity of the wicked.[122] Besides the customary responses known to us from Job and Wisdom Psalms, Sirach ventures in virgin territory on two fronts. The first is in the metaphysical realm, the second in the psychological. Sirach contends that creation itself rewards virtue and punishes vice, since God made the universe to consist of complementary pairs of good and evil. In addition, Sirach intimates that God punishes the guilty with excessive *Angst,* specifically in nightmares. But Sirach seems not to have been completely satisfied with such responses to the problem of evil; ultimately he abandons these arguments in favor of a mighty crescendo of praise for the creator of the universe (16:24-17:14; 42:15-43:33; 39:15-35). In each of these hymns creation and theodicy march hand in hand. In the same breath Sirach asserts that "The works of the Lord are all good, and he will supply every need in its hour" (39:33), and "No one can say, 'This is worse than that,' for all things will prove good in their season" (39:34; cf. 39:16-17). Such texts indicate that Sir. 18:1 accurately reflects the function of creation in the thought of Ben Sira ("He who lives forever created the whole universe; the Lord alone will be declared just"). One cannot miss the echo in the final clause of the oft-proclaimed "Just art thou, O Lord" within Israel's discussion literature. Here one moves barefoot and with bowed head, for we are privileged to witness the mighty struggle between God and a devotee who discovers the Lord as his enemy, and is nearly driven out of his mind. The combatant finds it difficult beyond imagination to give assent to the maxim that "God has made everything for its purpose (*lamma'anehû*), even the wicked for a day of trouble (he has made)," Pr. 16:4. Likewise, he even calls into question the notion of divine prescience actualized in the creative deed (Sir. 23:20). In short, creation theology functions as a defense of the justice of God; such a defense is necessitated by the threat of chaos in every dimension of life.

Creation and the Theological Task

If these conclusions are essentially correct about the function of creation theology within the argument over divine justice, I am now in a position to address the broader issue of authority in wisdom thought. Contrary to what would be expected, the wise men do not appeal to creation as direct authority for t eir counsel. On the other hand, the fundamental premise of their labor to understand the nature of reality is the orderliness of creation. This dependability is grounded in the creative act, at which time an order was established for all time. Creation, then, assures the wise person that the universe is comprehensible, and thus encourages a search for its secrets. Furthermore, creation supplies the principle of order that holds together the cosmic, political, and social fabric of the universe. When this assumed order gives way, appeal to creation surfaces explicitly in wisdom literature, for by this means the sage hopes to persuade himself and others that wholeness is available even when chaos reigns. But the difficulty of attaining the wholeness that has been postulated converts creation faith, once a comforting affirmation, into cause for anxiety and dismay. The final breakthrough comes when Sirach moves away from a rational defense of divine justice to a mighty crescendo of praise of the creator who has made all things in pairs, that is, good and evil. By this tour de force even the forces of chaos are *enlisted in the divine service,* so that both the original creative act and *creatio continua* bear witness to the justice of God.

Such an understanding of the function of creation theology in wisdom literature tends to confirm von Rad's thesis that creation plays a secondary role, although not in the sense in which he saw things. Whereas he thinks of creation as subservient to saving history, I believe creation belongs under the rubric of justice. The function of creation theology, in my view, is to undergird the belief in divine justice. Consequently, I agree with Schmid that creation belongs to the fundamental question of human existence, namely the integrity of God.[123] It would follow that traditions about creation are at the heart of the theological enterprise, and not on the outer fringes. In a word, the question of divine justice cannot be separated from that of creation, both in the sense of an initial ordering and continual creation in the face of defiant chaos within man and external to him.

So far these remarks have been restricted to the function of creation theology in sapiential thought. The evidence seems to demand a reexamination of the question of creation's role in non-wisdom texts. In studying the use of *bara'* in the doxologies of Amos and in hymnic texts in Deutero-Isaiah, I came to the conclusion some time ago that this root occurs predominantly within contexts of judgment.[124] I wish to take up that observation once again and to repeat the identification of doxology of judgment in a context of creation thought. In light of the above findings in wisdom literature, my earlier insight into the nature of the doxology of judgment would seem to be confirmed. In those texts, at least, creation and theodicy are interwoven from start to finish. Perhaps there is reason, therefore, to reassess Johannes Hempel's observation that Eve's response to the serpent is a theodicy of universal proportions,[125] coming as it does on the heels of the Priestly and Yahwistic creation narratives. It may turn out that Schmid is, indeed, correct in his judgment that Israel's "views of order and creation are two aspects of one and the same complex problem."[126] If so, we have returned to the state of research when Johannes Fichtner wrote his epochmaking study of Israelite wisdom,[127] even if by way of a long detour along paths carved out for us by von Rad. It remains now for us to investigate the theological significance of the interrelatedness of creation and retribution to which Fichtner called our attention four decades ago.[128]

Retrospect and Prospect

This analysis of the present state of research in the area of wisdom literature calls attention to the successes and failures of scholars in the twentieth century. I have the impression that a history of the interpretation of various wisdom books prior to 1900 C.E. would reveal two basic trends: (1) the attempt to bring wisdom thought into line with the more traditional biblical texts, and (2) the viewing of each literary complex in terms of what was desirable in any given era. The former tendency has recently been discussed by S. Holm-Nielsen,[129] who demonstrates the taming process to which Qoheleth was submitted in various early translations (LXX, Syriac, Vulgate) and in the writings of early Christian interpreters. The second trend, that of viewing a text through the mirror of one's own age, is beautifully documented by Nahum Glatzer in regard to the biblical Job.[130] The neglect of wisdom during the heyday of "salvation history" is still another manifestation of this tendency to read the text in light of one's special interests.

As I bring this survey to a close I am conscious of the poverty of our knowledge in so many areas of wisdom research. I have hardly touched upon five topics that will occupy the attention of scholars in the area of wisdom for years to come: (1) wisdom and myth/cult, (2) wisdom and apocalyptic, (3) the role of nature in wisdom thought, (4) intentional arrangement of larger collections of proverbs, and (5) other forms (omens,[131] school questions). As in the study of creation, so also in wisdom research, we stand at the beginning. Hopefully we do not stand before the door of biblical writ without a key.

NOTES

[1] G. Ernest Wright, *God Who Acts,* 1952, 104.

[2] The German edition appeared in 1957. The section has the title "Israel vor Jahwe," with Die Antwort Israels in parentheses.

[3] R. E. Murphy, "The Interpretation of Old Testament Wisdom Literature," *Inter,* 23(1969), 290; R.B.Y. Scott, "The Study of the Wisdom Literature," *Inter,* 24(1970), 41; A. M. Dubarle, "Où en est l'étude de la littérature sapientielle?," *EThL,* 44(1968), 417 ("Hardly an apt title, for the wisdom writings, which have no reference to a covenant between Yahweh and his people, can scarcely be considered the response to a summons").

[4] *Theology of the Old Testament,* II, III, 1967, 80-117.

[5] *Lehre und Wirklichkeit in der alten Weisheit,* 1958, 2. Gese refers to the observation of Walter Baumgartner, *Israelitische und altorientalische Weisheit,* 4, 10, 24 and "The Wisdom Literature," *The Old Testament and Modern Study,* 1951, 211.

[6] *Lehre und Wirklichkeit in der alten Weisheit,* 2.

[7] "Erwägungen zum theologischen Ort alttestamentlicher Weisheits-literatur," *EvTh,* 30(1970), 393-417, especially 416.

[8] See Brevard Childs, *Biblical Theology in Crisis,* 1972.

[9] Bertil Albrektson, *History and the Gods,* 1967, demonstrated the prevalence of this idea of divine action in history throughout the ancient Near East, thus undercutting the claim of uniqueness.

[10] Walter Brueggemann, *In Man We Trust,* 1972, indicates the theological timeliness of wisdom for the contemporary believer, although his account is admittedly onesided.

[11] "The Interpretation of Old Testament Wisdom Literature," 290.

[12] The Instruction of Amen-em-opet. Of the thirty sections in this Egyptian text, ten or eleven have more or less exact parallels in Pr. 22:17-24:22.

[13] *Die Weisheit Israels in Spruch, Sage und Dichtung.* Meinhold's discussion of wisdom is remarkably modern in some ways. His formal analysis of the literary types (fable, parable, allegory, proverb, or sentence) and the development of the literature from original two-lined sayings to series and larger units differs little from the latest studies in this area (von Rad, for example). Likewise his understanding of the date of the collections in Proverbs, Qoheleth, and Job is remarkably similar to most of the works since that time. Even the numerical values of the names Solomon and Hezekiah as 375 and 136(7) were thought to rest behind the number of proverbs in the two

major collections ascribed to Solomon and the Men of Hezekiah. But the modernity of Meinhold's book is not limited to literary analysis. On the contrary, Meinhold believed that wisdom extended beyond the four major wisdom writings to include Gen. 18 and related texts. Indeed, he defined wisdom so broadly that much of the book is devoted to a study of Israelite popular (folk) religion. Wisdom, he thought, takes for granted the prophetic adaptation of folk religion and divination. Meinhold also recognized the importance of Nature. He writes: "Yes, indeed, nature is a book that is rich in wisdom and instruction" (45). The international character of wisdom, too, was clear to Meinhold even at this time. He writes: "The walls of the Jewish church were not sufficiently high or strong to keep out the invasion of oriental and Greek wisdom." There is, however, one jarring note. Throughout the book Meinhold carries on a sharp polemic against Jewish egoism or self love, which he regarded as a theology that arose in the head rather than in the heart, and the individualism that rules out sonship in favor of servanthood.

[14] *Old Testament Theology,* I, 418, 428.

[15] "Method in Determining Wisdom Influence upon 'Historical' Literature," *JBL,* 88(1969), 130, 132. Ernst Würthwein, "Die Weisheit Ägyptens und das Alte Testament," in *Mitteilungen des Universitätsbundes Marburg* (1959), 69, describes wisdom literature similarly. He writes that these books are not only witnesses to an interesting cultural history, but constitute a theological debate over the deepest question of human existence, that of the understanding of God and man, the world and life. Von Rad's observation that "There is no knowledge which does not, before long, throw the one who seeks the knowledge back upon the question of his self-knowledge and his self-understanding" (*Wisdom in Israel,* 67) suggests that we are not as far apart as it appears at first glance. Compare also his additional comment, "In wisdom, however, man was *in search of himself* and took things into his own hands without being able to appeal to a specific, divine commission" (309, italics mine).

[16] "Bible, sagesse, science," *RSR,* 48(1960), 42-43.

[17] "Sagesse babylonienne et sagesse israélite," *Sciences Ecclesiastiques,* 14(1962), 309.

[18] *The Nature and Authority of Old Testament Wisdom Family Ethics: with Special Reference to Proverbs and Sirach,* unpublished diss., University of Melbourne, 1974.

[19] *The Intellectual Tradition in the Old Testament* (*BZAW,* 135), 1974. He thus takes seriously the objections of W. L. Lambert, *Babylonian Wisdom Literature,* 1960, 1 and H. Brunner, "Die Weisheitsliteratur," *HO,* 1 (1952), 90-110. Lambert calls the term a misnomer in Babylonian literature, while Brunner attempts to avoid the word "Weisheit" altogether.

[20] Notably Henri Frankfort, *Ancient Egyptian Religion,* 1948 and Hellmut Brunner, "Die Weisheitsliteratur," 90-110 for Egypt, and W. L. Lambert, *Babylonian Wisdom Literature,* 1, for Mesopotamia.

21 *Wesen und Geschichte der Weisheit* (*BZAW*, 101), 1966. Schmid demonstrated that there was a three-act drama in the wisdom of Egypt, Mesopotamia, and Israel: (1) the formulation of a composition, clothed in a historical garment of a specific time and place, (2) the dogmatic, static solidification, and (3) the testing of maxims and the selection of the ones that accord with personal experience.

22 Roland Murphy, "The Interpretation of Old Testament Wisdom Literature," 292 opts for theological anthropology, while John F. Priest, "Humanism, Skepticism, and Pessimism in Israel," *JAAR*, 36(1968), 311-326 prefers "sociology" (315).

23 The list of names is impressive, among whom are Paul Volz, Artur Weiser, Claus Westermann, Paul Humbert, and Heinz Richter.

24 As seen most clearly by C. Westermann, *Der Aufbau des Buches Hiob*, (*BhTh*, 23), 1956 and H. Gese, *Lehre und Wirklichkeit in der alten Weisheit*, 63-78.

25 For bibliography, see Scott, "The Study of Wisdom Literature," *Inter*, 24(1970), 23, n. 3, and Baumgartner, "Die israelitische Weisheitsliteratur," *ThR*, 5(1933), 259-261.

26 Walther Zimmerli, "Zur Struktur der alttestamentlichen Weisheit," *ZAW*, 51(1933), 177-204.

27 See Baumgartner, "Die israelitische Weisheitsliteratur," 270-279.

28 Gressmann, *Israels Spruchweisheit im Zusammenhang der Weltliteratur;* Baumgartner, "Die israelitische Weisheitsliteratur," 259-288 and "The Wisdom Literature," 210-237; Scott, "The Study of the Wisdom Literature," 20-45. See also the surveys of H. H. Schmid, "Hauptprobleme der altorientalischen und alttestamentlichen Weisheitsliteratur," *STU*, 35(1965), 68-74; Dubarle, "Où en est l'étude de la littérature sapientielle?" *EThL*, 44(1968), 407-419; R. E. Murphy, "Assumptions and Problems in Old Testament Wisdom Research," *CBQ*, 29(1967), 101-112; James L. Crenshaw, "Wisdom," in *Old Testament Form Criticism*, edited by John H. Hayes (*TUMSR*, 2) 1974, 225-264. R. B. Y. Scott gives another barometer by which to test the progress of scholarship in the area of wisdom, namely, the prominence of the term in periodic assessments of the state of Old Testament studies ("The Study of the Wisdom Literature," 24-25). The fact that H. J. Hermisson has been asked to write a new history of research in wisdom literature for *Theologische Rundschau* bears testimony to the progress that has occurred in this area.

29 "Edomitic Wisdom," *ZAW*, 44(1926), 13-25; Wisdom and Vision in the Old Testament," *ZAW*, 52(1943), 93-102.

30 "Ägyptische Parallelen zum AT," *ZDMG*, 63(1909), 531-539. We now know about a dozen Egyptian works belonging to the category of wisdom literature. Among the better known Instructions are: Ptahhotep, (for) Meri-ka-re, Amen-em-het, Hor-dedef, Ani, Amen-em-opet, and 'Onchsheshonqy. Only a few characteristic emphases of these instructions may be noted here. Ptah-hotep has a marvelous description of old age (cf. Qoh. 12:1ff.), a

warning against women, and an emphasis upon good speech. The Instruction for Meri-ka-re praises the upright of character over the sacrifice of an evil-doer, and encourages silence as a goal of the wise man. Ani emphasizes silence, and warns against women. Similarly Amen-om-opet stresses the silent one, enjoins care for the widow, and condemns the carrying off of landmarks. 'Onchsheshonqy indicates how deeply religious this literature becomes toward the end of the empire. Two texts express the despair created by social turmoil: A Dispute over Suicide and The Protests of the Eloquent Peasant. Still other texts set forth the superiority of the scribal profession to all others (In Praise of Learned Scribes; Satire on the Trades) or describe scribal characteristics (Divine Attributes of the Pharaoh).

[31] *Recherches sur les sources égyptiennes de la littérature sapientiale d'Israël*, 1929. Few today would endorse either the approach or the conclusions that Humbert drew, for they claim far too much and often fall into the area of universal human concerns. Still Humbert's work on the relationship between Amen-em-opet and the biblical Proverbs is decisive, in my estimation. In a concluding summary, Humbert writes that Egyptian influence can be' found in the following: the certain borrowing from Amen-em-opet; literary forms (the fiction of royal authorship; collections of maxims; a more or less philosophical dialogue with occasional narrative; the satire of trades and a panegyric of the sage; the description of the misery of old age); rhetoric and style (familial language with the address of a father to his son; parallelism in the gnomic genre; frequent use of imperatives; synonymous, antithetic and synthetic stichs; the role of comparison, etc.); expressions; images and conceptions (e.g., the heart being weighed in scales; the negative confession); pedagogical and moral ideas and principles of conduct (184).

[32] Etienne Drioton, "Sur le sagesse d'Aménémopé," *Mélanges bibliques rédigés en l'honneur de André Robert*, ed. Henri Cazelles, 1957, 254-280 and "Le livre des Proverbs et la sagesse d'Aménémopé," *Sacra Pagina*, I, 1959, 229-241; R. J. Williams, "The Alleged Semitic Original of the Wisdom of Amenemope," *JEA*, 47(1961), 100-106; B. Couroyer, "L'origine égyptienne de la sagesse d'Aménémopé," *RB*, 44(1963), 208-224.

[33] H. Brunner, "Gerechtigkeit als Fundament des Thrones," *VT*, 8(1958), 426-428.

[34] Baumgartner, "Die israelitische Weisheitsliteratur," 266.

[35] In addition to Humbert's epoch-making study, see Christa Bauer-Kayatz, *Einführung in die alttestamentliche Weisheit* (*BS*, 55), 1969 and *Studien zu Proverbien 1-9* (*WMANT*, 22), 1966; Schmid, *Wesen und Geschichte der Weisheit*.

[36] William McKane, *Proverbs* (*OTL*), 1970 has emphasized the importance of Egyptian Instructions for an understanding of Israelite proverbs. It is noteworthy that the Instruction of Ptah-hotep and the Instructions for King Meri-ka-re were intended for grown men upon whom the burden of counsel or rule had either fallen or was about to do so. This is in sharp contrast to

the usual assumption that Israelite wisdom was intended for adolescents facing sexual temptation and needing to learn how to cope with life.

[37]Erhard Gerstenberger, *Wesen und Herkunft des 'apodiktischen Rechts'* (*WMANT*, 20) 1965.

[38] For a discussion of this emphasis upon the hot tempered man and the silent one, see my essay "Method in Determining Wisdom Influence upon 'Historical' Literature," 133-134.

[39] *Qohelet und der alte Orient*, 1964.

[40] Gerhard von Rad, *Wisdom in Israel*, 1972, 17. The role of the wise courtier in ancient Israel has recently been studied by Walter Lee Humphreys (*The Motif of the Wise Courtier in the Old Testament*, unpublished diss., Union Theological Seminary, New York, 1970). Humphreys bases most of his analysis on analogy with Egyptian courtiers, and to some extent Sumerian and Babylonian. In the end he has to admit that "If material designed solely and exclusively for the courtier existed in Israel, it has not survived" (166).

[41] Henri Cazelles, "Les débuts de la sagesse en Israel," *SPOA*, 1963, 27-39.

[42] Jean Nougayrol, "Les sagesses babyloniennes: études récentes et textes inédits," *SPOA*, 47-50.

[43] R. Braun, *Kohelet und die frühhellenistische Popularphilosophie* (*BZAW*, 130), 1973 may reopen the whole question of Greek influence.

[44] *Weisheit im Wandel* (*BBB*, 37), 1971.

[45] Patrick W. Skehan, *Studies in Israelite Poetry and Wisdom* (*CBQMS*, 1), 1971, 172-236; James M. Reese, *Hellenistic Influence on the Book of Wisdom and its Consequences* (*AnB*, 41), 1970.

[46] *The Intellectual Tradition in the Old Testament*, 1974.

[47] "Jesaja unter den Weisen," *ThLZ*, 74(1949), 75-80; Whedbee, *Isaiah and Wisdom*, 1971, and Jensen, *The Use of tôrâ by Isaiah* (*CBQMS*, 3), 1973.

[48] Terrien, "Amos and Wisdom," *Israel's Prophetic Heritage*, edited by B. W. Anderson and Walter Harrelson, 1962, 108-115; Wolff, *Amos' geistige Heimat*, 1964 (*Amos the Prophet*, 1973).

[49] Crenshaw, "The Influence of the Wise upon Amos," *ZAW*, 79(1967), 42-52; "Amos and the Theophanic Tradition," *ZAW*, 80(1968), 203-215.

[50] Von Rad, "The Joseph Narrative and Ancient Wisdom," *The Problem of the Hexateuch and Other Essays*, 1966, 292-300, originally published in *SVT*, 1(1953); Whybray, *The Succession Narrative* (*SBTh*, 2nd ser., 9), 1968.

[51] Crenshaw, "Method in Determining Wisdom Influence upon 'Historical' Literature," 135-137.

[52] *The Intellectual Tradition in the Old Testament*, 89-91. Whybray suggests that my attack against his views is blunted by the fact that he has never said that wisdom was the exclusive background of the Succession Narrative. I find it difficult to understand in any other way the remark that the Succession Narrative was written by a teacher of the wisdom tradition (*The Succession Narrative*, 95).

[53] "Weisheit und Geschichte," *Probleme biblischer Theologie,* edited by H. W. Wolff, 1971, 136-154.

[54] J. L. McKenzie, "Reflections on Wisdom," *JBL,* 86(1967), 1-9; L. Alonso-Schökel, "Motivos sapienciales y de alianza en Gen 2-3," *Bib,* 43(1962), 295-316 (= "Sapiential and Covenant Themes in Genesis 2-3," in *Modern Biblical Studies: An Anthology from Theology Digest,* edited by D. J. McCarthy and W. B. Callen, 1967, 49-61).

[55] "The Origin of Humanism in Deuteronomy," *JBL,* 80(1961), 241-247; "Deuteronomy—The Present State of Inquiry," *JBL,* 86(1967), 249-262.

[56] " 'Wisdom' in the Book of Esther," *VT,* 13(1963), 419-455.

[57] *Old Testament Theology,* II, 1965, 301-315; *Wisdom in Israel,* 263-283. See also John G. Gammie, "Spatial and Ethical Dualism in Jewish Wisdom and Apocalyptic Literature," *JBL,* 93(1974), 356-385.

[58] "Magisch-Mantische Weisheit und die Gestalt Daniels," *UF,* 1(1969), 79-94.

[59] Von Rad's excursus on "Wisdom and Cult" did little more than whet the appetite of those who are interested in the subject (*Wisdom in Israel,* 186-189). One of my students, Leo G. Perdue, is currently completing a Ph.D. dissertation on the role of the cult in wisdom literature.

[60] For bibliography, see Crenshaw, "Method in Determining Wisdom Influence upon 'Historical' Literature," 129, n. 1 and Whybray, *The Intellectual Tradition in the Old Testament,* 1-2, n. 1.

[61] Crenshaw, "Wisdom," 226-264 (especially 229-262); von Rad, *Wisdom in Israel,* 24-50; Baumgartner, "Die literarischen Gattungen in der Weisheit des Jesus Sirach," *ZAW,* 34(1914), 161-198.

[62] W. McKane, *Proverbs,* 1970, 117-150 (particularly 122).

[63] *Der Maschal im Alten Testament* (*BZAW,* 24), 1913.

[64] *Studien zur israelitischen Spruchweisheit* (*WMANT,* 28), 1968.

[65] "Wise and Foolish, Righteous and Wicked," *VTS,* 23(1972), 146-165.

[66] *Die althebräische Literatur und ihr hellenistisch-jüdisches Nachleben,* (*HLW*), 1930, 44-56.

[67] W. Zimmerli, "Das Buch Kohelet—Traktat oder Sentenzensammlung?," *VT,* 24(1974), 221-230.

[68] *Die Geschichte der Synoptische Tradition* (*FRLANT,* 12), 1957, 73-74. H. H. Schmid takes over this distinction between constitutive and ornamental motifs (*Wesen und Geschichte der Weisheit,* 53-54) while H. J. Hermisson questions its value (*Studien zur israelitischen Spruchweisheit,* 139).

[69] *Proverbs.*

[70] Crenshaw, "Wisdom," 229-262.

[71] *Wesen und Herkunft des 'apodiktischen Rechts'.*

[72] *Recht und Ethos* (*StANT,* 15), 1966.

[73] *Studien zur israelitischen Spruchweisheit,* 113-136.

[74] *The Intellectual Tradition in the Old Testament,* 33-43. Even the evidence for schools in Egypt and in Mesopotamia is far from clear; see the

discussion· by Jacobsen, Landsberger, Wilson, Albright, Oppenheim, Speiser, Grene, Kramer, Parker, Seele, Hoselitz, Gelb, and Güterbock in *City Invincible: A Symposium on Urbanization and Cultural Development in the Ancient Near East* edited by Carl H. Kraeling and Robert M. Adams, 1960, 94-122. The connection between wisdom and schools has been affirmed by H. J. Hermisson: "Israelite wisdom has its center, its origin, and its places of cultivation in the Israelite school" (*Studien zur israelitischen Spruchweisheit,* 192) and by J. J. Van Dijk: "It is . . . highly likely that the school, if it did not actually create wisdom literature, held it in high esteem" (*La sagesse suméro-accadienne,* 1953, 23).

[75] *The Problem of the Hexateuch and Other Essays,* 69-74, 202-204.

[76] *In Man We Trust,* 29-47.

[77] Still another reading of the incidents is possible, and in my opinion more likely. Thus I see the first incident as David's cunning to save his skin. The second clearly implies that David cringed in fear for seven days, while the pouring out of the precious water was a shrewd move to bind himself more closely to his comrades. The so-called blank check in II Sam. 7 expresses the vested interests of a priestly group. Finally, David's freedom derives from the power of chieftainship and royalty, not from a knowledge that he is trusted by God.

[78] "David and His Theologian," *CBQ,* 30(1968), 156-181.

[79] "Die Weisheit Salamos," *ThLZ,* 76(1951), 139-144. Much has been made of the lists as an ordering of reality. This function is considered doubtful by A. Leo Oppenheim, *Ancient Mesopotamia,* 1964, 248.

[80] *Die Krise der Aufklärung in Israel,* 1952. My colleague, Lou H. Silberman, has pointed out to me the heavy freight borne by the word "Aufklärung." He questions the wisdom of using such a philosophical term to describe the ancient Israelite scene.

[81] *The Problem of the Hexateuch and Other Essays,* 293-294.

[82] K. Sethe, " 'Der Mensch denkt, Gott lenkt' bei den alten Aegyptern," *Nachrichten der Gesellschaft der Wissenschaft,* Göttingen, 1925, 141ff.

[83] *The Problem of the Hexateuch and Other Essays,* 299.

[84] Crenshaw, "Method in Determining Wisdom Influence upon 'Historical' Literature," 135-137.

[85] "The Joseph Story and Ancient Wisdom: A Reappraisal," *CBQ,* 35(1973), 285-297.

[86] *Ibid.,* 289.

[87] "Solomon and the Beginning of Wisdom in Israel," *VTS,* 3(1960), 262-279.

[88] "La Sagesse et la propagande juive à l'époque perse et hellénistique," *Werden und Wesen des Alten Testament, BZAW,* 66(1936), 148-154.

[89] For an analysis of this narrative, see my essay in *ZAW,* 86, (1974), 470-504 entitled "The Samson Saga: Filial Devotion or Erotic Attachment?"

[90] D. B. Redford, *A Study of the Biblical Story of Joseph (Genesis 37-50), VTS,* 20, 1970.

91 "Weisheit und Geschichte," 126-127; von Rad, *Wisdom in Israel*, 294-295; see also John L. McKenzie, "Primitive History: Form Criticism," *SBL Seminar Papers*, 1(1974), 87-99.

92 On class ethic, see Brian Kovacs, "Is There a Class-Ethic in Proverbs?," *Essays in Old Testament Ethics*, edited by James L. Crenshaw and John T. Willis, 1974, 171-189, and Hermisson, *Studien zur israelitischen Spruchweisheit*, 94-96.

93 Kovacs, "Is There a Class-Ethic in Proverbs?," 176. I am indebted to my student, Brian Kovacs, for the following discussion.

94 Robert Gordis, "The Social Background of Wisdom Literature, *HUCA*, 18(1943/44), 77-118.

95 Ephriam E. Urbach, "Class-Status and Leadership in the World of the Palestinian Sages," *Proceedings of The Israel Academy of Sciences and Humanities*, II (1966), 1-37.

96 Kovacs, 'Is There a Class-Ethic in Proverbs?," 178.

97 Georg Fohrer, "The Righteous Man in Job 31," *Essays in Old Testament Ethics*, 1-22.

98 "Is There a Class-Ethic in Proverbs?," 186.

99 "Zur Struktur der alttestamentlichen Weisheit." Zimmerli's understanding of wisdom as anthropocentric has been challenged by Hermisson and Schmid. The former writes that man is not the measure of all things, but is measured against the world in which he is placed (*Studien zur israelitischen Spruchweisheit*, 150-151). Schmid, on the other hand, claims that the center is not man but cosmic order, not anthropology but cosmology (*Wesen und Geschichte der Weisheit*, 197).

100 Crenshaw, *Prophetic Conflict (BZAW*, 125), 1971, 116-123 (Excursus B: "'eṣa and *dabar:* The Problem of Authority/Certitude in Wisdom and Prophetic Literature").

101 Most notably Schmid, *Wesen und Geschichte der Weisheit*, and *Gerechtigkeit als Weltordnung;* C. Bauer-Kayatz, *Einführung in die alttestamentliche Weisheit.*

102 *Revelation in Jewish Wisdom Literature*, 1946.

103 Murphy has observed that, if Gerstenberger and Audet are right about the intimate original connection between law and wisdom, Sirach's insight in associating the two was more brilliant than he realized ("The Hebrew Sage and Openness to the World," *Christian Action and Openness to the World*, 1970, 227).

104 *Wisdom in Proverbs, (SBTh*, 45), 1965, 104.

105 Murphy, "The Hebrew Sage and Openness to the World," 231.

106 "Ort und Grenze der Weisheit im Rahmen der alttestamentlichen Theologie," *SPOA*, 1963, 123 ("Die Weisheit des Alten Testaments hält sich ganz entschlossen im Horizonte der Schöpfung. Ihre Theologie ist Schöpfungstheologie"). See "The Place and Limit of the Wisdom in the Framework of the Old Testament Theology," 148.

[107] *Die altorientalische Weisheit in ihrer israelitisch-jüdischen Ausprägung* (*BZAW*, 62), 1933, 111. The two links mentioned are the absolute power of God and the idea of order. Fichtner discusses these under the rubrics of creation and retribution. Hans Heinrich Schmid, "Schöpfung, Gerechtigkeit und Heil: Schöpfungstheologie als Gesamthorizont biblischer Theologie," *ZThK*, 70(1973), 16 writes: "The fundamental theme of ancient Near Eastern views of creation was the question of a saving world, that is, of the existing understanding of a comprehensive righteousness." Schmid states further that "Views of order and of creation are two aspects of one and the same complex problem" (18). On this subject see H. P. Müller, "Wie Sprach Qohälät von Gott?," *VT*, 18(1968), 512-516.

[108] *Schöpfung und Chaos in Urzeit und Endzeit*, 1895; see now B. W. Anderson, *Creation Versus Chaos*, 1967.

[109] " 'Creation' Motifs in Ancient Hebrew Poetry," *CBQ*, 29(1967), 88-91. See also Claus Westermann, "Neuere Arbeiten zur Schöpfung," *VuF*, 14 (1969), 11-28 (especially 13). Westermann also notes that high cultures have three basic forms of traditions dealing with creation: "the narrative (myth), the praise of the gods (hymn), and wisdom" (17). He delineates four types: creation through the birth of gods, through battle, through a shaping or forming, and through the word (17).

[110] "The Theological Problem of the Old Testament Doctrine of Creation, *The Problem of the Hexateuch and Other Essays*, 131-143.

[111] "Schöpfung, Gerechtigkeit und Heil: Schöpfungstheologie als Gesamthorizont biblischer Theologie," 1-19.

[112] "The Traditions of the Establishing of the Earth in Deutero-Isaiah," *JBL*, 92(1973), 345-357.

[113] *Der Prediger* (*KAT*, 17), 1963, 229.

[114] Crenshaw, "The Problem of Theodicy in Sirach," *JBL*, 94(1975), 47-64.

[115] Idem, "The Eternal Gospel (Eccl. 3:11)," *Essays in Old Testament Ethics*, 23-55.

[116] On Qoheleth's use of the broken sentence, see H. P. Müller, "Wie Sprach Qohälät von Gott?," 507-521.

[117] See Hertzberg, *Die Prediger*, 152, for this reference, which I have not been able to verify on page 74 of Ranston's book.

[118] *Koheleth—The Man and His World*, 1951 (1968), 274-275.

[119] On these verses see Georg Sauer, *Die Sprüche Agurs*, 1963.

[120] "Wisdom Myth and Mytho-logy, an Essay in Understanding a Theological Tradition," *Inter*, 24(1970), 49-60.

[121] M. Sekine, "Schöpfung und Erlösung im Buche Hiob," *BZAW*, 77(1958), 220. According to Sekine, the second divine speech brings Job back into the realm of creation along with the original animals and accomplishes his new creation (221-222). Sekine thinks the central place of creation in Job is new to the Old Testament (222). For a similar understanding of

Job, see Norman C. Habel, "Appeal to Ancient Tradition as a Literary Form," *SBL Seminar Papers*, I, 1973, 46.

[122] For a detailed discussion, see my article entitled "The Problem of Theodicy in Sirach."

[123] Schmid, "Schöpfung, Gerechtigkeit und Heil: Schöpfungstheologie als Gesamthorizont biblischer Theologie," writes that creation is the framework within which historical views move (8), that the dominant background of all Old Testament thinking and faith is the idea of the comprehensive world order and with it creation faith in the wider sense of the word (11), and that creation faith is not a peripheral one in biblical theology, but in essence is its theme (15).

[124] Crenshaw, "*YHWH Šᵉba'ôt Šᵉmô:* A Form-Critical Analysis," *ZAW*, 81 (1969), 169-170. See my *Hymnic Affirmation of Divine Justice*, 1975.

[125] Cited in von Rad, *Genesis (OTL)*, 1961, 97.

[126] "Schöpfung, Gerechtigkeit und Heil: Schöpfungstheologie als Gesamthorizont biblischer Theologie," 18.

[127] *Die altorientalische Weisheit in ihrer israelitisch-jüdischen Ausprägung.*

[128] In this endeavor to comprehend the function of creation in wisdom literature one quickly sees the truth of Westermann's observation that "In the investigation of speech about the creator and creation we still stand entirely at the beginning" ("Neuere Arbeiten zur Schöpfung," 13). Similarly Martin Buber has written: "The biblical story of creation is a legitimate stammering account. . . . But this stammering of his was the only means of doing justice to the task of stating the mystery of how time springs from eternity, and world comes from that which is not world" (*On the Bible*, 1968, 11).

[129] "On the Interpretation of Qoheleth in early Christianity," *VT*, 24 (1974), 168-177.

[130] "The Book of Job and Its Interpreters," *Biblical Motifs*, edited by A. Altmann, 1966, 197-220.

[131] G. E. Bryce, "Omen-wisdom in Ancient Israel" *JBL*, 94(1975), 19-37, has taken an initial step toward understanding omen-wisdom in Israel.

SELECTED BIBLIOGRAPHY

Albright, W. F. "Some Canaanite-Phoenecian Sources of Hebrew Wisdom," *VTS*, 3 (1960), 1-15.

Alonso-Schökel, L. "Sapiential and Covenant Themes in Genesis 2-3," *Modern Biblical Studies: An Anthology from Theology Digest*, ed. D. J. McCarthy & W. B. Callen, Milwaukee, 1967, 49-61, [originally in *Bib.*, 43 (1962), 295-316.].

Alt, A. "Die Weisheit Salomos," ThLZ, 76 (1951), 139-144.

————. "Zur literarischen Analyse der Weisheit des Amenemope," *VTS*, 3 (1960), 16-25.

Anthes, R. *Lebensregeln und Lebensweisheit der alten Ägypter*, AO, 32.2 Leipzig, 1933.

Audet, J. P. "Origines comparées de la double tradition de la loi et de la sagesse dans le Proché-Orient ancien," *Acten Internationalen Orientalisten-kongresses*, 1, Moscow, 1962, 352-357.

Barton, G. A. *The Book of Ecclesiastes*, *ICC*, Edinburgh, 1908.

Barucq, A. *Le livre des Proverbes*, *SB*, Paris, 1964.

————. *Ecclésiaste*, *VS*, 3, Paris, 1968.

Bauckmann, E. G. "Die Proverbien und die Sprüche des Jesus Sirach," *ZAW*, 72 (1960), 33-63.

Bauer-Kayatz, C. *Einführung in die alttestamentliche Weisheit*, BS, 55, 1969,

————. *Studien zu Proverbien 1-9*, *WMANT*, 22, 1966.

Baumgartner, W. "Die israelitische Weisheitsliteratur," *ThR*, 5 (1933), 259-288.

————. "Die literarischen Gattungen in der Weisheit des Jesus Sirach," *ZAW*, 34 (1914), 161-198.

————. *Israelitische und altorientalische Weisheit*, SGV, 166, 1933.

————. "The Wisdom Literature," in *The Old Testament and Modern Study*, ed. H. H. Rowley, Oxford, 1951, 210-237.

Beauchamp, E. *Les sages d'Israel, ou le fruit d'une fidélité*, Québec, 1968.

Bic, M. "Le juste et l'impie dans le livre de Job," *VTS*, 15 (1965), 33-43.

Bissing, F. W. *Altägyptische Lebensweisheit*, Zurich, 1955.

Blank, S. H. "Wisdom," *IDB*, IV, 852-861.

Blieffert, H. J. *Weltanschauung und Gottesglaube im Buch Kohelet. Darstellung und Kritik*, Rostock, 1938.

Boer, P. A. H. de. "The Counsellor," *VTS*, 3 (1960), 42-71.

Boström, G. *Proverbiastudien. Die Weisheit und das fremde Weib in Spr. 1-9, LUA*, 30, 3, Lund, 1935.

Braun, R. *Kohelet und die frühhellenistiche Popularphilosophie, BZAW*, 130, 1973.

Brueggemann, W. *In Man We Trust*, Richmond, 1972.

――――. "Scripture and an Ecumenical Life-Style," *Inter*, 24 (1970), 3-19.

Brunner, H. *Altägyptische Erziehung*, Wiesbaden, 1957.

――――. "Der frei Wille Gottes in der ägyptischen Weisheit," *Les sagesses du Proché-Orient ancien-SPOA*, 1963, 103-120.

――――. "Die Lehre des Cheti, Sohnes des Duauf," *Äg-Forschungen*, H 13, Glückstadt und Hamburg, 1944.

――――. "Die Weisheitsliteratur," *HO*, 1, 2, Leiden, 1952, 90-110.

Bryce, G. E. " 'Better' Proverbs: An Historical and Structural Study," *SBL Seminar Papers*, 1972, 343-354.

――――. "Omen-Wisdom in Ancient Israel," paper read at the annual meeting of the SBL, Oct. 25, 1974, in *JBL* 94(1975), 19-37.

Buck, A. de. "Het religieus Karakter der oudste egyptische Wysheid," *NTT*, 31 (1932), 322-349.

Bückers, H. *Die unsterblichkeitslehre des Weisheitsbuches: Ihr Ursprung und ihre Bedeutung, AA*, 13, Münster, 1938.

Carmichael, C. M. "Deuteronomic Laws, Wisdom, and Historical Traditions," *JSS*, 12 (1967), 198-206.

Carstensen, R. N. *Job, Defense of Honor*, Nashville, 1963.

Causse, A. "La sagesse et la propagande juive à l'époque perse et hellénistique," *Werden und Wesen des Alten Testament, BZAW*, 66 (1936), 148-154.

――――. "Sagesse égyptienne et sagesse juive," *RHPR*, 9 (1929), 149-169.

Cazelles, H. "A propos d'une phrase de H. H. Rowley," *VTS*, 3 (1960), 26-32.

――――. "Les débuts de la sagesse en Israël," *SPOA*, 1963, 27-39.

Clarke, E. G. *The Wisdom of Solomon*, Cambridge, 1973.

Coats, G. W. "The Joseph Story and Ancient Wisdom: A Reappraisal," *CBQ*, 35 (1973), 285-297.

Conrad, J. "Die innere Gliederung der Proverbien," *ZAW*, 79 (1967), 67-76.

Cook, A. *The Root of the Thing. A Study of Job and the Song of Songs*, Bloomington, 1968.

Coppens, J. "Le messianisme sapiential et les origines litteraires du fils de l'homme danielique," *VTS*, 3 (1960), 33-41.

Coughenour, R. A. *Enoch and Wisdom*, unpublished diss. Case Western Reserve, 1972.

Couturier, G. P. "Sagesse babylonienne et sagesse israélite," *ScE*, 14 (1962), 293-309.

Crenshaw, J. L. "The Eternal Gospel (Eccles. 3:11)," in J. L. Crenshaw and J. T. Willis, eds. *Essays in Old Testament Ethics*, New York, 1974, 23-55.

———. "*eṣā* and *dabar*: The Problem of Authority/Certitude in Wisdom and Prophetic Literature" in *Prophetic Conflict, BZAW*, 124, Berlin, 1971, 116-123.

———. "The Influence of the Wise upon Amos," *ZAW*, 79 (1967), 42-52.

———. "Method in Determining Wisdom Influence upon 'Historical' Literature," *JBL*, 88 (1969), 129-142.

———. "Popular Questioning of the Justice of God in Ancient Israel," *ZAW*, 82 (1970), 380-395.

———. "Wisdom," in J. H. Hayes, ed. *Old Testament Form Criticism, TUMSR*, 2 (1974), 225-264.

Dahood, M. *Proverbs and Northwest Semitic Philology*, Rome, 1963.

———. "Canaanite-Phoenician Influence in Qoheleth," *Bib*, 33 (1952), 30-52, 191-221.

———. "Some Northwest-Semitic Words in Job," *Bib*, 38 (1957), 306-320.

Damon, S. F. *Blake's Job*, New York, 1969.

Daumas, J. "La naissance de l'humanisme dans la littérature de l'Égypte ancienne," *Oriens Antiquus*, 1 (1962), 155-184.

Davidson, A. B. *The Book of Job*, CBSC, Cambridge, 1951.

Delitzsch, F. *Proverbs of Solomon*, Edinburgh, 1875.

Dhorme, E. *Job*, London, 1967.

Dijk, J. J. A. van. *La sagesse suméro-accadienne. Recherches sur les genres littéraires des textes sapientiaux*, Leiden, 1953.

Di Lella, A. *The Hebrew Text of Sirach*, London, 1966.

Dillmann, A. *Hiob, KHAT*, Leipzig, 1891.

Donàld, T. "The Semantic Field of 'Folly' in Proverbs, Job, Psalms, and Ecclesiastes," *VT* 13 (1963), 285-292.

———. "The Semantic Field of Rich and Poor in the Wisdom Literature of Hebrew and Accadian," *Oriens Antiquus*, 3 (1964), 27-41.

Donner, H. "Die religionsgeschichtlichen Ursprünge von Prov. Sal. 8," *ZÄSpr*, 82 (1957), 8-18.

Driver, G. R. "Problems and Solutions," *VT*, 4 (1954), 225-245.

———, and Gray, G. B. *The Book of Job, ICC*, Edinburgh, 1921.

Drubbel, A. "Le conflit entre la sagesse profane et la sagesse religieuse. Contribution à l'étude des origines de la littérature sapientiale en Israël," *Bib*, 17 (1936), 45-70, 407-426.

Dubarle, A. M. "Où en est l'étude de la littérature sapientielle?," *EThL*, 44 (1968), 407-419.

———. *Les sages d'Israel, LD*, Paris, 1946.

Duesberg, H. et Fransen, I. *Les scribes inspirés*, Belgium, 1966.

Dürr, L. *Das Erziehungswesen im Alten Testament und in antiken Orient, MVÄG*, 36, 2, Leipzig, 1932.

Eissfeldt, O. *Der Maschal im Alten Testament, BZAW,* 24, Giessen, 1913.

Ellermeier, F. *Qohelet,* Herzberg am Harz, 1967.

Engnell, I. " 'Knowledge' and 'Life' in the Creation Story," *VTS,* 3 (1960), 103-119.

Erman, A. *Die Literatur der alten Ägypter,* Leipzig, 1923– *The Ancient Egyptians,* New York, 1966.

———. "Das Weisheitsbuch des Amen-em-ope," *OLZ,* 27 (1924), 241-252.

Feinberg, C. L. "The Poetic Structure of the Book of Job and the Ugaritic Literature," *BS,* 103 (1946), 283-293.

Fensham, F. C. "Widow, Orphan, and the Poor in Ancient Near Eastern Legal and Wisdom Literature," JNES, 21 (1962), 129-139.

Fichtner, J. *Die altorientalische Weisheit in ihrer israelitisch-jüdischen Ausprägung, BZAW,* 62, 1933.

———. *Gottes Weisheit,* Stuttgart, 1965.

———. "Jesaja unter den Weisen," *ThLZ,* 74 (1949), 75-80.

———. "Die Stellung der Sapientia Salomonis in der Literatur und Geistesgeschichte ihrer Zeit," *ZNW,* 36 (1937), 113-132.

———. *Weisheit Salomos, HAT,* 6, Tübingen, 1938.

Fohrer, G. *Das Buch Hiob, KAT,* 16, Gütersloh, 1963.

———. "The Righteous Man in Job 31," in *Essays in Old Testament Ethics,* 1-21.

———. *Studien zum Buche Hiob,* Gütersloh, 1963.

———. "Sophia ktl. B. Altes Testament," *ThWB,* 7, 476-496 = *Kittel's Theological Dictionary of the New Testament,* 1971.

Frankenberg, W. *Die Sprüche, HKAT,* 2, 3, 1 Göttingen, 1898.

Galling, K. *Die Krise der Aufklärung in Israel,* Mainz, 1952.

———. "Kohelet-Studien," *ZAW,* 50 (1932), 276-299.

———. *Der Prediger, HAT,* 18, Tübingen, 1969.

———. "Stand und Aufgabe der Kohelet-Forschung," *ThR,* 6 (1934), 355-373.

Gammie, John G. "Spatial and Ethical Dualism in Jewish Wisdom and Apocalyptic Literature," *JBL,* 93 (1974), 356-385.

Gaspar, J. W. *Social Ideas in the Wisdom Literature of the Old Testament,* Washington, 1947.

Gemser, B. "The Instructions of 'Onchsheshonqy and Biblical Wisdom Literature," *VTS,* 7 (1960), 102-128.

———. "The Spiritual Structure of Biblical Aphoristic Wisdom," *Adhuc Loquitur. Collected Essays of Dr. B. Gemser,* edd. A. Van Selms and A. S. Van der Woude, Leiden, 1968, 138-149.

———. *Sprüche Salomos, HAT,* 16, 1963.

Gerleman, G. *Studies in the Septuagint,* III: *Proverbs, Gleerup,* 1956.

Gerstenberger, E. *Wesen und Herkunft des 'apodiktischen Rechts', WMANT,* 20, Neukirchen, 1965.

———. "Zur alttestamentlichen Weisheit," *VuF.* 14 (1969), 28-43.

Gese, H. "Die Krisis der Weisheit bei Kohelet," *SPOA*, 1963, 139-151.
———. *Lehre und Wirklichkeit in der alten Weisheit*, Tübingen, 1958.
———. "Weisheit," *RGG*[3], 6, 1574-1577.
———. "Weisheitsdichtung," *RGG*[3], 6, 1577-1581.
Ginzberg, H. L. "Job the Patient and Job the Impatient," *ConJud*, 21 (1966-1967), 12-28.
———. *Studies in Koheleth*, New York, 1950.
———. "Supplementary Studies in Koheleth," *PAAJR*, 21 (1952), 35-62.
Glasser, E. *Le proces du bonheur par Qohelet*, Paris, 1970.
Glatzer, N. N. "The Book of Job and Its Interpreters," in A. Altmann, *Biblical Motifs*, Cambridge, Mass., 1966, 197-220.
———. [ed.] *The Dimension of Job*, New York, 1969.
Godbey, A. H. "The Hebrew Mašal," *AJSL*, 39 (1922-1923), 89-108.
Good, E. M. *Irony in the Old Testament*, Philadelphia, 1965.
Goodman, W. R. *A Study of I Esdras 3:1-5:6*, unpublished diss. Duke University, 1972.
Gordis, R. *The Book of God and Man*, Chicago, 1965.
———. *Koheleth—The Man and His World*, New York, 1951.
———. "The Lord out of the Whirlwind," *Jud*, 13 (1964), 48-63.
———. *Poets, Prophets, and Sages: Essays in Biblical Interpretation*, Bloomington, 1971.
———. "Quotations in Wisdom Literature," *JQR*, 30 (1939-1940), 123-247.
———. "The Social Background of Wisdom Literature," *HUCA*, 18, (1943/44), 77-118.
Gordon, E. I. "Sumerian Proverbs: 'Collection Four'," *JAOS*, 77 (1957), 67-79.
———. "A New Look at the Wisdom of Sumer and Akkad," *BO*, 17 (1960), 122-152.
———. *Sumerian Proverbs. Glimpses of Every Day Life in Ancient Mesopotamia*, Philadelphia, 1959.
———. "Sumerian Proverbs and Fables," *JCS*, 12 (1958), 1-21, 43-75.
Gowan, D. "Habakkuk and Wisdom," *Perspective*, 9 (1968), 157-166.
Greenstone, J. H. *Proverbs*, Philadelphia, 1950.
Grelot, P. "Les proverbes Araméens d'Ahiqar," *RB*, 68 (1961), 178-194.
Gressmann, H. *Israels Spruchweisheit im Zusammenhang der Weltliteratur*, Berlin, 1925.
———. "Die neugefundene Lehre des Amen-em-ope und die vorexilische Spruchdichtung Israels," *ZAW*, 42 (1924), 272-296.
Gunkel, H. *Die israelitische Literatur (Die Kultur der Gegenwart, 1, 7)*, Leipzig, 1925.
———. "Agyptische Parallelen zum AT," *ZDMG*, 63 (1909); 531-539.
Habel, N. "Appeal to Ancient Tradition as a Literary Form," *SBL Seminar Papers*, 1973, 34-54.
———. "The Symbolism of Wisdom in Proverbs 1-9," *Inter*, 26 (1972), 131-156.

Hain, M. *Rätsel,* Stuttgart, 1966.

———. *Sprichwort und Volkssprache. Eine volkskundlich-soziologische Dorfuntersuchung, Giessener Beiträge z. dt. Philologie* 95, Giessen, 1951.

Hamp, V. "Zukunft und Jenseits in Buche Sirach," in I. Nötscher, *Alttestamentliche Studien, BBB,* 1, Bonn, 1950, 86-97.

Harrelson, W. "Wisdom and Pastoral Theology," *ANQ,* 1966, 3-11.

Harrington, W. "The Wisdom of Israel," *IThQ,* 30 (1963), 311-325.

Haspecker, J. *Gottesfurcht bei Jesus Sirach, AnB,* 30, Rome, 1967.

Harvey, J. "Wisdom Literature and Biblical Theology (Part One)," *Bib Theol Bulletin,* 1 (1971), 308-319.

Hausen, A. *Hiob in der französischen Literatur,* Bern und Frankfurt, 1972.

Hempel, J. *Die althebräische Literatur und ihr hellenistisch-jüdisches Nachleben. Handbuch d. Lit. Wiss.,* Potsdam, 1930.

———. "Pathos und Humor in der israelitischen Erziehung," *Von Ugarit nach Qumran (Festschrift O. Eissfeldt), BZAW,* 77, Berlin, 1958, 63-81.

———. *Das Ethos des Alten Testament, BZAW,* 67 (1964, rev. ed.).

———. "Das theologische Problem des Hiob," *ZSystTh,* 7 (1930), 621-689, in *Apoxysmata,* Berlin, 1961, 114-173.

Herbert, A. S. "The 'Parable' (*Mašal*) in the Old Testament," *SJTh,* 7 (1954), 180-196.

Herder, J. G. *Spruch und Bild, insonderheit bei den Morgenländern, Werke,* ed. B. Suphan, Bd. 16, Berlin, 1887, 9-27.

Hermisson, H. J. *Studien zur israelitischen Spruchweisheit, WMANT,* 28 Neukirchen-Vluyn, 1968.

———. "Weisheit und Geschichte," *Probleme biblischer Theologie (Festschrift G. von Rad)* ed. H. W. Wolff, München, 1971, 136-154.

Hertzberg, H. W. *Der Prediger, KAT,* 1963.

Hölscher, G. *Das Buch Hiob, HAT,* 17, Tübingen, 1952.

Holm-Nielsen, S. "On the Interpretation of Qoheleth in Early Christianity," *VT,* 24 (1974), 168-177.

Horst, F. *Hiob (BKAT,* 16), Neukirchen-Vluyn, 1960-68.

Horton, E. Jr. "Koheleth's Concept of Opposites," *Numen,* 19 (1972), 1-21.

Hudal, A. *Die religiösen und sittlichen Ideen des Spruchbuches. Kritisch-exegetische Studie,* 1914.

Humbert, P. *Recherches sur les sources égyptiennes de la littérature sapientiale d'Israël,* Neuchatel, 1929.

———. "Le modernisme de Job," *VTS,* 3 (1960), 150-161.

Humphreys, W. L. *The Motif of the Wise Courtier in the Old Testament,* unpublished diss. Union Theol. Seminary, 1970.

Imschoot, P. van. "Sagesse et esprit dans l'ancien Testament," *RB,* 47 (1938), 23-49.

Irwin, W. A. "The Wisdom Literature," *IB,* 1 (1952), 212-219.

Jacob, E. "L'histoire d'Israel vue par Ben Sira," *Mélanges Bibliques. Rédigés en l'honneur de Andre Robert, Paris,* 1956, 288-294.

Jansen, H. L. *Die spätjüdische Psalmendichtung, ihr Entstehungskreis und ihr Sitz im Leben,*" *SNVAO,* 1937, 3.

Jensen, J. *The Use of tôrâ by Isaiah. His Debate with the Wisdom Tradition,* *CBQMS,* 3, 1973.

Johnson, A. R. *"Mashal,"* *VTS,* 3 (1960), 162-169.

Jolles, A. *Einfache Formen,* Halle, 1956.

Junker, H. *Das Buch Hiob, EB, Würzburg,* 1962.

Jung, C. G. *Answer to Job,* New York, 1960.

Keimer, L. "The Wisdom of Amen-em-ope and the Proverbs of Solomon," *AJSL,* 43 (1926-27), 8-21.

Kenworthy, A. W. *The Nature and Authority of Old Testament Wisdom Family Ethics: with Special Reference to Proverbs and Sirach,* unpublished diss. Univ. of Melbourne, 1974.

Kevin, R. O. "The Wisdom of Amen-em-ope and its Possible Dependence upon the Hebrew Book of Proverbs," *JSOR,* 14 (1930), 115-157.

Klostermann, A. "Schulwesen im alten Israel," in *Festschrift für Th. Zahn,* Leipzig, 1908, 193-232.

Koch, K. "Gibt es ein Vergeltungsdogma im Alten Testament," *ZThK,* 52 (1955), 1-42.

————., ed. *Um das Prinzip der Vergeltung in Religion und Recht des Alten Testament, Wege der Forschung,* 125, 1972.

Kovacs, B. W. "Is There a Class-Ethic in Proverbs?" in *Essays in Old Testament Ethics,* 1974, 171-189.

Kraeling, C. H. and R. M. Adams, eds. *City Invincible. A Symposium on Urbanization and Cultural Development in the Ancient Near East,* Chicago, 1960, 94-123 (Scribal Concepts of Education).

Kramer, S. N. " 'Man and his God.' A Sumerian Variation on the 'Job' Motif," *VTS,* 3 (1960), 170-182.

————. "Schooldays: A Sumerian Composition Relating to the Education of a Scribe," *JAOS,* 69 (1949), 199-215.

————. "Die sumerische Schule," *WZ Halle-Wittenberg,* 5, 4, 1956, 695-704.

Kraus, H.-J. *Die Verkündigung der Weisheit, BS,* 2 Giessen, 1951.

Kroeber, R. *Der Prediger, SQAW.* 13, Berlin, 1963.

Kuhn, G. *Beiträge zur Erklärung des Salomonischen Spruchbuches. BWANT,* 16. 1931.

————. *Erklärung des Buches Koheleth, BZAW.* 43, Giessen, 1926.

Kuschke, A. "Altbabylonische Texte zum Thema 'Der leidende Gerechte'," *ThLZ,* 81 (1956), 69-76.

Kuyper, L. "The Repentance of Job," *VT,* 9 (1959), 90-94.

Lagrange, M. J. "Le livre de la Sagesse. Sa doctrine des fins dernieres," *RB,* 16 (1907), 85-104.

Lambert, W. G. *Babylonian Wisdom Literature.* Oxford, 1960.

Lamparter, H. *Das Buch der Weisheit, Prediger und Sprüche, BAT,* 16, 1959.

Lang, B. *Die weisheitliche Lehrrede. Eine Untersuchung von Sprüche 1-7,* Stuttgart, 1972.

Lange, H. O. *Das Weisheitsbuch des Amenemope, Kgl.* Danske Vid. Selsk., Hist. fil. Med 11, 2, Kopenhagen, 1925.

Lapointe, R. "Foi et vérifiabilité dans le langage sapiential de retribution," *Bib*, 51 (1970), 349-368.

Larcher, C. *Études sur le livre de la Sagesse,* Paris, 1969.

Lebram, J. Chr. "Nachbiblische Weisheitstraditionen," *VT*, 15 (1965), 167-237.

————. "Die Theologie der späteren Chokma und häretisches Judentum," *ZAW*, 77 (1965), 202-211.

Leclant, J. "Documents nouvaux et points de vue récents sur les sagesses de l'Égypte ancienne," *SPOA*, 5-26.

Lindblom, J. *La composition du livre de Job,* Lund, 1945.

————. "Wisdom in the Old Testament Prophets," *VTS*, 3 (1960), 192-204.

Loretz, O. *Qohelet und der alte Orient,* Freiburg, 1964.

MacDonald, D. B. *The Hebrew Philosophical Genius,* New York, 1965 (repr.)

Mack, B. L. "Wisdom Myth and Mytho-logy," *Inter*, 24 (1970), 46-60.

Malchow, B. V. *The Roots of Israel's Wisdom in Sacral Kingship,* unpublished diss. Marquette Univ., 1972.

Malfroy, J. "Sagesse et loi dans le Deutéronome. Études." *VT*, 15 (1965), 49-65.

Marböck, J. *Weisheit im Wandel. Untersuchungen zur Weisheitstheologie bei Ben Sira, BBB,* 37, Bonn, 1971.

Marcus, R. "On Biblical Hypostases of Wisdom," *HUCA*, 23 (1950/51), 157-171.

Martin, G. W. *Elihu and the Third Cycle in the Book of Job,* unpublished diss. Princeton, 1972.

Martin-Achard, R. "Sagesse de Dieu et sagesse humaine chez Esaïe," *Maqqel Shaqedh (Festschift W. Vischer),* Castelnau, 1960.

Matenko, P. *Two Studies in Yiddish Culture,* Leiden, 1968 (Job and Faust, 75-162).

McGlinchey, J. M. *The Teaching of Amen-em-ope and the Book of Proverbs,* Washington, 1939.

McKane, W. *Prophets and Wise Men, SBT,* 44, 1965.

————. *Proverbs, OTL,* Philadelphia, 1970.

McKenzie, J. L. "Reflections on Wisdom," *JBL*, 86 (1967), 1-9.

Meinhold, H. *Die Weisheit Israels in Spruch, Sage und Dichtung,* Leipzig, 1908.

Michel, D. *Israels Glaube im Wandel,* Berlin, 1968.

Montgomery, J. W. "Wisdom as Gift. The Wisdom Concept in Relation to Biblical Messianism," *Inter*, 16 (1962), 43-57.

Morenz, S. "Ägyptologische Beiträge zur Erforschung der Weisheitsliteratur Israels," *SPOA*, 63-71.

Mowinckel, S. "Psalms and Wisdom," *VTS*, 3 (1960), 205-224.

Müller, H. P. *Hiob und seine Freunde, ThSt,* 103, 1970.

————. "Magisch-Mantische Weisheit und die Gestalt Daniels," *UF*, 1 (1969), 79-94.

————. "Wie Sprach Qohälät von Gott?" *VT*, 18 (1968), 507-521.

Munch, P. A. "Die jüdischen 'Weisheitspsalmen' und ihr Platz im Leben," *AcOr*, 15 (1936), 112-140.

Murphy, R. E. "Assumptions and Problems in Old Testament Wisdom Research," *CBQ*, 29 (1967), 102-112.

————. "The Concept of Wisdom Literature," in *The Bible in Current Catholic Thought*, New York, 1962, 46-54.

————. "A Consideration of the Classification 'Wisdom Psalms,' " *VTS*, 9 (1963), 156-167.

————. "Form Criticism and Wisdom Literature," *CBQ*, 31 (1969), 475-483.

————. "The Hebrew Sage and Openness to the World," in *Christian Action and Openness to the World* (Villanova Univ. Symposium, II, III, 1970), 219-244.

————. "The Interpretation of Old Testament Wisdom Literature," *Inter*, 23 (1969), 289-301.

————. *Introduction to the Wisdom Literature of the Old Testament*, Colledgeville, 1965.

————. "The Kerygma of the Book of Proverbs," *Inter*, 20 (1966), 3-14.

————. *Seven Books of Wisdom*, Milwaukee, 1960.

————. "The Wisdom Literature of the Old Testament," *The Human Reality of Sacred Scripture*, 1965, 126-140.

Nötscher, F. "Biblische und babylonische Weisheit," *BZ*, 6 (1962), 120-126.

Noth, M. "Die Bewährung von Salomos 'Göttlicher Weisheit'," *VTS* 3 (1960), 225-237.

Nougayrol, J. "Le version ancienne de 'juste souffrant'," *RB*, 59 (1952), 239-250.

————. "Les sagesses babloniennes: études récentes et textes inédits," *SPOA*, 1963, 41-50.

Nowack, W. *Die Sprüche, Prediger und Hoheslied übersetzt und erklärt, HAT*, 2, 3, Göttingen, 1898.

Oesterley, W. O. E. *The Book of Proverbs*, London, 1929.

————. *Ecclesiasticus*, Cambridge, 1912.

————. "The 'Teaching of Amen-em-ope' and the Old Testament," *ZAW*, 45, 1927, 9-24.

————. *The Wisdom of Egypt and the Old Testament*, London, 1927.

Orelli, C. von. *Die alttestamentliche Weissagung von der Vollendung des Gottesreiches in ihrer geschichtlichen Entwicklung dargestellt*, Vienna, 1882.

Otto, E. "Der Vorwurf an Gott," *Vorträge der orientalistische Tagung in Marburg*, 1950 (1951), 1-15.

Paterson, J. *The Wisdom of Israel*, Nashville, 1961.

Paulus, J. "Le thème du Juste Souffrant dans la pensée grecque et hebraique," *RHR*, 121-122 (1940), 18-66.

Peake, A. S. *Job, CB*, London, 1905.

Pedersen, J. "Scepticisme israélite," *RHPR*, 10 (1930), 317-370.

———. "Wisdom and Immortality," *VTS*, 3 (1960), 238-246.

Peters, N. *Die Weisheitsbücher des Alten Testamentes*, Münster i.W., 1914.

Pfeiffer, E. "Die Gottesfurcht im Buche Kohelet," *Gottes Wort und Gottes Land, Festschrift W. Hertzberg*, Göttingen, 1965, 133-158.

Pfeiffer, R. *Die religiös-sittliche Weltanschauung des Buches der Sprüche*, München, 1897.

Pfeiffer, R. H. "Edomitic Wisdom," *ZAW*, 24 (1926), 13-25.

———. "Wisdom and Vision in the Old Testament," *ZAW*, 52 (1934), 93-101.

Plöger, O. "Besprechung von U. Skladny, *Die ältesten Spruchsammlungen . . .*," *Gnomon*, 36 (1964), 297-300.

———. "Wahre die richtige Mitte: solch Mass ist in allen das Beste!" in *Gottes Wort und Gottes Land*, 1965, 159-173.

———. "Zur Auslegung der Sentenzensammlungen des Proverbienbuches," *Probleme biblischer Theologie*, 1971, 402-416.

Pope, M. H. *Job, AB*, Garden City, N. Y., 1965.

Porteous, N. W. "Royal Wisdom," *VTS*, 3 (1960), 247-261.

Preuss, H. D. "Erwägungen zum theologischen Ort alttestamentlicher Weisheitsliteratur," *EvTh*, 30 (1970), 393-417.

———. "Das Gottesbild der älteren Weisheit Israels," *VTS*, 23, 1972, 117-145.

Priest, J. F. "Humanism, Skepticism, and Pessimism in Israel," *JAAR*, 36 (1968), 311-326.

———. "Where is Wisdom to be Placed?," *JBR*, 31 (1963), 275-282.

Pritchard, J. B. ed. *Ancient Near Eastern Texts Relating to the Old Testament*, Princeton, N. J., 1955, 1969.

Rad, G. von. "Job XXXVIII and Ancient Egyptian Wisdom," in *The Problem of the Hexateuch and Other Essays*, Edinburgh & London, 1966, 281-291.

———. "The Joseph Narrative and Ancient Wisdom," in *The Problem of the Hexateuch and Other Essays*, 292-300.

———. *Old Testament Theology*, I, Edinburgh & London, 1962 (German edition, 1957).

———. "Some Aspects of the Old Testament World View," in *The Problem of the Hexateuch and Other Essays*, 144-165.

———. "Sprüchebuch," *RGG³*, 6, 285-288.

———. *Wisdom in Israel*, Nashville, 1972.

Rainey, A. F. "The Scribe at Ugarit. His Position and Influence, *Proceedings of the Israel Academy of Sciences and Humanities*, 3, 4, 1968, 126-146.

Rankin, O. S. *Israel's Wisdom Literature*, Edinburgh, repr. 1954.

Ranston, H. *The Old Testament Wisdom Books and Their Teaching*, London, 1930.

Reese, J. M. *Hellenistic Influence on the Book of Wisdom and its Consequences*, AnB, 41, Rome, 1970.

————. "Plan and Structure in the Book of Wisdom," *CBQ*, 27 (1965), 391-399.

Richter, H. "Die Naturweisheit des Alten Testaments im Buche Hiob," *ZAW*, 70-71 (1958-1959), 1-19.

————. *Studien zu Hiob, ThA*, 11, 1959.

Richter, W. *Recht und Ethos, Versuch einer Ortung des weisheitlichen Mahnspruches*, München, 1966.

Ringgren, H. *Word and Wisdom. Studies in the Hypostatization of Divine Qualities and Functions in the Ancient Near East*, Lund, 1947.

Röhrrich, L. "Sprichwort," *RGG*[3], 6, 282-284.

Roth, W. M. W. *Numerical Sayings in the Old Testament*, VTS, 13, 1965.

Rowley, H. H. *Job, NCB*, Great Britain, 1970.

Rudolph, W. *Vom Buch Kohelet*, Münster Westf., 1959.

Rüger, H. P. *Text und Textform in hebräischen Sirach*, BZAW, 112, Berlin, 1970.

Rylaarsdam, J. C. "Hebrew Wisdom," *Peake's Commentary on the Bible*, Edinburgh, 1962, 386-390.

————. *Revelation in Jewish Wisdom Literature*, Chicago, 1946.

Sanders, J. A. *Suffering as Divine Discipline in the Old Testament and Post-Biblical Judaism*, New York, 1955.

Sanders, P. S. *Twentieth Century Interpretations of the Book of Job*, Englewood Cliffs, N. J., 1968.

Sarna, N. "Epic Substratum in the Prose of Job," *JBL*, 76 (1957), 13-25.

Sauer, G. *Die Sprüche Agurs*, BWANT, 84, 1963.

Schechter, S. "A Glimpse of the Social Life of the Jews in the Age of Jesus the Son of Sirach," *Studies in Judaism*, 2nd Ser., Philadelphia, 1908, 55-101.

Schencke, W. *Die Chokma (Sophia) in der jüdischen Hypostatenspekulation: ein Beitrag zur Geschichte der religiösen Ideen im Zeitalter des Hellenismus*, 1913.

Schmid, H. H. *Gerechtigkeit als Weltordnung*, BhTh, 40, Tübingen, 1968.

————. "Hauptprobleme der altorientalischen und alttestamentlichen Weisheitsliteratur," *STU*, 35 (1965), 68-74.

————. *Wesen und Geschichte der Weisheit*, BZAW, 101, Berlin, 1966.

Schmidt, J. *Der Ewigkeitsbegriff im Alten Testament*, AA, 13, 5 Münster, 1940.

————. *Studien zur Stilistik der alttestamentlichen Spruchliteratur*, AA, 13, 1, Münster, 1936.

Schreiner, J. "Die altorientalische Weisheit als Lebenskunde. Israels neues Verständnis und Kritik der Weisheit," *Wort und Botschaft*, Wurzburg, 1967, 258-271.

Scott, R. B. Y. "Folk Proverbs of the Ancient Near East," *Transactions of the Royal Society of Canada*, 15 (1961), 47-56.

———. "Priesthood, Prophecy, Wisdom, and the Knowledge of God," *JBL*, 80 (1961), 1-15.

———. *Proverbs, Ecclesiastes, AB*, New York, 1965.

———. "Solomon and the Beginnings of Wisdom in Israel," *VTS*, 3 (1960), 262-279.

———. "The Study of the Wisdom Literature," *Inter*, 24 (1970), 20-45.

———. *The Way of Wisdom in the Old Testament*, New York, 1971.

———. "Wise and Foolish, Righteous and Wicked," *VTS*, 23 (1972), 146-165.

Sekine, M. "Schöpfung und Erlösung im Buche Hiob," *BZAW*, 77 (1958), 213-223.

Simpson, D. C. "The Hebrew Book of Proverbs and the Teaching of Amenophis," *JEA*, 12 (1926), 232-239.

Skladny, U. *Die ältesten Spruchsammlungen in Israel*, Berlin, 1961.

Smend, R. *Die Weisheit des Jesus Sirach, erklärt von R.S.*, Berlin, 1906.

———. *Die Weisheit des Jesus Sirach, hebräisch und deutsch*, Berlin, 1906.

Snaith, N. H. *The Book of Job, SBT*, 11, London, 1968.

Spiegel, J. *Die Präambel des Amenemope und die Zielsetzung der ägyptischen Weisheitsliteratur*, Glückstadt, 1935.

Sprondel, G. *Untersuchungen zum Selbstverständnis und zur Frömmigkeit der alten Weisheit Israels*, Göttingen, 1962.

Stamm, J. J. "Die Theodizee im Babylon und Israel," *JEOL*, 9 (1944), 99-107.

Steuernagel, C. *Die Sprüche, HSAT*, 2 Tübingen, 1922.

Story, C. I. K. "The Book of Proverbs and Northwest Semitic Literature," *JBL*, 64 (1945), 319-337.

Strack, H. L. *Die Sprüche Salomos, KKANT*, 6, 2, München, 1899.

Suys, E. *La sagesse d'Ani, AnOr* 11, Rome, 1935.

Talmon, S. " 'Wisdom' in the Book of Esther," *VT*, 13 (1963), 419-455.

Taylor, A. *The Proverb*, Cambridge, Mass., 1931.

Terrien, S. "Amos and Wisdom," in *Israel's Prophetic Heritage, Festschrift J. Muilenburg*, eds. B. W. Anderson and Walter Harrelson, New York, 1962, 108-115.

———. "Quelques remarques sur les affinities de Job avec le Deutéro-Esaïe," *VTS*, 15 (1965), 295-310.

———. *Job: Poet of Existence*, New York, 1957.

Thomas, D. W. "Textual and Philological Notes on Some Passages in the Book of Proverbs," *VTS*, 3 (1960), 280-292.

Thompson, J. M. *The Form and Function of Proverbs in Ancient Israel*, Leiden, 1971.

Thompson, K. "Out of the Whirlwind," *Inter*, 14 (1960), 51-63.

Toombs, L. E. "O.T. Theology and the Wisdom Literature," *JBR*, 23 (1955), 193-196.

Torczyner, H. = Tur-Sinai, N. H. "Proverbiastudien," *ZDMG*, 71 (1917), 99-118 and "Nachtrage und Berichtigungen zu meinen Proverbiastudien," *ZDMG*, 72 (1918), 154-156.

————. *The Book of Job*, Jerusalem, 1967.

Tournay, R. "Proverbs 1-9: A First Theological Synthesis of the Tradition of the Sages," *The Dynamism of the Biblical Tradition*, New York, 1967, 51-61.

Toy, C. H. *The Book of Proverbs, ICC,* 1899.

Tsevat, M. "The Meaning of the Book of Job," *HUCA*, 37 (1966), 73-106.

Urbach, E. E. "Class-Status and Leadership in the World of the Palestinian Sages," *Proceedings of the Israel Academy of Sciences and Humanities*, 2, (1966), 1-37.

Vergote, J. "La notion de Dieu dans les livres de sagesse égyptiens," *SPOA*, 159-190.

Vischer, W. "God's Truth and Man's Lie. A Study of the Message of the Book of Job," *Inter*, 15 (1961), 131-146.

————. *Der Prediger Salomo*, München, 1926.

Volten, A. "Der Begriff der Maat in den Ägyptischen Weisheitstexten," *SPOA*, 73-102.

————. *Studien zum Weisheitsbuch des Anii, Kgl. Danske Vid. Selsk, Hist. fil. Med.*, 23, 3, Copenhagen, 1937/8.

————. *Zwei altägyptische politische Schriften. Die Lehre für König Meri-kare . . . und die Lehre des Königs Amenemhet, An Aeg.* 4, Copenhagen, 1945.

Volz, P. *Hiob und Weisheit, SAT,* 3, 2, Göttingen, 1921.

Walcot, P. "Hesiod and the Instructions of 'Onchsheshonqy," *JNES*, 21 (1962), 215-219.

Walle, B. van de. "Problèmes relatifs aux méthodes d'enseignement dans l'Egypte ancienne," *SPOA*, 191-207.

Wallis, G. "Zu den Spruchsammlungen Prov. 10:1-22:16 und 25-29," *ThLZ*, 85 (1960), 147-148.

Weiden, W. A. van der. *Le livre des Proverbes. Notes philologiques, BO*, 23, Rome, 1970.

Weinfeld, M. "The Dependence of Deuteronomy upon the Wisdom Litera-ture," in *Yehezkel Kaufmann Jubilee Volume, Jerusalem*, 1960, 89-108.

————. "Deuteronomy. The Present State of Inquiry," *JBL*, 86 (1967), 249-262.

Weiser, A. "Das Problem der sittlichen Weltordnung im Buche Hiob," *Glaube und Geschichte im Alten Testament*, Göttingen, 1961, 9-19.

Werner, J. *Lateinische Sprichwörter und Sinnsprüche des Mittelalters aus Handschriften gesammelt, 2 Aufl. überarbeitet* von P. Flury, Darmstadt, 1966.

Westermann, C. *Der Aufbau des Buches Hiob, BhTh*, 23, 1956.

————. "Weisheit im Sprichwort," *Schalom (Festscrift A. Jepsen)*, Stuttgart, 1971, 73-85.

Whybray, R. N. *The Heavenly Counsellor in Isaiah xl 13-14, SOTSMS,* Cambridge, 1971.

———. *The Intellectual Tradition in the Old Testament, BZAW,* 135, Berlin and New York, 1974.

———. "Proverbs VIII 22-31 and its Supposed Prototypes," *VT,* 15 (1965), 504-514.

———. *The Succession Narrative, SBT,* 2nd Ser. 9, 1968.

———. *Wisdom in Proverbs, SBT,* 45, 1965.

Wied, G. *Der Auferstehungsglaube des späten Israels in seiner Bedeutung für das Verhältnis von Apokalyptik und Weisheit,* unpublished diss. Friedrich-Wilhelms Univ., Bonn, 1967.

Wildeboer, G. *Die Sprüche, KHCAT,* Freiburg, 1897.

Williams, J. G. "What Does It Profit a Man?: The Wisdom of Koheleth," *Judaism,* 20 (1971), 179-193.

Williams, R. J. "Scribal Training in Ancient Egypt," *JAOS,* 92 (1972), 214-221.

———. "Theodicy in the Ancient Near East," *CJTh,* 2 (1956), 14-26.

Wolff, H. W. *Amos' geistige Heimat, WMANT,* 18, 1964 = *Amos the Prophet,* Philadelphia, 1973.

Wood, J. *Wisdom Literature,* London, 1967.

Wright, A. G. "Numerical Patterns in the Book of Wisdom," *CBQ,* 29 (1967), 524-538.

———. "The Riddle of the Sphinx: The Structure of the Book of Qoheleth," *CBQ,* 30 (1968), 313-334.

———. "The Structure of the Book of Wisdom," *Bib,* 48 (1967), 165-184.

Würthwein, E. "Gott und Mensch in Dialog und Gottesreden des Buches Hiob," *Wort und Existenz,* 217-295.

———. *"Die Weisheit Ägyptens und das Alte Testament,"* Mitt. d. Univ.-bundes Marburg, 1958/59, H.3/4, 55-69 = *Wort und Existenz,* 197-216.

Zaba, Z. *Les maximes de Ptahhotep, Ed. de l'Acad. Tchech des Sciences,* Prag, 1956.

Ziener, G. *Die theologische Begriffssprache im Buche der Weisheit, BBB,* 11. Bonn, 1956.

Zimmerli, W. "Das Buch Kohelet—Traktat oder Sentenzensammlung?," *VT,* 24 (1974), 221-230.

———. *Das Buch des Predigers Salomo, ATD,* 16, Göttingen, 1962.

———. "Ort und Grenze der Weisheit im Rahmen der alttestamentlichen Theologie," *SPOA,* 1963 = "The Place and Limit of the Wisdom in the Framework of the Old Testament Theology," *SJTh,* 17 (1964), 146-158.

———. "Zur Struktur der alttestamentlichen Weisheit," *ZAW,* 51 (1933), 177-204.

———. "Die Weisheit Israels. Zu einem Buch von Gerhard von Rad," *EvTh,* 31 (1971), 680-695.

———. *Die Weisheit des Predigers Salomo,* Berlin, 1936.

Zimmerman, F. "Altägyptische Spruchweisheit in der Bibel," *ThGl*, 17 (1925), 204-217.

————. *The Inner World of Koheleth*, New York, 1973.

I.

THE ANCIENT NEAR EASTERN SETTING AND ISRAELITE WISDOM

SOPHIA
GEORG FOHRER

B. The Old Testament.

I. Terminology.

Since the LXX normally uses σοφία/σοφός for the Hbr. stem חכם, in essentials this alone need be considered. The verb חכם occurs 26 times (q 18, pi 3, pu 2, hi 1, hitp 2), חָכָם as adj. or noun occurs 135 times, the noun חָכְמָה 147 times and in the plur. חָכְמוֹת 4 [85] times. 73 instances are in the historical books (חכם 3, חָכָם 31, חָכְמָה 39), 41 in the prophets (חכם 1, חָכָם 24, חָכְמָה 16), 13 in the Psalms (חכם 4, חָכָם 2, חָכְמָה 7), [86] 180 in the Wisdom lit. proper (חכם 18, חָכָם 76, חָכְמָה 86), [87] and 5 in the other books. Thus about three-fifths of the total may be found in the Wisdom books. It is worth noting that in the historical books the words mostly denote technical or artistic ability (→ 484, 1 ff.) or cleverness and knowledge such as the wisdom of Solomon (→ 484, 24 ff.), more rarely magical craft, practical wisdom, and ethical or religious conduct (→ 486, 14 ff.). In the prophets they denote human ability of various kinds, the wisdom and the magicians of other nations; they are also found in criticism of wisdom and very rarely, and only in prophecy, in the context of eschatology, → 488, 30 ff. In the Wisdom lit. (→ 476. n. 87) the terms may sometimes be used for cleverness and prudence, but as in the Psalms they are employed in the main for rules of behaviour, for ethical or religious conduct. Qoh. stands apart, since it uses the words for the doctrinally clearly etched wisdom of the schools. In the few other instances the ref. is to magic or knowledge.

In the Aram. portions of the OT we also find the noun חַכִּים "wise man," which is used 14 times for men to whom one goes for the interpretation of dreams, and the noun חָכְמָה, which is used in Ezr. 7:25 for the Torah and elsewhere for the gift of interpreting dreams granted to Daniel.

The survey shows that the common translation "wise," "wisdom" is unfortunate and to a large degree inexact. It does justice neither to the broad range of the Hebrew terms nor to their precise meaning. If knowledge is presupposed in detail, this is not so much a deeper knowledge in the theoretical mastery of the questions of life and the universe as a solution of a practical kind on the basis of concrete demands. The reference is to prudent, considered, experienced and competent action to subjugate the world and to master the various problems of life and life itself. When detailed aspects are taken into account חכם means "cleverness and skill for the purpose of practical action." The fact that לֵב is often added [88] makes it plain that this is not a quality but can arise out of a feeling for the right

---

[85] Also in Prv. 14:1 instead of the adj. On חכמות as a plur. cf. for details E. Brønno, Stud. über hbr. Morphologie u. Vokalismus (1943), 187 f. This is probably a plur. of extension, intensity and majesty used as a title and denoting comprehensive, pure, authentic and supreme wisdom.

[86] Terms of the stem חכם are as much as possible avoided in Ps. because they became fixed quite early. Materially one group of Ps. is influenced by the Wisdom lit. or even belongs to it.

[87] Job, Prv. and Qoh.

[88] So Ex. 28:3; 31:6; 35:25; 36:1 f., 8; Job 9:4; 37:24; Prv. 10:8; 11:29; 16:21; "understanding" 1 K. 5:9.

thing which is fostered by traditional knowledge, education and personal experience. As it is with man, so it is with the gods and Yahweh, though one cannot say that one idea developed out of the other.

In keeping with this sense of חכם is the fact that the most common par. are derivates of בין "to perceive," "to understand (how to act)": נָבוֹן "perceptive," "skilled," [89] בִּינָה "insight," [90] and תְּבוּנָה "insight," "skill" (of the artisan). [91] Then we find derivates of ידע (→ I, 696, 17 ff.) emphasising either "understanding" [92] or "experience" (Dt. 1:13, 15), but also denoting the "skill" of the artist or magical "art." [93] The ref. is again to practical conduct when the following par. are found with terms derived from חכם: "uprightness," "honesty" Prv. 4:11, "to lead the heart along the right way" Prv. 23:19, and צַדִּיק "righteous," "pious" Dt. 16:19; Prv. 9:9; 23:24; Qoh. 9:1. One notes a similar connection in the antitheses: the "fool" (→ IV, 833, 31 ff.; 916, 30 ff.) is incapable of right action rather than stupid. [94] The corresponding terms relate less to thought and knowledge and more to action. Folly is disorder in a man's life which first finds expression in his conduct and then in imprudence and arrogance. [95]

II. Wisdom as an Ancient Oriental and Israelite-Old Testament Phenomenon.

On the one side the content of חכם is largely defined by a corresponding world of thought common to the ancient Orient, so that the terms, and the OT Wisdom books in which they mostly occur, belong to the circle of a Wisdom literature which in essentials is the same throughout the region. On the other hand the development was stronger in Israel than elsewhere and the international and supra-religious doctrine of wisdom in the true sense was both nationalised and also integrated into faith in Yahweh and adjusted to it.

1. Mesopotamia. In Mesopotamia there is no word corresponding to the Hbr. חכם. [96] Apart from the textually and philologically difficult Sumerian texts [97] Bab. has nēmequ "wisdom" and several adj. "wise" (enqu, mūdû, ḫassu, etpēšu). But these are

---

[89] Gn. 41:33, 39; Dt. 1:13; 4:6; 1 K. 3:12; Is. 5:21; 29:14; Jer. 4:22; Hos. 14:10; Prv. 1:5; 17:28; 18:15; Qoh. 9:11.

[90] Dt. 4:6; Is. 29:14; Job 28:12, 20; 38:36; 39:17; Prv. 2:3; 7:4; 9:10.

[91] Ex. 36:1; 1 K. 5:9; 7:14; Jer. 10:12; 51:15; Ob. 8; Job 12:12 f.; Prv. 2:2; 3:19; 15:1; 24:3.

[92] Jer. 4:22; Job 34:2; Qoh. 6:8, cf. also טַעַם "understanding," Prv. 26:16.

[93] 1 K. 7:14; Is. 47:10. דַּעַת "insight," Prv. 5:2; 15:2, 7; 21:11; "knowledge" Qoh. 1:18; "experience" Is. 33:6.

[94] With אֱוִיל "foolish," "stupid" cf. אֱוִלִי "inept," "unserviceable," while אַוֶּלֶת "(impious) folly" with עָשָׂה means "to act imprudently." כְּסִיל is religiously "bold" and "foolish" in practical matters. לֵץ "babbler," "mocker" (→ IV, 797, 24 ff.), is the man who demonstrates in his words his lack of acquaintance with what is right. נָבָל "vain," "foolish," means "without understanding" in mind or ethical conduct, נְבָלָה with "stupidity" is used euphemistically for serious sin. סָכָל is the one who acts "foolishly" (cf. the noun סִכְלוּת in Qoh.). From פתה I "to be inexperienced, misled," εὐ. is used for the simple and inexperienced young man who is easily led astray. Cf. also → I, 275, 43 ff.

[95] Cf. W. Caspari, "Über d. bibl. Begriff d. Torheit," NkZ, 39 (1928), 668-695.

[96] W. G. Lambert, Babylonian Wisdom Literature (1960), 1.

[97] J. J. A. van Dijk, La sagesse suméro-accadienne (1953), 17-21 thought he had found in Sumerian ME the central concept in the sense of an "immanence divine dans la matière morte et vivante, incréée, inchangeable, subsistante, mais impersonnelle," but this seems doubtful in the light of criticism, cf. T. Fish's review in Journal of Semitic Studies, 1 (1956), 286-288.

seldom used in the sense of OT Wisdom lit. [98] The ref. of "wisdom" is usually to skill in the cultus and magic, and the wise man is the initiate in these fields. In the text "I will praise the lord of wisdom" [99] the god Marduk is meant and his wisdom consists in skill in the rites of exorcism. The Accadian *hakâmu* "to grasp or understand something" is probably a West Semitic loan word, and, since it is synon. with *lamâdu* "to learn," it was probably adopted as a handy tt. [100]

Though the inclusive term is missing, there is a fairly extensive Mesopotamian lit. corresponding in content to the OT Wisdom books. [101] This is extant mostly in Accad., but much of it goes back to Sumerian traditions. Many collections of proverbs have been preserved in the Sumerian version (e.g., on school tablets), and these are usually grouped by the first characters. [102] Their authors obviously belonged to the same circle as those who created the Sumerian categorisation which made possible a systematic arrangement of the whole world of objects and experience. [103] In its practical use this arrangement is not explained rationally but illustrated by myths and poems which tell of the creation or restoration of order after chaotic relations. For the Sumerians the lists were a systematising supplement to the purely paradigmatic poems. The Babylonians and Assyrians adopted and developed them and there thus arose a whole branch of Wisdom lit. in the form of a cultural wisdom which received its definitive form esp. in the gt. series *ḪAR-ra* (*ḫubullu*) with 24 tables and thousands of entries. As these seek to master the world by means of the order of names, so the collections of proverbs try to grasp the regularity of life in order to be able to gair the mastery over it. Other texts, in the form of wisdom sayings, deal with ethical questions and impart practical counsel for a life which corresponds to the order of things and is thus successful. [104] Or else they tackle the problems which result from this view of life, [105] so that they might be regarded as precursors of the OT Job. [106] Finally one finds here traditional fables, disputes and debates and other wisdom texts which it is at times hard to classify by genre. [107]

2. Egypt. There is a clearer impulse towards development of the concept in Egypt. The norm of conduct which the wisdom doctrines seek to mediate is now described by the term *maat*. [108] This central word is not unequivocal and is hard to translate : usually "truth," better "right," "rightness," "primal order," "cosmic order." No distinction is made between divine and human or heavenly and earthly right and order, since there is

---

[98] Lambert, 99 mentions the wisdom sayings as a possible example, *Counsels of Wisdom*, 24 f.

[99] AOT, 273-281; J. B. Pritchard, *Ancient Near Eastern Texts²* (1955), 434-437.

[100] Cf. Ges.-Buhl, *s.v.* חכם.

[101] AOT, 284-295; Pritchard, 410 f., 425-430, 434-440; Lambert, *op. cit.*

[102] S. N. Kramer, "Sumerian Wisdom Literature. A Preliminary Survey," *Bulletin of the American Schools of Oriental Research,* 122 (1951), 28-31; J. J. A. van Dijk, *op. cit.,* 5-11 (bibl.); Pritchard, 425-427; E. I. Gordon, "The Sumerian Proverb Collections. A Preliminary Survey," *Journal of the American Oriental Society,* 74 (1954), 82-85; also "Sumerian Proverbs: 'Collection Four,' " *ibid.,* 77 (1957), 67-79; also "A New Look at the Wisdom of Sumer and Akkad," *Bibliotheca Orientalis,* 17 (1960), 122-152. Only a small portion has been published thus far, but it demonstrates the similarity to Prv.

[103] Cf. in detail L. Matouš, *Die lexikalischen Tafelserien der Babylonier und Assyrer in d. Berliner Museen,* I (1933); W. v. Soden, "Leistung u. Grenze sumerischer u. bab. Wissenschaft" in *Die Welt als Gesch.,* 2 (1936), 411-464, 509-557; also *Zweisprachigkeit in d. geistigen Kultur Babyloniens* (1960).

[104] Texts in Lambert, *op. cit.,* c. 4-5.

[105] Texts in Lambert, *op. cit.,* c. 2-3 (and perhaps 6).

[106] Cf. with further bibl. J. J. Stamm, *Das Leiden des Unschuldigen in Babylon u. Israel* (1948); A. Kuschke, "Altbabyl. Texte zum Thema: 'Der leidende Gerechte,' " ThLZ, 81 (1956), 69-76; Gese, 51-69. From the standpt. of form criticism, however, the texts are more like Ps. than Job and materially there are basic differences from Job as well as peripheral par.

[107] Cf. Kramer, *op. cit.;* van Dijk, *op. cit.;* Gordon New Look, 122-152.

[108] A. de Buck, "Het religieus karakter der oudste egypt. wijsheid," *Nieuw Theol.*

only one order obtaining equally throughout the world. The goal of wisdom teachings is to level the way for the order (maat) [109] which comes from God by transmission. With an almost total disregard for personal experience, which plays a big role in OT wisdom teaching, the wise teachers regard themselves as the faithful handers on of an objectively true order which has been present and valid for a long time. [110] As knowledge of the nature of this maat is transmitted, it is established and a condition of harmony is thus set up in state and society. Since maat as the right way of life is unchangeable, it applies equally and immutably to all those in the social group which is being addressed. The task of man is to subject himself to it and to see in it the criterion of wise action. The ideal of this man is the man of silence or — to use the term maat — of true silence — the person who is always master of the situation and who exercises self-control because he acts according to maat, restraining himself both outwardly and inwardly and avoiding all excitement. [111] His opposite is the heated person who is subject to his passions and uncontrolled. [112] Results correspond to conduct. If success and inner truth form a unity, it should not be overlooked that in part the basis of rules of behaviour is purely utilitarian. Profit and success beckon the obedient man, loss and damage threaten the transgressor. [113] But in part there is simply added instead : "For this is God's will," or : "This is an abomination to God." The two foundations belong together in Egypt. thought, for he who offends against maat also transgresses the divine will and consequently suffers loss.

Egypt. Wisdom lit. [114] influenced Israel more strongly than the incipient development of the concept. [115] Since maat embraces what are two different spheres in modern thought, cosmic order and the order of human life, two different genres are found in the Wisdom lit. : the serial knowledge of the Onomastica, [116] which is probably influenced by its Sumerian counterpart, [117] and the "teachings" or "instructions" [118] for which a fixed form developed [119] and of which we have seven in full or almost in full, another five in

---

Tijdschrift, 21 (1932), 322-349; H. Frankfort, Ancient Egypt. Religion (1948), passim; H. Brunner, "Die Weisheitslit." in Hndbch. d. Orientalistik, I, 2 (1952), 93-96; R. Anthes, "Die Maat des Echnaton v. Amarna," Suppl. Journal· of the American Oriental Society, 14 (1952); Gese, 11-21.

[109] Brunner, op. cit., 93: "As a goddess, Maat is found in the religious system of Heliopolis, where she is the daughter of the sun-god. She came down to men as the right order of all things in primal time. This order was disrupted by the wicked attacks of Seth and his companions, and restored by the victory of Horus. As the embodiment of Horus each new king at his coronation established this right order afresh, and a new state of Maat, i.e., of peace and righteousness, breaks forth."

[110] In keeping is the fact that in Is. 19:11 the advisers of Pharaoh explain their knowledge by the fact that they are students of the sages and kings of the past.

[111] Cf. also G. Lanczkowski, "Reden u. Schweigen im ägypt. Verständnis, vornehmlich des Mittleren Reiches," O. Firchow, "Ägyptologische Studien," Festschr. H. Grapow (1955), 186-196.

[112] Prv. 15:18; 22:24; 29:22 use חֵמָה for a "fiery" man, and Prv. 29:11 says that the fool lets his agitation increase while the wise man calms it.

[113] The full rejection of a utilitarian understanding by Gese, 7-11 goes too far.

[114] A. Erman, Die Lit. d. Ägypter (1923), 86-121, 238-302; R. Anthes, "Lebensregeln u. Lebensweisheit d. alten Ägypter," AO, 32, 2 (1933); AOT, 33-46; Pritchard, 405-410, 412-425, 431-434; F. W. v. Bissing, Altägypt. Lebensweisheit (1955).

[115] Esp. W. O. E. Oesterley, The Wisdom of Egypt and the OT (1927); P. Humbert, Recherches sur les sources égypt. de la litt. sapientiale d'Israël (1929); A. Causse, "Sagesse égypt. et sagesse juive," RevHPhR, 9 (1929), 149-169; S. Morenz, "Die ägypt. Lit. u. d. Umwelt," Hndbch. d. Orientalistik, I, 2 (1952), 194-206 (with bibl.); E. Würthwein, Die Weisheit Ägyptens u. d. AT (1960). K. Galling, Der Prediger, Hndbch. AT, I, 18 (1940), 47-90 pts. esp. to par. with the Egypt. pap. Insinger.

[116] A. H. Gardiner, Ancient Egypt. Onomastica (1947); H. Grapow, "Wörterbücher, Repertorien, Schülerhandschriften," Hndbch. d. Orientalistik, I, 2 (1952), 187-193.

[117] A. Alt, "Die Weisheit Salomos," Kleine Schriften d. Volkes Israel, II (1953), 95-97.

[118] The Egypt. title can denote "education," "instruction," esp. theol. teaching.

[119] Thus the usual title is : "Beginning of the instruction which X wrote for his son (pupil) Y."

fragments, and the titles alone of six or seven others. [120] We also find specific works which are not directly instructional but reflective or polemical, and which are traditionally reckoned in the Wisdom lit.

3. The Rest of the Ancient Orient. No Wisdom lit., or very little, has come down to us from the rest of the ancient Orient. [121] Israel, however, was acquainted with the wisdom not merely of the Babylonians (Jer. 50:35; 51:57; cf. Is. 44:25; 47:10) and the Egypt. (1 K. 4:30; cf. Gn. 41:8; Ex. 7:11), but also of other nations: the Canaanites (Ez. 28:3, 17: the Phoenicians gen.; Ez. 27:8: צמר probably Sumra, north of Tripoli, near Arvad; Zech. 9:2: Sidon), [122] the Edomites (Jer. 49:7; Ob. 8; Job 2:11), [123] and the people of the East in the district of Safa in northern East-Jordan (1 K. 4:30). [124] Though the wise men mentioned in 1 K. 4:31 — Ethan the Ezrahite, and Heman, and Chalcol, and Darda, the sons of Maho, are presumably Edomites or Canaanites, there are difficulties. [125] In addition to acquaintance and influence the dependence of the Israelite Wisdom teaching on that of the ancient Orient extends into the traditional texts of the OT. In Prv. 22:17-23:11 we have extracts from the Egypt. teaching of Amen-em-ope. [126] Prv. 23:13 f. is borrowed from the teaching of Achiqar. We have the words of Agur the son of Jakeh "the Massaite" [127] in Prv. 30:1-14 and the words of Lemuel the king of Massa in 31:1-9 — both belonging to tribes outside Israel. [128]

4. Israel. In spite of the uniform intellectual background חָכְמָה has many layers of meaning. Both its connection with the ancient Orient and also its distinctiveness may be observed at many stages of historical development.

a. On the basis of experience there has always been a practical acquaintance with the laws of the world and the activities of life. At all cultural stages man has seen it as his task to master his environment and to control his life in it. There has thus been a need to seek order and regularity in the various phenomena and events, to integrate oneself into this and to make use of it. This finds expression esp. in popular proverbs which

---

[120] For details cf. Brunner, 96-110; also B. Gemser, "The Instructions of 'Onchsheshonqy and Biblical Wisdom Lit.," *VT Suppl.,* 7 (1960), 102-128.

[121] In spite of its Syr. and Aram. form the book of Achiqar may go back to an Assyr. original.

[122] Cf. W. F. Albright, "Some Canaanite-Phoenician Sources of Hebr. Wisdom," *VT Suppl.,* 3 (1955), 1-15; also C. L. Feinberg, *Ugaritic Lit. and the Book of Job,* Diss. Baltimore (1945): C. I. K. Story, "The Book of Proverbs and Northwest-Semitic Lit.," JBL, 64 (1945), 319-337; M. J. Dahood, "Canaanite-Phoenic. Influence in Qoh.," *Biblica,* 33 (1952), 30-52, 191-221.

[123] R. H. Pfeiffer, "Edomitic Wisdom," ZAW, 44 (1926), 13-25; also "Wisdom and Vision in the OT," ZAW, 52 (1934), 93-101: also *Introd. to the OT* (1941), 678-683, has gtly. overestimated the influence of Edomitic thought on Israel.

[124] Cf. O. Eissfeldt, "Das AT im Lichte d. safatenischen Inschr.," ZDMG, 104 (1954), 88-118.

[125] Edomites: E. Meyer, *Die Israeliten u. ihre Nachbarstämme* (1906), 350; Canaanites: W. F. Albright, *Archaeology and the Religion of Israel* (1953), 127 f.

[126] Bibl. in B. Gemser, *Sprüche Salomos,* Hndbch. AT. I, 16 (1937), 9; O. Eissfeldt, *Einl. in d. AT²* (1956), 583, n. 1. The opposite view that Amenemope is dependent on Prv. (esp. W. O. E. Oesterley, "The 'Teaching of Amen-em-ope' and the OT," ZAW, 45 [1927], 9-24 etc.; R. O. Kevin, "The Wisdom of Amen-em-apt and its Possible Dependence upon the Hebr. Book of Proverbs," *Journal of the Society of Oriental Research,* 14 [1930], 115-157; O. Drioton, "Sue la Sagesse d'Aménémopé," *Mélanges bibl. André Robert* [1957], 254-280; also "Le Livre des Proverbes et la Sagesse d'Aménémopé," *Sacra Pagina,* I, *Biblioth. Ephemeridum Theologicarum Lovaniensium,* 12 [1959], 229-241) is les probable. Cf. P. Montet, *L'Égypte et la Bible* (1959), 111-128.

[127] Read הַמַּשָּׂאִי instead of "the oracle."

[128] Gemser, 81 and 83 ref. to par. Minaean-Sabaean names and other details and suggests an Arabian tribe. But W. F. Albright, "The Biblical Tribe of Maśśā and some Congeners," *Stud. Orientalistici G. Levi Della Vida,* I (1956), 1-14, thinks the ref. is to a semi-nomadic

embody knowledge and experience and transmit these to men so that they may draw conclusions from them regarding their conduct, 1 S. 24:14; Prv. 11:2a; 16:18; 18:12. The saying may be quite paradoxical, Prv. 11:24; 20:17; 25:15; 27:7. Thus insights are assembled and set alongside one another, even when they contradict one another, in an attempt to grasp the framework and boundaries of the orders, though without seeking to deduce general principles or to create a system. The gt. significance of such proverbs may be seen from the fact that a second line was often added later to bring out the application to human conduct, Prv. 25:23; 26:20; 27:20; Sir. 13:1.

b. In spite of what were probably earlier contacts with ancient oriental and Egypt. wisdom teaching, in the true sense it was during Solomon's reign that at court and in the developing establishment wisdom became native to Israel, and it was promoted at the school of wisdom which may be presumed to have existed at least in Jerusalem. [129] Hence it is not surprising that there is very common ref. to the wisdom of Solomon ($\rightarrow$ 462, 10 ff.), [130] which was that of ruler, judge, and scholar alike. [131] Nor need one be surprised that Prv. at least was ascribed to him as the model of the wise man. [132] The ancient ref. to his wisdom in 1 K. 4:32 f. gives fuller details : [133] "He spake 3000 proverbs, and his songs were 1005. And he spake of trees, from the cedar that is in Lebanon even unto the hyssop that springeth out of the wall ; he spake also of beasts, and of fowl, and of creeping things, and of fishes." If one allows for possible hyperbole and also for the ascription to Solomon (as absolute ruler) of things which applied to his age and reign in general, in form and content one may perceive two types of wisdom teaching : 1. the serial knowledge which arises out of the concern of wisdom for the phenomena of the plant and animal kingdoms, the Jerusalem lists apparently comprising 1005 or 3000 key-words [134] and relating to more than natural data, so that this might be better called cultural rather than nature wisdom ; 2. the practical wisdom which may be inferred from the specified form of proverb (מָשָׁל $\rightarrow$ V, 747, 18 ff.; 855, 5 ff.) and song [135] and which imparts prudent, moral and in many cases religious rules of conduct. [136] In Israel too, then, one finds the two main branches of ancient oriental wisdom teaching as these are found in Mesopotamia and Egypt ($\rightarrow$ 478, 7 ff.; 479, 20 ff.). Between them lies the riddle, which is related to wisdom in 1 K. 10:1 (cf. also Prv. 1:6), also the numbers saying and fable which probably developed out of the riddle. [137]

The situation in the 8th cent. is characterised on the one side by the fact that Isaiah

---

Aramaean tribe in the Syrian desert, the words of Agur and Lemuel being a slightly Hebraicised form of original Aram. texts of the 10th cent. or even earlier.

[129] Cf. K. Galling, Die Krise d. Aufklärung in Israel (1952), 5-10.

[130] 1 K. 2:6, 9; 3:12, 28; 5:9-11, 14, 21, 26; 10:4, 6-8, 23 f.; 11:41; 2 Ch. 1:10, 12; 2:11; 9:3, 5-7, 22 f.

[131] M. Noth, "Die Bewährung v. Salomos 'Göttlicher Weisheit,' " VT Suppl., 3 (1955), 225-237.

[132] Though his authorship of Qoh. seems to be a fiction of the writer's cf. 1:16 and other details. The songs of 1 K. 4:32 seem to be the basis for ascribing Cant. to Solomon.

[133] Cf. Alt, op. cit., though he wrongly relates the proverbs and songs to practical wisdom.

[134] Only occasionally is there further development of the proverbs and songs for special purposes, e.g., in the numbers sayings in Prv. and God's address in Job 38 ff.

[135] The wisdom song or poem can be called מָשָׁל in Ps. 49:4. Comparison of the poems in Job 18:5-21 and 20:4-29 is instructive since one may see that the second, as distinct from the first, is made up of proverbs or groups of proverbs. In 20:4-29 the description is not a connected composition. The sequence of strophes is capricious and the total impression is not uniform. Often independent sayings are adopted without being fused into the whole, v. 10, 16, 24 f.

[136] Cf. in this connection the distinctive salvation sayings ($\rightarrow$ IV, 365, 5 ff.) of the Wisdom lit. which in distinction from the בָּרוּךְ of the cultic blessing are introduced by אַשְׁרֵי.

[137] Cf. on this whole subject esp. J. Hempel, Die althebräische Lit. u. ihr hell.-jüd. Nachleben (1930), 44-56; J. Schmidt, Stud. zur Stilistik d. at.lichen Spruchliteratur (1936); A. R. Johnson, "מָשָׁל," VT Suppl., 3 (1955), 162-169.

thinks he must adopt a critical attitude towards the wise men with their apparently clever but in fact ruinous plans and measures. [138] It is plain that he has in view the ruling class, so that as in Solomon's time wisdom is the culture and morality of the official world in the broader sense. In keeping on the other side is the fact that acc. to the authentic-sounding superscription in Prv. 25:1 the whole collection Prv. 25-29 was made by the men of Hezekiah, king of Judah (c. 700 B.C.). In all probability this period was one when wisdom teaching played an important role in public life.

Only toward the end of the 7th cent. does the base seem to have broadened. Jer. 50:35 and 51:57 still ref. simply to the ruling class (in Babylon), but minor leaders are meant in Dt. 1:13, 15 and all who administer justice in 16:19. Jer. 8:8 f. speaks of the wise alongside the priests and the prophets, their task being to give counsel. Again Jer. 10:9 has, after 1 K. 7:14, the earliest use of חכם for manual skill, which is not commonly referred to before the post-exilic period. The constant expansion of the terms is a sign that from the later 7th century and on into the post-exilic age wisdom teaching was ceasing to be the culture and morality of the establishment and becoming an affair of broader circles with no social or sociological restrictions. It was transmitted and taught by a class of wisdom teachers whose typical representatives the author of Job used as models for the friends of Job and one of whom speaks in the author of the discourses of Elihu, 32-37. The pupil of Qoh. also calls the latter a teacher of this kind in 12:9-11, while in 2:14, 16 חכם is used as a tt. for the teaching sage, who is no longer judged so favourably, cf. later Sir. 39:1 f., 8; 51:23.

Underlying this wisdom teaching, which lives on from Solomon's time to a later age, though not without change, is an ideal of the culture and training of the whole man. Although, like proverbial wisdom, this has as its goal a cleverness and ability which can master the world, it is no longer seeking merely to establish the orders and laws of the world or life, but on this basis it is deliberately trying to educate men. Its ideal, like that of Egypt. teaching, is the cool person of Prv. 17:27 as distinct from the fiery man (→ n. 112, 116), the patient man as distinct from the wrathful (Prv. 14:29), [139] the self-possessed man who does not yield to searing passion (Prv. 14:30) but controls his emotions and impulses.

c. In post-exilic Israel with its profound intellectual developments the concept of wisdom was to a great degree thought out and used theologically among the so-called teachers of wisdom. Wisdom was regarded as a divine summons to man, as a means of revelation, as the great teacher of Israel and the Gentiles, and even as the divine principle set in the world at creation. All theological thinking thus became more or less wisdom thinking; at any rate, to a hitherto unknown degree, theology was unified and concentrated in the master concept of wisdom. [140] Apart from Prv. 1-9 and Job 28 there are hints of this in the inspired wisdom of Elihu, who by revelation and illumination knows that he possesses it (→ 493, 27 ff.), and also in the speech of God Himself in Job, in which the natural world, as God's creation, is at least initially brought into connection with the revelation made to man.

The incorporation of creation and revelation into this wisdom theology entails the inclusion of spheres which the cleverness and skill of cultural and practical wisdom had left on one side untouched. A comprehensive theological system is thus forged. [141] But in view of its unavoidable overemphases and inadequacies this system was almost bound to give rise to criticism, → 495, 20 ff. [142]

---

[138] Cf. J. Fichtner, "Jesaja unter d. Weisen," ThLZ, 74 (1949), 75-80.

[139] In gen. wrath is regarded as dangerous (→ V, 395, 14 ff.) because it is destructive and has evil effects, Prv. 6:34; 15:1; 16:14; 19:19; 27:4, because it questions God's righteous rule, Job 8:3, and because it undermines fear of God, Job 15:4. The angry man is thus compared to a fool, Prv. 14:17, 29.

[140] G. v. Rad, Theol. d. AT, I (1957), 439.

[141] v. Rad, 449: "It would thus seem that the later wisdom teachers must have had a very comprehensive and indeed encyclopaedic theology."

[142] The criticism was not, of course, because the system threatened to sever contact with

d. In this development a first evident mark of the wisdom of Israel is its nationalising and integration into the life of the people. On the one side this means that it gradually ceases to be a class affair and comes to correspond to the general human factor above all social and sociological boundaries. A sign of this is the adoption of many popular proverbs into collections like Prv. On the other side wisdom even in detail is adjusted to the situation in Palestine. Thus the onomasticon which underlies God's address in Job does not follow the Egypt. pattern but is shaped by the view of things and the details of geography, climate and zoology in Palestine, so that the examples selected correspond to the peculiarities of the Palestinian scene.

Another mark is the analogous religious concentration by which inter-religious wisdom is adjusted and subordinated to faith in Yahweh. This explains the great role played by ethical instruction and ethical or religious behaviour as compared with secular wisdom, and esp. the marked correspondence to the demands of Israel's belief in Yahweh. In particular one may note that not merely is the name of Yahweh often used rather than the general "God" or "Godhead," so that the God of creation and the cosmos is fully equated with Yahweh, but also that the "fear of Yahweh" is regarded as the beginning of wisdom.

The third mark is the comprehensive development of the concept with the help of חכם All the cleverness and skill needed for practical doing or non-doing, even in the most difficult and complicated matters, is expressed by the one stem, cf. also the opposite לֹא חָכָם "unwise" in Dt. 32:6.

III. The "Wisdom" (Sagacity and Knowledge) of Man.

1. Magic and Manticism.

In some instances the use of חכם corresponds to the Mesopotamian mode of expression. The Egypt. חכמים are similar to the magicians מְכַשְּׁפִים, Ex. 7:11. The חכמה of Babylon is its magical art, Is. 47:10, cf. v. 9, 12. The חכמים of Pharaoh are also similar to the priestly soothsayers חַרְטֻמִּים, Gn. 41:8, i.e., men who practise the mantic technique of knowing the future through interpretation of dreams. [143] Hence they are mentioned along with soothsayers [144] and those who seek oracles in Is. 44:25; חכם is a term for the one who pretends to know the background of events and also future events. Even animals — the ibis and cock [145] — have the ability to give advance notice of storms, Job 38:36. Similarly חכמים are later those who understand the times (Est. 1:13), i.e., astrologers who can foretell destiny on the basis of their knowledge of the stars, cf. the friends of Haman whom he asks concerning what will come to pass, Est. 6:13. [146] Thus the חכמים of Babylon are a college of soothsayers, magicians, and interpreters of dreams and signs, whom the king summons for the interpretation of his dreams, cf. Da. 2:27; 4:3.

2. Skill and Ability.

חכם is a man who has mastered something, even if it be only the doing of wickedness, Jer. 4:22. Thus magicians know and use their powerful formulae, Is. 3:3; Ps. 58:5, certain women know and use laments, Jer. 9:16, and priests know and use the Law of Yahweh,

---

Yahweh's work in history (v. Rad, 451) but because of the basic assertions and finally because of the very existence of a system, cf. Job and Qoh.

[143] Possibly Is. 19:12 is also referring to those who interpret the future.

[144] Read בָּרִים for the scribal error "empty chatter."

[145] Cf. on this G. Fohrer, Das Buch Hiob, Komm. AT, 16, ad loc.

[146] Neither v. is textually very certain. 1:13 may be referring to legal experts who know the laws (הַדָּתִים), while the ref. in 6:13 may be just to friends (cf. the versions).

which they are able to falsify acc. to their own will, Jer. 8:8 f. The word group is often used for technical or artistic skill. חכם is used of the accomplished artisan or artist (Ex. 36:8; 2 Ch. 2:12 f.) who has the masterly skill and artistic sense for any task (Ex. 31:3; 35:10, 31; 36:4; 1 Ch. 28:21), esp. in the sanctuary (Ex. 31:6; 36:1 f.) or in the making of idols (Is. 40:20). In this category one may include skilful metal-workers (1 Ch. 22:15; 2 Ch. 2:6), i.e., the smith (Ex. 35:35), worker in brass (1 K. 7:14) or goldsmith (Jer. 10:9), also the carpenter, or the weaver and dyer (Ex. 35:35) who can fashion materials of purple (2 Ch. 2:6) and make costly garments (Jer. 10:9) like those of Aaron (Ex. 28:3). חכמה is the skill of women at spinning (Ex. 35:25 f.), the business ability of the merchant (Ez. 28:3 f.), the knowledge of husbandmen concerning the work which has to be done (Is. 28:23-29), and the skill of sailors, which fails only in face of even mightier tempests, Ps. 107:27.

חכם often denotes the art of government. He who is master of this can become king even though he is poor (Qoh. 4:13), and he who is king needs it (2 Ch. 1:10). Part of it is the ability of the conqueror to subjugate peoples (Is. 10:13) or with diplomatic skill to propose a treaty (1 K. 5:7). Part of it is the ability to judge (1 K. 3:28), to separate the guilty ·from the community (Prv. 20:26), or to make a perspicacious resolve to build a residence (2 Ch. 2:11). The high officials of the king as חכמים are experienced in the art of government (Jer. 50:35; 51:57), whether they discharge specific tasks alone (Gn. 41:33) or impart political counsel (Is. 19:11). Finally every leader, even the most lowly, must have the appropriate ability, Dt. 1:13, 15.

3. Cleverness, Slyness and Cunning.

The ostrich, whose stupidity is proverbial, lacks wisdom (Job 39:15, 17), but other animals, even though small, act sensibly and with a view to self-preservation, so that "washed with all waters" they are exceedingly wise, Prv. 30:24-28. These examples show that חכם can be used for a non-moral cleverness and skill deployed in self-preservation. [147] Such cleverness or cunning is possessed by the woman who sends Joab to David artfully to secure favour for Absalom (2 S. 14:2) and also by the woman who treats with Joab and protects her district from destruction by offering the head of the rebel Sheba, 2 S. 20:16 ff. If this political wisdom serves to ward off a greater evil, the political cunning of the Egyptians hurts the unwanted Israelites by weakening their power through forced labour, Ex. 1:10; this is action in self-interest to the detriment of others. Cunning of this type is even more plain to see in the crafty counsel which Jonadab gave David's son Amnon to pacify his desire for his half-sister Tamar, 2 S. 13:3. David also suggests that Solomon should plot slyly and cunningly to bring about the destruction of Joab and Shimei ; as a wise man he will know how to do this, 1 K. 2:6, 9. Similarly in Job 5:13 the cunning in a bad sense are par. to the crafty נִפְתָּלִים with their wily machinations and crooked ways, cf. Dt. 32:5; Ps. 18:26; Prv. 8:8. Again, acc. to the view of Elihu the friends of Job had been grieved to find in Job a חכמה for which they were no match and which only God could overcome, i.e., a cleverness in the bad sense which continually evaded their arguments, Job 32:13.

4. Practical Wisdom.

חכמה is closely related to prudence, knowledge and reflection (Prv. 8:12) and in this sense it is best understood as the practical wisdom which is on top of life in all relations and situations. It is the skill of the helmsman תַּחְבֻּלוֹת (Prv. 1:5; 11:14), a technique

---

[147] Qoh. 2:19 is not unequivocal. The question is whether the heir is clever enough to administer and enjoy the inheritance left to him or whether he has the necessary business ability.

whereby one can make one's way through the perils of life to the desired goal. It knows wealth and poverty, [148] joy and pain, the necessity of work and the effect of friendliness, gifts, and bribes, Prv. 10:15; 12:25; 13:7 f.; 14:10, 13, 20; 15:13, 30; 16:26; 17:8; 18:16; 21:14. It knows the right attitude for the enjoyment of life and for dealings with others. [149] This prudence, taught by the example of the ant (Prv. 6:6), is what truly distinguishes man as his crown, Prv. 14:24. [150] With it a man realises that God rules the world (Dt. 32:29), is aware of all that happens on the earth, and can distinguish good and evil — like the angel of God acc. to the flattering statement of 2 S. 14:17, 20 — or he is at home in all knowledge (Da.1:4) and has understanding in all learning (1:17). Thus the lady at the court of Sisera's mother who tries to explain why Sisera has not yet returned is experienced in the ways of the world (Ju. 5:29), in contrast to the child which in the crisis of birth-pangs cannot find the way out at the right time (Hos. 13:13), or to the Edomites who do not see what Yahweh has in store for them even though disaster already looms (Jer. 49:7), or to the average man who dies unawares without noting in advance or even being conscious that his end has suddenly come, Job 4:21.

5. Culture.

Though man's higher culture is connected with חכמה in 1 K. 4:29 ff. it played a greater role than would be suggested by the OT tradition, which is not very interested in this. At any rate חכם describes the culture of the educated person. It finds primary expression in the onomastica of serial learning which were often used later as the basis of groups of proverbs or poems. These might embrace organic and inorganic nature, cf. Ps. 104; 148; Job 38:4-39:30; Prv. 30:15-33. Or they might relate to the earth and its peoples, cf. Gn. 10; 15:19 f. Or they might list specific types of men, cf. Job 24:5-8, 14-16a; 30:2-8. They are based on genuine observation which considers phenomena in the world from the standpt. of their difference from the observer and their mutual teleological relation. The goal is the practical one of mastering this world. This may be seen most clearly in Job 28 in the — vain — search for the final secret of the world whose possession will mean, not just theoretical knowledge, but practical control. There is, of course, little place for cultural wisdom in the OT writings. One can deduce Israel's attainments in this sphere only from the comparatively few pieces which use the materials of this wisdom, cf. Gn. 1:1-2:4a; Ps. 8:7 f.; 147; Job 28; 36:27-37:13; 37:15-18; 40:15-24; 40:25-41:26; Cant. 2:11-13a; 3:9-10; Qoh. 1:5-7; Δα. 3:52-90. [151]

6. Rules of Conduct.

חכם is often used for "rules of conduct" or "directions" for right conduct. When Elihu seeks to teach Job חכמה in Job 33:33 his aim is to give him rules of conduct and to lead him to do what is right. Acc. to Prv. 2:2 man lends his ear to חכמה when he listens to words and commandments, i.e., rules of conduct. Thus the task of the teacher of wisdom is to teach knowledge, to arrange sayings critically, so that from them will come חכמה as direction for proper behaviour. It is the task of writing fine and true sayings, Qoh. 12:9-11. As he himself possesses knowledge and prudence (Prv. 14:24) and is ready to be instructed (12:15), he imparts his insights to others (15:2, 7). The fool can pass as wise only so long as he remains silent ; once he tries to teach rules of life he betrays himself. Thus the *si tacuisses, philosophus mansisses* finds its counterpart in the OT, Prv. 17:28; Job 13:5. חכם is one who gives counsel עֵצָה as the priest does תּוֹרָה and the

---

[148] For details cf. Fichtner, 15-17.
[149] *Ibid.*, 17-23 for details."
[150] Read עָרְמָה for "riches."
[151] Later Sir. 39:26 ff.; 4 Esr. 7:39-42. Cf. esp. Alt, *op. cit.*; G. v.Rad, "Hiob 28 u. d. alt-

prophet דָּבָר (Jer. 18:18). But he himself listens to this counsel (Prv. 12:15) to which the man who lacks wisdom is referred (Job 26:3). If prudent and instructive words come thus from the heart (Prv. 16:23), and if anyone can give instruction thus (16:21), in distinction from ordinary speech this is not like "deep water" in a cistern which is no use to the thirsty but like a springing well which is of help to all who will drink of it (18:4). Even a wrathful king may be softened, since the proper rules of conduct can be conveyed to him (16:14). In distinction from the fool and the mocker the חכם listens to these rules and pays heed to salutary correction (15:12, 31), calming rather than intensifying his irritation (29:11), not causing a disturbance but pacifying others (29:8), not merely having enough for himself but feeding others by his instruction, i.e., leading them on the way to life (cf. 6:23; 10:17; 15:24 (on the way → V, 52, 25 ff.) and nourishing them with vital strength (3:18; 10:11; 13:14; 16:22 cf. the originally mythical metaphors of the tree of life and the water of life).

7. Ethical Conduct.

Directions and rules lead to the right conduct taught thereby, and this is also called חכם in Prv. 8:33; 19:20; 28:26. This grants understanding, but its practice also presupposes understanding. It is vain to try to achieve right conduct when there is no understanding, 17:16. Thus one must behave properly even in seeking and attaining right conduct. It is a matter of reverence and dedication, so that the mocker cannot reach the goal, 14:6. It is a matter of the inner disposition (16:23) which is not to be surrendered when one has it, 23:23. Seriousness is measured hereby, Qoh. 7:4. Thus one must be on guard against all that which wise ethical conduct would avoid (2:9-11) and which will corrupt it if one yields or falls victim thereto, [152] e.g., wine and strong drink (20:1), tippling and carousing (23:20 f.), bad company (2:12-15) and strange women (2:16-19; 5:1; 7:4 → IV, 731, 15 ff.; VI, 586, 5 ff.), [153] wealth (Ez. 28:16 ff. → VI, 39, 25 ff.; 324, 29 ff.) and unlawful gain (Qoh. 7:7), violent and passionate speech with no substance or truth (Job 15:2), taking the property of others, esp. by shifting landmarks or using false weights and measures, [154] partiality in judgment, giving or receiving of bribes, and false witness. [155] Right conduct is marked by uprightness and honesty (Prv. 4:11; 23:19). It involves the righteous and gentle treatment of the poor, widows and orphans [156] and a right attitude to parents and personal enemies. [157] It is the same as judgment (Ps. 37:30) and hence can distinguish between right and wrong and practise the right, Dt. 16:19; 1 K. 3:12. It consists in a life controlled by following wise rules (Prv. 2:2) or the divine commandments (Dt. 4:6). The divine Law, the Torah, can be regarded as the true source of sound ethical conduct, Ps. 19:7; 119:98. [158]

ägypt. Weisheit." *VT Suppl.*, 3 (1955), 293-301; H. Richter, "Die Naturweisheit des AT im Buche Hiob." *ZAW*, 70 (1958), 1-20; also R. B. Y. Scott, "Solomon and the Beginnings of Wisdom in Israel," *VT Suppl.*, 3 (1955), 262-279.
[152] → VI, 234, 29 ff.
[153] There are many warnings against illicit love, adultery and fornication, Prv. 5; 6:24, 25-35; 7:5-23. Adultery violates the marriage of another and is a trespass. Later we find religious and ethical motifs, Prv. 5:21-23, cf. adultery as a "heinous deed" (זִמָּה) in Job 31:11. Cf. Fichtner, 27 f.
[154] For details cf. Fichtner, 25-27.
[155] *Ibid.*, 28-30.
[156] *Ibid.*, 30-32.
[157] *Ibid.*, 33 f.
[158] The Law in the strict sense is not mentioned in Prv., Job, or Qoh., *ibid.*, 81-90.

8. Piety.

If חכמה as ethical conduct is often linked with religious ideas, the term can in several instances denote man's piety. As the unwise man offends against God (Dt. 32:6), so the חכם has the inner religious insight that God rules the world (Dt. 32:39). He understands the words of the prophets and the ways and gracious acts of Yahweh (Hos. 14:10; Ps. 107:43). He also perceives his own sin (Ps. 51:6) and the way in which life is circumscribed by God (Ps. 90:12). This type of insight breeds humility (Prv. 11:2; 13:10). But it is also the basis of true faith and trust (Ps. 90:12). [159]

חכמה is often connected with the fear of Yahweh. [160] In detail the two are not the same. According to Prv. 9:10 the fear of Yahweh is the beginning (תְּחִלָּה) of חכמה; according to Prv. 1:7; Ps. 111:10 it is the starting-point (רֵאשִׁית); according to Prv. 15:33 it is the chastisement which leads to חכמה. In Job 28:28, however, חכמה consists in the fear of Yahweh and in Prv. 14:16 the חכם is one who fears God, so that the two concepts are equated. On the other hand, in Prv. 2:6 man understands the fear of Yahweh and acquires the knowledge of God through the חכמה which is given to him, so that the fear of Yahweh here is neither the presupposition of pious knowledge nor is it equated with this; theologically defined חכמה raises the claim that it leads to God. The expression "fear of Yahweh or God," which is a favourite one in wisdom teaching, always denotes piety. It does not mean terror but religious awe which is offered to Yahweh as God or to any god by his devotees. It does not find expression in the cultus, which has a very minor role here. [161] It is the practical religion of what is done or not done day by day, i.e., ethical conduct (→ 486, 14 ff.; VI, 470, 41 ff.). He who practises the fear of Yahweh as practical piety (חכמה) has valuable insight (Ps. 111:10), so that the most important knowledge of life is attained in the sphere of right action rather than in that of the cultus or of thought. Hence Job 37:24 can say that God does not regard the חכמי־לב those who are skilled in wisdom or wise in understanding, but those who bring Him, the Lofty One, reverence. Similarly Prv. 3:7 contrasts wisdom in one's own eyes with the fear of Yahweh.

To the fear of Yahweh corresponds the non-doing of evil, Job 1:1; Prv. 3:7; 14:16. This negative mode of expression does not derive from the model of apodictic law with its categorical prohibitions, nor is the חכם hostile to evil as in prophetic theology. Rather he holds aloof from evil and carefully avoids it. This corresponds to the way of life and piety which is controlled by prudence and the sense of what is profitable, seeking to avoid all offences and to steer clear of all dangers.

---

[159] Cf. A. Weiser, *Die Psalmen*, II, *AT Deutsch*, 15⁵ (1959) on 90:12.

[160] Cf. "fear of God," e.g., Job 1:1. The shorter יִרְאָה occurs only in the speeches of Eliphaz in Job 4:6; 15:4; 22:4, the mere verb ירא only in Prv. 14:16.

[161] On the cultus and prayer, which by contrast plays a gt. role in Wisdom, → II, 797, 20 ff.; III, 239, 10 ff.; Fichtner, 36-46. v. Rad is quite wrong when he argues (*op. cit.*, 431) that the one instructed in wisdom was a member of the cultic community, that his life stood under cultic statutes, and that wisdom was limited to the ordering of life outside the cultus. In Prv. (apart from the later 3:9) 15:8, 29; 20:25; 21:3, 27; 28:9; 30:12 are more or less critical of the cultus, the emphasis is not on cultic action but on the uprightness of the worshipper, and what finally counts is prayer rather than sacrifice, Fichtner, 41 f. For the

In this light one may understand the proverbs which according to an originally Egyptian notion describe God as the One who weighs and tests the heart (Prv. 16:2; 17:3; 21:2; 24:12), which are aware of the pleasure or displeasure He takes in man's good or evil conduct (11:1, 20; 15:8 f., 26; 16:5, 7; 17:15; 20:10, 23; 22:11), and which refer to the limits sets for man's potentialities by God's intervention (16:1, 9; 19:21; 20:24; 21:30 f.). In the last resort this, too, brings it about that man's trust is set in Yahweh, 22:19.

9. Academic Wisdom.

Later, at least, the various aspects (→ 485, 33 ff.) form a great unity. In the later post-exilic age we find a theologically well-rounded body of instruction → 482, 31 ff. The impulse towards this was there from the outset, as may be seen from the ancient notes on Solomon's wisdom (→ 481, 9 ff.) in wich חכמה is almost a tt. already, and is certainly a tt. for comprehensive skill and learning (in distinction from the later period), cf. 1 K. 4:29 ff.; 10:4-8, 23; 11:41. Elihu speaks of the "wise" in Job 34:2, 34 more in the sense of an attitude to life, with a ref. to teachers of wisdom as well as to all those who live acc. to the principles taught. Job in 12:2 pours scorn on the self-assured conceit of his friends, who think they alone are the ones who possess all the wisdom alongside which no other attitude is possible; he suggests contemptuously that wisdom will perish with them, its only representatives. [162] More plainly Job 8:8 says that the content of wisdom is that "sought out" (חֵקֶר) by the fathers and in 11:4 the content of the preceding speech of Job is called "teaching" (לֶקַח). Qoh. esp. finds himself confronted by a closed body of teaching so that in him חכמה and חכם may be transl. academic wisdom and the academic teacher of wisdom (or wise man), e.g., 2:12 f., 14, 16, 21; 8:17. He, too, has learned it, has sought to establish all things by it, and is unceasingly concerned to attain the desired goal with its help, namely, the mastering and assuring of life by prudence, 1:13, 16. In fact wisdom has some advantages over folly. It can teach man not to find happiness in mere indulgence (2:3) and also to avoid obstacles (2:14). In the main, however, Qoh. is critical of wisdom (→ 495, 25 ff.); he is plainly referring to this wisdom of the schools.

10. Eschatological Blessing and Apocalyptic Endowment.

Twice חכמה is called an eschatological blessing. In Is. 33:6 חכמה and דַּעַת are Zion's riches of salvation and the fear of Yahweh is its treasure. In addition v. 5 refers to the right and righteousness with which Yahweh fills the city. Thus חכמה is used in the sense of the practical piety (→ 487, 1 ff.) which will be the wealth of Jerusalem in the age of eschatological salvation. According to Is. 11:2 the Spirit of Yahweh will fall on the Messianic ruler of the last time as a lasting possession; it is the spirit of חכמה, insight, counsel, knowledge, and the fear of Yahweh, but also of strength. The reference, then, is to the combination of חכמה in various forms with strength, as in Yahweh Himself according to Job 9:4; 12:13. This special and enduring endowment with the Spirit of Yahweh means that the mediated gifts both of wisdom in its various aspects and also of strength surpass the normal human measure, so that the Messianic ruler of the last days can be God's vicegerent and execute the divine will, with which he knows he is at one. The conditions which result in the eschatological reign are depicted in the following verses.

---

rest the natural incorporation of the wise man into the cultic community and its rules is an unproved presupposition.

[162] Cf. the debate between Aeschylus and Euripides in Aristoph. Ra., 868 f.

In Daniel we have the beginning of the fusion of later wisdom theology with apocalyptic. Daniel's חכמה differs from that which is proper to man. It does not merely surpass it (2:30); as a divinely given wisdom it is fundamentally different (5:11, 14). The secrets of the future are known to him by means of it.

IV. The "Wisdom" (Sagacity and Knowledge) of God.

1. God Possesses Wisdom.

חכם is ascribed to God more rarely than to man. 2 S. 14:20 says the angel of God is wise, and Job 15:8 speaks of the wisdom of His entourage. It is comparatively late, however, that God Himself is said to have wisdom. Apparently it took time before the Mesopotamian and Egypt. idea of gods of wisdom in various senses [163] and the Canaanite concept of the wisdom of El [164] could be integrated into the belief in Yahweh. Initially the presupposition that חכמה has its origin in God and is His possession tacitly underlies the description of it as God's gift to man, cf. already the story of Solomon and the Joseph cycle (→ 493, 8 ff.). Is. is more explicit. In debate with the supposedley clever politicians of his age he says in 31:1 f. that God, too, is חכם, and from the example of the farmer he shows that according to a given situation God can impart new and different counsel (עֵצָה) to His prophet, 28:23-29. Yet only later is it explicitly stated that חכמה is a possession and faculty of Yahweh, not with ref. to history, [165] but esp. with ref. to God as the Creator who has made all things wisely, i.e., with technical and artistic mastery, Is. 40:13 f., 28; Jer. 10:12; 51:15; Ps. 104:24; Job 26:12; Prv. 3:19 f., who understands how to make the clouds float in the sky even though they are laden with water, Job 37:16; cf. 36:29, and who counts them with a skilful hand so that they may come in due measure and do not bring too much or too little rain, 38:37. God's חכמה is also His mysterious action corresponding to man's ethical conduct according to the principle of retributive justice, 11:6. It is the codification of the principles of righteous human conduct in the law-code of Ezra (Ezr. 7:25) and the declaration of the mysteries of the future (Da. 2:20 f.; 5:11, 14). Since He has no rival with similar skill and ability among the peoples (Jer. 10:7), and since esp. He has the might and power to actualise what He has wisely thought out and skilfully planned (cf. the hymn of praise in Job 12:13 [166] and the bitterly ironical complaint of Job in 9:4), [167] no human understanding can stand against Him, Prv. 21:30. He confounds all the human cleverness which withstands His will, Is. 19:11-15; 29:14; 31:2 f.

2. God Attains and Creates Wisdom.

a. The poet of Job 28 uses חכמה for the principle which holds sway in all the world and in all life. Knowledge of this gives insight into all things and mastery over them. In opposition to the customary admonition to get חכמה (e.g., Prv. 4:5) the idea that man can control it is thus contested. [168] In spite of his Faustian urge

---

[163] For details Fichtner, 117 f.

[164] Gordon Manual Text, 51, IV 41; 51, V 65; 'nt V 38; cf. 126, IV 3.

[165] Cf. also J. Fichtner, "Zum Problem Glaube u. Gesch. in d. isr.-jüd. Weisheitslit.," ThLZ, 76 (1951), 145-150.

[166] Cf. Prv. 8:14 on personified חכמה.

[167] Job is not saying that respect is man's proper attitude in face of the absolute right of God (A. Weiser, Das Buch Hiob, AT Deutsch, 13² [1956], ad. loc.) but in justification of His complaint against God he is explaining why man can never be in the right.

[168] It makes no difference whether the song is a later addition put on the lips of Job in a rearrangement of the third round of speeches. Its negative judgment provides a reason

to know what it is that holds the world together at its core, [169] only God has found the way to wisdom, has attained it, sought it out, and used it in the creation of the world. Possession of הכמה, then, is not a theoretical knowledge of the world. It is practical control over it, vv. 25-27. Though הכמה is subject to God, being incorporated into His creative work and equated with the secrets of the divine creation, its original autonomy may still be glimpsed in the poem. It was a heavenly, pre-existent and independent entity side by side with God at a place to which God alone had access. It is not here a personified power of God or an independently evolved entity in the form of a hypostasis. [170] It is a material reality which is sought like other things (mineral wealth) and which has its own location like these. Now there is an element of speculation in this view, but it is also based on mythical notions. [171] In particular a Gnostic myth lies behind it ; this may be seen quite plainly both in this and later texts [172] → 507, 20 ff. The reference to this in Job 28 says that man's search for הכמה, for the secret of the world, has always been a vain one, and that it is subject to God's full disposal.

Other roots have been considered for the idea. Egypt and Babylon both spoke of an eternal divine wisdom which is proper to the gods or embodied by them or by hypostases or personifications. [173] An Iranian-Chaldaean origin has also been suggested, [174] cf. esp. personified piety (ārmaiti in the Avesta) [175] or personified religion and faith (daēnā in the Avesta), [176] or the Semitic goddess of love and heaven (Ishtar, Astarte), [177] or gen. an originally feminine deity which was co-ordinated with and subordinated to God and seen as an essential attribute. [178] There can certainly be no question of Gk. influence. [179]

b. As one of several elements the same myth stands behind the term הכמה in Prv. 1-9, the latest part of the book, in which several older sayings are employed in a new theological setting. [180] The main themes in this collection are an urgent and heart-felt commendation of both wisdom and the fear of God (1:7-9, 20-23;

---

for the addition in this case. The pt. of the poem is to explode once and for all the theology of the friends of Job and to repudiate their attempts to solve the riddle of human suffering. This does, of course, fit in with the supposed speaker (Job), who had first tried to solve his problem on the same premisses as those of his friends. The recommending of the fear of God in v. 28 seems to be a later addition and may be left out of account.

[169] O. Eissfeldt, "Religionshistorie u. Religionspolemik im AT," VT Suppl., 3 (1955), 94.
[170] Cf. esp. Schencke; J. Goettsberger, Die göttliche Weisheit als Persönlichkeit im AT (1919); P. Heinisch, Personifikationen u. Hypostasen im AT u. im Alten Orient (1921); also Die göttliche Weisheit d. AT in religionsgeschichtlicher Beleuchtung (1923); P. van Imschoot, "La Sagesse dans l'AT est-elle une hypostase?" Collationes Gandavenses, 21 (1934), 3-10, 85-94; Ringgren; R. Marcus, "On Biblical Hypostases of Wisdom," HUCA, 23, 1 (1950/51), 157-171.
[171] Baumgartner, 28, with ref. to Achiqar, line 95 (AOT, 458).
[172] Bultmann Hintergrund, 3-26.
[173] Baumgartner, 28.
[174] Reitzenstein Buch des Herrn d. Grösse, 46-58.
[175] Though cf. Bousset-Gressm., 520.
[176] Loc. cit.
[177] Boström, 12-14; W. F. Albright, From the Stone Age to Christianity (1949), 283 f. suggests an older Canaanite goddess of wisdom like the Mesopotamian Siduri Sabitu. But against this one must recall the different meaning of wisdom in Mesopotamia, → 477, 26 ff.
[178] G. Hölscher, Das Buch Hiob, Hndbch. AT, I, 17² (1952), 68.
[179] R. Kittel, Gesch. d. Volkes Israel, III, 2 (1929), 731 f.; E. Sellin, Gesch. d. isr.-jüd. Volkes, II (1932), 181.
[180] The claim of Albright, op. cit. (→ n. 177), 281 f., that Prv. 8-9 is Canaanite in origin is exaggerated. Linguistic echoes are due to the use of mythical ideas and creation statements.

2; 3:1-26; 4; 8; 9) and a warning against the strange woman (5; 6:20-35; 7). The two themes are often interwoven (2:16-19; 7:1-5; 9). חכמה, which in Job 28 is inaccessible to man, now speaks to him as teacher and revealer. This is made possible by the ideas of the Gnostic myth according to which חכמה seeks a dwelling among men, though in the myth it does not find this and returns to heaven; in Sir. 24:8 ff. it finds it in Israel and Jerusalem and in Sir. 24:23 ff. it can be equated with the Torah. In any case what it says to man is quite intelligible.

In Prv. 8:22-31, as in Job 28, חכמה is pre-existent and before all the works of creation. But it has no primal existence alongside God, who has to discover it. It was created first by Him and was then present at the further and true creation, not as a helper, but as a child playing in its father's workshop. [181] As God's favourite child (אָמוֹן v. 30) it played with creation and with man. [182] In distinction from Job 28 it is here a personal entity, created by God and having no part in creation. [183] God does not attain it; He creates it. The difference is due to the influence of a second myth, that of the primal man who was created before all worlds and who thus has a special wisdom of experience. By means of this myth, which is used in another way in Ez. 28:1-10, 11-19 and Job 15:7-8 as well (→ 493, 19 ff.), חכמה is personified. The point of the discussion is that חכמה shows its patent of nobility: [184] the older the nobility the higher it is in rank, and similarly, the older wisdom is, the more normative it is (cf. the argument in Job 15:7 f.). Thus the weight and authority of the address to man are enhanced.

חכמה is also personified in Prv. 1-9. She is a preacher in 1:20, a bride and wife in 4:6-9, a life-companion in 6:22; 7:4, a hostess in 9:1. As other personal metaphors show, these personifications are also figurative, cf. Is. 59:14; Ps. 85:10 f.; Prv. 9:13-18. Thus wisdom is no longer the neutral teaching passed on to man by the words of a sage; it summons man as a person, and it raises its voice like a prophet in the centres of public life in villages (1:20 f.) and at cross-roads (8:2). This pathos of prophetic proclamation is the third element in the current concept of wisdom (→ 493, 27 ff. on Elihu). Wisdom speaks with special authority. It invites and threatens. Like a prophet it sets man before the decision of life and death. [185] For it offers life, true, full and happy life in the OT sense, the life which is real salvation, 3:18, 22; 4:13, 22 f.; 8:35; → II, 845, 33 ff.; 851, 17 ff. In this respect it is the revelation of God's will to man. Hence man must track it down (2:4), find it (3:13), woo it (4:7), accept the invitation which it offers to the feast as beloved (4:6 ff.), sister, or bride (7:4). For in so doing man accepts God's will and does it, so that God is well-pleased with him (8:35). That this applies not merely to Israel but to man generally may best be seen from 8:1--21. In its metaphors and modes of expression all this is again influenced by the mythical concept of חכמה seeking a dwelling and union with man. [186] The fact that this con-

---

[181] Gemser, op. cit., 39.

[182] The later Jewish transl. of אָמוֹן in v. 30 as "master builder" rests on later ideas → n. 291. In the LXX God is made the subj. of v. 31.

[183] The apparently divergent statement in Prv. 3:19 f. is due to the fact that an older proverb is present here which uses חכמה in the technical-artistic sense.

[184] G. Wildeboer, Die Sprüche, Kurzer Hand-Comm. AT, 15 (1897), 27.

[185] On good and evil → III, 478, 22 ff.

[186] In this light it is clear that חכמה is not the rival of 'Αφροδίτη παρακύπτουσα who through strange women entices the Israelites to take part in aphrodisiac cults (as suggested by Boström, 127-147).

cept is adopted soberly and in a way which is not detrimental to faith in Yahweh is based on the fundamental theological understanding, which is marked by incorporation of the prophetic element. [187]

V. The Origin and Source of Sagacity and Knowledge.

1. The Tradition of the Fathers.

In distinction from the teaching tradition of Egypt, tradition is only one source of sagacity and knowledge in the OT. The Egypt. situation is excellently characterised in Is. 19:11 when Pharaoh's advisers say that they are students of the sages and kings of former times to whom many of the teachings may be traced back; they draw exclusively on the tradition of the fathers. The friends of Job do this too, but for them tradition is not the only source of their counsel. This is in keeping with all instruction in Israel, which lays special emphasis on introduction to the traditions of the fathers. [188] Bildad appeals to the teaching of former generations because these are superior to the experience of an individual or a single generation, Job 8:8-10. Eliphaz appeals to the teaching tradition which lives on into his own generation and is confirmed by it, and which is pure and unperverted because of the absence of aliens from other tribes or countries at the time of its origin, 15:19 f.

2. Personal Experience.

A second source of knowledgeability is the experience a man gathers in the course of life. This is why old men are usually regarded as the repositories of wise experience with an adequate insight into things, Job 12:12; 15:10; 32:7; cf. Ez. 7:26. Along these lines Eliphaz appeals to what he has perceived and discovered, 8:4; 5:3, 27; 15:17, so that he can pass it on in the instruction of others. Job adduces his own very different experience, 21:6. Qoh. in particular either refers to his own perceptions and experiences or depicts them, e.g., 1:13a, 16-17a; 2:1, 3a, 4-8, 12a, 24; 3:10 f., 16; 4:1, 4a, 7. In form-critical analysis this element is one of the factors in many of the statements in Qoh., which are constructed acc. to the schema of gathering experience — result (a proverb as basis or confirmation). [189]

3. Means and Methods.

The two means to mediate sagacity and knowledge to others, or learn them oneself, on the basis of tradition and experience are instruction and correction (→ II, 473, 25 ff.; V, 604, 30 ff.), cf. Prv. 19:20; 21:11. The ref. may be to simple teaching (Prv. 4:11; 9:9; 13:14; Ps. 105:22) as one has converse with the wise (13:20). It may be loving (31:26), but it may also take the form of correction (9:8), censure (Qoh. 7:5), or the rod (Prv. 29:15). It takes place by means of מָשָׁל (Prv. 1:1, 6) and דָּבָר (1:6; 22:17) and other forms of address, e.g., 1:6. Since the wise man can understand hard sentences and give their interpretation (פֵּשֶׁר) for the learner (Qoh. 8:1) his words have the same function as the ploughman's goad and smite like nails which are driven in (12:11). If

---

[187] On the many contacts with Is. (esp. 40-66), Jer. and Dt. cf. for details A. Robert, "Les ttaches littéraires bibl. de Prv. I-IX," *Rev. Bibl.*, 43 (1934), 42-68, 172-204, 374-384; also 4 (1935), 344-365, 502-525.
[188] Cf. Ex. 13:8 ff.; Dt. 4:9; 6:7, 20 ff.; 11:19 ff.; Jos. 4:6 f., 21; Ps. 78:5 ff.; cf. L. Dürr, *Das Erziehungswesen im AT u. im Alten Orient* (1932), 107 f.
[189] Qoh. 1:12-15; 1:16-18; 2:1-11, 12b (threefold sequence); 2:12a, 13-17 (twofold sequence ut altered); 3:16 f.; 4:1-3; 4:4-6; 4:7 f.; with double experience 2:24-26; 3:10-15 (in 3:1-15).

this instruction is not enough there is chastisement (Prv. 8:33; 13:1) and the rod (29:15). Knowledge develops with great labour and many blows; this was perhaps the original pt. of the proverb which is used in a different sense in Qoh. 1:18.

4. The Gift of God.

a. If a man usually acquires sagacity and knowledge from tradition and experience by the way of learning and chastisement, there is also the possibility of extraordinary endowment with the gift of חכמה; this is a divine endowment, even though it takes place only in specific instances. God endowed special men in this way, e.g., Joseph in Gn. 41:16, 38 f., Joshua by the laying on of the hands of Moses in Dt. 34:9, Solomon in 1 K. 3:12, 28; 5:26; 10:24; 2 Ch. 1:12, and Daniel in Da. 1:4, 17, 20; 5:11, 14. One may refer similarly to individual prophetic inspiration in Jer. 9:11 and the experience of nocturnal revelation by Eliphaz in Job 4:12-21, and cf. too artistic ability in Ex. 28:3; 31:3, 6; 35:31; 36:1 f. and skill in husbandry in Is. 28:26. The oldest instances are in the story of Solomon, the Joseph cycle, and Is. 28:26, the others being later, cf. also Ps. 60:7; 94:10; 119:98; Prv. 28:5; Qoh. 2:26. In Job, too, God gives wisdom (11:6; 38:36) or keeps far from it (17:4). The gen. view is espoused here that God gives a measure of חכמה to man but that this cannot compare with His own, so that many things appear wonderful and mysterious to man, 42:3.

b. The situation is different when in accordance with the myth of the primal man (cf. Ez. 28:1-10, 11-19) someone might claim that he was born before the rest of creation and that as the oldest he was thus the wisest man, or that like the primal man he was admitted to the heavenly counsel and thus shared something of the divine חכמה, Job 15:7 f. cf. Jer. 23:18, 22. Only thus can he be superior to the teachings of tradition or the experience of the ancients. These conditions naturally do not apply to Job, so that Eliphaz is using the originally mythical ideas as fig. comparisons to beat down what seems to him to be the presumptuous presentation of Job.

c. In later wisdom teaching we find another view which first comes to the surface in the speeches of Elihu in Job 32-37. The knowledge and teaching which Elihu possesses and wants to impart is described by him as דֵּעַ ("knowledge") in 32:6, 10, 17; 36:3 (fem. plur. דֵּעוֹת 36:4); materially, however, this is the same as חכמה. The rare word denotes either God's own knowledge (37:16; 1 S. 2:3; Ps. 73:11) or that imparted by Him (Is. 28:9; Jer. 3:15) and has been deliberately selected for Elihu's speeches in order to show from the very outset that Elihu is conscious of having God's own knowledge and the knowledge imparted by Him. [190] This is why he says that he has it "from afar," i.e., in view of the par. "creator," from God, 36:3. It has been mediated to him by God's "spirit" and "breath" so that he has not had to garner the experiences of a long life or to learn the tradition of the fathers; in spite of his youth he is wise because by inspiration he has received divine wisdom as an enduring possession, 32:7-10. The view of Elihu, then, is that חכמה is first God's possession. He then claims that it neither remains hid from man (Job 28) nor is mediated only in specific cases but that it has been granted to him gen. and in toto. What he has received is his "portion" (32:17) of the totality of divine wisdom and this is enough to give a full answer to Job and his friends. This knowledge is sinless (33:3, probably based on Zeph. 3:9) and perfect or — as the plur. form is designed to show — comprehensive and unsurpassable, 36:4. Acc. to the serious and by no means ironical view of the author of the speeches, what Elihu teaches is the final conclusion of divine wisdom. Elihu thus claims for himself the same dignity of supernatural illumination and direct inspiration as the prophet. He stands alongside the

---

[190] In keeping is the fact that Elihu uses the more common דַּעַת only when he says that Job or the sinner does not have wisdom or knowledge, 34:35; 35:16; 36:12.

prophet or in his place, and even surpasses him inasmuch as the inspiratory Spirit fills him wholly and permanently. [191]

Along these lines the figuratively personified חכמה of Prv. 1-9 is the mediator of revelation in the sense that in her proclamation she is like a prophet and can claim supreme authority, revealing God's will to man, offering man life, and regarding acceptance as that of the divine will → 491, 31 ff. Eschatological Messianic חכמה and apocalyptic חכמה (→ 488, 30 ff.) are also viewed as a permanently granted possession.

VI. Value, Result and Criticism of Sagacity and Knowledge.

I. Value and Result.

Instruction in sagacity and knowledge is as profitable to the pupil as a springing well compared to a cistern with deep standing water, Prv. 18:4. The teacher who instructs in rules of life is as valuable to his listeners as a ring and jewel of gold, 25:12. Wisdom is a costly treasure (21:20); indeed, it is more precious than treasure (3:15; 8:11; cf. Job 28:15-18). For חכמה protects and delivers a man (Prv. 2:8, 20) so that he avoids obstacles (Qoh. 2:14, 16), steers clear of trouble (Prv. 14:3), masters every difficulty (Qoh. 8:5), escapes the snares of death (Prv. 13:14) and evades misfortune (28:26). Positively wise conduct profits a man (Prv. 9:12), so that he may expect success (Qoh. 9:11a) and great prosperity (Job 22:25; cf. 5:12; 6:13; 11:6) and reach the goal of his way (Prv. 14:8). He achieves honour (Prv. 3:35) and is blessed (12:18), for חכמה builds up (14:1) and achieves lasting results (24:3). Not mere knowledge, but practically applied sagacity and understanding are strength, 21:22; Qoh. 7:19; 9:15. Sometimes we read of their value for others. In particular the father or teacher rejoices in the one who has become wise (Prv. 10:1; 15:20; 23:15, 24) and he can give an answer to those who scorn him as a poor teacher, Prv. 27:11.

One can hardly overlook the fact that this view of life has a certain utilitarian or eudaemonistic aspect. It is not for nothing that in Job the value of piety is often weighed by wise counsellors (22:2 f.; 35:6-8) and Job is attacked for contesting this (34:9; 35:3) or he himself suggests that only sinners dispute it, 21:15. [192] Conduct not only has its origin in a basic attitude; it also seeks a specific end and result. This is true not least in the חכם as sagacity and knowledge for the purpose of a specific manner of life. The two are inseparably related; prudence and understanding are always directed to a particular result. Yet as compared with pure utilitarianism a distinction is to be made. There is no essential difference or antithesis between the inner worth of a deed in act or conduct as such and its outer result. [193] The two are one and the same when the חכם seeks to know the orders in the world and in life so that he may subjugate the world and master life. Thus Job's friends constantly exhort him to submit to the orders and to integrate himself into them; this is the proper inner attitude which leads to right conduct and guarantees outer success, so that fresh salvation beckons him on. It is true, of course, that God's address says of this cosmic order (עֵצָה) that as a divine order it is unfathomable to man. Hence Qoh. 3:1-15 draws the conclusion that there can be no assurance as to the success of human action.

---

[191] He thus claims he should be heard like a prophet (32:10) and believes that he has better arguments to present than Job's friends in the difficult situation (32:14). He must speak unconditionally as a vessel of the divine Spirit (32:18-20) since the Spirit compels him to speak like a prophet, cf. Jer. 20:9.
[192] Cf. the ethical final clauses → III, 330, 13 ff.
[193] So rightly Gese, 7-41.

The order of the world and of life is never abandoned by God; it is established and upheld by Him. He is thus pleased with prudent, intelligent or pious integration into it and displeased with attacks upon it. Acc. to His retributive justice He thus grants to the חכם prosperity and success as blessing and salvation, but evil to the fool and evil-doer. Thus the two-sided belief in retribution is a basic pillar of practical wisdom → IV, 711, 7 ff. Acc. to this conviction a good act will always issue in good and a bad act in evil. Wisdom teaching stands or falls with the principle that man's conduct and state correspond. This correspondence is not, of course, mechanical, but goes back to God, who necessarily acts thus in accordance with His righteousness. [194] If the facts seem to be against this, the suffering of the innocent can be explained by saying that he endures the fate of man who is imperfect and inadequate by nature (Job 4:17-21) or that God uses suffering to educate him (5:17; 33:13-24). The prosperity of the wicked is said to be one of appearance only, since in reality he is plagued by many torments, Job 15:20-22. In the case of both there is a glance beyond individual life to retribution visited on children, Ps. 37:25; Job 5:4 f.; 18:19; 20:10; 27:14; Prv. 13:22; 20:7. Finally, this view leads to a developed doctrine of retribution in which every sin bears a specific penalty and a line is drawn from the effect (good fortune or ill) to the cause (piety or sinfulness). This shows plainly the value and result of prudent and instructed conduct in the ethical or religious sense.

2. Criticism.

If earlier criticism of חכמה is directed against pagan soothsaying or the art of interpretation (Gn. 41:8; Is. 44:25), then against the ostensibly clever politicians of Jerusalem (Is. 5:21; 29:14; 31:1-3), at a later date it is focused on the comprehensive and established system of teaching.

Qoh. grants that academic wisdom has a relative value (2:3, 14. 16; 4:13; 10:12), but in the last resort he does not think it brings any real advantage (2:15; 9:11a), since it is no better than equally ineffectual folly (1:16 f.; 6:8). Thus it is useless from the standpt. of possessions, which one must leave behind, so that all one gets from them is trouble, 2:21. It is also valueless in face of death, which smites all men impartially, 2:15 f. (cf. Ps. 49:10), and which, since one can neither anticipate it nor avoid it, forms an impenetrable frontier for the wisdom of the schools. Another frontier is woman (not just the strange woman of Prv.), who ensnares and seduces the wise man, so that he forgets his life-principles and his concern for the shaping of life becomes illusory, if God so wills, 7:26. The fate of the wise does not depend, as their teaching maintains, on their just and pious conduct, but is prepared already in God's hand in a way which cannot be fathomed or known, 8:17; 9:1. The only option, then, is to live actively and enjoy to the full the share of life granted, 9:7-10. [195]

If in spite of this plea for an active enjoyment of life Qoh. does not try to shape life constructively but recommends an acceptance of the portion of life given, and above

---

[194] The roots lie in the original idea that every act creates a sphere which surrounds man for good or ill, so that by its very character a good act has good results, while a bad one is destructive. At most only the relics of this view are to be found in Yahweh religion, as against J. Pedersen, *Israel*, I-II (1926), 336-377; K. H. Fahlgren, *Sedaqa nahestehende u. entgegengesetzte Begriffe im AT* (1932), 4; K. Koch, "Gibt es ein Vergeltungsdogma im AT?" ZThK, 52 (1955), 1-42. The almost magical and mechanical equation of good act and success, bad act and disaster, is here completely subordinate to the personal sway of Yahweh and His retributive righteousness. Cf. the discussion in Gese, 42-50; H. Graf Reventlow, "Sein Blut komme über sein Haupt," VT, 10 (1960), 311-327.

[195] This criticism is itself criticised in Qoh. 12:12-14, where the author sees a danger for the student in the gt. no. of books with their many different opinions. That Qoh. is in view may be seen from the fact that his divergent view is comprehensively interpreted and corrected. Qoh. is now championing an ethics grounded in God's commandment and the concept of final judgement on the hidden deeds of men.

all a marked restraint, the author of Job wrestles with the doctrine of retribution in an attempt to achieve a new structure of life which will lead to true human existence beyond mere living. If this is not to be found in the traditional teaching of Job's friends, which is proved. false by Job [196] and rejected as sinful by God (42:7 f.), [197] neither is it to be found in the Promethean-Titanic pretension of Job, who at first tries to snatch his good fortune from God, protesting his blamelessness and opposing God in an attempt to triumph over Him, 31:35-37. Real understanding is gained only from personal encounter with God. Right conduct consists in humble and devoted silence on the basis of rest in God. This is rooted in the experience that the destiny of man rests on the puzzling and inscrutable but purposeful acts of God. It is rooted in the assurance of fellowship with God, which outweighs all else, 40:4 f.; 42:2-3, 5-6. Is. 51:7 f. and Ps. 73:25-28 are to the same effect. Hence man must not glory in his own wisdom but only in the knowledge of Yahweh, i.e., in fellowship with the God who rules the world and men, and in the life which is ordained by Him, Jer. 9:22 f.

SOLOMON AND THE BEGINNINGS OF WISDOM IN ISRAEL

R. B. Y. SCOTT
Montreal

The traditional connection of the name of Solomon with books of Hebrew wisdom and poetry raises a series of related problems. It is quite out of the question that the king was in fact the composer of the whole book of Proverbs, of Ecclesiastes and Wisdom, of psalms canonical and extra-canonical: how then did his name come to be attached to them? If—as appears likely—the ultimate origin of this literary convention is the statement of 1 Reg. v 12 that "he uttered three thousand proverbs, and his song(s were) a thousand and five" [1]), what reliance can be placed on this claim? Does it mean no more than that Solomon was credited with these accomplishments because wisdom literature and poetry flourished at his court and under his patronage [2])? Are the accounts of Solomon's superlative wisdom and fame a legendary embellishment of history? If so, what was the historical basis of these accounts, and when and why did the embellishment take place? How is this picture of Solomon's wisdom as intellectual brilliance and literary productivity to be related to the quite different interpretation of it—as discernment to render justice—in the famous story of the dream at Gibeon?

Many scholars seem to accept almost at its face value the story in 1 Reg. v 9-14 of Solomon's superlative literary gifts and fame, and hence have no difficulty in regarding him as the earliest patron, and indeed the fountain-head, of Israelite wisdom. EISSFELDT, for example, speaks of the "ganz richtig festgehaltenen Tatsache, dass Salomo an seinem Hof die Weisheitsdichtung gepflegt hat und auch selbst auf

---

[1]) LXX "five thousand".

[2]) R. EISLER draws attention to the parallel claim of Ashurbanipal to have written the tablets of his library; *AJSL* 42 (1926), p. 73, note 1. He says that Nabù gave him wisdom, and he acquired the arts of reading and writing; cf. D. D. LUCKENBILL, *Ancient Records of Babylonia and Assyria*, ii, secs. 767, 934, 986.

diesem Gebiet sehr fruchtbar gewesen ist" [1]). Similarly BAUMGARTNER in his 1951 survey of recent studies in the Wisdom Literature comments that "there is now again more disposition to treat seriously the ascription of both (Prov. x 1—xxii 16 and xxv—xxix) to Solomon" [2]). Most historians of Israel and commentators on the Wisdom books allow a greater or lesser degree of historical substance to the Solomonic tradition [3]), but there remains considerable scepticism about the antiquity and reliability of the more extravagant accounts of Solomon's wealth and wisdom. CAUSSE calls these "le mirage salomonien", and H. WHEELER ROBINSON says of Solomon's "posthumous reputation for wisdom" that "it is not easy to decide just where the historic Solomon ends and the legendary accretions begin" [4]). SKINNER, who accepts the tradition of Solomon's wisdom as substantially historical, nevertheless acknowledges that the description of it in 1 Reg. v 9-14, "with its backward look to the shadowy personages of a hoary antiquity .... can hardly have come from an ancient source" [5]). ALBRIGHT infers that Solomon's literary production, of which "nothing seems to have been directly preserved, ... was more prolific than inspired" [6]).

---

[1]) O. EISSFELDT, *Einleitung in das Alte Testament*, p. 527.

[2]) W. BAUMGARTNER, in *The Old Testament and Modern Study* (ed. H. H. ROWLEY), p. 213.

[3]) Cf. *inter alia*, E. SELLIN, *Geschichte des israelitisch-jüdischen Volkes*, i, p. 197; ii, p. 179; C. F. KENT, *History of the Hebrew People*, 13th ed. (1916), p. 184-187; R. KITTEL, *Geschichte des Volkes Israel*, 2nd ed. (1909), p. 231-232; A. T. OLMSTEAD, *History of Palestine and Syria*, p. 341; J. SKINNER, *I and II Kings* (Century Bible), p. 97; O. S. RANKIN, *Israel's Wisdom Literature*, p. 6; B. GEMSER, "Sprüche Salomos", *HAT*, p. 2; W. BAUMGARTNER, *TR* N.F. 5 (1933), p. 270; H. M. ORLINSKY, *Ancient Israel*, p. 85; E. SELLIN, *Einleitung in das Alte Testament*, 8th ed. (1950), ed. L. ROST, p. 156; W. A. IRWIN, in *The Interpreter's Bible*, p. 179. This view is stated more tentatively by T. H. ROBINSON, *History of Israel*, i, p. 242; M. NOTH, *Geschichte Israels*, (2nd ed. 1954) p. 200-201; H. R. HALL, *Ancient History of the Near East*, 7th ed. (1927), p. 433; and A. ALT, *TLZ* (1951), p. 139-144.

[4]) A. CAUSSE, *BZAW* 66, p. 148 ff.; H. WHEELER ROBINSON, *History of Israel*, p. 69-70.

[5]) J. SKINNER, *op. cit.*, p. 97. Cf. also I. BENZINGER, "Die Bücher der Könige", *KHAT*, p. 23-24; H. MEINHOLD, *Die Weisheit Israels*, p. 6; W. O. E. OESTERLEY, *ZAW* N. F. 4 (1927), p. 17; R. H. PFEIFFER, *Introduction to the Old Testament*, p. 383, 645; J. A. MONTGOMERY, ed. H. S. GEHMAN, "The Books of Kings", *ICC*, p. 107, 129; A. BENTZEN, *Introduction to the Old Testament*, 2nd ed. (1952), ii, p. 172. It is striking that J. FICHTNER, "Die altorientalische Weisheit in ihrer israelitisch-jüdischen Ausprägung", *BZAW* 63 (1933) does not seem to mention Solomon's name, except in the title of Sap. Sol.!

[6]) W. F. ALBRIGHT, *From the Stone Age to Christianity* (1940), p. 224.

I

The traditional connection of the name of Solomon with Israelite gnomic literature rests on two biblical foundations: the descriptive narratives in 1 Reg. v 9-14 and x 1-10, 13, 23-24; and the titles in Prov. i 1, x 1 and xxv 1 [1]). The ascription to him of Ecclesiastes and Wisdom, like the fantastic developments of later Jewish and Muslim legend, is based unquestionably on these passages and supplies no independent evidence. In fact, the title in Prov. i 1 (or, more exactly, in i 1-6) [2]), is itself dependent on x 1 and xxv 1, as is clearly shown by the inclusion also in the book of sections credited to other authors [3]). This biblical evidence must be examined closely to see if it merits the confidence or the scepticism with which it has been viewed by different scholars. Before this is done, we may note certain general considerations of historical probability which appear to support the biblical tradition.

In the first place, it seems unlikely that the focusing of Wisdom on Solomon, as of the Law on Moses and the Psalms on David, could be entirely without foundation. Though, as ELMSLIE says, "one suspects that the King's reputation for sagacity may have been enhanced by his royal estate, and that .... we see him through the haze of grandeur, ... the tradition of his wisdom stands, and like all firm traditions has a basis in fact" [4]). The basis in fact may have been far removed from the fanciful accounts given in 1 Reg. v and x, but "there must have been some reason for connecting wisdom with Solomon in this way" [5]).

The reason may well have been the known connections of the king with the Egyptian court, where wisdom literature had flourished since the days of the Middle Kingdom or before [6]). "That the practice of wisdom found a home at Solomon's court is made the more likely", says BAUMGARTNER, "by the latter's strong leaning toward the Egyptian monarchy" [7]). GEMSER argues further that the deliberate cultivation of Wisdom in Jerusalem began with Solomon's estab-

---

[1]) The writer of Eccles. assumes the Solomonic tradition, and poses as the king though without mentioning his name.

[2]) Cf. R. H. PFEIFFER, op. cit., p. 645.

[3]) xxii 17-xxiv 22, and xxiv 23-24, to "the Wise"; xxx 1-33 to Agur ben Jakeh, and xxxi 1-9 to king Lemuel.

[4]) W. A. L. ELMSLIE, Studies in Life from Jewish Proverbs, p. 71.

[5]) W. O. E. OESTERLEY, The Book of Proverbs, p. xxii.

[6]) Cf. J. B. PRITCHARD, Ancient Near Eastern Texts, p. 412-424.

[7]) BAUMGARTNER, op. cit., p. 213; cf. TR N.F. 5 (1933), p. 270.

lishment of a corps of officials on the pattern of the Egyptian court, whether or not the king himself engaged in literary composition [1]). ALT's argument is more substantial; noting the remarkable fact that the subject matter of the proverbs attributed to Solomon in 1 Reg. v 13 is the non-human natural world, whereas in the book of Proverbs it is human life and experience, ALT suggests that so unexpected a representation must have had firm roots in credible sources utilized by the editors of Kings. The analogy of the encyclopaedic nature-wisdom of Egypt and Mesopotamia, and the fact that in Egypt at least this was a living phenomenon at that time—as witness the Onomastikon of Amenope—lend support to the tradition [2]). The same may be said of VON RAD's view that the Joseph story, with its interest in Egypt and its portrait of the hero as exhibiting the qualities prized by "the older wisdom", is a product of a kind of *Aufklärung* under the early monarchy [3]).

Certainly it must be acknowledged that the assertions of 1 Reg. v 9 ff. and x 1 ff. that Solomon (or his court) was famous for developing Wisdom on the Egyptian model are not, on general historical grounds, improbable. It must be pointed out, however, that the Pharaoh's daughter was only one of Solomon's many wives, even if the principal one. This marriage, even with the dowry provided by Pharaoh and the private palace provided by Solomon [4]), is a slim basis for speaking of the latter's "strong leaning toward the Egyptian monarchy" in culture as well as in politics. The gods to whom his wives are said to have turned away Solomon's heart in his old age [5]) were not gods of Egypt. They did, however, include gods of the Sidonians, with whom, through Hiram of Tyre, Solomon's relations are much better documented than are his relations with Egypt [6]). The influence of Egypt, says OESTERLEY, "might have been indirect, through the Phoenicians, or direct, through the friendly relations between the royal houses". But OESTERLEY goes on to say, "While

---

[1]) B. GEMSER, "Sprüche Salomos", *HAT*, p. 2. Cf. H. GRESSMANN, *ZAW*, N.F. I, p. 282; SELLIN, *op. cit.*, ii, p. 197; 1 Reg. iv 1-6.

[2]) A. ALT, "Die Weisheit Salomos", *TLZ*, 76, p. 139-144.

[3]) G. VON RAD, *Josephgeschichte und ältere Chokma*, Congress vol., Copenhagen S.V.T. I (1953), p. 120-127. MAX WEBER, *Ancient Judaism*, p. 199, adds that "the short story of Joseph .... indicates .... relations to the temple priesthood of Heliopolis, the main seat of Egyptian wisdom".

[4]) 1 Reg. ix 16, 24, iii 1.

[5]) 1 Reg. xi 5, 7, 33.

[6]) Cf. 1 Reg. v 15-32, vii 13-14, ix 10-14, 26-28, x 11, 22.

the possibility is recognized, it must be held to be improbable that
at this period the Israelites were influenced by Egyptian religious or
literary thought; for the soil was not yet sufficiently receptive" [1].

II

The only evidence which directly links the name of Solomon with
the introduction of Wisdom literature in Israel consists, as already
noted, in the narratives of 1 Reg. v and x, and in the titles in Prov.
x 1 and xxv 1. [2]). The latter, in fact, would be meaningless apart from
the existence of some such tradition of Solomon's wisdom as is presented in the former, though not necessarily so extravagantly stated.
PFEIFFER remarks that the "Book of the Acts of Solomon" mentioned
as a source in 1 Reg. xi 41 "was based partly on folk tales and the
writer's fancy" [3]). The romantic and fanciful elements are clearly
those which have to do principally with Solomon's proverbial glory
and wisdom. Yet it is on these passages alone that the repute of
Solomon as founder and patron saint of the Wisdom literature in
Israel ultimately depends.

The key passage is 1 Reg. v 9-14, where Solomon's wisdom is
defined as intellectual superiority and universal knowledge, sur-
passing the traditional lore of Egypt, of the desert Arabs and of the
Edomites [4]), and resulting in the production of three thousand
proverbs and vast numbers of songs. While these six verses have a
certain completeness in themselves, the story of the Queen of Sheba
in x 1-10, 13 is their natural sequel. A third short passage, x 23-25,
lays emphasis on a feature common to all three,—the universal fame
of the king's superlative wisdom. In these two passages in chapter x
this wisdom of Solomon is linked in the exuberant description with
material prosperity and magnificence as its natural counterparts.
Since these additional features appear also in iv 20, v 1, 4-5, and since
v 10-11, 14 so closely resemble x 23-24, and v 6 resembles x 26, it
is natural to associate the accounts of Solomon's political supremacy
in iv 20, v 1, 4-5 with those of his world famous wisdom in v 9-14.

---

[1]) W. O. E. OESTERLEY, ZAW N.F. 4 (1927), p. 16-17.
[2]) Chron. adds no independent information of value; the narrative of 1 Reg.
v 9-14 is ignored. On the important differences between the M.T. and LXX in
1 Reg. 1-11, see below.
[3]) PFEIFFER, op. cit., p. 383.
[4]) On Heman and Ethan as Edomite sages, cf. R. H. PFEIFFER, ZAW N.F.
3, p. 14.

In other words, it seems that the claim that the king was supreme among contemporary sages on the international scene, and was the author of thousands of proverbs and songs, is but one element in a cycle of folktales of the glory of Solomon.

It is noteworthy that, when the theme of the king's wisdom as encyclopaedic knowledge is resumed in x 1-10, 13, in the story of the Queen of Sheba, it is once more associated with a description in superlative terms of Solomon's wealth and magnificence. Chapter x 23-24, furthermore, repeats the thought and language of v 14; especially if we read in x 24, with LXX, "all the kings of the earth". There is something quite distinctive about the picture of people and queens coming from the ends of the earth to Solomon's presence to "hear his wisdom" [1]), and also about the intimate association in these stories of wealth and wisdom as characteristic of his glory [2]), The bliss of his subjects, the far extent of his dominions, the power of his chariot force, the superlativeness and fame of his intellect, the incomparable splendour of his court, the vast size of his harem,—all this in manner and conception is of one piece. It is surely significant that such extravagant descriptions of royal magnificence are found elsewhere in the Bible only in Esth., Dan. i-vi, and Chron. The pomp and splendour of courts and palaces are the subjects of midrashic tales in Esth. and Dan. i-vi, and in these pictures the wise men at the royal court are a frequent feature [3]). The Chronicler makes a fabulous character of David, as this folklore in the first Book of Kings makes of Solomon: David musters armies of fantastic size; like Solomon, his fame is world wide, and his riches— including three thousand talents of Ophir gold—are enormous [4]).

The extent of this element of folklore in the account of Solomon's reign in the first Book of Kings is a point to be considered. It has often been noted that the extravagant statements in iv 20, v 1, 4-6, about the extent and prosperity of Solomon's kingdom, disrupt the sequence and alter the tone of their context. The LXX preserves, as a sequel to iv 7-19, a shorter text in a more natural order,—v 7-8, 2-3. This is followed by a shorter form of M.T. v 4 [5]), which in turn introduces the "wisdom" passage, verses 9-14, with which we are

---

[1]) Cf. v 14, x 1, 8, 24.
[2]) Cf. v 1, 4-6, 9-14, x 4-7, 23-25, xi 1, 3.
[3]) Cf. Esth. i 13, vi 13; Dan. i 4, 20, v 11-12, etc.
[4]) 1 Chron. xii 23-37, xiv 17, xxix 3-5.
[5]) A clear case of homoioteleuton, pace MONTGOMERY, op. cit., p. 132.

chiefly concerned. The verses intruded in M.T. into this shorter text, i.e., iv 20, v 1, 4-6, clearly belong with v 9-14 [1]). In chapter x, verses 1-10, 13-15, 20b-25, 27 are of the same genre [2]). In addition, the words "And Solomon son of David reigned over Israel and Judah in Jerusalem", which occur at the beginning and the end respectively of the LXX insertions at ii 35 and ii 46b, and which have no exact counterpart in M.T., may belong to the folktale cycle [3]).

The literary and linguistic affinities of this material are with post-exilic, rather than with pre-exilic, writings. In addition to the general impression of lateness created by the grandiose imagination of the writer or writers, and the parallels already noted with Esth., Dan. i-vi and Chron., there is more precise linguistic evidence to the same effect:

iv 20, v 15—"*Judah and Israel*" (in this order, as designation of the whole people); elsewhere only in 2 Chron. xvi 11, xxv 26, xxviii 26, xxxii 32.

iv 20—"*eat, drink, and rejoice*" (the verbs '*kl, šth šmḥ*, thus co-ordinated); elsewhere only in Eccles. viii 15; cf. Eccles. ii 24, iii 13; Esth. ix 17-19, 22.

v 1, 4, x 1, 24, 25—Aramaizing use of participle for finite verb, with or without *hāyâ*.

v 4—"*beyond the river*"; the reference clearly is to the area *west* of the Euphrates, as sixteen times in Esr.-Neh. and not elsewhere. (In Jos. xxiv 2, etc., the reference is to the area *east* of the Euphrates).

v 9—"*understanding*" (*t'bûnâ*); a word found chiefly in Prov. and rare in pre-exilic writings.

v 9—"*largeness of mind*" (*rōḥab lēb*); the closest parallel is the late Ps. cxix 32. *lēb* with the meaning "mind, intelligence" is commonest in Prov.

v 11—"*be wise*" (*ḥākam*); almost all the twenty-seven occurrences of this verb are post-exilic.

---

[1]) Of this material only v 4ac appears *here* in LXX; however, iv 20, v 1ac, 4, 5 (plus "eating and drinking"), 6, 1ab are found in the long insertion which follows ii 46b in LXX. The inclusion of v 6 with the legendary material may be questioned on account of its obvious dependence on the annalistic record in x 26; but *all* the folklore elements may be said to be imaginative developments of a more sober tradition.

[2]) Note that x 26 is in LXX followed by the equivalent of v 1a.

[3]) Apparently as its opening sentence. In the first instance it follows a composite verse, ii 35a, 46c, 35b. In the second instance it replaces iii 1 which, *in M.T.*, follows directly on ii 46c. The form of the sentence is related to xi 42, iv 20 and v 5.

v 11—"*Ethan, Heman, Calcol, Darda*"; proper names found elsewhere only in 1 Chron. ii 6 and derived psalm titles (Pss. lxxxviii and lxxxix).

v 13—"*trees*"; Burney [1]) remarks that the plural use is mostly late or poetical.

x 2, 10, 25—"spices" (*b^eśāmîm*); of the twenty-five occurrences of this word outside this chapter, twenty-two are in "P", Cant., Esth. and Chron.

x 3—Nip'al of '*lm*, of hidden knowledge, is found again only in "P", Iob, Eccles. and the Chron. parallel.

x 8—"*happy!*" (*'aśrê*); commonest in late Pss. and Prov.

x 15—"*governor*" (*peḥā*); of twenty-three occurrences outside this passage, at least nineteen are post-exilic.

The internal evidence that these accounts of Solomon's wisdom and glory are legendary and late is supported by several indications that they were not part of the original Deuteronomic edition of the Book of Kings. The textual disorder which accompanies the appearance of this material in 1 Reg. v, already noted [2]), is exemplified further where it appears again in chapter x. The first part of the story of the Queen of Sheba, x 1-10, interrupts the continuity of ix 28—x 11-12, and similarly the last named verses separate x 1-10 from its conclusion in x 13. In the LXX textual tradition ix 15, 17-22 have been transferred to follow x 22; x 26 is a variant of M.T. v 6, and is followed by the equivalent of v 1a. It is of interest that the parallel in 2 Chron. ix 25-26 agrees at this point with the LXX of Kings. Evidently the text of Kings was still fluid when the Old Greek translation was made. The disorder noted may be due to the insertion of the folklore material at different points in existing parallel textual traditions. In both M.T. and LXX this material is patently intrusive [3]).

A fundamental difference in viewpoint between the midrashic tales of Solomon's glory and the Deuteronomic context in which they are now found lies in the interpretations given of the king's traditional wisdom. Three distinct interpretations appear, of which the second is consequent upon the first, and the third upon the second. These are:

---

[1]) *Op. cit.*, p. 52.

[2]) LXX includes v 9-10 in the apparently miscellaneous matter inserted after ii 35; and also, in a second long insertion after ii 46b, all of iv 20-v 6 together with v 9 (abbreviated) and some other material.

[3]) Cf. Montgomery, *op. cit.*, p. 126 (commenting on iv 20-v 14) "a *pot-pourri* of material bearing on the reign, much of it duplicated in cc. 9 and 10. Evidently Heb. Kings early underwent transformations".

1) Wisdom as *the ability of the successful ruler*. This occurs in two contexts in the narratives of Solomon's reign, 1 Reg. ii 1-2, 5-9 and v 15-26. In the first of these the moribund David speaks of his son as "wise" in the unspecialized sense of "competent, knowing what to do", like Joseph in Gen. xli 33, 39, and able rulers in general [1]). The Deuteronomic intrusion in ii 3-4 makes it clear that the remainder of ii 1-9 belongs to a pre-Deuteronomic introduction to the story of the summary executions in ii 28-46. In any case, the "wisdom" spoken of has nothing to do with the making of proverbs, nor is it unique with Solomon, even in degree.

The second passage, v 15-26, also shows marks of the intrusion of editorial material, verses 17-19, 21, into a pre-Deuteronomic narrative which reads consecutively without the interpolated speeches. The editorial verse 21 clearly echoes the Deuteronomic language of the speeches in Solomon's dream (iii 5-15), and the word "wise" here takes its colour from that earlier passage. On the other hand, "wisdom" in v 26, as the context makes clear, is the competence in negotiation and administration which marks the successful ruler. It is to be noted that it is *this kind of wisdom* which is said to have been promised to Solomon; apparently a reference back to the source underlying the present account of the dream which is in distinctively Deuteronomic language [2]).

2) Wisdom as *the insight to distinguish right from wrong*, with the resulting *ability of a judge to render true justice*. This is one particular quality of a successful ruler, and so may be seen as the special emphasis of the Deuteronomic editor. He has made it the theme of his re-writing of the dream story, and has appended as an illustration of such judicial wisdom the old folktale of the two mothers [3]). The translation "govern" for *lišpōṭ* in iii 9 is too broad; that the particular capacity to judge justly is in question is clear from the specifications in verses 9 and 11, as well as from the concluding words of

---

[1]) Cf. F. BROWN, S. R. DRIVER, C. A. BRIGGS, *Hebrew and English Lexicon of the Old Testament*, p. 314. It is possible but less likely that the meaning here is "shrewd, cunning".

[2]) MONTGOMERY, *op. cit.*, p. 107, agrees with KITTEL that the incident of the dream at Gibeon "is in origin an early, practically contemporary story", but assigns its present form to late editors. C. F. BURNEY, *Notes on the Hebrew Text of the Books of Kings*, p. 28-32, demonstrates conclusively that in its present form the story is thoroughly Deuteronomic in tone and style.

[3]) MONTGOMERY, *op. cit.*, p. 109, cites a close parallel from Indian lore, and notes that GRESSMANN has assembled twenty-two such parallels.

the appended illustration. It is all the more curious that this aspect of royal wisdom is not referred to again after chapter iii.

3) Wisdom as *intellectual brilliance and encyclopaedic knowledge*, especially of the world of nature other than man. This picture of Solomon's wisdom as given in v 9-14, and x 1-10, 13, 23-24, is the basis of his repute as founder of the Wisdom literature. If the Deuteronomic editor who composed the speeches in Solomon's dream had intended to include in the subsequent narrative these pictures of the king as the supreme sage of mankind, he could hardly have restricted his definition of wisdom to the rendering of true justice. But, on the other hand, the legend could easily have developed from the words of Yahweh's promise in the dream, iii 12-13: "I give you a wise and discerning mind, ... also .... both riches and honour, so that no other king can compare with you".

One notable characteristic of the Deuteronomic editing of the material concerning Solomon's reign is the composition of speeches in the editor's distinctive style [1]). It is therefore important that the speech of the Queen of Sheba in x 6-9 does not resemble the other speeches in this regard, although x 9 seems to be patterned on Hiram's benediction in v 21 [2]). The Deuteronomic editor and his sources show no acquaintance with the legendary material, whereas the latter at almost every point can be recognized as an imaginative development of the promise in iii 12-13 of wisdom, riches, and honour beyond compare.

A further piece of evidence that the passages which thus glorify Solomon are post-Deuteronomic interpolations is the fact that the definitely Deuteronomic editorial and source material does *not* glorify the king unduly, except as builder of the Temple and as displaying judicial wisdom. Only once, in the language of the dream at the commencement of his reign, is it said that Yahweh was pleased with him. On the other hand, Solomon is admonished and warned

---

[1]) Cf. ii 3-4, iii 6-14, v 3-5, 7, vi 12-13, viii 14-30, 46-61, ix 3-9.

[2]) *yᵉhî bārûk* is found elsewhere only in Prov. v 18; Ru. ii 19 (Jer. xx 14 is not a real parallel); *ḥāpēṣ b*, followed by infin. does not appear in any Deuteronomic context; *nātan* for "set" (on a throne) is not used elsewhere in Kings, contrast 1 Reg. ii 24; the fem. infin. cstr. of *ᵓhb* is used once thus in Deut. vii 8, but contrast Deut. iv 37, etc.; to "love Israel forever" *sounds like* Deut., but apparently is not found there; *śîm lᵉmelek* (cf. *nātan lᵉmelek*, 2 Chron. ix 8) is in contrast to the *Hipᶜil* of *mlk* used in the Deuteronomic prayer at iii 7. In contrast to these many differences in a single verse it should be observed how closely the language of Hiram's benediction in v 21 resembles that of the prayer in iii 6-9.

repeatedly, in anticipation of his defection from Yahweh [1]). The rebel Jeroboam is even promised the legitimate succession upon the same conditions as Solomon. The narrative of Rehoboam's disastrous meeting with the northern tribesmen at Shechem (a calamity which the editor regards as divinely ordained), reflects not only on the young king but on his father.

Again, the law of the kingship in Deut. xvii 14-20 unquestionably forbids a later monarch to pattern himself on Solomon. These verses imply that it was Solomon's misfortune (and perhaps his excuse?) that he did not have available a copy of the law of Moses for study. The king is commanded to be literate, and there is not the slightest suggestion that Solomon was remembered for his wisdom as well as for his horses, his wealth and his wives. All this is hard to reconcile with knowledge by the Deuteronomic writers of the lavish adulation of Solomon's wisdom found in 1 Reg. v 9-14. In fact it must be asserted unequivocally that this passage and its portrait of Solomon as the wisest of men and the author of proverbs of encyclopaedic wisdom is late and largely imaginary. It is a quite insufficient foundation for the far-reaching conclusions with respect to the Wisdom literature which have been built upon it.

III

The second piece of biblical evidence upon which rests the traditional connection of Solomon with Wisdom writings is found in the titles of collections of proverbs at Prov. x 1 and xxv 1. The bodies of material which follow these headings—Prov. x 1 - xxii 16, and xxv 1 - xxix 27—are the only writings to which Solomon's name is attached which have the slightest claim to be dated before the Exile, let alone in the early monarchy [2]). It is therefore important to decide what weight can be laid on the descriptions of these collections as "proverbs of Solomon", and what is meant by the reference to the literary activities of "the men of Hezekiah".

The phrase "Proverbs of Solomon", like the phrase "Psalms of David", is of so indeterminate meaning as to be valueless as evidence of authorship. It may be simply a conventional term for proverbs

---

[1]) ii 3-4, iii 14, vi 11-13, ix 3-9, xi 1-40.

[2]) EISSFELDT, op. cit., dates Eccles. in the 3rd cent. B.C.; Prov. i-ix in the 4th or 3rd; Cant. in the 3rd; Sap. Sol. and Pss. Sol. in the 1st cent. The titles of Pss. lxxii and cxxvii are obviously late inferences from the content of each.

of a particular type (cf. "a Miltonic Ode") or of a historic era (cf. "Elizabethan poetry") known familiarly by a famous name associated with it [1]). At the same time it must be admitted that ascription of authorship (whether justified or not) is the most probable meaning, if only because the post-exilic folktale in 1 Reg. v 9-14 claims this specifically. Since the title in xxv 1 appears to *look back* to Hezekiah's age, it does not prove that the ascription of proverbs to Solomon was a convention as old as, or older than, Hezekiah.

The added information, however, that the collection beginning with xxv 1 consists of proverbs "which the men of Hezekiah king of Judah *brought forward*" [2]), is interesting and probably significant. BARNES sees here "strong evidence not lightly to be set aside" that the tradition of Solomon's authorship of collections of proverbs was accepted in the days of Hezekiah [3]). This is a possible explanation, though, as noted already, the heading may mean no more than that these proverbs were "Solomonic" in some general sense. More important is the mention of Hezekiah's scribal establishment. Since no tendentious purpose can be suspected in the mentioning of the otherwise unknown "men of Hezekiah", this is first-rate evidence that an organized literary wisdom movement existed at Hezekiah's court and under his patronage. The king's men *transcribed, published,* or *carried forward from tradition* a collection of maxims which, *in this later editorial title,* are designated "proverbs of Solomon". There is a double ambiguity: just as the phrase may *or* may not indicate authorship, so it may *or* may not imply that the association of proverbs with the name of Solomon existed before Hezekiah's time. The significant point is that such an association did exist *at that time,* when a literary wisdom movement and a court scribal establishment were to be found at Jerusalem under royal patronage.

It is a remarkable fact—particularly remarkable if Solomon had been in fact the founder and patron of Wisdom literature in Israel—that

---

[1]) Cf. SELLIN-ROST, *op. cit.*, p. 157; S. R. DRIVER, *Introduction to the Literature of the O.T.*, 9th ed. (1913), p. 407.

[2]) *Hipʿil* of *ʿtq*; A.V. "copied out"; R.S.V. "copied"; PFEIFFER, *op. cit.*, p. 645, "collected". The lexicons of BROWN, DRIVER and BRIGGS and of KÖHLER and BAUMGARTNER propose the meaning "transcribe", as in late Heb.; this meaning does not occur elsewhere in the O.T. The only other appearances in the O.T. of this verb. in Hipʿil, viz., Gen. xii 8, xxvi 22; Iob ix 5, xxxii 15, support for this context in Prov. the meaning "bring forward", i.e., "bring forward from the past", "transmit", "transcribe".

[3]) W. E. BARNES, *The First Book of Kings* (Camb. Bible), p. 38.

"the wise" as a class or profession do not once appear *during or after* Solomon's reign, until the time of Isaiah and Hezekiah. Then they come on the scene quite definitely, are recognized as leaders of society in Jeremiah's time, and, like Solomon himself, are credited with collections of proverbs [1]). It is true that, earlier, two female sooth-sayers are mentioned and called "wise women", but there is no indication that they had anything to do with literary wisdom. It is true, also, that the quotation of folk proverbs in the early histories points to a popular gnomic tradition stretching far back into the past [2]). But there is nothing whatever in the records to suggest the continuous existence since the time of Solomon of a school of literary wisdom in Israel [3]). As has been shown, the fabulous tales of Solomon's own wisdom are of little, if any, historical worth.

This is not to suggest for a moment that the traditions of Solomon's glorious reign had no foundation in fact. Quite the contrary! It was a period of remarkable social and political development, of economic organization and expansion, of centralized power, court life, and international relations. Above all there were the great building enter-prises of palaces and temple and chariot cities, visible evidences of Solomon's power and glory remaining to later generations. It is no wonder that tales of that glory were kept alive through the long centuries after that glory had departed [4]). A selection of them—in a post-exilic form—were inserted into the Deuteronomist's account of Solomon's reign. A pre-exilic form of the same tales of Solomon's glory and wisdom may have come from the scribal school of Heze-kiah.

Hezekiah was the first king since Solomon who could claim to be the sole Israelite monarch. Several lines of evidence suggest that he set out to foster a national revival, taking Solomon as his model. In particular, he became a patron of wisdom literature, more effective

---

[1]) Jes. v 21, xxix 14, xxxi 2; Jer. viii 8-9, ix 23, xviii 18; Prov. xxii 17, xxiv 23.

[2]) 2 Sam. xiv 2, xx 16; 1 Sam. x 12, xxiv 14; 1 Reg. xx 11, etc.

[3]) The one possible exception to this categorical statement is the Joseph story with its "wisdom" characteristics, as VON RAD has pointed out; see above, p. 274. It is debatable how much older than the eighth century the Joseph story is; in any case it is not nearly as old as Solomon's reign.

[4]) NOTH, *op. cit.*, p. 187-188, identifies the "Book of the Acts of Solomon" (1 Reg. xi 41) as containing the factual material on the reign, and distinguishes from this "noch einige Anekdoten, wie sie offenbar über Salomo noch lange im Umlauf waren. Diese Anekdoten haben Salomos Reichtum und Weisheit zum Gegenstand".

though less famous than his predecessor. As GEMSER says, commenting on Prov. xxv 1, "Der Regierung Hiskias, also der Zeit Jesajas, ist ein solches Unternehmen, das die Schätze der Tradition sichern wollte, wohl zuzutrauen. Die assyrische Bedrohung Judas und die Abwendung der Gefahr, die Berührung mit den grossen Kulturmächten der Zeit und die nationale Wiedergeburt — das alles hatte zur Folge, dass sich das Volk auf seine geistigen Güter besann, und das um so mehr, als nach dem Falle Samariens .... Juda das Erbe des Nordreichs antrat" [1]).

Although since 722 most of the territory of northern Israel had been organized as an Assyrian province, at least part of the tribal lands of Benjamin was under Hezekiah's control [2]). If the account in 2 Chron. xxx of the invitation to the northern tribes to resume the practice of pilgrimage to Jerusalem is substantially true, the intended result would be as much political as religious (as Jeroboam I had foreseen long before). The editor of Kings credits Hezekiah with military prowess, though he gives but one example of it [3]). The Chronicler, on the other hand, concludes his account of the crisis of 701 with the assertion that the Lord similarly saved Hezekiah from *all* his enemies. He adds that (like Solomon!) Hezekiah had peace on all sides, received tribute and universal admiration, and possessed riches and honour and treasuries and store-houses and cities [4]). Most important of all in the eyes of this writer were Hezekiah's measures to cleanse the temple and restore the full glories of worship; here the comparison with Solomon becomes quite specific,—"since the time of Solomon .... there had been nothing like this in Jerusalem" [5]).

The restricted interests of the Chronicler are perhaps responsible both for the extravagant language used about Hezekiah's power and glory, and for his omission of any reference to certain other parallels to the Solomonic tradition of which we hear in the prophecies of Isaiah [6]). This evidence is much more important than the Chronicler's

---

[1]) GEMSER, *op. cit.*, p. 73.

[2]) Cf. SELLIN, *Geschichte*, i, p. 268-269, citing Micah's addresses to Judah as "Jacob" and "Israel". Cf. Mich. iii 9-12.

[3]) 2 Reg. xx 20, xviii 7-8. Perhaps the revolt against Assyria was thought to have been successful, in view of xix 21-37. The editor's text could hardly have included xviii 14-16, which is omitted in the parallel text in Jes. xxxvi.

[4]) 2 Chron. xxxii 22-23, 27-29; cf. 1 Reg. v 1, 4, 14, x 21-25. Hezekiah's wealth is testified to also in Jes. xxxix.

[5]) 2 Chron. xxix 3-36, xxx 13-27.

[6]) The records of Hezekiah's reign in 2 Reg. xviii-xx consist chiefly of excerpts from an earlier Book of Isaiah. Apart from this Isaianic material, 2 Reg. tells us

because it is contemporary, but also because it is *incidental*, i.e., it is not coloured in order to highlight a theme. Three interrelated features which appear in Isaiah's picture of Hezekiah's reign recall three similarly interrelated features of the Solomonic tradition: (i) intercourse with Egypt, with resulting strong Egyptian political and cultural influence on the Jerusalem court; (ii) unusual prominence in the scene of horses and chariots as the basic military arm, and as a symbol of glory; (iii) the power and influence at court of organized "Wisdom"; in this case not so much in the person of the king [1]) as in "the wise" as a professional group, and in the person of court secretaries like Shebna [2]). The first two of these are of interest chiefly as further evidence that Hezekiah may have thought of himself as reviving through imitation the ancient glories of Solomon. The third bears more directly on the thesis of this paper.

It is altogether to be expected that the political and economic expansion of Hezekiah's reign should have been paralleled in the cultural sphere. This showed itself in religious expansion, iconoclastic reform, and measures to restore the prestige of the temple. It is evidenced also in the literary developments of which there are many indications, and particularly in the new prominence in Israel of literary Wisdom. The religious and the literary movements may, indeed, have been closely associated, particularly if BENTZEN is correct in surmising that a scribal school was installed in the temple at Jerusalem, as at Mari and elsewhere [3]). BENTZEN also refers with approval to the suggestion of NYBERG that the end of the eighth century was a time when oral traditions were being fixed in writing as a result of the realization—following the catastrophe to Samaria—that Israel's traditions were in danger of perishing.

The most concrete piece of evidence for this literary renaissance is, of course, the reference in Prov. xxv 1 to the literary undertaking of the "men of Hezekiah" [4]). PEROWNE recalls the view of SAYCE

---

only of the king's iconoclasm, his rebellion against Assyria (with no details), his Philistine conquests, and his feats of hydro-engineering.

[1]) Though A. COHEN, *The Proverbs*, p. 166, comments on the "fine style" of Hezekiah's message in 2 Reg. xix 3. The fact that the king here originates, or quotes, a proverb, is also of interest. There seems no reason to question that this contemporary record reproduces Hezekiah's words with substantial accuracy.

[2]) For (i), cf. Jes. xix 1-15, xx 1-6, xxx 1-7, xxxi 1-3, xxxvi 4-10. For (ii), cf. Jes. ii 7, xxii 18, xxx 16, xxxi 1-3, xxxvi 8-9. For (iii), cf. Jes. v 21, xxix 14, 15-16, xxx 1, xxxi 2, xxii 14, xxxvi 3, 22.

[3]) BENTZEN, *op. cit.*, p. 171-172; ii, p. 173.

[4]) This use of the word "men" in the sense of "professional servants", "fol-

that this title points to the existence of a royal library at Jerusalem, and Hezekiah has even been called "a Jewish Ashurbanipal" on the basis of it [1]). Although it is too much to claim that the attribution to Hezekiah in Jes. xxxviii 9 of the following psalm establishes his authorship, the very fact that his name could be attached to it shows that he was associated in the popular mind with literary activity. Unlike Moses, David and Solomon, moreover, Hezekiah did not move in the mists of remote antiquity. He is the *only* pre-exilic king after Solomon whose name has literary associations, and these are with both psalmody and wisdom writings.

The evidence, indeed, is quite sufficient to show that the reign of Hezekiah was a time of literary activity in Judah. It is the most probable time for the bringing together of northern and southern historical traditions, prophetic records and psalm collections. The reference in Prov. xxv 1 to Hezekiah's scribal school as engaged in the collection and publication of proverbs is only one of several indications that the Wisdom movement had become influential both in culture and in politics. Jes. v 21 tells us that self-styled "wise men" and sceptics are in positions of authority. In the oracles of Isaiah found in xxix 13-14, 15-16, xxx 1-5 and xxxi 1-3 the prophet makes it plain that "the wise" are a coherent party influential at court, working for a calculated pro-Egyptian political policy which ignores the prophet's call to trust in Yahweh. Very pointedly Isaiah threatens disaster, since those who rely on horses and chariots do not consult Yahweh, "though *he too* is wise!".

It is striking, too, how Isaiah pours his scorn on the wise men of Egypt on whom their opposite numbers in Judah modelled themselves: "How can you say to Pharaoh, I am a son of the wise, a son of ancient kings?" [2]) Is it unlikely that these "wise men" of Judah also claimed an inheritance going back to "ancient kings", and thus built on the tradition of Solomon's success as a ruler the legend of his accomplishments as a sage?

The close relationships of nascent Israelite literary wisdom in this

---

lowers" (cf. "David's men", 1 Sam. xxiii 3, 5; "Abner's men", 2 Sam. ii 31) tells against the emendation in 1 Reg. x 8 of "happy are thy men!" to "happy are thy wives!" (with LXX). The latter would be an incongruous remark in the circumstances; no oriental would suggest that Solomon maintained his harem in order to admire his wisdom.

[1]) T. T. PEROWNE, *Proverbs* (Camb. Bible) p. 156; E. SELLIN, *Introduction to the O.T.* (tr. W. MONTGOMERY), p. 209; cf. BENTZEN, *op. cit.*, ii, p. 173.

[2]) Jes. xix 11.

period with the ancient wisdom tradition of Egypt are demonstrated by the evidence of direct dependence in at least one instance.
It is now generally agreed that the section entitled "the words of the
wise" in Prov. xxi 17 — xxiv 22 is directly or indirectly dependent
upon "The Instruction of Amen-em-opet", an Egyptian literary
work of 1000-600 B.C. [1]). Possibly there is some significance in the
fact that this section of Proverbs is separated by only one small
collection (xxiv 23-34) from the collection attributed to "the men of
Hezekiah" (xxv—xxix). "Dass die spätere Königzeit den Amen-en-ope
als Lehrmeister gehabt hat, ist jetzt über allen Zweifel sicher be-
wiesen", concludes SELLIN-ROST [2]).

The familiarity in Isaiah's time, not only of wisdom as an organized
social phenomenon, but of gnomic literary forms, is evident from that
prophet's own use of these. In Jes. xxviii 23-29, the Parable of the
Farmer, the oracle is in the manner of the Wisdom teachers. The
form of address recalls Prov. v 1 and xxii 17; and the rhetorical
questions Iob xv 2-3. For the dependence of human upon Divine
wisdom, cf. Iob xii 7-26; Prov. viii. Again, in Jes. xxxii 1-8 the
prophet promises the fruits of royal justice and the discomfiture of the
fool and the knave; for the matter we may compare Jes. xi 1-9, but
the manner is that of Prov. viii 15-21 and xvi 10-15. Just as in Jes.
v 1-7 the prophet adopts the rôle of the singer of vintage songs, so
here he takes the role of the wisdom teacher. In each case it must
have been because the respective figures were thoroughly familiar
to his audience.

Two minor pieces of evidence may be appended in support of the
thesis that Hebrew literary Wisdom received its first great impetus
as a result of Hezekiah's efforts to renew the vanished glories of
Solomon. The first is the prominence at court of the professional
scribe, Shebna. In Jes. xxii 15-19 he is royal chamberlain, and is
denounced for the pride which he exhibited in the possession of
"splendid chariots", and the preparation for himself of a princely
"tomb on the height" [3]). Clearly such a man was in a position of
power. Even when (apparently) in xxxvi 3 he has yielded the superior

---

[1]) Cf. PRITCHARD, *op. cit.*, p. 421; W. O. E. OESTERLEY, *ZAW* N.F. 4 (1927),
p. 16 ff.; BENTZEN, *op. cit.*, ii, p. 172-173; H. H. ROWLEY, *Growth of the Old
Testament*, p. 141; R. H. PFEIFFER, *Introduction to the Old Testament*, p. 648.

[2]) *Op. cit.*, p. 156.

[3]) The interesting possibility that this tomb has been identified is discussed
by N. AVIGAD, *Israel Exploration Journ.*, iii, p. 137-152.

office to Eliakim, as Isaiah predicted would happen, Shebna the scribe is still one of the principal royal ministers.

Finally, there is a further reflection arising from the law of the kingship in Deut. xvii 14-20, which has already been discussed in another connection [1]). It is a well known principle of law that a practice is not forbidden by law unless the situation demands it, i.e., unless the practice exists or the act has been done. Whom did this law have in mind, when it forbade the king to pattern himself on Solomon, unless it be Hezekiah? The Deuteronomic code was almost certainly formulated in the 7th century, after Hezekiah's reign. This law, however, could hardly have had in mind Hezekiah's successor Manasseh, who imitated and surpassed Solomon only in his cruelty and oppression.

IV

We seem now to be in a position to answer the questions raised in the opening paragraph of this paper, if not with full assurance, at least with a high degree of probability. Though general historical considerations do not preclude, but rather favour, the connection with Solomon of the origins of literary wisdom in Israel, the ostensible biblical evidence for this in the first Book of Kings is post-exilic in date and legendary in character. The legend is based on the promises which, in 1 Reg. iii 12-13, accompany the Deuteronomic editor's interpretation of Solomon's wisdom as judicial discernment.

The first real impact of Egyptian Wisdom on Israel, with evident results in Hebrew literary production, seems to belong to the reign of Hezekiah. This is suggested by Prov. xxv 1, supported by the other lines of evidence which have been enumerated above. If "proverbs of Solomon" were so called before this time, there is no substantial evidence to show when and how this came about. The reason may lie in the existence of popular tradition based on Solomon's known relations with Egypt, and on the visible remains of his magnificent buildings. In any case, the tradition seems to have been cultivated deliberately by Hezekiah as part of his grandiose plans to restore the vanished glories of Solomon's kingdom, for in Hezekiah's reign appear the first clear evidences of Hebrew Wisdom as a significant literary phenomenon.

---

[1]) See above, p. 281.

SOLOMONIC WISDOM*

By ALBRECHT ALT, LEIPZIG

For Johannes Herrmann on his 70th birthday

The author of the Deuteronomistic History describes the wisdom of
Solomon by contrasting the king's achievements with those of other peoples and of their most famous sages and also by indicating the number
and contents of the proverbs and songs that derive from Solomon (I Kings
5:9-14 [English, 4:29-34]).[1] The extent to which the author is personally
involved in forming these sentences is just as difficult to determine as is
the question about the type of tradition on which he might have drawn.
Did he have available some narrative[2] similar to those about Yahweh's
equipping Solomon with wisdom (I Kings 3:4-15), about his juridical
verdict in the lawsuit between the two women (I Kings 3:16-28), and
about the visits of the Queen of Sheba (I Kings 10:1-10, 13)? And were
these narratives perhaps already joined together in a literary structure,
from which he first had to free them in order then to distribute them
throughout his own account of the reign of Solomon? Or does that description rather derive, whether by direct or indirect means (such as by
way of the "Book of the History of Solomon," cited in I Kings 11:41),
from statements of the official court annals? For its general formulation
does not correspond to the Israelite narrative structure with its normal
basis in concrete and individual events, so it might be based on, e.g., an
official entry about a collection of wisdom proverbs and songs composed
either by Solomon himself or on his behalf.[3] There is virtually nothing to
be gained here by pursuing further these and other possibilities concerning

*Originally published as "Die Weisheit Salomos," ThLZ LXXVI (1951), 139-
144. Translated by Douglas A. Knight, Assistant Professor of Old Testament,
Vanderbilt University.

literary derivation. In my opinion a definite decision cannot be reached, given the present state of affairs.

In any case, however, considering what the author of the Deuteronomistic History has to say about the subject matter of Solomonic wisdom, it is very improbable that he could have made these statements by himself without support of a pre-given tradition. For he writes about the king: "He spoke of trees, from the cedar that is in Lebanon to the hyssop that grows out of the wall; he spoke also of beasts, and of birds, and of reptiles, and of fish" (I Kings 5:13 [English, 4:33]). It is thereby maintained that this wisdom refers—predominantly if not exclusively—to the phenomena of the plant and animal world in a way not to be found in the biblical book of Proverbs and in Sirach, the typical representatives of normal Israelite wisdom. To be sure, these books are obviously not entirely devoid of references to the state of affairs in the extra-human sphere of nature, especially in the kingdom of animals. But they occur relatively seldom and are never mentioned for their own sake, rather serving always to illustrate truths which are valid for human life and according to which each person should act. This entirely human-oriented wisdom of life characteristic of the normal Israelite collections of proverbs stands in quite distinct contrast to nature wisdom, of which the Deuteronomistic History or, better yet, its "Vorlage" speaks with reference to Solomon. Thus in my opinion one does violence to the peculiarity of the statements in I Kings 5:13 [English, 4:33] if, in the interest of compatibility with those other collections, one follows the frequent attempt[4] to understand them as if Solomon's proverbs and songs about plants and animals are only envisioned as occasional allusions to extra-human phenomena that parallel human life.

It becomes less objectionable to attribute to Solomonic nature wisdom such a special position in comparison to the wisdom of human life found in the collections of proverbs if one considers that the Old Testament retains a few (though not many) poems of greater or lesser size which certainly attest to a cultivated nature wisdom. I do not however wish to include here the isolated plant fables appearing in the narrative literature, such as that of Jotham (Judges 9:8-15), since they only constitute a transferral of human conditions into an extra-human sphere in order ultimately to make some didactic point for humanity. In contrast, the speeches of God in the book of Job with their poetic descriptions of natural phenomena and especially of animals (Job 38-41) certainly belong here. This also is primarily true for a few numerical proverbs which are grouped together at a rather hidden place in the book of Proverbs and in which comparison is made of strikingly similar matters in diverse areas of nature, above all in the animal world (Prov. 30:15f., 18-20, 24-28, 29-31).[5] For in these passages genuine observations of nature are treated throughout from the perspective of the difference of these phenomena from those in the human sphere, and yet at the same time from the perspective of their meaningful order with respect to each other.[6] Consequently one cannot dispute the fact that there was a special *Gattung* of nature wisdom in Israel, out of which a type of *Mirabilienliteratur* could develop and apparently did in fact develop, though which in the canonized tradition of the Old Testament was almost totally suppressed by the mass of wisdom literature about human life. Yet the diversity of the contents and especially of the forms of expression in the portions retained can perhaps give us a certain impression of the once rich life of this *Gattung* in Israel. Its just-mentioned fate in the last stages of the history of Israelite literature gives support, in my opinion, to the likelihood that its heyday was not later, but rather earlier than that of the wisdom about human life which eventually gained almost sole dominance. However, considering the impossibility of dating even those passages available to us, we are prohibited from attempting to determine their chronology more precisely. From our vantage point, even the origins appear necessarily to remain in the dark.

Thus our discussions to this point have gained us no more than a certain possibility that the details of the Deuteronomistic History regarding Solomonic wisdom are reliable, and I would not know how to elevate this possibility to the rank of full certainty on the basis of the Old Testament alone and without the assistance of daring constructions of questionable worth. To be sure, those details certainly do not intend for the wisdom of Solomon to be regarded as an isolated fact in the intellectual history of Israel, but rather consciously and emphatically put it in a much wider framework: "Solomon's wisdom surpassed the wisdom of all the people of the East, and all the wisdom of Egypt. For he was wiser than all other men, wiser than Ethan the Ezrahite, and Heman, Calcol, and Darda, the sons of Mahol; and his fame was in all the nations round about" (I Kings 5:10f. [English 4:30f.]). There is little significance in the fact that we know absolutely nothing of the persons named here individually and that we cannot even determine whether the author considers them as contemporaries of Solomon.[7] On the other hand, it is very important for us to note the matter-of-fact way in which he applies the standard of foreign wisdom to Solomonic wisdom, although he is thoroughly convinced of the superiority of the latter. For he would hardly have considered such a comparison appropriate if he had regarded nature wisdom, of which he considered Solomon to be the recognized master, as a peculiar possession of Israel, and not rather a common property which also the sages of other nations were in competition to foster and advance. Thus the situation in the field of nature wisdom in the ancient Orient was apparently no different from that in the area of wisdom about human life. And there can no longer be any doubt as to the international character of the latter, now that a whole series of pertinent older and younger works, especially from Egypt, have joined the literary monuments in the Old Testament and now that it has been demonstrated that one of these works, the Instruction of Amenemope, has in fact a direct literary relationship to the biblical book of Proverbs. If that is the case, then we are not only justified but even obligated to be on the watch for extra-Israelite evidences of nature wisdom in the ancient Orient, and furthermore to see whether these then can help us render a more definitive judgment on the reliability of the details about Solomonic wisdom in the Deuteronomistic History.

Regarding substantive relationship as well as chronological proximity we have now available for comparison a piece of Egyptian literature that only a few years ago, through the masterful publishing and editing of Sir Alan H. Gardiner, was made as understandable as could be expected, considering the incomplete and defective nature of the manuscripts discovered to date: the so-called Onomasticon of Amenope, from the period around 1100 B.C.[8]

The intention of this piece is stated quite well in the superscription, which has fortunately been preserved: "Beginning of instruction . . . on all that is, which Ptah created and Thoth recorded, on the heavens and what belongs in it, on the earth and what is in it, what the mountains spew forth, and what the flood covers with water, on all things on which Re' shines, and on all that which becomes green on the earth." This statement of purpose corresponds to what begins forthwith and fills the whole writing: an enumeration of beings and things of the heavens, the waters and the earth, of divine and royal persons, courtiers, officers, professions, classes, tribes and types of people (including those outside of Egypt), of cities of Egypt itself, of buildings and their parts, of estates, of types of grain and their products, of foods and drinks, of parts of an ox and types of meat—altogether 610 entries preserved, without even reaching the end of the piece in its original length. As can be seen from this description of the contents, the work constitutes no more and no less than an attempted encyclopaedia of all knowledge, be it only in the form of a listing of key words in a relatively substantive order, whereby no less attention is paid to the beings and things of extra-human nature than is given the phenomena of human life. At no point is there an intrusion of rules in the sense of Egypt's ancient and richly developed wisdom about life; in fact nowhere in the whole writing is even a sentence formed. It is all the more noteworthy that the title includes the identifying word "instruction" (sb'j.t), just as is the case for books on wisdom about life.

Even the existence of this one work would suffice to prove that the "instruction" of the Egyptians, despite all the predominance of wisdom about life, nonetheless did not entirely neglect observations on nature. This is further confirmed by another writing, about half a millennium older but of shorter length, which in the same dry enumerative style begins with plants and animals and nowhere speaks of human categories.[9] Therefore the Egyptians must have had a tradition for this *Gattung* of wisdom literature, which however was flexible enough to be able to adjust when necessary to changing interests and to the increase or loss of knowledge.

As an example of this, the older writing just mentioned contains a list of fortifications of the Middle Kingdom in Nubia, which do not recur in the work of Amenope,[10] whereas this latter piece contains a long list of names of tribes, regions and localities in Libya, Asia Minor, Syria and Palestine, many of which did not become known to the Egyptians until the period of the New Kingdom; in contrast, Nubia is significantly ignored.[11] Even in the cases where both writings treat the same matters, the details are too divergent to allow us to assume that the younger piece might have been literarily dependent on the older one. So for the present the findings suffice only to establish the presence of the *Gattung* in the Egyptian literature of the second millennium B.C.;[12] further insight into its history and especially into its origin will have to await the discovery of additional texts.

Unfortunately under these conditions the question must also remain unanswered as to whether the *Gattung* in Egypt appeared autochthonously or under foreign influence. This question is all the more significant since such encyclopaedic lists had for a long time belonged to the common stock of learned literature in that other ancient civilization of the Near East, Babylon.

Soon after their invention of writing, but at least by the beginning of the third millennium B.C., the Sumerians, true to their characteristically ordered thinking, launched this "enumerative science". It was later appropriated and further developed by the Akkadians until around the middle or second half of the second millennium, when it obtained its final canonized form, especially in the great series ḪAR-r a = ḫubullu with its twenty-four tablets and its thousands of entries.[13] And even if the Sumerians produced their lists originally, as it seems, only for the purpose of collecting and organizing their cuneiform signs, apparently very soon this was accompanied also by the aim to express through the ordering of these signs the internal connection of the words and of the beings and things that they signified. And thus by bringing together these logical catalogues of signs and words for the individual categories of beings and things, eventually a delineation of the whole world in the multitude of its phenomena came into being. This encyclopaedic purpose remained quite unmistakable in the later forms of these lists up until their canonization, and it failed to be realized only in those cases where special catalogues for certain categories (e.g., the gods) were developed and canonized separately.[14] In Babylon just as in Egypt it was understood that the lists should contain only designations of beings and things, hence only *substantiva*. The Akkadians adopted the original Sumerian lists, and this accounts for the texts with the Sumerian words in one column and their corresponding Akkadian signs beside them.

It is quite possible historically, at least for the second millennium B.C., that there might have been a connection between the very similar products of this "enumerative science" in Babylon and Egypt—especially since the Egyptians in that period could have become acquainted with the pertinent works of Babylonian literature and thus been induced perhaps to imitate them. For beginning at some indeterminate time, probably quite near the start of the second millennium, the Babylonian script and language radiated so widely and intensively, especially toward the West, that even the pharaohs had to use this script and language in conducting their diplomatic correspondence with the great and small rulers in Asia Minor, Mesopotamia, Syria and Palestine—as the archives from Amarna and Boghazköi indicate. Consequently also Babylonian literary works reached the Western lands, and among them were the enumerative pieces which could serve an important function for those interested in learning the script and language of the old civilization of the East. Thus the archaeological digs at Ugarit on the Syrian coast in particular have uncovered numerous tablets and fragments of tablets containing lists, generally those of the canonical series ḪAR-r a = ḫubullu, at times only with the Sumerian text, sometimes Sumerian and Akkadian, one time even Sumerian and Hurrian.[15] But there are also fragments of such tablets from the cuneiform archive of Amenophis IV in Amarna, thus from Egypt itself;[16]

so the only question that remains is when this importation from Babylonia to the kingdom of the pharaohs might have begun. Considering analogous imported finds from the same place of origin, one should hardly be surprised, in my opinion, if future discoveries in Egypt would show that this influx began during the Middle Kingdom, i.e. at the beginning of the second millennium.[17] It does not necessarily follow from these circumstances, however, that the Egyptians were initially inclined to produce lists in their own script and language simply because they had become aware of similar lists from Babylon; similar needs experienced independently of each other at the Euphrates and at the Nile could have elicited the same literary *Gattung*. But even then we cannot dismiss a certain influence exerted by the Babylonian works with their long and established tradition on the Egyptian onomastica, especially the younger ones.[18] And if even that should not prove accurate, it nonetheless remains established that toward the end of the second millennium B.C. this *Gattung* of wisdom was definitely alive in quite similar form in both Babylonia and Egypt, canonized in the former while still productive in the latter.

Now naturally it may at first appear quite risky for me to hypothesize that Solomonic wisdom and the little amount of comparative literary products retained in the Old Testament might be related to the stated works of Babylon and Egypt. For at least their form shows no obvious relationship whatsoever between the two: According to the Deuteronomistic History Solomon's wisdom yielded "3000 proverbs and 1005[19] songs" (I Kings 5:12 [English, 4:32]), whereas the consistent, inflexible enumerative style of the Babylonian and Egyptian lists has nothing to do with proverb and song. But what they have in common is a specificity of content through their striving after the greatest possible comprehension of beings and things of the natural world, and it is irrelevant whether Solomon's wisdom was really restricted to the kingdom of plants and animals as the wording of the tradition says (I Kings 5:13 [English, 4:33]), or whether these realms are mentioned only as examples taken from the total area of nature. In my view, there is a satisfactory historical solution for this tension between substantive correlation and formal differentiation: Presumably in his activity within the area of wisdom, on the one hand Solomon remained true to the content of the pre-given tradition of Babylonian and Egyptian "enumerative science". But on the other hand he preferred to give it an entirely altered form—be it at his own initiative or on the basis of some precedence—by expanding the bare enumerations into whole series of proverbs and songs about the traditionally treated beings and things.[20] This innovation did not remain restricted to form alone since the intruding art of poetic description necessarily led to a presentation of relationships in the natural world which could in no way be expressed by means of the prosaic enumerative style of the old lists. And with this advance the wisdom of Solomon indeed superseded all of its predecessors, and its reputation of uniqueness was thus justified historically. Though Babylonian and Egyptian wisdom persisted throughout in its traditional schema of pure "enumerative science",[21] the postulated innovation by Solomon created a totally different framework for Israelite wisdom, in which it long could have enjoyed considerable freedom to move and develop, had not the preponderance of wisdom about human life soon caused it to languish, as mentioned above.

It cannot be denied that this hypothetically inferred process of Solomon's alteration of an old literary *Gattung* accords well with the picture we gain from other traditions about his endeavors and accomplishments. In every respect he is eager to extend culturally the influence of the Palestinian-Syrian empire inherited from his father David, and thus to elevate this new political entity to the position of equal partner with the older kingdoms in the power system of his time. It was quite consistent with this that he became engaged in the international competition concerning wisdom, and if he succeeded in developing and fostering a new *Gattung* that surpassed the old traditional products of his neighboring competitors, then he could certainly be persuaded that he had gained for himself significant prestige also in other areas. We must perhaps leave the question unanswered as to whether the Babylonian or the Egyptian models influenced him more or whether in fact he considered only one of these groups to the exclusion of the other. In light of the whole situation however he was probably stimulated more by Egypt, where the encyclopaedic nature wisdom at the time of Solomon (as evidenced by the then young but highly regarded and often copied Onomasticon of Amenope) was much more of a living entity than the already hardened and canonized tradition of the Babylonians.[22] Solomon had apparently appropriated much else in other respects (especially in the area of political structures) from Egypt, the closest old civilization.[23] However, since we have seen that the literary products of the Babylonian and Egyptian "enumerative science" were, at least in their form, so similar as to be almost interchangeable with each other, it is only of secondary importance whether Solomon was primarily or exclusively influenced from the one side or the other. Rather, what is much more decisive for our understanding of history is the fact that the postulated foreign influence—even at a point as far removed from the central spiritual character of the Israelite people as were this observation and comprehension of the natural world—did not take the form of mechanical appropriation and imitation of the progress of older civilizations, but instead led to the rise of a new literary *Gattung* and thereby to Israel's further emancipation from the heritage of the past.

NOTES

[1] The author of the Chronicler's History has taken almost nothing from this section (cf. II Chron. 9:22-24).

[2] So Noth, *Überlieferungsgeschichtliche Studien I* (1943), p. 110 [2nd ed., 1957, p. 68].

[3] Compare the statement in Prov. 25:1 about a collection of proverbs made by the "men of Hezekiah king of Judah."

[4] So Kittel in his commentary, *ad loc.;* similarly Meinhold, *Die Weisheit Israels* (1908), pp. 9f.

[5] Eissfeldt, in his *Einleitung in das Alte Testament* (1934), p. 93, rightfully associates these numerical proverbs with I Kings 5:13. On their form, cf. Bea, *Biblica* 19 (1938), p. 444; 21 (1940), pp. 196ff.

[6] The reflection on nature in the book of Koheleth (especially in Chapter 1), which is almost despairing about the possibility of comprehending any reasonable order in the world, is also a quite different matter since it practically forgoes any observation and presentation of individual phenomena in the extra-human sphere of nature.

[7] There is nothing to be gained by considering what is later said about these persons (I Chron. 2:6,8; 6:18,29, etc.; Psalm 88:1; 89:1).

[8] Gardiner, *Ancient Egyptian Onomastica* (1947), I, pp. 24ff., and II, pp. 1ff. One of the longer manuscripts (Papyrus Hood) was published long ago (Maspero, *Journal asiatique* 8. Sér. 11 [1888], pp. 250ff., 309ff.), while the longest one (Glossar Golénischeff) was only known in part (Golénischeff, *ÄZ* 40 [1903], pp. 101ff.).

[9] Ramesseum Onomasticon (Pap. Berlin 10495); Gardiner, *op. cit.*, I, pp. 6ff.

[10] Edited by Gardiner, *JEA* 3 (1916), pp. 184ff.

[11] Cf. Alt, *Schweizerische Theol. Umschau* 20 (1950), pp. 58ff.

[12] At the present only insufficient fragments of a third text of the same *Gattung* are available (Spiegelberg, *Rec. de trav.* 19 [1897], pp. 92ff.; Gardiner, *op. cit.*, I, pp. 64ff.).

[13] The best overview of the existence and history of this *Gattung* of Babylonian literature is to be found in v. Soden, *Die Welt als Geschichte* 2 (1936), pp. 417ff. On the canonical series, cf. also Matouš, *Die lexikalischen Tafelserien der Babylonier und Assyrer in den Berliner Museen*, I (1933), pp. 1ff.

[14] Basic works on canonical lists of gods has been done by Zimmern, *Zur Herstellung der grossen babylonischen Götterliste A n = (ilu) Anum* (1911); additional material in v. Soden, *op. cit.*, pp. 440ff. (also on the older lists of gods).

[15] Virolleaud, *Syria* 10 (1929), Tablet LXXVII, Nos. 4ff.; Thureau-Dangin, *ibid.* 12 (1931), pp. 225ff.; 13 (1932), pp. 233ff.

[16] Amarna No. 345ff. Knudtzon; Gordon, *JEA* 20 (1934), p. 138; *Orientalia* N.S. 16 (1947), pp. 1ff. [unavailable to me]. The above mentioned canonical series is apparently missing in these fragments.

[17] Cf. especially the depository of Tod from the time of Amenemmes II (Bisson de la Rocque, *Tôd* [1937], pp. 113ff.; Vandier, *Syria* 18 [1937], pp. 174ff.).

[18] In this regard it is noteworthy, e.g., that the encyclopaedic lists in Babylonia and also in Egypt do not contain catalogues of gods. Cf. above, p. 76. —The best evidence for the considerable contact between both bodies of literature during the New Kingdom is to be seen in the fragment of a cuneiform list of Egyptian words from Amarna (Smith, Gadd and Peet, *JEA* 11 [1925], pp. 230ff.; Albright, *ibid.* 12 [1926], pp. 186ff.).

[19] LXX: "5000".

[20] Thus the amazingly high number of proverbs and songs attributed to him can simply be explained on the basis of the multitude of beings and things which were to be considered according to the tradition of the *Gattung*, even in its newer form.

[21] The rich literary tradition of Babylonia and Assyria in the first millennium B.C. shows that during that period only the older canonical lists continued to be transmitted, recopied, and to some extent also supplied with commentary. For the later period of Egypt we lack at present sufficient material for comparison.

[22] A new matter needing investigation is the extent to which one needs to take account of a direct influence of Babylonian culture and literature on the life and thought at the royal courts of Palestine during the period of Solomon, considering that further to the north on the Phoenician coast a move toward cultural autonomy had been in process for centuries and that in the Syrian interior the influx of Arameans had significantly disrupted the old connections.

[23] Cf., e.g., de Vaux, *Revue biblique* 48 (1939), pp. 394ff.; Begrich, ZAW N.F. 17 (1941), pp. 1ff.

EGYPTIAN WISDOM AND THE
OLD TESTAMENT*

By Ernst Würthwein

The *rediscovery of the ancient Near East* may be considered one of the most interesting events in modern historical research. While our knowledge of the ancient peoples who lived in Mesopotamia and along the Nile, in Syria and Asia Minor had previously been quite meagre, that situation altered radically as archaeological research began in those regions in the nineteenth century and a wealth of heretofore unknown materials of the most diverse sorts came to light. Among these, texts—written on papyrus, clay tablets and other material—which had survived the millennia proved to be especially instructive, and were now accessible as authentic records to the first ranks of scientific investigation. New branches of science, egyptology and cuneiform studies arose and made available the new-found documents of historical, religious, juridical, economic and other contents, whose number, already almost incalculable, still continues to grow. Thus, direct and extremely vivid insights into every area of the life of these ancient peoples became possible as a result. The limits of our historical understandings, in the broad sense of the word, were pushed back by millennia. The process itself has become familiar to a wide public through popular scientific publications, so that I may content myself here with a brief allusion to it.

The rediscovery of the ancient Near East also served to show the OT in a new light. Israel, whose literature handed down through the OT had until then been considered incomparably old, now proved itself in truth to be a new-comer among the peoples of the ancient Near East. That in many

*Originally appeared as "Die Weisheit Ägyptens und das Alte Testament; Rede zur Rektoratsübergabe am 29. November 1958," *Schriften der Philips-Universität Marburg*, Vol. VI (Marburg: N.G. Elwert Verlag, 1960). Translated by Brian W. Kovacs, Associate Professor of Sociology, Centenary College of Louisiana, Shreveport.

respects it stood under the spiritual influence of those cultures could not be denied. Did that mean, however, that it was almost fully devoid of any originality, as a certain school contended in the famous Babel-Bibel controversy? Matters are more complicated and more deeply entangled. Doubtless, Israel opened itself to outside influences, but it equally abruptly rejected and opposed what it perceived to be incompatible with its beliefs. For example, it could take over the god El from the Canaanite pantheon and identify him with its God Yahweh, through which the former acquired new characteristics. The god Baal, however, whose orgiastic cult was seen as abominable, it virulently detested along with his followers and persecuted them cruelly at times. It is part of the essence of OT faith that it "bears a polemical and usurping character, that it does not remain static, but lives in constant dialogue, takes hold of assimilable thoughts, concepts and ideas out of other religions and, transforming them, incorporates them into itself," [1] but also clearly rejects what would endanger it. This entire living process is more comprehensible to us today than ever before, when the sayings of the OT can be confronted with archaeological material and texts from its surroundings.

II

The so-called *OT wisdom* portrays a particular kind of segment from this problem area. In that, it concerns a specific literary form with quite definite features of form and content, which is represented in the OT by the books of "Proverbs," "Job," "Qoheleth," and a few Psalms, in the post-canonical literature by "Jesus Sirach" and other literary works; I must limit myself, in this address, to the OT itself.

This literature goes back to a specific class, the so-called wise, who are mentioned between priests and prophets at Jer 18:18 in an enumeration of the authoritative classes in the spiritual life of Israel, which gives clear evidence that they were so acknowledged.

The OT tradition of King Solomon, whose wisdom was famed to be greater than that of all the sons of the orient and than the wisdom of Egypt (1 Kings 5:10), is considered its most luminous representative, shrouded in legendary fame. This comparison with wisdom outside of Israel is significant. While one perceived the law given to Israel and the word of God mediated through its prophets as incomparable, he also knew: there is wisdom outside of Israel as well. Indeed, it is clear to us today that Israelite-Jewish wisdom forms only a branch of the universal ancient Near Eastern wisdom. In particular, since the 1870's, so many Egyptian wisdom teachings from the period of about 2800 up to 100 B.C. have become known, that we can construct a clear picture of the nature and appearance of Egyptian wisdom.[2] Certainly, there was a wisdom literature in Babylonia and Assyria as well, though the remaining fragments provide no such clear picture as for Egyptian wisdom. As in other areas (e.g., in the organization of the state and the kingship ritual), the influence of Egypt was also more intense that that of other cultures. This was proven decisively in the 1920's, when the Instruction of Amenemope, which originated in the first half of the first millennium B.C., was published and a portion of the Book of Proverbs, viz. 22:17-23:10, was discovered to be dependent upon it. This discovery threw significant light on the entire form.

When Israelite tradition tied wisdom in a special way to King Solomon, to that extent it happened to hit on something right, since in his time for the first time the pre-conditions were given for an influx, particularly, of Egyptian wisdom. His father David had created an empire with which the other nations had to reckon. Political and economic connections with the surrounding world were established, an Egyptian princess moved into Jerusalem as the wife of Solomon. Magnificent structures designed by foreigners rose in Jerusalem; a brilliant court life unfolded according to foreign patterns. At the royal court of Solomon and his successors, foreign or foreign-trained scribes were inevitable as higher officials, diplomats, etc. Thus, even in the cultural realm, there came about a departure from the narrowness and isolation of ancient Israelite life, at least at the royal court and its environs. There, too, wisdom found its first place of cultivation as well as its students among the youths who were destined for official careers; but later, especially in the post-exilic period, it encompassed wider circles. A new, foreign spirituality thus gained a foothold in Israel. Just as what was set in motion under Solomon later led to serious problems in the area of politics, religion and social life, so too the assimilation of wisdom contained the stuff of conflict and possibilities for momentous developments. To my mind, the seed has already been sown here for the teachings of retribution characteristic of late Jewish nomism.

III

We shall now attempt briefly to characterize wisdom. It concerns a *practical* wisdom, a wisdom which wants to help man to master life successfully. It does that by setting up rules in the form of proverbs:

> Like a city with torn-down walls
> is a man without self-control. Prov 25:28

or formulated as admonitions:

> Do not presume to honor before the king
> and do not put yourself in the place of the great;
> for better that one should say to you: come up here,
> than that one should set you down before a noble. Prov 25:6f.

How one gets through life successfully is shown in sayings concerning domestic, professional, public life, concerning conduct toward friends and enemies, wife and children, superiors and inferiors, in family and society. The wise do not approach life as either alien or frightening. They are of the opinion that it proceeds according to fixed laws and that one can discern these laws after the fact and organize them into an elegant pattern so that he can master life with their help.

In that connection, there is also no lack of religious sayings. The "fear of God," i.e. piety, is proclaimed the beginning and fundament of wisdom. One could attempt to assemble such and similar kinds of sayings in order to project from them a theology of wisdom. This venture, however, would hardly lead us to the heart of wisdom. There seems to me to be an alternative, more productive question, concerning the understanding of God, world, man, that stands behind wisdom and that is presupposed as the well-established foundation of all endeavors beyond further reflection or discussion. Only when we have managed to grasp that understanding of existence and that feeling of life which guides the wise, will we achieve an adequate understanding of the individual, yet quite diverse, sayings which encompass the height and the depth, the exalted and the trivial. Thus, we shall now turn to the Egyptian wisdom.

IV

Earlier research, whose views are still influential today, generally tended to perceive a kind of secular book of etiquette in the *Egyptian instructions*. Moreover, since hardly any admonition fails to make reference to what excellent success adherence to it will bring along with it, the wisdom books appear to be instructions for ambitious youths who want to establish careers and attain the highest possible level within the Egyptian hierarchy of officialdom. Even when truth and righteousness are recommended, they are to be understood pragmatically. Whoever strives for them finds them to be advantageous to him in his way of life as a means of advancement. No wonder that wisdom literature is considered thoroughly secular and from a religious perspective rather impoverished. One first believes he becomes aware of deeper more pious and moral tones in the late wisdom teaching of Amenemope from the first half of the first pre-christian millennium. It is significant enough that Oesterley[3], e.g., would like to trace this uniqueness of Amenemope's back to Israelite influence. So little do people attribute original religious character to an Egyptian wisdom book. This view, however, is not true to the actual content of the Egyptian instructions. More recent studies, among which I call special attention to those of the Egyptologists de Buck and Brunner and of the religious historian Henri Frankfort[4], have shown that a thoroughly religious understanding of life and world stands behind the often utilitarian-sounding counsels.

One must immediately state that the ancient cultures knew no such distinction between worldliness and religion as is familiar to us. Religion reached into every area and all things have a religious dimension. Thus, it would be notable if the Egyptian wisdom were to bear the secular character which some scholars have attributed to it. Actually, one misses the implication of many sayings if he does not sufficiently attend to their religious presuppositions. And, indeed, it is the concept of *Maat* which has decisive significance for Egyptian wisdom. Here, it is basically a question of a central concept in the Egyptian view of life and world. We have no word in our modern languages which can adequately render the content of Maat, because Maat is at once a cosmological and ethical idea. It may be translated as "truth," "rightness," "justice," "primordial order." "As a goddess, Maat belonged to the Heliopolitan religious system, where she appeared as the daughter of the sun-god. She came down to men in the beginning as the proper order of all things. Through the evil assaults of Seth and his comrades, this order was upset, but restored through the victory of Horus. As the embodiment of Horus, each new king renews this right order through his coronation; a new state of Maat, i.e. of peace and righteousness, dawns." [5] Frankfort defines this Maat in the following words: Maat is "the divine order erected at the time of the creation; this order is manifest in nature through the normal course of events; it is manifest in society as righteousness; and it is manifest in the life of the individual as truth." [6]

The goal of the wisdom instructions is nothing less than this Maat, "which derives from god, thus is fully removed in its nature from all human influences . . . thereby paving the way for it to be transmitted on." [7]

Therefore, one wants to establish a harmonious situation in state and society and help the individual to the best-possible state of fortune.

How did the Egyptian teachers of wisdom attain knowledge of Maat, the divine order? They were nowhere commissioned, like the OT law-giver and prophet, through transcendent revelation; they have, "rather, read Maat from the course of this world and . . . dressed it in an attractive style for their sons." [8]

As god-given order, Maat has claim on absolute validity. It is said of her, that she is powerful, she is immense, she endures. Life, fortune, prosperity, each is only possible in that one joins himself to her. Whoever goes in opposition to her is like one who swims against the stream; he cuts himself off from the fountain of life. He will have no success in everyday life, and can expect no mercy from the judges at the judgment of the dead. On the other hand, the normal consequence of Maat is life, prosperity. "Maat is great, and its appropriateness is lasting; it has not been disturbed since the time of him who made it, (whereas) there is punishment for him who passes over its laws. It is the (right) path before him who knows nothing. Wrongdoing has never brought its undertaking into port. (It may be that) it is fraud that gains riches, (but) the strength of Maat is that it lasts." [9] Following it brings profit, even in the other world: Whoever comes to the judges of the dead without sin "will be like a god in the kingdom of the dead, freely proceeding like the blessed dead." [10]

A fixed order thus lies at the base of life and to observe it is the beginning of wisdom. Once that becomes clear, then some counsels also acquire a deeper significance that might appear to us at first glance as reprehensible opportunism. Hence, e.g., a demeanor toward superiors is commended that one might well term base servility: "Keep your face down until he greets you, and speak only when he has greeted you. One does not know what evil is in his heart. Laugh when he laughs. That will please his heart and what you do will be agreeable." [11] As a result, one may be tempted to find here the speech of a shrewd and crafty courtier. But it would be wrong. The superior in Egypt obviously has a higher, to some extent god-given authority. Hence, it is of great significance that one respect him—not only for the sake of his person; insofar as one honors him, one observes the order. To despise him would mean to disturb the order, the Maat, and whoever disturbs Maat brings about his own cutting-short: it remains, but the rebel perishes because of his opposition to it.

Since the way of Maat undoubtedly leads to life, to success, and since this way is teachable and learnable, it remains within man's power to structure his life toward the good. Whoever patterns himself according to the rules of wisdom will lack for nothing. Thus, the feeling of security which appears to us in this literature. Man lives "in a world that is neither antagonistic nor ultimately problematic." [12] If only man goes the right way, then all external circumstances will also work propitiously for him.

What significance does the deity have for this order? God appears in the Egyptian wisdom first as the one who gave the right order and through it ordered all of life, and second as the one who in omniscience and righteousness saw that this order was kept protected. He punishes whoever violates it; he rewards the followers, the "ones who hear." This applies as much to this life as to life after death. Thus, in the "Instruction for King Merikare," even the king—a god-king!—is admonished to do right so long as he exists on earth with the explanation that the hour can come unforeseen when his deeds will be judged. "And he is a fool who despises the judges of the dead."

God's activity thus takes place entirely in the context of firmly-established, unchangeable order. Even the deity cannot step outside of it, because he cannot act against his own laws. When it says in the Instruction of Ptahhotep, "what men prepare for never occurs; what god commands, occurs," it does not mean a sovereign, arbitrary act of god. Rather, if man attempts, in madness, to burst through the barriers of divine commands, he must come to ruin on god's determination to carry out his laws. [13]

The concept of a righteous order which governs life is absolutely basic to the Egyptian teachers of wisdom. Even if an occurrence in this world should raise some questions about righteousness, they can always be allayed by reference to retribution in the next world. Therefore, the problem of the righteousness of god can never be so clearly perceived as in Israelite religion where, as is well known, belief in a survival into the next world only quite late played any role. In sum, the understanding of existence of the Egyptian wisdom instructions can be characterized as follows:

1. Life proceeds according to a fixed order.

2. This order is teachable and learnable.

3. Man is thereby handed an instrument with which to determine and secure his way through life. Because,

4. God himself must pattern himself according to this order, this law.

Hence, the Egyptian wisdom is most closely bound up with the religiously-determined understanding of world and life. Belief in a god-given order is not only ornament, but fundament, upon which the undertaking of the wisdom teacher depends. Even where this order is not expressly mentioned, belief in it is presupposed. Above all, it gives the sayings their deeper sense.

V

When wisdom, first within courtly circles, was taken over *into Israel,* people may not have been conscious of its ideological and religious content. But it was there and it proved itself to be effective. What is remarkable in the entire process is not that some individual phrases were taken over from the Egyptian wisdom teachings, but rather that people grew up through them into the implicitly maintained understanding of existence. That people affirmed the possibility of securing human life and worked intensely toward its realization. Thus there developed a type of man who was new to Israel and whose self-confidence must have been offensive to the genuine-Israelite faith, which prophetic criticism also confirms (e.g. Is 5:21; 29:14; Jer 4:22; 8:8). We shall make the special position of wisdom with the OT clear through several points.

a.) Like the Egyptian, Israelite teachers of wisdom speak of a moral *lawfulness* which governs life. Whoever is good and upright, his life proceeds in well-being and security; but the wicked person meets misfortune of every sort:

> No ill befalls the righteous,
>> but the wicked are filled with trouble. Prov 12:21 [RSV]
> The house of the wicked will be destroyed,
>> but the tent of the upright will flourish. Prov 14:11 [RSV]
> The righteous has enough to satisfy his appetite,
>> but the belly of the wicked suffers want. Prov 13:25 [RSV]

This connection between deed and consequence is extraordinarily narrow. It is almost a question of an internal regularity which could best be compared to natural law. The well-known picture of Psalm 1 is especially striking: as a tree that is sufficiently well-watered turns green and bears fruit, so the upright person flourishes. That is a law that obtains in the nature of the matter. Therefore, the older Israelite wisdom also entirely avoided speaking of a retributing Power in this connection. In the preceding examples, which could easily be multiplied, no such entity is mentioned. Nevertheless, that may remind one very much of the Egyptian teaching concerning Maat. One could still assume that the Israelite wisdom teachers saw Yahweh himself as the guarantor who assured that the moral order of life remained intact, just as god is sometimes mentioned in the Egyptian wisdom in just such a context.

If life proceeds according to that internal regularity postulated by wisdom, then particular possibilities result for man. Actually, wisdom has very high regard for a person's power. All of those goods of life, highly treasured in Israel as throughout the ancient Near East, he can attain and secure for himself: long life in good health until he dies old and sated with life, flourishing flocks of children who guarantee continuance of the family, material possessions, honor and reputation. One need only make use of that regularity according to which life proceeds, must prove himself to be upright: then will, indeed then can all the rest not fail. Thus, a person has the power to structure his life toward success and good fortune. He can also earn the blessing of God.

In that connection, there is only silence about what otherwise has such central significance in the OT and which we must regard as authentically Israelite. At the focal point of almost every book of the OT stands the covenant people Israel, and what it is and what it should become is a product of its history. It is the nation with whose fathers God made his covenant, to whom he gave promises and on whom he laid responsibilities, whom he led out of Egypt through the wilderness and into Palestine, and in whose history he is continually present with his grace and his mission, his salvation and his judgment. When one reads the wisdom literature, one almost gets the impression that its author knew nothing at all of these matters. It seems to have little meaning for them, at least as we must interpret it, that these things should have anything concrete to do with Israelites. Within the OT, that is highly unusual. Only its foreign origins and the resulting entirely different conceptual orientation toward the unhistorical individual person make it conceivable that wisdom for so long a time overlooked the central themes of Israelite religion. What correlates with that—which is of special significance—is the fact that the relation between human act and divine blessing is determined completely differently from that in genuine Israelite Yahwistic faith. In the traditions of the Israelite twelve-tribe coalition, covenant and law are most closely bound up with each other. In fact, the relationship is such that the law is subordinated to covenant. Thus, the Decalogue begins with a reference to the continuing covenant and Yahweh's activity: "I am Yahweh your God who brought you out of Egypt," and only then do the commands follow which Yahweh places on his community. There are commandments of Yahweh to Israel because of the fact that there is a covenant. Not the reverse: commandments do not create covenant. Further, the blessing of Yahweh does not follow from fulfillment of the commands; it precedes instead. And, the law has only *the* intent of insuring the exclusivity of the relationship between God and nation, i.e. to prevent any sort of departure from faith in the *one* God and covenant partner.[14] "Thus, even in the OT laws —and indeed especially in Deuteronomy—the divine blessing is a gift, which was *prior* to the law and its fulfillment, and therefore independent of it also, which is certainly assured through fulfillment of the law but which cannot first be earned." [15]

It was a momentous alteration of this conception when wisdom aroused the impression that a person might be able to strive for and attain the divine blessing in and of himself and outside of the covenant. Perhaps that was Egyptian thinking, but not genuine Israelite.

b.) Now, wisdom's understanding of existence also has important consequences for the *idea of God*. God's working can only unfold within the bounds of that regularity which governs the totality of life. Correspondingly, Yahweh appears in wisdom first and foremost as retributor:

> A bulwark to him who walks in innocence is Yahweh,
>   but consternation for the evil-doers. Prov 10:29[16]
> A good man obtains favor from the Lord,
>   but a man of evil devices he condemns. Prov 12:2 [RSV]

Thus, God is the guarantor of that order which interpenetrates all of life. Through it, however, he himself is bound: even the deity cannot set aside the law which governs all of life. His power is limited to taking care that it retains its validity by means of proper retribution. Hence, Yahweh becomes a calculable God because he is bound to a determinable law in his dealings.

There is no time to show in detail how wisdom's notion of God stands in extreme tension to that of the rest of the OT. It is quite clear that the God of the covenant, whose realm above all is history and before whom nations are like drops in a bucket (Is 40:15), is entirely different in his entire fundamental conception from the God of wisdom who acts as retributor in the life of the individual. This retributive God, in his activity, is clear, rationally comprehensible, calculable—so to speak, without being a puzzling enigma. However, the God who called forth one people from the circle of nations and dealt with them specially is ultimately incomprehensible in his purposes. Sovereign, he disposes over man who is like clay in the hand of the potter before him (Jer 18:6; Isa 45:9; 64:8); he is also sovereign in his grace: "I am merciful to whomever I wish to be merciful, and I have pity on whomever I wish to have pity." (Ex 33:19)

It is not surprising that in Israel it came to controversy with this wisdom founded upon alien presuppositions. It becomes literarily comprehensible for us in the books of Job and Ecclesiastes, for which the Hebrew term is Qoheleth, which belong to the OT's late period.[17]

VI

As we concern ourselves now with Ecclesiastes (Qoheleth), we must establish that he vehemently contested the understanding of existence of wisdom in part of his aphorisms, and quite obviously as a man who himself had gone through wisdom and for whom, as a wisdom teacher, the school-tradition of his class had been called into question.

a.) As the *ethical order of life* was applied, according to which every earthly event should work out, he observes that it proves itself nonexistent in reality:

> There is something empty which happens on earth:
> There are righteous who meet with
> What the wicked deserve.
> And there are wicked who meet with
> What the righteous deserve.
> I say: This too is empty. (8:14)

How offensive these sayings of Qoheleth were perceived to be by a Judaism that had made wisdom's teaching of retribution its own as an important dogma is seen by the fact that in 8:12f. glosses were added that should correct Qoheleth's heresies.[18]

Even in the fact of *death*, the wise had maintained man's relative power: whoever is upright assures himself of long life, the wicked must die prematurely. Qoheleth had observed, however, that the reality appeared otherwise:

> Both have I seen in the days of my empty life:
> There are righteous who perish in their righteousness,
> And there are godless who live long in their wickedness. (7:15)

The wisdom teachers wanted to take the sting out of the difficult problem of death by making a distinction between the death of the righteous and the death of the wicked. To Qoheleth's clear gaze, however, it proved to be an illusion. Death is death—it is the same for all, for righteous and wicked, for pure and impure, for those who sacrifice as for those who do not, for those who take vows as for those who foreswear them:

> That is evil by everything that happens under the sun:
> That all meet *one* fate,
> and indeed: their end is with the dead.[19] (9:3)

b.) Whoever so reveals the order of life postulated by wisdom to be a fiction will also re-evaluate *man's possibilities*. Wisdom maintains that all possibilities are open for the person who treads upon the stage of life. It is up to him to determine his own destiny. Qoheleth, however, contests this exalted freedom and power. It has long since been disposed concerning man, his destiny is fixed:

> What happens is long since determined,
> determined what a man will be.
> And he cannot go into court
> With him who is stronger than he. (6:10)

Correspondingly, human deeds do not admit of calculation to what result they will lead. Entirely other than human factors decide:

> Once again I saw under the sun:
> Not the swift win the race,
> Nor the heroes the battle,
> Nor the wise bread,
> Nor the understanding riches,
> Nor the knowing favor.
> Rather, all meet time and chance. (9:11)

And now the worst is that man does not know his time; he fumbles in the dark, and suddenly jt lays hold of him:

> For man does not know his time:
> Like fish caught in a net,
> Like birds caught in the snare,

Thus the children of men will be ensnared
In an evil time,
When it suddenly overtakes them. (9:12)

Thus, while human life appears to the wise comprehensible, clear even, because it proceeds according to fixed laws and is therefore calculable; for Qoheleth, it is obscure, dark, because governed by an alien purpose. When, however, an unknown factor is everywhere determinative, how shall a person know, with regard to the future, what is "good"? Hence, Qoheleth's question:

Yes, who knows what in life is good for a man
As long as the days of his empty life continue,
Which he passes "in the" shadows?
Yes, who can tell a man
What will be after him under the sun? (6:12)

Still another place shows how uncertain, ridiculous, any calculation portrays life for Qoheleth:

Throw your bread into the water,
Still, you can find it after many days.
Give portions to seven or eight,
Still you do not know what evil may come upon the earth. (11:1f.)

If one throws his bread into the water, he thinks it is lost. But it must not be so. If one puts his money in seven or eight different places, then he acts cautiously. According to human reckoning, he will preserve his money in at least a couple of places. However, that must not be so! "Whether one does something completely foolish or entirely thought-out: the former can turn out well, the last can be useless; it does not depend on someone's willing or pursuing, one can never calculate how an event will turn out." [20]

How far removed we are in all these sayings from the secure, spontaneous act, like wisdom's feeling of life that trusts the ordered process of life. Precisely in that antipathy, however, we sense that Qoheleth formulated his views obviously with a glance toward wisdom. They contain an indirect polemic.

c.) That also applies, now, to the sayings that he produced concerning

God. In. wisdom, God functioned principally as righteous retributor. "The world is order, cosmos, even God conforms to these laws and does not overstep them. He is the crowning and guarantor of this order, whose inner structure is accessible to the observation of the wise." [21]

Within this order, God and man work together. Wherever man goes the right way, God takes care that he attains the proper success. That Qoheleth, conversely, asserted the determinedness of man, we have already seen. But God, so he continues, is entirely free in whatever he does:

> Because to a man who pleases him
> He gives wisdom, knowledge and happiness.
> To whoever displeases him, he gives the toil
> Of gathering and heaping up,
> And giving it to whoever pleases him.
> That too is empty and straining after wind. (2:26)

Here, God appears entirely sovereign, bound to no consideration of human endeavor or a moral order. Qoheleth, however, does not feel himself driven now to protest against God, whose caprice, or better enigmatic character, he has recognized, as Job did. He only confirms it. This confirmation, though, means a total denial of the image of God in wisdom.

God's conduct, which man cannot reduce to any simple formula therefore, is inalterable:

> I recognized: Everything God does,
> It is for eternity.
> To that there is no adding,
> From it there is no taking away.
> God has done it that man might fear before him. (3:14)

It is impossible to influence God's actions. Man must accept it as inalterable, conclusive. As a result, he becomes conscious of how powerful and sovereign this God is in his acting and how much man is different from him. The result is that fear of this God overtakes man. He has wished it so. Now, wisdom literature often talks of the fear of God; but it is something well-tempered: reverence, piety. For Qoheleth, though, it has other, more original features. "Fear is a constitutive moment in Qoheleth's portrait of God. As a consequence, the idea of the fear of God has recaptured much of its original freshness, the mysterious awe before an overwhelming force, as opposed to ḥokmah (= wisdom)." [22]

Just as God is powerful and sovereign, he is unsearchable in whatever he does:

> He has made everything beautiful for its time . . .
> Only that man might not comprehend
> The work that God does from beginning to end. (3:11)

In every event, God is decisive. But, wisdom's pretentious assertion to have comprehended the internal structure of the world's course, proves as a result to be frivolous. "God does not permit his secrets to be found out. Man can only take what God gives him. But he has not stood in the divine council." [23]

Here, Qoheleth collides with the central claim of the Wise and the most important presupposition of their enterprise. Thus, it is entirely understandable that he does not content himself with mere antitheses but crosses over into outright polemic in which he calls the opponent by name:

> I saw in every deed of God
> That man could not comprehend
> The work that occurs under the sun.
> Even though man exerts himself
> To search it out, he does not find it.
> Even when the *wise man* claims to comprehend it,
> He can not find it out. (8:17)

In spite of the efforts and the claim of the wise, God shows himself to be unsearchable, veiled. "The God whom Qoheleth faces, is the hidden God, only the hidden one." [24]

To summarize, we can say that Qoheleth sought to prove wisdom to be a confusion at decisive points. In opposition to the bright picture they paint of life proceeding in the harmony of act and consequence, he assiduously emphasized the dark sides. He showed man his limitedness: matters have already been disposed concerning him, God has determined his fate, while man himself fumbles in the darkness, not knowing in whatever he does how it will turn out for him. And the end is the same death for all.

Above all, however, Qoheleth conceived God entirely differently from the wise; he saw him in his power and sovereignty and in his wholly-otherness, which makes him completely unintelligible to man. To the extent that Qoheleth diligently emphasized this aspect of God, he showed that he had clearly perceived the weakest point—from the point of view of Israelite faith—in wisdom: the impotence of God. Thus, Qoheleth brought into play in his own sayings significant features of the OT view of God, and one can say on the basis of this observation that he has made himself the advocate of the OT belief in God. On the other hand, something decisive is lacking. Qoheleth removes God so far from man that trust in him is hardly possible any more, and scarcely even prayer. Hence, caution is advised toward God in visiting the Temple, prayer and vows (5:1ff.). Is that conceivable on the basis of the OT? One might well conclude that the developing crisis of wisdom apparent in Qoheleth is not determined by OT faith alone, although this has proven a vital part of it. The way he conducts the debate shows Qoheleth to be a thinker of great individuality whose spiritual attitude one might want to make intelligible by reference to Greek spirituality. But, repeated attempts to prove conclusively a Greek source for Ecclesiastes have not yet succeeded.

VII

Like Qoheleth, the dialogue and divine speeches of the *Book of Job* must also be understood as a debate with wisdom. The discussions which are conducted between Job and his friends revolve about three themes which are decisive for wisdom: about the law of harmony between deed and consequence, about the possibilities of man and about the governance of God. That the three friends move entirely within the paths of the wisdom teachers in their expositions of these three question areas is readily apparent to anyone who reads at all into their speeches. Because of time considerations, we must forego here any detailed proof. But even for Job himself, it is true that he argues from afar on the basis of a dialogue with the fundamental views of wisdom. It should indeed have been the case that God acts as the righteous retributor in the way wisdom maintains. But because it is not so, one must protest against this God, call him to account. Only the divine speeches move beyond this understanding of God.

According to the self-portrait he gives in chs. 29-31, Job was a man after the wise's own hearts: he led a life of justice and righteousness, and received good fortune and wealth. That seemed to him to be thoroughly in order, and he believed himself to be secure in his life's fortunes. Then, misfortune broke upon his life without any perceptible reason and proved the principles by which he had lived up till then to be illusion. Where his misfortune was concerned, he had to dispute with utter determination that he had merited it: the moral order of the world maintained by the friends, and in which he himself had believed in better days, had broken down. But not only in his case does it happen; as he goes on in ch. 21, there is— what could never be, according to the teachings of the wise—a good fortune of the godless, and life's course is filled with difficult puzzles.

Job can only see the cause for it in God. He does not doubt for a moment that God is the lord of man and his life and that from his hand comes everything that happens to a man. But how does God prove himself to be now toward man? That he is a righteous retributor is a belief that Job must let drop because it seemed impossible to him to interpret his suffering on that basis. He himself has experienced how God, in power and freedom, not to mention arbitrarily, acts toward man:

> He snatches away, who can hinder him?
> Who says to him: What are you doing? (9:12)

God acts irresistibly, in absolute sovereignty. There are no limits to his activity: no external ones, because no one can oppose him, to hinder him. But also no internal one, because he does whatever he wishes without being bound through any ethical principle; and no one can call him to account.

That thought is so contradictory to wisdom that one can only interpret these sayings from the Book of Job as a direct polemic against wisdom whose view of the God-man relationship is thus proven to be internally untrue, unrealistic. In this, Job argues not only from the experience of his own life, but also refers to the irresistible omnipotence of God in nature (9:5-7) and in the life of nations (12:14-25). Here, he assiduously raises the frightening, destructive, enigmatic side of God. With real delight, he confronts the harmless contingent God of his friends, who reigns only within the scheme of the dogma of retribution, over against the dreadful, sinister, threatening God shown him through nature and history. In fact, he does not shrink from attributing to him thoroughly demonic characteristics:

> Thus is everything one! Therefore I declare:
> Innocent or guilty, he destroys.
> If "his" scourge suddenly kills,
> He laughs at the fears of the guiltless.
> The earth "he gave" into the hand of the wicked,
> He veiled the face of its judge. . . . (9:22-24)

Can faith in an ethical world-order which offers man security, this trust in God, be more cruelly shattered than it is here?

In these and similar sayings, Job is concerned with destroying the in-offensive image of God of his friends which is identical with that of wis-dom—to expose the vacuity of their naive-optimistic understanding of existence which proclaims man's power. God is overwhelming, and man completely relinquishes his will in good and evil.

On the other hand, admittedly there is no lack of words of trust, in which Job clings to God. Precisely because he alone is powerful, he be-comes the ultimate refuge of the suffering and despairing man. Still, one can hardly be permitted to find the solution to Job's problem in such sayings because at the same time he adjudges the divine speeches of chs. 38-41 to be a later addition.

Taken by itself, the dialogue, i.e. chs. 3-37, offers no solution at all. What Job says concerning God is too much the antithesis of wisdom's view to be able to touch the reality of God. This last only becomes ap-parent when God manifests himself in the thunderstorm and answers Job (chs. 38-41). It is instructive and significant there how the poet worked with the traditional materials of wisdom. The rhetorical questions, with which God makes the questioner Job into the questioned and finally calls him into question, derive their stylistic form from the Egyptian wisdom school.[25] Equally, the content of the divine speeches which take their subject matter from the extensive realm of nature hark back to the "onomastica," name-lists, of Egyptian science which served in the cur-riculum of the wise's scribal schools. In Job 38ff., however, their intent has been totally changed. "While those (Egyptian) lists arose from and were produced by the intense capacity of human knowledge to gain control over nature, the poet of Job transformed that [literary] form entirely into the spirit of the OT so that it served him as proof of the limits of human knowledge over against the overwhelming divine creative power and wis-dom in nature." [26] Hence, even at this point, the disagreement with wisdom is clearly at work.

The divine speeches counterbalance the preceding sayings about the relation of God and man since they place Job before God who is visible in his creation and at the same time incomprehensible. The introductory question:

Who is this who declares (God's) counsel as darkness? (38:2)

is directed toward making Job conscious of his situation as a man. The excursion through creation, put as questions which are to be interpreted as variations of that basic question, show him to be limited in time, power, knowledge and ability before that God who is active in all and from the beginning, eternally reflecting, and incomprehensible.

If, however, the relationship of God and man is to be seen in this way, then the claim of the wisdom represented by the friends to comprehend the entire course of life including him who stands over it and to perceive it in its regularity is thereby set aright just as in Job's denial. In the face of this God, there is neither claim nor protest. Therefore, Job surrenders:

See, I am too small, what can I reply to you? (40:4)

And further:

I had known that you could do everything;
Nothing that you intend is impossible for you.
From hearsay I had heard of you;
Now, however, have my eyes seen you.
Therefore, I recant and repent in dust and ashes. (42:2, 5, 6)

The culmination of the OT faith is thus not an order like "Maat" which binds God and man in the same way, but rather a personal God who stands over against the world and the individual person as *Lord*.

VIII

What we have seen is a significant and instructive example of Israel's encounter and controversy with oriental cultures. In some circles, it opens itself to them with a certain joyfulness and gives them room within it. Then, however, some become conscious of the alienness of this spirit and must set themselves off from it on the basis of what is Israel's own: its belief in a sovereign God who cannot be understood nor reckoned according to human criteria but who is and remains wholly other and incomprehensible to human understanding. Thus, the wisdom books—Proverbs, Ecclesiastes, Job—are not only witnesses to an interesting cultural history, but a theological controversy over the profoundest question of human existence, the question of the understanding of God and man, world and life. The question poses itself to every one of us as well. The various answers we sketched are possibilities for us, too. Whether we adopt one of them and if so, which, is a decision that lies beyond our [purely] scientific undertakings.

NOTES

[1] J. Hempel, *ZAW* XIII (1936), pp. 293f.

[2] A pleasant overview of the surviving instructions is given by H. Brunner, *Handbuch der Orientalistik* I, 2 (1952), pp. 96ff.

[3] Oesterley, *ZAW*, IV (1927), pp. 9ff.

[4] A de Buck, "Het religieus karakter der oudste egyptische wijsheid," *Nieuw Theologisch Tijdschrift* XXI (1932), pp. 322ff. Brunner, *Handbuch*, pp. 90ff. *Idem, Altägyptische Erziehung* (1957), *passim.* H. Frankfort, *Egyptian Religion* (1948), pp. 59ff.

[5] Brunner, *Handbuch*, p. 93.

[6] Frankfort, p. 63.

[7] Brunner, *Handbuch*, p. 93.

[8] *Ibid.*, p. 95.

[9] Instruction of Ptahhotep (5th dynasty, about 2400 B.C.), 95ff. Translation according to Wilson in Pritchard, *ANET* (2d ed.; 1955), p. 412. Wilson's translation of Maat is "justice."

[10] Instruction for King Merikare (10th dynasty, the end of the 3d millennium B.C.), 57. Translation [German] according to von Bissing, *Altägyptische Lebensweisheit* (1955), p. 55.

[11] Ptahhotep, 120ff.; von Bissing, p. 46.

[12] Frankfort, p. 60.

[13] Brunner, *Handbuch*, p. 98. This interpretation of Brunner's is unquestionably preferable to that of those who want to find our "Man proposes but God disposes" in the statement of Ptahhotep.

[14] M. Noth, *Die Gesetze im Pentateuch* (1940), p. 42 (*Gesammelte Studien* [1957], p. 70).

[15] *Ibid.*, p. 83 (*Ges. St.*, p. 132).

[16] Emended text; cf., B. Gemser, *Sprüche Salomos, HzAT* (1937), pp. 42f.

[17] Even in Proverbs, some sayings already appear which could be interpreted as a reference to a divine authority independent of any human activity and could be meant as a dispute with wisdom's view of God (e.g. 16:1, 9; 21:30f.; cf. H. Gese, *Lehre und Wirklichkeit in der alten Weisheit* (1958), pp. 46ff.). But, apart from the fact that they partially admit of another interpretation as well, their value should not be exaggerated. They depict marginal phenomena and cannot really rectify the portrait of God which finds its expression in the overwhelming majority of sayings (cf. also W. Zimmerli, *ZAW* X (1933), pp. 189ff. [See Section III of Zimmerli's article which appears elsewhere in this volume]).

[18] Cf. K. Galling in Haller-Galling, *Die Fünf Megilloth, HzAT* (1940), pp. 80f.

[19] On the restoration of this text, see Galling, p. 80.

[20] H. W. Hertzberg, *Der Prediger, KAT* (1932), p. 174.

[21] W. Zimmerli, *Die Weisheit des Predigers Salomo* (1936), p. 11.

[22] Blieffert, *Weltanschauung und Gottesglaube im Buch Kohelet* (Rostock Dissertation; 1938), p. 56.

[23] Hertzberg, p. 88.

[24] Galling, p. 62.

[25] G. von Rad, *SVT* III (1955), pp. 293ff.

[26] A. Weiser, *Das Buch Hiob, ATD* (2d ed.; 1956), p. 243.

THE INSTRUCTIONS OF 'ONCHSHESHONQY
AND BIBLICAL WISDOM LITERATURE

B. GEMSER

Groningen

Four times the wise men and *wisdom of Egypt are referred to in the Old Testament*. In Gen. xli 8 in the story of Pharaoh's dreams the king sent and called for all the soothsayer-priests of Egypt and all its wise men to get the interpretation of what troubled his spirit. In Ex. vii 11 when Aaron cast down his rod before Pharaoh and it became a serpent, the king summoned the wise men and the sorcerers; and they also, the soothsayers (or magicians) of Egypt, did the same by their secret arts. Magic art rather than what we understand by wisdom is here their field of action. Nearer to our concept comes what is mentioned in 1 Kings v 10 (trl. iv 30) about king Solomon: that his wisdom surpassed the wisdom of all the people of the East (the *benê qèdem*) and all the wisdom of Egypt; what is meant by this follows from the reference in the second next verse to the three thousand proverbs and a thousand and five songs which king Solomon is said to have uttered and that he spoke of the trees and the beasts and the birds and the reptiles. Here wisdom includes apparently moral precepts as well as knowledge of nature and its phenomena. [1]) The only pericope in which some nearer acquaintance with the Egyptian wise men is revealed, is Isaiah xix 11-15 in a prophecy of doom over Egypt in which as in a mocking song is said: "Utterly foolish are the princes of Zo'an, the wise counsellors of Pharaoh give stupid counsel [2]). How can you say to Pharaoh, "I am a son of the wise, a son of ancient kings"? This utterance proves that during the viiith or viith century B.C. [3]) the close connection between or

---

[1]) On the meaning of the last reference see A. ALT, "Die Weisheit Salomos", *Theologische Literaturzeitung* 76 (1951), S. 139-144 = *Kleine Schriften zur Geschichte des Volkes Israel*, II (1953), S. 90-99; and also M. NOTH, "Die Bewährung von Salomos 'Göttlicher Weisheit' ", in *Wisdom in Israel and the Ancient Near East*, Supplement Vetus Testamentum, Vol. III, Leiden, 1955, p. 225 f.

[2]) Or according to 1Q Isa: "its wise men give Pharaoh stupid counsel".

[3]) The authenticity of vss. 1-15 is usually doubted; but even in the younger

even the indentity of the wise men of Egypt and its princes and kings of old was well known in Israel. But there is in the Old Testament no mention at all of the names of these teachers nor of the titles and contents of their writings. [1])

It had to last until the second part of the xixth century A.D. before any *original Egyptian wisdom text* came to light, and by far the majority of the now available books of "Instructions" have been discovered and published in this our xxth century. In 1952 HELLMUT BRUNNER could write in *Handbuch der Orientalistik* [2]): "Aus der Zeitspanne von rund 2800-100 v. Chr. sind uns sieben Lehren ganz oder fast vollständig überkommen, von fünf weiteren liegen Bruchstücke vor, während wir von sechs oder sieben anderen nur die Titel kennen". In my commentary on the Proverbs of Solomon, published in the Dutch series *Tekst en Uitleg* in 1928, I could already make use of these seven entirely or nearly complete "Instructions" [3]). They are in chronological order: The Instruction of Ptah-hotep, vizier of king Issi or Izezi from the Old Kingdom, vth Dynasty; The Instruction for Meri-ka-ré from his father, king Cheti/Achthoes II, of the xth Dynasty, the period of transition from the Old to the Middle Kingdom; The Instruction of Amen-em-hét, king of the xiith Dynasty, for his son Sesostris I; from the same period the Instruction of the scribe Cheti, the son of Duauf (for a long time the name has been read inversely Duauf, the son of Cheti) [4]); originating from the New Kingdom is the Instruction of the scribe

---

second part of the chapter the vss. 18 and 19 f. have to be dated before the reformation of Josiah, cp. E. SELLIN-L. ROST, *Einleitung in das Alte Testament*, Leipzig, 1950, S. 102 f.

[1]) The discovery of the close, often literal resemblance between the Instructions of Amen-em-ope(t) and Prov. xxii 17 —xxiii 11 in 1923/1924 (see my *Spruche Salomos*, in *Handbuch zum Alten Testament* ed. by O. EISSFELDT, Tübingen, 1937, S. 65 ff.) and the instructive study by G. VON RAD, *Josephgeschichte und ältere Chokma, Suppl. Vetus Testamentum*, Vol. I (Congress Volume Copenhagen 1953), Leiden, 1953, p. 120-127, as well as the many similarities between single proverbs in the wisdom books of Egypt and Israel (See my *De Spreuken van Salomo* I, *Spreuken* II, *Prediker, Hooglied*, in *Tekst en Uitleg*, ed. F. M. TH. BÖHL and A. VAN VELDHUIZEN, Groningen, 129, 1931, and *Sprüche Salomos*, passim) prove beyond doubt that at least some of the wise man of Israel were acquainted with the works, teachings and ideals of Egypt's sages.

[2]) *Handbuch der Orientalistik*, her. v. Bertold SPULER, Ier Band, *Ägyptologie*, 2ter Abschnitt, *Literatur*, "Die Weisheitsliteratur", Leiden, 1952, S. 90-110.

[3]) See my, *De Spreuken van Salomo*, I, in *Tekst en Uitleg*, p. 11 and *passim*; for Duauf, ib., p. 10,12 (77, 114, 162).

[4]) For Cheti's Instruction cp. the new treatment by Hellmut BRUNNER, *Die Lehre des Cheti*, Ägyptologische Forschungen, Heft 13, 1944.

Anii, of the second half of the xviiith Dynasty; the Instruction, so wellknown since 1923 because of its close relation to Proverbs xxii 16 ff. of Amen-em-ope(t), high official, "Overseer of the Soil, and Overseer of Grains", dating somewhere from the times of the xxiith-xxvith Dynasties; and lastly the Instruction named after the mediator in the acquisition of the document for the "Rijksmuseum van Oud-heden te Leiden" Papyrus Insinger, also called "Das demotische Weisheitsbuch" from late Persian or early Ptolemaic times. [1]) In his above-mentioned survey HELMUT BRUNNER gives a very elucidating, short characterization of all these seven works.

Of the but *fragmentarily preserved wisdom books* the Instruction for Ka-gemni, purporting to have been written at the royal command by the vizier of king Huni and probably dating from the end of the iiird or from the ivth Dynasty, is often included in the series, because although only the end of the book is preserved, its contents and concluding narrative are of importance, and it is found on the same papyrus as the Instruction of Ptah-hotep. [2]) In 1940 the opening lines of the Instruction of Hor-dedef or Djedef-hor, hereditary prince and son of king Khufu/Cheops of the ivth Dynasty were published [3]); although only the short title of the collection and a few lines with sayings of the composer have been preserved on the two ostraca on which they are written, the find is important because Djedef-hor was already known in tradition as a famous ancient wise man, having become as legendary for his wisdom as the great Imhotep from the time of king Djoser. So these "miserable remains" as John A. WILSON calls them, provide at present the oldest textual witness of Egyptian wisdom literature. I would like to remark here that one of the precepts of this Instruction which reminds of a passage of Ptah-hotep's book, finds a parallel in Solomon's Proverbs. It reads: "If thou art a man of standing and foundest [a household, *take*] thou a wife as *a man of feeling*, and a male child will be born to thee. Thou shouldest build thy house for thy son (in) the place where thou art . . . ". A passage in Ptah-hotep opens almost identically: "If thou a art man of standing, thou shouldest found thy household and love thy wife at home as is fitting". The short collection Prov. xxiv

---

[1]) FR. W. Frhr. VON BISSING, *Altägyptische Lebensweisheit*, Zürich, 1955, S. 91 calls it "Das demotische Weisheitsbuch des Phibis, Sohnes des Tachospalen".
[2]) Papyrus Prisse, cp. G. JÉQUIER, *Le Papyrus Prisse et ses variantes*, Paris, 1911.
[3]) H. BRUNNER, *Handbuch der Orientalistik*, S. 97; JOHN A. WILSON in JAMES B. PRITCHARD, *Ancient Near Eastern Texts*, Princeton, 2nd ed., 1955, p. 419.

24 ff. has in vs. 27 a precept of almost the same tenor: "Prepare your work outside, make things ready for you in the field; and after that build your house", i.e. found a household of your own; the proposed insertion of the words *tiqqaḥ lĕkâ iššâ*, so that the second half reads: "and after that take a wife and build your house", finds ready support in the Egyptian versions, at least as far as the meaning of the expression "build your house" is concerned.

The *latest* and by no means insignificant *addition* to the series of Egyptian wisdom books, also providing important new material for comparison with Old Testament *ḥokmâ*-literature forms the *Instruction of 'Onch-sheshonqy*. It is preserved on Papyrus No. 10508 of the collection of the Department of Egyptian Antiquities in the British Museum, acquired in 1896; the late Herbert Thompson Professor of Egyptology in the University of Cambridge, S.R.K. GLANVILLE, has edited it under the name "The Instructions of Onchsheshonqy" as Vol. II of the Catalogue of Demotic Papyri in the British Museum, as recently as 1955. Part I contains Introduction, transliteration, translation, and notes, Part II the Plates. It was a tragic coincidence that the editor died a fortnight after his work had been published by The Trustees of the Museum. The proposed Vocabulary will, I understand, be completed by his pupil Mr H. S. SMITH of Cambridge, already mentioned in the Acknowledgments of the work. Dr B. H. STRICKER, conservator of the Egyptian Department of the "Rijksmuseum van Oudheden" at Leiden, gave a translation in Dutch with Introduction in the "Jaarbericht No. 15" of the "Vooraziatisch-Egyptisch Genootschap Ex Oriente Lux", published in May last year, 1958, p. 11-38 [1]). Dr STRICKER writes in his Introduction: "It happens only too rarely, that the Egyptian literature, as we know it to-day, can be enlarged by a newly-discovered document, and still more rare is the case that such a document at the same time contains a text that is readable and intelligible to everyone. Such a happy event we welcome in the publication of GLANVILLE's posthumous work". The text consists of twenty-seven and a half columns and is complete except for some lacunae, especially in the first two columns, and a damage at the top of the papyrus by which

---

[1]) STRICKER renders the author's name as Anchsheshonq.

It seems that this newly published work has not yet drawn much attention, neither among students of Egyptian nor of Biblical wisdom. Hellmut BRUNNER refers to it only in a footnote of his work *Altägyptische Erziehung*, Wiesbaden, 1957, S. 8, A. 14, 2.

one or more, but not many lines at the beginning of each of the twenty-eight columns have been lost. The text is written in a fine, clear hand, so similar to that of the two well-known demotic papyri, the Strasbourg *Petubastis* [1]) and what GLANVILLE calls "the Leiden Wisdom Book (Pap. Insinger)", which are generally considered to have been written by the same scribe, that at first sight it looked as though the same scribe wrote all three texts. But detailed study has shown that there are too many smaller or greater differences in handwriting and also some in grammar to substantiate this meaning. As date of the MS the editor supposes on palaeographical grounds late Ptolemaic times. The date of the composition itself is put by the editor in a very careful weighing of arguments as probably in the vth century B.C.; the personal names in the introductory Narrative represent the Late Pharaonic period; it may be that this narrative is simply a literary device; the collection of precepts itself may then be of an earlier date; but it seems that there are in the Instructions themselves some references to the imprisonment of the author as related in the Introductory Narrative (Col. 8, lines 9 f. and Col. 26, l. 1-8) which would mean that the two parts of the book have to be considered contemporary. The book seems to be an original demotic composition, not hieratic; which, as the editor declares, in the light of our present knowledge of demotic seems to make it improbable that the text was composed before the vth century. I intend to come back to this point later on; for the time being I want to remark that this dating puts the Instruction of 'Onchsheshonqy in the available series of Egyptian wisdom books on the penultimate place, as the youngest before the Leiden wisdom book of Papyrus Insinger.

As to *the contents* of this remarkable text, the first five of its twenty-seven and a half columns of not much more than twenty-six lines each contain the introductory narrative. It is an interesting story, reflecting the position of officials at the court of the Pharaoh, and the intrigues in which they so easily could become involved. Such a thing happened to the pretended or real author of this Instruction, 'Onchsheshonqy, priest of Rē at Heliopolis, while he resided at Memphis at the invitation of the friend of his youth, the court-physician Har-si-esi. This man takes part in a conspiracy against the life of the Pharaoh (unfortunately the name of the king is never

---

[1]) W. SPIEGELBERG, *Der Sagenkreis des Königs Petubastis*. Demotische Studien, Heft 3, Leipzig, 1910; cp. GLANVILLE, *l.c.*, p. xi, n. 1.

mentioned). Har-si-esi's plans are being overheard while he explains them to 'Onchsheshonqy, the king is informed, and after Har-si-esi 'Onchsheshonqy also is summoned before the royal court. He, presumably rightly, declares that he is innocent, and even has tried to dissuade his friend from taking part in the conspiracy. After Har-si-esi with all his people and all the conjurers have been thrown into the fire of an altar, built at the door of the royal palace, 'Onchsheshonqy is being taken to prison. When, on the occasion of the anniversary of the accession of Pharaoh, all the other prisoners are being released, but not 'Onchsheshonqy, he understands that his imprisonment will last long, probably lifelong, and he asks the favour of a writing-palette and a roll of papyrus, that he may write a book of instruction for his young son, whom he has not been able to instruct so far. Informed of his request, the Pharaoh consents to his being given a writing-palette, but not a roll of papyrus. Thereupon 'Onchsheshonqy, took the pot-sherds of the jars in which he received his daily ration of wine, and wrote upon them the Instruction for his son. It is not related that the pot-sherds reached their destination regularly or at all; but it is said that their contents were being reported to Pharaoh and his great men daily. Whether, as in the case of Ahiqar, the wise counsellor of Sennacherib [1]), 'Onchsheshonqy, after having been in danger of being executed at the royal command, was also in the end rehabilitated, the story does not tell. The lamentation at the end of the narrative, which in more than thirteen lines, all of them beginning with the same words: "When Rē is angry with a land", pictures the calamities caused by the divine wrath (Col. 5), is certainly meant to influence and convince of his innocence not only the invoked God and all the people who find the pot-sherds, (Col. 4, lines 19-21) but also the king and his counsellors.

The *translations* of GLANVILLE and of STRICKER *differ* in many cases and respects. As a non-Egyptologist I feel quite incompetent to give preference to one of them in general and especially in individual difficult readings. It makes a difference in the ethics of the work if one reads with GLANVILLE (Col. 8, l. 9 f.): "Do not follow after a scribe when they take him to prison; follow after him when they take him to his tomb", or with STRICKER:" Do not with draw your hand from a scribe when they take him to prison; if you withdraw your hand from him, they take him to his tomb". GLANVILLE translat-

---

[1]) Cp. H. L. GINSBERG in PRITCHARD's A.N.E.T., p. 427 ff.

es (Col. 11, l. 20): "A bull is not born of a bull", STRICKER: "A bull is not born as a bull". Again a question of different ethical standard is presented by GLANVILLE's rendering (Col. 15, 1:14): "Do not commit a robbery of which you will be convicted", as compared with STRICKER's: "Do not commit robbery; later on you will be discovered". It makes some difference if one is being advised: (Col. 16, l. 15): "Do not laugh at instruction", or being warned: "Don't mock at a cat". A statement like: "All neighbours are welcome in a house; thieves are not welcome" (Col. 20: l. 15) shows a different social milieu as when one hears: "All kind of cattle are received in a house; a thief is not received". In the passage on the different and often anomalous allotments of fate in GLANVILLE's version (Col. 26, l. 3-8): "There is one who gains (wealth) without seeking (for it)", the tragic note of STRICKER's rendering is missing: "Many a one saves without finding".

Cases in which STRICKER's *translation* seems to me more to the point are the following. GLANVILLE has (Col. 7, l. 19 f.): "The little man who behaves arrogantly is greatly detested. The great man who behaves modestly is highly respected."; STRICKER: "The miserable one, whose pride is great, his stench spreads itself. The man of distinction, whose pride is small, his praise spreads itself". Over against GLANVILLE's rendering (Col. 19, l. 6): "If a *bulṭi* (a Nile-fish) gives way to its rival the fish perish as a result", STRICKER gives the better understandable: "If a bird takes away the place of another bird, it must give up a feather". In the same column, line 10 GLANVILLE translates: "Do a good deed (only) to throw it into mid-river, and it is extinguished when you find it"; STRICKER's version gives more sense: "Do a good deed and throw it into the river; when this dries up, you shall find it". The proverb Col. 22, l. 6 which GLANVILLE leaves incomplete: "He who makes love to a woman in the street with his purse . . .", STRICKER thinks himself able to give in full as: "He who makes love to a woman in the street, his purse is cut open at its side". In the same column, line 16 GLANVILLE reads: "If you are hungry, eat your (own) filth, (and) you will (soon) be satiated by the filth of it"; as is already indicated by the three words which GLANVILLE inserts between brackets, this rendering is uncertain; STRICKER's translation again gives better sense: "If you are hungry, eat what you detest; when you are satiated, detest it again". Column 23, line 19 is given in GLANVILLE's edition as: "The guests(?) are those who sit in the houses, it is the musicians who are making merry (?)", while

STRICKER translates: "The architects build the houses, the musicians inaugurate them". This rendering is supported by the two following sayings: "The frogs are those who praise Hapi (i.e. the inundation); it is the mice which eat the emmer. The oxen are those who procure the barley and the emmer, it is the asses who consume it"; all three proverbs seem to be variants of the truth: "One sows and another reaps" (John iv 37).

But on the other side there are ample cases in which GLANVILLE's *renderings* seem to be *preferable*. The person who stands in contrast to the wise man and the prudent woman is always called in GLAN-VILLE's version: "the fool" (Eg. *lḫ*; e.g. Col. 6, 1. 14; Col. 18, 1. 9 et passim); why STRICKER always translates: "the hypocrite", is not clear and it fits not so well in the context. GLANVILLE's rendering: "the blessing" (Eg. *rnn.t*) in the group of proverbs Col. 8, lines 17-23, gives a better meaning and preserves the ancient colouring to my mind better than STRICKER's "prosperity". GLANVILLE has kept himself nearer to the original without sacrificing English idiom where he preserves more truly the original order of words in groups of proverbs with the same initial words or expressions (e.g. Col. 10 lines 11-25 "Oh may . . ."; Col. 13, 1. 13 f. "Do not get . . ."; Col. 20, lines 22-25 "The waste of . . ."; Col. 21, lines 1-12 "There is no . . ."; Col. 26, lines 4-6. "There is . . ."). Also in individual cases GLANVILLE often seems preferable. I mention Col. 11, 1. 9 f.: "Do not hurl a lance (?) if you are not able to control its flight. He who raises a dyke to the sky—it will fall upon him." STRICKER translates: "Do not hurl a lance if you are unable to hold its shaft. Who spits at the sky, before him it (the spittle) falls down (again)". GLANVILLE's version (Col. 12, 1. 12): "Foolishness does not occur in a house where a wise man is", seems more acceptable than STRICKER's: "The affairs of a hypocrite do not prosper in the house where a wise man is staying". Certainly more sense gives GLANVILLE's proverb (Col. 18, 1. 11): "The children of the fool wander in the street; those of the wise man are by his side", than the strange reading of STRICKER: "The children of the hypocrite wander in the street, the children of the wise man are in his belly". And as a last example, Col. 21, 1. 20 f.: "Better a statue of stone for a son than a fool. Better to be without (a brother) than to have a brother who is evil", compares favourably over against STRICKER's rendering: "Better a statue of stone than a hypocritical son. Better nothing than a crime". Future study of the text by Egyptologists will certainly clear up many of

these discrepancies; suggestions of Old Testament scholars may
perhaps be of some use in comparing Biblical evidence.

The *form of the single proverb* in this collection (which contains more
than 550 sayings, i.e. about 22 chapters of the length of the Biblical
Book of Proverbs) is the usual one in wisdom literature, although
the differences with Old Testament *mešalîm* are often remarkable.
Already the frequency of proverbs consisting of only one line and
grammaticaly one short sentence, is a distinctive difference. There
are apodictic precepts like: "Do not be put out by thing(s). Do not be
dissatisfied with your occupation (Col. 6, l. 23 f.). Do not bother about
(or trust) a fool. Do not bother about the property of an idiot (Col. 7,
l. 6f.). Do not neglect to serve your God. Do not neglect to serve your
master. Do not neglect him who serves you (ib., l. 14-16). Learn how
to approach Pharaoh. Learn how to sit in the presence of Pharaoh.
Learn to observe (STRICKER: Learn the constitution of) the sky. Learn
to observe (or Learn the constitution of) the earth (Col. 25, l. 10-13)".
Equally numerous are statements like: "The blessing of a district
is a lord who executes justice. The blessing of a temple is a priest
(STRICKER: its purity). The blessing of an acre is the actual working
of it. The blessing of a store-house is in stocking (STRICKER: sustain-
ing) it. The blessing of a safe is cash in hand (STRICKER: the management by one hand). The blessing of property is a prudent woman
(STRICKER: the management by a prudent woman). The blessing of a
wise man is his speech (Col. 8, l. 17-23). The personality [1]) of a man is
(STRICKER: is determined by) his family. The personality of a man
is his strength(?). The personality of a man (shows) in his face. The
personality of a man is (determined by) one of his members" (Col. 11,
l. 11-14). Also exclamations or wishes occur, e.g.: "Oh may the
flood-water not fail to arrive ! Oh may the fields not fail to be green !
Oh may the poor plot of land be the one which grows fodder in
abundance ! Oh may a cow (STRICKER: the womb) receive her bull !
Oh may the moon succeed (STRICKER: receive) the sun and not fail
to rise ! Oh may life always succeed death !" (Col. 10: l. 17-20, 24 f.).

Most frequent however are sayings of so-called *synthetic parallelism*,
in which the grammatical sentence runs through both parts of the
proverb, and the second half implements the first (cp. Biblical Prov.
x 18, 26; xi 7, 8, 22, 31). I quote: "Serve your (?) God, that he may

---

[1]) Eg.: ¦*my.t*, also translated with "character", and synonym of *ḫ't.t* "heart,
innermost", see Aksel VOLTEN, *Das demotische Weisheitsbuch*, Kopenhagen,
1941, S. 75 f.

protect you. Serve your brothers, that you may have a good reputation. Serve a wise man, that he may serve you. Serve him who serves you. Serve any man, in order to find profit. Serve your father and your mother, that you may go and prosper (Col. 6, l. 1-6). Do not send in your affair a maid-servant, for she takes care only of her own interests (STRICKER's translation). Do not send (GLANVILLE: consult) a wise man in a small matter, when a large matter is at hand (STRICKER: will rest). Do not send (consult) a fool in a large matter when there is a wise man whom you can send (or: consult)" (Col. 6, l. 12-14).

It is remarkable that there are so *few* proverbs *with antithetic parallelism*. This is a very definite difference with Biblical wisdom, where the putting together of contrasting sentences is very customary (esp. in Prov. x-xv and xxviii, xxix). I noted only nine cases in which a proverb from the outset clearly is conceived as an antithesis. I quote: "A thief steals by night; he is found in the day time. Give a prudent woman a hundred pieces of siver; do not accept two hundred from a foolish one. The children of the fool wander in the street; those of the wise man are by his side. Take the rich man to your house, take the poor man to your boat. The way of God is open for everyone, (but) the blockhead does not know how to find it. Choose a prudent husband for your daughter, do not choose for her a rich husband." (Col. 14, l. 11; Col. 18, l. 9, 11, 23; Col. 23, l. 12; Col. 25, l. 15; cp. also Col. 13, l. 2, 6; Col. 26, l. 9; and in STRICKER's translation Col. 26, l. 14 f.: "Otherwise the disposals of God, otherwise the thoughts of man"). Contrasting effects are also discernible in the proverbs of the type "Better . . . than", e.g. "Better dumbness than a hasty tongue. Better sitting still than carrying out an inferior mission (STRICKER). Better to live in your (own) small house than to live in the large house of another. Better a small property which has been acquired (STRICKER) than a large property which has been squandered" (Col. 15, l. 16 f.; Col. 23, l. 8 f.; cp. also Col. 21, l. 20-22, see above p. 109). The same effect lies in the already mentioned proverbs on the theme "One sows, another reaps" (Col. 23, l. 19-21, above p. 108 f.).

About the same number of cases occur in which the antithesis is extended over two separate sayings, e.g.: "The little man who behaves arrogantly is greatly detested. The great man who behaves modestly is highly respected (Col. 7, l. 19 f., see above p. 108). Do not undertake expense until you have set up your storehouse. Undertake expense according to your means (Col. 9, l. 24 f.; see further Col. 15, l. 11 f.; Col. 18, l. 7 f., 16 f.; Col. 19, l. 22 f.; Col. 22, l. 10 f.; Col. 25,

l. 18 f.). This is often more a matter of arrangement than of structure of single proverbs.

Single proverbs containing *a synonymous parallelism* seem totally absent, or in any case very scarce in 'Onchsheshonqy's collection. The type is well-known in Biblical wisdom; I refer only to such Biblical sayings as: "A liberal man will be enriched, and he who waters will himself be watered. He who troubles his household will inherit wind, and the fool will be servant to the wise. From the fruit of his words a man is satisfied with good, and the work of a man's hand comes back to him. The evil bow down before the good, the wicked at the gate of the righteous" (Prov. xi 25, 29; xii 14; xiv 19). It is again a different case when separate proverbs with more or less the same contents are placed next to one another, of which there are quite a number of instances in 'Onchsheshonqy's book. I cite: "Do not say 'young man' to one who has grown up. Do not despise a man who has grown up (Col. 7, l. 21 f.). Do not speak hastily lest you give offence. Do not say the first thing that comes into your head (ib., l. 23 f.). [1])

In this lacking of sentences intended to cover two lines of synonymous parallelism and in the scarcity of antithetic parallelism one is inclined to see a less developed form of wisdom than in the well-balanced, more elaborated pattern of most of the Biblical Proverbs.

Comparisons are fairly frequent. I cite: "Do not purify yourself with water only; the river flows down (even) for the stone (Col. 17, l. 12 f.). Beer matures (only) on its mash; wine matures until it has been opened (STRICKER: by not opening it; Col. 19, l. 22 f.). The hissing of a snake is more significant (STRICKER: has more effect) than the braying of a donkey. A snake which is eating, has no venom. The waste of a donkey is carrying bricks. The waste of a boat is carrying straw (Col. 20, l. 9, 13, 24 f.). A slip of the tongue in the royal Palace is (like) a wrong turn of the helm at sea. A cat which loves fruit, hates him who eats it. Do not drink water from a well and (then) throw the pitcher back into it. Belly of a woman, heart of a horse (Col. 23, l. 10, 15, 23 f.) When a donkey runs with a horse, it takes over its pace. When a crocodile wants a donkey, it puts on a wig (STRICKER). Man is still more inclined to copulate than a donkey; his purse restrains him (STRICKER). A woman is a quarry; the first-comer exploits her (STRICKER). A good woman of noble character

---

[1]) Other instances are Col. 9, l. 16f.; Col. 11, l. 8 f.; Col. 12, l. 17 f.; Col. 15, l. 5 f.; Col. 16, l. 21 f.; Col. 17, l. 10 f., 12 f.; Col. 18, l. 16 f.; Col. 19, l. 11 f.; Col. 21, l. 15 f., 18 f.

is like food coming forth in hunger-time (STRICKER), (Col. 24, l. 7, 8, 10, 20 f.).

The style forms of *admonition or precept* ("Mahnwort") and *statement* ("Aussagewort") are both represented and alternate. I counted about two hundred and fifty-eight of the first form and two hundred and seventeen of the second, or two hundred and thirty seven if sayings in the form of a wish ("Oh that .. !) are included. Sometimes a whole column or the greater part of it consists of admonitions (e.g. Col. 6; 7; 9; 16; 17), sometimes however the same is the case with statements (e.g. Col. 20; 21; 23; 24; 26).

A *principle or system of arrangement* is not discernible in 'Onchsheshonqy's book of proverbs. This is remarkable in view of the rather late date of this collection and when compared with the Leiden Wisdom Book (Pap. Insinger) for which Aksel VOLTEN has proved a very definite and conscious composition throughout [1]). Also the Instructions of Amen-em-ope(t) are well divided in their thirty chapters, each of them containing sayings on more or less one subject. Anything of this kind is lacking in 'Onchsheshonqy's collection, which is rightly characterised by GLANVILLE as "An Anthology of Proverbs". There are however rudiments of grouping of different kinds. Several times sayings beginning with the same initial words or expressions are coupled together, without further connection as far as concerns the material contents. Little words like negatives, conjunctions, pronouns serve as connective links. Thus the negation "Not" (Eg. *m- 'r*) in the sense "Do not" (Col. 6, lines 10-24; almost the whole of Col. 7 and about half of Col. 9; Col. 12, line 1-7; Col. 13, l. 13 f.; Col. 14 l. 19-23; almost the whole of Col. 16; Col. 17, lines 1-17; Col. 28, l. 2, 4 f., 7-11). An other expression is "There is" (Eg. *wn* or *wn p nt*; Col. 26, lines 3-7, 17 f.), and "He who" (Eg. *p nt*, ib., l. 19-21); also "There is no" (Eg. *mn* or *mn p nt*, Col. 21, lines 1-12. There is a group of twenty sayings beginning with the exclamation or wish "Oh, may" (Eg. *hmy e*; stretching from Col. 10, line 11 until Col. 11, line 4). That there is deliberateness in this grouping together can perhaps also be deducted from the frequent exaggeration in the manuscript of the size of the first sign or group of signs in each line, especially where this grouping is discernible (cp. also GLANVILLE, p. xi). A less formal principle of grouping is the one after ideas, like "Better . . . than" (cp. above, p. 109, 111) and "Otherwise are" (above p. 111). Thus

---

[1]) See Aksel VOLTEN, *l.c.*, S. 122 ff.

there is a small collection beginning with the imperative "Serve" (Col. 6, l. 1-5), or "Do not send" (ib., l. 12-15), or "Do not long for" (ib., l. 16 f.), "Do not pamper" (ib. l. 18 f.), "Do not instruct" (Col. 7, l. 4 f.), "Do not bother about (or trust)" (ib. l. 6 f.), "Do not conceal" (ib. l. 8-10), "Do not run away" (ib., l. 11 f.), "Do not neglect (STRICKER: hesitate)" (ib., l. 14-17).

The lamentation at the end of the Introductory Narrative, with its opening words "When Rē is angry with a land" repeated at the beginning of at least thirteen lines, is a kind of transitional form to those passages where a grouping by definite subjects is found. Mention has already been made of the group of ten sayings with the idea of wherein the "blessing" of a locality, building, person etc. exists (Col. 8, l. 17 until Col. 9, l. 4). A group of five sayings is concentrated on the interesting idea of a man's "personality" (Col. 11, l. 11-14), another of four on what "the waste" is of a thing, an animal, a person (Col. 20, l. 22-25). Interesting is also the group of four in which the donkey plays a role and is a symbol (Col. 24, l. 7-10). Fairly large is also the collection in which woman is the main topic (nine proverbs, Col. 25, l. 14-23, except l. 16). Capital (or wealth) and expenses are the combining idea in Col. 9, l. 19-22, 24 f.; borrowing money in Col. 16, l. 9-11. What kind of persons are of no use is enumerated in the three lines 22-24 of Col. 24. Antithesis forms the connection between the two proverbs: "There is no wise man who comes to grief. There is no fool who finds reward" (Col. 21, l. 7 v.).

It is remarkably rare to find synthetical grammatical periods or lines of thought running through more than one line; of these I encountered only two instances; the one on the conduct towards a friend of youth: "if you keep company (STRICKER: grow up) with a man and are on good terms with him (STRICKER: and come to wealth with him), do not leave him when he fares badly; let him attain his house of eternity (unconcerned); his heir (STRICKER: who comes after him) will make provision for you" (Col. 17, l. 18-20). The other instance is about annoyance or insult and its bad effects (Col. 22, l. 21-25; in which a further subtlety is the six times using of the verb ḫpr "to occur"): "Do not insult (STRICKER: annoy) a nobleman (STRICKER: a man of the multitude, the common people); when insult occurs, fighting occurs; when fighting occurs, killing occurs; killing does not occur without God knowing; nothing occurs except what God ordains".

In view of all these formal characteristics of this Egyptian wisdom book, it must be said that the hokmatic sentences of the *Old Testament*, even in those parts where sayings of only two coherent members prevail, represent a much *more developed art* of proverbial literature, not to speak of the chapters with larger units as Prov. xxv-xxix, and the treatises on definite subjects which form the main contents of Prov. i-ix and Qoheleth.

The proverbs of 'Onchsheshonqy show *a rural background*; their imagery is derived from a life with nature and in the country-side. Although the Introductory Narrative is set in towns and at and around of the royal court, it is not the world of court-officials and scribes in which the proverbs themselves have their setting. This again is a remarkable difference with wisdom books such as the Leiden Papyrus Insinger and the Instructions of Amen-em-ope(t), and even most of the Egyptian proverbial literature. Here the resemblance with most of the Biblical proverbs forces itself upon the reader, especially as far as the older collections Prov. x-xxii 16 and xxv-xxix are concerned [1]). The observation of the sky and of the earth is recommended (Col. 25, l. 12 f.; cp. above p. 110); the North-wind is mentioned (Col. 23, l. 5); the seasons are to be taken in consideration: "Do not say 'It is summer'; there is winter (to come). He who does not gather wood in summer, will not be warm in winter" (Col. 9, l. 16 f.). I have cited already proverbs in which the inundation of the Nile and perhaps the dykes are mentioned (Col. 10, l. 17; col. 23, l. 20; col. 11, l. 10, see above p. 109); cp. also: "When the Nile rises, it distributes to everyone (STRICKER: it is a frontier to everyone; Col. 18, l. 24). He who cannot keep his eye on the river, let him give his mind to the water pots" (Col. 22, l. 17). Crocodiles are a part of the imagery, as in Col. 22, l. 8 and 15: "When a woman likes a crocodile, she takes on its character. A crocodile does not catch a townsman" (cp. also Col. 10, l. 4 f. and Col. 24, l. 8, see above p. 114). It speaks of fish (Col. 18, l. 25) and fishermen: "The fisherman casts of from shore (or with STRICKER: casts out his net on board ship) without being able to say 'God will dispense to every house' (STRICKER: in ignorance, considerating that God sends to every house; Col. 11, l. 15, cp. also Col. 26, l. 15, above p. 111, and about a boat Col. 20, l. 25, above p. 112). Fields and farmwork are often mentioned, e.g.: "Do not say 'My land flourishes' (STRICKER: is

---

[1]) Cf. my *De Spreuken van Salomo*, I, p. 22 f. and *Sprüche Salomos*, in *Handbuch zum Alten Testament*, her. v. O. EISSFELDT, 1937, S. 47, 49.

now grown over); do not fail to inspect it (Col. 9, 11). Do not build
a house on agricultural land (Col. 14, l. 22; cp. also Col. 8, l. 19;
Col. 10, l. 18 f., see p. 110). When you are working on the land, do not
do anything deceitful" (?; STRICKER: anything wrong). Interesting
is that although writing is mentioned first, the other occupations for
the son are all of the rural kind in the proverb Col. 17, l. 23: "Let
your son learn to write, to plough, to fowl (STRICKER: to fish) and
to trap according to the season of the year (STRICKER: so that in a
year in which the inundation withdraws itself, he gets profit of what
he performs)." On dung speaks Col. 17, l. 24, on ploughing Col. 9,
l. 14: "Do not say 'I have ploughed the field but it has not paid';
plough again, it is good to plough" (cp. also 20, l. 7). Of the planting
of trees knows Col. 20, l. 4: "End by planting any tree, begin by
planting a sycamore". Corn and straw and wheat-harvest are referred
to: "If you are trading in straw when it is wanted, do not go round
offering corn" (Col. 15, l. 22; also Col. 24, l. 18). Beer and wine and
their treatment are distinguished Col. 19, l. 22 f. (seen p. 112). Of the
work of the weaver tells Col. 20, l. 5. Snakes are a frequent occurrence:
"Do not kill a snake and leave its tail (Col. 11, l. 8). He who has been
bitten of the bite of a snake, is afraid (even) of a coil of rope" (Col. 14,
l. 14; cp. also Col. 20, l. 9, 13, see p. 112). The tame and the wild animal
appear in the contrasting pictures: "When a man smells of myrrh, his
wife is a cat in his presence (STRICKER: stands before him as). When
a man is sick (STRICKER probably better: is in difficulties) his wife
is a lioness in his presence" (Col. 15, l. 12). Roads are often unsafe:
"Do not take the road without a stick in your hand" (Col. 17, l. 14).
Especially the domestic animals figure largely in these instructions:
"Do not neglect (STRICKER: understimate) a matter if it concerns
a cow (Col. 9, l. 8). If a cow is stolen from the field, its owner must be
fought with (?) in town (Col. 19, l. 4; cp. also Col. 9, l. 23, Col. 23,
l. 11 and the already mentioned Col. 10, l. 20; Col. 11, l. 20, Col. 23,
l. 21, see p. 110, 108, 109). Also the donkey is an integral part of man's
daily life. "Do not let your donkey kick at the palmtree (STRICKER: Do
not fasten the your donkey's leg . . .) lest he shake down its fruit (?;
STRICKER: lest he shakes it to and fro; Col. 11, l. 18). A beam is not
loaded on a donkey (Col. 22, l. 7; cp. further the already mentioned Col.
20, l. 24; Col. 23, l. 21, and the small collection Col. 24, l. 7-10, see p. 109,
114). The horse occurs two times in already given sayings (Col. 23, l. 24;
Col. 24, l. 7). The cat performs, except in the contrast to the lioness
just mentioned and in Col. 16, l. 15 already refered to (above p. 108),

in Col. 23, l. 15: "A cat which loves fruit, hates him who eats it (STRICKER: Although a cat likes fruit, she hates however him who eats it). From STRICKER's translation one gets the impression that the town figures rather frequently in 'Onchsheshonqy's book; GLANVILLE however gives a somewhat different picture by rendering the Egyptian *tme* more often with: village or district [1]), which seems to fit better in many cases. He certainly sums up the impression of the whole of the book well when he remarks (Introduction, p. xv): "Our text is written by a man who understands country life and is familiar with the proverbial wisdom and pithy sayings of the peasant. Again and again his images are taken from the farm or from nature— *to a degree which is perhaps unique in Egyptian literature of any kind"* [2]).

As far as concerns the contents of the proverbs or *the subjects* on which the author wants to give instruction, *the relation to Divinity* is, although not the main item, not unfrequently referred to. I counted twenty-four sayings in which God or the God (*p ntr*) occurs, another two with "the Great God" (Col. 8, l. 6; Col. 14, l. 17), one with Re (*P-R'*; Col. 25, l. 4) and one with Thoth (Col. 10, l. 12). Here we find the well-known phenomenon in wisdom literature that the separate gods of the pantheon are hidden behind the conception of Divinity in general ("das Numinose, das allgemein Göttliche" as Hellmut BRUNNER calls it, l.c., p. 96). In remarkable contrast to the proverbs themselves, the Introductory Narrative mentions Rē several times (Col. 2, l. 9, 22; Col. 3, l. 4, 13 f.; Col. 4, l. 19-21; Col. 5, l. 1-13) of which two times together with "the Gods who are with him", and once moreover with "Neith-Oury, the Mother, the great Goddess" (Col. 3, l. 4) [4]). In the lamentation on the theme "When P-Re is angry with a land" (Col. 5, l. 1-13) the main thought is that thereby the *ma'at*, the right order in human society [5]) is disturbed and human

---

[1]) Cf. Col. 8, l. 17; Col. 9, l. 3; Col. 15, l. 15; Col. 18, l. 13; Col. 19, l. 4; Col. 21, l. 24 f.; Col. 22, l. 15; Col. 27, l. 13.

[2]) Spacing by myself.

[3]) Col. 6, l. 1; Col. 7, l. 14; Col. 11, l. 15, 21, 23; Col. 14, l. 10; Col. 16, l. 14; Col. 18, l. 15. 17; Col. 19, l. 14; Col. 20, l. 6; Col. 21, l. 10; Col. 22, l. 24 f.; Col. 23, l. 12, 14; Col. 25, l. 4, 5; Col. 26, l. 8, 14; Col. 27, l. 12, 14, 21; Col. 28, l. 10.

[4]) If the reading Col. 1, l. 19 is right, it would seem, in comparison with Col. 3, l. 13 f., that the author identifies Rē and "the God".

[5]) On the important conception of *ma'at*, see the literature advanced by VON BISSING, *Altägyptische Lebensweisheit*, S. 178, A. 12; also BRUNNER, *Handbuch der Orientalistik*, S. 93-96 and Hartmut GESE, *Lehre und Wirklichkeit in der alten Weisheit*, Tübingen, 1958, S. 11-21.—To such anomalous circumstances refer also Col. 19, l. 6, 13, 14; Col. 20, l. 22-25; Col. 22, l. 7; Col. 25, l. 10-13.

relations are turned topsyturvy. Only once the expression *ma'at* is mentioned in the proverbs themselves: "Speak Truth to all men; let it be a very part of your speech (STRICKER: let it be identified with your mouth; Col. 13, l. 15). God is the sovereign disposer of all: "Every good deed is (from) (STRICKER: All success lies in) the hand of God (Col. 20, l. 6). All have a portion of the fate from God (STRICKER: All are in the hand of the fate of God; Col. 26, l. 8; cp. l. 14, above p. 111). A certain religious fatalism or determinism is discernible in these and other sayings, like in the above mentioned passage on insult, on which follows fighting, thereupon killing: "And killing doesn't happen without God knowing; nothing happens except what God ordains" (see p. 114). If a woman is at peace with her husband, it is the will (STRICKER: the decrees) of God (Col. 25, l. 5). His predelection as well as his rejection decides:"Every hand is stretched out to God, but He accepts (only) the hand of his beloved (Col. 23, l. 14). Do not dwell in a house, which is cursed by God, lest his wrath turns against you (Col. 27, l. 14 STRICKER). In the Introductory Narrative the accused friend of the author excuses his conspiracy against Pharaoh with the words: My great Lord! On the day on which Rē commanded me to do well, He put good furtune for Pharaoh in my heart; on the day on which Rē commanded me to do which was grievous, He put evil fortune for Pharaoh in my heart" (Col. 3, l. 13-15). The precept to serve God (already in the first line of the collection of the proverbs; Col. 6, l. 1; Col. 7, l. 14, see above p. 114, 110) gets an opportunistic tone in its context[1]). Pure piety is expressed in sayings like: "Make sacrifice and libation before God, and let the fear for Him be great (STRICKER: become great) in your heart. Do not pray to God (STRICKER: for an oracle) and neglect what He says (STRICKER: and tresspass his command). Do not say '(Now that) I have this wealth I will serve neither God nor man'. Wealth is perfected in the service of God, the one who causes (it) to happen (STRICKER: Wealth comes to an end, fear of God generates new (wealth)) (Col. 14, l. 10; Col. 16, l. 14; Col. 18, l. 16 f). Trust in God is recommended in the passage Col. 11, l. 21-23 in which a kind of theodicy is touched upon: "Do not say 'The sinner against God (STRICKER: Gods enemy) lives today', but look to the end. Say (rather) 'A fortunate fate is at the end of old age' (STRICKER: Speak of prosperity only at the end of life). Put your affairs in the

---

[1]) See however on opportunism the view of GESE and others, below p. 122.

hand of God". God will call to account: "There is none who deserts his travelling companion whom God does not hold to account for it (Col. 21, l. 10). A good deed turns aside the punishment of the Great God (STRICKER: even of a great god; Col. 14, l. 17). I quoted already (p. 111): "The way of God lies open for everyone". "God looks into the heart" says Col. 26, l. 11. Rather touching the collection closes with the word of comfort: "Do not be weary of crying to God, for He has his hour for hearing the scribe" (Col. 28, l. 10).

Towards *the king*, in the Introductory Narrative called "the image of the Sungod" (Col. 2, l. 9), respect and reverence is prescribed and the right behaviour in his presence is recommended, but the number of proverbs in which the king figures (I counted six: Col. 9, l. 7; Col. 16, l. 16; Col. 23, l. 10; Col. 25, l. 7, 10 f.) appear inconsiderable in comparison with the many cases in which the king is mentioned and the great respect in which he is held in the Biblical wisdom books[1])

Also towards the master or *the superior* in rank and position a respectful attitude is advised. I quote only: "Do not take liberties with your superior. Do not neglect to serve your master. Do not sit down beside your better. Do not talk too much in the presence of your master" (Col. 7, l. 13, 15; Col. 13, l. 23; Col. 17, l. 25). The old man too has to be respected: "Do not speak of an old man as of a lad. Do not despise an old man in your yeart" (Col. 7, l. 21 f., STRICKER).

Especially *the parents* are to be held in esteem, father as well as mother. I cited already Col. 6, l. 6: "Serve your father and your mother, that you may go and prosper". "Do not open your heart to your wife or to your servant. Open it to your mother, ..." says Col. 13, l. 17 f. Children have to be brought up strictly: "Do not let your school-boy son approach the door of the storehouse in a lean year" (Col. 16, l. 3). They must learn to work (above, p. 116). "Better a statue for son than a fool" (above, p. 109). The responsibility of the parents is great: "A guard (STRICKER: a regent) who robs— his son is a poor man" (Col. 11, l. 17). Children have to be treated equally: "Do not prefer one of your children to another ..." (Col. 13, l. 11); and have to be respected themselves: "Do not laugh at your son in the presence of his mother lest you learn the (small) size of his father" (Col. 11, l. 19).

With *women* and the right estimation of them the author had apparently most trouble. There are more than fifty sayings which refer to

---

[1]) See my *Sprüche Salomos*, S. 37 f., 49, 51.

them. That there are different women is accepted in proverbs like:
"Do not speak scorn of a loved woman. Do not speak praise of a
detested woman. Do not marry a sour (STRICKER) woman" (Col. 22,
l. 10 f.; Col. 24, l. 6). Against the bad ones a whole short collection
warns (Col. 25, l. 19-22). Woman is pictured as dependent, unself-
reliant, unsteady, fickle (Col. 20, l. 19; Col. 22, l. 8; Col. 15, l. 11 f.,
see above p. 115, 116). Her sexuality is accentuated, often in coarse
language (Col. 20, l. 23; Col. 21, l. 4; Col. 22, l. 4; for Col. 23, l. 24
and Col. 24, l. 20 see above p. 112). She cannot be trusted even in
material things: "Let your wife regard your wealth; do not trust her
with it. Do not trust her (even) with her provisions for (STRICKER:
during) one year" (Col. 12, l. 13 f.). "A woman is a danger (STRICKER:
cɜlamity), . . . she does not part with a tree without having disfigured
it (Col. 25, l. 9). Over against these rather unkind judgements stand
fortunately a number of appreciations, like the following: "The blessing
of property is a prudent woman" (Col. 8, l. 22, see above p. 110).
"Give a prudent woman a hundred pieces of silver, do not accept
two hundred from a foolish one" (Col. 18, l. 9, see p. 111). I quoted
already the comparison of the good woman with food coming forth
in time of hunger (Col. 24, l. 21, above p. 112). That happy relations
can exist in marriage is known and longed for: "Oh that the heart of
a woman and the heart of her husband should be free from animosity"
(STRICKER: May the heart of a man be the heart of the woman, that
they stay far from strife; Col. 25, l. 14). "Choose a prudent husband
for your daughter, do not choose for her a rich husband. If a woman
is at peace with her husband they shall never fare badly" (Col. 25,
l. 15, 18). In the education of the children she plays an important role:
"Do not marry an impious woman, lest she give your children a
bad upbringing" (Col. 25, l. 17). It seems even as if child-bearing
is not her only task and value: "Do not abandon a woman of
(STRICKER: in) your household because she has not conceived a
child" (Col. 14, l. 16). In Biblical wisdom the warnings against the
bad woman are no less frequent and stringent, especially against the
iššāh zārāh, "the strange woman" (Prov. ii 16 ff.; v; vi 24 ff.; vii; xxii
14), and Qoheleth can be cited for contrasting verdicts (vii 26; ix 9);
but, notwitstanding all appreciation of the prudent woman and good
mother in Egyptian wisdom literature, the Instructions of 'Onchsheshonqy confirm strongly the impression that the height of the Israelitic
conception is not reached [1]).

---

[1]) See my *Sprüche Salomos*, S. 53, 85.

One cannot say that the background or *mood* of the author is pessimistic although the circumstances as related in the Introductory Narrative might make one expect as much. Pessimistic statements on woman, as cited above (Col. 12, l. 13 f; Col. 13, l. 16-18; Col. 25, l. 9) are contradicted by appreciations. Col. 12, l. 19 says: "Even the benevolent master will kill to please himself (STRICKER: until he gets rest)". "Do not go to your brother if you are in trouble; go to your friend" (Col. 16, l. 4). "Do not be too trusting lest you become poor", says the proverb following a warning against lending money without security" (Col. 16, l. 21 f.). "Inspect your house twice every hour that you may catch the burglar" (STRICKER: and you will find that you are robbed; Col. 17, l. 22). That one sows and another reaps (Col. 23, l. 19-21) and that God hears his favourite (Col. 23, l. 14) has already been mentioned. The future is unpredictable: "No man knows the day of misfortune. Do not delay to get yourself a tomb on the hill; you do not know the length of your life" (Col. 12, l. 3, 5). The author knows of the ingratitude of men and of bitter experiences, but it does not cast him down: "if you do a kindness to a hundred (GLANVILLE: five hundred) men and one of them recognizes it, a part is not perished. Do not be despondent when you are in distress (STRICKER: when you get bitter experiences); your end is not made (yet)" (Col. 14, l. 9; Col. 18, l. 21; cp. Col. 11, l. 21-23 above p. 118). *Rather* an *optimistic* view of life appears in other proverbs as well. "Do not be distressed so long as you have (something). Do not be worried as long as you have something. Do not be put out by things. Do not be dissatisfied with your occupation" (Col. 6, l. 21-24). "Do not be faint-hearted when you are in trouble and do not long for death (STRICKER). He who lives, his seed flourishes. There is none wretched except him who has died" (Col. 19, l. 15-17). The well-known current wisdom doctrine is expressed in the antithesis: "There is no wise man who comes to grief; There is no fool who finds reward" (Col. 21, l. 7 f.).

Usually Egyptian wisdom is said to represent *class-ethics* [1]). This is empathically denied by Hellmut BRUNNER, *Altägyptische Erziehung* 1957 and GESE, *l.c.*, S. 30 [2]). Although not very frequently, there are

---

[1]) See my *Sprüche Salomos*, S. 6.
[2]) Hellmut BRUNNER, *Altägyptische Erziehung*, Wiesbaden, 1957, S. 2 f., 5-7, 31, 116-123 (against class-ethics and utilitarianism in Egyptian wisdom); also GESE, *l.c.*, S. 30: "Die ägyptische Instruktion gibt keine Standesethik für den Schreiber, sondern ist grundsätzlich eine Lehre für die Erziehung eines jeden im Volke . . . Die Bezeichnung der ägyptischen Weisheitslehre als Standesethik ist abzulehnen".

several proverbs in 'Onchsheshonqy's collection, which savour this
kind of ethics more or less clearly. I cite: "Take the rich man to your
house, take the poor man to your boat. If a poor man says 'I will kill
you', he will kill you in truth. If a rich man says 'I will kill you', lay
your head on his doorstep" (Col. 18, l. 23, 7 f.). "Give one loaf to your
labourer, take two from his shoulders (STRICKER: receive two from
the work of his arms). Give one loaf to the man who does the work,
give two to the man who gives the orders" (Col. 22, l. 20 f.). "Do not
ridicule your master in the presence of a poor man" (Col. 17, l. 17).
If STRICKER's translation is right, the following sentences belong
to the same category: "Do not take a slave (GLANVILLE: a youth) for
your companion (Col. 13, l. 24). Do not send a maidservant in your
affairs, for she has only her own affairs at heart (Col. 6, l. 12, cp. above
p. 111). If a woman is of more noble birth (GLANVILLE: arrogant)
than her husband, let him leave the way free for her" (Col. 27, l. 7). [1])

Utilitarianism or eudemonism, usually accepted as a definite feature
of Egyptian and Babylonian as well as of Biblical wisdom [2]), is
impassionedly denied in Egyptian teaching by GESE. He speaks of
"die eudämonistische Fehl-interpretation der ägyptischen Weisheit"
(*l.c.*, p. 7-11), and cites with full approval FRANKFORT's explanation
that at the common root of the frequent and narrow connection of
action and effect lies the concept of harmony with the divine order
(*ib:*, p. 14, n. 4). We should add something foreign to Egyptian
thinking if we should assign effect and action to two different categories. It would take too far to go into this controversy more deeply
at present. One cannot, however, fail to get the impression from
'Onchsheshonqy's Instructions that the good or bad effect of action
or conduct is frequently and openly represented as its motive force.
The collection opens with the already mentioned group of six admonitions each of them beginning with "Serve . . .", and each of
them has a reference to the effect: "Serve your God, that He may
protect you. Serve your brothers, that you may have a good reputation. Serve a wise man, that he may serve you. Serve him who serves
you. Serve any man in order to find profit. Serve your father and your

---

[1]) Also Col. 28, l. 7 f may belong here if STRICKER's rendering is followed:
"Do not be too often speaking about your . . . to the man of the multitude, that
you not come to shame. Do not be too often speaking (words of praise) to the
man of the multitude, that he not go to ruin by rebuke".

[2]) See my *De Spreuken van Salomo*, I, p. 27 and for Qoheleth my *Spreuken* II,
Prediker en Hooglied van Salomo, Tekst en Uitleg, Groningen, 1931, p. 58, 62, 100.

mother, that you may go and prosper" (Col. 6, l. 1-6). I quoted already Col. 15, l. 14: "Do not commit a robbery of which you will be convicted (see p. 108). The promising first half of the saying: "Do not conceal yourself from a stranger who comes from elsewhere", disappoints in the second half: "if there is nothing in your hand, there (may) be something in his" (Col. 16, l. 19). I cited the proverb running to over three lines on fidelity to the friend of youth (Col. 17, l. 18-20): the last line again spoils its high ethics by saying: "his heir will make provision for you". "Be modest", says line 26 of the same column, "that your reputation may increase in the hearts of all men". "Do not be greedy, that you may not be denied (STRICKER: abused). Do not be mean, that you may not be disliked" (Col. 21, l. 15 f.). If there is no utilitarian sentiment in the following three proverbs, one would ask what is the meaning of the word: "There is no use in my son if I do not make use of his earnings (?). There is no use in my servant if he does not do my work. There is no use in my brother if he does not pay attention to my troubles" (Col. 24, l. 22-24).

One is even inclined to speak of *opportunism* in sayings like the following: "Do not take legal action against your superior unless you are sure of success (Col. 8, l. 11; cp. also lines 9 f. in GLANVILLE's translation, see p. 107). Do not make a vehement accusation against a man (STRICKER: Do not direct biting words towards a man) if you cannot make him give way (STRICKER: unless you can overcome him thereby; Col. 12, l. 22). If you are trading in straw, when it is wanted you do not go round offering corn" (Col. 15, l. 22, see p. 116). GLAN-VILLE himself speaks of cynicism in explaining the proverb: "If you are powerful throw your deeds (STRICKER: your books) into the river; if you are weak throw them also" (Col. 18, l. 6; cp. his note 222 on p. 75: "Perhaps the most cynical verse in the whole of the In-structions . . . The powerful man will not need legal documents to back his claim; the small man will find them useless"). Scarcely less cynical is to my mind Col. 19, l. 25: "When you are given a loaf for stupidity, let teaching be an abomination to you".

In strange contrast to these examples of eudemonism and worse are not a few sayings of a really high and *pure ethical character*. Col. 6, l. 8 reads in STRICKER's translation: "Be small of pride, but great of soul (GLANVILLE: magnanimous) that your heart gains beauty". Again in STRICKER's rendering Col. 12, l. 4: "Do not trust your people to him who has never known adversity". "Do not be afraid to do something which you are justified in doing" (Col. 15, l. 13). The wife of a subordinate, the impoverished friend, even the entreating enemy are recommended for fair dealing: "Do not take liberties with a woman whose husband is subordinate to you (Col. 17, 1. 3, 18). When you enemy entreats you do not conceal yourself from him" (Col. 19, 1. 5). The disinterested, unselfish good deed is recommended: "Do not say 'I did a service to this man, but he did not thank me for it'. There is no good deed except the good deed which you do to the man who has need of it" (Col. 15, 1. 5 f.). "Let your good deed reach him who has need of it. Do not be mean; wealth is no security" (STRICKER: possession does not let itself be kept; Col. 12, 1. 17 f.). The negative golden rule is expressed in Col. 15, 1. 23: "Do not do what you dislike to someone, and so cause another to do it to you". I quoted already the precept of always speaking the truth, which reads together with its preceding line: "Do not acquire (STRICKER: Do not speak with) two voices. Speak truth to all men; let it be a very part of your speech" (Col. 13, 1. 14 f., cp. p. 118).

In reading through the pages of 'Onchsheshonqy's collection one is frequently *reminded of* similar thoughts, concepts and expressions in *Biblical wisdom*. Following the order of the Book of Proverbs, I refer to eight subjects. The warning against intercourse with the wife of another man (Prov. vi 20-35 and passim) is repeatedly expressed: "Do not make love to a married woman. He who makes love to a married woman, is killed on her doorstep. Do not marry a wife whose husband is alive, lest you make for yourself an enemy" (Col. 23, 1. 6 f.; Col. 8, 1. 12; cp. Col. 21, 1. 18 f.). The typical presupposition of the indocility of the fool (Prov. ix 7-12, cp. my *Sprüche*, S. 41; also Eccl. x 15) is shared by the Egyptian wise: "Do not instruct a fool, lest he hate you. Do not instruct him who will not listen to you. Do not bother about a fool (Col. 7, 1. 4-6). 'It irks me what they do' says the fool, when he is instructed (Col. 10, 1. 6). Another's instruction (STRICKER: the lesson learnt by another) does not touch the heart of a fool; that which is near his heart is near his heart" (Col. 27, 1. 10). The promise of one's house being established for ever, assured to the righteous in Biblical Proverbs, is given to the wise in the Egyptian book: "The wise master who is merciful (STRICKER: who gathers counsel) —his house is established for ever" (Col. 12, 1. 9). Looking at or awaiting the end of a man's way and conduct, so often advised in Solomon's sayings, e.g. xiv 12 f.: "There is a way which seems right to a man, but its end is the way of death. Even in laughter the heart may ache, and the end of joy (may be) grief" (cp. also v 4,

11; xvi 25; xx 21; xxiii 13, 32; xxiv 19 f.; xxv 8; xxix 21), is recommended Col. 11, l. 21: "Do not say 'The sinner (?) against God (STRICKER: God's enemy) lives to-day', but look to the end". The knowledge that man proposes but God disposes (cp. Prov. xvi 9, 33; xix 21; xx 24) is not only clearly expressed in the Instructions of Amen-em-ope(t) (xix 14-17; xxii 5 ff.; xxiii 8 ff.), but according to STRICKER's translation also by 'Onchsheshonqy: "Otherwise are the disposals of God, otherwise the thoughts of men" (Col. 26, l. 14). For the turning upside-down of relations in human society the Israelite wise man is just as afraid as the Egyptian; compare Prov. xix 10: "It is not fitting for a fool to live in luxury, much less for a fool to rule over princes" (also xxx 21-23 and Eccl. x 5-7) with 'Onchsheshonqy's lamentation on when Rē is angry with a land, Col. 5, l. 1-13; I quote: "When Rē is angry with a land he exalts its humble people and humbles its mighty people; . . . he appoints its scribe to minister to it; . . . he appoints its washerman as hierogrammatist (STRICKER)", lines 9, 12 f. The passage against slackness in helping those in distress, Prov. xxiv 10-12: "if you show yourself slack in the day of distress, your strength (will be) small (when you need it). Rescue those who are being taken away to death; hold back those who are stumbling to slaughter, etc. . ." finds a ready commentary in STRICKER's translation of Col. 8, l. 9 f.: "Do not withdraw your hand from a scribe when they take him to prison; if you withdraw your hand from him, they take him to his tomb" (cp. above, p. 107). Of the twice occurring Biblical proverb: "He who digs a pit will fall into it" (Prov. xxvi 27; Eccl. x 9), the first part appears literally in Col. 26, l. 27 (the second half is illegible).

It is remarkable that an equal number of similarities present themselves between the small Biblical *Book of Ecclesiastes* and 'Onchsheshonqy's collection. The lament of Qoheleth that he must leave all the results of his toil to the man who comes after him; and who knows whether he will be a wise man or a fool (ii 19; cp. vi 2; Ps. xxxix 7; Luke xii 20), may be compared with the short collection Col. 23, lines 19-21 already referred to above, p. 108 f.). The evil which Qoheleth has seen: "Folly is set in many high places, and the rich sit in a low place. I have seen slaves on horses, and princes walking on foot like slaves" (x 5 f.), is the same which 'Onchsheshonqy ascribes to the wrath of Rē (above, p. 125, 114, 107). The proverb on the digger of a pit, occurring Eccl. x 8, is followed by the sentence: "He who quarries stones is hurt by them", which resembles remarkably Col. 22, l. 5:

"He who shakes the stone —it will fall upon his foot". The rather difficult saying of Eccl. x 15: "The toil of a fool wearies him, so that(?) he does not know the way to the city", is not explained by the contents of Col. 23, l. 12, but the same expression of "not finding the way" occurs there when it says (in STRICKER's translation): "The way of God is open for everyone, the good-for-nothing (GLANVILLE: blockhead) does not know how to find it". The often and differently explained words of Eccl. xi 1 f.: "Cast your bread upon the waters, for you will find it after many days", has a remarkable parallel in 'Onchsheshonqy's saying: "Do a good deed and throw it (GLANVILLE: only to throw it) into the river; when this dries up you shall find it" (Col. 19, l. 10; see above p. 108). In the light of this, it seems probable that the spirit of enterprise recommended in the whole of Eccl. xi 1-6 [1]) includes also, although not exclusively, the doing of good deeds. The verses 4-6: "He who observes the wind will not sow; and he who regards the clouds will not reap. As you do not know the way of the wind nor (how) the bones (are formed?) in the womb of a woman with child, so you do not know the work of God who makes everything. In the morning sow your seed, and at evening withold not your hand; for you do not know which will prosper, this or that, or whether both alike will be good", these verses certainly mean all kind of activities also of the economic kind. They resemble: Onchsheshonqy's advice: "In fair weather or foul, wealth increases (only) by making the most of it. (Good) fortune will not happen to you; (good) fortune is given to him who seeks it (Col. 8, l. 13 f.). Of related tendency is the already cited proverb: "The fisherman casts off from shore (or: casts out his net from on boardship) without being able to say 'God will dispense to every house' " (Col. 11, l. 15; see above p. 115). The *bêth 'ôlām* of Eccl. xii 5 as name of the grave appears in the passage of three lines quoted above on fidelity to the friend of youth: "Let him attain his house of eternity (unconcerned)" (Col. 17. l. 18-20). These many similarities do let one ask if in Qoheleth an Egyptian background or at least some connection with Egyptian wisdom is not likely. Outside the wisdom books but of clear proverbial character is Jeremiah's metaphor: "Can the Ethiopian change his skin?" (xiii 23); 'Onchsheshonqy gives the answer: "There is no negro who lays off his skin (STRICKER; GLANVILLE reads: who bares the breast?; Col. 21, l. 5).

---

[1]) See my *Spreuken* II, *Prediker* etc., p. 133 f.

The *great importance* however of the discovery of the Instructions of 'Onchsheshonqy lies to my mind in the fact that *although in date the latest but one* of the nine now extant complete or nearly complete wisdom books it nevertheless shows a *definitely less developed* character in form as well as in content. Already Ptah-hotep has units and paragraphs of greater length and is clearly divided into thirty-seven chapters. In Meri-ka-re five constituent parts are apparent, each one with its own character. Longer paragraphs are also found in Amen-em-het and Cheti. Even Anii, although according to GLANVILLE (Introduction, p. xii) close in spirit with 'Onchsheshonqy, has next to smaller also greater sense-units ("Sinnsabschnitte"). Amen-em-ope(t)'s Instructionbook as well as the Leiden Papyrus Insinger, both nearest in time to 'Onchsheshonqy, exist of definitively and deliberately composed chapters with sayings centered around a special subject. Strophic composition can be distinguished in both. Each chapter has a heading which is a more or less constituent part of the contents. But about 'Onchsheshonqy GLANVILLE rightly wrote: "There is no orderly organization in 'Onchsheshonqy's Instructions, still less explicit into chapters ... The treatment is rather haphazard ... It is as if 'Onchsheshonqy really had written what came into his mind, day by day; for the story says that what he wrote was taken daily to be read to Pharaoh and his court. . . Essentially there is no logical order to these precepts" (*l.c.*, p. xiii).

As to content the position is similar. Already Ptah-hotep wants not only to instruct the ignorant about wisdom but also about the rules of good speech. It reads in its title: "The beginning of the expression of good speech". Cheti especially exalts the art and the office of the learned scribe over against all other preoccupations, particularly all crafts. All the other wisdom books are clearly products of well developed scribal and literary art. Although 'Onchsheshonqy's proverbs cover, as GLANVILLE puts it; "the whole range of proverbial utterance, from the colloquialism of contemporary experience and oral tradition to the literary cliché", the first kind definitely prevails. And "though 'Onchsheshonqy's aphorisms sometimes have an epigrammatic quality which is perhaps not found elsewhere in Egyptian, they have none of the poetic refinement of Amenemopé's" (GLANVILLE, p. xiv).

Especially in religious and ethical respects there is a remarkable difference already with many of the older wisdom books but very salient in comparison with Amen-em-ope and Insinger. The short but informative characterization of these two latest wisdom books by Hellmut BRUNNER (*l.c.*, p. 106-109) reveals a height of religious feeling, ethical sentiment and rational power of abstraction which puts them at the top of all the preceding works of this kind. 'Onchsheshonqy's Instructions however are "sharply differentiated from those of the Papyrus Insinger", as GLANVILLE rightly formulates, "by their lower moral standard, and above all by a lack of any of the philosophical concepts which seem to be at the back of Insinger" (*l.c.*, p. xiv).

All this means *a warning* against constructing an evolutionary straight line of development of Egyptian wisdom and proverbial literature. Its less developed products do not necessarily stand at the beginning. They can accompany and be contemporary even with the highest specimens of thought and feeling. Flourishingperiods may be·followed by times of decline. And towards the end of a culture less developed forms and products may appear next to the most elaborate and refined ones. One has to keep in mind also that in different circles and layers of society different forms of thought and expression have been in vogue. As far as Egypt is concerned, the impression gained by the discovery of 'Onchsheshonqy's wisdom is corroborated by a small collection of proverbs (three columns of of forty-three sayings in all) from the second or first century B.C. on the so-called Demotic Papyrus Louvre 2414, which resemble very much our collection. [1])

The lesson learnt by the extant Egyptian wisdom literature and especially by the discovery of the Instructions of 'Onchsheshonqy has its significance also for the dating and the reconstruction of the history of Biblical proverb books and collections. Here too more developed forms and thought are not necessarily younger and later than the more simple ones. The combination of more elaborate meditations and treatments of subjects as in the first half of the Book of Ecclesiastes with groups of simple and short proverbs in the second half is not so strange in the light of what we know possess of Egyptian collections and does not compel to the separation in time and authorship of the various contents of this book. Ancient history is apparently not much less rich and varied than that of our modern Western world.

---

[1]) See Aksel VOLTEN, *Die moralischen Lehren des demotischen Pap. Louvre* 2414 in *Studi in memoria di Ippol. Rosellini*, Vol. II, Pisa, 1955, p. 269-280.

WIDOW, ORPHAN, AND THE POOR IN ANCIENT NEAR EASTERN LEGAL AND WISDOM LITERATURE

F. CHARLES FENSHAM

IN ANY civilized modern state the rights of widow, orphan, and the poor are protected. This protection is in many cases seen as a product of religious zeal and regarded as a religious duty. Indeed, the whole idea of Muslim charity, one of the pillars of that religion, is born from a realization of this duty. This religion requires kindness to orphans and widows and charity to the poor.[1] The same idea is present in Christianity. Through the influence of Christianity orphanages were erected for the protection of orphans and special laws were promulgated to protect the weak. It is thus of some interest to trace the roots of this disposition back to history, almost into the dark ages of prehistory.

The protection of widow, orphan, and the poor was the common policy of the ancient Near East. It was not started by the spirit of Israelite propheticism or by the spirit of propheticism as such.[2] From the earliest times on a strong king promulgated stipulations in connection with protection of this group. Such protection was seen as a virtue of gods, kings, and judges. It was a policy of virtue, a policy which proved the piety and virtue of a ruler. Great Mesopotamian kings like Urukagina, Ur-Nammu and Hammurapi boast in their legal inscriptions that they have accomplished this principle. Success was not possible if this principle was not carried through. It is also obvious that this policy was closely connected to social reform or a new legal promulgation. In bad times, in

times of decay, the protection of widow, orphan, and the poor was neglected. Widows, orphans, and the poor were sold as credit-slaves[3] and kept in a state of slavery for a lifetime. To obliterate this abuse, laws and also religious pressure were used as compulsory methods to protect the rights of this group.

The policy of protection of the weak occurs also in the wisdom literature of the ancient Near East. There exists a close link between style and contents of wisdom literature and the ancient legal codes. The wisdom literature was used as didactic material to instruct people how to behave.[4] Legal material, on the other hand, comes with a casuistic stipulation on a transgression of normative conduct prescribed by wisdom literature. The punishment on the transgression is prescribed in the second part of the stipulation. Wisdom literature, optimistic or pessimistic, gives us a policy of conduct. It is noteworthy that this policy bears a close relation to certain parts of the prologue and epilogue of legal codes. To see how close this connection is we may turn to the Old Testament tradition concerning the combination of sound, impartial judgment and wisdom in the person of Solomon.[5] It is

---

[1] Alfred Guillaume, *Islam* (1954), p. 64.

[2] Cf. G. Lanczkowski, "Ägyptischer Prophetismus," *ZAW*, LXX (1958), 38.

[3] Cf. I. Mendelsohn, *Slavery in the Ancient Near East* (1949), pp. 14 ff., 19 ff., 23 ff.; cf. also my "A Few Aspects of Legal Practices in Samuel in Comparison with Legal Material from the Ancient Near East," *Studies in the Book of Samuel* (1960), pp. 19 ff.

[4] Cf. H. Gese, *Lehre und Wirklichkeit in der alten Weisheit* (1958), pp. 5–6, for a definition of the *Gattung* of wisdom literature taken over from Van Dijk. E.g. exhortation concerning moral life and a maxim concerning the norm for morals and prudence. Cf. also S. du Toit, *Bybelse en Babilonies-Assiriese Spreuke* (1942), pp. 128 ff.

[5] For the evaluation of wisdom and Solomon cf. J. Bright, *A History of Israel* (1959), pp. 198–99.

therefore not surprising to find the policy of protection of widow, orphan, and the poor present in both legal and wisdom literature. We have narrowed the scope of our study down to these two genres of literature, because to include cultic psalms and prophetic literature would take us too far afield. It will suffice to draw attention to the fact that the plea of prophets for restoration of morality and protection of the weak points to times of absolute decay and negligence of the commonly accepted policy of the gods and strong kings; in case of the Israelite prophets, from the principles of the religion of Yahweh.

MESOPOTAMIA

We turn in the first place to Mesopotamia. The oldest witness to the policy is present in the reformatory measures taken by Urukagina, king of Lagash in the Ur I period, approximately 2400 B.C. .We read that mighty people were not allowed to do injustice to the orphan and widow.[6] The stipulations of this reformatory action were regarded as a treaty between the god, Ningirsu and Urukagina. The mention of Ningirsu is surprising, because in later texts the protection of the weak is connected to the sun-god, Shamash or Sumerian Utu (Babbar).[7] Our knowledge of early Sumerian religion is, however, too fragmentary to make any far-reaching conclusions. All we know is that some connection existed between Ninurta, the weather god, and Ningirsu.[8] In the legal code of Ur-Nammu (ca. 2050 B.C.) recently discovered by S. N. Kramer in the Istanbul

Museum, the same idea as in the case of Urukagina is present, viz. in the prologue the protection of orphan, widow, and the poor (man of one shekel) is mentioned. The tablet is unfortunately broken and it is impossible to ascertain to which god the execution of justice is ascribed.[9] It is interesting to note that the idea of protection is placed in the prologue where the religious background and general policy of the king is stated. A very important occurrence of this policy is found in the famous Code of Hammurapi (CH) (1728-1686 B.C.). In the prologue there is reference to justice executed by the king and the statement is made that the strong are not allowed to oppress the weak,[10] so that the sun (Utu-Shamash, god of justice) may rise over the people.[11] Almost the same statement is made in the epilogue, but an important addition is present, viz. that justice might be given to the orphan and the widow.[12] Lower down in this inscription Shamash is called in to maintain justice in the land. A few observations can be made at this stage. Important is the fact that Shamash is called judge of heaven and earth. This means that religious and social ethics are closely connected here.[13] The protection of the weak is regarded vertically and horizontally. The vertical protection comes from the god Shamash, which therefore falls in the religious sphere, while the horizontal protection comes from the king, the substitute of the sun-god, which thus falls in the social sphere. This was the case with divine and royal policy, but is there any indication that the protection of widow and orphan was carried through in practical

---

[6] A. Deimel, "Die Reformtexte Urukaginas," OR, Vol. II (1920). Cf. for a translation by Moortgat Scharff-Moortgat, Ägypten und Vorderasien im Altertum (1950), pp. 242–43.

[7] Cf. F. M. Theo de Liagre Böhl, Godsdiensten der Wereld, I (1948), 119, and his very important article "De Zonnegod als Beschermer der Nooddruftigen," Opera Minora (1953), pp. 188–206. I want to thank him for drawing my attention to this article.

[8] Cf. J. Bottéro, La religion babylonienne (1952), p. 45.

[9] Cf. S. N. Kramer, Scientific American (Jan. 1953) pp. 26–28, and History Begins at Sumer (1958) pp. 91 ff.

[10] Cf. A. Deimel, Codex Hammurabi, III (1950) dan-nu-um, en-ša-am a-na la ḫa-ba-li-im.

[11] CH. §§ 37–41.

[12] Cf. Meek's translation in Ancient Near Eastern Texts (1955), pp. 164, 178.

[13] Cf. Böhl, "De Zonnegod," p. 193.

(f.) In his admirable study on Old Babylonian law of inheritance Klíma proves
that this question must be answered in the
affirmative. When a woman married a
husband in Mesopotamia, she had left the
house of her father and had no right whatever remaining. She had also no right of
inheritance of the property of her husband.
Yet she was not left without anything. In
CH §§ 171–74 it is stipulated that she must
receive the *šeriktu* and a gift of her husband
(*nudunnú*) and has also the right to stay
in her husband's house. A difference is
made between a first wife (*hi-ir-tum*) and a
widow (*almattum*), but in every case she
was left with sufficient protection to ensure
a comfortable life.[14] Credit-slavery was a
common phenomenon in Mesopotamia.
This was usually inflicted on the poor or in
certain circumstances on widows and
orphans. One of the most humane laws of
CH was promulgated to limit the severity
of credit-slavery. In §§ 117–18 it is stipulated that credit-slaves must be released
after three years, a very narrow limitation
of the period of slavery in comparison with
e.g., the Hebrew law where the period is
six years.[15] This limitation was fixed to
discourage credit-slavery and the exploita-
tion of the poor and unprotected.

The idea that the poor man is protected
by Shamash and that this is expected as a
way of life amongst his people, occurs frequently in Babylonian wisdom literature.[16]
In the great majority of these texts reference is made to the poor in general but not
specifically to the widow and orphan.[17]
In the Babylonian Theodicy (± 1000 B.C.
according to Lambert), where a discourse
takes place between a friend and a sufferer,
the sufferer contrasts in ll. 265–75 the
greedy life of the strong man with that of
the weak whom he oppresses. In a pessimistic mood he shows that the strong man
is assisted and enjoys success, while the
weak has to suffer.[18] The friend answers
the sufferer by pointing out that from the
creation of mankind they had been so perverse that the cause of the rich was advanced and the harm of the poor man
plotted.[19] Conduct over against the feeble
and downtrodden is prescribed in the
Babylonian precepts and admonitions, also
called the Proverbs of Utnapishtim. Kindness must be shown to the feeble, and
sneering at the downtrodden is forbidden.
A transgressor of this way of life must expect punishment from Shamash.[20] Another
interesting piece of evidence is the bilingual (Sumerian and Akkadian) hymn
possibly addressed to Ninurta, in which
various forbidden things are mentioned.
In l. 11 the matter of oppression of the
poor is stated.[21] Interesting is the possibility that this tablet was intended as a
hymn to Ninurta. The fact that some connection existed between Ninurta and
Ningirsu and that the latter was linked
with the reformatory measures of Urukagina points to the probability that these
gods were regarded in some places of
Mesopotamia as protectors of justice. A
very important text is the hymn to the
sun-god, Shamash, where assistance to the
weak is mentioned as pleasing to

---

[14] J. Klíma, *Untersuchungen zum altbabylonischen brecht* (1940), pp. 52 ff.

[15] For a discussion of these stipulations cf. Driver, "Code of Hammurabi," §§ 117–19, *SPKD* (39), pp. 65–75; W. F. Leemans, *The Old-Babylon Merchant* (1950), p. 17, note 60; F. R. Kraus, *Ein ikt des Königs Ammi-Saduqa von Babylon* (1958), pp. 167–72.

[16] Cf. the latest works on Sumerian and Baby-lonian wisdom, Van Dijk, *La sagesse suméro-accadi-ne* (1953); A. M. van Dijk, "Culture sumérienne bible," in *L'Ancien Testament et l'Orient* (1957), pp. 17 ff.; S. du Toit, *op. cit.*; and the admirable work W. G. Lambert, *Babylonian Wisdom Literature* (1960); F. M. Böhl, "De Zonnegod."

[17] In *Shurpu*, II, 19, 45, 46 reference is made to a widow, but the position is not clear, cf. Du Toit, *op. cit.*, p. 162.

[18] Cf. Lambert, *op. cit.*, pp. 86–87, Gese, *op. cit.*, pp. 51 ff.

[19] Ll. 276–86. Cf. Lambert, *op. cit.*, pp. 88–89.

[20] *Ibid.*, pp. 100–01 and also B. Gemser, *Spreuken II, Prediker, Hooglied van Salomo* (1931), pp. 51 ff.

[21] Lambert, *op. cit.*, p. 119.

Shamash.[22] In another passage the cry of the weak for help and justice is mentioned.[23] It is obvious that the assistance of the poor was regarded as a virtue. Very important is the fact that kings were called on to carry through this policy. Hammurapi is pictured in front of Shamash in a gesture of adoration on the stelas on which the laws are inscribed. Another example can be mentioned, viz. the foundation inscription of Iaḫdun-Lim of Mari, discovered in 1953 by Parrot and published by Dossin. This inscription is dedicated to Shamash, who is called king of heaven and earth, judge (*ša-pi-iṭ*) of gods and men.[24] This discovery proves beyond doubt that a sanctuary of Shamash at Mari existed from the earliest times.[25] Important for our purpose is the fact that Shamash is called "judge" with a pure West Semitic word, viz. *šapiṭu*. Words derived from the same stem were used to connote the judicial activities of a king in favor of widow and orphan, as we shall see further on.

EGYPT

Our material concerning widow, orphan, and the poor is much more restricted in Egyptian literature. This is due to the fact that no legal code has as yet been discovered, while the extant demotic code is still unpublished.[26] The absence of a legal code is attributed by various scholars to the fact that the word or command (*mdw*, *wḏ*) of the reigning king was regarded as actual law and no written law could have existed beside it.[27] This is, however, a hypothesis which is not yet proved.

If we turn to the existing material, a few interesting things turn up. The protection of the weak was also the ideal of kings and nomarchs (rulers of a district). At the beginning of Dynasty XII there lived a nomarch named Ameny who boasted that he ruled his province with justice, respecting the poor man's daughter and the widow.[28] If we take a glance at the occurrence of this ideal and policy in the wisdom literature, it is obvious that the ideal of respecting the rights of the weak, widow and the orphan flourished in times of decay or at the beginning of a new period. We have ample evidence of this policy at the end of the First Intermediate Period and the beginning of the Middle Kingdom ($\pm$ 2000 B.C.). In the didactic discourse of the Eloquent Peasant, the peasant says to Rensi, the chief steward: "Because thou art the father of the orphan, the husband of the widow. . . ."[29] This statement by the peasant is of the utmost importance, because a married woman had no legal personality after her husband's death, as was also the case with minor orphans. It was, thus, the duty of the king or nomarch to protect their rights in the same way as the father of the family should have done. In the Instructions of Merikare the conduct of a king against his people is prescribed. One of the maxims indicates that, if the king desires long life on earth, he must not oppress the widow and annex the property which someone has inherited from his father.[30] The latter part of the maxim clearly refers to the orphan. Another text which originated not long after this is the Instructions of King Amenemhet. In Pap. Millingen 1:6–7 the

[22] Cf. *ibid.*, pp. 132–33 (ll. 99–100) and Böhl, "De Zonnegod," p. 203.

[23] Lambert, *op. cit.*, pp. 134–45 and Böhl, *op. cit.*, p. 204.

[24] G. Dossin, L'inscription de fondation de Iaḫdun-Lim, roi de Mari, *Syria*, XXXII (1955), 12.

[25] Dossin, *op. cit.*, pp. 1–2.

[26] To be published by Girgis Matta, as Professor W. F. Albright has informed me.

[27] Cf. J. A. Wilson, *The Culture of Ancient Egypt* (1956), p. 49.

[28] Cf. Sir Alan H. Gardiner, *Egypt of the Pharaohs* (1961), p. 129.

[29] For the text cf. E. Suys, *Étude sur le conte du fellah plaideur* (1933), pp. 24–25 and *8; for a translation, J. A. Wilson, *ANET*, p. 408 and cf. Lanczkowski, *op. cit.*, p. 38.

[30] Aksel Volten, "Zwei altägyptische politische Schriften," *Analecta Aegyptiaca*, IV (1945), pp. 22–23.

great acts of the king are enumerated. One of these is charity to the poor and the elevation of minors.[31] Emphasis on this policy and ideal is quite understandable when we take into consideration the confusion and abuse of the general rights of the people during the First Intermediate Period. The following quotation may suffice: "A man smites his brother, his mother's son. Men sit in the bushes until the benighted traveller comes, in order to plunder his load. . . . He who had no yoke of oxen is now possessor of a herd," etc.[32] In bad times the weak were unprotected and the widow and orphan bereaved of their rights. With the Eleventh and Twelfth Dynasties mighty kings stepped in and widow, orphan, and the poor were not mentioned in wisdom literature until the Twenty-first Dynasty ca. 1000 B.C. It is true that during the Second Intermediate or Hyksos Period chaos ensued, but a very important difference is to be noted, because this chaos was not instigated by a social revolution as in the First Intermediate Period, but came mainly from outside. It is true that during the Thirteenth Dynasty and later, numerous petty kings ruled in different parts of Egypt, but this is only a proof of weakness and not of a social upheaval and drastic changes.

Unfortunately the reformatory measures taken by Haremheb after the decay during the Amarna Period, which are inscribed on defective stela from Karnak, are so difficult to interpret that no evidence can be gleaned from them.[33] The famous Instructions of Amenemope originated 1000 B.C. Here again there is concern for the oppressed and disabled. A maxim declares that the oppressed must not be robbed and that no harshness may be inflicted on the disabled.[34]

We have ample evidence that kings and rulers were encouraged to protect the weak. Is there any religious connection between this policy and the Egyptian gods? Surprisingly enough this connection existed and the sun-god, Re, or his supplanter, Amon, was regarded as protector of the weak par excellence.[35] In a Late Egyptian text, Anastasi II, 6:5 ff. Amon-Re is called vizier of the poor. His judgment is impartial.[36] This text has clearly something in common with the above mentioned material in the Instructions of Merikare. The obligation felt by the king toward the god, to act righteously toward the poor, the widow, and the orphan, is expressed in Papyrus Harris I, where Rameses III boasts to the god Ptah that he has given special protection to widows and orphans.[37] This protection is also reflected in the few legal documents of inheritance at our disposal. It is obvious from certain testaments that the wife of the deceased had also the right of inheritance. Obviously enough each of the children of the deceased obtained his part of his father's property.[38]

In spite of the lack of legal material and the fact that we have mainly used wisdom literature as our source, the parallel trend between Mesopotamian policy of the protection of the weak and that of Egypt is clear. It is regarded as a virtue of kings and rulers and as an important part of the duty of the sun-god. As in Mesopotamia the

[31] Ibid., p. 107.
[32] Gardiner's translation in op. cit., p. 109.
[33] Ibid., pp. 244–45.
[34] Cf. A. E. Wallis Budge, The Teaching of Amen-

em-apt (1924), p. 188, and Wilson in ANET, pp. 421–24 for a good translation. The book of Lange was not available.
[35] For a discussion cf. J. H. Breasted, Development of Religion and Thought in Ancient Egypt (1912) pp. 353 ff.
[36] Cf. for the text A. H. Gardiner, Late-Egyptian Miscellanies, "Bibliotheca Egyptiaca," VII (1937), p. 16; a translation by R. A. Caminos, Late Egyptian Miscellanies (1954), pp. 9–10.
[37] Cf. Günther Roeder, Die ägyptische Götterwelt (1959), p. 55.
[38] Erwin Seidl, Einführung in die ägyptische Rechtsgeschichte bis zum Ende des Neuen Reiches (1951), pp. 57–58.

religious ethics are closely intertwined in Egypt with the social ethics. It is to a certain extent, however, possible to trace the social policy of protection back to its very roots in Egyptian history. The conception of social justice started probably with the First Intermediate Period when almost a reversion of social classes took place.

UGARIT

Unfortunately no legal code or wisdom book is found in the Ugaritic literature which gives us a clear picture of Canaanite culture before the Iron Age. There is, however, in the epic of Aqhat something worthy of mention. While Daniel the king was waiting for the god of crafts, Kothar-waḫasis, to bring a bow for Aqhat, his son, he was busy judging (the stem *ṭpṭ*) the cause of the widow and orphan. Ginsberg translates:

Straightway Daniel the Rapha-man,
Forthwith Ghazir the Harnam[iyy]-man,
Is upright, sitting before the gate,
Beneath *a mighty tree* on the threshing floor,
Judging the cause of the widow,
Adjudicating the case of the fatherless.[39]

Again the judgment in favor of widow and orphan is idealized. Important is the fact that the stem *ṭpṭ* is used to connote the exercising of justice.[40] We have seen above that this West Semitic stem is used to characterize the judicial activity of Shamash over gods and men. The idea of protection and of judging the case of the weak was, thus, not unfamiliar to the Western Semites.

THE OLD TESTAMENT

Now we have to turn to the Hebrew world, where references to the protection of widow, orphan, and the poor are numerous. Professor Böhl protested against the

fact that H. Bolkenstein in his book *Weldadigheid en Armenzorg* ("Charity and Care for the Poor") gives a few pages to Egypt and Israel and does not mention anything about Mesopotamia.[41] It is true that other scholars working on social problems in the Old Testament have totally neglected the parallel material from Mesopotamia and Egypt. We can not agree e.g. with H. Bruppacher that compassion for widow and orphan is something unique in the Old Testament over against other literatures.[42] A welcome new interpretation is presented by C. van Leeuwen with necessary references to extra-biblical material, although the full scope of this material is not used.[43] It is, however, not our purpose to discuss the rich literature of modern scholars which grew around the concept "poor." The more important works are ably discussed in a study of J. van der Ploeg in *Oudetestmentische Studien*.[44]

We desire to start our study with a discussion of certain trends of Psalm 82 which gives us the clue to a better understanding of the position of widow, orphan, and the poor in Israel. The interpretation and date of this psalm offers severe difficulties and is differently interpreted by modern scholars.[45] Various scholars place it in the period between the seventh and fourth centuries B.C.[46] This is not the place to argue on

---

[39] H. Ginsberg in *ANET*, p. 151. Cf. for the text Gordon. *Ugaritic Manual* (1955), p. 179.

[40] Cf. my "The Judges and Ancient Israelite Jurisprudence." in *Die Oud Testamentiese Werkgemeenskap in Suid-Afrika* (1959), pp. 15–17.

[41] Böhl, "De Zonnegod," pp. 194–95.

[42] H. Bruppacher, *Die Beurteilung der Armut im Alten Testament* (1924), p. 16.

[43] C. van Leeuwen, *Le développement du sens social en Israel avant l'ère Chrétienne* (1955), e.g. p. 27 when the Code of Hammurapi is used.

[44] Cf. J. van der Ploeg, "Les pauvres d'Israel et leur piété," *OTS*, VII (1950), 237–42.

[45] We refer to the "*Thronbesteigung*" theory of Mowinckel, where this psalm is interpreted in light of the battle myth in which Yahweh annually overcomes the rival gods of foreign nations. Cf. S. Mowinckel *Das Thronbesteigungsfest Jahwäes und der Ursprung der Eschatologie* (1920), pp. 67 ff. For a comprehensive analysis of modern interpretations cf. H.-J. Kraus *Psalmen*, II (1960) and J. Ridderbos, *Die Psalmen* II (1958), pp. 325–27.

[46] Cf. G. Ernest Wright, *The Old Testament against its Environment* (1950), p. 37, although he admits that there is no certain means to date it.

possible dates and interpretation of this psalm, but to my mind it is perfectly clear that it is strongly influenced by Canaanite mythology which is to a certain extent purged to fit in with Israelite conceptions and also to show the absolute domination of Yahweh over the heathen gods.[47] The possibility is not excluded that it was also used shortly after it was purged as a kind of missionary poem to convince the Canaanites that Yahweh is a God of justice and no other is beside him. The important part for our study is vss. 3–4 in which God challenges the gods to give justice (stem *shāphaṭ*) to orphans and the poor and to save the wretched from the power of the evildoers. The gods fail to accomplish this command and the verdict of death is pronounced over them. The last verse of the psalm brings to God the victorious command to give justice to the world. Out of this we may deduce that the only One who can give justice and deliverance to the weak is God. The God of Israel is regarded as the only true judge and protector of the weak. The important difference between this conception and that of Mesopotamia and Egypt is that the exercising of justice is narrowed down to one God and all the others are excluded. In light of this must we proceed to the legal and the wisdom literature.

In the Covenant Code we have two distinct pronouncements on justice to widow, orphan, and the poor. Oppression of widow and orphan is forbidden in Ex. 22:21–24 and a severe punishment is pronounced. In 23:6 the command is given not to abuse the rights of the poor. The style of both is apodictic as a direct command from God to his people.[48] The vertical line is drawn and closely linked up with the horizontal responsibility to the poor. There is, furthermore, a special interest in the fate of the widow and orphan in Deuteronomy. In Deut. 10:18 the protection of this group is linked with the Supreme Judge, Yahweh, who is not willing to accept bribery, but willing to do justice to widow, orphan, and *ger* (stranger). This text is the basis for all the later stipulations in this group. In Deut. 14:28–29 the command is that widow and poor must be allowed to feast on the tithes. In 16:11, 14 the Israelite receives the command to let the widow, orphan, and *ger* partake in his feasts. In 24:17–22 special stipulations concerning this group are made, e.g., the rights of the widow must not be abused, and furthermore, food must be left on the land for them.[49] In 27:19 a person who abused the rights of *ger*, widow, and orphan is cursed. Every time the lead is given, Yahweh gives justice to this group and everybody has to do likewise. Something extraordinary in the Old Testament in contrast to other literatures is the balanced view on this policy. The command is given to execute justice to the weak, but at the same time the warning is given not to favor the poor in spite of their guilt (Ex. 23:3, Lev. 19:15). In the Covenant Code as in CH a protective measure is taken against the abuse of credit-slavery. In the Covenant Code it is stipulated that a credit-slave must go free after six years.[50] The just execution of this stipulation was neglected in times of decay as is illustrated by Jeremiah in the time of Zedekiah.[51]

---

[47] Cf. for the Canaanite background R. T. O'Callaghan, "A Note on the Canaanite Background of Psalm 82," *CBQ*, XV (1953), 311–14.

[48] Cf. for stylistic analysis A. Alt, *Die Ursprünge des israelitischen Rechts* (1934). Alt's view that the apodictic style is typically Israelite is challenged by a few scholars, e.g. Landsberger and Meek; B. Lands- berger, "Die babylonische Termini für Gesetz und Recht," *SPKD* (1939), p. 223, n. 19; T. Meek, *ANET*, p. 183, n. 24. The latest article on the subject is by Stanley Gevirtz, "West-Semitic Curses and the Problem of the Origins of Hebrew Law," *VT*, XI (1961), 137 ff. and p. 138 for a criticism of Alt's view.

[49] Robert North, S. J., *Sociology of the Biblical Jubilee* (1954), pp. 118–19.

[50] For a discussion cf. my "A Few Legal Aspects," p. 20.

[51] Cf. M. David, "The Manumission of Slaves under Zedekiah," *OTS* (1948), pp. 63–79.

An interesting and illuminating discussion of the legal status and the protection of widow and orphan in Bedouin society in comparison with Israelite society is given by Samuel Nyström.[52] He points out that widows and orphans are legally protected, because the widow has the right to go back to the house or family of her father. The same is applicable to the orphans. If the nearest relatives are dead, they have the right to claim protection from remote relatives. Insofar the position in Bedouin society. Do we have the same kind of conception in Israelite and Near Eastern circles? The whole idea of the levirate marriage is important, of which the Book of Ruth is sufficient evidence. The difference between the Bedouin idea and that of Israel is that in Israel (as in Mesopotamia) the widow was assimilated to the family of her husband and not to that of her father. A woman was usually sent back to the house of her father in certain circumstances, e.g., when she was divorced by her husband on legal grounds, and she had the right to reclaim her dowry which she had received from the house of her father. M. David, however, makes the point that a widow in the ancient Near Eastern connotation means that she or her children has no direct family ties. He holds the view that the common practice was that the wife of a deceased man and her children must go back to the house of her father, where they are protected.[53] This view is in accord with the common practice in Bedouin society. The problem, however, is not solved. What about the levirate marriages? Was this marriage only contracted when the widow had no remaining family ties? The position becomes a little more illuminated when we bear in mind that the married wife was bought by her husband from the house of her father (bride's price in Akkadian *tirḫatu* and in Hebrew *mahor*). After her husband's death his family had the right to keep her in the family or else they would suffer damage.[54] This is the basis of levirate marriage, as is also the case with the other kind of levirate in which the husband of a deceased wife has the right to marry one of her sisters.[55] In the case of Naomi and Ruth, the former went back from Moab to her own people for protection, the latter accompanied her and was allowed before her marriage to Boaz to enjoy the favors of a widow as prescribed in Deuteronomy (24:17–22).[56] In other words, Ruth was regarded as a widow according to law until she was assimilated to the family of Boaz.[57] We may argue, however, that Ruth might have had no family ties. We have one case in the Old Testament where the levirate took place in spite of family ties. In the story of Tamar we have evidence that the levirate marriage was contracted; but after the death of Onan, Tamar's second husband, brother of Er, her former husband, Judah had sent her back to the house of her father until the youngest son should reach marriageable age (Gen. 38). We have, thus, definite evidence to the fact that a widow was allowed to go back to the house of her father in certain circumstances and with the consent of the head of the family of her deceased husband. I do not think that with all this evidence we can narrow the meaning of widow and orphan down to people without family ties.[58] It is true that the common policy of protection was mainly concerned with the poor widow and

[52] Samuel Nyström, *Beduinentum und Jahwismus* (1946), pp. 139–47.

[53] M. David, *Vorm en Wezen van de Huwelijkssluiting naar Oud-Oostersche Rechtsopvatting* (1934), pp. 7–9.

[51] Cf. e.g. P. Koschaker, *Quellenkritische Untersuchungen zu den altassyrischen Gesetzen* (1921), p. 46.

[55] *Ibid.*, p. 47.

[56] Cf. for the legal position in Ruth, M. David, *Het Huwelijk van Ruth* (1941), *passim*.

[57] For stipulations concerning levirate in Israel cf. Deut. 25:5 ff.

[58] Also against J. Pederson, *Israel*, I–II (1926) 44–46.

orphan, but it may also include those who were temporarily without legal protection as was the case with Ruth.

The prescribed way of life in Old Testament wisdom literature takes care of the weak. It is definitely regarded as the policy of God to protect the widow and poor. God maintains the borderline of a widow's property (Prov. 15:25). Anybody who abuses the rights of widow, orphan, and the poor acts contrary to the will of God. The oppressor of the weak reproaches his maker (Prov. 14:31). The oppression of widow, orphan, and the poor is carried out by evildoers and, according to a pessimistic attitude, they are prosperous in spite of their sins (Job 24:1-4). Anyone who assists the weak will receive blessings from the Lord. The man who gives bread to the poor (Prov. 22:9), who has compassion with the weak (Prov. 19:17) is blessed by God. A command is issued to respect the rights of this group. E.g., one is forbidden to enter the property of the orphan, viz. to claim it as his own (Prov. 3:10).[59] Another command, also in the corpus related to Amenemope, is not to rob the poor because of his poverty (Prov. 22:22, cf. Amenemope, Chap. 2:IV).[60] Another important fact is that in Old Testament wisdom literature the protection of the poor is described as a virtue of kings (Prov. 29:14)

[59] Some scholars conjectured ʿolām to ʾalmānā. Cf. C. Toy, *Proverbs*, "ICC" (1948), pp. 431–32; but cf. Toit, *op. cit.*, p. 161. B. Gemser, *Sprüche Salomos*, "AT" (1937), pp. 66–67 accepts ʾalmānā because of parallel with Amenemope VII.

[60] The whole question of the relation between v. 22.17 ff. and Amenemope is very difficult. The majority of scholars hold the view that the author of v. 22:17 ff. borrowed from Amenemope. Cf. A. Erman, "Das Weisheitbuch des Amenemope," *OLZ*, VII (1924), 241–52; H. Gressmann, "Die neugefundene Lehre des Amenemope und die vorexilische Spruchdichtung Israels," *ZAW*, XLII (1924), 272– Other scholars hold the opposite view, that Amenemope borrowed from Israelite wisdom. Cf. W. E. Oesterley, *The Wisdom of Egypt and the Old Testament* (1927); recently E. Drioton, "Sur la sagesse d'Aménémopé," *Mélanges bibliques rédigés en l'honneur de André Robert* (1957), pp. 254 ff.

This policy was regarded as the will of God, the virtue of kings, and the duty of the common people. The execution of the policy is embodied in the Old Testament legal literature. Severe punishment is pronounced on those who have transgressed this principle. In the wisdom literature protection of the weak is regarded as the correct way of life.

CONCLUSIONS

We have remarkable similarities and analogies between the conception of protection of the weak in Mesopotamian, Egyptian, and Israelite literature. Still some minor differences occur, as we have pointed out in a few cases.

1. The basic conception in all the literature discussed is that the protection of the weak is the will of the god. In polytheistic religions this characteristic is ascribed to a special god in the pantheon; in Mesopotamia Shamash, the sun-god, is regarded as the protector of the poor, although in some instances Ningirsu and Ninurta are mentioned. This divine protector is also held as judge of heaven and earth, of gods and men. In Egypt the protection is also ascribed to the sun-god, Re (or Amon-Re). He is also held as judge. In one special text, the Destruction of Mankind, he is shown as the one who exacts punishment on mankind and orders Hathor to obliterate the human race.[61] In some circles Ptah is regarded in the same role as god of justice. Yahweh is described in Old Testament literature as the protector of the weak par excellence. With direct apodictic style of command and prohibition Yahweh takes the weak under his protection. This is one of the important ethical doctrines of the Old Testament, but definitely not unique in comparison with conceptions in neighboring cultures. The only basic difference

[61] Cf. J. Vandier, *La religion égyptienne* (1949), pp. 37–38.

is that Yahweh is regarded as the only protector. He is even placed in opposition to the gods of foreign nations and hailed as the only true Supreme Judge of the world (Ps. 82). This fact might have been emphasized annually by a cultic festival. In all the material discussed the vertical line is drawn to emphasize the protection. This was done to sanction the protection of the weak in society.

2. The principle of protection of the weak is regarded in Mesopotamian, Egyptian, and Israelite literature as the virtue of a great king. The king was the direct representative of the god on earth. In some cases he was regarded as a substitute for the god, but still a human being, as in Mesopotamia. In other cases he was regarded as a divine being, as in Egypt, where the king was the son of the sun-god. In Israel he was regarded as the representative of Yahweh with granted powers to rule the nation. The close link between the god and the king is obvious from the above-mentioned examples. Therefore, if protection of the weak is the will of the god, it is the duty of the king to execute it in practical life. In the early Israelite community this was done almost in the way of a Bedouin sheikh who sits down to hear the complaints of his people. Cf. e.g. in II Sam. 14 in which David listened to the complaints of the woman of Tekoah. In later Israelite times the principle of protection of the weak was abandoned by kings and this was more than any thing else responsible for the ethical and moral preaching of the prophets on this point. The kings had failed in one very old, deeprooted principle, viz. to protect as representative of God the widow, orphan, and the poor (Isa. 1:17).

3. The general conception of protection of the weak is, furthermore, expanded as a common way of life of ordinary people. They have to respect the rights of the poor or else receive punishment, if no through legal means, then through dire punishment of the god. That these right were abused is true especially of decade society as in the First Intermediate Perio of Egypt and in Israelite society during th times of the prophets. The vertical com mand and prohibition by the god is to b executed in horizontal relations.

4. The similarities are not restricted t common policy but are also observable i parallel ideas. Thus a clear parallel betwee the Babylonian Theodicy and Job exist The Babylonian sufferer complains tha the strong man succeeds in oppressing th poor, and the weak has to suffer. Th complaint originated out of the pessimist conception that the evildoer succeeds, b the pious is oppressed without hope assistance.[62] The same idea occurs in th Book of Job where the sufferer complain about acts of oppression by evildoe exacted on orphan, widow, and the poo He says: "Yet God layeth not folly them" (AV). Another parallel is that long reign of life is promised to the king man (judge) who protects the weak. Th appears in the Maxims of Merikare, th Hymn to Shamash, and in Proverbs. Another similarity occurs in the hymn Amon-Re in which he is regarded as th vizier of the poor whose judgment is i partial. In the Hymn of Shamash the jud is encouraged to be impartial in his jud ment, as this would be pleasing to Sh mash. The same idea occurs in Deut. 10: where the impartial judgment of Yahw is stressed. An interesting parallel betwe Egyptian and Israelite material is t following. The Maxims of Merikare forbi one to eject another from the property his father, referring here to the orpha The same idea occurs in Prov. 23:10 whe

---

[62] Cf. Gese, *op. cit.*, pp. 62 ff.
[63] Volten, *op. cit.*, pp. 22–23, Lambert, *op. c* pp. 132–33, and Prov. 29:14.

ne is forbidden to enter on the property f the orphan.

5. The attitude taken against widow, rphan, and the poor is to be looked at om a legal background. These people had o rights, no legal personalities, or in some ases possibly restricted rights. They were lmost outlaws. Anyone could oppress 1em without danger that legal connec- ons might endanger his position. To store the balance of society these people ust be protected. Therefore, it was ecessary to sanction their protection by rect command of the god and to make it e virtue of kings.

It is, however, surprising at what early age in the history of the ancient Near East the compulsion was felt to protect these people. I do not think that it is correct to speak of borrowing of ideas con- cerning our subject. It was a common policy, and the Israelites in later history inherited the concept from their forebears, some of whom had come from Mesopo- tamia, some had been captive in Egypt, and others had grown up in the Canaanite world. In the Israelite community this policy was extended through the en- couragement of the high ethical religion of Yahweh to become a definite part of their religion, later to be inherited by Christians and Muslims.

UNIVERSITY OF STELLENBOSCH
STELLENBOSCH, SOUTH AFRICA

II.

THE ESSENTIAL STRUCTURE OF WISDOM THOUGHT

CONCERNING THE STRUCTURE OF OLD TESTAMENT WISDOM*[1]

By WALTHER ZIMMERLI

Whoever has read even a single page into Prov is impressed how a total disposition toward life[2] is bruited about here with considerable emphasis. It bears a thoroughly distinctive stamp (of the wise); the assertion is that it is the proper solution to the question of life. The spurious solution (the fools' conduct) is sharply delineated alongside the right.

Not only is the answer to any question significant, but also the way the question is put. For a prior judgment lies behind the form of every question: naturally of special significance where it concerns the totality of a life-attitude and thus incorporates a pre-understanding of all of life, as it does here. The task of the discussions which follow, therefore, is to see, behind the emphatically propounded solution, the question which precedes it, and to discern the kind of previous judgment which it passes on life.

In Proverbs, it may seem difficult still to hear the question because every effort is applied here toward construction of the answer, out of the wholly optimistic conviction they know the solution. By contrast, the examination of Qoheleth is essentially easier. Through the solution of resignation found here, the unresolved question shows through from every side. Qoheleth has a certain answer, a certain attitude in life as an answer, but the positive emphasis is lacking. The problem has not been resolved; he advocates an emergency solution that is not entirely satisfactory. (The course of the investigation will make it apparent that the way the question is put is identical in its basic structure for Proverbs and Qoheleth: a point the following remarks will assume without further proof.)

*Originally published as: "Zur Struktur der alttestamentlichen Weisheit," ZAW X:3 (1933), pp. 177-204. Translated by Brian W. Kovacs, Associate Professor of Sociology, Centenary College of Louisiana, Shreveport.

When we speak of the "central question" of wisdom hereafter, it should be taken to mean: How does the wise man formulate that question to which the answer is his conduct through life? What is the focus of his existence? In terms of what question does he understand his life? What is the problem from which Qoheleth withdraws in resignation, that Proverbs believes with unbroken optimism to have solved? [3]

This prompts us to seek some formulation of this question in wisdom's own words, in which this question manifests itself. Significantly, such a statement is found in Qoheleth. For Qoheleth, the question remains unsolved, so he must content himself with having formulated it; Prov has resolved it, the question is settled and not formulated any more. Qoheleth (1:3) conceives the question which impels him in the words mh ytrwn l'dm bkl ᶜmlw. If one breaks down Qoheleth's pessimistic predisposition to this question and conceives it, on the basis of an optimistic attitude, as a question that anticipates a positive response, then one has a good formulation of what is the driving motive behind the wise's entire disposition: mh ytrwn l'dm (cf. 3:9; 5:15b; 6:8; also 2:22; 10:10f.).[4] If the optimistic tone of normative wisdom is imputed to him, then in the same way Qoh 2:3—I reflected . . . ᶜd 'šr 'r'h 'y zh ṭwb lbny h'dm 'šr yᶜsw tht hšmym (Hertzberg: . . . that I might see what good fortune is for the children of men); similarly 6:12 mh ṭwb l'dm bḥyym. See also n. 28 below.

The formulations universally show the anthropological position from which the question is put (ṭwb l'dm; ytrwn l'dm etc.). It is a question of people whose human possibilities should be established. Further, it must be carried forward in an equally more clearly limited way: the question's orientation cannot be raised above its anthropological point of origin; it has its center of gravity in the individual unhistoric person toward whose good fortune it asks. Therefore, it should be identified by a clearer word than anthropocentric.

Through the juxtaposition of another possible attitude, this point becomes clear. One could imagine an anthropological point of departure that would immediately lead to the question of orders within which man is fixed—a self-understanding of man that would show him directly subject to determined orders. In concrete terms: when he asks the anthropological question, OT man immediately understands himself as a member of Yahweh's covenant people Israel. Therefore, the question is stated forthwith in another formulation: how am I to organize my life as a member of the covenant people, as a part of this order which is set over me, within which I find myself and which obligates me?

It is no coincidence that Proverbs and Qoheleth (as well as Job) entirely lack reference to man as a member of the covenant people; instead, the neutral term 'dm appears very frequently to designate the subject of the wisdom saying (45 times in Prov and esp. 49 times in Qoh, along with ḥy 9 times, on that see below [Section VI]). That thoroughly corresponds with wisdom's way of putting the question. It is autonomous man—not apprehended nor enslaved by any prior order—who wants to organize freely from himself outwards and to assess the world.

The objection here will run: man is still only a subordinate, which means man and not God, creature and not Creator, therefore subject and not free —rather in the sense of Is 31:3 or of Ezekiel, who uses the word man quite frequently (95 times) in the distinctive form "son of man" in this sense of inwardly subordinate and dependent. Other places can be adduced where this creatureliness of man before God is delineated in all clarity, like Prov 15:11; 16:1; 20:12; 21:2; 22:2 etc.; or like 1:7 where the fear of God is unmistakeably put at the beginning. It seems to force us to the proposition that, even for the wise, recognition of an order binding man stands at the beginning, the most encompassing order of Creator and creature—even if one cannot speak of covenant and historical election here either. Hence, the proposition of a radically anthropocentric point of departure is not possible.

It will nevertheless be maintained here that, seen structurally, it is a question of secondary elements in these sayings which stress man's subordination. These notions play no role at all at the point of origin, at the initial point of self-understanding where the question arises how life is to be understood.[5] Wisdom's way of putting the question does not take this limitation into consideration at all; it is only "figured in" subsequently; it is a part of the over-all context of the answer to the question asked.

It might be natural to rely on the historical genesis of the wisdom literature for proof of the proposed opinion. What might be doubtful in terms of the biblical literature which is currently before us becomes undeniably clear in the light of the early history of wisdom. Wisdom grows up out of the ancient court wisdom of life. Out of an aristocratically insular class morality of the scribal and priestly strata in Egypt and Babylon, it spread throughout the breadth of the nation in an Israel that was more democratic—and equipt with a similar script—though admittedly without being able to cast off the last remnants of its aristocratic origin (Sir 38:24ff. or in its later development, the wise man is the person versed in the Law, as opposed to the *am ha-aretz;* scholar—cf. Strack, *Einleitung in Talmud und Midrasch,* 5th ed., p. 62 n. 1). What the driving question is here, however, the structure of this aristocratic Egyptian precursor does not leave in doubt for a moment. It is not the question of that order within which man finds himself set, nor of the obligation resulting from it; rather, it is the question, How do I make use of the bounds fixed about me to my own advantage (cf. Qoh 4:13f.)? It is the experienced and shrewd courtier who speaks.[6]

One could seek to prove the opinion stated by referring to this origin of wisdom. In reality, however, this allusion can prove no more than a possibility. It is possible that, in terms of its fundamental question, wisdom remained unchanged in its transition into Israel. It is just as possible, however, that here history made use of its right to re-organize, introducing an internal shift in the wisdom sayings during their passage into the Israelite spiritual world.

A convincing reply to the question is only possible on the basis of the entire disposition of the Israelite wisdom sayings which are before us.

The question should be stated once again in its completely fundamental breadth, Does the "central question" of wisdom grow up out of knowledge and recognition of a fixed, binding obligation—above the question arose concerning the broadest tie of creature to Creator—whose realization in practical conduct is now in question? Or, is the contention right that it is a question which originates with the individual person, ultimately being oriented around him alone?

II

For a reply to this question, we are now led to a more basic kind of consideration. Where determination means a fixed order, there can be detailed discussions about the exact interpretation of that determination. Implicit within any such determination, however, there will always be the essential character of authority which limits any discussion.

This demand for authority, though, does not seem to correspond badly with wisdom. Not only is the entirety of wisdom admonition repeatedly referred to as torah (1:8; 3:1; 13:14; 28:4, 7 *et passim*)—with the same designation as the Law which is authoritative admonition *kat 'exochēn*—the correspondence also appears in the designation of individual admonitions of the wise, when they often occur as commands mswt (2:1; 3:1; 4:4; 6:23 *et passim*).[7]

One would like to clarify completely the distinction between Law's command and wisdom's command by ascribing regulation of the relationship to God to the Law, while conceiving the statements of wisdom as guides through the "secular world" (so e.g., Kuhn, *Beiträge zur Erklärung des Salomonischen Spruchbuches,* 1931, pp. 2f.). This external distinction is by no means satisfactory, however. Rather, the inner essence of the command must be compared, the one with the other. Here, we are interested in the inner nature of the wisdom command.

The question of the command's legitimation is decisively important for establishing this inner nature. To what does it appeal when it attributes obedience to men?

Beyond the purely external terminological similarity to the Law, there seems to be a series of additional features which confirm the authoritative character of the wisdom command. Again and again, it is stressed that everything depends on "hearing" [8]—the high value of the 'zn šmᶜt is underscored a number of times (15:13; 25:12) since 'zn above all is the principal entrance for wisdom. Wisdom's precept can be simply termed leqaḥ (that which is to be accepted 1:5; 4:2; 9:9; 16:21, 23; in another sense 7:21); obedience to the wise commandment can be designated lqḥ (cf. lqḥ mṣwt 10:8 etc.). Moreover, when the picture of education in the Egyptian scribal schools[9] is considered, and certain aphorisms of Proverbs concerning the education of the young man to wisdom are compared with it (13:24; 22:15; 29:15; 23:13f.; and to the last see Aḥikar 81f.)[10], then they seem to round out the picture of how wisdom-precept is authoritative-command in the strictest sense.

The question of the commandment's internal legitimation would then be answered corresponding to the literal sense of mṣwh, that the precept receives its validity from the authority who enunciated it. Sufficient justification for obedience to the command would lie in general recognition of this authority, which one might well find in personified wisdom as one of the beings closest to the deity.

Nevertheless, closer examination advises against this obvious shortcut on weighty opposing grounds, though it certainly retains some validity for a later period (that of the identification of Law with wisdom which is not yet present however in Prov 1-9).

One factor in this connection: nothing is said, in the older texts, of the personified wisdom which would issue the commands. The precepts are put solely in the mouth of the deity.[11]

More important, even the authoritative character of the wisdom rules— and thus the conception of these rules as real commands, as they must appear after being called mṣwt—cannot withstand closer examination. Numerous observations substantiate this.

The frequent reference to wisdom rules as ᶜṣh must certainly catch one's eye (21:30 ᶜṣh parallel to ḥkmh and tbwnh; 8:14; 12:15; 20:5 *et passim*). Translated, ᶜṣh means counsel. If we take it in the literal sense, however, "counsel" implies that the principle of conduct proceeds amidst consultation with the particular well-being of the man before it. This interpretation is confirmed by other observations. Many sections of Proverbs draw a picture of the wise man whose first rule is never to act on his initial impulse, but to restrain himself, to wait, to reflect, until the right moment and the right counsel is there.[12] A command appears categorical; counsel is debatable. It should be considered and pondered. It should be clear before it is transformed into deed. Thus, obedience is not the virtue of the wise, in terms of a general inculcation of hearing, but dᶜt and tbwnh—the latter not in the sense of a Hosea or Jeremiah as dᶜt 'lhym, as an inner deference to God, but as the ability to ponder, facility at reflection. Hence, the requisite human disposition can be called ᶜrmh and mzmh—both terms which stand on the verge of cunning or cleverness, understood *in malam partem*.[13] tḥblwt should also be placed here, though it is not unambiguous[14] in its derivation (1:5; 20:18; 24:6 tḥblwt ršᶜym; 12:5).

A further point follows here: counsel stimulates reflection and independent decision. Authority disposes without further justification. A glance at the exterior form of the sayings in Proverbs leads to the surprising conclusion that the direct instruction form largely does not occur at all. One could begin reading at 10:1. One would first come across a direct command at 13:20—admittedly, a textually doubtful place.[15] In spite of its imperatival dress, 14:7 is hardly an admonition, if the text is even in good order; cf. BH. The first trouble-free established text with a direct admonition appears at 16:3—and it is omitted from the LXX. Continuing within the second proverb collection (10:1-22:16), we find only 19:18, 20, 27 (meaning unclear); 20:13 (v. 16, like 14:7, should not be included here in spite of imperatival appearance), 22; 22:6, 10. The direct admonition occurs more frequently in chs. 25-29, but compared to the total number of verses, it is so infrequent as to be virtually negligible (25:6f., 8, 9f., 16, 17, 21f.; 26:4, 5; 27:1, (2), 10, 11, (13-20:16), 23ff.; 29:17). Only in the collections in 22:17-ch. 24 is it more frequent, and chs. 1-9 are almost exclusively in the outward form of the admonitory address.

Thus, from a purely external point of view, we have two forms of wisdom saying: the admonition addressed specifically to the individual

(16:3), and the simple aphorism which we term for short "proverb." How are these two forms of the wisdom saying internally organized in comparison to each other? Note that the wisdom saying appears in Proverbs in the dress of the mśl (See Eissfeldt, *Der Maschal im AT*, 1913; Hempel, *Die althebräische Literatur* (Handbuch der Literaturwissenschaft, ed. by O. Walzel), 1930ff., pp. 44ff.; G. Boström, *Paronomasi i den äldere hebreiska Maschalliteraturen*, Lund 1928).

It would seem at first that a whole series of direct admonitions would be transformed into ordinary sayings without any great difficulty. Out of 16:3, for example, "Commit (reveal?) your work to Yahweh, and your plans will be established"—"Whoever commits his work to Yahweh, his plans will be established." Or 19:20. "Listen to advice and accept instruction, that you may be wise at your end" (or, in your ways; cf. BH)—"Whoever listens to advice and accepts instruction will be wise at his end." Also, see e.g. 20:13; 25:16, 17, 21f.; 26:4, 5 etc. And vice versa, an admonition is readily at hand for many sayings and can be made to complement without difficulty. For 10:2a for example (unrighteous treasures are quite useless). "Do not aspire to unjust profit, because treasures unrighteously acquired confer no utility" (see 23:4, 5). Or, for 10:3a ("Yahweh will not allow a righteous person [or, the soul of a righteous person] to go hungry"). "Devote yourself to righteousness, because Yahweh will not. . . ." The existence of an inner relationship between the two is unmistakeable.

Insight into the nature of this relationship is facilitated by the fact that these two forms are often found joined together in Proverbs into a verbal unity; for example, in 23:20f., 26f.; 24:15f., 19f. The first verse or stichos contains the admonition, while the ky need only be dropped from the succeeding verse to convert the latter into an entirely correct saying-form of mashal (Cf., e.g., 23:27a in the two verses at 23:26f. with the "saying" at 22:14; 24:20b in 24:19f. with 13:9b.)

It is clear how the admonition anticipates restraint and legitimation in the concluding saying, which discovers some kind of relationship within the experience of life. Insight into this relationship—the knowledgeable calculation of consequences which the commanded or forbidden action should carry with it, "according to experience"—in the last analysis should be the motive which spurs the person who is addressed into action, or which keeps him from acting.

The bringing together of both aphorisms can come about externally through various forms. In commanding or admonishing, the expected outcome (the goal to be attained) is most frequently introduced through ky (22:17-18, 22-23; 23:6-7, 10-11, 26-27; 24:1-2; 27:23-24ff). It also recurs throughout chs. 1-9, e.g. 1:8-9, 15-17. The outcome is less frequently introduced simply by waw (16:3a-b; 29:17aa-abb) or by lamedh plus the infinitive (2:12, 16), while in 3:8 the outcome merely is placed unconnected in a new sentence alongside the command. Moreover, a stressed final connection (by means of lm^{c}n) also occurs somewhat infrequently between the command and the saying which calculates the consequence (19:20a-b). In prohibitions, on the other hand, the warning is introduced through pn, when not by means of ky (24:17-18; 25:8a-b, 9-10, 16a-b, 17a-b; 26:4a-b, 5a-b etc.).

Other sayings might be ventured with respect to the relationship of admonition to proverb. The two should not be regarded as equivalent. In the oldest collection in chs. 10ff. (Hempel, *Altheb. Literatur,* p. 51, may be more correct in his assessment than Fichtner, *Altor. Weisheit,* p. 8), only 10 of the 375 sayings are pure admonitions (perhaps only 8 originally; discounting 20:16, then only 7). In the collection in chs. 25-29, only 15 of 127 sayings-units have direct admonitions (not counting 27:13-20:16, only 14); in ch. 30, 4 of 13; I count 25 admonitory units in the 33 within 22:17-ch. 24. Chs. 1-9 and the sayings of Lemuel are almost exclusively admonitions.

This clearly shows, therefore, the development from proverb toward admonition. More exactly, the ad hominem expression appears more and more in place of the proverb which the old collections almost exclusively employ: the neutrally formulated sentence that states an experiential relationship from which a rule of conduct can usually be inferred straightforwardly. The command's anchorage in the general experiential rule, however, is not given up. In chs. 1-9, it still seems to be a direct stylistic rule that the common statement of experience be appended to the units of admonition which have to some extent attained considerable scope here. (E.g. 1:19 within 1:8-19; 1:32 [33] in 1:20-33; 2:21f. in 2:1-22; 3:1ff. includes shorter units of admonition and explanation similar to ch. 24; 3:1-2, 3-4, 5/6a-b, 7-8, 9-10, 11-12;[16] 3:32-35 in 3:21-35; 4:18, 19 in 4:10 [1?]-19; 5:21-23 in 5:1-23. The formal distinction becomes much less clear thereafter, but the content relationship between admonition and the general statement remains no less significant.)

Thus, one may well speak of a formal development of the mashal from Prov 10ff. up through Prov 1ff.: a stylistic change to the admonition, to the "commandment-saying." An inner shift of tone, however, does not go hand in hand with it. The point of departure remains the proverb which formulates a common rule of experience. Rather, the development should only be described as making explicit the implication, already lying hidden within the saying, that one should consider the facts of experience given in the saying when he acts.

A few verses still remain to be examined which contain direct admonitions without any explanation or reference to the outcome; e.g. 19:27 (content unclear, textually corrupt); 24:27, 28, 29; 27:2; 31:8f. etc. They are very few. Most still refer back in some sort of covert fashion to the success one will have, the goal one can attain, the danger he will escape— hence, presupposing implicitly just such an experiential statement. (Cf. 22:6; 23:13f., introduced in 24:12b by means of a direct questioning phrase; 27:10 [if it was originally complete in this form; otherwise, a simple admonition]; 20:22 hidden within a new admonition). The remaining couple of cases, however, where even this hidden presupposition cannot be inferred do not amount to a new type which devolved from the others. Rather, especially since in terms of content they keep entirely within the framework of the other proverbs,[17] we shall interpret them on the basis of the others and may perceive in them simply a shortened form of the expression. In each instance, justification through the experiential should be appended in thought; half has been omitted for sake of brevity. The inner relationship between admonition and saying in Prov undergoes no further shift in these places.

This overview of the formal structure of wisdom discourse now provides clear evidence for the validity of the thesis stated initially: one cannot speak of wisdom commandment in the strict sense. Wisdom admonition lacks authoritative character. Its legitimation does not come about through any appeal to some authority.

Authority can only be conceived of personally. Examination of the form of wisdom discourse has shown that the admonitory saying refers the person who is called upon back to an impersonal experiential statement. Motivation to obey the admonition rests in the application of this experiential rule to the individual.[18]

Authority rules categorically. Counsel is debatable. This was said before in discussing designation of command as counsel. That has been thoroughly confirmed here. When authority governs, its entire interest is that the commanded act and no other occur in that way and no other. The crucial point lies at the formal moment of obedience; beyond that, authority does not reflect at all on the inner relationship between the obedient individual and the content of the command. The admonitory-saying of the wise is entirely different. Here, everything is directed toward man's finding a relationship to the inner sense of the "commandment" in freedom. Hence, it is not the categorical demand for such a realizeable deed and no other, but rather constant clarification of the "precept" through the justification attached. Everything does not depend on the action's being carried out that and no other way, but on acting out of proper reflection (basic reflection on consequences which are set in motion "according to experience"). The crucial point, therefore, lies behind the instruction's wording in the justification, in the experiential clause, which a person should calculate in, which he should consider, and out of reflection upon which he should act. Concrete conduct is set fundamentally free.

This is made exceptionally clear by the section at 26:4/5. "Do not answer the fool according to his folly, so that you be not made like him yourself."—"Answer the fool according to his folly, so that he may not appear wise in his own eyes." As universally applicable precepts, two such immediately juxtaposed yet expressly contradictory instructions as these would be an absurdity. Taken as counsel, the consideration—upon which it principally depends—set forth here has a certain validity in any case. In the concrete individual situation, the reader is left free to decide for the one or the other side.[19]

However paradoxical it may sound, if one thinks of the places which enjoin ·one to drum wisdom into the youth and which esteem the šmᶜ, which one can straightforwardly translate as obey, the sage is nevertheless a person who is free to decide at that moment on the basis of his own reflection, one who is freely "knowing," ·i.e. a man entrusted with the rules of experience.

The answer to the question of the internal legitimation of the wisdom statement insofar that it takes the form of a "command" is given along with the preceding. In its wording, the "precept" contains no authorization; it receives this only by referring back to the clause of common experience which should be intelligible to the person. It is never unconditional, rather always and only a conditional command. Obedience to the precept does not occur for the sake of some personal connection between the preceptor and the one who is addressed. Above all, it is no obedience of will to will. Instead, it is a free disposition of the hearer on the basis of the relationships and principles pointed out to him.

III

The investigation of the wisdom admonitions of Proverbs has resulted in the finding that they already reflect in their external form a characteristic deficiency in authority. None of the admonitions is firm, each succumbs to pressure and pulls back to the justification which stands behind it (saying-form which contains an experiential clause). This finding is, from the outset, not very propitious for the contention that the "central question" of wisdom grows out of a primary knowledge and recognition of a fixed order.

Here, however, we must go beyond the common basic assertion and look at the material more precisely. The reference to fixed orders upon which the "dependency" of human existence is based could certainly be concealed within the general statements and experiential rules which the "aphorisms" of Proverbs proffer; so that one can merely speak of an inadequacy of Proverbs' expressive form. An example makes this clear.[20] To the precepts, "fear Yahweh and desist from evil" (3:7b), "honor Yahweh out of your possessions" (3:9a), "trust in Yahweh with all your heart . . ., in all your ways acknowledge him" (3:5f.), the justification could follow, "because he is your creator," or "because you are his creation and such has he commanded you." Then, the proposed thesis would be untenable. Instead of that however, the justifications read (attached here in the form of a consequence in a future final-clause—the whole character of wisdom permits us actually to speak of a justification here; cf. II), "it will be healing to your body" (read lš'rk) and tonic to your bones" (3:8 to 3:7), "your granaries will be filled with grain (thus G; MT "with satisfaction") and your wine presses will overflow with new wine" (3:10 to 3:9), "he will smooth your ways" (3:6b to 3:5, 6a). One could multiply the examples which show that in exactly those places where we most expect some reference to a fixed order and authority by reference to Yahweh as the justification to an admonition, we do not find the creative, ordering God, but rather the God who rewards in the consequence of man's upright conduct (conversely, punishing the fools and the godless) therefore who gratifies human wishes (cf. 8:35 or perhaps even the second halves of verses 3:32, 33 which sound so unconditionally authoritative in their first halves). The preceding examples from chs. 1-9—the most recent, most religiously animated collection which presents the most highly developed sayings (God and wisdom) and which is very obviously preferred to the other collections as an interpretative canon—are instructive for the understanding of the religious admonitions. We are justified in interpreting the quite laconic and therefore ambiguous sayings of chs. 10ff. which are in the short mashal form on the basis of the explicit sayings in chs. 1-9.

"Whoever derides the poor slanders his Creator" (17:5), "an abomination for Yahweh are different weighing stones and a deceptive scale is not good" (20:23), "an abomination for Yahweh are men with base hearts, but his pleasure are those who walk blamelessly" (11:20). Statements like the preceding, which occur repeatedly (cf. as well 11:1; 12:22; 15:8, 9; 16:5; 17:15; 20:10) seem quite unequivocally to confirm the subjugation of everyday existence to God and to demonstrate the original theocentric orientation of the wise's sayings in that they denote obedience to God's commands as rṣwn and disobedience as twᶜbt yhwh.[21] Is it also true, however, that we should group all further statements of the wise about this center and on that basis interpret them as admonitions which would bring the divine orders of the world (compassion, due moderation, irreproachable ways etc.) into their own for the sake of the God who ordained them? So that in twᶜbt- or rswn-yhwh, the ultimate and most profound motives which determine the wise's conduct should be acknowledged? The finding from Proverbs 1-9 advises us not to infer the answer to the question of the relationship of the wise to God from these sayings. A group of sayings—also rather more numerous—leads to another answer to the question. Aphorisms like 12:2, "a good man obtains favor (rṣwn) from Yahweh," and 18:22, "whoever has found a wife has found good and obtains favor (rṣwn) from Yahweh," already show a shift within the word rṣwn. rṣwn yhwh steps out of the theocentric orientation which it possessed in the earlier examples into man's intelligibility and valuation. "Pleasing to God", which bore absolute character in theocentric consideration, becomes in human perspective a "very great value,"[22] with which man reckons and which he regards as something he "receives" from God (wypq 8:35; 12:2; 18:22), which at 11:27 has obviously already been completely separated from God and become an individual value among other values—"whoever seeks good (perhaps to be emended with G to ḥrš devises) finds favor" (cf. also 8:35 rṣwn myhwh parallel to ḥyym (see below), 18:22 parallel to ṭwb-something good).[23]

This same twist which the word rṣwn shows here appears in the greater part of those proverbs which speak of the relationship to God. 10:3, "Yahweh does not let the upright hunger." 10:22, "Yahweh's blessing makes rich." 14:26, "in the fear of Yahweh is strong assurance." 14:27, "the fear of Yahweh is a fountain of life" (cf. 10:27; 19:23). 22:4, "the reward of humility and the fear of Yahweh (read wyr't yhwh, cf. BHK) is riches and honor and life." In no way is the transcendent position of God infringed upon; the creative might of Yahweh is all the more often stressed (see above). However, Yahweh, the fear of Yahweh and the blessing of Yahweh are not ultimate, insubstantiable dimensions which a person confronts in a final decision, beyond any further analysis, when he seeks to understand his life. They are given immediacy for him; the decision for or against is obviated through mediate concepts like satisfaction, riches, life, assurance, honor (see below). Without going into these dimensions further at this point (see below [Section VI]), one thing is nevertheless confirmed: these are ideas which are entirely oriented toward man and his individual possibilities in existence. The man-based perspective becomes clear through them. These mediating concepts should seize man; here man is spoken to in terms of his fundamental question; on the basis of this, he is moved to action.[24]

Wisdom does not intend the totally Incalculable by its concepts of God, which appears wherever the notion of God is earnestly viewed as that of the Lord and Creator, but rather the calculable side with respect to which man can "conduct" himself, where he can bring forward his question and get a response. God is seen from man's viewpoint, and his conduct (drk yhwh 10:29) is evaluated against the worth that it can have for man—to state it rather crassly.

Even the warmly religious sayings which already resonate with other tones that later sayings still more strongly emphasize should not obscure the fact that this basic structural pattern is not given up with the biblical Proverbs. Even 16:3, "commit (or, with S T V, reveal) your works to Yahweh" (the verse is omitted in G, though), continues, "then will your plans be established." Or 20:22b, "wait for Yahweh, he will help you" (on chs. 1-9, see above). And one must understand in the preceding sense places which may also bear interpretation in the sense of defenselessness before God, according to which God as Lord actually has the first word and would not be some factor in a calculation based in human interest. 21:31, "a horse is made ready for the day of battle, but in Yahweh lies the outcome (tšwᶜh)." Even here, there is still talk of tᵉsuᶜah (cf. 16:20; 19:14, 21). And even 21:2, 30 cannot be raised above this restriction. They, too, are not meant in that radical way which would destroy the human position. That a boundary has admittedly been reached in these verses is clear.

The conclusion which is significant for Israelite circumstances stands,

that the obvious reference to the Creator's authority does not follow as
the express justification for sayings which deal with man's conduct with
respect to Yahweh, but instead they appeal to man's interest in a veiled
form as the ultimately decisive factor. As a result, the concept of man's
creaturely subjection cannot stand structurally at the beginning.

IV

In the very sayings concerning the relationship to God where we most
expected to come across the primary acknowledgement of a supra-indi-
vidual determination by a higher authority, the absence of any such
authority turned up. Even the justificatory clauses in the admonitions
(aphorisms) lack any conclusive appeal to a fixed order and are oriented
toward the individual I and its advantage.

This inner structure of the wisdom saying can be illuminated from
another side. There is a very popular form of indirect admonition that
recurs often throughout Proverbs and Qoheleth which introduces with the
word ṭwb what is represented as valuable and worth striving for. In and
of itself, this ṭwb is, to begin with, open to interpretation from both sides.
Should a greater number of verses appear like 18:5, s't pny rs⁰ l' ṭwb (cf.
20:23 or 24:23-28:21)—the designation of man as lpny h'lhym ṭwb or
lpnyw 7:26; 2:26 which occurs twice in Qoheleth also belongs here—so
that one could identify in them a type of wisdom saying, then a thorough-
going examination must begin here whether such an arrangement of the
good and not good, simply asserted or justified by reference back to the
deity, does not tacitly refer back to the basic presupposition of a binding
order.

Now, however, quite another connection is characteristic for these ṭwb-
sayings. "Better little in piety than great riches in uncertainty (unrest),"
15:16. "Better a table with herbs in love, than a fatted ox with hate,"
15:17 (cf. 3:14; 8:11, 19; 12:9; 16:8, 16, 19, 32; 17:1; 19:1, 22; 21:9,
19; 25:7, 24; 27:5, 10; 28:6). "Better a handful in peace than both
handsful in affliction and straining after wind," Qoh 4:6 (cf. esp. 7:1, 2,
3, 5, 8 [twice], 11 emended text etc.—17 times in all).[25]

Thereafter, the other form of the ṭwb-saying developed as the archetype
of that mashal in which good and better are weighed against each other
in both stichoi.[26] Here it is not significant that these were soon applied in
the realm of what to our minds is the morally neutral (25:7) or in the
ethical (19:1).[27] What is decisive is that wisdom could have developed
this type of mashal out of itself. Consequently, one would expect it to

show the structural impress of wisdom especially clearly. Accordingly, there must be a weighing off of good and better; the setting up of a scale of value is the form of speech concerning the good—we might better say concerning what appears valuable to it—appropriate to wisdom. This gradation of good and better, however, contradicts an idea of the good which norms itself on some authoritative standard.

Wherever sure determinations stand at the beginning, good and evil are always somehow bound up with obedience and disobedience. But obedience and disobedience are absolute antitheses which tolerate no relativization. A structure which proceeds from the acknowledgement of determined orders would not develop out of itself as the archetype of its saying the form of weighing and relative comparison.

On what, however is ṭwb normed if the ṭwb lpny h'lhym (to employ generally the formulation which, to be sure, in Qoh 7:26 is applied to man) is rejected as not distinctive of the structure of wisdom?

Insofar as we respond to this question, we arrive once more at the point from which we departed, at Qoheleth's formulation mh ṭwb l'dm bḥyym, 6:12. This formulation can be taken here in terms of a profounder understanding; it must converge with what has just preceded. When the point toward which the ṭwb is directed—in the question of the individual elemental values of life (esp. so in Proverbs) as well as in the comprehensive conception of Qoheleth where the question mh twb, mh ytrwn is directed toward the whole life—is recognized as man, then that irresistibly fits together with the prevailing knowledge which admits of increase and decrease.

A ṭwb which is normed on an order which overarches man and binds him to obligation will necessarily bear an absolute character. A ṭwb which is oriented about man himself and his personal inclinations in the same way can have no absolute character from internal necessity; it will necessarily admit a greater and a lesser.

That gives us the right to find in the (ṭwb) l'dm, which often recurs in Qoheleth[28] but which is never so expressly formulated in Proverbs, the word which resolves the wisdom sayings of both works.

Everywhere there is talk of ṭwb (ṭwbh) and where values and strengths in life (bḥyym Qoh 6:12) are identified, compared and evaluated, we may expand the correlative point as (ṭwb) l'dm. That is the basic question of wisdom, that out of this more or less implicit central point, free, unbound and self-determining man should scrutinize his life and world according to their possibilities—not according to duties, but rather first and foremost according to their possibilities.

V

What has been called heretofore wisdom's "central way of putting the question" solely on the basis of its formal relationship can now be expanded, however, in terms of its lineaments of content without great difficulty.

For the wise, it is a question of man and his possibilties in the world. In its most basic form, the question may be formulated as, "How do I as man secure my existence?"

This question is easily heard as a starting point to some meshalim. With what warm sympathy does 3:23f. depict this "assurance of the wise." "Then will you go your way in confidence and your foot will not stumble, when you sit (MT lie down) you will not be overtaken by fear (on phd, see below), when you lie down your sleep will be pleasant" (cf. also hlk bth 10:9; škn bth 1:33; bth "be secure" used absolutely 11:15; 28:1; mbth ʿz 14:26). Even the warnings against false security (14:16; bth blbw 28:26; ʿz mbthh 21:22) are intended as preparation for the proper confidence. Piety is esteemed as the proper "stronghold" of man (sgb 18:11; 29:25). The origins of welfare and peace (šlwm 3:2, 17), help (tšwʿh or yšʿ 11:14; 21:31; 24:6; 20:22; 28:18), shelter (mhsh 14:26) are investigated and penetratingly laid out—what actually has permanence (the house of the righteous has permanence ʿmd 12:7; cf. also 27:4; 29:4; kwn 4:26; 12:3; 16:3, 12; 24:3; 25:5; qwm 15:22; 19:21; (24:16 see Qoh 4:10)), eternal permanence indeed (kwn lʿd 12:19; 29:14; yšwd ʿlm 10:25; cf. 10:30). Not in the sense of orders to which man is subordinate, but in the sense of possibilities according to which man comprehends in free choice, to which he can conform in the interest of his own security.

Death stands as a dark boundary on the edge of all human existence. Therefore, we should not be surprised to come upon mention of this opponent even in wisdom, and to hear hidden in back of some wisdom sayings the question, "How do I preserve my existence in the face of death?"

Ever anew, a wild profusion of sayings betray this innermost visage. In the first collection, chs. 1-9, association with the harlot is above all depicted as the way to death (2:18; 5:5, 23; 7:27). By reference to the risk of death, more general sayings counsel against derelictions of the wisdom admonition (8:36; 13:14; 15:10; 19:16), of righteousness (12:28 emended text, cf. BHK; 10:2; 11:4, 19), of the fear of God (14:27). Unjust profit (21:6 emended text, cf. BHK), royal displeasure (16:14 in a pale use of the image of the angel of death), indeed even offenses of the tongue (18:21) and sloth (21:25) can bring about death.

In place of dying, a variety of expressions mention being killed (hrg 1:32; 7:26), perishing ('bd 1:32; 11:10; 19:9; 21:28; 28:28, occasionally in connection with tqwh 10:28; 11:7), being rooted out (nkrt 2:22 parallel to yšḥw; 10:31; in connection with tqwh 23:18; 24:14). Or, they speak of endangering the npš (1:19; 6:32; 8:36; 29:24); death the adversary is picturesquely described as the place of shadows (2:18; 9:18; qhl rp'ym 21:16), as the insatiable (27:20; 30:16 corrected text), the life-devouring (1:12) š'l (punishment for concourse with the harlot 5:5; 7:27, for folly 9:18; 15:24; and for inexperience 23:14); dying is shown as extinguishing the lamp (13:9; 20:20; 24:20; cf. Qoh 11:8 "days of darkness").

Now, it should be noted that all these sayings do not mean death as a necessary fate (Qoh 3:2 ᶜt lmwt), but intend premature death[29] as reaction brought about by human conduct (Qoh 7:17 lmh tmwt bl' ᶜtk). Death is one element within the broad answer to human activity which operates principally through the law of retribution, which is elsewhere depicted, without explicit mention of death, as the misfortune which suddenly befalls one ('yd 1:26f.; 6:15 pt'm ybw', see 24:22; 27:10), sudden terror (pḥd pt'm 3:25; pḥd rᶜh 1:33), the day of wrath[30] (11:4, see v. 23; 16:4 ywm rᶜh, cf. Qoh 9:12). The disaster which suddenly befalls one and which is variously described as terror (mḥth 13:3 *et passim*), stumbling (ksl noun 16:18; verb 4:19; 24:16), tottering (mwt 10:30; 12:3), falling (npl 11:5, 14, 28; 17:20; 28:10, 14, 18), being shattered (nšbr 6:15; 29:1) and being taken captive (nlbt 10:8) in the snare and the grave (mwqš (lnpš) 22:25; 29:25, swḥh 22:14; 23:27; cf. šḥt 26:27) moreover includes a series of other misfortunes which betake man, like disgrace (6:33 ngᶜ wqlwn . . . hrph and as an amplication of the preceding (v. 32) mšḥyt npšw), scorn (bwz 18:3 along with qlwn . . . hrpp), poverty (13:18) and want (28:22). Among these destroyers of human fortune, death is to be understood as the epitome of misfortune. And, just as human misfortune can be avoided through man's proper conduct, so this death can be avoided.

It is worthwhile to clarify the distinctiveness of this interpretation of death completely. Death is neither that which burdens every human life with complete dubeity nor the inevitable barrier which is set against every human being as the ultimate and ineluctable peril; instead, even the notion of death is apprehended within the network of calculation. It is divested of its incalculability because only that segment is seen which man can control by means of his conduct. Its final keenness is taken away from it since this ponderable segment, by means of the concept of retribution, becomes a dimension at man's disposition.

The objection will be raised here that peaceful acceptance of natural death in old age is particularly characteristic of OT thought, so that a common OT theme appears here that occurs every bit as much in prophetic and legal piety. But, "when two say the same, they still don't say the same thing." This conception of death acquires a specific meaning purely within the structural context of wisdom.

In the context of a self-understanding which interprets man's life in terms of God in one's limited determinacy and creatureliness, this understanding of death fits in without difficulty. Even man's death is just an expression of this sort of determinacy, and is a point at which man's specific inner being becomes apparent.[31] On the other hand, where, as in wisdom, life is understood on the basis of the man who seeks security for himself, death must be by far the most disruptive element. If the concept of man's security is thought through radically to its end, in the way wisdom lays it out, then it must butt against this barrier.

In Qoheleth, we have this situation before us. Qoheleth, who thinks through to the end wisdom's way of putting the question much more decisively and more courageously, must confront this adversary death.

True, even with him, we still come upon much customary, traditional wisdom material[32] as well as finding the familiar prudently-moderated representation of death found in normative wisdom. Avoidable death, against which one is warned in 7:16f. as being the consequence of all-too-great righteousness and wisdom—as well as all-too-great unrighteousness and folly—is clearly distinguished within Qoheleth's own sharper formulation, lmh tmwt bl' ᶜtk (7.17; cf. 7:15 'bd). But this admonition, which contrasts with Proverbs' admonitions particularly in the greater clarity of thought, but not in content, does not comprise Qoheleth's completely distinctive radical consideration of death.

Rather, this comes through in other places. In the context of the pessimistic (v. 9) accounting in 3:1-9, 3:2 gives voice to the painfully-perceived inevitability of dying: birth has its time, death has its time.[33] And, the clearly-confessed collapse of the wise's understanding of life, according to which human life can be secured, according to which two groups of people, wise or fool, differ from one another in the fact that the wise man is skilled in this security while the fool is not—the collapse of this understanding of life is admitted in 2:16, "how the wise man along with the fool," cf. 9:3. Or, applied somewhat differently, this knowledge of the limitation of all human wisdom through reality of death is expressed in 2:18f. (the impotence over the question of succession, "who knows whether he [the successor] will be a wise man or a fool.").

Here, in terms of a certain suffering for an honest view of life, the great adversary has hoved into the field of view, before which the self-understanding of the wise must break down, where it changes into a new understanding of life (cf. the reversion to the theocentric life-understanding in the Book of Job when met with reality experienced in its unintelligibility, as suffering),[34] when it does not wish to prolong its life in the resigned-broken attitude of a Qoheleth.

If the view is traced back from here to the normative wisdom sayings of Proverbs, then we find the attitude identified initially confirmed anew in their orientation to the problem of death. Not only is the pursuit of man's security revealed in the way death is observed and all means are sought-out to overcome it, but directly within the treatment of the concept of death itself, the wise man has already secured himself before venturing into the danger-zone of this concept. By tacit agreement, death only comes as far into the field of view as it is amenable to calculation. The wise speak only of the "when" of death; the "what" of death is glossed over[35]; because, wherever a wise man should happen to overstep the constantly stressed rule of security, *mēden agan* (see esp. Qoh 7:16f.), with a radical way of putting the question, there he falls into the abyss of this conception.

VI

In its negative form, the question of security—the central question on the basis of which the wise man arranged his life—may be stated thus, "How do I keep myself from misfortune, especially from premature death?" The positive way of formulating the "security question" of the wise results from a simple change of sign, "How do I improve my existence through life and good fortune?" Just as in the former misfortune and death are internally co-ordinated with one another, so in the latter are good fortune and life.[36]

Human good fortune, more exactly described as riches (c̆sr 3:16; 22:4 *et passim;* hwn 8:18; 'ṣrt 8:21 *et passim*), satiation (see the frequent appearance of the verb sb^c; šqwy 3:8), health and healing (rp'wt 3:8; mrp' 4:22; 13:17; 16:24; 29:1), joy (noun and verb smḥ 10:28; 29:2, 3 *et passim*), honor (very frequent), peace (šlwh 17:1; see nwḥ 29:17) etc., finds its pinnacle in long life. "An honorable crown is gray hair," 16:31; see 20:29. So greatly does life (ḥyym) stand out as the highest form of good fortune, that it has already been straightforwardly proposed to translate ḥyym simply with fortune (Baudissin, *Festschrift Eduard Sachau*, Berlin 1915, pp. 143ff., "ATliches ḥajjim 'Leben' in der Bedeutung von 'Glück' "). Actually, for some places in Proverbs, this translation would be quite satisfactory, but it is discouraged by the fact that then the fundamental relationship to the concept of life, which is quite distinctive of OT perception, would be missing.[37] Further, the uniqueness of this concept is to be described analogously to the concept of death.

Places like 10:30 ("the upright will not waver into eternity"), together with the utilization of the mythological images of the tree of life (3:18; 11:30; 13:12; 15:4) and the fountain of life (10:11; 13:14; 14:27; 16:22) which certainly intended the radical question of eternal life free from death in their mythological origins,[38] admittedly may suggest that the radically-put question of life be found within wisdom. Even here, however, the striking fact is simply confirmed that while the question of life is put quite at the center and mythological images of life are taken over, still the mythos' question of eternal life—which actually would have to be asked with greater urgency by a wisdom with so clearly an anthropocentrically-oriented attitude (see the analogous explanations on the question of death above [Section V])—is merely filled out from an optimistic disposition. Just like the concept of death here the question of life within the normative wisdom of Proverbs is obscured at its dangerous points out of an instinctive caution, even though within mythos whose imagistic language has been taken over it is fully stated, even though wisdom's point of departure, the question "how do I make myself secure?" would seem to demand the taking-over of the unaltered question. By means of this diminution, the "life" question is rendered harmless; "life" can now be talked about quite emphatically; time-limited life is now at one's disposal (by means of the law of retribution)[39]; one knows the "way to life" ('rḥ[wt 1]ḥyym 2:19; 5:6; 10:17; 15:24; drk ḥyym 6:23), points of departure for life (twṣ'wt ḥyym 4:23), and knows how the number of life's years (šnwt ḥyym 3:2; 4:10; 9:11) and the length of one's days ('rk ymym 3:2, 16; 28:16; see the presupposed positive wisdom sayings in Qoh 7:15; 8:12f.) are to be attained.[40]

Through Qoheleth, who displays the resultant break-down of the concept, it becomes possible to test the validity of this interpretation of the conception of life in wisdom. It must immediately be apparent that, for him, any emphatic application of the idea of life is totally lacking. The fact, obvious even to him, that a man reaches an advanced and fortunate old age—which Proverbs usually esteems emphatically as ḥyym—is only described by Qoheleth in the restrained terms 'ryk (ymym), 7:15; 8:12f. That is no coincidence. The use of the word ḥyym which repeatedly recurs (2:3, 17; 3:12; 5:17, 19; 6:12 [twice]; 8:15; 9:3, 9 [three times]) clarifies this. While Proverbs perceives ḥyym as riches, blessing and good fortune, as growth and expansion, it is exactly the reverse in Qoheleth. Even the adjective ḥy (in Proverbs, only at 1:12 in the context of a metaphor) does not mean one liberated from confinement into freedom, but one determined to die, and is best translated by "mortal." 4:2, "the dead and the living who still (ᶜdnh) live." 7:2, "(in the house mourning) the living take it (death) to heart." And 9:4, where, clearly, life seems to be immediately confronted with death ("better a living dog than a dead lion"), goes on, "because the living know that they must die" (v. 5).[41] And in quite the same way, "life," wherever it is discussed, is perceived as restriction and limitation which makes human existence hopeless. One need only look at the outward expression. Even this is directed toward laying out the hopeless narrowness which is an immediate part of life. Hence, man's life is rather circumspectly rendered, in plerophorism, "the (limited) number of the days of their (his) lives" 2:3; 5:17, or in the same sense "the days of his life" 5:19[42]; 8:13[43].

6:12 is quite significant, where the word "life" slips by Qoheleth without any qualification ("who knows what is good for man in life?"), and he then immediately counters any misunderstanding through the addendum which follows (viz. "in the number of the days of his vacuous life, which he passes like a shadow" mšpr ymy ḥy hblw, so also 9:9 kl ymy ḥyy hblk and 7:15 ymy hbly). One cannot speak more plainly than in this double placement of accents: numbered, vacuous. And the accent, destined to die, in 9:3 is put on the word "life," "the heart of the children of men is full of evil, and folly is in their hearts in their lifetime and their end (thus reading according to Σ, cf. BHK) is with the dead." Thus, Qoheleth can arrive at the, for the—thought-world of wisdom—unheard-of saying, "therefore, I hated life," 2:17.

It has always been a vexation, and given rise to many source-analyses, that Qoheleth took over so much traditional wisdom material into his "instruction" along with that of his own disposition. Even in the course of investigating his concept of death, we came up against the traditional consideration of death next to Qoheleth's own particular position. Therefore, it is highly instructive that we find utterly no evidence of the customary view of life which one would certainly expect to be mentioned because it is everywhere so important. It is meticulously suppressed by Qoheleth. Here, therefore, we have to acknowledge a limit to the taking over of traditional materials. So many sayings which otherwise stand in tension with Qoheleth's other opinions are still taken over, yet Qoheleth cannot speak of "life" in the old way. Therein lies an indirect reference to the central position which the concept of life holds in wisdom. This life which is the greatest human security as wisdom teaches it here is revealed to be an illusion through the radical questioning of Qoheleth. Not only is it incalculable for man (collapse of the world's rationality and the law of retribution), but it is above all unattainable for man. Not only is the modus of life's apportionment missing (how is life apportioned?), but the tacit presupposition completely carried through in Proverbs that man's existence in "life" is above all assurable collapses in the discovery that life is not breadth, increase and security, but rather barrier, way to death and peril.

At this juncture, out of Qoheleth's sayings concerning "life," we must look back one more time. Viz. in Qoheleth, we come up against sayings like 5:17 where it is said of life (the number of the days of life) that God has given them. Or 8:15, where it talks of "the days of his life that God has given him under the sun." In the same way, 12:7 belongs here, "the spirit (= life) returns to God who gave it." [44] These places, together with others like 1:13; 3:10; (hᶜnyn 'šr ntn 'lhym; ᶜnyn rᶜ ntn 'lhym)[45], compel us to state the question quite earnestly here at the end of the road: Does not knowledge of this God-established human existence still stand as the operative point of departure for Qoheleth wholly at the center of his disposition toward life? Does he not reckon from the very beginning on with this divine determination of life tht hšmš; therefore, is it not also permissible here to speak of a radically anthropocentric self-understanding? Has not the circumscription been realized here at the end, that man interprets his life on the basis of creaturely obligation?[46]—So that the fear of God (5:6; 7:18; 8:12f.) is to be understood as the simple articulation of a self-understanding that is fundamental (Odeberg). It is important not to gloss over this question because on it depends the entire self-understanding of wisdom heretofore laid out.

Qoheleth "acknowledges" the divine-determinedness of all existence, stressing with great clarity that it takes away man's discretion. But even though this is so centrally important to him, his innermost disposition is not based on the "recognition" of this fact. At base, Qoheleth rebels against this fact; that he finally acquiesces and that his instructions contain the recognition of this situation, admonition to the fear of Yahweh, cannot detract from this innermost point of origin. A man whose life-understanding started out with the "acknowledgement" of the God-determinedness of existence, could not place this which is given by God (2:24 myd h'lhym hy'; 2:26 wlḥṭ' ntn ᶜnyn . . . l'dm stwb lpnyw ntn ḥkmh) under judgment (gm zh hbl" 2:26). 2:24-26 is only the clearest formulation of what lies throughout the entire book: the extreme formulation of all of life, together with Qoheleth's solution—this formulation Qoheleth never ventures—together with the fear of God is hbl wrᶜwt rwḥ. That all of life can be placed under judgment in this way—indeed, in a place where its divine facticity is specifically stressed—reveals that Qoheleth's ultimate criterion is something quite different from divine facticity and the fulfillment of the duty implicit in this God-determinedness: it is the criterion of mh ytrwn l'dm. Only in this way is his pessimistic and negativistic attitude explicable. In the precept of the fear of God there does not lie a joyfully affirming volition which flows from man's innermost self-understanding, but rather the instruction, founded on the basis of an understanding of the world, toward conduct most conducive to human fortune. The following would lie in the direct line of Qoheleth, "curse God (who has given you all of existence' affliction and the confinement of life) and die" (Job's wife Job 2:9). But because Qoheleth does not wish to die, or at least wants to defer death as long as possible (lmh tmwt bl' ᶜtk 7:17), he is forced to traverse the way of the fear of Yahweh.[47]

Qoheleth senses in the world's divine conditioning the irrational, incalculable hard boundary of his will to life. The conflict between both dimensions (divine determination and human life-will) makes it quite evident that Qoheleth's own striving originates somewhere else than in divine order. This conviction is far less apparent in Proverbs, where both dimensions intermingle harmoniously and without conflict. This harmonious and unconflicting intermingling, however, is the hallmark of normative wisdom (just as much in Egypt as in Israel). Our description, which has endeavored to preserve wisdom's vitally important anthropocentric-eudämonistic point of departure which also manifested this importance in the case where conflict arose, could clearly only have carried this through against the contradictory background of thinking tightly oriented around God; within such an orientation, there is no place for human fortune. But it would leave behind a false impression if it were not also stressed in conclusion, quite emphatically, that this antithesis did not exist in the consciousness of the wise.

The wise man perceives no separation between his attitude and the divine conditioning of the world. God's claims need not be called into conflict with those of man. Rather, it is his belief that man's requirements in life are best cared for within the divine order of the world, and that man's real claim on advantage will be entirely satisfied through willing participation in the world's divine ordering. Even God comes into his own when man pursues his fortune (along the right path). And so vice versa, even man comes to his good fortune the best and surest if he fears God.

VII

The formulation of the question in terms of which the wise man gains practical mastery over his life has, in its basic outline, been laid out.

A more extensive description would now have to educe the answer the wise man finds.

As a result, it would once again have to show the uniquely rational violation of the whole of reality which became clear to us in terms of his conceptions of God, and of death and life. The wise man approaches, not only these dimensions, but the entire world with the claim that he comprehends it in the intelligible laws of its operation. Thus, for the wise man, the whole world arranges itself into a scale of value within which every entity has its place, from the immensity of God who is acknowledged as the highest value (even God's inscrutability is so ordered in e.g. 16:33; 20:24; just the same as the king's calculability is figured in 25:3) down to the minute values of good fortune belonging to petty life (joy, satisfaction, happy countenance etc.). Therefore, it is the wise man's business to have this scale of values readily at hand.

Further, it would set out the rules which the wise man has recognized in the course of events; it would have to show their diversity and inner dissimilarity, from the outward rules by which success is regulated up to the statement of proper retribution. Within OT normative wisdom, it would have to show how the doctrine of retribution attained such a dominant position that it breaks every other rule. When a secular experiential rule (e.g., riches are power) competes with the moral retributive rule, the moral rule of retribution wins in every instance (concerning the significance of the distinction between "moral" and "secular" rules, see above, n. 27). Only the rules of success through moderation and of restraint can sporadically maintain preferential positions for themselves (e.g. in the question of surety, or Qoheleth's moderation of righteousness etc. 7:16ff.).

It would have to point up to the naive optimism and the unhistorical approach to life as necessary emanations from this basic rationalistic attitude.

Finally, it would portray man as he is re-formed in reaction to this conception of the world: the wise man in his exalted consciousness of power which is conveyed to him in wisdom as the capacity to comprehend and assess the world, and the pointedly religious veneration which he finally (1-9) offers to this wisdom according to which humanity is divided into two groups for him, the wise and the fools. It would have to describe the imperceptible transition from wise man into righteous (fool into the unrighteous man) that goes hand in hand with the exalted position of the moral retributive law.

I must content myself, however, with these few references.
(Completed 1 August 1933)

NOTES

[1] The normative form of the wisdom teaching, whose purest exemplar is found in the Solomonic book of aphorisms (abbr. Prov), forms the basis of the following analysis. Closely related to it is the "instruction" of Qoheleth (abbr. Qoh), which still has distinctively individual features. It is extensively relied upon in what follows, while the formally more remote Book of Job is referred to only very occasionally. The greater number of quotations are from Prov; for those from Qoh etc. the Book is specifically mentioned in the citation.

[2] By which is meant that within the colorful diversity of individual proverbs, a unified understanding of life is nevertheless expressed. The question deals with this ultimate unity.

[3] At least for the overwhelming majority of their sayings; the beginnings of a problematic attitude appear e.g. in 30:1ff.

[4] The wise's orientation to the question becomes especially clear if we accept Hertzberg's correction within 10:10b (Der Prediger, 1932; KAT XVI 4): hakiš-ron wyitron. While in 5:10, there is the simple substitution of the synonym kišrōn for yitrōn (mh kišrōn 1"), here we would have intensification through a doubling of the expression (but, admittedly, Frankenberg, Podechard).

[5] For Qoh, one might best ask whether, in the way the question is put here, knowledge of man's limiting "determinedness" already makes itself felt— here admittedly in the antithesis between God and man's impotence and limitedness in the face of his unrelatedness to God's plans. Cf., e.g., Odeberg's conception of the tḥt hšmš (Hugo Odeberg, Qohaelaeth: a Commentary on the Book of Ecclesiastes, Uppsala 1929: "sublunar world," the world of limitation is known in its determination by God; in the recognition of his insignificance as part of the divine order, man finds access to the "better life." The meaning of life "self-evidently centres in God" (92). "God is the centre of his life" (93). In spite of the pessimistic shift, one can still recognize the original normative orientation to the question of wisdom even here. This will be demonstrated below in detail. See esp. [Section VI].

[6] Cf. R. Anthes, Lebensregeln und Lebensweisheit der alten Ägypter, 1933 (AO 32, 2). On the wisdom of the Old Kingdom: . . . Basic tone of the instruction: Be submissive, do not put yourself in opposition to the order, thus will you get ahead (p. 13). This eudämonistic feature also characterized all the Egyptian wisdom literature which followed (this is not made clear enough in Anthes who principally notes the increasing differentiation and ethicizing). The Instruction of Amenemope still purposes "to guide rightly on the way of life and keep him (the person) sound . . . on earth (title) and "bring luck" (Ch. 1 according to Erman, OLZ XXVII (1924), col. 242). Cf. also L. Dürr, Das Erziehungswesen im Alten Testament und im antiken Orient (MVAG 36, 2), 1932, p. 48ff.

[7] The places in question have been dealt with by Fichtner (*Die altorientalische Weisheit in ihrer israelitisch-jüdischen Ausprägung, BZAW* 62, 1933), pp. 82ff. Fichtner covers the interpretation of torah and miṣwah in Prov and Qoh by "wisdom-instruction" and "wisdom-command." The appearance of dabar, also dealt with by Fichtner in the same work, leads to terminological contact with the no-less "authoritative" prophetic word. For the word of wisdom going about in the dress of prophetic authority, reference is principally made to 1:20ff., which appears to have the literary form of a rebuke or threat. (For this sort of element in Sirach, see Baumgartner, *ZAW* 34 (1914), pp. 186ff.

[8] Just as in the Egyptian wisdom. (P. Humbert, Recherches sur les sources égyptiennes de la littérature sapientiale d'Israël, 1929, pp. 35f., 69f.)

[9] Erman-Ranke, *Ägypten und ägyptisches Leben in Altertum*, 1923, pp. 374ff. Dürr, *Erziehungswesen*, pp. 20ff. (For Assyro-Babylonian, cf. pp. 71ff.)

[10] Cited from Gressmann, *AOTB²* (Texts, p. 457). Reference should be made here to the frequent appearance of the word mwśr which can occasionally become an exact synonym for ḥkmh when used absolutely (5:23 antithetically parallel to 'wlt). yśr is the word which is used to designate corporal punishment (1 K 12: 11, 14). The root ykḥ is similarly used (twkḥt).

[11] This is meant literally. However much wisdom most highly esteemed the fear of God and however often the twᶜbt yhwh is introduced as sufficient basis for observance of a prohibition and rṣwn yhwh for obedience to a command, a clear formulation of the command of wisdom as command of God never appears, in sharp contrast to the Law and the prophets. That betrays an unspoken recognition of the difference between God's (Yahweh's) word and the word of wisdom.

[12] One could add Qoh 5:1, 3f. as an especially typical example—because it deals in particular with conduct toward the deity. An instructive example as well because it has an exact parallel in the Law at Dt 23:22-24; a comparison of the diction in both locations is quite informative as to the nature of both complexes. Qoh 5:3a verbatim like Dt 23:22a. Then, however, the justification of the command: In Dt, the absolute saying, claim of God, sin, totalities ultimately normed to God's will; for Qoheleth, the softened "no pleasure is in the fool" (hence no pay as well) and then the relative, not absolutely qualified ṭwb-saying (see below, [Section IV]).

[13] Both expressions appear in this sense only in 1-9: mzmh 1:4; 2:11; 3:21; plur. in 5:2; 8:12; ᶜrmh 1:4; 8:5, 12. mzmh is used in Prov 10ff. only in the customary sense of 'yś (or, bᶜl mzmwt), 12:2; 14:17; 24:8. Cf. also the LXX translation where ᶜrmh is given by panourgia; the Vulgate uses astutia in 1:4; 8:5.

[14] "Art of navigation(?)" (Frankenberg on 1:5). Keeping the metaphor, we could relieve the ambiguity of the expression by rendering it, "art of tacking." The translation "art of navigation" is suggested by the LXX which translates

1:5; 24:6 (20:18 is omitted in LXX) kubernesis, 12:5 kurebneo. The hypo-thesis that the Greek translation, indigenously Egyptian, thus worked out of living tradition is strengthened especially by the fact that we often find the topics of sailing, pilots, steersman and proper navigation in Amenemope. Title: Instruction . . . to steer the heart away from the evil (cf. chs. 2,7,9,11,29); 18: . . . Man's tongue is (indeed) the helmsman of (his) ship, though the Lord of All is his pilot. 26: A pilot who keeps watch from afar, who does not let his ship founder (according to Erman, *OLZ*). Since this topic otherwise does not appear in Prov, one might with some justice find it tacit within tḥblwt.

¹⁵ K: halok et-ḥokamim waḥᵃkam. Q: holek et-ḥakamim yiḥᵉkkam. So also S T V. G^B(N) reads sumporeuomenos sophsis sophos ese. G^N*(second red. from the 7th. cent.)A gives somporeuomenos . . . estai. The earliest G therefore had the irre-concileable text hwlk wḥkm before him, which now leads to the question which of the words has undergone corruption. A look at the parallel half of the verse wrᶜh ksᵛylym yrwᶜ and comparison with the rest of Prov leads me to the position that wḥkm should originally have read yḥkm. (Contra BHK [the fol-lowing citations are always to the second edition], Kautzsch⁴ [Steuernagel], with Frankenberg.)

¹⁶ In place of the admonition, a "praise of good fortune (saying of blessing" ('šry) is found in 3:13-14ff. On the basis of its form, it can be considered mid-way between saying and admonition because it makes a simple statement (Happy is, blessed is . . .) into an emphatic encomium, a summons of praise, and thus achieves the character of a summons even without direct address. On the basis of its spiritual disposition, it fits closely together with wisdom. It is a significant occurrence that, among the narrative writings—Dt 33:29 belongs among the Psalms—'šry appears only in the narrative concerning the Queen of Sheba I K 10:8 = 2 Chr 9:7). It formulates the major concern of wisdom (Who is fortunate? on which see the exposition below), which is usually dealt with in Prov through sober reasoning, in a hymnically intensified form. Thus, this "encomium of happiness" often occurs in Prov with 'šry sometimes placed at the beginning 3:13; 8:34; 28:14 (8:32b; Qoh 10:17), sometimes later 14:21; 16:20; 29:18. (This later placement of 'šry, which occurs only in Prov, can only be considered a distortion of the pure form which the emphatic initial placement of "happy is" certainly demands. This distortion can be explained from the reasoning-attitude of Prov, which forces the sequence cause-effect even upon the internally transformed, stratified saying in hymnic form: cause—ob-serve an instruction; effect—it is well with him 29:18b). Naturally however, this form had its principal place in the wisdom psalms (1:1; (32:1); 112:1; 119: 1, 2; 128:1, 2) and, beyond that, extensive application in the Psalter. On occurrences in Sirach, see Baumgartner, *ZAW* 34 (1914), p. 167.

¹⁷ On ᶜd ḥnm 24:28 (which can be read ᶜd hms according to G, BHK; cf. 3:31 'yš ḥmś), cf. 12:17; 14:5; 19:5; 24:28. On the prohibition of paying-back

the evil 24:29; cf. 20:22; in a somewhat different sense 25:21f.; on the prohibition of self-glorification 27:2; perhaps 25:6f.

¹⁸ This lack of authority is immediately perceptible right where wisdom attempts to appear with a personal claim (personification in 1-9) in the same way that prophetic announcements of atonement and judgment appear to man (see n. 7 above). Two things are noticeable in this section. First, the odd neutrality with which the "calamitous outcome" is depicted. After the personal summons, "heed my reproof" (1:23), and the personal reproach, "you have rejected all my counsel" (1:25), one expects then the continuation, "therefore will I punish disobedience, I will bring misfortune upon you." Instead, it says most impersonally "when your calamity comes . . ." (26, 27). The punishment of the un-wise (pty) does not consist of an unexpected personal in-breaking of wisdom behind which man perceives the wounded authority, but rather in the course of events which man could actually have foreseen. The only thing that wisdom itself does in this punishment is to look upon him "laughing" (1:26), but merely to observe. And the second. The rebuke which begins so personally, seemingly from the most vital personal capacity to seize man in direct address, flags in its second half and finally drops out of direct address imperceptibly into a "speech concerning" man and world (vv. 27/28ff.), a sign of the artificiality of the selected form. No uniquely decisive words—obedience, repentance, judgment—are involved here, but general, eternally valid considerations.

¹⁹ Qoh 7:3/9 can be referred to further here. Here, too, this inner fredom of the wisdom admonition arises in the contradictory admonitions—"Better is displeasure than laughter, because when the face is displeased, it does the heart good" and "Do not be ready in your spirit to haste to displeasure, for displeasure rests in the breast of the fool"—and the verses are more than simply "symbolic of the unsystematic ·naive' composition of Qoh" (Hertzberg, 127). We find the classic expression of this inner line of structural development for wisdom, however, in the Babylonian "Dialogue between a master and his servant" (*AOT²*, pp. 284ff.), which reveals the proximity of the danger of falling into an unproductive featureless sophism.

²⁰ Principal importance attaches to sayings concerning the relationship to God.

²¹ The paralleling of rṣwn and twᶜbh is only found in (10) 11-15 (1:1, 20; 12:22; 15:8), which supports the isolation of 10-15 as originally a component collection, Fichtner 74).

²² A. Schulz, *Der Sinn des Todes im AT* (Verzeichnis der Vorlesungen an der Akademie zu Braunsberg im Sommerhalbjahr 1919), p. 32 attaches to 8:35 the translation "prosperity, fortune."

²³ An analogous development of the word twᶜbh cannot be proven. The absolute use of the word twᶜbh in 21:27; 28:9; (26:25) can very easily be interpreted in the sense twᶜbt-yhwh.

²¹ Internally continued within this saying is what was superficially described as "being evident to man" in Section II (above). Why are the experiential clauses intelligible to the wise man? What is the reason why he is affected and, beyond mere insight and taking-cognizance, is spurred into action. It lies in the fact that all the sayings—this is especially characteristic of the Yahweh-sayings which are under consideration here—tacitly array themselves around a focal point, the question of human existential possibility (life and the fortunes of man, see below). And this question is wisdom's central question; here it is seized and activated; here, out of vision comes conduct (out of the saying, the admonition).

²⁵ With Qoheleth's resigned reversion, the same type is found in 6:8. On the displacement of ṭwb through ytrwn which is completed here, see n. 28. In Amenemope, this form also appears frequently. See chs. 6 (3 times), 13 (twice), 22. The saying doublet, "better is bread with a joyful heart than riches with sorrow" (chs. 9 and 13), shows moreover that there is an older material involved, available to and adapted by Amenemope.

²⁶ In its brief form, this juxtaposition can even take place within the stichos itself Prov 19:22b; 27:10c, so that the other stichos then either presents a second comparison in parallel form Prov 8:19 (= 3:14 transposed form), contains the justification of the saying in the first stichos (Qoh 7:3), or simply continues the saying (Qoh 7:11 emended text; 9:16, 18; Prov 8:11). On the other hand, the normal form can be the simple comparison of both stichoi (ṭwb . . . mn, thus esp. Prov, see 12:9; 15:16, 17; 16:8 et passim, but also Qoh 4:6, 13; 5:4; 7:2, 5). Finally, in Qoh appears the decomposition of the strict mashal form into prose, 4:3; 6:3; 9:4; see also 3:22. On the appearance of this form in Sirach, see Baumgartner, ZAW 1914, p. 167.

²⁷ Differentiation of the purely secular rule of utility, the moral rule and the religious rule does not depend upon the essence of wisdom; rather, what is significant for it is that it sets all three groups of rules equal and only quantitatively establishes gradations among them. "The fear of God is the first and most important (rʾšyt) thing in wisdom" (1:7). Classification according to the various groups of admonition in recent studies of wisdom takes this point of view, working from the outside in, without ever laying out this fact clearly enough.

²⁸ Here, too, obviously, apart from the pessimistic tone which it bears in Qoheleth. So it is with ṭwb l(bny h)ʾdm in 2:3; 6:12; 8:15. 2:24a is either to be changed directly to ṭwb lʾdm or, along with 3:12 (ṭwb bm), it is to be understood in the same sense (i.e., the ṭwb bʾdm). 1:3 uses lʾdm in any case right alongside ytrwn, which is intermittently used almost as a synonym (5:15, lw). 3:9 has it in a somewhat unique way ytrwn hʿwsh; 2:11 ʾyn ytrwn tht hšmš is intended in almost the same sense. See also 6:11 ytr lʾdm, ytr is used as a direct synonym for ṭwb in 7:11, the conventional lʾdm here is poetically

paraphrased by lr'y hšmš (on 6:8, see n. 25 above). Finally, reference should be made to the pallid formula mh hwh l'dm 2:22. See also kśrwn, n. 4 above).

[29] On which see Schulz, esp. pp. 31ff.

[30] Here, the concept of Yahweh as retributor is particularly remote. It means: the day on which retribution occurs—which man expects on the basis of experience.

[31] See the words of Shenki [ET- Siduri] in the Old Babylonian recension of the Gilgamesh Epic (C Col. III 3ff.): "When the gods created men, they set aside death for mankind, life (however) they kept hold of" (according to *AOT²* p. 194). In the OT, see Gn 3:19; 6:3. That the mention of the divine determination is tied up here both times with the concept of sin witnesses to the depth of the self-understanding which is expressed by the OT in these places, though in mythological garb. Precisely the clearly seen, but agonizingly perceived, barrier of death was connected up with the mysterious knowledge of guilt before the holy. So also in Ps 90. n. 40 below will make mention of the fact that still another line of the OT belief in God appears in this connection between life and death.

[32] For this "school tradition" within which Qoheleth lives and with which he disagrees, see Galling, *ZAW* 1932, pp. 276ff.

[33] Even in 12:1ff., this tone occurs with sensitivity (cf. v. 8). Similarly, in 9:10 Sheol as the limit of all wisdom, and 8:8—there is no power over the day of death.

[34] Hempel, *Zeitschr. f. syst. Theol.*, Jahrg. 6 (1928/9), pp. 621ff. The theological problem of Job. Esp. pp. 675ff.

[35] The significance of this fact comes specially to light in view of the contention that, within the wise's observations of life, the question of the 'hryt, the "end," that a thing will take, obviously places a meaningful role (the "end" of concourse with the harlot 5:4, 11; of wine 23:32; of disputes 25:8; see, further, 14:12, 13; 16:25; 20:21; 29:21 (meaning unclear); as well as 1:19 perhaps 'hrwt should be emended to 'hryt; while in 19:20 'rhtyk should be read instead of 'hrytk). It follows that one may regard the concept of 'hryt for the end of human life; that would necessitate a look at the inevitable boundary of death, which would give the concept of 'hryt a dangerous sound. It is significant for the basically optimistic attitude of Proverbs that the concept of 'hryt is specialized in another direction; used absolutely, it can acquire the meaning "a good end" (23:18 = 24:14, see BHK on the text, 'hryt parallels tqwt) so that it immediately casts a threat toward the evil person, "the evil man will receive no (good) end" (parallel to, "the lamps of the godless will be extinguished") 24:20.

[36] When Fichtner, p. 64, identifies "life" as the "content of retribution" then that is an impossible restriction. Life is a comprehensive objective of the wise,

the way of retribution is only an individual path to this goal, even if the most important.

³⁷ See Dürr, *Leben*, pp. 2ff.; Sellin, *Beiträge zur israel. u. jüd. Religions-geschichte*, Heft 2 (1897), pp. 56ff.

³⁸ Cf. the tree of life in paradise and the anxious statement of Yahweh, ". . . that he (the man) should only not stretch out his hand and also take from the tree of life, and he eat and live forever" (Gn 3:22), or Gilgamesh's quest for life.

³⁹ Here, too, is a place where reference must be made to the sayings which appear with the greatest frequency and in terminological variety which deal with the question of "being saved." They are to be understood quite analogously to the sayings about "life." "The upright man is saved from affliction and the godless steps into his place." 11:8; ḥls also 11:9. Much more frequently nṣl 2:12, 16; 6:3, 5; 10:2; 11:4, 6; 12:6; 19:19; 23:14; occasionally also nṣr in this meaning 2:8, 11; 4:6; 20:28. In addition to which mlṭ 11:21; 19:5; 28:26 (see Qoh 7:26; 8:8); nqh which is sometimes parallel to it should be included here as well on the basis of the close connection between sin and punishment in Proverbs, 6:29; 11:21; 16:5; 17:5; 19:5, 9; 28:20. Finally, reference should also be made to the analogous use of šmr 2:8; 3:26; 6:22; 14:3 corrected text, see BHK. This preferentially turns up in word-play, in which šmr is occasionally replaced by nṣr, "his life preserves (šmr) who guards (nṣr) his mouth" 13:3; this mashal is expanded in 21:23; see also 16:17; 19:16, "who keeps (šmr) a precept guards (šmr) his life."

⁴⁰ Other mention of ḥyym is this emphatic sense of "increase of life" and good fortune, also 3:22 (parallel ḥn); 4:22 (parallel to mrp); 8:35 (parallel to rswn); 11:19; 12:28; 18:21 (parallel to mwt); 10:16; 14:30; 15:31; 16:15; 19:23; 21:21; 22:4. Without this emphatic augmentation, only 27:27 life-sustenance; 31:12 lifetime.

⁴¹ Otherwise, ḥy appears at 4:15; 6:8; 10:19.

⁴² Here it is quite clear: whoever receives riches from God and the possibility to enjoy them will also be helped so that he will not as often think of his limited days. Even if in another sense, 11:8 also speaks of the "thinking about the day of darkness." 6:1ff. is to be understood in the same way where as a result it might appear that value is attributed to a life that is allowed to enjoy good fortune. It is just the relative value that one could forget the ymy ḥyym by good fortune; and they remain ymy ḥyym (or ymy šnyw 6:3) even if they be 2000 years (6:6).

⁴³ 3:12 may also be interpreted in the same way.

⁴⁴ It is notable that it is often said of life that God has given it, but never death. The latter is—inasmuch as in the "gift of God" of limited life, death remains implicit as divine ordinance—always quite neutrally and impersonally described as fate that simply happens (mqrh 2:14; 3:19; 9:2 where in the

previous verse it is said that all men are in God's hand; *et passim*) as "time and chance" which "happen to everyone" (9:11, see Budde in Kautzsch[4]). Here, the same direction may appear within the portrait of Yahweh that Bruppacher has pointed up for the position of poverty (*Die Beurteilung der Armut im AT*, 1924, esp. pp. 24ff.—poverty is not founded in the will of God). Yahweh is the God of power and life and "death is no part of the creative order" (also Gn 3 etc., it is punishment, not originally the will of God, see above, n. 31). This genuinely Israelite perception which struggles through to clear expression in Wisdom of Solomon in connection with the belief in resurrection (1:13 "God has not made death and has no joy in the destruction of the living"; 14 ". . . he has created everything for existence . . ." quoted after Kautzsch, *Apokryphen*. But see also Ez 18:23) hindered Qoheleth in articulating what he would actually have to say, that God has ordained man to die. The sharpest saying which Qoheleth ventures is that ᶜnyn (rᶜ) comes from Yahweh, 1:13; 3:10.

[45] Still other sayings, in a broader sense, are also to be included here: 2:24ff. eating and drinking and the goods of life myd 'lhym hy'; 3:13 mtt lhym hy'; riches are the gift of God 5:18.

[46] "Consider your creator (read br'k) . . ." 12:1. See also Hertzberg, *Kommentar* pp. 37ff. which would assert a direct dependence on the biblical creation narrative.

[47] What is of specifically OT character in both pieces (Job, Qoheleth) is that atheism, the simple rejection of a judging God or the contention of his impotence, does not appear above the horizon. Cursing would, here as there, bring about as a consequence immediate death through the might of God. In the preceding is also the answer to Odeberg's thesis (see above n. 5). Equally, affinity and difference may be significant to Hertzberg's conception (esp. pp. 32ff.).

VII

THE SPIRITUAL STRUCTURE OF BIBLICAL
APHORISTIC WISDOM

A Review of Recent Standpoints and Theories

BEREND GEMSER

The Tenakh scholar of Swiss origin, Walther ZIMMERLI, at present Professor at Göttingen University, enriched the literature on Biblical Wisdom with a penetrating, acute and lucid study already twenty-eight years ago. It is his article in the *Zeitschrift für die Alttestamentliche Wissenschaft*, Vol. 61, 1933, entitled: 'Zur Struktur der alttestamentlichen Weisheit'. By 'Struktur' he does not mean so much the literary forms of the shorter or longer units among the utterances of ancient Israel and its wise men, but mainly their inner, spiritual structure, their main theme, their centre of interest, the question proper which they put to life and its phenomena and about the powers and forces which govern and regulate it. It is chiefly the Book of Proverbs of Solomon and the Book of Qoheleth to which he dedicates his attention. His results and statements in their main features are the following.

The central question of the wisdom of Proverbs and Qoheleth is: *mā ṭōb lā'ādām* or *mā yitrōn lā'ādām*; their starting-point is anthropological, even anthropocentric; their centre of gravity lies in the individual man and his happiness, apart from his historical ties and without consideration of fixed orders in which he is set, the individual, unhistorical man (as ZIMMERLI puts it), not as a member of the people of the Covenant nor as a creature faced with the Creator. Their driving question is not the order in which man is put and the duty ensuing therefrom, but: 'How can I make the most of life?'

A second structural point which ZIMMERLI stresses is: the word of wisdom is not an authoritative command, but an advice, and therefor discussable. Advice, *'ēṣā* means that the instruction is subjected to the approval, the consent of man, who is supposed to be free in his decision to follow it up or to reject it after considering its pros and cons. Most of the utterances of wisdom show therefore the form of statements ('Aussagen') and not of admonitions ('Mahnungen'). The instructions of wisdom do not contain in themselves full plenary power ('Vollmacht'); no imperative personal authority stands behind them. Even the proverbs with religious contents do not, according to ZIMMERLI, contain a reference to a set order, to the authority of God as last instance. The *mᵉšālīm* which put the question: 'What is good?' do not ask for a *summum bonum*, nor for a good founded in or based on the will of God, but must be explained after the *tōb min* construction and present or intend a gradual, relative, preferable good.

Materially the central question is: 'How can I as man insure my existence?" Expressions like *bātaḥ, mibtaḥ, niśgab, ʿāmad, kūn, nimlaṭ, hinnāṣēl, tūšiyyā, tᵉšūʿā* occur time and again. Behind all these lies hidden the question: 'How can I preserve my existence from death?' In wisdom literature death too is caught in the network of calculation, not taken in its ultimate, problematical, mysterious character, but as premature, violent death avoidable by human conduct. Positively the central question reads: 'How can I enrich my existence with happiness, prosperity and longevity?". Life in its earthly, worldly fullness is the target, life not in its radical sense, but as a good of which man himself can dispose.

Thus normal ancient Israelitic wisdom had a fundamentally rationalistic attitude; the whole world (even included life and death and Providence) can be known in the calculable laws of its course. Such an attitude involves a naïve optimistic outlook and an unhistorical approach of life.

As far as known to me, this conception of the essence of Hebrew wisdom has not been seriously challenged before the appearance of the standard work of the Heidelberg professor Gerhard VON RAD, *Theologie des Alten Testaments*, I, München 1957 and the 'Habilitationsschrift' of the young scholar

Hartmut GESE, submitted in the same year to the Evangelical Theological Faculty of the University of Tübingen under the guidance of the wellknown professors Karl ELLIGER and Arthur WEISER, published in 1958, entitled *Lehre und Wirklickeit in der alten Weisheit*. In my commentaries on Proverbs in the Netherlands series *Tekst en Uitleg*, Groningen 1929 and 1931 as well as in the German *Handbuch zum Alten Testament* under the editorship of Prof. Otto EISSFELDT, Tübingen 1937, (esp. p. 53 f., 57-59, 63) I have not shared ZIMMERLI's views, but the Netherlands work has appeared before his article and in the very compact German one there was little opportunity for going into discussion with the author.

How unopposed ZIMMERLI's results have been accepted in many circles is shown by a doctor's dissertation, defended before the Evangelical Theological Faculty of the University of Münster, Westfalen, by a minister of the church, E. G. BAUCKMANN, in 1958, entitled: 'Die Proverbien und die Sprüche von Jesus Sirach. Eine Untersuchung zum Strukturwandel der israelitischen Weisheitslehre', published in the *Zeitschrift für die Alttestamentliche Wissenschaft*, Vol. 72, 1958. BAUCKMANN apparently accepts all the main theses of ZIMMERLI on the authority, form and central question of the more ancient Israelitic wisdom as represented in Solomon's Proverbs, with which he then confronts the Proverbs of ben Sira. Ben Sira tries to combine the teaching of Wisdom and of the Torah; this objective involves a change of inner structure; and the author of the thesis comes to the conclusion that ben Sira has not so much taken over together with the letter of the Torah its spirit also, but that he has impressed on the Torah the stamp of wisdom; the Torah has lost its original character and function of authoritative, regulative order for the people of the Covenant; it has become itself wisdomteaching and wisdom has become a form of theologizing.

A diametrically opposite standpoint is taken by VON RAD, although not expressed in a polemic antithetical way. This scholar distinguishes 1) the older wisdom of Israel as represented mainly in Proverbs, ch. x ff., which he calls 'experimental wisdom', 2) 'theological wisdom' as found in Prov., ch. i-ix and related passages in post-exilic literature, and 3) finally the sceptical wisdom of which Qoheleth is the principal mouthpiece, the wisdom with tragic outlook and undertone.

Characteristic of wisdom is according to VON RAD its proceeding from the elementary experiences of daily life and thereby learning to master life. For that purpose there is in wisdom an unceasing observing and listening whether here and there in the confusion of events there can not be detected some law and order, some system and arrangement. Human language itself is already a means of ordering, arranging, objectivizing and conjuring observed phenomena. Especially a mashal is a systematizing pronouncement, conjuring and mastering life's phenomena. Empirical gnomic apperception is one of man's main forms of thinking. It is based on the obstinate presupposition of a hidden order. Especially in the similes, metaphors, parables and in the numerical proverbs this seeking after order, similarity, relation, analogy, secret connection is apparent. Wisdom already in its most ancient appearance is a penetrating will towards rational clearing up and ordering of the phenomena of the world and of human life.

The place for training and studying, for cultivating and fostering wisdom was chiefly the royal court where the prospective officials had to be formed and educated; in Israel probably just as in ancient Shumer and Akkad, also the gatherings and schools of the wise men and teachers of youth. Thus a more specialised aim of busying oneself with wisdom ensued, resulting in a didactic tone and form. It was not considered to be the duty of the wise to instruct his pupils in matters of religious belief and creed and cult; his domain was that of everyday life and human society; questions of belief emerge for them only at the borderlines of their range of vision. The wise men, however, did not keep separated the various spheres of life. The morally good and the useful were identical for them. Their conviction was twofold: whosoever is good, is such not in an isolated existence, but always for other people, for society also; secondly: man by his actions becomes involved in a relation and connection of fate; action puts into operation a movement for good or for evil for the agent as well as for his environment. Everywhere in wisdom there is a quest and search for hidden law and order.

In the mainly later, the theological phase of its history wisdom becomes the divine appeal to man, the mediator of divine revelation, the educator of peoples, especially of Israel, and the divine principle of the creation. Thus almost the whole of late-Jewish theologizing becomes more or less chokmatic, and wisdom extends its province of inquiry and contemplation to all the areas of life of the universe. She is less interested in the traditions of Israels history and religion than in the miracles of creation, its riddles and regularities, its systematism. Consequently an all-embracing, encyclopaedic theology arises, but always connected with a very practical application; its cosmological pronouncements serve as premise and legitimation of its appeal to listen and to follow up its precepts.

GESE in his afore-mentioned dissertation as private University lecturer in Tübingen confronts Israel's wisdom with the teaching of the Egyptian wise men, and sees fundamental as well as formal similarities between both. He comes to the conclusion that in both literatures the teachings of wisdom are an attempt to interpret the world as order. He opposes vehemently the interpretation of Egyptian and Israelite wisdom-teaching as eudaemonistic or utilistic; its aim is not to become successful in life, but result and action are considered as a unity; the finality of an action is not to be confused with its norm. This norm in the individual as well as in the universal sphere is *ma'at*, translated as 'truth' and 'right', but most appropriately by 'world-order'. Not so apparent, but none the less fundamental is the idea of the world as order in Israelite wisdom, especially in its doctrine of the correspondence between action and its result (either good or bad), in the life of the individual as well as in society and state life, an order which in often hidden, and of which man can not dispose, but which is nevertheless to be supposed and accepted and taken into account. The correspondence and connection of action and result is not necessarily seen as personal, divine retribution, but in terms of the belief in a personal, just and judging God it assumes this aspect.

GESE sees as the specific contribution of Israel's wisdom-teaching the conviction that God dispenses of good and evil to man independently of human plans and conduct and toil, independently also of the order of correspondence between action and result. It is God himself who determines *mišpāṭ* and grants *ṣedāqā* as sovereign and supreme ruler of the universe and of human life.

In his rather small book with its well-composed way of argument and plenty of sound remarks and felicitous formulations, entitled *Revelation in Jewish wisdom Literature,* published in 1946, just in between the appearing of the studies of ZIMMERLI and VON RAD, J. COERT RYLAARSDAM of the University of Chicago investigates how and when Hebrew wisdom, which in its beginnings does not seem to have possessed a religious or national character of its own, has become conscious of divine revelation as the source of its understanding of life, its aims and its limitations. Important for our subject is his stressing of the concurrence in all periods of the two convictions: that man has to seek wisdom empirically and rationally by his own human experiences, observations and investigations, but also that as the source of wisdom is in the Deity, wisdom is at the same time a prerogative and gift of God. Significant also is RYLAARSDAM's pointing to the correspondence (albeit with characteristic minor differences) between wisdom-teaching and the preaching of Deuteronomy and the Deuteronomistic historiographers as well as of the great prophets of Israel, a correspondence of belief in 1) a moral order of universe and history, in reward and punishment, 2) their world-affirming outlook and eschatology and 3) the virtues and spiritual attitude which they recommend. There certainly is in later times an increasing emphasis on the necessity and significance of divine revelation and guidance in the search for wisdom, but the balance and concurrence of divine initiative and enlightment on the one side and human ratio and effort on the other side were never totally absent or wholly disturbed.

It is impossible in the time at our disposal to go into all the relevant questions and statements. Only three of the more important problems will be discussed.

The first is the question of the authority with which wisdomteaching confronts its audience. ZIMMERLI has formulated it in a clear and definite way in stating: The word of wisdom is not an authoritative commandment, but it is an advice, and therefore discussable; it is offered, submitted to the considerations and the free choice of the addressed. It seems to me that this statement finds its origin in a much too modern, western way of the thinking, and that it is connected with the German translation of *'ēṣā*, namely 'Rat'. If one investigates the passages of Tenakh where the root *yā'aṣ* and its derivations *'ēṣā* and *mō'ēṣā* occur—MANDELKERN's Concordance enumerates 80 passages for the verb (including the participle *yō'ēṣ*), 88 for the substantive *'ēṣā* and 7 for *mō'ēṣā*—an almost totally different impression forces itself upon the reader. There are, especially in the narrative parts undoubtedly several cases where *yā'aṣ* and *'ēṣā* have the meaning of consultation and deliberation, of submitting private personal opinion to the discussion with and the choice of men of equal or higher or related status, as e.g. in the story of the maltreatment of the Levite and his concubine at Gibeah with the ensuing discussion in the congregation at Mizpah (Judges xix 30; xx 7), or in the case of the advice of the royal counsellors Ahithophel and Hushai to the rebellious Absalom (II Sam. ch. xv-xvii), and in the narrative of king-designate Rehoboam's consultations with the two groups of court advisers (I Kings xii), but even in the last two cases there lies in *'ēṣā* a strong element of authority, when it is said of Ahithophel: 'In those days the counsel which Ahithophel gave was as if one consulted the word, the oracle of God' (II Sam. xvi 23), and when Rehoboam's loss of ten out of the twelve tribes is attributed to his rejecting the counsel of his father's counsellors.

'To walk in one's counsel' is the same as 'to walk in one's ways', as is stated in the passage in II Chronicles xxii 3-5, where Ahaziah of Judah, the son of Jehoram and Athaliah is criticized for following the counsel and example of the house of Ahab, just as the prophet Micah announces divine judgement against his people because 'you have kept the statutes of Omri and all the works of the house of Ahab and walked in their counsels' (Micah vi 16).

In the Bileam-pericope we hear this seer saying to the king of Moab: 'Behold I am going to my people, $l^ekā$ $'i^c\bar{a}ṣekā$ $'aṣèr$ $ya^ca\dot{s}è$ $hā^c\bar{a}m$ $hazzè$ $l^camm^ekā$ $b^e'ah^arīt$ $hayyāmīn$ (Numb. xxiv 14), and in Deutero-Isaiah's prophecy, ch. xliv 24, God is represented as introducing himself as the one 'who confirms the word of his servant and performs ($yaślīm$) the counsel of his messengers'. In these passages 'counsel' has the meaning and authority of a divine message, and counseling means announcing God's plan and decision.

Isaiah the first who more than any prophet makes use of wisdom-forms in his preaching, often announces the $^ca\dot{s}at$ $'a\d{d}ōn\bar{a}y$ which never means a discussable advice but always a resolute decision and purpose (Is. v 19; xiv 24, 26 f.; xix 17; xxiii 1; xxviii 29; also xlvi 10 f.). The Messiah of ch. ix 5 and xi 2 is the $p\grave{e}l\grave{e}'$ $y\bar{o}^c\bar{e}ṣ$ because he is endowed with a spirit of counsel and strength(!). Often the expressions 'counsel' and 'strength' alternate; other synonyms are $r\bar{a}ṣ\bar{o}n$ (xlvi 10 f.) and $t\bar{u}\dot{s}iyy\bar{a}$ 'effective, wellbeing promoting action' (Is. xxviii 29; Prov. viii 14; Job xii 13).

There is scarcely a difference of authority in Jer. xviii 18 between the counsel of the wise, the torah of the priest and the word of the prophet, no more than in Ez. vii 26 between the vision of the prophet, the torah of the priest and the counsel of the elders; there is a difference in form, but hardly in authority.

Johannes PEDERSEN in his famous standardwork *Israel, Its Life and Culture*, Oxford University Press, London, 1940, has stressed already this authoritative element of the Israelitic meaning of counsel on every page where he mentions this conception (Vol. I/II, p. 128-130, 183 f., 241 f., Vol. III/IV, p. 13, 72 f., 90 f., 120, 626), and the Leiden Professor P. A. H. DE BOER in his penetrating study 'The Counsellor' in the 65th birthday volume *Wisdom in Israel and in the Ancient East*, presented to Professor H. H. ROWLEY (Suppl. Vetus Testamentum, Vol. III, Leiden, 1955, p. 42-72) provides a wealth of material from Tenakh as well as from Israel's 'Umwelt' and later Jewish literature reaffirming this sense. The counsels of wisdom are not advice offered without obligation to the free discussion and decision of the addressed, they claim to be listened to and followed up and put into practice.

But—and this is our second question—from where do they derive this authority? ZIMMERLI says: 'Autorität is nur personenhaft zu denken' ('Authority can only be thought of in terms of personality'). I am afraid that also in this statement the modern, Western way of thinking and logic plays too great a role. GESE has proved from Egyptian texts and recent studies of Egyptologists that Egyptian thinking and moralising, even the whole of Egyptian political and social life, was permeated and governed by the idea of *ma'at*, 'world-order, the right order'. VON RAD has gone still further back in human history and pointed out that already in language itself, the more so in proverbial expression, the search for a hidden order in universe, nature and human experiences is apparent, and that it is this order which is thought of as regulating and determining the conduct of men and its consequences. Almost day by day it becomes clearer that also in Shumerian and Babylonian thinking and teaching the concept of the divine order and norm (Shum. *me*, Akk. *parşu*) is of fundamental importance (cp. J. J. A. VAN DIJK, *La sagesse suméro-accadienne*, Leiden 1953, p. 17 ff.; Edmund I. GORDON, *Sumerian Proverbs*, University of Pennsylvania, Philadelphia 1960, Collection Two, 1, p. 176 ff. cf. also Collection One, 1, p. 40).

216

In the interesting report of a symposium by six American scholars and students of the Ancient Orient J. A. WILSON, ed., *Authority and Law in the Ancient Orient* (Suppl. Journal of the American Oriental Society, Nr. 17, Baltimore, 1950) the authority of impersonal Law and World-order is stressed time and again. I quote only what E. A. SPEISER says about Mesopotamia: 'Total law (*kittum û mēšarum*) was impersonal and above the crown' (p. 13).

Parallel and intertwined with this universal ancient Oriental belief in an impersonal, yet authoritative world-order was the conviction that wisdom was a prerogative and gift of the gods; wisdom and word, intelligence and speech were even, in Egypt as well as in Babylonia and Ugarit, thought of as personal divine beings. No wonder that in ancient Israel with its fundamental belief in a personal, even one personal Deity wisdom was seen as one of the most essential qualities of God, and the teachings of wisdom as the expressions of his will. It may be that in the older wisdom texts Israel's particular faith does not find such an overall and deliberate expression as in the younger products; but the pictures of the ideal, prudent and successful man in the old narratives of Joseph and of the young David, which VON RAD rightly classifies under the older Israelite wisdom conception, prove that this image is inconceivable without the essential trait of the *yir'at 'adōnāy* or *yir'at 'elōhîm*. And it is his torah (not in the narrower sence of written law, but in the all-embracing one of divine instruction) which comes to man through prophet, priest and wise man, through elders and ancient tradition, through counsellors and teachers of the people and through the parents; even their, the parents' advice and guidance can therefore be called *tōrā* (Prov. i 8; vi 20; xxxi 26) and *miṣwā* (vi 20).

Our third and last question is: Is there then no definite and characteristic difference between the words of the prophet, the torah of the priest and the counsel of the wise? And if not, why are these spiritual leaders of the people distinguished so clearly and why are their teachings usually expressed by

different terms? RYLAARSDAM who stresses the correspondence between the prophets and the wise in the contents
of their teachings, distinguishes their outlook (as he calls it)
and idea of revelation very well by calling the prophets' a
vertical conception of revelation and that of the wise a horizontal; the prophet is conscious of the direct and often unexpected word of God in his mind, even in his ears, the sage
derives his knowledge of the divine will by studying daily
human experience and the way of life in nature and history.

But why then all those motivations in the advices of the
wise, all this referring to and falling back on general experimental statements, why this dominating of 'Aussage' over
against 'Mahnung', this as ZIMMERLI calls it 'stets Durch-
sichtigmachen des Gebotes durch die beigefügte Begründung'
(making the command transparent by giving reasons)? There
is a somewhat overstrained logical conception of command in
ZIMMERLI's and BAUCKMANN's argument: Command is
command, is apodictic, has to be obeyed without further
consideration and deliberation. This is not the way in which
Israel's law-teachers, prophets and wise men consider the
situation. Undoubtedly God's commandments have to be
obeyed. But all these three groups of spiritual leaders try to
persuade their people by motivating (not so much the contents
as well as the following up of) the divine commandments.

In my lecture before the Copenhagen Congress of the
International Organization of Old Testament Scholars in
1953, *The Importance of Motive Clauses in Old Testament Law*
(Suppl. Vetus Testamentum, Vol. I, p. 50-66) I have collected
and explained this frequent phenomenon in the different law-
codes of Tenakh. May I cite just one sentence from it: 'The
motive clauses with their appeal to the common sense and to
the conscience of the people disclose the truly democratic
character of their laws, just as those (the motivations) of the
religious kind testify the deep religious sense and concentrated
theological thinking of their formulators' (p. 63; in this volume
p. 111).

The law-book of Deuteronomy, but also the exhortations of

the great prophets abound with motivations and with references to the blessings or curses which will follow the obeying
or rejecting of them, without detracting anything from the
authority and validity of their instructions. It is only natural
that particularly the wise men and teachers of the younger
generation make use of this pedagogic method.

In a small symposion on the wisdom of Israel between
Professor ZIMMERLI and GALLING of Göttingen University,
Professor VAN DER WOUDE of Groningen and myself, held in
Groningen in 1961 ZIMMERLI wholeheartedly dropped his
view of a eudaemonistic objective of Proverbs, and declared
that today he would formulate many of the statements of his
former, youthful article more cautiously, although he would
stick to his view of the anthropological design of wisdom and
thence an element of aiming at success and prosperity. This
clarification is very welcome. One cannot take the sceptical
meditations of Qoheleth as the only fitting key to the whole
of Israels wisdom teaching; Qoheleth is rather an extreme
consequence of one of the aspects of the method used by
the wise to make their counsels acceptable and attractive for
their youthful audience and for the mass of their people in
their everyday life. *Rē'šīt ḥokmā yir'at 'ªdōnāy* (Ps. cxi 10)
remains the keyword of Israels wisdom, *rē'šīt* in its twofold
sense of basic principle as well as of the best fruit of wisdom.

QUOTATIONS IN WISDOM LITERATURE

By ROBERT GORDIS

Jewish Theological Seminary of America

TWENTY-ONE centuries ago Ben Sira said, "Turn aside to me, ye fools, and tarry in my house of study" (Ecclus. 51.23), an invitation which readers have accepted with alacrity, despite the uncomplimentary epithet. That much has nevertheless remained unclear, both in the contents and the structure of the Wisdom literature, is largely due to the failure to recognize clearly the existence of two schools of Wisdom, or, more accurately, of one school with a group of dissidents on the fringe.

The main school of Wisdom, whose literary monuments are the Books of Proverbs and Ben Sira, and, in a derivative sense, the Wisdom of Solomon, was concerned with the practical *Hokmah*. It was fundamentally conventional in its viewpoint; its function was to teach men, and particularly the youth, the arts and wiles of practical living. It emphasized such matters as the necessity for labor, the importance of foresight, and the need of frugality. It preached adherence to moral and religious standards, because it sincerely felt that honesty is the best policy.

It is true that even among these Sages the metaphysical urge was not absent. They hypostasized Wisdom, as in the great hymn in Proverbs, chapter 8:

The Lord made me as the beginning of His way,
The first of His works of old . . .

but that was Wisdom as an idea and an ideal. The *Hokmah* they taught their disciples was definitely mundane. It was

123

sane, and it was workable. Therein lay its abiding value and its equally evident limitations.

Among those who had been trained in the Wisdom academies were a few bolder and more speculative minds, the authors of Job, Koheleth and Proverbs 30. The same gift of observation which the conventional Wise Men applied to the practical problems of the individual, these thinkers utilized in dealing with profounder issues, the meaning of life, the secret of happiness, the problem of suffering, the reward of virtue and the nature of death. They were the devotees of the higher or speculative Wisdom. They were unwilling to deny patent facts or base conclusions on insufficient evidence. They therefore found themselves frequently at variance with the religious and moral teaching of their day, including that of their own teachers in the academies of Wisdom.

The Wise Men of the dominant school applied reason to mundane affairs, but, in the field of religious thought, they were content to accept the ideas laid down by the Torah and Prophets and expounded by the recognized teachers of the day. Their attitude was aptly summarized by Ben Sira:

> What is too wonderful for thee do not search,
> And what is hidden from thee do not seek,
> Observe only what is permitted thee,
> And have no concern with mysteries. (Ecclus. 3.20 f.)

But for these few bolder spirits, there were no barriers, no forbidden territory. On the great, fundamental issues they were unable to accept the easy comfort of a religious tradition, nor did they claim the divine inspiration of prophecy. They knew only what was revealed to them by their own observation and reflection. That they were doomed to the dissatisfaction of perpetual uncertainty goes without saying.

For this very reason there is deep human interest in their lives. They were men of the transition, when one system of ideas was dying and another powerless to be born. Thus they lacked the sublime confidence of the Prophets in the ultimate triumph of justice in the world. Moreover, they opposed the conventional theory that suffering is invariably the penalty and the evidence of sin. In this last respect, these Sages were in advance of their contemporaries. In other regards, they were more conservative than their generation. For example, they rejected the new ideas of a future life and of retribution after death, which were making headway among the masses, as an answer to the problem of suffering (Job 14.14–19; Eccl. 3.19–21).

In sum, the relationship of these unconventional Wise Men to the culture of their day was essentially complex. Within their world-view were elements of the completely conventional, the modified old, and the radically new. They doubtless accepted many aspects of the practical Wisdom as expounded in the schools, where they were educated and perhaps themselves taught. In this role of teachers of Wisdom they probably contributed original sayings of their own, which were not different in form or spirit from that of their more conventional colleagues. Other ideas they accepted in modified form, while still others they opposed entirely.

The complexity of their viewpoint must necessarily be reflected in their writings, for "style is the man." By postulating such an ambivalent attitude for Koheleth toward the dominant Wisdom, we gain in an understanding of his work. He was in the school and yet not quite of it, a devotee of the practical Wisdom, like the compiler of Proverbs, and, at the same time, the confirmed opponent of many of its basic assumptions. Failure to recognize this truth has created untold theories, that offer unwitting testimony to

222

the truth of the contention that "of the making of books there is no end, and much talk is a weariness to the flesh" (Eccl. 12.12).

Thus, in the eighteenth century, the view was prevalent that the book of Koheleth is a dialogue between a refined sensualist and a sensual worldling, or between a pupil and a teacher, or a record of conflicting views of academies of learned men.[1] Another way of accounting for the apparent contradictions of the book is the theory, first suggested by Van der Palm, adopted by Graetz, and elaborated by Bickell, that the book was written on leaves that were subsequently disarranged. More recently, the theory of composite authorship was tentatively advanced by Haupt, and worked out by Siegfried, who divided the book among nine authors.

Today the regnant theory is less extreme. It argues that the essentially heterodox and unconventional writings of Koheleth were subjected to wide and persistent interpolation, in order to make them acceptable to the orthodox. Jastrow finds over 120 interpretations in a book of 222 verses; Barton claims that a Hasid glossator is responsible for 15 important additions, and that a *Hokmah* interpolater is the author of 30 more, aside from many minor changes Volz eliminates an equal number of passages, which do not, however, coincide with Barton's. Eissfeldt protests against the assumption of composite authorship, and assumes only nine pious additions. However, he saves the authenticity of the text, only by assuming that there is no clear-cut, integrated philosophy in Koheleth, merely a series of rambling reflections that often contradict one another.[2]

---

[1] So Döderlein, Tyler. Cf. Barton, *ICC on Ecclesiastes*, p. xxi.

[2] Barton, op. cit.; Jastrow, *The Gentle Cynic* (Philadelphia, 1919), pp. 245-55; Volz, "Hiob und Weisheit" (in *Die Schriften des A. T.*, Göttingen, 1921), pp. 235; Eissfeldt, *Einleitung in das A. T.* (Tübingen, 1934), p. 558.

In Job, too, most scholars, when baffled by apparent irrelevancies and contradictions, have excised countless stichs and verses as interpolations and transposed many others.[3]

Several factors have complicated the understanding of the style of these masterpieces. Elsewhere, we have called attention to an important characteristic of the style of Koheleth, his unconventional use of the conventional religious vocabulary of his day.[4] In this paper, we shall attempt to demonstrate another element in the style of Ecclesiastes and Job — the use of quotations.[5] A few general considerations must preface a more detailed analysis of this usage.

While it is true that in prophetic literature the entire discourse of the prophet is the word of God, literary quotations, as such, are rare. Though each prophet has undoubtedly learned much from his predecessors, his inspiration is essentially a unique and personal quality, the product of an ecstatic communion with God. His message is not the result of study and argument, and needs no logical demonstration. It bears its assurance of truth in its conviction that "thus saith the Lord."

[3] Duhm, *Das Buch Hiob erklärt* (1897) passim. Driver-Gray, *ICC on Job*, (1921) more conservatively, eliminate about 30 verses in the first 23 chapters of Job (Vol. I, p. xxxvii, n. 1, and pp. xlix f.). Torczyner (*Das Buch Hiob*, Vienna, 1920), whose procedure is extremely arbitrary, emphasizes that he does not excise any passage from the book; he merely rearranges several hundreds of them (Preface, p. viii). (For a recent criticism of Torczyner's method, see Prof. Kemper Fullerton, "Job, Chap. 9 and 10" in *AJSL*, Vol. LV (July, 1938) pp. 263–7). Cf. also David Yellin, חקרי מקרא איוב (Jerusalem, 1927), who rearranges Chap. 7, 19 and 20 completely.

[4] "Cynic's Progress, a Reinterpretation of Ecclesiastes" in *Opinion* (New York), February, 1937, pp. 17–21.

[5] A somewhat similar treatment of quotations, though differing radically in approach and considerably in details, appears to our knowledge only in Ludwig Levy, *Das Buch Qoheleth* (Leipzig, 1912), pp. 57–9. Our own results are based on a completely independent investigation of the material. For purposes of comparison, Levy's conclusions have been added in our footnotes.

In Wisdom, however, the situation is otherwise. Here there is no supernatural revelation, merely patient observation used as the basis for reasonable conclusions. Each generation of Sages find in the extant proverbial literature of the past a body of truth, created by their predecessors, whose observations on life have approved themselves to their colleagues.[6]

The universal human character of Wisdom is such that its material may be drawn even from non-Jewish sources or concern itself with non-Jewish figures like Job.[7] Koheleth belongs to the Wisdom school. We may therefore expect to find proverbs quoted in his notebook, as in any other work of the Sages.

Nor is it merely these a priori considerations that make quotations in the Wisdom literature likely. We have at least one indubitable instance, which reveals the form in which these quotations are couched. In Eccl. 4.8 we read:

יֵשׁ אֶחָד וְאֵין שֵׁנִי גַּם בֵּן וָאָח אֵין לוֹ וְאֵין קֵץ לְכָל־עֲמָלוֹ גַּם
עֵינָיו (כ׳) לֹא־תִשְׂבַּע עֹשֶׁר וּלְמִי אֲנִי עָמֵל וּמְחַסֵּר אֶת נַפְשִׁי
מִטּוֹבָה גַּם־זֶה הֶבֶל וְעִנְיַן רַע הוּא.

There is one that is alone, and he hath not a second; yea, he hath neither son nor brother; yet is there no end of all his labour, neither is his eye satisfied with riches:

[6] See the brief but suggestive treatment in Max L. Margolis, *The Bible in the Making* (Philadelphia, 1922), pp. 61-6, 78-82.

[7] Cf. the Proverbs of Amenemope, the Ahikar romance and the biblical references to the wisdom of Egypt, and the sons of Kedem (I Kings 5.10 f.). On the other hand, Ethan, Heman, Calcol and Darda, referred to there, are almost certainly identical with the Judahites Ethan, Heman, Calcol and Dara of the Zarah clan mentioned in I Chron. 2.6. Their "wisdom" consisted essentially of their musical attainments, as evidenced by the references to the Temple guilds of Heman and Ethan (Ps. 88.1; 89.1; I Chron. 15.17, 19, as well as I Chron. 25.1, 6; II Chron. 5.12; 35.15, where Jeduthun appears in place of Ethan). The material from Ugarit is affording a great deal of evidence as to Canaanite sources for Wisdom literature. Prof. W. F. Albright goes so far as to postulate a Phoenician-Canaanite origin for *Hokmah* as a whole (*JBL*, LVII, (June, 1938), 221).

nor does he say "for whom then do I labour, and bereave my soul of pleasure?" This also is vanity, yea, it is a grievous business.

Here we find no external signs of a quotation but rather an abrupt transition. In fact not only quotation marks but an entire clause, given above in italics, must be supplied in order to indicate which words are being cited. Elsewhere in Ecclesiastes and Job, too, these characteristics of abrupt transitions and even contradictions, without any connecting words or other formal sign of a quotation, reappear. It may easily be paralleled by examples from biblical and rabbinic literature.[8] Such quotations can be recognized only by internal evidence and a sympathetic understanding of the writer's personality.

That quotations are an important element in Koheleth's style, seems to us an assured fact. Nevertheless, we are well aware that the assumption of a quotation in any given passage is a hypothesis, as to the plausibility of which opinions will naturally differ. Rather than burden the dis-

---

[8] Cf. Ketubot 13.3:

בנכסים מועטים הבנות יזונו והבנים יחזרו על הפתחים אדמון אמר בשביל שאני זכר הפסדתי

"When an inheritance is small, the daughters are to be supported and the sons go begging from door to door." Admon says "*A son might argue under these circumstances* 'Shall I suffer because I am a male?'" Here the words in italics, which are essential to the sense as indicating a hypothetical quotation, are lacking in the Hebrew and must be supplied by the reader.

A similar instance occurs in Abot 2.4:

אל תאמר דבר שאי אפשר לשמוע שסופו להשמע

"Do not say something which cannot be understood, *thinking* 'it will ultimately be understood.'" (so Bertinoro, Maimonides). It should, however, be noted that though this seems to be the original reading, the text of the *Mahzor Vitry* differs from it. Cf. Taylor, *Sayings of the Jewish Fathers* (1st edition, Cambridge, 1877), p. 44.

Examples of similar quotations without an introductory formula are common in Psalms. Cf. the standard commentaries on such passages as 2.2; 4.7b (which is a quotation from a source different from the quotation in stich a); 8.4 f.; 10.4 (cf. 10.13); 22.9; 22.24 f.

cussion at each point, we prefer to make the general qualification here that each of these suggestions is advanced
tentatively. In the last analysis, the test of their value
will be the same as that applied to all sound exegesis — the
cumulative evidence of usage, and the degree of coherence
and intelligibility gained for the text.

We are now in a position to analyze the various categories
of quotations in Ecclesiastes and Job.

A. The simplest type of quotation is the *straightforward
use of proverbs, with which the author agrees*. Even the most
unconventional thinker will recognize the value of the practical counsel given in the book of Proverbs. The most confirmed cynic will agree that

> By slothfulness the rafters sink in;
> And through idleness of the hands the house leaketh,
> (Eccl. 10.18)

or suggest that it is wise to diversify one's undertakings:

> Cast thy bread upon the waters,
> For thou shalt find it after many days. (Eccl. 11.1)

Exactly as in any other Wisdom book, like Proverbs and
Ben Sira, the notebook of Koheleth registers proverbs of
the conventional mode. That these are generally excised
by modern scholars like Siegfried, McNeile, Haupt and
Barton, though with no unanimity, is due to a rigid view
of his personality, that declares that if Koheleth be unconventional he must be an iconoclast throughout, perpetually
at war with conventional ideas. Actually, he may not
merely be quoting these proverbs with approval, but may
have composed them himself.

Particularly congenial to the pessimism of Koheleth
would be a statement like 7.3, which he inserts in his notebook:

Sorrow is better than joy, for by sadness of countenance
the understanding improves."[9]

At times, Koheleth appears to buttress his argument by
a proverb, part of which is apposite, while the rest of the
saying, though irrelevant, is quoted for the sake of completeness, a literary practice of writers in all ages. The use
of quotation marks will serve to make the matter clear.

Be not rash with thy mouth and let not thy heart be
hasty to utter a word before God; For God is in heaven,
and thou upon earth; therefore let thy words be few.
For "a dream comes through much business; and a fool's
voice in many words."[10]

Since Koheleth was himself a product of the Wisdom
academies, it is usually impossible to determine whether
the proverbs we encounter in his writings are quotations
or are original with him. At times, however, some characteristic fillip of style stamps a passage as indubitably
original.

Thus 11.4 seems a typical quotation, but all the earmarks
of Koheleth's personality are to be seen in the ironic comment that precedes it (v. 3). His thought seems to be that

---

[9] Barton interprets the verse to mean that there is a moral purpose
to suffering, an idea foreign to Koheleth's viewpoint, and he therefore
follows Haupt in eliminating it as a gloss. Levy sees in it a quotation
from an ascetic. The sense, however, is related to that expressed in
1.18: בְּרֹב חָכְמָה רָב כָּעַס "In much wisdom is much vexation." It therefore follows that a melancholy exterior is a sign of inner understanding.
On the latter passage, see our paper in *JBL*, LVI (1937), 323 ff.

[10] Eccl. 5.1, 2. The entire section 4.17–5.6 is excised as the work of
the Hasid glossator by McNeile, while vv. 5.1–2 are regarded as the
product of K5 by Siegfried. Haupt however regards 4.17, 5.1 as genuine,
but eliminates 5.2. Barton accepts the entire section except 5.2, 6a.
Volz eliminates vv. 1–2 as an "unimportant proverb." Actually terms
like כְּסִיל, עִנְיָן, חֵפֶץ and the general viewpoint expressed are completely
in accord with what we should expect of Koheleth, and there is no
convincing reason for doubting the genuineness of the passage. Levy
does not recognize 5.2 as a proverb, which seems evident by its parallel
structure.

the events of nature will take place without man's assistance, and there is therefore no justification for idle gazing:

> If the clouds be full of rain,
> They empty themselves upon the earth;
> And if a tree fall in the south, or in the north,
> In the place where, the tree falleth, there shall it be.
> He that observeth the wind shall not sow;
> And he that regardeth the clouds shall not reap. (Eccl.
> 11.3, 4)

Incidentally, the unity and integrity of the passage seems
clear from its chiastic structure, for 3a and 4b deal with
cloud and rain, while 3b and 4a are concerned with the
wind uprooting a tree.[11]

Other examples of the straightforward use of proverbs
in Ecclesiastes are to be found in 7.4, 7; 8; 10.2, 8, 9, all of
which may be original epigrams of Koheleth.

In Job, too, instances of proverbial quotations are occasionally met with.[12]

B. Even more strikingly characteristic of Koheleth's
style is his *use of a proverb as a text,* which he then elaborates
in his own unique manner. Here, too, it cannot be determined whether the proverb is a quotation from the conventional *Hokmah* literature or was composed by Koheleth,
himself a teacher of Wisdom. Thus, a typically abstemious
and moralizing doctrine is sounded in Eccl. 7.2a:

---

[11] There is therefore no need to remove v. 4 as a gloss with Siegfried,
Haupt, McNeile and Barton. Levy takes v. 3 as a quotation, but in a
widely differing sense. According to him, it is a counsel of quietude,
which Koheleth rejects in v. 4. That Koheleth would urge "the strenu-
ous life" does not seem to accord with his general view as to the futility
of labor and skill, to which he refers again and again (cf. 2.18–24; 4.4–8;
5.12–16; 6.1 ff.).

[12] In addition to the passages discussed below, Job 2.4 may fall within
this category. The cryptic verse 17.5:

לְחֵלֶק יַגִּיד רֵעִים וְעֵינֵי בָנָיו תִּכְלֶינָה

is perhaps best taken as a folk-saying: "He invites his friends to a feast,
while the eyes of his own children fail with longing." So, essentially,
Budde ad loc. See Driver-Gray, *ICC*, Job, vol. I, pp. 151–2, for a full
discussion of this difficult passage.

It is better to go to the house of mourning
Than to go to the house of feasting . . .

a warning against the revelry and immorality of the house
of mirth. But Koheleth gives it a darker undertone:

For that is the end of all men,
And the living will lay it to his heart.[13] (Eccl. 7.2b)

Examples of this use of proverb as text with ironic comment are plentiful. Thus a proverb extols the virtues of
cooperation. Koheleth approves the sentiment, but for
reasons of his own:

"Two are better than one; for they have a good reward
for their labor." For if they fall, the one will lift up his
fellow; but woe to him that is alone when he falleth, and
hath not another to lift him up. Again if two lie together,
then they have warmth; but how can one be warm alone?
And if a man attack him that is alone, two shall withstand him; and a threefold cord is not quickly broken.[14]
(Eccl. 4.9–12)

The teachers of morality emphasized that love of money
does not make for happiness. This idea is expanded by
Koheleth through the characteristic reflection that strangers
finally consume the substance of the owner, an idea to which
he refers again and again (cf. 2.18 ff., 4.7 ff.):

"He that loves silver will not be satisfied with silver,
and he that loves riches will have no increase." This also
is vanity, for when goods increase, they that eat them
are increased; and what advantage is there to their
owner, save beholding them with his eyes? (Eccl. 5.9 f.)

---

[13] Levy takes the entire verse as a quotation of an ascetic, but is
unable to explain why, if Koheleth is opposed to its theme, he quotes
it at all. Levy overlooks the fact that Koheleth's counsel of joy as the
highest good flows from a profoundly tragic conception of life. We have
sought to reconstruct his spiritual history in the paper referred to in
note 4.

[14] While Siegfried, McNeile and Haupt eliminate these verses as
glosses, Barton justly remarks, "it is an open question whether Koheleth
himself may not have introduced them" (op. cit., p. 110). Levy sees
no quotation here at all.

The Book of Proverbs counsels submission to political authority:

Fear, my son, God and king, and meddle not with those who seek change. (Prov. 24.21)

Koheleth repeats this idea but with his tongue in his cheek:

I counsel thee; keep the king's command,
And that because of the oath of God.

Submit to the king because of your oath of fealty, but also, he adds as an afterthought:

Forasmuch as the king's word has power;
And who may say unto him: "What doest thou?" (Eccl. 8.2-4)

because the king is powerful enough to crush you.

Similarly, to maintain oneself in an atmosphere of political tyranny and intrigue requires skill in choosing the proper occasion. That idea Koheleth appends as a comment to a perfectly moral utterance about the virtues of obedience:

"Whoever keeps the commandment shall know no evil" but a wise man's heart discerns the proper time. For every matter has its proper time, for man's evil is great upon him. (Eccl. 8.5-6)[15]

In addition to these examples which mirror the political conditions of Koheleth's time, several interesting instances of his use of conventional *Hokmah* material in the field of religion and philosophic speculation are apparently to be met with.

For example, Koheleth is not disposed to deny altogether that retribution overtakes the sinner. Yet, in many instances, the righteous and the wicked are treated alike. At other times, punishment is meted out to the sinner, but

---

[15] These verses are excluded as the work of the Hasid glossator by McNeile, Barton, Volz and Eissfeldt (loc. cit.). Levy, on the other hand, takes the entire passage, vv. 2-8, as a quotation, with a loss, it seems to us, in the piquancy of the passage.

only after a long delay, which affords him the opportunity and the incentive to sin.

These two limitations on Divine justice are referred to in an interesting passage, 8.11–14, the center of which (vv. 12b, 13) is a quotation of the traditional view, from which Koheleth dissents. There is therefore no need to eliminate vv. 11–13 as a gloss.[16] Our rendering is as follows:

> Because the sentence against an evil deed is not exe-
> cuted speedily, therefore the hearts of men are encouraged
> to do evil, because a sinner does evil a hundred times,
> and God is patient with him; although I know the view
> that "it shall be well with them that fear God, because
> they fear Him, but it shall not be well with the wicked,
> neither shall he prolong his days, like a shadow, because
> he does not fear God."

[16] These verses, 11–13 inclusive, are attributed to the Hasid glossator and deleted by Siegfried, Haupt, McNeile and Barton, largely because of v. 12, while Volz and Eissfeldt eliminate vv. 12, 13. Practically all translations and commentators seek to connect 12a and 12b, in accordance with the masoretic punctuation, which places a full stop at the end of v. 11, and a secondary pause (*Athnah*) at the middle of v. 12 (לו). They therefore follow the Vulgate *attamen* and render the opening אֲשֶׁר in v. 12a as "although." This, in spite of the fact that the opening אֲשֶׁר in v. 11 is given correctly as "because." They therefore render "Although a sinner does evil exceedingly, and prolongs his days, nevertheless I know that it shall be well with those who fear God," etc. (Barton).

We believe that the opening אשר in v. 12, like אשר in v. 11, is to be given as "because," and v. 12a continues the idea expressed in v. 11, while v. 12b introduces the contrary and conventional view as a quotation.

It may be added that the usual interpretation suffers from several linguistic difficulties. There is no warrant for אֲשֶׁר meaning "although" and Hitzig, Delitzsch and Wright correctly render it as "because." Moreover, on the accepted view, כִּי גַם is made to introduce the principal clause of the sentence and the principal idea. However, its usage elsewhere (in Eccl. 4.14), as well as that of the equivalent conjunction, גַם כִּי, is invariably that of a subordinating conjunction = "although" (Isa. 1.15; Hos. 8.10; 9.16; Ps. 23.4; cf. also Prov. 22.6; Lam. 3.8). In our rendering, it introduces a genuine subordinate clause (vv. 12b, 13) subordinate logically as well as grammatically. It may be noted that our rendering agrees with that of Ludwig Levy.

> There is a vanity which is done upon the earth: There are righteous men, who are rewarded according to the work of the wicked; and again, there are wicked men, who are requited according to the work of the righteous — I say that this also is vanity.

Koheleth would undoubtedly agree with the universal view that life on any terms is preferable to death. Yet his general intellectual conviction as to the futility of living impels him to a comment, which ostensibly justifies, but actually undermines, the entire proposition.

> "Indeed he who is joined to all the living has hope, for a living dog is better than a dead lion." For the living know that they shall die; but the dead know nothing, neither have they any reward; for their memory is forgotten. Their love, their hatred and their envy, all is long perished, nor have they any longer a share in any thing that is done under the sun. (Eccl. 9.4–6)

Another instance where the "comment" explicitly refutes the "text" is to be found in 2.13, 14 where two traditional proverbs are quoted and opposed:

> I have seen that "Wisdom excels folly as light excels darkness." "The wise man has his eyes in his head, but the fool walks in darkness." But _I_ know that one fate meets them all.[17]

These examples of proverbial sayings used as the basis of more or less extended comment must suffice here.[18]

Whether these proverbial sayings, which serve as "texts," are quotations from other _Hokmah_ writers, or are original with Koheleth, cannot be determined, especially since gnomic literature is particularly apt to swallow up the

[17] Here vv. 13, 14a are omitted by Siegfried, but retained by Barton. Levy takes v. 14 as a conventional proverb, but not v. 13, an alternative procedure which is almost equally satisfactory.

[18] Treatment of such passages as (a) 7.1a, 1b; (b) 7.5 f.; (c) 7.19 f.; (d) 11.1 f., as well as the extraordinarily interesting section 3.17 f., must be reserved for a projected Commentary on Ecclesiastes.

individual in the anonymity of the mass. It would seem that 9.4 is more likely to be original than 2.13, 14, because of the trenchant style of the former passage.

Yet the issue is not so fundamentally important as it may appear. For there can be no doubt that the proverbs represent the substance, if not the phraseology, of conventional lore and that the comment is indubitably Koheleth's own.

C. Another noteworthy device by which Koheleth expresses his divergence from commonly accepted views is the use of *contrasting proverbs*. As is well known, proverbs frequently contradict one another. "Fools rush in where angels fear to tread" is opposed by the saw "To hesitate is to be lost." The beautiful sentiment "Absence makes the heart grow fonder" is bluntly denied by the saying "Out of sight, out of mind."

The compiler of Proverbs was aware of this tendency when he quoted these two maxims in succession:

> Answer not a fool according to his folly, lest thou also be like unto him.
> Answer a fool according to his folly, lest he be wise in his own eyes. (Prov. 26.4, 5)

Job and Koheleth use the same device, but for their own purposes. They quote one proverb and then register their disagreement by citing another diametrically opposed thereto.

No theme was dearer to the hearts of the instructors of youth than that of the importance of hard work. Koheleth expresses his doubts on the subject by quoting the conventional view and following it by another proverb of opposite intent.[19]

---

[19] For the conventional view cf., among other passages, Prov. 6.6–11; 10.4; 12.24, 27; 13.4; 19.24; 24.33. Koheleth's attitude is expressed in 2.18 ff.; 4.4 ff.; 5.12 ff.; 6.1 ff.

"The fool foldeth his hands together, and eateth his
   own flesh."
"Better is a handful of quietness, than both hands full
   of labour and striving after wind." (Eccl. 4.5, 6)

That Koheleth favors the second view is proved by its
position as a refutation after verse 5, by the characteristic
phrase, "vanity and chasing of wind," and by his oft-
repeated view of the folly of toil in a meaningless world.[20]

Like all the Wise Men, conventional or otherwise,
Koheleth has a prejudice in favor of wisdom as against
folly. He himself tells how the wisdom of one poor man
proved more efficacious than a mighty army. Yet he knows,
too, how little wisdom is honored for its own sake, and
how one fool can destroy the efforts of many wise men.
These ideas seem to be expressed in some reflections, consisting of brief proverbs contradicted by others.[21]

I thought "Wisdom is better than prowess" but "the
   wisdom of the poor man is despised and his words
   are not heard."
"Wisdom is better than weapons of war." But "one
   fool destroys much good."[22] (Eccl. 9.16, 18)

[20] Vulgate, Ibn Ezra, and Levy supply "saying" after v. 5, thus making v. 6 the opinion of the fool, who prefers indolence to labor. This
solves the contradiction of vv. 5 and 6, to be sure, but places Koheleth
in the position of urging hard work, which is highly unlikely. See note
26 above. Barton's elimination of 4.5, as the gloss of the *Ḥokmah* inter-
polator, deprives the passage of the unique flavor of its author's personality.

[21] So Levy. Barton, following Siegfried and Haupt, considers 9.17–
10.3 *Ḥokmah* interpolations. Volz eliminated 9.17, 18a as "unimportant
proverbs." Such a procedure fails to reckon with the fact that Koheleth
was himself a member of the *Ḥokmah* school. Verse 9.17, regarding the
value of quiet speech, is a conventional utterance completely in accord
with the unimpassioned spirit of Koheleth's reflections, and there is
no good reason for doubting its authenticity.

[22] The root חטא, as Barton (op. cit., p. 165) notes, means "to miss,
make an error" and refers here to intellectual slips, so that to Koheleth
it is almost identical with כסיל. So too חֹטָאִים in 10.4 refers to errors
committed by a courtier before a ruler, and not to sin in the moral or
religious sense.

Here, the latter proverbs, in which Koheleth expresses his own standpoint, are undoubtedly of his own composition. The former proverbs, from which he dissents, may be quotations, or, as seems more probable, original restatements by Koheleth of conventional *Hokmah* doctrines.

The recognition of this device in Job (15.9, 10) helps to explain an otherwise abrupt transition. Throughout the argument Job's friends have insisted that they possess superior wisdom because of their greater age:

> What knowest thou, that we know not?
> What understandest thou, which is not in us?
> With us are both the gray-headed and the very aged,
> Much older than thy father in days. (Job 15.9, 10)

Job denies this principle, by citing it in one proverb and refuting it by another. Here, too, the use of quotation marks and an introductory formula would make the connection clear.[23]

> *You say* "With aged men is wisdom and length of days
>   is understanding"
> *I say*   "With Him is wisdom and might; He hath
>   counsel and understanding." (Job 12.12, 13)

Per se, the second proverb merely asserts God's wisdom; but by being placed in juxtaposition to v. 11, it serves to undermine the doctrine of the superiority of the aged. The relationship between these two verses is aptly illustrated by another passage of similar import from the Elihu

---

[23] Driver-Gray, *ICC Commentary on Job*, Vol. I, p. 116 f., quote this interpretation, but do not accept it "because the antithesis is formally unexpressed." The evidence adduced in this paper of the frequent absence of such formal signs should be sufficient to modify this judgment. Siegfried and Duhm omit these verses — an easy escape from the difficulty which solves nothing. Some scholars take v. 12 interrogatively, "Have the aged men wisdom, and length of days understanding?" (Volz, Ball) or adopt the even more violent expedient of prefixing לא "The aged have not wisdom," etc. (Jastrow)! Budde stands alone in recognizing that v. 12 is a quotation of the traditional view, refuted in v. 13.

speeches. Like Job, Elihu is impatient with the pretensions
of the elders to superior wisdom. He also quotes the accepted opinion as to the relation between age and wisdom
and then proceeds to refute it. He does so, however, not
by a proverb, but by a comment. Here the transition is
clear because of the use of the introductory words: (v. 7,
אָמַרְתִּי; v. 8, אָכֵן).

> I thought "Days should speak, and many years should
>   teach wisdom."
> But it is the spirit in man and the breath of the Al-
>   mighty, that gives understanding. (Job 32.7, 8)

D. While proverbs are not lacking in the Book of Job,
quotations as a rule take a form different from those in
Ecclesiastes. The author of Job is not a philosopher coolly
discussing opinions in his study. He is a man who thinks
and feels deeply, and whose glowing passion has created a
poem rather than a dissertation. Job has no need to quote
the conventional doctrines on reward and punishment from
other literary sources, for they are being expounded in his
very presence by the Friends. In his zeal to attack their
views and defend his own, Job has occasion to quote and
even misquote the utterances of his adversaries, as men
have always done in controversy. Since these quotations
too are marked by no external signs, they have frequently
been misunderstood and removed from the text.

Chapter 21, vv. 19–34, supplies an excellent illustration.
Here commentators have resorted to excision and emendation, in order to make the passage intelligible.[24] These

---

[24] The variety of views may be studied in Driver-Gray, Budde and
Ball. A brief selection is here given. Thus v. 22 together with v. 21b,
23–26 is eliminated by Volz. Ball emends v. 22a to read: הֲלֹא אֵל יְלַמֶּד־
דָעַת "Shall not El teach knowledge?" This he interprets (p. 293) to
mean that Job argues, "Should we not rather observe what God actually does rather than assert a priori notions of what he ought to do?"
This seems far-fetched.

In order to bring v. 30 into harmony with Job's views, scholars have expedients become unnecessary if we recognize that here, at the end of the Second Cycle of speeches, Job restates no less than four arguments of the Friends and refutes each in turn:

I.   The Friends argue that the sins of the fathers will be visited upon the children. This is the position of Bildad:

> His children shall be hungry and calamity shall be
> ready for his fall. (Job 18.12)

This view, eminently satisfying in the old days of group solidarity, was becoming increasingly unattractive with the emergence of the individual personality in Hebrew thought. In 21.19a, Job quotes this view; in vv. 19b–21, he refutes it.

II.   Another argument of the Friends is that God is too exalted for human comprehension and hence beyond man's criticism. This is a favorite theme of Eliphaz, as in 4.17 and 15.14:

> "What is man that he be pure and how can he born of
> woman be just?
> Behold he does not trust his holy ones and the heavens
> are not pure in his eyes."

God's greatness is emphasized from a slightly different viewpoint in 15.8:

> Dost thou hearken in the council of God?
> And dost thou gather wisdom to thyself?

generally accepted the emendations of לְיֹום into בְּיֹום and יוּבָלוּ into יֻצָּל (Siegfried, Beer, Steuernagel, Budde, Volz), reading the verse:

כִּי בְיֹום אֵיד יַחָשֶׂךְ רָע בְּיֹום עֲבָרֹות יֻצָּל

"In the day of calamity the sinner is spared,
In the day of wrath he is saved."

Ball objects that these changes are graphically too extreme and reads:

כִּי מֵאֵיד יַחָשֶׂךְ רָע וּבְיֹום עֲבָרָה יִפָּלֵט

"That the bad man is kept from calamity
And in the day of wrath he escapes."

Aside from linguistic difficulties, these changes are entirely unnecessary, if the passage is understood as a quotation.

This view Job paraphrases in 21.22:

> Shall any one teach God knowledge?
> Seeing that He judges those on high?

He then proceeds to refute this conception of God's perfect dealings with man, but not by a direct attack. Instead, Job paints an unforgettable picture of reality, emphasizing the contrast between the ease of the wicked and the bitter lot of the just during their lifetime, while even in death there is no just retribution, for they both meet the same end (vv. 23–26).

III. The Friends have delighted to point out that while the sinner may seem to be well entrenched in his prosperity, calamity suddenly comes upon him, destroying his habitation and leaving nothing to mark the site of his former glory. This position has been emphasized by Eliphaz (in 5.3 ff.; 15.32 ff.), Bildad (8.22; 18.5–21), and Zophar (11.20; 20.26):

> I have seen the foolish taking root;
> But suddenly I beheld his habitation cursed. (5.3)
> They that hate thee shall be clothed with shame;
> And the tent of the wicked shall be no more. (8.22)
> For the company of the godless shall be desolate,
> And fire shall consume the tents of bribery. (15.35)
> He shall have neither son or son's son among his people,
> Nor any remaining in his dwellings. (18.19)

Job quotes this favorite doctrine of the Friends in the form of a rhetorical question addressed to him (v. 28):

> "Where is the house of the prince, or where the tent
> of dwelling of the wicked?"

Then, taking the rhetorical question at face value, he proceeds to reply sarcastically that any passer-by can point out the mansion of the oppressor standing unharmed in all its glory! (vv. 27–28)

IV. The Friends insist that punishment ultimately overtakes the sinner, no matter how long the delay.

Koheleth had already pointed out that this delay in punishment encourages men to commit crime (Eccl. 8.11 ff.). Job, however, is concerned with the injustice involved. He quotes the opinion of the Friends (v. 30) but insists that justice demands an immediate punishment of the sinner. Instead, Job says, the transgressor lives a life of ease, and to cap it all is buried with pomp and ceremony at the end (vv. 30–34).[25]

The entire passage understood in this light is a striking example of effective argument, marked by passion, irony and logic:

19. A. "God stores up his iniquity for his children" . . .
         Let Him recompense *him*, that *he* may know it!

20.   Let his own eyes see his destruction,
         And let him drink of the Almighty's wrath.

21.   For what concern has he in his house after him,
         Seeing the number of his months is determined?

22. B. "Shall anyone teach God knowledge?
         Seeing he judges those on high?" . . . [26]

[25] The use of quotations in chap. 21 has been partially recognized. Thus, v. 19a is taken as a quotation by Budde and by Driver-Gray, who follow the English version and prefix "Ye say" and apparently by Ball (*Book of Job*, 1922). Verse 22 is similarly treated by Hitzig, but the consensus of scholarly opinion has not hitherto inclined to this view. The satiric intent of vv. 28 f. has been overlooked, and v. 30 has proved another stumbling-block. See Driver-Gray, op. cit., for an excellent conspectus of the interpretation on these passages. On the other hand, Yellin, op. cit., p. 52, renders vv. 19, 22 and 30 as do we, but takes v. 28 differently.

[26] Verse 22b may possibly be rendered differently, as follows:
    "Shall any one teach God knowledge
    And shall he judge the All-High?"
i. e., can any human being presume either to instruct or to judge God. This rendering has the advantage of giving a better parallelism to the verse. For רָמִים as an epithet of God, we may perhaps compare the biblical use of עֶלְיוֹן (Num. 24.16; Deut. 32.8; II Sam. 22.14; Isa. 14.14; Lam. 3.35, 38; and very frequently in the Psalms, 91.1, 9; 92.2 and often). Cf. also the very common title גָּבוֹהַּ "The All-High" in rab-

23.   One dies in his full strength,
           Being wholly at ease and secure.

24.   His pails are full of milk,
           And the marrow of his bones is moistened.

25.   And another dies in bitterness of soul,
           And has never tasted any joy.

26.   Together they lie down in the dust,
           And the worm covers them over.

27.   Behold, I know your thoughts.
           And the devices by which you do me violence.

28.   C.   If you say: "Where is the house of the prince
           And where is the tent of dwelling of the wicked?"

29.   Haven't you asked the passers-by,
           You cannot deny their tokens!

30.   D.   "Indeed the sinner is saved for the day of
              calamity,
           And will be led forth to the day of wrath."

31.   But who shall declare his way at once,
           And for what he has done — who will requite him?

32.   For he is borne to the grave,
           And keeps watch over his tomb.

33.   The clods of the valley are sweet unto him,
           And all men draw after him,
           And before him an innumerable host.

34.   How then do you comfort me with vanity?
           And your answers remain only a betrayal. (Job
           21.19–34)

   E.   Another form of quotation in Job may be described
as *oblique restatement*. At times, Job cites the opinion of

binic literature, probably a development from the usage in Ps. 138.6.
Note also the use of רָם in Isa. 57.15: כִּי כֹה אָמַר רָם וְנִשָּׂא שֹׁכֵן עַד וְקָדוֹשׁ
שְׁמוֹ. The plural רָמִים would be analogous to similar epithets, as קְדֹשִׁים
when applied to God (see Ehrlich, *Randglossen*, on Hosea 12.1; Prov.
9.10).

the Friends, not literally but ironically, in a form bordering on parody. Failure to recognize this fact has vitiated many attempts to interpret chapter 12, one of the most striking utterances of Job. Thus of a chapter of twenty-five verses, Grill and Siegfried eliminate twenty-two while even Driver-Gray delete nine of that number.[27]

A clue to the understanding of the chapter is to be found in vv. 7, 8:

וְאוּלָם שְׁאַל נָא בְהֵמוֹת וְתֹרֶךָ   וְעוֹף הַשָּׁמַיִם וְיַגֶּד־לָךְ
אוֹ שִׂיחַ לָאָרֶץ וְתֹרֶךָ   וִיסַפְּרוּ לְךָ דְּגֵי הַיָּם

It is obvious by the singular verbs and suffixes (וְתֹרֶךָ ,שְׁאַל, שִׂיחַ ,לָךְ) that Job cannot be talking to his Friends, whom he always addresses in the plural (cf. 6.21–20).

The passage 12.7–8 is actually *a restatement by Job of the Friends' admonition to him.* In 12.5 he has declared

לַפִּיד בּוּז לְעַשְׁתּוּת שַׁאֲנָן נָכוֹן לְמוֹעֲדֵי רָגֶל

that the secure can afford to look with contempt on the sufferings of their fellow men. Then follows his recapitulation of the Friends' position as he sees it. They have had to admit the prosperity of the wicked (v. 6), but have sought, in effect, to deflect his attention elsewhere, by calling on Job to admire God's perfection as reflected in the natural order (vv. 7 f.; cf. 5.9 ff.; 11.7 ff.):

Who doeth great things and unsearchable,
Marvelous things without number;
Who giveth rain upon the earth,
And sendeth waters upon the fields;

---

[27] Siegfried omits 12.4 to 13.1; Grill (*Zur Kritik der Komposition des Buches Hiob*) omits 12.4 to 13.2. Driver-Gray delete 12.4–12, (op. cit., vol. I, p. 111). Volz leaves only five verses in Job's speech (12.2, 3, 11, 12; 13.2), and transfers the remainder (12.4–10, 13–25; 13.1) to Zophar in chap. 11 (op. cit., p. 39 f.). Jastrow (*Book of Job*, Philadelphia, 1920) omits vv. 4c, 5 in part, 6c, 10, 12, 13, 17–19, 22, 23, and 25. Ball removes 4c, 6, 10 (doubtfully), and 13. Budde, on the other hand argues forcefully against Grill and Siegfried's procedure (*Das Buch Hiob*, ad loc.; also *ThLZ*, 1891, no. 2).

So that He setteth up on high those that are low,
And those that mourn are exalted to safety. (Job
5.9, 10, 11)

Job meets this attempt to sidetrack the argument by replying that there is nothing new in the idea of the power and greatness of God (vv. 9–10); in fact, he can and does portray God's might far more effectively than the Friends (vv. 11–25). All this, he repeats, he knows as well as they (13.1, 2). Yet he still adheres to his desire to argue with the Almighty. (13.3).

A translation of the salient sections of the passage will demonstrate its unity and power and clarify the process of thought:

4.   A mockery have I become to His Friend,
     who calls to God and is answered, a mockery to the
     perfect saint!

5.   For calamity there is contempt, in the mind of the
     secure, prepared for those whose feet stumble.

6.   *You admit*, "The tents of the robbers are at peace,
     and the dwelling places of those who anger God, who
     hold God in their hand."

7.   "But," *you say*, "ask the cattle to teach you,
     and the fowl of the heaven to tell you.

8.   Or speak to the earth that it instruct you
     and let the fish of the sea declare to you."

9.   Who knows not in all this,
     that the hand of the Lord has made it!

10. In whose hand is the soul of every living thing
     and the spirit of all human flesh.

11. Indeed the ear tests words
     as the palate tastes its food.

12. *You say* "Wisdom is with the aged and understanding
     with length of days."

13. *But I say* "With *Him* is wisdom and strength
     His are counsel and understanding."
14. Behold He destroys and it cannot be rebuilt.
     He imprisons a man and he is not released.
15. He shuts up the waters and they dry up
     or He sends them forth and they overturn the earth,
     etc.

— — — — — —

13.1. Behold all this my eye has seen, my ear has heard
       and understood.
   2. What you know, I know also; I am not inferior
       to you.
   3. But *I* will dispute with the Almighty and desire to
       argue with God!

— — — — — —

That Job exaggerates and misstates the position of his
opponents is inherent in the very nature of things. Mark
Anthony's oration in *Julius Caesar* is merely an ironic
restatement of Brutus' judgment on the dead tyrant — a
restatement that proves its undoing.

Through this study of quotations in Wisdom Literature
we hope to have gained a better understanding of many
difficult passages in Ecclesiastes and Job. In addition, we
are led to recognize the essential unity and genuineness of
the received text, and are thus enabled to see Koheleth
steadily and see him whole. Above all, we begin to appreciate the agonizing conflicts of these spirits, who wrestled
with eternal problems in the conviction that nothing less
than the truth was worthy of their God.

244

THE RIDDLE OF THE SPHINX: THE STRUCTURE
OF THE BOOK OF QOHELETH

ADDISON G. WRIGHT, s.s

Qoheleth is one of the most difficult books in the Bible, and it has long been an enigma and a source of fascination for its readers and students. In 1898 Plumptre wrote: "It comes before us as the sphinx of Hebrew literature, with its unsolved riddles of history and life,"[1] riddles such as the title "Qoheleth" which the author assumes, the date and place of composition, the language, the unity of authorship, the structure, genre, message and background of the book, indeed the reasons for its very presence in the biblical canon. In this century there has been a growing consensus of scholarly opinion on positions connected with a few of these issues (title, date, background, presence in the canon). Among recent commentators there has also been a trend away from the earlier assessments of Qoheleth as a hedonist or pessimist or skeptic or agnostic, and a trend toward a more balanced view which does justice to Qoheleth as a man of faith and which realizes that no single label expresses the complexity of his thought; but there is still a lack of agreement on what the dominant note is that Qoheleth strikes. So we have advanced a certain distance since Plumptre, but the basic problem of the book remains: its seeming lack of order and of progression of thought, as well as its alternation of orthodox and of heterodox statements sometimes to the point of apparent contradiction. It is only when the principle underlying this maze can be established with evidence sufficiently objective to give some promise of a consensus, that we will have the requisite data to move ahead with confidence to attack the remaining and major problems (message, genre, and unity) and to solve the essential riddles.

The present writer believes that the principle underlying this maze is not to be sought in multiple authorship, or in an appeal to a "dialectic" mode of thought or to Qoheleth's supposed vacillating attitude toward tradition (now standing with it, now against it), but that the principle is to be sought in the area of structure. He believes that the book is in fact structured and that the key to that structure is to be found in three successive patterns of verbal repetition in 1,12-11,6. When these patterns are taken as indicating the framework of the book and when that framework is brought to the material as an overlay as it were, there emerges out of the apparent disorder a straightforward presentation of a very simple theme, albeit somewhat reduced in content from what has previously been

---

[1] E. H. Plumptre, *Ecclesiastes* (*Cambridge Bible*; Cambridge, 1898) 7.

seen as the message of the book. The following pages elaborate on these assertions and present the evidence upon which they are based.

Previous Views on the Structure

In the past, two positions, *grosso modo,* have been taken with regard to the structure of Qoheleth. One position is that there is no plan; one cannot make an outline. Impressed by the disorder, these commentators have concluded that it would be to force the material if one tried to show order and overall sequence of thought, and they have concluded that the respectful approach to the work is to isolate units or themes or even authors, and to view the book as a collection like Prv or as assorted observations around the theme that all is vanity and other secondary ideas. The words of Delitzsch well represent this position: ". . . a gradual development, a progressive demonstration, is wanting, and even the grouping together of the parts is not fully carried out; the connection of the thoughts is more frequently determined by that which is external and accidental, and not infrequently an incongruous element is introduced into the connected course of kindred matters. . . . All attempts to show, in the whole, not only oneness of spirit, but also a genetic progress, an all-embracing plan, and an organic connection, have hitherto failed, and must fail."[2] This view is espoused in one form or another by a large number of commentators and is the prevailing opinion.[3]

[2] F. Delitzsch, *Commentary on the Song of Songs and Ecclesiastes,* trans. by M. G. Easton (Edinburgh, 1891) 188.

[3] Thus C. H. H. Wright, *The Book of Koheleth* (London, 1883); G. Wildeboer, *Der Prediger* (*Kurzer Handkommentar zum AT*; Frieburg, 1898); Plumptre, *op. cit.*; A. H. McNeile, *An Introduction to Ecclesiastes* (Cambridge, 1904); V. Zapletal, *Das Buch Kohelet* (Freiburg, 1905); G. A. Barton, *The Book of Ecclesiastes* (*ICC*; New York, 1908); G. C. Martin, *Proverbs, Ecclesiastes and Song of Songs* (*Century Bible*; Edinburgh, 1908); M. Jastrow, *A Gentle Cynic* (Philadelphia, 1919); A. L. Williams, *Ecclesiastes* (*Cambridge Bible*; Cambridge, 1922); A. Allgeier, *Das Buch des Predigers* (*Die Heilige Schrift des AT*; Bonn, 1925); G. Kuhn, *Erklärung des Buches Koheleth* (*BZAW* 43; Gressen, 1926); B. Gemser, *Prediker* (Groningen, 1931); K. Galling, "Kohelet-Studien," *ZAW* 50 (1932) 276-99; *id., Die fünf Megilloth* (*HAT*; Tübingen, 1940); A. D. Power, *Ecclesiastes* (London, 1952); R. H. Pfeiffer, *Introduction to the Old Testament* (London, 1952) 724; R. Gordis, *Qoheleth—The Man and His World* (New York, [2]1955); E. Jones, *Proverbs and Ecclesiastes* (*Torch Bible Commentaries*; London, 1961); W. Zimmerli, *Das Buch des Predigers Salomo* (*ATD*; Göttingen, 1962); E. T. Ryder, "Ecclesiastes," *Peake's Commentary on the Bible,* eds. M. Black and H. H. Rowley (London, 1962); H. W. Hertzberg, *Der Prediger* (*Kommentar zum AT*; Gütersloh, [2]1963); O. Eissfeldt, *The Old Testament: An Introduction,* trans. by P. R. Ackroyd (Oxford, 1965) 493-94; R. B. Y. Scott, *Proverbs. Ecclesiastes* (*Anchor Bible*; New York, 1965); A. Barucq, *Ecclésiaste* (*Verbum Salutis*; Paris, 1968).

Another position is represented by those who feel that the book must have some unity or progression of thought and who have attempted to offer an outline, e.g., Bea,[4] H. L. Ginsberg,[5] and some of the commentaries.[6]

[4] A. Bea, *Liber Ecclesiastae* (Romae, 1950) :
  1,2-3 Theme
  1,4-2,26 Neither the study of nature nor pleasure nor wisdom satisfies man
  3,1-7,24 Wisdom cannot solve the enigmas of life
  7,25-9,17 Study of the practical utility of wisdom
  9,18-12,8 Practical advice
  12,9-13 Epilogue

[5] H. L. Ginsberg, *Studies in Koheleth* (*Texts and Studies of the Jewish Theological Seminary of America*, XVII; New York, 1950) 1-11; *id.*, "Supplementary Studies in Koheleth," *Proceedings of the American Academy for Jewish Research* 21 (1952) 35-62; *id.*, "The Structure and Contents of the Book of Koheleth," *Wisdom in Israel and in the Ancient Near East*, eds. M. Noth and D. W. Thomas (*VT[S]* 3; Leiden, 1955) 138-149 :
  A. 1,2-2,26 All is vanity and man's only profit is using his goods
  B. 3,1-4,3 All happenings are foreordained but never fully foreseeable
  A'. 4,4-6,9 } are complementary to A and B
  B'. 6,10-12,8 }

[6] F. Hitzig, *Der Prediger Sulomo's* (*Kurzgefasstes exegetisches Handbuch zum AT*; Leipzig, 1847) 125-126 :
  1,1-4,16 Theoretical foundation
  4,17-8,15 Rejection of false advice
  8,16-12,14 Qoheleth's advice

C. D. Ginsburg, *Coheleth* (London, 1861) :
  1,2-11   Prologue
  1,12-2,26 Investigation of pleasure and wisdom
  3,1-5,19 Investigation of toil
  6,1-8,15 Investigation of riches and prudence
  8,16-12,7 Résumé and conclusion
  12,8-12 Epilogue
and similarly, O. Zöckler, *Ecclesiastes*, trans. W. Wells (New York, 1870).

J. F. Genung, *Words of Koheleth* (Boston, 1904) :
  1,2-11   The fact and the question
  1,12-2,26 An induction of life
  3,1-22   Times and seasons
  4-5   In a crooked world
  6,1-7,18 Fate and the intrinsic man
  7,19-9,10 Avails of wisdom
  9,11-11,6 Wisdom encountering time
  11,7-12,7 Rejoice and remember
  12,8-14 The nail fastened

E. Podechard, *L'Ecclésiaste* (*Études Bibliques*; Paris, 1912) :
  1,2-3   Theme of the book
  1,4-11   Preliminary consideration
  1,12-2,26 Vanity of wisdom and of pleasures
  3,1-22   Vanity of man's efforts

The results have been quite disparate, and this lack of agreement has been viewed by many as the final and conclusive evidence if more were needed that there is indeed no plan in the book to begin with. These attempts at

4,1-5,8	Diverse anomalies in human society
5,9-7,12	Vanity of riches
7,13-9,10	Virtue is unable to assure happiness
9,11-11,6	Effort and talent are unable to assure success
11,7-12,8	Conclusion
12,9-14	Epilogue

and similarly D. Buzy, *L'Ecclésiaste* (*La Sainte Bible*, Pirot-Clamer; Paris, 1946).
A. Vaccari, *Institutiones biblicae* (Romae, 1935) II, 77:

1,4-3,15	The vanity of the transitory effects of effort
3,16-5,19	The vanity of evil in society
6-7	The vanity of the insatiableness of desires
8,1-11,6	The vanity of the uncertainty of the future
11,7-12,8	Conclusion

A. Miller in H. Höpfl, *Introductionis in sacros utriusque testamenti libros compendium,* (Romae, ⁵1946) II, 328:

1,4-2,26	
3,1-7,29	Three series of reflections
8,1-10,20	
11,1-12,7	Conclusion

J. J. Weber, *L'Ecclésiaste* (Paris, 1947):

1,1-11	Introduction
1,12-2,26	Investigation of wisdom and pleasure
3,1-22	The powerless efforts of man
4,1-6,9	Diverse anomalies in society
6,10-9,10	Assorted reflections on life
9,11-11,8	The disproportion between effort and success
11,9-12,14	Conclusion

R. Pautrel, *L'Ecclésiaste* (*BJ*; Paris, 1948) sees eight vanities discussed in two parts:
Part I

1,4-11	Prologue on ennui
1,12-2,26	The good life
3,1-22	Death
4,1-5,8	The individual lost in the collectivity of society
5,9-6,12	Money

Part II

7,1-7	Prologue on laughter
7,8-8,15	Belief in a sanction during life
8,16-9,10	Love does not satisfy
9,11-11,6	Chance
11,7-12,8	Old age

H. Lamparter, *Das Buch der Weisheit: Prediger und Sprüche* (Stuttgart, 1955):

1,3-2,26	
3,1-7,24	Three series of sayings
7,25-12,7	
12,8-14	Epilogue

outlines, with few exceptions,[7] have been largely the "this is how I read Qoheleth" sort of thing with no evidence offered aside from the critic's assurance that he sees a sequence of thought. The writer has no desire to add one more attempt of that kind here; rather he is speaking out of another tradition of criticism,.a sort of third approach to Qoheleth that is beginning to form.

In the field of literary criticism, the twentieth century has seen the development of a new school known as the New Stylistics or the New Criticism. It is a term which describes a great variety of literary critics, but the distinguishing features of all of them are: (1) a trend away from the psychological, historical, and biographical approaches to literature; (2) a placing of the point of departure for criticism in the work itself; and (3) a careful verbal and structural analysis.[8] The elements of the method are not new; but the emphasis is new, the explicit and single-minded manner in which the work is done is new, and the interest in structure is thoroughly modern and corresponds to structural preoccupations in many of the sciences today.

The New Criticism in its pure form is of course a reaction to other schools of criticism and needs to be balanced by them, especially (for our

---

O. S. Rankin, "Ecclesiastes," *The Interpreter's Bible*, 5 (New York, 1956) :

    1,2-4,3   Qoheleth's world outlook
    4,4-9,16 A wise man's experiences
    9,17-12,7 Concluding advice

C. Siegfried (*Die Sprüche, Prediger und Hoheslied* [*Handkommentar zum AT*; Göttingen, 1898]), who considers the book in its present form to be the product of nine authors, provides a plan for the *Grundschrift*.

[7] C. D. Ginsburg (*op. cit.*, 17) constructs his plan on the basis of the recurrence of the advice to enjoy the fruits of one's labor in 2,26; 5,17-19 and 8,15, and interprets these as the conclusions of sections. Weber (*op. cit.*, 222) views the repetitions of that same idea in 2,26; 3,22; 6,9; 9,7-10 and 11,8 as marking the ends of sections. Pautrel (*op. cit.*, 12), who simply states that there are initial and concluding formulae, apparently builds in part on the occurrences in 2,26; 3,22; 6,9; 8,15 and 9,7-10. Hitzig (*op. cit.*, 125-26) based his plan on the change to an imperative in 4,17 (similarly Castellino below) and on the repetition of the enjoyment idea in 5,17-19; 8,15 and 9,7-10. None takes into account all of the occurrences of the idea, and each sees its appearance in 3,13 as not significant.

[8] P. Guiraud, *La stylistique* (Paris, 1961) and G. Watson, *The Literary Critics* (Harmondsworth, 1962) briefly survey the school in its European and American forms. A handbook that synthesizes much of the trend is R. Wellek and A. Warren, *Theory of Literature* (New York, ³1962). Further bibliography can be found in each. Examples of work in the same spirit in biblical criticism are the studies of Muilenburg and Alonso-Schökel (on Hebrew poetic and prose selections), Galbiati (on Ex), Lamarche (on Zech 9-14), Vanhoye (on Heb), Reese and the present writer (on Wis), and much of the *redaktionsgeschichtlich* work on the Gospels.

purposes) whenever it exhibits a tendency to view as secondary the meaning the author intended to give his work. In addition, many feel that its close analysis and dissection leave a piece of literature lifeless, and they heartily agree with T. S. Eliot's sneer that it is "the lemon-squeezer school of criticism."[9] Here surely it is a question of judgment as to the suitability and potential of the method for the study of a given work, and undoubtedly it is also and ultimately a matter of taste. Of special value for the exegete, though, is the school's emphasis on structural analysis. Reading in context is universally recognized as the cardinal rule of objective exegesis, but the ascertaining of context in the past has been all too often something less than objective. The New Stylistics can shore up this weakness.

With regard to structural analysis in its restricted sense, i.e., the isolating of the plan of a work, the New Critics observe that there are two methods which can be used. One which they do not employ and which might be called the subjective method is to go immediately to the thought of a work and attempt to describe the sequence of ideas by translating them into an outline. The method has the advantage of being direct (one immediately produces that which is desired, the outline), but it has the disadvantage of being quite open to subjectivity in that the logical development seen by the critic may not be the logic of the author at all. One may well mistake topic sentence for development or development for topic sentence, and, of course, one such alteration and the thrust of the material of that particular section becomes different for the reader from what the author intended. Sometimes, too, our thought patterns may prevent us from seeing any plan at all in works that are indeed structured. This is generally the method that has been used on Qoheleth in the past (and on many other biblical books) and the variety of outlines that have been produced bears eloquent witness to the subjectivity of this approach.

The other procedure and the one pursued by the New Critics is what we might call an objective method.[10] It must remain vague in its formulation so as to be flexible, but essentially it is to put attention, first of all, not on the thought but on the form. The critic looks for repetitions of vocabulary and of grammatical forms and thus seeks to uncover whatever literary devices involving repetition the author may have used, such as inclusions, *mots crochets,* anaphora, chiasm, symmetry, refrains, announcement of topic and subsequent resumption, recapitulation, etc. In this way too he

---

[9] T. S. Eliot, *On Poetry and Poets* (New York, 1957) 125.

[10] For a discussion of this aspect of criticism see L. Alonso-Schökel, *Estudios de poética hebrea* (Barcelona, 1963) 309-336; "Poésie hébraïque," *VDBS* 8 (Paris, 1967) 85-90 and the bibliography in each.

discovers indeliberate repetitions that might provide a key to the thought and its emphases, and he becomes aware of clusters of vocabulary which may indicate blocks of material. The critic also looks for changes: changes of genre, person, mood, etc., all of which are potential indicators of seams between units. He searches for numerical patterns which the author may have impressed upon his work for one reason or another and which can provide clues to the author's conception of the plan of the work. The critic then brings whatever patterns there are to the thought and evaluates as significant those patterns that coincide with breaks in the thought and with conceptual units, and in that way gradually develops an outline. The subjective element is by no means removed entirely, but it is considerably lessened in that one is dealing with objective indices of structure in the work itself. And where there is a multiple convergence of indices in conjunction with breaks in the thought, the conclusions can approach a certitude.[11]

There have been two studies of Qoheleth in the spirit of the New Stylistics. One is the work of Oswald Loretz, *Qohelet und der alte Orient*,[12] which is an analysis of the book's style and themes. With regard to the plan, Loretz seems to have started with a proneness to be easily convinced that the book is not structured and that the key to its understanding lies in a study of interwoven themes. This apparently has led him to utilize the data of his analysis[13] more as a microstylist concerned with vocabulary and motifs than as a macrostylist concerned with overall structure. In any event he does not see a plan in the book.

The second study in the spirit of the New Criticism is to be found in a recent article of George Castellino[14] which is addressed solely to the ques-

[11] For example, in Wis (which is a virtual textbook case because of the multiple literary devices used by the author) the limits of sections are marked with inclusions and at the same time with *mots crochets*. Frequently the sections thus indicated are paralleled with others and this symmetry further confirms the division into units and also indicates their arrangement into larger groupings. Finally, the number of verses in each unit is proportioned to the number of verses in the neighboring unit on a fixed ratio obtained from additive series, and this proportioning is carried out in a pyramid fashion so that the same patterns are found ultimately in the major divisions of the book. The discovery of these interlocking patterns provides the final confirmation of the structure. Cf. "The Structure of the Book of Wisdom," *Bib* 48 (1967) 165-184; "Numerical Patterns in the Book of Wisdom," *CBQ* 29 (1967) 524-538.

[12] Freiburg, 1964.

[13] In a work as large as Qoheleth it is of course necessary to make a selection of the vocabulary to be analyzed. Unfortunately as it turned out Loretz overlooked one key word, *mṣ'*, and so its patterns did not figure in his study.

[14] "Qohelet and His Wisdom," *CBQ* 30 (1968) 15-28.

tion of structure. The method that Castellino wished to apply is sound. He goes immediately to the external form of the book and subjects it to analysis. He looks to repetitions and changes of verb forms. He observes that the book starts out with reflections on human life in the first person singular and that this pattern obtains all the way to 4,16. At 4,17, however, there is the abrupt change to the imperative for eight verses and, while this is not sustained and Qoheleth falls back again occasionally into the I-narrative, Castellino (as did Hitzig a century ago)[15] sees a different kind of discourse from there on. He thus divides the book into two parts: 1,1-4,16 and 4,17-12,12. As supporting evidence he offers the patterns of occurrence of five words and phrases in parts one and two. He sees the first part of the book as a negative appraisal of life upon which appraisal Qoheleth passes judgment in part two in a more positive and orthodox manner.

There are two problems with Castellino's proposal. First of all, the plan does not match the thought. There is no major break at 4,17, because the positive advice offered by Qoheleth in 5,17-19 has already been given in 2,24 and in 3,12-13, and the negative appraisal of life in 1,1-4,16 is continued in 5,12-6,9. Secondly, the objective data upon which the analysis is based are meager. No evidence at all is offered for the analysis of 4,17-12,12; it is the subjective method that is used. Statistics on vocabulary occurrence are difficult to interpret and need considerable reinforcement by other data before anything approaching certitude can be reached. The only "other data" offered are the changes of person in 4,17-5,7,[16] and these, viewed in complete isolation from all that follows, do not necessarily prove anything; as it turns out the book is constructed on other patterns, and the change in person at 4,17 is in fact of secondary significance for overall structure. Despite its shortcomings, however, the writer is deeply indebted to Castellino's article, because through it he became interested in the problem and was alerted to a meaningful pattern of repetition in 1,12-6,9; once entry was gained to the plan in that way, the solution of the rest of the riddle soon followed.

The Analysis

Let us remove from consideration for the moment 1,1 (the title of the book) as well as 1,2-11 on the endless round of events, etc.; it is generally acknowledged that the book gets underway in 1,12. In 1,12-15 there is an introductory statement and it ends with "all is vanity and a chase after wind," plus a proverb. This is followed by a second and parallel introduc-

---

[15] See note 7 above.

[16] If 12,9-14 is from the hand of the editor, the repetition of "fear God" in 5,6 and 12,13 is not significant structurally.

tion in 1,16-18 and this ends with "a chase after wind," plus a proverb. Qoheleth then tells in 2,1-11 how he tested pleasure-seeking, and this section ends with "all was vanity and a chase after wind." He then takes up in 2,12-17 the "wisdom, madness and folly" of 1,17 and tests them and finds no advantage to wisdom, and this paragraph ends with "all was vanity and a chase after wind." So there is a double introduction and then two paragraphs which are a development on them. These four units are generally recognized, and it is generally recognized that there is a development of thought up to this point. It is generally seen that these four paragraphs end with "(all is vanity and) a chase after wind," but as far as the present writer knows no one has ever pursued the pattern further in seeking a plan. In the spirit of the New Criticism let us pursue it further. The phrase occurs five more times: 2,26; twice together in 4,4-6; once in 4,16 and again in 6,9, and there it ends, never to be repeated in the remaining six chapters of the book. If we follow the analogy of the first four sections and let these subsequent occurrences of the phrase mark the ends of units also, they mark off four additional sections in a short-long-short-long arrangement: 2,18-26; 3,1-4,6; 4,7-16; 4,17-6,9. (The two occurrences of the phrase in 4,4-6 are taken together as marking the end of one section.) Are these meaningful units? In these four sections and only in these four sections the author evaluates the results of man's toil (an idea taken up from 2,10-11), and 24 of the book's 35 occurrences of the stem 'ml are here. In this material he in fact makes four observations on the results[17] of man's toil (2,18-26; 3,1-15; 4,7-9; 5,12-6,9), and each of the four sections, marked out by the pattern, contains *one* of these observations plus digressionary remarks suggested by the discussion of toil (see below). Moreover, three of the four sections begin with the "toil" idea; only 4,17-6,9 inserts digressionary remarks at the outset. So the verbal pattern coincides with a thought pattern and alerts us to the fact that the main subject of 2,18-6,9 is "toil."

There is, then, a continuity of thought from 1,12-6,9. In these chapters Qoheleth is reporting the results of his investigation of life undertaken to "understand what is best for men to do under the heavens during the limited days of their life" (2,3). He begins with a double introduction (1,12-15; 1,16-18), and then evaluates pleasure-seeking (2,1-11), wisdom (2,12-17), and finally the results of toil in four sections (2,18-6,9). The evaluation repeated at the end of each section is that it is a vanity and a chase after wind. These eight units are tied together not only by the repetition of the evaluation but also by an interlocking arrangement whereby

---

17 The little paragraph on toil in 4,4-6 is a secondary remark on the source of toil and is not part of the main discussion on the results of man's labor.

once the series begins, each section picks up an idea mentioned two units earlier. The "wisdom, madness and folly" of 2,12-17 resumes 1,17; "toil" in 2,18-26 picks up that idea from 2,10-11; "one fate" in 3,19 resumes 2,14; the problem of a man having no one with whom he can share the fruits of his toil in 4,7-16 picks up the idea of leaving the fruits of one's toil to another in 2,18-26; "oppression" in 5,7 resumes the same idea in 4,1; 5,11 recalls 2,23; and the idea of the non-satisfaction of riches in 5,9 resumes 4,8 (from the immediately preceding section in this final instance).

Running through these four sections on the vanities connected with toil there is another and related idea: there is nothing better for man than to eat and drink and enjoy the fruit of his labor (2,24; 3,13; 3,22; 5,17). This is the only advice that Qoheleth feels he can offer on what is good for man to do. When he gives the advice, he also remarks that the ability to enjoy is a gift of God (2,24-26; 3,13; 5,18), and at the end of the fourth section he elaborates on that idea. He points out that there are problems even with the advice to enjoyment: God does not give some men the power to enjoy the fruit of their labor (6,1-6); moreover, the appetite of man is never satisfied (6,7-9). And on this note the four sections on toil end. So there is not only a continuity of thought in 1,12-6,9, but there is also a development with regard to the enjoyment idea insofar as the advice is offered four times and then is heavily qualified in the last section.

In 6,6-9 some phrases recall earlier remarks: all go to the same place (cf. 3,20; 2,14-16); man's appetite is not satisfied (4,8; 5,9); what advantage does the wise man have over the fool (2,12-17). Perhaps this is a summing up, and 6,9 marks a major break in the book. The cessation here of "this is vanity and a chase after wind" creates a presumption to that effect, and the final qualification of the enjoyment idea reinforces that presumption. The following lines therefore deserve close scrutiny because they may be the beginning or even the introduction to the next part of the book.

The lines in question are simply 6,10-12, for immediately following them is a collection of proverbs (7,1ff.). In these three verses two ideas are repeated from the first part (what is, is [cf. 1,9.15; 3,15], and the vanity of many words [cf. 4,17-5,6]), and then a conclusion is drawn from the observations up to this point: who knows what is good for man to do (cf. 2,3; 2,24; 3,12; 3,22; 5,17) and who can tell him what will be after him (cf. 3,22). Is any of this vocabulary taken up again in the material that follows? In 8,7 there is a similar expression: "he does not know what is to be, for who can tell him how it will be"; but this does not seem to have any significance in that it is isolated and does not constitute the beginning or end or the theme of the passage in which it occurs. If we go further, though, we find something which looks quite significant indeed. The words "do not know" and "no knowledge" start occurring with great frequency after 9,1: in 9,1.5.10.12; 10,14.15; 11,2; and three times in 11,5-6; and this brings us right up to the poem, at the end, on youth and old age (11,7-12,8). The occurrence of "do not know" in 9,5 and its threefold appearance in 11,5-6 mark the ends of sections. If we let the others in between also mark the ends of sections, we get six units (9,1-6; 9,7-10; 9,11-12; 9,13-10,15; 10,16-11,2; 11,3-6). Each one deals with one aspect of the "what comes after" problem, and each says that man does not know (see below).

What about chs. 7-8? The pattern of the verb "not know" in chs. 9-10 calls attention to a similar pattern with the verb "not find/who can find" in chs. 7-8. It occurs in 7,14.24.28 (*bis*) and finally three times together in 8,17 at the very end of ch. 8. The first one marks the end of a section as does the triple repetition in 8,17; and if we let the others mark the ends of sections on an analogy with them and with the verb "to know" in chs. 9-10, we get four sections each containing traditional wisdom material and a subsequent comment on it; each one deals with one aspect of the "what is good for man to do" problem, and each says that man cannot find out[18] (see below).

So, to recapitulate, there is the eight-fold repetition in 1,12-6,9 of "vanity and a chase after wind," marking off eight meaningful units which contain eight major observations from Qoheleth's investigation of life, plus digressionary material. A secondary motif runs through the sections on toil (the only thing that he can find that is good for man to do is to enjoy the fruit of his toil), and at the end even this is shown to have limitations. Where this pattern ceases in 6,9 there follows immediately the introduction of two new ideas: man does not know what is good to do nor what comes after him; and another verbal pattern begins. The first idea is developed in four sections in 7,1-8,17. The end of each unit is marked by the verb "find out" and the final section ends with a triple "cannot find out" (8,17) in an *a b a* arrangement (*lō' yûkal hā'ādām limṣô' . . . weʾlō' yimṣā' . . . lō' yûkal limṣô'*). The second idea is developed in six sections in 9,1-11,6. The end of each unit is marked with "do not know" or "no knowledge" and the final section again ends with a triple "you do not know" (11,5-6) and again in an *a b a* arrangement (*'ênekā yôdēaʿ . . . lō' tēdaʿ . . . 'ênekā yôdēaʿ*). When this pattern ends we are right at the beginning of the generally recognized unit on youth and old age at the end of the book.

[18] Save in the first section. Here the effect of the whole section is to say that man cannot find out, but the verb "find," marking the end, is used in the sense of "find fault" with God (see below *ad loc.*).

Because of the convergence of indices, it seems almost certain that the patterns uncovered are a deliberate device utilized by the author to provide the main structure of the book. There are three successive patterns embracing exactly all the material between the initial (1,2-11) and concluding poems (11,7-12,8). Where one pattern ends the next begins. The patterns suggest that the book is divided into two main parts (1,12-6,9; 6,10-11,6) and the thought is also thus divided: in the first part Qoheleth is concerned with the vanity of various human endeavors, and in the second part with man's inability to understand the work of God. Each of the two halves indicated has an announcement of its topics at the beginning (1,12-18; 2,3 and 6,10-12) and does indeed pursue those topics. In the second half of the book there is a bipartite construction, and the two parts are paralleled to each other in structuring techniques even down to the triple ending in an *a b a* arrangement. Throughout the book the patterns coincide with meaningful units in the thought (see below). Finally the units match the thought in a repetitive manner and this adds further weight to the argument. If each section indicated by the pattern were on a different topic, the plan would be less certain. But it is a case of verbal repetitions marking out and exactly coinciding with repetitions of ideas. Eight sections are indicated in 1,12-6,9 and each is a part of Qoheleth's investigation of the vanity of various features of life, and only there is that investigation found. In chs. 7-8 four sections are indicated and each is a critique of traditional advice on what is good for man to do; and when the vocabulary repetition ("to find out") stops, so does the idea. In 9,1-11,6 six sections are indicated and each is a repetition of the problem of what comes after; and when the vocabulary repetition ("to know") stops, so does the idea.

Perhaps there are additional indices reinforcing the above, for it may be that Qoheleth used inclusions. There are repetitions in each section which could be so interpreted. What makes one hesitant to affirm their existence is the large amount of vocabulary repetition in the book, and the fact that sometimes the first part of a potential inclusion stands in from the beginning of its section some distance. But in some of the units the repetitions are striking[19] and do invite one to see the repetitions in other sections as inclusions. We shall indicate these possible inclusions below, but they do not constitute the essential argument.

There follow below an outline and a brief paraphrase of each unit of the

---

[19] E.g., *'ên qēṣ lᵉkol*, 4,8 and 16 (the only occurrences of *qēṣ* in the book, save in the editor's epilogue [12,12]); *yôm . . . yôm*, 7,1 and 14; *heḥākām*, 8,1 and 17; *gam 'ahăbâ gam śin'â*, 9,1 and 6; *'ir*, 9,14 and 10,15; *'ereṣ*, 10,16-17 and 11,2; *ma'ăśêh hā'ĕlōhim*, 7,13; 8,17; 11,5.

book to show the train of thought indicated by the structure. The writer is convinced that the patterns discovered should be the basis of future exegesis of the book, and that the material falling in each indicated unit should be interpreted in that context. He is not necessarily convinced that in each case he has captured the correct interpretation, but he wishes to begin that task.

Outline

TITLE (1,1)

POEM ON TOIL (1,2-11)

I. QOHELETH'S INVESTIGATION OF LIFE (1,12-6,9)

DOUBLE INTRODUCTION	(1,12-15)*	
	(1,16-18)*	
STUDY OF PLEASURE-SEEKING	(2,1-11)*	*ends with
STUDY OF WISDOM AND FOLLY	(2,12-17)*	"(vanity and)
STUDY OF THE FRUITS OF TOIL		a chase after
ONE HAS TO LEAVE THEM TO		wind"
ANOTHER	(2,18-26)*	
ONE CANNOT HIT ON THE RIGHT		
TIME TO ACT	(3,1-4,6)**	
THE PROBLEM OF A "SECOND		
ONE"	(4,7-16)*	
ONE CAN LOSE ALL THAT ONE		
ACCUMULATES	(4,17-6,9)*	

II. QOHELETH'S CONCLUSIONS (6,10-11,6)

INTRODUCTION (6,10-12): man does not know what God has done, for man cannot find out what is good to do and he cannot find out what comes after.

A. MAN CANNOT FIND OUT WHAT IS GOOD FOR HIM TO DO

CRITIQUE OF TRADITIONAL WISDOM		
ON THE DAY OF PROSPERITY		
AND ADVERSITY	(7,1-14)*	
ON JUSTICE AND WICKED-		*ends with "not
NESS	(7,15-24)*	find out/who
ON WOMEN AND FOLLY	(7,25-29)**	can find out"
ON THE WISE MAN AND THE		
KING	(8,1-17)***	

B. MAN DOES NOT KNOW WHAT WILL COME AFTER HIM

HE KNOWS HE WILL DIE; THE DEAD KNOW NOTHING	(9,1-6)*	
THERE IS NO KNOWLEDGE IN SHEOL	(9,7-10)*	*ends with "do not know/no knowledge"
MAN DOES NOT KNOW HIS TIME	(9,11-12)*	
MAN DOES NOT KNOW WHAT WILL BE	(9,13-10,15)**	
HE DOES NOT KNOW WHAT EVIL WILL COME	(10,16-11,2)*	
HE DOES NOT KNOW WHAT GOOD WILL COME	(11,3-6)***	

POEM ON YOUTH AND OLD AGE (11,7-12,8)

EPILOGUE (12,9-14)

Summary of the Book

1,12-15. Qoheleth begins by stating that he has studied all that is done on earth and he has found that *all is vanity and a chase after wind*. He closes the section with a proverb to the effect that the situation cannot be changed (cf. 3,14-15; 6,10, where the same idea marks the beginning of the second half of the book; 7,13). Possible inclusions (henceforth *Incl.*): *na'ăśâ taḥat/šenna'ăśû taḥat* in 13 and 14.

1,16-18. Qoheleth has studied wisdom and folly and concludes that the acquisition of wisdom is a *chase after wind*. He closes this second introductory section, as the first, with a proverb and it serves to explain his conclusion. Incl.: *weḥôsaptî/yôsîp . . . yôsîp; ḥokmâ; wādā'at/da'at; harbēh/berōb* in 16 and 18. There is a partial chiastic arrangement in the two introductions: (a) "I applied my mind" (13); (b) "I have seen everything" (14); (b) "I have acquired great wisdom . . . my mind has had great experience" (16-17); (a) "I applied my mind" (17). Perhaps it is simply a chiasm; perhaps the "I applied my mind" is an inclusion tying the two introductions together.

2,1-11. Qoheleth studied pleasure-seeking to see what is good for men to do. He undertook great works and did not deprive himself of any pleasure, but he found that *all was vanity and a chase after wind,* for there was no gain. Incl.: *beśimḥâ . . . ûleśimḥâ/śimḥâ . . . śāmēaḥ* in 1-2 and 10; *hebel* in 1 and 11; *ma'ăśay* in 4 and 11; *'āśâ* in 2-3 and 11.

2,12-17. The author takes up the "wisdom, madness and folly" of 1,17 and presents the results of his study of that aspect of life. He found that, despite the traditional teaching on the superiority of wisdom (2,13-14a), both the wise and the fool suffer the same fate, so what is the value of wisdom (14b-15)? "This also is vanity" (15) is a divider.[20] The idea of one fate is developed (16) and the conclusion stated—"*all is vanity and a chase after wind.*" Incl.: *ḥokmâ . . . heḥākām/heḥākām* in 12-14 and 16; *hakkᵉsîl* in 14 and 16; *'aśûhû/šenna'āśâ* in 12 and 17.

2,18-26. Qoheleth resumes the idea of toil from 2,10-11, and presents the first of four sections on the results of toil. Here he observes that the fruits of one's toil must be left to another, and who knows if he will be a wise man or a fool (18-19). "This also is vanity" in 19 is a divider. In any event the fruits must be given to one who did not work for them (20-21). "This also is vanity" in 21 is a divider. What does a man have from his work but pain and vexation and loss of sleep (22-23). "This also is vanity" (23) is a divider. There is nothing better for a man to do than to find enjoyment in the fruit of his toil, but enjoyment is something God-given and uncertain (an idea to be developed in 6,1-6) and thus it too is *vanity and a chase after wind.* Incl.: *ḥokmâ; da'at; yittᵉnennû/lātēt* in 21 and 26.[21]

3,1-4,6. Qoheleth presents (perhaps from traditional wisdom) the 14 opposites which have their time (2-8) and immediately applies them to the subject of toil. There is no profit in toil because God has established a time for everything and then has put timelessness in man's heart. Hence man has no sense of the right time to act, and so his toil is fruitless or chancy (9-11). There is nothing better than to find enjoyment in the fruit of one's toil (12-13). We cannot change what God has done (14-15). Incl.: *'āśâ . . . 'āśâ hā'ĕlōhîm/ya'aśeh hā'ĕlōhîm . . . hā'ĕlōhîm 'āśâ* in 11 and 14.[22]

While on the subject of time, Qoheleth adds a further observation (3,16-4,3). There is injustice in the world (16). According to the traditional wisdom, since there is a time and place for everything, then for every

[20] Except in 2,1, "this (also) is vanity/all is vanity/all that comes is vanity" is not only an evaluation, but it also has a structural function as a sort of quarter or half divider within a unit. Cf. 2,15.19.21.23; 3,19; 4,8; 5,9; 6,2; 7,6; 8,10.14; 11,8.

[21] V. 26a is taken in a non-ethical sense (so Barton, Gordis, Ryder, etc.). Qoheleth's judgment that even enjoyment is vanity (26b) is based on the uncertainty of it. This idea will be developed in 6,1-6 and the same judgment repeated in 6,9.—It may be noted that this first section on toil (2,18-26) is strongly tied to the preceding section on wisdom and folly (2,12-17) by the *mots crochets* "hate," "wise," and "fool" in 16-17 and 18-19.

[22] If there are inclusions, the 14 opposites stand outside of them in the manner of a text cited for the sake of subsequent comment.—We have put 3,14-15 with the preceding rather than with what follows on an analogy with 2,24; 3,22; and 5,17 where the advice to enjoyment is followed by remarks to the effect that man should accept what God does.

work there is a judgment (17).²³ But the author remarks that, not only cannot man predict the times of the opposites in 2-8, he has no grounds for predicting even that there will be a judgment, for man appears to be no different from the beasts in life or in death (18-21). So there is nothing better for man than to enjoy his works, for he has no way of knowing anything of the future to help him determine what else might be good to do (22; the latter is a major thought in the second part of the book, cf. 6,12; 9,1-11,6). In fact, in view of all the evil done on earth, the only ones more fortunate than those who are alive with regard to the knowledge of the future are those not yet born, who have not yet seen the evil done under the sun (4,1-3)! Incl.: *rā'itî/rā'â* in 3,16 and 4,3; *hamma'ăśeh* in 3,17 and 4,3.²⁴

The author returns to the topic of toil, the idea of oppression in 4,1, perhaps, suggesting the envy from which all of man's toil stems (4,4-6). This too is *vanity and a chase after wind*; and by juxtaposing two proverbs, Qoheleth urges not indolence but a handful of quiet, rather than two hands full of toil which is a *chase after wind* (4,4-6). Incl.: *'āmāl* in 4 and 6. Perhaps *'āmāl* in 3,9 and 4,6 is an overall inclusion for the whole section.

4,7-16.   Qoheleth presents his third observation on the results of toil: the problem of the "second." He points out that sometimes a man is alone and has no second one (son or brother) who will benefit from the riches gained by his toil (7-8). "This also is vanity" (8) is a divider. There follows a series of traditional sayings on "two are better than one" (9-12); and this is followed by an obscure example (13-16) which is related to the problem of the second (cf. *haššēnî* in 4,15) and perhaps challenges the "two is better than one" idea: the old and foolish king is perhaps a man who indeed has a "second" after him, but the second turns out to obscure the king's memory.²⁵ *This also is vanity and a chase after wind.* Incl.: *'ên qēṣ l^ekol* in 8 and 16.

4,17-6,9.   This final section on toil begins with a collection of wisdom material on the folly of many words (4,17-5,6). This theme appears again in 6,11 (the introduction to the second part of the book) and toward the end of the second part in 10,12-15; cf. also 12,12. Incl.: *dābār . . . d^ebārēkā*

---

²³ Emending in 3,17 MT *šām* to *mišpāṭ* with CCD. In any event, this is the sense of the sentence.

²⁴ It may be that there are two paragraphs here, 3,16-22 (Incl.: *rā'itî/rā'itî . . . lir'ôt* in 16 and 22; *hamma'ăśeh/b^ema'ăśâ(y)w* in 17 and 22), and 4,1-3 (Incl.: *wā'er'eh/rā'â; na'ăśîm (na'ăśâ) taḥat haššāmeš* in 1 and 3).

²⁵ This interpretation would see *taḥtā(y)w* in 4,15 as referring to the king, *lipnêhem* (temporal) in 16 as referring to the king and the heir, and *bô* in 16 as referring to the old king. If *bô* refers to the heir, then perhaps the story is about two men who try to go it alone.

. . . *b^erōb d^ebārim/d^ebārîm harbēh* in 5,1-2 and 5,6. As Gordis has noted, Qoheleth at times cites "a proverb, part of which is apposite, while the rest of the saying, though irrelevant, is quoted for the sake of completeness, a literary practice common to writers in all ages."[26] This practice is evident here as well as in 5,8-12; 7,1-12.19-21; 8,1-5; 9,13-11,4.

Qoheleth then sets up the ideas that will provide the basis for his final remarks on toil and enjoyment by assembling four pieces of traditional wisdom (5,7-11). Vv. 7-8 are used here as a picture of a hierarchy of greed and of acquisition of goods, and v. 9 states the insatiableness of man's appetite. "This also is vanity" (9) is a divider. The acquisition of goods is often accompanied by the loss of goods (10) and by the loss of enjoyment (11). He then takes up the ideas of acquisition and loss of goods and observes that sometimes a man will accumulate riches and then lose them and have nothing to show for his toil. He repeats for the fourth time that the only good he has been able to discover for man to do is to find enjoyment in the fruit of his toil (5,12-19). Incl.: *b^e'inyan/ma'ănēhû*[27] in 13 and 19; *'āmāl* in 14 and 18.

The author points out, however, that there is a serious problem even with this advice (as he has already hinted in 2,24-26 and in his characterizing of enjoyment as a "gift" of God in 3,13 and 5,18). Resuming the loss of enjoyment idea from the beginning of the section, he observes that sometimes God does not give a man power to enjoy the fruit of his toil (6,1-2). "This is vanity" (2) is a divider. The evil of such a situation is developed in 3-6. Incl.: *rā'îtî/rā'â* in 1 and 6.

Finally Qoheleth takes up from the beginning of the section the idea of the insatiableness of man's appetite (6,7). In this regard what advantage does the wise man have over the fool (8a), especially if the wise man be poor and have little to satisfy any desires (8b). Better is enjoyment of what is at hand than the wandering of desire (a paraphrase of Qoheleth's advice to enjoy the fruits of one's toil), but this too is judged a *vanity and a chase after wind* (9), because a man may not be given the power to enjoy (6,1-6) and because his appetite is insatiable (6,7-9). On this note the first half of the book ends. Incl. for 6,7-9: *nepeš* in 7 and 9; for 4,16-6,9: *r^e'ût 'ēnā(y)w/mar'ēh 'ēnayim* in 5,10 and 6,9. Some phrases recall earlier remarks: all go to the same place (cf. 2,14-16; 3,20); man's appetite is never satisfied (4,8; 5,9); what advantage has the wise man over the fool (2,12-17).

6,10-12. The introduction to the second half of the book. What God has

---

[26] Gordis, *op. cit.*, 101. He gives a parallel example from Egyptian literature.
[27] Thus LXX, Coptic, Syro-Hexaplar, Vulgate.

done is fixed (cf. 1,9; 1,15; 3,15) and man cannot dispute with him; there is vanity in a multiplicity of words (cf. 4,17-5,6). For who knows what is good for man to do, and who can tell him what the future holds in store. Incl.: *nôdā'/yôdēa'* in 10 and 12. There are three interrelated ideas here, but the basic one is that man cannot ascertain what God has done (cf. 3,11), for this idea runs throughout this second half (7,13; 8,17; 11,5). This inability on the part of man is manifested in two ways: in his inability to find out what is good to do (developed in four sections in chs. 7-8) and in his inability to know the future (developed in six sections in 9,1-11,6).

7,1-14. Qoheleth assembles a number of proverbs keyed to the word "good," i.e., proverbs which offer advice on what is good for man to do. "This also is vanity" in v. 6 is a divider as usual and separates the proverbs into two groups.[28] The first group extols the advantages of sorrow and adversity, but the effect of the second grouping is to point out the corruptibility of the wise man in the face of adversity. He may become impatient (8), angry (9), complaining (10), and may not possess anything to enjoy, even though wisdom may prolong his life (11-12). The juxtaposition of the two groups speaks for itself, and Qoheleth simply states that what God has done cannot be changed. He offers his usual advice to enjoy the good day; on the evil day one should consider that God has made the evil day as well as the good, so that man *may not find* fault with God.[29] Incl.: *yôm . . . yôm* and *tôb . . . tôb* in 1 and 14.

7,15-24. Qoheleth cites advice (16-18) on what is good for man to do in view of the problem of retribution, and adds three more sayings (19-22) to the effect that wisdom is good but the righteous man is never totally just (thus explaining 16-18). Perhaps the arrangement of 16-18 is Qoheleth's, perhaps it is prior to him. In any event he has tested it all and found it not helpful. The secret of what God has done is too deep and who can *find it out?* Incl.: *tithakkam/'ehkāmâ* in 16 and 23.

[28] The connection of "this also is vanity" (6) with the surrounding material has long been a problem. That MT may have suffered damage at this point could be argued from breaks in the text here in 4QKoh (cf. J. Muilenburg, "A Qoheleth Scroll from Qumran," *BASOR* 135 [1954] 26-27). But, as Muilenburg observes, the breaks could simply be erasures and the text need not have diverged in any way from MT. If we take into account the structural function of "this also is vanity" as a divider separating the proverbs into two opposing groups, and if we let it refer to 1-6 and see its explanation in 7-12, MT makes very fine sense as it stands.

[29] *'al-dibrat šellô' yimṣā' hā'ādām 'aḥărā(y)w me'ûmâ.* The translation, "find fault with him," already probable on linguistic grounds (cf. Symmachus; Rashi; Williams; G. R. Driver, "Problems and Solutions," *VT* 4 [1954] 230; Ryder; CCD), is further supported by the fact that the theme of "what comes after" is taken up only in 9,1-11,6 and is absent from the conclusions of the four sections in chs. 7-8. The appearance of the idea in 8,7 is secondary and is not a main point.

7,25-29. As Qoheleth tries to add up the sum of things, he investigates the traditional wisdom on the folly of women (26) and that it is good to escape them. But he *did not find* the sum in that material either. In fact he found that men were scarcely better than women with regard to folly. Incl.: *ḥešbôn/ḥiššᵉbōnôt* in 25 and 29.

8,1-17. The author cites the traditional advice that it is good to listen to the wise man and obey the king (1-6a). Yet, he observes, the wise man in fact does not know the essential answers nor does the king deliver from the essential evils, and man lords it over man to his hurt (6b-9). Incl.: *šilṭôn/šālaṭ* in 4 and 9; *ra'* in 5 and 9.

Taking up the idea of wickedness from v. 8, Qoheleth presents the problem of retribution once again (10-12a),[30] cites the traditional doctrine (12b-13), but observes that it is not always borne out in fact (10-14). "This also is vanity" (14b) is a divider. He commends enjoyment once again, but confesses three times that man *cannot find out* the work of God (15-17), and this ends the first part of the second half of the book. Incl.: *yôdēa'/lāda'at* in 12 and 17. *Heḥākām* in 1 and 17 is the overall inclusion for the section, and *ma'ăśēh hā'ĕlōhîm* in 7,13 and 8,17 is an inclusion tying together the four sections of chs. 7-8.

9,1-6. Qoheleth begins to develop the second idea of the introduction (6,12): man does not know the future (what will be after him). He recalls the traditional teaching that the just man is in the hand of God (1a), but he observes that the just man cannot figure out whether God's sentiments toward him are favorable or unfavorable, and he is always uncertain whether he will meet good or evil in the future. For both the just and the wicked have one fate; in this life the same things happen to each, and afterward they both die (1b-3). But, he observes, citing two proverbs, it is better to be alive than dead (4), for as far as knowledge of the future is concerned man at least knows that he will die; the dead *do not know* anything of what is done on earth after them (5-6). Incl.: *yôdēa'* in 1 and 5; *gam 'ahăbâ . . . gam śin'â* in 1 and 6.

9,7-10. The author once again commends enjoyment. Man knows that this is his portion in life, for since he is permitted it, God must have approved it. He urges that whatever man does he do it with all his might, for there is *no knowledge* or work or thought or wisdom in Sheol. Incl.: *ma'ăśeh* in 7 and 10. But this is all man knows of the future, and in the next four sections Qoheleth cites the wisdom material itself to show that man does not know his time, and does not know what will happen for evil or for good.

---

[30] "This also is vanity" (10) divides the observation into two parts as usual.

9,11-12. The deserving do not receive their due. Rather everyone is subject to a time of misfortune, and a man *does not know* when that time will be. V. 12aβ-b may be a proverb. Incl.: *ēt* in 11 and 12b.

9,13-10,15. Man does not know what will come after him. This section consists mainly of previously independent units of wisdom material arranged to create a picture of the uncertainty of the future. At the end of the collection there is also inserted the idea once again of the folly of many words (cf. 4,17-5,6; 6,11). The section is developed in four parts. (a) 9,13-10,1. The future is uncertain because of the vulnerability of wisdom to neglect and folly. Incl.: *ḥokmâ* in 9,13 and 10,1. (b) 10,2-7. Traditional wisdom, which attempts to predict what one will find "on the road" (2-3) and which offers advice on how to keep wise men in high places (4), does not always work out. The images of the "high places" and the "road" are retained and the refutation in 5-7 is given in those terms. Incl.: *hōlēk/hōlᵉkîm* in 3 and 7. (c) 10,8-11. Proverbs arranged in chiastic fashion present six pictures of the unexpected or of the possibility of accident.[31] Incl.: *nāḥāš* and *yiššᵉkennû/yiššōk* in 8 and 11. (d) 10,12-15. Many words are foolish, for *no man knows* what is to be and who can tell him what will be after him. Incl.: *dibrê/dᵉbārîm* in 12 and 14. The overall inclusions for the section are *dābār* in 9,16-17 and 10,12-14; *'îr* in 9,14 and 10,15.

10,16-11,2. Traditional material is assembled to show that man does not know what evil may happen. There is the possibility of evil even among nobility (16-17) to the detriment of the land (18) and the depletion of state funds (19). Evil can result from even the most careful speech (20). Venture forth, but do not put all the eggs in one basket because you *do not know* what evil may happen (11,1-2). Incl.: *'ereṣ* in 10,16-17 and 11,2.

11,3-6. What is to happen will happen (3). He who is cautious will never act (4). Venture forth in spite of the uncertain. As you *do not know* how the spirit comes to the child in the womb, so you *do not know* the work of God and you *do not know* what good will happen (5-6). Incl.: *yiṣrā'/zᵉra'* et-zar'ekā in 4 and 6. Perhaps the triple *'ênᵉkā yôdēa'* . . . *lō' tēda'* . . . *'ênᵉkā yôdēa'* is an inclusion with *'ēn yôdēa'* in 9,1 and *yāda'* in 6,10-12. Once again *ma'ăśēh hā'ĕlōhîm* in 11,5 recalls the same phrase in 7,13 and 8,17. It may be that *ṭôbîm*, the last word in 11,6, is intended as an inclusion with *ṭôb* in 6,12 or 7,1.

---

[31] 10,10a is obscure. The context (the uncertainty of the future) suggests that it is a picture of iron sharpened beforehand but accidentally blunted, and that we should read *wᵉhû' lᵉpānim* (with CCD). The other problems in the text (the subjects of the verbs, the nature of the *pi'el*, the pointing of *qlql* and its meaning) leave room for a variety of translations.

The Two Poems

There remains to discuss the introductory (1,2-11) and concluding (11,7-12,8) poems which stand outside of the structure described above.

In the introductory piece, " 'vanity of vanities,' says Qoheleth, 'vanity of vanities; all is vanity' " (1,2) is an overall inclusion for the book with 12,8 as is generally recognized. The question in 1,3, "What does a man gain by all the toil at which he toils under the sun," provides the context in which 1,4-11 is to be read. There follows a poetic section in 3-8 with a subsequent prose comment in 9-11. The poetry is probably to be divided into two sections: 4-6 on the endless round of events (Incl.: *hôlēk* in 4 and 6 [*bis*]), and 7-8 on the lack of progress in nature and in man's speech, sight, and hearing (Incl.: *mālē'*/*timmālē'* in 7 and 8). The comment of 9-11 states that there is nothing new, and if something seems to be new, it is because one doesn't remember the previous occurrence. Moreover, the same lack of remembrance will obtain in the future (Incl.: *hyh* in 9 and 11). Thus there is no profit in toil because nothing is gained, neither progress, novelty, nor remembrance.

The closing poem reinforces Qoheleth's advice on enjoyment. It begins with a prose introduction (11,7-8) which summarizes this final section: enjoy the light, and (as an incentive for enjoyment) remember the darkness that is coming. "All that comes is vanity" (8) is a divider. This advice to enjoy and remember is then developed in a two-part poem: enjoy your youth (11,9-10; Incl.: *bᵉyaldûtèkā*/*hayyaldût* and *libbᵉkā*/*millibbekā* in 9 and 10)[32] and remember your grave[33] (12,1-7; Incl.: *bôrᵉkā*/*habbôr* in 1 and 6; *wᵉšābû*/*wᵉyāšûb*[34] . . . *tāšûb*). The second part of the poem is structured by the repetition of "before" (*'ad 'ăšer lō'*) in 12,1.2.6 and this yields three sections: (a) a general characterizing of old age as the unwelcome time of life (1); (b) old age is the winter of life (2-5); (c) four

---

[32] Perhaps *hābel* at the end of 11,10 is a divider.—The admonition in 11,9 that God will bring one to judgment appears to clash with the previous remarks on judgment in 3,16-21 and 8,10-14. But Qoheleth is a believer and he believes that God is acting; he simply is confessing that he cannot find out what God is doing in his day. And this obtains for God's justice as well. Qoheleth affirms it in principle (11,9), but in the main part of the book he questions it in its manifestations.

[33] Reading *bôrᵉkā* with Galling and Scott. MT "remember your creator" has always been felt to be foreign to the context, for according to 11,8 what is to be remembered is the darkness to come. If 12,1 is the opening line of the second part of the poem as seems indicated by the repetitions "enjoy" (11,8 and 9) and "remember" (11,8 and 12,1), and if 12,1 is meant to state the theme of the second part as 11,9a does for the first part, then the difficulty becomes acute. If the author is using inclusions, *bôr* in 1 would go nicely with *bôr* in 9, and this may explain the choice of the word.

[34] MT *wᵉyāšōb*.

images of death and the conclusion (6-7). 12,8 provides the overall inclusion for the book with 1,2, and the epilogue is from the hand of the editor.

The two poems, then, single out and express in an arresting way two main thoughts of the book: what profit is there in toil (the point of four of the six sections on vanity in the first half), and the advice to enjoyment (the only good that Qoheleth can find for man to do).

Conclusion

If the above analysis is correct, the book speaks more clearly, but at the same time says much less, than we previously thought. The idea of the impossibility of understanding what God has done (which was always seen as *a* theme) is in reality *the* theme, and it is built on the vanity motif prominent in the first part of the book. The only advice offered is to find enjoyment in life and in the fruit of one's toil while one can (2,24; 3,12-13; 3,22; 5,17-19; 7,14; 8,15; 9,7-9; 11,7-12,8), to venture forth boldly in spite of the uncertain (9,10; 11,1.4.6), to fear God (5,6; 11,9), not to work feverishly (4,4-6), not to put all the eggs in one basket (11,2), and not to waste words trying to puzzle things out (1,18; 4,17-5,6; 6,10-11; 10,12-15). The "be not too just, be not too wicked" advice in 7,16ff., frequently seen as a major thought of Qoheleth, is not Qoheleth's message at all, but is something he judges not helpful. Similarly, the various collections of proverbs are not "Qoheleth's favorites" offered by way of advice as previously treated, but they are either cited to be criticized or they are arranged and juxtaposed to produce various negative effects.

In 12,9 the editor remarks that Qoheleth taught the people knowledge and he weighed, scrutinized, and arranged many proverbs. If this analysis is correct, Qoheleth was an extremely skillful arranger of proverbs, and there is a greater depth of meaning to the editor's remark than we had hitherto suspected.

ADDISON G. WRIGHT, S.S.
St. Mary's Seminary
Roland Park
Baltimore, Maryland

JOB xxxviii AND
ANCIENT EGYPTIAN WISDOM
1955

GERHARD Von RAD

Commentators have always agreed that Yahweh's speech in *Job* xxxviii is a superb poem. No progress has, however, been made on the form-category of the speech since Gunkel first instituted the form-critical method. In subject-matter, this account of the wonders of creation clearly has much in common with hymns. It has also been thought that there might be some connection between the interrogative form of *Job* xxxviii and the rhetorical questions often found in hymns.[1] The interrogative style used in hymns is nevertheless quite distinct from the style of the present passage. It is admittedly a rhetorical device in both cases, but in hymns it is the human worshipper who asks the questions, whereas here he is the person to whom they are put. Furthermore, the fact that *Job* xxxviii-xxxix consists entirely of questions from beginning to end precludes us from regarding it as a hymn. We must attempt to approach the problem from a different angle.

The *Onomasticon* of Amenope (edited with a commentary by Sir Alan Gardiner), is recognised as an encyclopaedic scientific work, a "compendium concerning all that Ptah created, the heavens and their appurtenances, the earth and all that is in it". The work mentions other objects, persons, offices, professions, tribes, Egyptian cities, and so on, simply listing a series of nouns or short phrases in each case. The work as preserved to us enumerates six hundred and ten items.[2] It is only the beginning of the list which interests us here, and it might well be useful to compare the list of cosmological and meteorological items in Amenope with that in Yahweh's speech in *Job* xxxviii.

1. H. Gunkel and J. Begrich, *Einleitung in die Psalmen*, pp. 54ff.
2. A. H. Gardiner, *Ancient Egyptian Onomastica*, London 1947.

267

Onomasticon of Amenope

1. Heaven
2. Sun
3. Moon
4. Star
5. Orion
6. Great Bear
7. Pavian
8. "The strong one"
9. Boar
10. Storm
11. Orcanus
12. Dawn
13. Darkness
14. Sun
15. Shade
16. Sunlight
17. Sun's rays
18. Dew
19. ?
20. Snow (?)
21. Rainstorm (?)
22. Primaeval ocean
23. "Flood" (Nile)
24. Rivers

Job XXXVIII

12. Morning
13. Dawn
16. Sea
    Primaeval ocean
17. Underworld
    Darkness
18. Earth
19. Light
    Darkness
22. Snow
    Hail
24. "Wind"
    East wind
25. Torrential rain
    Thundercloud
28. Rain
    Dewdrops
29. Ice
    Hoarfrost
31. Pleiades
    Orion
32. Mazzaroth

Ben Sira XLIII

1. Firmament
   Heaven
2. Sun
6. Moon
9. Stars
11. Rainbow
13. Lightning
14. Clouds
15. Cloud
    Hail
16. South wind
17. Thunderstorm
    Whirlwind
19. Hoarfrost
20. Ice
22. Dew
23. Rahab
25. Sea monsters

Psalm CXLVIII

1. Heaven
3. Sun
   Moon
   Stars
4. Heaven
   Heavenly ocean
7. Sea monsters
   Primaeval ocean
8. Fire
   (? lightning)
   Hail
   "Ice" (LXX)
   Stormy wind
9. Mountains
   Hills
   Fruit-trees
   Cedars
10. Wild beasts
    Cattle
    Reptiles
    Birds
11. Kings

Song of the Three Children

36. Heaven
37. (Angels)
38. Heavenly ocean
40. Sun
    Moon
41. Stars
42. Showers
    Dew
43. Winds
44. Fire
    Heat
47. Nights
    Days
48. Night
    Darkness
49. Cold
    Heat
50. Frost
    Snow
51. Lightnings
    Clouds
52. Earth
53. Mountains
    Hills

25. Sea
26. Waves
27. Great Sea
28. Lake
29. Spring
30. Pool (?)
31. Delta
32. Water
33. Pond
34. Front
35. Rear
36. Well
37. Fount
38. ?
39. Riverbank
40. ?
41. Current
42. Fountain
43. Streams
44. Flood
45. ?
46. Currents
47. Water-hole
48. ?
49. Banks
50. ?

Bear
34. Clouds
   Waterfloods
35. Lightning
36. Ibis
   Cock
37. Clouds
   Heavenly
      water-skins
39. Lion
   Young lion
41. Raven

Job xxxix
1. Mountain goat
   Hind
5. Zebra
9. Wild ox
19. Horse
26. Hawk

Peoples
Rulers
Judges
12. Young men
   Maidens
   Old men
   Children

54. Vegetation
55. Fountains
56. Sea
   Rivers
57. Whales
   Sea monsters
58. Birds
59. Wild beasts
60. Cattle
61. Israel

Comparison is actually possible only from *Job* xxxviii.12 onwards, since verses 4-11 deal with the creation of the world by Yahweh and with the battle against chaos which is wholly foreign to Egyptian thought. The *Onomasticon*, on the contrary, contains no theological or mythological introduction, but confines its attention to the bare enumeration of cosmographical data. Thus there is nothing in Amenope corresponding to the first part of Yahweh's speech.

What then are we to think of the series of phenomena depicted by Amenope and by *Job* xxxviii.12ff. respectively? We certainly cannot claim any precise parallelism. The correspondences begin only with Amenope 12, and even these are far from exact. Nevertheless, the two texts approximate very closely at those points where they enumerate meteorological phenomena: snow, hail, wind, and so on.[3] This is also true of the constellations, although in Amenope they are significantly listed at the beginning, whereas in *Job* they interrupt the enumeration of meteorological phenomena almost as if there had been an interpolation in the text at this point (*Job* xxxviii.31-32). Certainly we are not in a position to say that *Job* xxxviii shows literary dependence on Amenope, although there is undoubtedly some connection between the two texts.

It may be that there existed some other *Onomasticon* which was used by the composer of Yahweh's speech in *Job*. The Rameses *Onomasticon*, for example, contains lists of plants, minerals, birds, fishes, and animals.[4] In contrast to this, *Job* xxxviiiff. confines itself to the enumeration of heavenly phenomena, and then suddenly switches to a list of animals from xxxviii.39 to xxxix.26. That this list is itself not original is clearly indicated by the interpolation here of birds; but doubtless this is to be expected in a poetic work. The fact that in *Job* we have a free poetic composition naturally means that the original material has been thoroughly worked over stylistically. The poet was thus at liberty to follow up the associations which arose continually in his mind as he worked. The wonder is rather that the technique of enumeration should have been so firmly maintained in the poem. It is only in the second half of

---

3. Amenope nos. 12-23, *Job* xxxviii.22-29.
4. Gardiner, *Ancient Egyptian Onomastica*, pp. 7ff.

Yahweh's speech that the poet gives free rein to his descriptive imagination.

Since we are doubtless still far from having proved our case, we plead in aid a further passage, the Creation Hymn of Ben Sira xliii. 1 ff. Compared with the unrelieved interrogative style of *Job* xxxviii, the form of the sentences in this passage is freer and more varied. None the less, there can be no doubt that this poem, too, follows a pattern which was already laid down. The pattern begins with the heavenly bodies and works its way round to the various natural climatic phenomena, the underlying scheme being rather more easily discerned than it is in *Job* xxxviii. Yet once again we must not deceive ourselves regarding the extent to which this example depends upon an Egyptian model.

There can, of course, be no question of either of our Hebrew texts depending in any direct, literary sense upon an Egyptian *Onomasticon*. We may nevertheless assert that such encyclopaedic works found their way into Israel, and that Israel also learnt to compile scientific lists of cosmic and meteorological phenomena as well as of the animal kingdom. In compiling their instructional poems, therefore, the wisdom-writers, well-versed in all kinds of learned literature, had the comparatively easy task of going through this long-established scheme of current scientific learning, and of putting into poetry the somewhat prosaic tabulations. The procedure in Ben Sira xliii. 1 ff. is thus basically the same as that in the πατέρων ὕμνος of Ben Sira xliv-xlix. One is a learned account of racial history, the other a scholarly natural history—both in poetic form.

As our next example let us consider *Ps.* cxlviii. This begins with an exhortation to praise Yahweh. The first creatures bidden to praise him are the heavenly ones. They are, of course, outside the scope of the onomastic encyclopaedia. Yet when the hymn moves on from the heavenly beings to cosmological and meteorological phenomena, it falls almost at once into the traditional learned pattern, and, as in the *Onomasticon* of Amenope, leads on from the heavenly bodies to the meteorological occurrences of the earth below.

This section is of particular interest to us at this point, because it goes much further than either *Job* xxxviiiff. or Ben Sira xliii in the material it uses. The section as a whole is

271

much less full, and, as in the meteorological section, enumerates fewer instances. At the same time it includes more categories: fruit-trees, wild and domestic animals, reptiles, and birds. This series is reminiscent of the Rameses *Onomasticon*, which begins with an almost completely unreadable list of plants and liquids before going on to birds, fishes and animals.[5]

By contrast, *Ps.* CXLVIII.11ff. corresponds almost exactly with the arrangement of the Amenope *Onomasticon*, which starts with the heavens and goes on to the weather, the earth and thence to the king, to officials, and to various professions. In verse 12 we come to a section concerning young men, maidens, old men, and children which Gardiner classes under the heading "types of human being", and at this point the affinity with the *Onomasticon* is particularly striking. The corresponding passage from Amenope reads as follows:

295.	Man
296.	Youth
297.	Old man
298.	Woman
299.	Young woman
300.	Various persons
301.	Boy
302.	Child
303.	Lad
304.	Girl

For our last example it will be well worth while to consider the Benedicite (*Song of Three Childr.* vss. 35-68).[6] It is difficult to fix the date of this passage, which was undoubtedly in origin an independent poem, and not a composition expressly written for interpolation into the *Book of Daniel*. It could well be of the same period as *Ps.* CXLVIII, which it closely resembles but to which it certainly owes nothing, maintaining its own distinctive characteristics throughout as against this psalm. It is therefore interesting to see that here the weather, the mountains, and the hills are followed by a short list of terrestrial water-formations, the fountains, seas, and rivers of verses 55f. There is nothing

5. Gardiner, *Ancient Egyptian Onomastica*, p. 37.
6. Cf. the form-critical analysis made by C. Kuhl, *Die drei Männer im Feuer*, *BZAW* No. 55, 1930, pp. 90-100.

especially striking about the passage itself, except that the *Onomasticon* of Amenope contains a similar but much more detailed list of terrestrial water-formations in which *inter alia* seas, rivers, and springs are mentioned. On the other hand the Benedicite contains features which could find no place in the Egyptian list, such as angels (vs. 37) and sea monsters (vs. 57).[7]

The problems thus opened up have numerous ramifications. We ought no doubt to start with the details in order to ascertain in what respects the pattern which was taken over in Israel was modified or extended as a consequence of topographical or climatic conditions. We ought also to establish the extent to which the pattern has influenced Old Testament hymnody as a whole. Above all we ought to consider the theological implications of the fact that Israel adapted this somewhat arid scientific material to the purposes of the worship of Yahweh.[8]

Let us, however, go back to our starting-point in *Job* xxxviiiff., for we have still reached no conclusions with regard to the form-category of Yahweh's speech itself. The further problems which this raises cannot be solved by regarding the passage as a hymn, for we know of no hymns which consist wholly of rhetorical questions. Could this curious form, which seems to be unique in Israel's literature, be in some sense a derivative of ancient Egyptian wisdom literature?

Let us turn our attention to the well-known polemical writing in which the scribe Hori makes a literary onslaught upon his colleague, called Amenemope. This document, usually known as *Papyrus Anastasi I*, after the only complete extant manuscript, dates from the time of Rameses II (1301-

7. [The original German uses throughout the text of the Benedicite found in the edition of Rahlfs, which includes interpolated verses omitted in *RV*. The author dismisses these verses as spurious, on the authority of Rothstein, in Kautzsch, *Apokryphen und Pseudepigraphen*, Leipzig 1900, Vol. 1, p. 182, and the text and numbering of verses in the present translation is therefore that of *RV.—Tr.*]

8. Since this was written, my assistant, K. Baltzer, has drawn my attention to a list in *IV Ezra* vii.39ff.: "neither sun, nor moon, nor stars, nor clouds, nor thunder, nor lightning, nor wind, nor rainstorm, nor fog, nor darkness, nor evening, nor morning, nor summer, nor spring, nor heat, nor winter, nor ice, nor frost, nor hail, nor storm, nor dew, nor noonday, nor night, nor shining, nor twilight, nor light . . ." The series is interesting in that it shows that such compilations existed in Israel in non-poetical material. The question as to whether this list is related to *Gen. I* calls for a separate study.

1234 B.C.), the time of that Indian summer of Egyptian wisdom writing in which it made its mark upon Israel. Only one section of this extensive document is of interest to us here—the well-known passage on Syria, so valuable for our understanding of the historical geography of pre-Israelite Palestine. Here, in this one single instance (ch. XVIII, vs. 9 to ch. XXVIII, vs. 1), we find precisely similar rhetorical questions, and in such profusion that the whole passage forms an almost unbroken succession of such questions. "Hast thou not gone to the land of the Khatti, and hast thou not seen the land of Upe?" So the series begins. "Come teach me about Berytus"; "Where is the road to Aksaph?" "Pray instruct me as to the mountain of User. What is its peak like?" "Hast thou not gone to the land of Takhsi?"[9]

These are but a few examples. There are in all about fifty such questions. Let us compare these with the questions in *Job* XXXVIIIff.: "Where were you? . . . Tell me" (vs. 4); "Surely you know!" (vs. 5); "Have you commanded?" (vs. 12); "Have you entered?" (vs. 16, 22); "Have the gates . . . been revealed to you?" (vs. 17); "Have you seen?" (vs. 17, 22); "Have you comprehended?" (vs. 18); "Where is the way?" (vss. 19, 24) and so on.

No further demonstration is needed to show that the form is identical in both cases. The close relationship of the *form* of the two texts is to be clearly seen in the phrase "Tell me", used once in *Job* (vs. 4) and three times in *Anastasi I*, and even more particularly in the questions "Hast thou not gone?" "Where is the road?" These two questions are, of course, meant to be taken literally in the papyrus, whereas in *Job* they refer to the "storehouses of the snow" (vs. 22) or the "gates of darkness" (vs. 17), and can be understood only figuratively.[10]

The stylistic form of these ironical questions in the papyrus, as well as in Yahweh's speech in *Job* is doubtless purely a literary device, but we may reasonably ask whether this was always so.

9. Erman, *The Literature of the Ancient Egyptians*, Eng. tr. by A. M. Blackman, London 1927, pp. 228ff.; cf. J. B. Pritchard, *Ancient Near Eastern Texts*, London 1955, pp. 477f.

10. The authors of *Job* and *Papyrus Anastasi I* are, of course, widely removed from one another in date, but this form-category used in wisdom literature shows a quite extraordinary persistence. The "professional satire", fashionable in Egypt in the time of the Middle Kingdom, is still found in Ben Sira (ch. XXXVIII, vss. 24ff.).

Is it not conceivable, indeed probable, that this form of rhetorical question (or, more exactly, catechetical question) originally had its own actual situation in life, and only subsequently acquired literary status? Wisdom-teaching belongs to the world of education, and is part of the learned instruction given to those destined for high office.

Let us look once again at the questions of *Papyrus Anastasi I*:

> Pray instruct me as to the mountain of User. What is its peak like?
> How is Byblos built?
> Where is the river Litani?
> How does one cross the Jordan?
> How does one by-pass Megiddo?
> Put me on the road to Hamath.
> When one goes to Adummim, in which direction does one turn?
> How many miles is it from Raphia to Gaza?

Can there be any doubt that these were at one time questions actually asked in the schools? Was not this the method by which young scribes, the future governors of provinces, were taught and examined in the geography of Egypt's neighbours?[11] One has only to look at the opening sentence of the passage, "Come here to be questioned", or the closing words "Answer me now!" Naturally this does not apply to the questions in Yahweh's speech, which are couched in a more literary and poetical form.

Looking back over our findings, however, we find that our conclusions on *Job* xxxviii still pose a disturbing problem. We saw that in listing the phenomena of the cosmos and of nature, *Job* xxxviiiff. follows an established pattern, which derives ultimately from Egyptian wisdom-literature as exemplified in the *Onomastica*. We also saw that the catena of questions in Yahweh's speech corresponds very closely with the ironical questions of *Papyrus Anastasi I*, which itself goes back to the

---

11. A special problem arises with regard to the questions, "Have you gone?" "Have you not been?" and the like. Were these in fact school questions? Did the teacher seek to make his instruction vivid by the pretence that his pupils had actually seen the places concerned? It may perhaps rather be that such questions represent a literary development of this form-category.

catechetical mode of instruction in ancient Egyptian scribal schools. How does it come about, however, that the form of *Job* xxxviiiff. reflects at the same time two quite distinct form-categories, as if the composer of the speech were dependent upon both the pattern of the *Onomastica*, and the interrogative style of satirical works? What has a learned onomasticon in common with a polemical satire? Perhaps a very great deal!

We need only ask where Hori acquired all this knowledge with which he now bullies his colleague, to his pedantic self-satisfaction. What text-books would the wisdom-teachers have taken as the basis of their instruction, other than their own learned works—in this case, their onomastica? The *Onomasticon* of Amenope contains in one particular passage (nos. 250-70) a whole list of Palestinian names, and gives a very fair impression of what the original of *Anastasi I* must have looked like.[12]

There is nothing to be said for the view that the outstanding knowledge of Palestinian geography displayed by the writer of the papyrus is based on personal experience, unless, that is, we regard both the style and the content as exclusive and peculiar to Hori himself. If, however, we accept that he is copying and parodying the instructional method of the classroom and cate-chising his opponent like a schoolboy, it becomes much more probable that he is simply going through the lists of a text-book.

In the nature of things it would be difficult to prove this conclusively from the text, although Gardiner has in fact made a comparison between the onomastica and this part of the papyrus.[13] An exact investigation of this text from all extant copies with regard to the grouping of localities lies beyond the scope of our present study, but such an analysis would add greatly to the probability that an earlier list had been used as copy, since it would reveal gaps and omissions in the lists of names. Ought we not, however, to regard this type of literature much more as a conventional form based upon an established text? If we do, the personal contribution of the writer would be much less considerable, as regards both style and material, than it is usually thought to be. If the author of the Egyptian polemical work had catechised his colleague not on his geo-

12. A. Alt, *Syrien und Palästina im Onomastikon des Amenope, Kl. Schr.*, I, pp. 231ff.
13. Gardiner, *Ancient Egyptian Onomastica*, p. 4, n. 1.

graphy but on his cosmological and meteorological knowledge, we should have had an exact parallel to *Job* xxxviii.[14]

14. It is unnecessary to cite in this connection the Babylonian and Assyrian lists (cf. L. Matouš, *Die lexicalischen Tafelserien der Babylonier und Assyrer*, 1933), since the order of the items in these lists is quite different. The characteristic arrangement, passing on from the heavens and heavenly bodies to meteorological phenomena and then to the earth itself, is known only in Egyptian texts and in Israelite material derived from them. Even the Ras Shamra lists offer no comparable parallels.

An understanding of these correspondences may help in assessing the onomastica and their purpose. We underestimate the learned character of these compilations if we think of them only as spelling-books for use in scribal schools (cf. Erman, *The Literature of the Ancient Egyptians*, pp. 190ff.). It is highly improbable that the wisdom writers of Israel based their poetical instructional compositions on spelling-books!

III.

WISDOM AND THE
THEOLOGICAL TASK

Where Is Wisdom to be Placed?

JOHN F. PRIEST

IN a monograph published over ten years ago, reprinted a number of times, and justly well known and highly influential, G. Ernest Wright addresses himself to the nature of biblical theology as recital. In the course of suggesting a tentative program for the presentation of biblical theology so understood, he notes: "In any outline of biblical theology, the proper place to treat the Wisdom literature is something of a problem."[1] Although in this monograph and elsewhere Wright has made some excellent suggestions regarding the nature of Israel's Wisdom and its place in Old Testament theology, a survey of the more widely circulated books on Israel's religion and theology from the mid-nineteenth century to the present accentuates the problem to which Wright refers and indicates that the question, "Where is Wisdom to be placed?", remains a very live one.

Raising this question does not imply that Wisdom is ignored by writers on Old Testament theology. Rather, the question indicates that the Wisdom literature remains rather awkwardly and uneasily related to what is commonly considered the main thrust of the biblical message. Rylaarsdam, in his exceedingly valuable work on the Wisdom literature, puts the matter this way, "This striking neglect of Jewish history and religion by the canonical wisdom writers clearly indicates that the Hebrew Wisdom movement had not yet been integrated into the national religion."[2] And it is quite commonly stated that the canonical wise men had no real interest in Law, as formally defined, or worse still from the perspective of Old Testament theologians, no interest in election and covenant.[3] Sometimes this deficiency is minimized by asserting that the sages did not ignore these matters because they were unimportant but because they were dealt with elsewhere and the wisdom writers thus intentionally limited themselves to a narrower sphere of concern.[4]

This narrower sphere provides the way by which the wisdom literature is usually related to the theology of the Old Testament. There is little need for extensive documentation of this point for it is so widely held as to be almost axiomatic. H. Wheeler Robinson expressed the view concisely when he defined Wisdom as "the discipline whereby was taught the application of prophetic truth to the individual life in the light of experience."[5] My own

JOHN F. PRIEST is Associate Professor of Old Testament Studies at the Hartford Seminary Foundation, Hartford, Connecticut. His article is based on a paper read before the Annual Meeting of the National Association of Biblical Instructors at Union Theological Seminary, New York, December 29–30, 1962.

[1] G. Ernest Wright, *God Who Acts*, London: SCM Press, 1952, p. 115.

[2] J. Coert Rylaarsdam, *Revelation in Jewish Wisdom Literature*, Chicago: University of Chicago Press, 1946, p. 20.

[3] E. g. James Muilenburg, *The Way of Israel*, New York: Harper, 1961, p. 98. This view is commonly presented in standard works.

[4] Cf. Gerhard von Rad, *Theology of the Old Testament*, vol. I (E.T.), New York: Harper, 1961, p. 435; W. O. E. Oesterley, *The Book of Proverbs*, London: Methuen and Co., 1929, pp. ix f.

[5] H. Wheeler Robinson, *Inspiration and Revelation in the Old Testament*, London: Oxford University Press, 1946, p. 241.

Old Testament professor, writing for a popular audience, put it this way, "The Sages wer the spiritual middlemen who mediated the exalted doctrines of the prophets and interprete them in terms of common life and experience. They succeeded where the prophets failed they reached the common people."[6] Oesterley perhaps states it most bluntly of all when h views the task of the wise men as "the religious education of adolescents."[7] This under standing stresses the function of Wisdom as applying religious truth to the affairs an concerns of everyday life and particularly as individualizing the message of the prophet which was originally addressed to the community as a whole.

Generally considered to be more significant theologically are those cosmological an cosmogonic speculations which loom larger in the non-canonical materials but which ar found in Prov. 8:22 ff., Job 28, and perhaps in some of the "Wisdom" additions to th prophetical books. On this point writers on Old Testament theology[8] devote considerabl space to Wisdom as personalized, mythologized or hypostatized. The importance of thi concept for Old Testament theology, for post-Biblical Judaism and for early Christianity is rightly to be stressed, but to focus upon it as the primary theological contribution of th wisdom literature requires dismissing as theologically irrelevant the bulk of that literatur since so little of the canonical material deals even obliquely with the subject.

In both of these cases — individual application of prophetic teaching and Wisdom a hypostatic speculation — there is the tacit assumption that the Wisdom literature belong to the later periods of Israel's history and that most of it is indeed post-exilic. We mus return to this assumption later, but before so doing it is necessary to speak briefly abou the nature of wisdom itself in Hebrew thought and to set forth, equally briefly, the mos commonly accepted views of the development of the literature which deals primarily wit that wisdom.

It is usually agreed that in early Israel and the Near East in general wisdom wa originally a very practical affair. A study of the word, and its contexts, in the Old Testa ment illustrates the wide diversity of concerns with which wisdom was associated an there is no gainsaying that often these concerns are quite down to earth. As a "very prac tical thing wisdom was a means to an end. Wisdom meant capacity: to be wise is to posses the requisite capacity for a particular task."[10] This type of wisdom clearly was "tha sagacity and common sense which enabled man to live a happy and prosperous life."[11] Thi understanding of wisdom is assumed to have been the dominant view in the earliest perio of Israel's life and quite often it is seen as representing a secular approach to the world Gunkel[12] insisted very strongly on the secular nature of Israel's early wisdom and he i

[6] John Paterson, *The Book That Is Alive*, New York: Charles Scribner's Sons, 1954, p. 66. Though o some points I depart from his interpretations I am deeply indebted to Dr. Paterson for first stimulating m interest in the Wisdom Literature and offer this article as a modest token of my esteem for his 75th birth day which occurred in 1962.

[7] Oesterley, *op. cit.*, p. lxi.

[8] E. g. Walther Eichrodt, *Theologie des Alten Testaments*, vol. II (2nd ed.), Berlin: Evangelische Ver lagsanstalt, 1948, pp. 42 f.; Edmund Jacob, *Theology of the Old Testament* (E.T.), New York: Harper, 1958 pp. 118 ff. See especially the bibliography on p. 120 which deals exclusively with hypostatization.

[9] Cf. especially Rylaarsdam, *op. cit.*, pp. 99–118; also a full treatment of the subject with special refer ence to the prologue of John, Rendel Harris, *The Origin of the Prologue to John's Gospel*, Cambridge, Cam bridge University Press, 1917.

[10] Paterson, *op. cit.*, pp. 50 f.

[11] Julius A. Bewer, *Literature of the Old Testament*, New York: Columbia University Press, 1933, p. 310

[12] Hermann Gunkel, "Vergeltung," *Religion in Geschichte und Gegenwart* (2nd ed.) vol. V, Tübingen J. C. B. Mohr, 1931, col. 1532.

llowed by many writers who maintain that this was true not only in Israel but in the hole international wisdom movement in the Near East.

In this light wisdom is seen as serving a largely utilitarian function, negating or at ast tacitly ignoring the role of God in the world and in human affairs. In this period, it said, "the wisdom seeker must rely entirely on his natural human equipment."[13] As time ent on, this secular appeal to a strictly utilitarian approach wore thin. The sages did not bandon their attempts to interpret life's meaning in terms of their traditional understanding f wisdom, but they added a new dimension to it, the religious. "The leaders of the movement discovered that religion and its foundations are valid and important in a rational, ritical outlook upon the world and they began to find the deep bases of reason and ethics."[14] his religious foundation of wisdom is summed up in the well known phrase, "The fear of e Lord is the beginning of wisdom."

This religious wisdom was, in its early period, essentially optimistic. The universe as orderly and moral because the God behind it willed it to be so. The sages were confident at they could discover enough of the way that the universe operated to teach men the uiding principles by which life was to be lived and which would result in success and appiness. The great divide in mankind could be spoken of as between the righteous and he wicked as well as the earlier and still used division between the wise and the fool. The ay of wisdom was the right way of walking before Yahweh.

But questions emerged. Did life, the observable phenomena, always work out in accord vith the teaching, the principles? Were the lives of all men explicable in the strict application of the teachings of the sages? There were two results of these inquiries. On the one and there was a loss of belief in the dependability of life and the consequent assertion that ife was meaningless or, and this amounts to the same thing, unknowable. On the other and the questioning resulted in a new orientation for life's meaning which transcended he moral, optimistic outlook of the sages without remaining in the abyss of the pessimist. This orientation finds life's meaning neither in principles nor phenomena but in a vital eligious faith in a living God.

Yet, it can be seen that neither the pessimism of Koheleth nor the "existentialism" of ob left a deep impress on the life of Judaism and thus wisdom "to survive as a living force n Judaism . . . had to undergo a more thorough acclimation to the doctrines of election and ovenant."[15] In this acclimation wisdom was nationalized and became more and more dentified with the Torah itself or took on an eschatological and/or mythological role in osmological speculation. Thus the movement which had begun as a secular, humanistic pproach to life at long last was thoroughly accommodated into the religion of revelation.

A similar internal development in the wisdom movement has been detected in Egypt 'wherein the confident affirmation in the worldly order of the Old Kingdom is replaced y a period of doubt and searching for a new way and finally by one in which trust in a esourceful and gracious divine power dominates."[16] And the extant Babylonian materials an be classified in a not dissimilar manner.[17]

---

[13] Rylaarsdam, *op. cit.*, p. 67.

[14] *Ibid.*, p. 32.

[15] G. Ernest Wright, "The Faith of Israel," *Interpreter's Bible*, vol. I, New York: Abingdon-Cokesbury, 952, p. 382.

[16] Thomas O. Lambdin, "Egypt: Its Language and Literature," *The Bible and the Ancient Near East*, Garden City: Doubleday, 1961, pp. 292 f.

[17] Cf. W. G. Lambert, *Babylonian Wisdom Literature*, London: Oxford University Press, 1960, pp. 1–18.

The view outlined above is widely held and it would be foolish to dismiss it. Nor do desire to dismiss it out of hand for it is the view I have held and taught, but it does see that it is subject to serious modification. First of all, there is no universal agreement tha Israelite wisdom ever was secular, if indeed that term would have made any sense in th ancient Near East. Competent scholars have disagreed with the positing of any secula period of Israel's wisdom, maintaining that the wise men held implicitly from the beginnin religious views which "in all they wrote hallowed what we call worldly wisdom and whic sanctified common sense,"[18] and that from the beginning "The quest for wisdom is th quest for the meaning of life."[19] Such a quest is religious and not secular.[20]

This contention gains support from a look at Egypt and Babylon, Israel's close con nections in the wisdom movement. Even if, and this is by no means beyond dispute,[21] ther was a movement from the secular to the religious in the wisdom literature of these countries such a shift had already taken place by the 15th century at the latest, well before the incep tion of Israel's wisdom. Therefore by the time the borrowing process began some element of both Egyptian and Babylonian wisdom were on a solid religious footing. It seems quit unnecessary to assume that Israel's had first to borrow the earliest foreign materials an then repeat the same process of development through which they had gone.

Careful study of Proverbs seems to indicate that it is simply impossible to demonstrat that the earliest strata are secular and the latest religious. Even in Ben Sira, admittedly lat and often used as the chief example of the equation of Wisdom with Torah, maxims appea which, if they had been found in Proverbs would have been assigned to the earliest strat since they are obviously "secular" in content and orientation.[22] It is not to be denied tha in Ben Sira wisdom is at times equated with Torah, but the total picture in the book i much more complex.

Is it possible to propose a view which will do justice to the more widely held positior of development from secular to religious, through questioning to nationalization, and a the same time avoid what seems to be an unnecessary schematization which forces some o the data into somewhat unnatural settings? I believe that it is and that such a view will als provide a more comprehensive approach to the role of Wisdom in Old Testament theology

The chief problem of relating wisdom to an Old Testament theology seems to sten from the absence of the distinctive themes of election and covenant and the distinctiv institutions of the cult in the wisdom materials. Further, wisdom is hardly considered t play a distinctive role in the creative period of Israelite theology, for wisdom arrives some what tardily on the scene. This lateness is, so it is claimed, verified literarily by the de

---

[18] Oesterley, op. cit., p. lvi.

[19] Bernhard W. Anderson, *Understanding the Old Testament*, Englewood Cliffs: Prentice-Hall, 1957 p. 465.

[20] Cf. the strong statement by Oliver S. Rankin, *Israel's Wisdom Literature*, Edinburgh: T. and T Clark, 1936, p. 69: "We have no reason to assume, in the absence of actual evidence, that at any tim there was in Israel a purely secular proverb literature . . . from the very outset in Israel's wisdom writing the religious sanction of right conduct, the motive supplied by the idea of God's blessing and cursing wa present." Cf. also H. W. Robinson, op. cit., p. 252: "Behind the ethical aphorisms . . . there is almost alway present a confidence that Yahweh is active in man's life."

[21] Cf. Rankin, op. cit., pp. 70 ff. and Lambert, op. cit., p. 1. The latter relates early Babylonian wisdon to the cult rather than to morality but this is nevertheless "religious."

[22] E. g. many of the maxims of Ben Sira, especially in chapters 7, 8, 31, 32, though many other scattered throughout the book, are "secular." Interestingly, the "secular" and "religious" sayings will ofter be found side by side. This is highly significant in an overall assessment of the Wisdom Literature but w cannot detail the issue here.

endence of the wise men on the prophets in their function of individualizing the prophetic messages, and by the lack of particularity in wisdom, resulting from the stress on the doctrine of creation, which is itself a late theological formulation in Israel.

But as Toombs has commented, "as long as Old Testament theology is represented exclusively in terms of the history, institutions and cultus of the Hebrew people, it will exclude the wisdom literature by definition."[23] And long ago, Sellin, apropos the Wisdom literature, wrote "that the intellectual life of Israel was much richer and more many sided than we are apt to imagine from attending too exclusively to the evidence of the prophetic and historical writings."[24] Consequently the problem may reside not in the aberrance of wisdom but in too rigid an interpretation of Old Testament thought in terms of election and covenant — or even with the addition of the cultic elements.

The question can also be asked, is wisdom's alleged dependence on the prophetic messages universally valid? It has been argued that in some instances, both with respect to style[25] and content[26] the borrowing went the other direction. The doctrines of retribution, social concern and polemic against sacrifice are to be found both in prophetic and sapiential materials and there is no overwhelming evidence for the necessary priority of one over the other. Nor does stress on the individual necessarily mean that Wisdom is late for there is a great deal of arguing in a circle employed to demonstrate that the community takes complete precedence early and that the individual emerges only later.

In the other near Eastern religions the individual had already arrived on the scene before Israel's beginnings and pre-eminently in the wisdom literature of those religions. Careful attention to the history of religions and cultural anthropology also could caution against a too facile denigration of the individual. Lest this be taken as arguing exclusively from non-Israelite sources, one might note that in Deuteronomy the preaching is directed to the individual as he lives in community[27] and that in the earlier historical narratives again and again the individual plays a distinctive role both as an actor on the stage of history and as a being addressed personally by God and personally responsible to Him. Indeed the so-called history of salvation begins in earnest with the call and response of Abraham, an individual. Even if the Exodus tradition is prior to the patriarchal narratives, the latter were considered of singular importance by the 10th century, on any score an early individualization. Thus there is no mandatory reason to view concern for and address to the individual a late development.

What then of the connection between wisdom and creation as against the "earlier" concern with the saving history? Persuasive arguments have been put forward that on form-critical grounds and from an examination of the prophetic emphases Israel's creation faith is subsequent in time to faith in the saving history. Indeed von Rad maintains that in Old Testament thought, "Israel only discovered the correct theological relationship of the two when she learned to see creation too as connected theologically with the saving history."[28]

---

[23] Lawrence E. Toombs, "Old Testament Theology and the Wisdom Literature," *JBR* XXIII (1955), p. 195.

[24] Ernst Sellin, *Introduction to the Old Testament*, (E.T.) New York: Doran, 1923, p. 207.

[25] Johannes Lindblom, "Wisdom in the Old Testament Prophets," *Wisdom in Israel and the Ancient Near East* (Supplement to *VT*, 1955), pp. 192–204.

[26] Rankin, *op. cit.*, pp. 53–76; Hugo Gressmann, *Israels Spruchweisheit*, Berlin: Karl Curtius, 1925, p. 56 f.; Johannes Fichtner, *Die altorientalische Weisheit in ihrer israelitischen-jüdischen Ausprägung*, Giessen: A. Topelmann, 1933, pp. 111 ff.; Jacob, *op. cit.*, pp. 119, 263.

[27] Cf. von Rad, *op. cit.*, p. 226.

[28] *Ibid.*, p. 136.

In his examination of creation faith in Deutero-Isaiah and in the priestly account of creation he concludes that creation is seen as a prelude to redemption, or better still, as an act of redemption in itself. That Yahweh is Creator is a soteriological statement. He goes on to say that in the Wisdom literature, at a later period, "Creation was in reality an absolute basis for faith, and was referred to for its own sake altogether and not in the light of the other factors of the faith."[29]

But, as von Rad himself notes, in some of the Psalms which may very well be early or at least are not particularly late, Creation is referred to in connection with the saving act of Yahweh in Israel's history. It seems equally clear that in some other Psalms, equally early, this creation faith appears quite independently of any mention of the saving acts.[30] Also, in at least two specific places in the oldest strata of Proverbs, Yahweh as creator is extolled.[31] Thus even if the "faith in the first article"[32] were peculiar to the Wisdom tradition it is not necessarily a very late tradition because of that.

As a matter of fact the Creation faith is by no means limited to the Wisdom tradition in the earlier periods. Indeed in the piece of literature widely regarded as the oldest in the Old Testament, the song of Deborah, reference to Yahweh as Creator is unmistakable.[33] Israel's creation faith is ancient indeed. To allow this, however, does not necessarily rule out the priority of faith in the saving history and it would still be possible to see Creation faith as a prelude to redemption, a soteriological event. But it does require seeing a conjunction of creation and salvation at a very early date. Further, it suggests that if the Creation faith is indeed the particular concern of the Wisdom tradition, that since that faith is ancient so also is the tradition.

Can we properly speak of Wisdom literature at so early a period as is implied above. A number of scholars have drawn a distinction between the age of wisdom in Israel and the age of Israel's Wisdom literature. While there is little doubt that the editing of these books is post-exilic and that they have much post-exilic material, it is likely that Proverbs in particular contains much pre-exilic material, some of it from a quite early period in the life of Israel.[34] Albright has suggested that the borrowing from Amen-em-ope may

---

[29] *Ibid.*, p. 139.

[30] Dating the Psalms is notoriously difficult and much depends on presuppositions about the relative dating of the content; e. g. no monotheism before II Isaiah, monotheism in a certain psalm, therefore, psalm is post II Isaiah. This method often results in a sterile circularity which deadens Old Testament research. Personally I am convinced of a pre-exilic date for both Ps. 8 and Ps. 19:1-6, which clearly stress creation faith. Even if this be disallowed, the early dating for Ps. 29 is clear and Martin Noth, *History of Israel* (E.T.) New York: Harper, 1960, p. 39, suggests that Ps. 104 came to Israel "through the mediation of the bronze age cities [of Canaan]."

[31] Prov. 14:31; 20:12.

[32] Otto Procksch, *Theologie des Alten Testaments*, Gütersloh: C. Bertelsmann, 1950, p. 400 so characterizes the theology of the Wisdom Literature.

[33] A critic of this paper raised the question of reference to Yahweh as Creator in the Song of Deborah. Jud. 5:20 f. certainly asserts Yahweh's rule over nature in that he uses the natural forces to fight Sisera. Rule over may not be unambiguously equivalent to creation of but I think that this criticism and my reaction to it gets to the heart of the problem of considering creation faith in the Old Testament. Far too often much significance has been given to creation faith until it was *explicitly* avowed. My contention is that both creation faith and salvation-history are implicit long before either becomes doctrinally formulated. In this light implicit assertions predicated on creation faith, such as Amos 4:13; 5:8; and Gen. 14:22 (which I take as a very early independent narrative) are valid witnesses to the antiquity of Israel's creation faith.

[34] Cf., e. g. William F. Albright, "Canaanite-Phoenician Sources of Wisdom Literature," *Wisdom in Israel and the Ancient Near East*, pp. 1–15; H. Cazelles, "A propos d'une phrase de H. H. Rowley," *Ibid.*

well have been as early as the 10th century[35] and that there remains in Proverbs a real nucleus from the age of Solomon.[36] Is the tradition which makes Solomon the patron saint of the Wise Men entirely a pious fiction? Since Israel's wisdom is related to the international wisdom movement, the ascribing of the two oldest strata in the book of Proverbs to Solomon and the men of Hezekiah appears significant. We know that just during those two reigns there was the most intercourse between the court at Jerusalem and the court of the Pharaohs.[37] Since Egyptian wisdom activity was centered around the court it is perhaps not altogether non-historical to attribute a certain amount of literary activity to Israelite wisdom circles just at those two times. One might note in passing that these two periods roughly parallel the two great moments in pre-exilic "prophetic" thought, the period of the Yahwist and the 8th century prophets Amos, Hosea and Isaiah of Jerusalem. Did perhaps two divergent religious traditions flourish simultaneously and together express something of the totality of Israelite faith which either, taken separately, would not do?

Perhaps this unduly schematizes the situation and one needs rather to look for a common religious tradition in early Israel from which prophets, priests and wise men selected specific emphases without necessarily rejecting those emphases chosen by the other groups. This view allows for the growing recognition of the close interaction between prophet and priest and also permits an understanding of materials common to both prophet and sage without assuming the dependence of the one on the other. This view requires a much broader definition of the wisdom tradition than has been common,[38] and one which speaks

---

pp. 26–32; C. I. K. Story, "The Book of Proverbs and Northwest Semitic Literature," *Journal of Biblical Literature*, LXIV (1945), pp. 319–337.

[35] Albright, *op. cit.*, p. 6.

[36] *Ibid.*, p. 13. This nucleus might have been transmitted orally but it should not be overlooked that "writing" was one of the stocks in trade of the wise men. Sigmund Mowinckel, *Prophecy and Tradition*, Oslo: Jacob Dybwad, 1946, p. 33, notes that "It appears as if in ancient times recording has been mainly used for some special kinds of literature, such as laws *and wisdom*" (italics mine).

[37] Cf. R. B. Y. Scott, "Solomon and the Beginnings of Wisdom in Israel," *Wisdom in Israel and the Ancient Near East*, pp. 262–279, esp. 276–279. Scott concludes that "the tradition [of Solomon and wisdom] seems to have been cultivated deliberately by Hezekiah as part of his grandiose plan to restore the vanished glories of Solomon's kingdom, for in Hezekiah's reign appears the first clear evidence of Hebrew wisdom as a significant literary phenomenon" (p. 279). One might rather conclude that Hezekiah repeated what he knew to have been true in Solomon's time. On the presence of wisdom in the Solomonic period, cf. Albrecht Alt, "Die Weisheit Salomos," *Theologische Literaturzeitung*, LXXVI (1951), cols. 139–144; Noth, *op. cit.*, pp. 218–224. Von Rad, *Der Heilige Krieg im Alten Israel*, Göttingen: Vandenhoeck and Ruprecht, 1951, p. 39, comments on the era of Solomon as a "typical Enlightenment" which he attributes, in part at least, to "the influx of international wisdom." Noth's comments, *op. cit.*, pp. 220–223 on the influence of the wisdom movement on the rise of historical writing are highly suggestive, for it is widely held that the wise men had little interest in history. Fichtner, "Zum Problem Glaube und Geschichte in der israelitischen-jüdischen Weisheitliteratur," *Theologische Literaturzeitung*, LXXVI (1951), cols. 145–150, has questioned this assumption in a most constructive way. I would suggest, more strongly than Fichtner appears to do, that a thorough study of Ps. 78, which clearly combines wisdom motifs and historical concerns, may prove illuminating for this problem. Otto Eissfeldt, in "Das Lied Moses Deuteronomium 32:1–43 und Das Lehrgedicht Asaphs Psalm 78," *Berichte über die Verhandlungen der Sächsischen Akademie der Wissenschaften zu Leipzig*, phil.-hist. Klasse, vol. 104, part 5, pp. 36 f. suggests a date of c. 930 B.C. for the Psalm.

[38] Cf. von Rad, *Theology*, p. 428: "Any sound discussion of Israel's wisdom means taking the concept as broadly as it was indeed taken. For her, thinking in terms of wisdom was something common to humanity. Wisdom had to do with the whole of life and had to be occupied with all its departments. It was most unfortunate that in the past the Old Testament wisdom was thought of more or less as the product of an exclusive theological school."

more properly of wisdom traditions.[39] A part of the problem in interpreting the role of wisdom is the failure to recognize the divergent wisdom traditions which are but imperfectly combined in the extant literature. This view would recognize that the later sages, teachers par excellence, did act as spiritual middlemen for the prophets, but it would also recognize that not all sapiential material is to be so interpreted. Such a broad approach might also permit us more properly to deal with certain extant Hebrew material which in fact does display a marked "humanistic" if not secular approach. For while I would contend for an early "religious" wisdom in Israel, the presence of more humanistic observations in all periods is undeniable.

Though by spatial limitation this paper can be but a preface to a prolegomenon one specific point may be mentioned as the particular contribution which further examination of the wisdom literature may provide for an understanding of Old Testament theology more inclusive than any survey which deals exclusively with election and covenant can indicate. This broader view is specifically related to the thought which emerges from a consideration of Yahweh as Creator which consequently viewed man as individual, as human being, not simply as member of the covenant community. This provided a universal as well as a particularistic motif in Israel from the beginning. It also indicates that an attitude toward nature which can hardly be called a natural philosophy but which takes quite seriously the role of nature as a medium of revelation was as integral to native Israelite thought as the prophetic view of history as the dominant medium. This is not to say that the wise men identified God with the natural forces nor that they neglected completely the historical sphere as an area of investigation.[40] By the same token it is appropriate to remember that the prophets with all their concern for history were not oblivious to Yahweh's wonder and workings in the realm of nature. What is being argued is that Israel's total understanding of Yahweh's self disclosure included nature, derived from the Creation faith, and that any account of Old Testament theology must recognize that element as existing in Israel from the very beginning of any formal expression of faith.[41]

All this in no way denies the validity of election faith, of covenantal theology, of *Heilsgeschichte*. Nor does it necessarily imply that these emphases were not the most creative and enduringly important elements in Israel's faith. But it does immeasurably broaden our apprehension of the scope of Israel's awareness of the significance of Yahweh for the totality of existence. Further, it points toward a more comprehensive approach to Israel's understanding of the nature of revelation. It also opens the way to fitting the wise men and their work into their proper niche in the total theological thought of Israel. For in their own way the wise men were media of revelation, just as were the prophets and the priests.[42] If they did not so explicitly claim "inspiration" it was because their apprehension of God lay within the human sphere of man's God given capacities. Their creation faith with its consequences was no less faith because it looked upward rather than receiving a word directly from above. Finally, though I do not read the Old Testament in any narrow Christological sense, does this view perhaps enable us to perceive even more fully the climax of God's dealings with Israel in Him who is the Word of God and the Wisdom of God?

---

[39] A too much neglected study of this point was made by Paul van Imschoot, "Sagesse et Esprit dans L'Ancien Testament," *Revue Biblique*, XLVII (1938), pp. 23–49. Though I do not fully accept his division of the wisdom movement into two parts — aristocratic and popular — it seems that the direction of his thought is indispensable for a proper understanding of the complexity of the extant wisdom materials.

[40] Cf. Fichtner's article cited in n. 37 and Ben Sira 44–49.

[41] I should stress again (cf. n. 33) that recognition must be given to the probability that both "creation faith" and "salvation history" underwent long periods of development before either became a fixed doctrine.

[42] Cf. H. W. Robinson, *op. cit.*, pp. 231–261.

Popular Questioning of the Justice of God in Ancient Israel*

By J. L. Crenshaw

(Vanderbilt Divinity School, Nashville, Tenn. 37203)

The task of justifying the ways of God to man has become "a universal religious nightmare"[1]; the problem is not so much the justification of God in the face of actual suffering as it is the *reconciling of evil* with the knowledge that God intends *salvation for mankind*[2]. In essence theodicy is the search for a solution to the problem of meaning[3], an undertaking that did not begin with modern man, the so-called fourth man, creature come of age[4].

Neither the ancient Israelite nor his Mesopotamian neighbors shied away from the above-mentioned task[5], even if for the former one admit the correctness of the charge of a "conspiracy of silence"[6] on the occasion of the death of Josiah. One might with some justification contend that the conspiracy of silence characterizes contemporary biblical scholars, inasmuch as attempts to wrestle with the problem of theodicy are few indeed. Apart from some discussion in exegetical studies of Job and theological examination of the problem of evil, three special treatments of theodicy have broken the silence of ignorance or timidity. The first, W. Eichrodt's "Vorsehungsglaube und Theodizee im Alten Testament"[7], is a masterful affirmation of

---

* The presidential address delivered to the Southern Section of the Society of Biblical Literature on Mar. 28, 1969, at the University of South Carolina, meeting jointly with the American Academy of Religion, Southern Section, and the Southern Humanities Conference.

[1] This is the task envisioned by J. Milton in: Paradise Lost. The Psychologist C. G. Jung has observed that theodicy "is no longer a problem for experts in theological seminaries, but a universal religious nightmare" (Answer to Job, 1969, 174).

[2] A. Jäger, Theodizee und Anthropodizee bei Karl Marx, SchTU 37 (1967), 14—23 ("Theodizee ist nicht so sehr eine 'Rechtfertigung' Gottes angesichts des faktischen Leides, als vor allem die 'Rechtfertigung' des Übels im Gegenüber zum Wissen um Gottes Heil für den Menschen", 14).   [3] Ibid.

[4] See K. H. Miskotte, When the Gods Are Silent, 1967, 1—7 and passim, for discussion of this terminology.

[5] The peculiar failure of Egypt to wrestle with the problem of theodicy has been explained by the fact that the idea of justice as *right* rather than as *favor* never seems to have spread to Egypt, and by the centrality of the belief in immortality (R. J. Williams, Theodicy in the Ancient Near East, Canadian JIh 2 [1956], 18f.). It is customary to call attention to "The Complaints of the Eloquent Peasant," "The Prophecy of Nefer-rohu" [ti], and "A Dispute over Suicide," but the difference between these and Israelite and Mesopotamian literature is great.

[6] S. B. Frost, The Death of Josiah: A Conspiracy of Silence, JBL 87 (1968), 369—382 ("... the silence following the death of Josiah which is so profound is the silence of the historiographers", 381).   [7] Festschrift O. Procksch, 1934, 45—70.

God's providence as proclaimed both explicitly and implicitly in the Old Testament, together with a reminder that the Israelite refused to solve the problem of evil by rational theories, choosing rather (1) the prophetic message of the God who comes (II Isa II Zech Ps 22 23-32); (2) the escape to the immediate experience of God's nearness (Ps 73, even in the presence of death; Jer 15 15-21 Ps 16 [Ps 17 15 and 63 4 come close; Job 3—21 attempts this unsuccessfully]); and (3) creation faith, an affirmation of a wondrous creation before which creaturely silence is mandatory (Job 38—41)[8]. Eichrodt clearly perceives that the *word of God* in this context, an *addressing of man* by God even in wisdom literature, implies that suffering can only be solved from revelation. The import of the divine creative word is also recognized by J. J. Stamm, whose "Die Theodizee in Babylon und Israel"[9] calls attention to the striking similarities between Job and *The Babylonian Theodicy*, neither of which judges God at the bar of reason. Rather Job pays heed to the revelatory word of the Creator, while the Babylonian sufferer trusts in the religious experience of past generations. In a word, the appeal to revelation or tradition falls far short of a theodicy, the resolution of the problem by human reason[10]. The existential character of the problem of evil does not escape Stamm's vision, for he notes that a crisis of faith rather than intellectual curiosity or literary artistry rests behind the ancient Near Eastern attempts to deal with the problem of theodicy[11]. The purely religious nature of these ancient probings is also grasped by R. J. Williams, whose "Theodicy in the Ancient Near East"[12] discusses the basic literary tradition pertinent to his subject and suggests that the intermediary for whom Job longed, the impartial judge who would even call Yahweh to task, was none other than the Canaanite Baal[13]

---

[8] Ibid. 64—70. The emphasis is upon the necessity for wonder, not man's nothingness. A. Heschel, Man is not Alone, 1951, 11 ff., replaces Kant's moral imperative with one of wonder, arguing that a capacity for radical amazement separates man from beast.

[9] Jaarbericht Ex Oriente Lux 9 (1944), 99—107.

[10] Ibid. 101. 107. N. H. Snaith, The Book of Job, 1968, 33, points to the prophetic influence upon Job, and argues that *The Babylonian Theodicy* served as a model for the biblical work (21—27).

[11] Ibid. 99. For a superb discussion of the crisis through which wisdom passed, see H. H. Schmid, Wesen und Geschichte der Weisheit, 1966, 74—78. 131—140. 173—195. J. Priest, Humanism, Skepticism, and Pessimism in Israel, JAAR 36 (1968), 321, suggests that Ezekiel's stress upon the transcendence of God and Deuteronomy's elevation of a "Book" contributed to the crisis from which skepticism arose.

[12] Op. cit. 14—26.

[13] Ibid. 24. The argument rests on the parallel with the Baal and Anat epic (ANET 140), which Ginzberg translates by "So I know that triumphant Baal lives, That the prince, lord of the earth, exists!"

If the literature of ancient Israel and Mesopotamia wrestling with the problem of evil cannot be described as theodicy in the sense intended by Leibniz or Kant, perhaps the re-orientation suggested by A. Jäger[14] in the direction of anthropodicy has merit. The crucial question for man is not "How can one reconcile the existence of God with the presence of evil?" but "What positive meaning for man can be had in the face of the tentacles of death?" If this be a proper assessment of our situation, one can approve wholeheartedly the desire of J. Priest to elevate anthropology, or as he prefers, sociology, to at least equal position with theology in Old Testament scholarship[15]. The fruits of such a perspective await our plucking, but Priest's interpretation of Job from the standpoint of the nagging question, "Why am I?", and of Qoheleth as a denial of meaningful history, indicates that a refusal to eat from this tree is folly rather than wisdom. In an article in JBL, I have described wisdom literature as Israel's quest for self-understanding in terms of things, people and God[16], and am now prepared to maintain that the question of meaning is more basic than that of God, indeed that biblical man's point of departure was not God but self. In essence, the God question is secondary to self-understanding[17].

I. INITIAL RUMBLINGS: A FAMINE IN THE LAND OF PROMISE

Whether theodicy or anthropodicy be the term to describe our present task, the intention is the same, namely to examine the evidence for initial rumblings in Israel indicative of difficulty in answering the question of meaning, to look closely at the literary deposit expressive of a volcanic eruption (Job and Qoheleth) and to consider the alternative methods of dealing with a loss of meaning, specifically the escape to the comforts provided by religion and the flight from God by the stout-hearted.

The use of the expression "famine" above implies that there once was plenty, indicates that the initial rumblings are the result of a privation. But privation from what? From a belief in the efficacy of good works! So long as ancient man thought of the gods in terms of

---

[14] Op. cit. 19.

[15] Op. cit. 311—326.

[16] J. L. Crenshaw, Method in Determining Wisdom Influence upon "Historical" Literature, JBL 88 (1969), 129—142.

[17] This suggests that Old Testament theology should begin with man rather than God as is common in the works adopting a systematic principle. Heschel op. cit. 129 observes that "The Bible is not man's theology, but God's anthropology, dealing with man and what he asks of him rather than with the nature of God." Also pertinent to this discussion is Heschel's reminder that our "self-concern is a cupful drawn from the spirit of divine concern" (145).

impersonal force, caprice was anticipated and tolerated. However, once personal categories were applied to the gods, man came to expect them to behave in a manner that was humanly predictable, even though free to act in a high-handed fashion on occasion[18]. The belief in the efficacy of good works was characteristic of all three segments of Israelite society. In a recent book entitled "Gerechtigkeit als Weltordnung", H. H. Schmid has demonstrated that basic to the wisdom of the ancient world was the conviction that the Creator had established the universe in an orderly fashion, that a principle of the right or appropriate deed held the created order together, and that man's purpose was to act in harmony with this principle at all times. Although going by different names (*Maat* in Egypt, *ME* in Mesopotamia, *ṣăddîq* in Israel), this principle was thought to have been guaranteed by the king and to have encompassed the areas of law, wisdom, nature (vegetation), warfare (victory over enemies), cult (sacrifice), as well as kingship[19]. Any action that was not in accord with the governing principle of the universe was thought to have upset the balance of nature, to have reintroduced an element of chaos into the created order, hence to be deserving of punishment or death. Conversely, the appropriate deed was rewarded, since it sustained the universe, so that religion became highly utilitarian.

The prophetic theology, with strong ties to covenantal and holy war traditions, was equally positive in the view that the good deed was rewarded. In reality, the basis of a covenantal (or treaty) relationship is a promise that accord with the stipulations of the covenant will bring blessings while a breach of the agreement calls upon the heads of the rebellious all the curses spoken or unspoken. When this is kept in mind, the prophetic theology within individual oracles and in the Deuteronomic history is completely understandable. Furthermore, the holy war traditions, particularly the comforting "Fear not, for I am with you", and the memory of theophanies for judgment upon enemies[20], coupled with the conviction of Israel's chosenness and uniqueness contributed to the belief that obedience would not pass unnoticed by God. Priestly religion, too, supported the view that good men fare well in this life, both in its relationship with magic and with law. The presupposition of the cultic act was that the deity could be moved, whether automatically or by proper conduct matters little as far as the principle is concerned, while the codification of law rests on the premise that God has declared his will for man and will, by the use of the stick or the carrot, punishment or reward, see

---

[18] W. G. Lambert, Babylonian Wisdom Literature, 1960, 6ff.

[19] Gerechtigkeit als Weltordnung, 1968, 15—77 and passim.

[20] H. D. Preuss, . . . Ich will mit dir sein!, ZAW 80 (1968), 139—173, and J. L. Crenshaw, Amos and the Theophanic Tradition, ibid. 203—215.

that it is carried out. Even if we refuse to join K. Koch in affirming a "sphere of destiny" in which the deed activated a principle that guaranteed punishment for transgression[21], and prefer rather H. Graf Reventlow's view that God's freedom transcends any such nexus of guilt and punishment[22], the point still stands that priest, prophet and wise man labored under the assumption of a correlation between good conduct and earthly reward.

Undergirding this belief in the efficacy of the good deed was ancient man's sense of solidarity, the corporate merging of the one and the many, making possible the conviction of imputed merit and guilt, and providing a convenient explanation for any divergence from the principle of retribution. But in Israel this balloon was punctured as a result of the rise of a wealthy class and urban culture, the valiant effort to patch the holes by the great prophets succeeding only in increasing the sense of guilt felt by those who refused to sacrifice private interests for the welfare of the group. Even the classical prophets contributed to the breakdown of the correlation between good conduct and reward, both in affirming the grace of God despite Israel's rebellious response, and in making grandiose claims not borne out in actual history, then in escaping to the safe position of expectancy. Both the emergence of false prophecy and the never-fulfilled eschatological hopes (or those only partially fulfilled, as in the case of II Isaiah) set the stage for complete loss of faith on the occasions of the death of Josiah, the fall of Jerusalem and collapse of the Davidic dynasty despite II Sam 7 and numerous psalms expressing the conviction that Yahweh has established David's throne for eternity.

Such a crisis was not, however, unique to Israel, as H. H. Schmid, "Wesen und Geschichte der Weisheit" has discerned so clearly[23]. Rather both in Egypt and in Mesopotamia wisdom's claims were challenged because of a failure to accord with human experience, particularly during subjugation by enemies who either did not know about the principle governing the universe or did not give any credence to it. Nevertheless, the crisis was more acute in Israel because of the deep *personal relationship* between her and Yahweh, a bond best described by marital or familial imagery, and not even approximated by the conviction of non-Israelites as early as the Sumerians

---

[21] Gibt es ein Vergeltungsdogma im Alten Testament?, ZThK 52 (1955), 21.

[22] Sein Blut komme über sein Haupt, VT 10 (1960), 311. H. Gese, Lehre und Wirklichkeit in der alten Weisheit, 1958, 45—50, emphasizes Yahweh's freedom from any principle of order. W. Brueggemann, Tradition for Crisis, 1968, 78 f., calls attention to Hosea's radical departure in asserting that the blessings promised in Lev 26 and Dtn 28 for covenant obedience will befall the *disobedient*!

[23] See note 11.

that the people are the apple of the deity's eye[24]. In Israel the loss of the corporate sense does not begin with Jeremiah and Ezekiel, whose intention was to encourage a generation upon whom the crisis had fallen, but at least as early as the Davidic and Solomonic decisions to alter tribal boundaries, maintain a mercenary army, and ape the ways of neighboring powers. We should expect, therefore, to discover within literature as early as the Davidic era echoes of rumblings brought on by a famine in the land of promise, the inevitable disparity between religious claims and actual experience.

The Yahwistic narrative bears witness to such concern over the conduct of God in the face of extreme wickedness. The account of Abraham's intercession for a doomed Sodom and Gomorrah, although no attack against collective guilt, dares to entertain a radically new understanding of God's righteousness (Gen 18 17-33). The Yahwist recognizes that there is more injustice in the death of a few innocent people than in the sparing of a guilty multitude; his question, however, is "To what limits is the application of this principle subject?" Or put another way, "What determines God's judgment on Sodom, the wickedness of the many or the innocence of the few?" The guilt of the city is beyond question, but the narrator pushes Yahweh to the point of admitting that a very small number of innocent people could spare a great host, so willing is He to save. The fact that Sodom and Gomorrah are inhabited by non-Israelites indicates just how far Yahweh will go in overlooking sin for the sake of a few righteous; Sodom becomes a "pattern of a human community toward which Yahweh's eyes turn in judgment" (G. von Rad). The subsequent angelic removal of all "righteous" people from the doomed cities protects Yahweh from the accusation of injustice, even if the Yahwist did not press God to an admission that one innocent person could spare the city (cf. Am 9 10, where a distinction is made between the guilty and innocent and only the former punished)[25].

Similar rumblings may lie behind the Yahwistic portion of the incident of the golden calf in Ex 32 (25-35). Couched within the Deuteronomic concern for Yahweh's reputation, promise to the fathers and repentance (7-14), this narrative lays stress upon the wrath of God despite the intercessory pleadings of the innocent Moses who dares to lay his life on the altar, hence provides a sort of corrective to anyone who might be disposed to press the principle enunciated in the narrative about Sodom and Gomorrah to his own advantage.

---

[24] S. N. Kramer, Sumer, Int DB IV 1962, 463, and Stamm op. cit. 105—107.

[25] G. von Rad, Genesis, 1961, 204—209, and J. Skinner, Genesis, 1910, 305. H. Gunkel, The Legends of Genesis, 1964 (originally in 1901), 60, writes that the story teller hides from us the most important point in this narrative, Abraham's thoughts while viewing the smoke from Sodom.

In this instance Moses is assured that Yahweh will punish the guilty, little comfort before the brandished swords of the levites, who presumably join Aaron in guilt but escape punishment. The God who can order mass homicide is also capable of carrying out the test of Abraham's faith in the Elohistic narrative of Gen 22. But even here there is a growing suspicion that the demand of human sacrifice is unbecoming to God.

Once the justice of God was questioned, even if obliquely, the everpresent lament intensifies in pathos, for the expressions of confidence lose something of their force. Jeremiah's poignant cry for justice may begin with the conventional confession of God's righteousness (12 1), but the prophetic accusation that Yahweh prospers the wicked, and the divine oracle of hatred for a covenanted people (12 2-13) indicate the shallowness of the claim. Jeremiah's contemporary, Habakkuk, affirms God's justice, however, even in the face of all evidence to the contrary; the final hymn is almost unsurpassed in the Old Testament for grandeur of faith despite one's external situation (cf. Dan 3 16-18). Habakkuk vows that even starvation will not prevent him from rejoicing in God (3 17-19); nevertheless, the perversion of justice and failure of God to respond when the cry of oppression storms the gates of heaven are not nullified by promise of action in the future. The deepest cry of anguish comes, however, not from a prophet, but from a cultic liturgy agonizing over the failure of God to keep his promise to David. Composed of an ancient hymn on the mercies of Yahweh as seen in his victory over Chaos and the election of David, a prophetic oracle promising the permanence of the Davidic dynasty, and a lament over the collapse of that line, psalm 89 may be Israel's reaction to the death of Josiah[26]. Regardless of the historical situation calling forth the psalm, the disparity between God's promise and the reality of the situation finds no rational resolution, and must be stated with a bleeding heart[27]. Little wonder, therefore, that a volcanic eruption takes place, that out of this agony come two masterpieces of the human spirit, Job and Qoheleth.

II. VOLCANIC ERUPTION: JOB AND QOHELETH

Y. Kaufmann has described the concerns of theodicy as threefold: (1) the origin of natural, or primary evil, (2) of religious evil,

---

[26] H. J. Kraus, Psalmen, II 1966, 615—625, and A. Weiser, The Psalms, 1962, 590—594.

[27] Weiser op. cit. 593 writes: "Man is not able to resolve by his own thinking the contradiction between the promise and the actual state of affairs; he can only state that contradiction with a bleeding heart; . . . "

and (3) of moral evil[28]. While Job focuses upon the problem of moral evil, both in its social and divine manifestation, and Qoheleth draws attention to natural evil, particularly death, it was left for the apocalyptic author of II Esdras to wrestle with the issue of religious evil, the weakness of Israel apropos foreign empires (cf. Gen 11 and origin of *idolatry*).

Although the biblical Job may be *sui generis*, at least as far as literary classification is concerned, it is but one of several attempts to grapple with innocent suffering in the ancient Near East[29]. At least three solutions to the problem are manifest: (1) man is congenitally evil; (2) the gods are unjust; and (3) our knowledge is partial. The fragmentariness of human understanding was a necessary corollary of the belief in the hiddenness of God, the *Deus absconditus* expressive of true mystery (the *numinous*), but also of his refusal to be controlled by anyone who knows *hă-šem*, the Name. The partiality of man's knowledge lent credence to the suggestion that innocent suffering was disciplinary, purgative even, and to the much later belief that all would be set right in a future existence.

The declaration of man's congenital sinfulness goes back to Sumerian times; S. N. Kramer renders the pertinent passage

> "Never has a sinless child been born to its mother,
> ... a sinless workman has not existed from of old."[30]

Similarly the *Babylonian Theodicy* affirms that

> "Narru, king of the gods, who created mankind,
> And majestic Zulummar, who dug out their clay,
> And mistress Mami, the queen who fashioned them,
> Gave perverse speech to the human race.
> With lies, and not truth, they endowed them forever."[31]

In full agreement with such sentiment was Eliphaz, Job's miserable comforter, for from him we hear

> "Behold, God puts no trust in his holy ones,
> and the heavens are not clean in his sight;
> how much less one who is abominable and corrupt,
> a man who drinks iniquity like water!" (15 15f.; cf. 4 17)

Likewise Bildad wishes to view man in terms of his own stature; he exclaims

---

[28] The Religion of Israel, 1960, 332.
[29] Lambert op. cit. 21—91. 139—149 and J. Pritchard, ed. ANET, 1955, 434—440.
[30] Man and his God: A Sumerian Variation of the "Job" Motif, in: Wisdom in Israel and in the Ancient Near East (SVT 3, 1960), 170—182, especially 179.
[31] Lambert op. cit. 89.

"How then can man be righteous before God ?
How can he who is born of woman be clean ?
Behold, even the moon is not bright
    and the stars are not clean in his sight;
how much less man, who is a maggot,
    and the son of man, who is a worm !" (25 4-6)

Similarly the accusation of the gods as unjust occurs in extra biblical literature as well as in Job, indeed is the presupposition of the works. This comes out most strikingly, however, in "The Babylonian *Pilgrim's Progress*", to use W. G. Lambert's title for *Ludlul bēl nēmeqi*, where the sufferer complains that he is being treated like an impious one who has neglected prayer, sacrifice, holy days, reverence, God even[32], and in the *Dialogue of Pessimism*, where such a recognition of the injustice of God lies behind the despair[33]. In Job, too, the justice of God comes under attack, indeed gives way before the might of Titanic Job (9 22-24 24 1-12).

The incompleteness of human understanding, celebrated in the majestic hymn of Job 28, is emphasized in "The Babylonian *Pilgrim's Progress*" and *The Babylonian Theodicy*. The former complains

"I wish I knew that these things were pleasing to one's God !
What is proper to oneself is an offense to one's god,
What in one's own heart seems despicable is proper to one's god.
Who knows the will of the gods in heaven ?
Who understands the plans of the underworld gods ?
Where have mortals learnt the way of a god ?"[34]

The Babylonian Theodicy expresses the same sentiment, even if admitting that savants attain to wisdom:

"O wise one, O savant, who masters knowledge,
In your anguish you blaspheme the god.
The divine mind, like the center of the heavens, is remote;
Knowledge of it is difficult; the masses do not know it."[35]

It is quite clear that Job is at one with the extrabiblical parallels in the solutions provided. This is true even when one appeals to the theophany as the final resolution of Job's situation, for the same answer is found in "The Babylonian *Pilgrim's Progress*", where Marduk comes to the sufferer and removes all adversity. In view of this affinity between Job and similar works, the assumption of the uniqueness of Job as to *Gattung* is open to question. But what are we to

---

[32] Ibid. 39.
[33] Ibid. 145—149.
[34] Ibid. 41.
[35] Ibid. 87.

call Job? A *rib*, answered lament, *Streitgespräch*, or what? The kinship with the covenant lawsuit, indeed the legal background, of Job has long been recognized. When one admits the close relationship between law and wisdom championed by E. Gerstenberger[36], the thesis that Job is a *rib* becomes quite possible, as Stamm has already perceived[37]. On the other hand, H. Gese's contention that Job is a paradigm of an answered lament[38] presents serious difficulty, inasmuch as the framework of Job differs radically from that of laments, and even the poetic *dialogue* stands out both in mood and complexion. More attractive than either, however, is the view that Job is a *Streitgespräch*, a controversy dialogue. Such disputations are well known to wisdom literature from its earliest manifestation; their form consists of a mythological introduction followed by a debate between two contestants, the resolution of which is determined by divine judgment[39]. However, the prophetic *Streitgespräch*, which differs as to intensity of argumentation and purpose, namely self-vindication of the prophet, has contributed to the genre as found in Job, and explains the kinship with II Isaiah. In Job the mood differs from the calm, almost playful, wisdom discussion of the relative value of things, animals or professions; rather Job employs the controversy dialogue as a weapon of warfare, his own vindication being at stake. In reality, then, Job is rooted in wisdom and prophetic theology, both as to literary genre and final resolution of the problem by a theophany. The key to Job, at least from this perspective, is the emotional outburst of 13 16 ("This will be my salvation, that a godless man shall not come before him"). Since God comes to Job, he has been vindicated, the problem of meaning is no more, for all things fall into place when in the presence of the Creator of the ends of the earth. For the author of Job, meaning is theological — nothing else matters, neither love (for wife, children, friends), nor desire for earthly goods.

Qoheleth can find no such meaning anywhere; this author is convinced that life is empty, vain, profitless. Neither material possessions, human friendship, nor religious devotion alter the fact that nature is oppressive, that death is the negation of all good, that God is therefore untouched by the plight of creatures. What, then, is man to do? Qoheleth advises him to find some pleasure in wife and children, and to work with dignity, in this way postponing death as long as possible. In Qoheleth there is a challenging of the power of human reason,

---

[36] Wesen und Herkunft des "apodiktischen Rechts", 1965, and: Covenant and Commandment, JBL 84 (1965), 38—51.

[37] Op. cit. 104 (with a reference to an article in: Der Grundriß 5 [1943], 1 ff.).

[38] Op. cit. 63—78.

[39] Lambert op. cit. 150—211.

Zeitschr. f. alttestamentl. Wiss., Band 82, 1970   26

298

a recognition of the bankruptcy of wisdom. In Job and in Qoheleth we discern a failure of nerve, the one rational, the other theological[40]!

In the presence of volcanic fire as seen in Job and Qoheleth, and following the leads suggested by each, two responses are possible: (1) repentance, confession of God's justice despite everything, that is, an affirmation of meaning (Job); and (2) despair, criticism of God for not caring, the denial of divine justice, hence of meaningful existence (Qoheleth). Both responses characterize the popular reaction to the disparity between the promises of faith and the realities of experience.

III. SURVIVAL OF A FAITHFUL FEW:
THE DOXOLOGY OF JUDGMENT

The confession of God's justice in the presence of a sentence of death appears in various strata of biblical literature, all of which date from the period of crisis surrounding 587 B. C. and its sequel. The vocabulary of this confession and the act itself led F. Horst to the conclusion that there was within sacral law of Israel (and related peoples) a ceremony in which the guilty person was admonished to give glory to Yahweh (Josh 7 19 Job 4—5 Jer 13 15f. I Sam 6 5 Ps 118 17-21 I Chr 30 8 (LXX) Am 4 6-13 9 1-6), that is, to confess that the Lord is just even when demanding the death penalty[41]. To the literature associated with this occasion Horst gave the title "Doxology of Judgment". His suggestion has been endorsed by G. von Rad and R. Knierim, both of whom provide additional passages to be understood from this perspective (I Kings 8 3 Ezr 10 7ff. Dan 3 31-34 Neh 9 Ezr 6 Dan 9 Isa 12 1f. [von Rad] Ps 16 56-60 29 1-9 89 7-15 118 17-21 Mi 1 1 Isa 6 3 [Knierim])[42]. In a work in ZAW[43] I have sought to demonstrate that the doxology of judgment and prophetic recitation of disciplinary punishment characteristic of ancient days of penitence gave way in the exilic and post-exilic community to hymnic confessions concluded by the refrain "YHWH Ṣᵉbaʾôt Šᵉmô" (Jer 10 12-16 31 35 51 15-19 Isa 51 15), and finally to cultic confessional prayers (Dan 9 Neh 9 Ezr 9 Jer 32). The centrality of creation faith in these passages is occasioned by the knowledge that it is the Creator who

---

[40] For recent discussions of Qoheleth's manner of speaking about God, see H. P. Müller, Wie sprach Qohälät von Gott?, VT 18 (1968), 507—521, and E. Pfeiffer, Die Gottesfurcht im Buche Kohelet, in: Gottes Wort und Gottes Land (Festschrift für H. W. Hertzberg), 1965, 133—158.

[41] Die Doxologien im Amosbuch, ZAW 47 (1929), 45—54 (Gottes Recht, 1961, 155—166).

[42] G. von Rad, Old Testament Theology, 1962, 357ff., and Knierim, The Vocation of Isaiah, VT 18 (1968), 56.

[43] YHWH Ṣᵉbaʾôt Šᵉmô: A Form-Critical Analysis, 81 (1969), 156—175.

calls all men to judgment, and the striking association of *bara'* and a theophany for judgment indicates that a new look at the role of creation faith in Israelite thought is mandatory. The peripheral place of creation faith in the Old Testament does not grow out of a refusal to take nature seriously. On the contrary, B. Albrektson[44] has laid to rest (once for all, it is hoped) the one-sided emphasis upon God's action in history as opposed to nature as the distinctive of Israelite thought. While it is true, as von Rad has advocated so ably[45], that the Canaanite threat to the moral integrity of Yahwism constituted a barrier to adoption of creation faith, an obstacle overcome only by II Isaiah's stroke of genius in utilizing the Canaanite mythologem to interpret the event of the exodus, nevertheless there must be a better reason for the Israelite hesitance to place creation at the center of his faith. I would venture to propose another possibility: the close association of creation faith with a theophany for judgment was out of place in Israel until the crisis of meaning emerged, the awareness that judgment had fallen. Out of reflection upon the implications of a final judgment came the necessity to postulate a doctrine of creation as central to Yahwism. In a word, such judgment of all mankind can only come from the Creator of all[45a]: Against this setting the declaration that Yahweh is *ṣǎddîq* must be understood (Jer 12 1 Ps 119 137 Ezr 9 15 Neh 9 8. 33 Ex 9 27 Zeph 3 5 Lam 1 18 Dan 9 14 II Chr 12 6; cf. II Kings 10 9).

A related literary phenomenon has come to the attention of S. Frost, who refers to "asseveration by thanksgiving" as a special means of magnifying God's justice even in the context of adversity[46]. Such asseverations of thanksgiving Frost identifies in prophetic and psalmodic literature mostly from the *crisis period* of Israelite faith under discussion here (Isa 42 10-13 44 23 49 13 25 1-5 12 1b-2. 4b-6 Hos 13 4 Jer 20 7-13 Ps 118 21 116 5 54 8-9 (Heb.) 86 8-13 57 22). These positive affirmations of God's justice, like the doxology of judgment and confessional prose prayers interspersed throughout Old Testament literature, are but the Joban popular response to the volcanic eruption in Israelite society. Small wonder that a note of expectancy comes to dominate post-exilic literature, for this surrender before the God who comes in judgment must be rewarded, since the justice of God is boldly asserted, hence the eschatological expectation of Hag, Zech, and Mal falls upon ears atune to this frequency. However, such escape by means of an anticipated coming of God in judgment and,

---

[44] History and the Gods, 1967.
[45] The Theological Problem of the Old Testament Doctrine of Creation, in: The Problem of the Hexateuch and other Essays, 1966, 131—143, originally in: BZAW 66, 1936.   [45a] For further discussion, see my article referred to in note 43.
[46] Asseveration by Thanksgiving, VT 8 (1958), 380—390.

26*

through punishment, in love was not the only one open to Israel; Qoheleth was not entirely devoid of disciples, although few have been aware of it.

IV. JUDGMENT THROUGH FIRE:
THE POPULAR DENIAL OF MEANING IN LIFE

In the past, far too little attention has been given to the actual religion of the "man in the streets" in ancient Israel, the spotlight of scholarly scrutiny being turned on the officially sanctioned religion of Israel. There is a growing recognition of the necessity for taking a closer look at Israelite religion as it really was rather than as it was hoped it would be. It is interesting that the study of Amos has led G. Farr and C. J. Labuschagne in this direction, the latter of whom has promised a monograph on what he calls para-theology[47]. In an attempt to solve the enigma of false prophecy I have been forced to take seriously the popular beliefs that constituted a live option for the man of faith. In fact, I would even suggest that the study of prophecy in general and of false prophecy in particular has moved in the direction of taking seriously the voice of the people. Prophetic research began with an emphasis upon the great individualist, ethical monotheist, ecstatic, only later to shift away from the man to his message, both as to its character as doom only or weal *and* woe, and the traditions employed by the prophet. The next logical step, it seems to me, is to discuss the hearers, to discern what they contributed to the dialogue. Fortunately, the voice of the people is not altogether hidden from us; we possess a special source for this phenomenon, namely the prophetic quotations of the oral response to their message. H. W. Wolff's masterful "Das Zitat im Prophetenspruch"[48] provides a useful point of departure, but much more needs to be done. On the basis of prophetic quotations, I would venture to describe Israel's popular religion in terms of arrogant confidence, spiritual insensitivity, taunting defiance, remorseless despair, painful query and historical pragmatism. I shall here limit myself to a glance at some of the evidence for the last two characteristics, painful query and historical pragmatism. The claim that Yahweh was merciful, compassionate, and slow to anger was questioned in Jeremiah's day by those who feared that God's anger would last forever (3 4-5a).

---

[47] Farr, The Language of Amos, Popular or Cultic?, VT 16 (1966), 312—324, and Labuschagne, Amos' Conception of God and the Popular Theology of his Time, in: Studies on the Books of Hosea and Amos, 1964/65, 122—133. Th. C. Vriezen, The Religion of Israel, 1967, 20, writes that a hard core were faithful as in Isaiah's day, "while the great mass of the people must undoubtedly have trimmed their sails to the wind".

[48] Gesammelte Studien zum Alten Testament, 1964,36—129, originally Beih EvTh 4,1937.

Ezekiel's contemporaries complained that "The days grow long, and every vision comes to nought" (12 22), in fact, questioned the justice of God ("The way of the Lord is not just" 18 25). Likewise Malachi's opponents complained that "Everyone who does evil is good in the sight of the Lord, and he delights in them" (2 17), "It is vain to serve God. What is the good of our keeping his charge" for "evildoers not only prosper but when they put God to the test they escape" (3 12. 15). This painful questioning of God's justice was supplemented by historical pragmatism; the people demanded that God repay their goodness, and when he did not, they turned to other gods or to their own desires. This can be seen in the demand that Yahweh "speed his work that we may see it" (Isa 5 19), and the report that the worship of the queen of heaven paid higher dividends, hence the adulation of Yahweh would be sheer folly (Jer 44 16-19). In the light of this evidence, one must object to the usual assumption that belief in the efficacy of good works, what E. M. Good calls the magical assumption in religion[49], was of popular origin and typifies the faith of the masses as opposed to that of the religious establishment. No longer ought we to say that the dialogue in Job is an attack on popular religion[50]; on the contrary, both this questioning of God's justice and Qoheleth's denial of any meaning in life have more affinity with popular religion than with official Yahwism. This kinship is particularly noticeable in the prophetic *Streitgespräch*.

On the basis of II Isaiah, J. Begrich has observed that the *Streitgespräch* emerged from the concrete situation of the prophet and assumed the form of question and answer, claim and counter-claim[51]. E. Pfeiffer's analysis of the discussions in Malachi indicates that three stages are evident: (1) the initial statement; (2) the objection by the partner in the discussion; and (3) the defense of the original statement, together with the conclusion[52]. My own study of the controversy dialogue has convinced me that it is a weapon of warfare, a self-vindication of the prophet. Accordingly, stylistic devices of rhetorical question and citation of popular theology draw attention to the radicality of the prophetic message, which is reinforced by rational argumentation based on human nature and experience, together with invective and threat. The pedagogic value of the disputation is minimal, owing to the great gulf between prophet and people, a chasm enlarged by abusive language. In essence, the defense of God's justice prominent in prophetic disputations is an effort at self-vindication, a burning issue after the emergence of false prophets.

[49] Irony in the Old Testament, 1965, 196—240.
[50] Against G. A. Larue, Old Testament Life and Literature, 1968, 296, and Stamm op. cit. 103.   [51] Studien zu Deuterojesaja, 1963, 48—51, originally in BWANT 25, 1938.
[52] Die Disputationsworte im Buche Maleachi, EvTh 19 (1959), 546—568.

A thoroughgoing analysis of the disputations that pertain to the justice of God cannot be attempted here, but a few observations are in order. In Mi 2 6-11 the popular demand that the prophet preach *šalôm* is based on the belief that God does not punish his covenant people, and the prophet is forced to defend God's justice. Again, the well known parable of the farmer in Isa 28 23-29, where the point is made that the farmer does the proper thing at the right time, must be interpreted against the backdrop of a denial of the justice of God, as W. Whedbee's recent Yale Dissertation on "Isaiah and Wisdom" has recognized[53]. Here Isaiah is assuring the people of God's justice by promising that God acts in a manner appropriate to the occasion. Likewise, the prophet attacks those who ask, "Who sees us? Who knows us?" by employing a *Streitfabel* calling attention to the absurdity of the clay complaining that the potter has no understanding (29 15f.). A similar questioning of the justice of God prompts II Isaiah to praise the Creator as one who does not faint or grow weary, who is unsearchable in understanding, hence the claim that "My way is hid from the Lord, and my right is disregarded by my God" is thought to have no real content. Finally, Malachi addresses himself to the popular rejection of God's justice, suggesting that those who deny that God is just or ask "Where is the God of justice?" can find comfort in the expected coming of the messenger of the Lord who will refine Israel's priesthood, indeed, that those who advocate that serving God is vain should take note of the fact that God is keeping a book of remembrance so that eventually there will be a distinction between the righteous and the wicked, and the saints will tread down the sinners on the day when Yahweh acts (2 17—3 5 3 13—4 3). Are Job and Qoheleth to be silenced so easily? Is there not more integrity in the popular questioning of the justice of God than in Malachi's affirmation of it[54]?

EPILOGUE: THE RESPONSIBILITY FOR HONESTY

It would be interesting to pursue the variations of the Joban theme in "Paradise Lost", where one finds God's honor saved at man's expense, "J. B.", where human love provides the hope for one who had discovered that God does not love, but *is*, whereas we *do* love, and Jung's "Answer to Job", where the eternal gospel that one *can* love God but *must fear him* is altered little by the participation

---

[53] 1968, chapter II.

[54] Heschel op. cit. 132 reminds us that "even the cry of despair: There is no justice in heaven! — is a cry in the name of justice that cannot have come out of us and still be missing in the source of ourselves".

of God in the enigma of human suffering[55]. However, I wish to conclude by raising for your further reflection some questions growing out of this discussion. To what extent are religious leaders responsible for what the masses are asked to believe? When grandiose theological claims are made, must their promulgator assume the responsibility for loss of faith that results when the promises do not materialize? Are prophets culpable for having thought more about vindicating themselves before their attackers than about real communication? Does every appeal to a future act of God cast a positive vote for the Marxist claim that religion is an opiate of the people[56]? Which, then, is preferable, the creed of the blind man ("I have been young, and now am old; yet I have not seen the righteous forsaken or his children begging bread", Ps 37 25), or that of the heart of stone ("It is hopeless, for I have loved strangers, and after them I will go", Jer 2 25 b)?

A final thought. Is the current emphasis on wisdom literature indicative of our inability to take revelation seriously any more? Now that we can no longer say *kō 'amăr 'ᵃdonai* ("Thus hath the Lord spoken") are we reduced to *šᵉmă' bᵉni mûsăr 'abika* ("My son, listen to your father's advice")? Has the crisis that confronted Job and Qoheleth invaded the ranks of Old Testament scholarship? Shades of Qoheleth! Is there nothing new under the sun[57]?

Die Behauptung der Gerechtigkeit Gottes in Israel durch Priester, Prophet und Weisen konnte angesichts der tatsächlichen Erfahrung nicht aufrechterhalten werden. Erste Fragen, wie sie in Gen 18 Ex 32 Jer 12 Hab und Ps 89 erhoben werden, führen sowohl zu mutiger Behauptung (Hiob) als auch zu abweichenden Meinungen (Kohelet) — beides Antworten auf das Versagen von Theologie und Weisheit, die mit a) Gerichtsdoxologien und Versicherungen der Rechtschaffenheit und b) Zitieren volkstümlicher Antworten auf die prophetische Botschaft fortfuhren.

L'affirmation en Israël par prêtres, prophètes et sages de la justice divine ne pût être maintenue sans autre, confrontée à la réalité. Des questions premières, telles qu'on les trouve en Gen 18 Ex 32 Jér 12 Hab et Ps 89 conduisent aussi bien à une affirmation courageuse (Job) qu'à des positions différentes (Qoheleth). Ces réponses à la défaillance de la théologie et de la sagesse ont fait avancer le débat a) par des doxologies de la justice et la promesse que Dieu fera droit aux siens b) en citant les réactions populaires à la prédication prophétique.

---

[55] Jung op. cit. 169 ("That is the eternal, as distinct from the temporal gospel: one can love God but one must fear him") and A. MacLeish, J. B., 1956, 151 f. (Sarah: "You wanted justice and there was none ... only love". J. B.: "He [God] does not love. He is." Sarah: "But we do. That's the wonder").   [56] Jäger op. cit. 22.

[57] H. H. Schmid, Hauptprobleme der neueren Prophetenforschung, SchTU 35 (1965), 142, asks some pertinent questions about what is meant when the sage learns from experience what prophets proclaim as revelation. This line of thinking opens all sorts of possibilities for Old Testament scholarship.

Wisdom and Vision in the Old Testament[1]

By **Robert H. Pfeiffer**, Harvard University.

(Cambridge [Mass.], 57 Francis Avenue.)

The religion of Israel was not, until the reformation of Josiah in 621 B. C., substantially different from the religions of the nations whose territory adjoined the land of Canaan. The conception of Jehovah held by David and Ahab was so strikingly similar to the conception of Chemosh held by Mesha, king of Moab, that JULIUS WELLHAUSEN could wonder why Jehovah, and not Chemosh, eventually came to be regarded as the sole God of heaven and earth.

The pages of the O. T. contain the record of the rise of Jehovah from the level of a localized deity of a mountain, of a nation, and of a country, to the position of the universal deity of all nations and of the physical world; they picture the development of a religion national in scope and ritualistic in character, which gradually became a worship in spirit and in truth. In a historical process of this magnitude and significance we can scarcely hope to discover *all* the factors that contributed some of the energy required for this spiritual ascent; however the determination of the outstanding forces that lifted the religion of Israel out of the atmosphere of commonplace to that of eminent distinction, should not prove to be beyond the realm of possibility.

The critical investigation of the O. T. during the last century has correctly recognized in the prophetic movement the first outstanding factor in the religious progress of Israel. But, if I am not mistaken, there is a second factor the significance of which has not been sufficiently emphasized, namely the wisdom literature of the O. T. In radically different manner, prophecy and wisdom gave to the religion of Israel a universal scope and a spiritual character: prophecy gave a moral content, wisdom an intellectual content, to the traditional worship and belief.

True, such idealistic tendencies were not entirely unprecedented: Egypt and Babylonia had their prophets and sages whose high moral teaching and bold speculations rank high among the spiritual achievements of our ancient forebears. But somehow, these seeds that could have conceivably matured in movements vast enough to stir the soul of mankind, failed to bear fruit. In Egypt, Ikhnaton in the 14th Century B. C. envisioned a single god of all the world, a god strong in might and benevolent in temper; but the seed of this noble faith fell upon stony ground and among the weeds, bearing but scanty fruit. A powerful priestly hierarchy, with a prestige and authority scarcely inferior to those of the throne, effectively controlled the currents of thought in ancient Egypt and Babylonia, preventing the fruition and spread of any ideas deemed inimical to the priestly

---

[1] Opening address at the Harvard Divinity School, September 26, 1933.

control of the masses. Within the ranks of the priesthoods of the valleys of the Nile and of the Euphrates scholarship flourished, but the conclusions, as well as the objectives, of research were mapped out in advance.

Israel, on the contrary, offered a more fertile ground for religious experimentation. For the priestly class, even in its heyday in the time of Christ, never achieved a despotic authority and at no period of its history attracted to its ranks the very best minds of the nation. In Egypt the priests of Amon could easily dispose of the brilliant speculations of Ikhnaton, incorporating therefrom into their systems only what suited their purposes; but though Amaziah, the priest of Bethel, could silence Amos and ban him from the kingdom, only one century later the priests of Jerusalem adopted the heresies of Amos and of the later prophets and, through the publication of Deuteronomy, gave them official standing in the new national religion.

In spite of their conservative attitude, the Jewish priests were carried away first by the tide of the prophetic ideals of social justice and spiritual religion, and later by the tide of philosophic speculations tinged with heresy. Whether under the pressure of public opinion or of that of inner conviction, the priests of Jerusalem allowed the germination of those tenets of prophecy, in 650 B. C., and of wisdom, in 450 B. C., that eventually stripped their class of true religious leadership by enhancing the prestige of the synagogues at the cost of that of the temple: unwittingly the Jerusalem priesthood, by incorporating prophetic ideas into Deuteronomy and tenets of wisdom into the Priestly Code two centuries later, signed its own death warrant and, notwithstanding the pomp and circumstance of the last century of its history, it ceased to exist after the destruction of the temple in 70 A. D.

Although the priests of Jerusalem were not as dynamic as the prophets nor as profound as the sages, they furthered religious progress by giving official recognition to prophecy in Deuteronomy and to wisdom in the Priestly Code. The most significant difference between these two great charters of Judaism lies not in the ritual prescriptions but in the conception of God. In Deuteronomy Jehovah is the sole God of Israel; in the Priestly Code Jehovah is the sole God in existence, the God of all nations, the God of heaven and earth. The ouverture of Deuteronomy is the Ten Commandments, the sublime and final summary of prophetic theology and ethics; the ouverture of the Priestly Code is the first chapter of the Book of Genesis, an equally sublime condensation of the doctrines of the sages. In Deuteronomy the origin of the world is not taken into consideration, whereas the Priestly Code begins with the words, "In the beginning God created heaven and earth". In Deuteronomy the motivation for the observance of the Sabbath is the deliverance from Egypt; in the Priestly Code it is the rest of God on the seventh day of creation. In other words, the speculations of the wise men concerning the nature and origin of the world, which are given so prominent a place in the Priestly Code, are beyond the mental horizon of the compilers of the Deuteronomic Code. Philosophical wisdom, of which no trace can be detected in Israel's literature prior to the Exile, becomes an integral element in Judaism in the two centuries separating the writing of Deuteronomy from the publication of the Priestly Code. It was during this period that the Jews, always prone to trace the origin of their institutions to a remote antiquity, began to regard Solomon as the first and greatest of their wise men.

Before attempting to determine the influence of Hebrew wisdom on the religious thinking of the Jews, let us inquire into its sources and determine its fundamental teachings.

In the First Book of Kings (5 10; Engl. 4 30) we read that „Solomon's wisdom excelled the wisdom of all the Children of the East, and all the wisdom of Egypt". Legendary as this post-exilic statement is, it is significant: in asserting that Solomon's wisdom surpassed that of the Edomites and of the Egyptians, the author unwittingly suggests not only that these two nations were known to be the chief exponents of wisdom in the part of the world known to the Jews, but also, by implication, that they were the teachers of the Jews in this field. Although the wisdom literature of the Edomites must have been notable for its high quality, since it is here given precedence over that of the Egyptians and is praised elsewhere in the O. T., it was completely lost unless, as I believe, some of its most notable productions found their way into the pages of the O. T [1]. Conversely not only much of the Egyptian wisdom literature has survived, but recent discoveries have furnished documentary proof that Prov 22 17— 23 14 is a summary of the Maxims of Amen-em-ope.

The Egyptians were justly proud of their wisdom, and traced its origin to no less a personage than Imhotep, the great architect who, about 3000 B. C., invented the terraced pyramid; although his writings are lost, we still have the admonitions of Ptahhotep dating less than four centuries after his time.

The contribution of Egyptian literature to the wisdom of the O. T. can be summed up in three points.

1. God is the creator of heaven and earth. No traces of this conception can be detected in the O. T. before the sixth century, when it appears prominently in the Book of Job and in the Second Isaiah. In Egypt, conversely, a thousand years before Moses, the author of the Admonitions for King Merikere wrote as follows, "Men, the flock of God, are provided for (?). He made heaven and earth at their desire. He checked the greed (?) of the waters, and made the air to give life to their nostrils. They are his own images, proceding from his flesh." One could nearly think that these words stand in the O. T.; and even more so in the case of the admirable Hymn to Aton, the life giving sun-god, written by Ikhnaton in the 14th Century and paraphrased in the 104th Psalm: "Creator of the

---

[1] See my article, "Edomitic Wisdom" (ZAW 44 [N. F. 3], 1926, 13—25).

germ in woman, maker of the seed in man, giving life to the son in the body of his mother, nurse even in the womb, giver of breath to animate everyone that he maketh! . . . How manifold are thy works! They are hidden from before us, O sole God whose powers no one possesses. Thou didst create the earth according to thy heart when thou wast alone: men, all cattle great and small, all that are upon the earth, that go about their feet; all that are on high, that fly with their wings. . . ." A few centuries later, a humble scribe in the Theban necropolis, prayed to Amon, "who maketh the people and the birds to live, who supplieth the needs of the mice in their holes, the worms and the insects likewise". Have we not here, in this grandiose conception of the deity and of its creative work, in the notion that men and animals alike are animated by the breath emanating from the same God, in the humble recognition of man's inability to comprehend the manifold works of God, have we not here the source of some of the basic principles of the theology of the Book of Job?

2. A philosophical pessimism runs through the writings of the Egyptian sages, as later through the Book of Job, a sense of the fragility and futility of human life, a brief span filled with misery followed by the darkness of death. The theme of the Song of the Harper is the familiar, "Let us eat and drink for to-morrow we die." „Those who once built houses—their places are no more, what has become of them? No one comes back thence to tell how they fare, to tell what they need, to apease our heart, until ye approach the place to which they have gone." But such is the sadness of life and such is the sinfulness of mankind that to some, as to Job, death itself, with all of its mystery and terror, seemed to be the only release from suffering beyond endurance. After depicting the rapacity, greed, heartlessness, and wickedness of mankind, the Misanthrope concludes his Dialogue with his soul with a wistful expression of his longing for death: "Death stands now before me like healing to one who is ill; . . . like the fragrance of myrrh, like sitting under the sail on a windy day; . . . death stands now before me, as a man longs to see again his house, after having been many years in captivity."

3. And finally the ethical teaching of the Egyptian sages presents striking parallels to the rules of conduct that occupy such a prominent place in the wisdom literature of the O. T. It is true that not seldom the Egyptian sages, like the authors of some of the Proverbs of Solomon, concern themselves with trivial matters of etiquette, such as the proper manners at the table, or the advantages of tactfulness with one's superiors; again their advice is at times merely the teaching of common sense or the counsel of self-interest, as when Ani, like the author of Prov 7, warns the young man against the snares of the woman from abroad, whose husband is away on a journey. But it cannot be gainsaid that occasionally (as, for instance, in the speeches of the Eloquent Peasant) Egyptian wisdom approaches the sublimity of the moral code of the 31st chapter of the Book of Job, the ethical high-water mark of the O. T.

5. 6. 1934

The influence of Egyptian ideas on the Book of Job, the Proverbs of Solomon, and some Psalms can hardly be disputed; there are however no clear traces of it before the 6th Century, although the earliest document of Hebrew wisdom is dated three centuries earlier, I refer to the myths of beginnings in the first eleven chapters of the Book of Genesis. The pessimistic view of human life, the interest in philosophic problems, and the conception of the deity as inimical to mankind are totally at variance with the views and mental attitude of the Israelites; these, and other, considerations have led me to the conclusion that this ancient document was not written by an Israelite, but probably by an Edomite[1].

Like the Book of Job, the stories of the creation of Adam and Eve and of the Garden of Eden assume the unity of the human race and its close kinship with the animal kingdom, they betray a pessimistic outlook on human existence, whether in city, farm, or wilderness, and regard knowledge as the most precious, as well as the most elusive, aim of mankind. The myth of the Garden of Eden is the epic of a battle between man and an unfriendly deity. The God that created Adam expected him to live like one of the beasts, even though he was their superior in some respects, and to find companionship among them. The prime concern of the deity is to safeguard its own superiority with respect to man: Adam is placed in the Garden to dress it and to keep it, but is not allowed to partake of the fruit of the tree of knowledge (the deity actually goes so far as to deceive Adam by telling him that he would die on the day that he would eat therefrom). The eating of the fruit of the tree of knowledge in open defiance of the deity gives to Adam and to his descendants the capacity for culture: man progresses on the road of civilization in opposition to a deity jealous of its prerogatives and anxious to keep man on the level of uncouth barbarism; impelled by an irresistible urge originating in the eating of the forbidden fruit, man advances to an ever higher civilization, overcoming obstacles, meeting tragedy, increasing in wickedness as he becomes more refined: godless and bold, he cannot do otherwise.

The God of Adam and Eve has as little in common with the God of Israel as the deity of the Book of Job. Although superficially there seems to be no similarity between that philosophical discussion and the naïve myths of Genesis, both works are animated by the same protest against the divine indifference to human suffering, by the same sense of "impendent horrors, threatening hideous fall"; both the editor of the stories of Genesis and the author of the Book of Job clothed their philosophy in ancient folk-tales, not unlike Plato, who used traditional myths to express some of his deepest thoughts. It is of course obvious that in theological and philosophical depth, in scientific knowledge of nature and its laws, of living beings and their mode of existence, the Book of Job differs from Genesis as

---

[1] See my article, "A Non-Israelitic Source of the Book of Genesis" (ZAW 48 [N. F. 7], 1930, 66—73).

Zeitschr. f. d. alttest. Wiss. Bd. 52 1934   7

309

the full bloom differs from the bud; the emphasis is also different: in Genesis the theme is the origin and early stages of human culture; in the Book of Job it is the place of man in a world ruled despotically by an omnipotent deity, a deity whose actions disclose neither justice nor love in its dealings with mankind.

The author of the Book of Job attempted valiantly, but in vain, to solve a problem of theology that has scarcely been brought nearer a final solution by later thinkers down to our day and which may in fact be insoluble, being, in the words of WINDELBAND, "the squaring of the circle in the realm of religious conscience". It is the problem of theodicy, the reconciliation of the deity of religious longing with the deity of metaphysics, of the God of justice and lovingkindness with the absolute ruler of the world, whose blind fury slays, with indifferent unconcern, the innocent together with the wicked.

Possibly through personal experience and undoubtedly through observation, the poet became keenly aware of the misery of human existence, unrelieved by any hope of heavenly bliss after death. Clothed with clay, crushed before the moth, born in a world of overwhelming grandeur but indifferent to his fate and deaf to his appeals, man's only hope is the assurance that the ruler of the world hears his cry with a sympathetic ear. But the voice that answers Job out of the whirlwind merely rebukes his impertinence in attempting to understand the ways of God and points out the admirable order regulating the course of all phenomena, an order that discloses a supreme wisdom, transcendent and mysterious, utterly beyond the capacities of human understanding. Unable to comprehend the ways and purposes of God, man should resign himself to his fate and practice justice and mercy, without hope of reward, without fear of punishment, in obedience to the dictates of his conscience, which Job terms a covenant which man makes with himself.

The religious emotions of the author of the Book of Job recoiled with horror from the ultimate conclusions of his argument, for in strict logic nothing was left but the inference that the Almighty is a cruel despot tormenting him without reason. Such a thought seemed more dreadful than death. With the desperate frenzy of a drowning man, Job grasps any bits of the wreckage of his faith that were still floating around him. There are occasional glimmers of faith and hope in the book, there are fleeting visions (which his reason would regard as utterly fanciful) of a God of justice vindicating his right against the God of power; and we may surmise that these moments in which the clouds seemed to lift disclosing his future justification, even though after his death, saved the distracted mind of the poet from the darkness of insanity.

The theological edifice which the explosion of the Book of Job had wrecked to its very foundations was rebuilt by the prophets and wise men of Judaism, beginning with the Second Isaiah; only one author in the O. T. refused to lend his hand to the work of reconstruction: nay, in contemplating the ruins, he concluded that the destruction had not been sufficiently through and that those

very fragments, that had offered Job a foothold and had been skilfully utilized by the Jewish builders, were indeed less than worthless.
The man who dared draw the ultimate conclusions from the premices
and arguments of Job veiled his identity under the puzzling name
of Ecclesiastes. The agnosticism and pessimism of the Book of Job
had been tempered by some faint glimmers of faith; Ecclesiastes was
a cynic devoid of illusions, whose teaching is summed up in the
words, "Vanity of vanity, saith the Preacher, vanity of vanities; all
is vanity". His point of view was skepticism as BERTRAND RUSSELL
understands it, namely the doctrine "that it is undesirable to believe
a proposition when there is no ground whatever for supposing it
true".

Judaism did not take Ecclesiastes seriously, contenting itself with
editing and re-editing his book with pious annotations; but even so,
learned opinion was long divided in regard to the canonical status
of the book. The Book of Job however could not be disposed of
in such an offhand manner; one might easier ignore a hurricane
than the vehemence of its onslaught upon the traditional orthodoxy:
"And, behold, there came a great wind from the wilderness, and
smote the four corners of the house."

The repercussions of the brilliant heresies of Job reached far
and deep; in defending itself from their radicalism Judaism was
forced to retreat, abandoning traditional positions that proved to be
strategically untenable. I can only mention three aspects of the
revolution which the doctrines of Job wrought in the theological
thinking of Judaism.

1. The conception of God as the creator of the world, for which
the author of the Book of Job was probably indebted to Egyptian
wisdom, proved to be the keystone that completed the theological
arch well begun, but left unfinished, by the pre-exilic prophets.
Amos and his successors had been the heralds of a God of righteousness and power, active among all nations in upholding justice and
honesty, destroying His own people, on account of its ineradicable
wickedness, through Assyria, the rod of his anger. But the prophets
had not regarded their God as the creator of heaven and earth,
they hat not extended the realm of his activity beyond the human
world to include the creation and upholding of all that exists. It
was the Second Isaiah, at the same time a pupil of the prophets and
a reader of the Book of Job, that made the great discovery that
Jehovah, the prophetic God of justice and love, and the Almighty,
the creator and upholder of the world so brilliantly portrayed in the
Book of Job, were one and the same God, nay the only true God[1];
his faith can be summed up, with Professor GEORGE F. MOORE, in
the words, "Israel's god is the only God; the almighty is the saviour
of his people". Thus Judaism adopted the conception of God as the
creator of the world, rejecting at the same time with the greatest

---

[1] See my article, "The Dual Origin of Hebrew Monotheism" (Journal of Biblical
Literature 46 [1927], 193—206).

7*

vehemence the corollary that Job had not been able to avoid, namely that like nature, which is the work of His hands, the deity is not concerned with the fate and with the conduct of individuals and of nations. The speeches of Elihu, inserted into the Book of Job, and some Psalms and Proverbs take issue with the doctrine of God's indifference to human affairs; but no one refuted it with more elo-quence that the Second Isaiah in those classic words, "Why sayest thou, O Jacob, and speakest, O Israel; 'My way is hid from the Lord, and my judgement is passed over from my God?' Hast thou not known? Hast thou not heard, that the everlasting God, the Lord, the creator of the ends of the earth, fainteth not, neither is he weary? . . . He giveth power to the faint; and to them that have no might he increaseth strength." But religious controversies are not always conducted with such dignity and urbanity; the 10th Psalm is an example of the bitter invective to which some Jews resorted in combating Job's doctrine of the divine indifference to man, a view which to them (v. 4) was the equivalent of rank atheism[1].

2. In the 28th Chapter of the Book of Job. wisdom is the rational plan of creation, a sort of diagram of the world according to which God created all that exists; this cosmic wisdom is accessible only to God, it is not found in the land of the living: it is a sort of noumenon conceiled behind the veil of the phenomena. But again Judaism refused to admit that an impassable gulf separated the realm of God and of ultimate reality from that of human beings. Just as the transcendent deity of Job became the God in whose communion the Psalmists found their deepest joy, the God who was with them even though they walked through the valley of the shadow of death, in like manner the inaccessible cosmic wisdom of Job 28 is described by the author of the 8th Chapter of the Book of Proverbs as stan-ding at the crossroads and teaching men how to live, although it had been born before the world was made and had witnessed the creation of heaven and earth. This personification of the abstract wisdom of the Book of Job seems to be the first step in the deve-lopment of the Jewish doctrine of intermediaries between God and the world which, fertilized in the Wisdom of Solomon and in Philo with the Greek doctrine of the logos, evolved eventually to Christian Gnosticism.

3. And finally Judaism strove to overcome the pessimistic mood, resulting from the sense of human insignificance and from the doc-trine of God's indifference to human fate, which pervaded the Book of Job. In bringing God into close contact with man Judaism at the same time exalted human nature. What is man? Job answers that he is a worm, the 8th Psalm that he is a creature but little inferior to the angels, a being under whose feet God had placed all things. On the other hand, deaf to the incontrovertible arguments

---

[1] "In the pride of his countenance [the wicked] does not investigate; all this thoughts (amount to this), 'There is no god'."

of Job, Judaism clung with desperate tenacity to the doctrine that God rewards and punishes human deeds on this earth and that therefore piety brings tangible compensation, — until the tragic experiences of individuals and of the nation vindicated Job's conclusions and proved, beyond the shadow of a doubt, that the meek seldom inherited the earth, which fell, as often as not, into the hands of unscrupulous scoundrels. In this emergency, when the validity of their religion was in question, the Jews, like Job, abandoning the solid ground of reality, set sail for the alluring regions of fancy. Job, against all evidence of fact and reason, had found temporary solace in the dream that God would some day, even though he be dead, vindicate his innocence. Jewish apocalypse, recognizing that the present world is inherently and incurably evil, envisioned a future world, ushered in through the intervention of God, in which all hopes were realized. Apocalypse is always Utopian; its god, like Job's god of the future, is the god of wishes and of illusions; the specifications of the ideal world of eschatological expectations have no relation with the possibilities of actual reality[1]. Job seems to have entertained the chimerical hope that he himself, after his own death, would witness his own vindication on earth; Daniel went one step farther and boldly asserted that "many of them that sleep in the dust of the earth shall awake, some to everlasting life, and some to shame and everlasting contempt". Such fanciful dreams are not without danger; Job vividly describes the caravans lured to their ruin, in the pathless desert, by a mirage; Ecclesiastes, no sooner had Daniel portrayed the day in which the dead would arise out of their graves, hastened to denounce the visionary character of this hope by pointing out that death is indeed the end, for "then shall the dust return to the earth as it was: and the spirit shall return unto God who gave it". And yet it cannot be denied that blissful illusions, such as those of Job and of Daniel, not seldom prove to be effective opiates for patients whose condition is beyond rational cure.

Israel's outstanding contribution to human culture is that conception of God which was substantially adopted from Judaism by Christianity and Islam. The world owes therefore a conspicuous debt of gratitude to those three men of genius that were chiefly responsible for charting the course of religious though in tho O. T. and thus transformed the national god of the Israelites into the deity of universal scope and unspotted moral character. These three thinkers, whose views were regarded as heresies during their time, are Amos, the author of the Book of Job, and the Second Isaiah.

Amos was the exponent of Jehovah's sway over all nations, the author of the Book of Job was the exponent of God's sway over nature, and the Second Isaiah, by combining these two notions, became the first exponent of monotheism in the O. T.

---

[1] See J. WELLHAUSEN, Israelitische und Jüdische Geschichte. 7. Auflage, Berlin 1914, p. 195 f.

[Completed 30. Oct. 1933.]

THE PLACE AND LIMIT OF THE WISDOM IN THE FRAMEWORK OF THE OLD TESTAMENT THEOLOGY

by PROFESSOR WALTHER ZIMMERLI

THE faith of the Old Testament has its origin in the fundamental fact that God encountered Israel in the midst of history. The preamble of the decalogue mentions it: 'I am Yahweh thy God, which brought thee out of the land of Egypt, out of the house of bondage.' From this beginning Israel knows that her God encountered her not in a reaction but in a free divine action in history. Through this action He laid hold upon Israel, called her and made her His people. At a later time this previous deed of God came to be designated by the term 'election of Israel'. The powerful word-event of Old Testament Prophecy made plain once more this structure of God's action: Yahweh, the God who addresses Israel in and through history by the word of His messengers and who is not only reacting against Israel's sin but acting by His free grace, proves to be the God who stands by the independence of His election.

At the same time God reveals Himself to be the holy Lord. God's covenant with Israel was never without the law of covenant. So the history of Israel was always linked with the question of obedience or disobedience. Once more we have to mention the prophets. They declare that God is jealous about His holy command in His history. Or we may formulate the matter thus: they announce His holy command as contained within His history.

What has been said so far relates to the two central canonical parts of the Old Testament, namely, the Law and the Prophets. Now we turn to the phenomenon of Wisdom which in Old Testament literature is represented by the book of Proverbs, by Ecclesiastes, by some Psalms and by parts of the book of Job, all of which form part of the third division of the canon. I intend to confine my discussion of Wisdom to Proverbs and Ecclesiastes.

These books maintain that Wisdom literature in Israel had a definite historical point of entrance. The main title of Proverbs says that Solomon was the author of the book of Proverbs. Ecclesiastes also claims the fiction of Solomonic origin. We hear from 2 Kings 5.9-14 that Solomon cultivated the literary form of proverbs. The statement of Prov. 25.1, that the proverbs which follow it were copied by the men of Hezekiah, king of Judah, also leads to the court of Jerusalem. But it seems that literary Wisdom was spread also in a wider circle of educated people in Israel. The courtly origin of literary Wisdom may explain the international relationship of Wisdom. The discovery of an Egyptian original of Prov. 22.17-23.12 in the Teaching of Amenemope made very clear this international character of Wisdom. The insertion of two royal wisdom-collections from the Arabic Massa into Prov. 30-31 also bears witness to this international character of Wisdom.

This leads immediately to a first point that we have to establish about the structure of Wisdom: Wisdom has no relation to the history between God and Israel. This is an astonishing fact. The establishment of a relationship between history and Wisdom might well have been deduced from the report of 1 Kings 3.4-15. This chapter tells us about a dream of King Solomon, the son of David, at Gibeon. Solomon asks God because of God's grace to his father to give him wisdom to judge the people of God. Wisdom is here to be understood as a gift that is given to the son of David on behalf of Israel, the people of God. We might think here of God's covenant with Israel. That there is neither in the Proverbs nor in Ecclesiastes an attempt to take this way of thinking makes clear that wisdom has its own structure which is not altered even when wisdom is integrated in Israelite thinking. Wisdom has to do with man (*'āḏām*). People and king are mentioned in so far as they are sociological factors in mankind. Proverbs sometimes speaks about people (*'am*).[1] But this people is never the people as the elect of Yahweh. Proverbs and Ecclesiastes speak more than once about the king.[2] But the king is never the anointed king of God's people Israel and the son of David, who received God's special promise. If we compare the historical work of the Deuteronomistic writer or the words of the prophets, we can see very clearly the difference between them and the words of the wise man.

[1] Prov. 11.14, 14.28, 28.15, 29.2.
[2] Prov. 14.28, 35, 16.10, 14f etc.; Eccles. 4.13, 5.8 (RV 5.9), 8.2, 4 etc.

If we now try to characterise the theological attitude of Wisdom, we must say: Wisdom thinks resolutely within the framework of a theology of creation. That is confirmed by the fact that God, whom the Proverbs cite by His proper name Yahweh, while Ecclesiastes speaks about 'God' (*'elōhîm*), never appears as the 'God of Israel' nor as the 'God of the Fathers' nor as Yahweh Zebaoth, whereas occasionally He can be named 'Maker' or 'Creator'.[1]

I do not overlook that there are also formulations in which the special language of Israel appears. We find, for instance, the saying 'inherit the land'. If it should be suggested, as has been done,[2] that this saying is Deuteronomic, we may turn the tables and ask if there are not in Deuteronomic paraenesis elements of Wisdom language. Again we may find clearly Israelite thinking represented by the Israelite redactor of Prov. 22.22ff, who adds to his Egyptian model, the text of Amenemope, that God will plead the cause of the poor. In 23.11 God is the redeemer (*gō'ēl*) of the fatherless. But all these borrowings never lead to a clear reference to the history of God and Israel.

But now we have to characterise Wisdom more precisely in the field which we have defined. Recent research into Wisdom has rightly underlined that it is not possible to understand Wisdom as a purely profane doing, which shows man as a being who is free from all commitment. Egyptian Wisdom shows that Wisdom lives in the sphere of a comprehensive faith of an order that can be characterised by the conception of divine *ma'at* (truth).[3] But having secured this insight we must ask what is a more precise understanding of the Wisdom structure. Is Wisdom to be described simply as the preaching of the worship of *ma'at*? Does Wisdom intend some kind of service of God—the God behind *ma'at*? If we accept this understanding, do we not alter the central aim of both Egyptian and Israelite wisdom? Do we not confuse Wisdom's honouring of the sphere of *ma'at*, in which Wisdom lives without doubt, with the real intention of Wisdom?

We see in the preamble of Ptahhotep as in that of Heti and Amenemope, that Wisdom—though it knows the religious

---

[1] Prov. 14.31; 17.5; Eccles. 12.1.
[2] J. C. Rylaarsdam, *Revelation in Jewish Wisdom Literature*, 1946, 23.
[3] H. Brunner, *Handbuch der Orientalistik*, I, 2, 1952, 93-96. H. Gese, *Lehre und Wirklichkeit in der alten Weisheit*, 1958.

world of order, in which it lives—has very practical aims. 'The teaching of life, the testimony for prosperity, all precepts for intercourse with elders, the rules for courtiers, to know how to return an answer to him who said it, and to direct a report to one who has sent him, in order to direct him to the ways of life, to make him prosper upon earth.'[1] The Israelite translator of this preamble of Amenemope adds to his model the remark: 'That thy trust may be in Yahweh.'[2] But in adding this statement he does not change the whole teaching of Wisdom into an instruction of trust in God, as for example the paraenetic part of Deuteronomy does. This addition does not alter the primary character of Wisdom as an attitude of prudence. Wisdom is *per definitionem taḥbūlôth*, 'the art of steering', knowledge of how to do in life, and thus it has a fundamental alignment to man and his preparing to master human life.

G. von Rad speaks in his *Theology of the Old Testament* in an impressive manner about the phenomenon of language. Language is a primary phenomenon of Wisdom.[3] It is a first process in mastering the world around us. The sapiential *taḥbūlôth* is to be understood on the same lines. It also aims at mastering the reality which encounters us. From Egypt we have cataloguing compendia, which enumerate the things of the world in long series of words. The Onomasticon of Amenope claims to enumerate 'all, that is, that Ptah created and Thot recorded—the heavens and all that belongs to them, the earth and all things on it'.[4] Similarly Solomon's wisdom enumerates the things 'from the cedar, that is in Lebanon, even to the hyssop that springeth out of the wall' (2 Kings 5.13, EVV. 4.33). In enumerating all these things Wisdom orders and controls the world. The history of the form of the *māšāl* makes quite clear that Wisdom has to do with two elementary spiritual functions: (1) The word of statement (*Aussagewort*) apprehends the facts of reality and establishes them in perceiving and enumerating them. The word 'establish' can be understood in a very verbal sense. The things which are elusive, that seem to be so mobile

---

[1] J. B. Pritchard, *Ancient Near Eastern Texts*, 1955, 421.
[2] Prov. 22.19.
[3] G. von Rad, *Old Testament Theology*, vol. 1, 418f. Also W. Zimmerli, 'Die Weisung des Alten Testamentes zum Geschäft der Sprache' (in *Das Problem der Sprache in Theologie und Kirche*, ed. by W. Schneemelcher, 1959).
[4] A. Alt, 'Die Weisheit Salomos' (in *Kleine Schriften zur Geschichte Israels*, 2, 1953, 90-99, esp. 94).

that they cannot be grasped, are seized, stopped, established. Then (2) the word of admonition (*Mahnwort*) on the other hand applies what was previously established to man. In the form of an imperative or jussive it says how man has to behave and how to do right *vis-à-vis* what has been established. Also if we are careful not to jump to conclusions about literary priorities, it is clear from the facts that the explicit rule of life is built upon to the observation of facts. Otherwise we see that the desire to lay down fixed rules of life was always a motive for finding better knowledge of the reality of the life. The emphasis of paraenesis always belongs to the pathos of Wisdom.

The world-wide horizon of sapiential series of words, which aims at mastering the reality of the world and which also is to be found behind the description of the creation in the book of Job[1] cannot, however, conceal that ultimately all sapiential knowledge of the world aims at showing how man should live. We can see this even in the late Wisdom of Ecclesiastes. Here 1.3-11 seems to speak of pure natural phenomena; the way of the sun, the wind, the water. But here also the emphasis is upon man: the word, which can never be spoken finally, the eye, that never can see all that it wants to see. So the maxim 1.3-11 begins quite rightly with the anthropological question: 'What profit hath a man of all his labour, wherein he laboureth under the sun?' And then follows the statement of the transitoriness of all the generations.

What is the relevance of all these observations for the theological structure of Wisdom? They show that man, God's creature, is not only a passive creature, but goes out actively. Certainly he is a man who might seek his place in the created world. The attitude of hearing and asking must always form part of his behaviour. But more than that: Wisdom shows man as a being who goes out, who apprehends through his knowledge, who establishes, who orders his world. The way he walks in it is intended to be a way of progress. It aims at avoiding danger, to be a way of ascent. In Proverbs and in Ecclesiastes the tendency towards a professional career is not so pronounced as in Egyptian wisdom. But here also the way of Wisdom is a way in which man seeks to gain his life—certainly not in insolent

---

[1] G. von Rad, 'Hiob 38 und die altägyptische Weisheit' (in *Wisdom in Israel and in the Ancient Near East*, Suppl. to *Vetus Testamentum*, 3, 1955, 293-301).

haughtiness, but in respect for the surrounding world of order, even the order of the divine world. The Israelite who knows the Creator knows the fear of God: 'The fear of the Lord is the beginning of knowledge.' But here also Wisdom is more than mere unreflecting fear of God. Here also it is will and comprehensive ability to direct the whole of life. 'Fear of God' is doubtless the highest maxim, the queen of all the rules of direction. But even that highest maxim is seen in the context of a possibility of direction. It is incorporated into the whole of Wisdom recommended by the wise man.

We have now to ask about the legitimacy of such behaviour in the framework of Old Testament faith, which is rooted in the historical encounter of Yahweh and Israel. Is there in the creed of Israel a place in which man is permitted—not as a son of Abraham and Jacob, but purely as man—to tackle his life in the manner indicated?

In this concern we cannot here overlook what the primeval history in the Book of Genesis says. The Old Testament does not only speak about the encounter of Yahweh and Israel in the midst of history; beyond this, Yahweh who encountered Israel is also shown as the Creator of heaven and earth, who called man into life from the beginning and who dealt with man. It does not matter that Israel formulated this faith relatively late and used cosmogonic material from its environment in formulating its faith in creation. More important is it to see how Israel speaks about the inner meaning of this event. Israel's faith must understand the creation of man by God as an event in which God bestows on man a great gift. Here we feel that the understanding of creation is deeply influenced by the manner of Israel's encountering God in History. But in giving His gift to man God empowers him with a striking independence. The primeval history of J (Yahwist) states that God allowed man to be in His good garden, paradise, and to eat all its fruit except the fruit of one single tree—the sign of his obedience. It tells that God showed to man all the beasts that He created, and allowed him to give them their names. To name somebody is a king's privilege. In giving them their names, man seizes this part of the created world, orders it, refuses it—accepts finally the wife (*'iššāh*) as a being belonging to him.[1] The P

---

[1] Gen. 2.19-23.

(priestly writer) is far more abstract, logical and precise. He states that the creator blesses man and gives to him the right of rule: 'Be fruitful and multiply and replenish the earth and subdue it; and have dominion over the fish of the sea, and over the fowl of the air, and over every living thing, that moveth upon the earth.'[1]

We have put the question whether there is a human right to go out to master the world. The Torah answers this question by its recital of the creation. Explicitly it is stated that man's going out is not against God's will. God authorises man's going out by His own word and blessing.

So we have found the place where Wisdom is to be seen in the framework of Old Testament Theology. It seems to me, that from here it is possible to understand some peculiarities of biblical Wisdom. First of all I remember what has often been called the eudaemonism of Wisdom.[2] Wisdom often recommends the blessing which man can obtain by following the rules of its teaching, and warns against the harm which punishes the man who disregards them. 'The righteousness of the upright shall deliver them. But they that deal treacherously shall be taken in their own mischief' (Prov. 11.6). In the light of Gen. 1 there is here not an ungodly arbitrary appropriation of prosperity and success but a tendency to approach the blessing which God connected with wise—and i.e., according to Prov. 1.7, in faithful—behaviour of man. In Egypt the wise man pays attention to the rules of *ma'at*. In Israel Wisdom has a peculiar affinity to God's command. Even if there is no simple identification of the commandment of the covenant and the rule of wisdom, the older wisdom cannot overlook the revealed will of God. Scholars have always noted the frequent occurrence in Proverbs of the notions of wicked and righteous—notions originally connected with the law. 'Wise' can be replaced by 'righteous', 'fool' by 'wicked'.

On the other side it becomes clear that the admonition of the teacher of wisdom is not to be confused with the commandment of the law-giver of the covenant. The apodictic law of the covenant decrees authoritatively in case of need in announcing

[1] Gen. 1.28.
[2] J. Fichtner, 'Die altorientalische Weisheit in ihrer israelitisch-jüdischen Ausprägung', *BZAW* 62, 1933, 75-79.

the curse against disobedience. The admonition of the wise man remains in the framework of counselling. The wise man is *yōʿēṣ* 'counsellor' who wants to persuade by the weight of his arguments and the evidence of his counsel.[1] The motive clauses which follow the admonition in the enlarged wisdom-style give clear evidence for it. Counsel affords a certain margin of liberty and of proper decision. Certainly we cannot say that counsel has no authority. It has the authority of insight. But that is quite different from the authority of the Lord, who decrees.

So the weighing of the different possibilities always belongs to the behaviour of the wise man. It leads to the form of the sapiential comparative *māšāl*-sentence. The prophet who starts from the law of the covenant says: 'He hath showed thee, O man, what is good and what does Yahweh require of thee . . .' (Mic. 6.8). Wisdom shapes the weighing-comparing *māšāl*-sentence. This form often occurs in Ecclesiastes, especially in 7.1-14, where the maxims treat the question: What is good? But it can also often be found in the Proverbs: 'Better is a dinner of herbs, where love is, than a stalled ox and hatred therewith' (15.17).

It is a consequence of all this that wisdom includes a strange inner tension. Its theology of creation knows clearly that the reality to which it has access is always subordinate to God's will. In the Proverbs we often hear: 'Man thinks, God directs.'[2] God controls and reserves his right to decide even where man thinks that his own way is quite right.[3] In God's hand is the heart of the king.[4] He keeps His secret to Himself.[5] 'There is no wisdom nor understanding nor counsel against the Lord' (21.30).

But at the same time man knows that God authorises him to go out into the world, to observe, to establish the things of the world. Establishment begins in the field of man's work and reward. It is concerned with power and influence. But also the field of interhuman relations, the order of honesty and dishonesty, truth and falsehood, rightdoing and wrongdoing is cleared up. Here also matters are established. What is obscure

---

[1] 2 Sam. 17.1-14. Cf. also P. de Boer, 'The Counsellor' (in Suppl. to *VT*, 3, 1955, 42-71).
[2] Prov. 16.1, 9, 19.21.
[3] Prov. 16.2, 21.2.
[4] Prov. 21.1.
[5] Prov. 25.2.

is illuminated by the instruction of divine commandments. It seems to me that we can hear the language of the priestly world, when the Proverbs speak of an abomination (*tô'ēbhāh*) to God,[1] and when on the other hand they speak of God's pleasure (*rāsôn*)[2] and of what is clean (*tāhôr*).[3] In the language of concrete instruction Wisdom establishes what is good and where man has a right to wait for the blessing of God. By his orientation to the fixed order the wise man is able to say where God will reward,[4] where he will punish,[5] where he will hear,[6] where the Omniscient will act.[7] Because he knows the illumination, which God gives through his commandment, the wise man is able to encourage confidence in Him.[8] He can praise the blessing which results from man's fear of the Lord.[9]

That is the way in which Wisdom investigates the world. The older Wisdom of Prov. 10-31 does so in a quite undogmatic manner. It has no comprehensive reflection on the function of its own power. The aspect changes in Prov. 1-9. Now begins a fundamental reflection on Wisdom. There emerges a knowledge of the significance of Wisdom in its essential nature, and expression is given to the praise of Wisdom. I do not think that we should speak of a deeply changed structure of the 'counsel' of the wise man. But now Wisdom is seen as a personal being, who encounters man with authority. It is quite characteristic that the same Wisdom, which assists God's creation (3.19f, 8.22ff) unexpectedly stands before man to lay the cloth and to invite him to its meal (9.1ff). Or elsewhere it encounters man in the squares of the town like a preacher of repentance (1.20ff). Wisdom offers blessing to man. The man who follows its way receives this blessing.

What was the outcome of this development? Besides the perception that all that happens comes from the decision of the creator, there arose a whole complex of principles, through which security is promised to the man who wants to master his life. To him who follows Wisdom, the promise is given: 'Then shalt thou walk in thy way securely and thy foot shall not

---

[1] Prov. 17.15, 20.10.   [2] Prov. 11.1, 20, 12.22.
[3] Prov. 15.26.   [4] Prov. 12.2.
[5] Prov. 15.25, 16.4.   [6] Prov. 15.29.
[7] Prov. 15.3 (11).
[8] Prov. 16.3, 20, 18.10, 20.22, 22.19, 28.25, 29.25.
[9] Prov. 10.27, 14, 26f.

stumble' (3.23). 'Whoso hearkeneth unto me shall. dwell
securely' (1.33). In all these principles the God who acts by
His freedom runs the risk of being pushed back in favour of a
God who can only react in the setting of the order known by the
wise man. The friends of Job show this God very clearly in
their speeches to Job. But is this really the world of reality?
And is Wisdom really Wisdom apart from reality?

Wisdom seeks to be a human art of life in the sense of mastering life in the framework of a given order in this life. It is an
unfailing evidence of the anthropological starting-point of Wisdom that it is precisely in its field that the question of theodicy
(in which God is challenged by man) arises more emphatically
than anywhere else in the Old Testament. The Wisdom texts
of Job, Psalms 37, 49, 73 and Ecclesiastes can prove it. We do
not have time here to follow further this lawsuit, in which God
is challenged by man. I wish to look at Ecclesiastes. Here the
inner problem of Wisdom in the setting of an Old Testament
Theology openly arises and the limits of Old Testament Wisdom
are clearly indicated.

Ecclesiastes is a wise man, who emerges from the world of
Wisdom. His whole book shows it and the word of the first
epilogue in 12.9 confirms it explicitly. But at the same time
Ecclesiastes is keenly debating the average wisdom, which
thinks that Wisdom is a possible enterprise which can afford to
man real insight and security of life. In 8.17 Ecclesiastes
maintains the inscrutability of God's deeds. When he says in
this connexion: 'Yea, moreover though a wise man thinks to
know it, yet shall he not be able to find', he openly challenges
his adversary, against whom he debates. Ecclesiastes, the wise
man, is in conflict with the Wisdom of schools.

But Ecclesiastes is a wise man also in the following sense. He
emerges from an explicit theology of creation, which is in no
way connected with the encounter of God and Israel in history.
That is all the more striking, inasmuch as there are many indications that Ecclesiastes knew even the combined text of Gen.
1-3 and for that matter, I suppose, also the whole Pentateuch.
But for his thinking the only thing that is important is that God
has created the world. 'He made it beautiful in his time', says
Ecclesiastes in 3.11, which unmistakably reflects Gen. 1. God
also determines all that happens even today. Long ago he

determined it, says 3.14 in emphasising sharply this theology of creation.

Ecclesiastes does not speak about free election and grace in the history of God's dealings with Israel. But he knows also, that the creator sends man into the world to subdue it. But man's going out into the world 'in wisdom' is according to Ecclesiastes a fruitless pain, even a pain under a curse. 'I applied my heart to seek and to search out by wisdom concerning all, that is done under heaven; it is a sore travail that God hath given to the sons of men to be exercised therewith' (1.13).

In his attempt to master the world 'by wisdom', which means 'by knowledge and active life', he encounters the reality of the creator more clearly than any other Israelite wise man before him. Everywhere he meets with a reality that is determined and cannot be apprehended. Behind all this determination and all this ability not to be apprehended it is God, who cannot be scrutinised, who is free, who never reacts, but always acts in freedom. This reality finds its hardest expression in the fact of death. In a manner hitherto unheard-of in the Old Testament, Ecclesiastes sees death as the power that takes away the power of the whole creation and even of man's Wisdom. The fact that every man's hour of death is incalculable gives full evidence of God's majesty and freedom. The secret of God is inaccessible to man. 'As thou knowest not what is the way of the wind nor how the bones do grow in the womb of her that is with child, even so thou knowest not the work of God, who doeth all' (11.5).

Behind the reflection about death lies a peculiar doctrine of 'falling time'. Ecclesiastes discovers the time, that means the connexion of every event in the world with its '*ēth*, its proper time. The majesty of the Creator is revealed by the fact that the '*ēth* of every event is at His disposal. Even the older Wisdom reflects about the problem of due time. 'A man hath joy in the answer of his mouth and a word in due season (*b*ᵉ*ittô*), how good is it', says Prov. 15.23. To perceive the favourable time to act is the sign of real Wisdom. The Egyptian Ptahhotep speaks about the acting in due time that alone brings success for example on the occasion of an invitation into the house of a superior one. 'Let thy face be cast down until he addresses thee, and thou shouldst speak only when he addresses thee. Laugh after he laughs, and it will be very pleasing to his heart and what thou mayest do will be pleasing to the heart. No one can know what is in the heart.'[1] In his encounter with reality Ecclesiastes has totally lost the belief that man could be anywhere master of time. In a quite self-torturing way he speaks about the abandonment of man to the power that alone disposes of the time. 'I returned and saw under the sun, that the race is not to the swift, nor the battle to the strong, neither yet the bread to the wise, nor yet riches to men of understanding, nor yet favour to men of skill; but time and chance happeneth to them all. For man also knoweth not his time; as the fishes that are taken in an evil net and as the birds that are caught in the snare, even so are the sons of men snared in an evil time, when it falleth suddenly upon them' (9.11f). Yet the most inward, most personal emotions of man are determined by God. 'Whether it be love or hatred, man knoweth it not' (9.1).

Therefore man being quite unprotected has to surrender to what is given to him. That is the conclusion which the admonition of Ecclesiastes reaches. It is God who gives. Twenty-five times Ecclesiastes uses the verb *nāthan*, 'give'. Twelve times God is the subject of this giving.[2] God also gives good things and joyfulness. But He gives them of His own will. So man should seize what God gives in every moment and be glad of the portion that God gives. The word *ḥēleḳ* 'portion'[3] bears in the sayings of Ecclesiastes an accent of limitation. God gives only a portion. The Whole He retains in His hand.

In speaking like this Ecclesiastes returns unexpectedly to a genuine element of Israel's faith. God gives of His free will. Through his sapiential encounter with the reality of the world Ecclesiastes caught sight of the freedom of God, who acts and never reacts. He feels this freedom of God as a painful limitation of his own impulse to go out into the world by wisdom and to master the world. Nevertheless he holds unswervingly fast to the creator, who alone has power to allot and to dispose of the times. The face of the creator is in Ecclesiastes' mind not transformed into that of a demon. Ecclesiastes endeavours to stand although he is broken down.

So in a double sense Ecclesiastes fulfils the task of revealing

[1] Pritchard, op. cit., 412.
[2] Eccles. 1.13, 2.26 (twice), 3.10, 11, 5.17, 18 (RV 5.18, 19), 6.2, 8.15, 9.9, 12.7, 11.
[3] Eccles. 2.10, 21, 3.22, 5.17, 18 (RV 5.18, 19), 9.6, 9 (11.2).

the limit of Wisdom in biblical theology. Ecclesiastes is the frontier-guard, who forbids Wisdom to cross the frontier towards a comprehensive art of life. He secures the right interpretation of the sentence: 'The fear of the Lord is the beginning of knowledge.' He never means that fear of God can be integrated to Wisdom as an instrument of Wisdom—even though 'fear of God' might be highly honoured and might get the best seat at the table. He who fears God knows that God is the Lord, and that, if it is God's will, even the highest human Wisdom can break down and can become deep foolishness. The fear of God never allows man in his 'art of directing' to hold the helm in his own hands. Wisdom, which for Ecclesiastes elsewhere 'excelleth folly' (2.13), is possible when it is willing to seize only the portion and not the whole—when it is willing to enjoy the gift that God gives today and will not try to make God's promise an item in the calculation of man's life. The fear of God remains open to God Himself—the free and living God. Hence Ecclesiastes reminds Wisdom of its place before the creator.

But at the same time the Wisdom of Ecclesiastes reminds us by remaining cool behind the full message of election and grace in the Old Testament of a limit of Wisdom in another direction. The sapiential theology of creation can gain full life only when it dares to believe that the creator is the God who in free goodness promised Himself to His people. Israel became acquainted with this God, who is faithful to His people through judgment and wrath, when it encountered God in history. In the framework of an Old Testament Theology, the sapiential theology of creation will be recalled to the God who joined Himself to His people by His encounter with them in history. 'They shall be my people and I will be their God, saith the Lord God' (Ezek. 37.23). When Wisdom appropriates only this 'portion'; then the Wisdom of the fear of the Lord will find its limit as well as its fulfilment.

IV.

THE LITERARY HERITAGE OF THE WISDOM TRADITION

III

A SINGLE EDITOR FOR THE WHOLE BOOK OF PROVERBS

PATRICK SKEHAN

This article will not pretend to be exhaustive in treating the text of a book which has some very puzzling sections (Prov 6:1-19; 9:7-12; 22:17-24,34; 30:1-33); it intends nevertheless to re-examine the question of the unity of the Book of Proverbs. This can only mean proposing again the hypothesis that the author of chs. 1-9 is the sole editor for substantially all of the Book, and studying the evidence which would currently lend support to such a position. The writer believes that he has lately advanced the literary analysis of Prov 1-9 to a point not previously attained;[1] and that in so doing, he has established the fact that the author of this section paid constant and careful heed to the external, artificial structure of his composition. The leading ideas of the same author and certain features of his style are easily discernible; and it remains therefore to be seen how far the rest of the Book in its present form may safely be ascribed to an editor with identical interests and a similar manner of composition.

1. Preliminary Considerations

It is customary to divide Proverbs into eight, or nine, or ten sections. The present writer proposes to treat rather of four large blocks of text (1-9; 10:1-22,16; 22:17-24:34; 25-29), in each of which he sees an artificial unity which it is more than plausible to ascribe to the same hand. We may begin by eliminating from immediate discussion certain small sections. The alphabetic poem about the woman of valor (31:10-31) might easily be the work of the editor in question; it is, however, a self-contained unit which has no necessary bearing on the problem of the book as a whole. Proverbs 31:1-9 is ascribed to a non-Israelite origin in the text itself; whether this be fact or literary device, the language marks off this section from the rest. Proverbs 30:1-6 is of a similar character,[2] and should also be kept separate. In the remainder of chapter 30, there is a deliberate gathering of numerical

---

[1] In "The Seven Columns of Wisdom's House in Proverbs 1-9," *CBQ* 9 (1947) 190-198, reproduced above pp. 9-14.

[2] This supposes the reading of Prov 30:1 as *neʾûm ha-geber: lāʾ ʾîtay ʾēl; lāʾ ʾîtay ʾēl weʾûkal*, closer to Aramaic than to Hebrew: "(Mortal) man says: I am not God; I am not God, that I should be able ...," following the view of C. C. Torrey, proposed at the American Oriental Society meeting of 1940. Only so does the text become understandable in itself and with what follows.

proverbs: 30:7-9, based on the number 2, and the following six sections, each based on the number 4: 30:11-14,15b-16,18-19,21-23,24-28,29-31. We may see in the *ḥidôt* of Prov 1:6 a suggestion that the editor we are discussing gathered together the numerical proverbs. However, such an arrangement is to some extent speculative; and it is proposed to draw from this material at the moment only one pertinent observation: these numerical proverbs, and the alphabetic poem, help us to justify *a priori* the expectation that a discoverable artificial number will serve as the controlling element in other sections of the book where unity of some kind was intended by an editor.

Proverbs 1-9 has been discussed in the earlier article alluded to above. The discovery of a deliberate pattern of 7x22 lines for chapters 2 to 7 is the one quite new element which now prompts re-examination of our data regarding the rest of the Book. The writer does not pretend to be able to establish a unique plan which will account for chs. 1 and 8-9 as well as the 7-columned structure of 2-7. That such a plan existed, he thinks altogether probable; nor is he inclined to suppose any basic disarrangement in the extant text: only that it was intended to conform to a design of some kind, and that we have lost the key to it. In the absence of such a key, the sections of Prov 1-9 which are outside the "seven columns" can only be examined by the internal criteria which have been in use all along. By such a test, only Prov 9:7-9,11,12 are clearly without any appropriate context. In this they are similar to Prov 6:1-19, for which the external structure they disturb combines with the internal criteria to show them out of place. Prov 9:10 is exempted from a like judgment because it forms a complementary, balancing element six lines (and one unified "stanza") from the end of these chapters, to the similar single line Prov 1:7, six lines (and again one "stanza") from the beginning. Hence in addition to chs. 1 and 8, the writer would ascribe to the original author of this section Prov 9:1-6,10,13-18 in that order.[3]

It has been said very often that Prov 10:1-22,16 form one comprehensive collection of "Solomonic" proverbs put together from two main portions— roughly Prov 10-15 and 16:1-22:16—either or both of which may have had a previous independent history. It has also been noted, though a number of commentators ignore the fact, that the entire collection consists of precisely 375 single-line proverbs, and that the numerical value of the Hebrew name Solomon in the title "Proverbs of Solomon" (10:1) is likewise 375.[4] The

---

[3] For the placing of Prov 6:1-19 and the rationale of the structure in 9,7-12, see *CBQ* 29 (1967) 166-67, 169, reproduced below pp. 31-32, 34-35.

[4] So, e.g., by C. Steuernagel, in Kautzsch-Bertholet, *Heilige Schrift des Alten Testaments* (Tübingen, 1923) 2, 278.

reader can judge for himself of the likelihood of mere coincidence in a case of this kind.[5] Whatever that likelihood might be, it is in fact eliminated from consideration when we combine this datum with facts pertaining to the subsequent sections of the book. The block of text beginning with 22:17 is intended by its author to consist of thirty sayings, according to the true text of 22:20, where the number is explicitly mentioned.[6] In addition, the collection which embraces Prov 25-29 is governed by a title describing it as Solomonic proverbs "which the men of Hezekiah, king of Judah, copied out" (25:1). The significant word here is Hezekiah, whose numerical value in Hebrew is 130.[7] The number of proverbs in the section is close to this. This series of facts can mean only that each of the three sections named is governed by a specific number, for the extent of what it contains; and the identity of technique in building these sections is the first consideration to which we may appeal for evidence that the same individual built each and all of the collections.

2. Proverbs 10:1-22:16

We may now examine this largest collection to see whether there are within it any traces of editorial activity that might tell us something about the compiler. In a collection such as this, there are three obvious places to look: the beginning, the end, and the point in the middle where the two lesser collections are joined together. The end of the whole collection seems in no way noteworthy for any special features of its arrangement. At the beginning, there are suggestions of a desire to integrate the collection with the material in chs. 1-9. At least, the bulk of those chapters is addressed to a youth spoken of as "my son"; and 10:1, with its antithesis of the wise and the foolish son, suggests that the same reader is still intended. Then also the contrast between the "just" and the "wicked" in four of the first seven proverbs, employing the same terms which are habitual in the "seven columns" (cf. 2:20-22; 3:32-34; 4:14-19,18; 5:21-23) betokens a continua-

---

[5] It is not here intended to affirm that all 375 proverbs have been preserved to us textually intact; but whatever injuries, and perhaps subsequent repairs, the text may have undergone have left untouched both the substantial integrity and the precise original extent of the collection.

[6] The number 30 as the correct reading for MT *šilšôm* (*ketib*) or *šālišîm* (*qere*) here was rather widely accepted before the discovery of the Wisdom of Amenemope, the Egyptian book in thirty explicitly indicated "chapters," which has a definite literary relationship with this part of Prov. That discovery places the reading itself beyond doubt, however one may explain the relationship between the two books.

[7] According to MT *Ḥizqiyāh*; the form intended is, however, *Yeḥizqiyāh* with a numerical value of 140, the number of lines in the section; see *CBQ* 29 (1967) 173-74, reproduced below p. 44.

tion of the same interest. Besides, 10:1-2 are substantially duplicates (at most, deliberate variants) of 15:20 and 11:4 respectively, and thereby suggest that editorial selection has been at work.[8]

It is when we proceed to a study of the central portion of the collection, however, that the hand of a recognizable editor seems plain. The customary point at which commentators divide the text is after ch. 15; and in fact, on a purely numerical division, 16:4 is the central proverb of the 375. The distinctive characteristic of the six prior chapters (10-15) is the persistence of antithetic parallelism in the individual proverbs; this feature is prominent in the text as far as 15:32, only one verse from the end of ch. 15. Also, the first time that a direct precept occurs, as distinct from the preceding proverbs which are descriptive or non-preceptive in character, is at 16:3 (though 13:20 and 14:7 are sometimes cited, neither is convincing). It seems to the writer, however, that the compiler's, or editor's work can be traced back to Prov 14:26, for the following reasons. The actual departure from consistent use of antithetic parallelism begins at just this point. In what precedes, out of 141 proverbs, only nine may be cited which seem to lack this feature. Of the nine, 10:26 and 11:22 contain a complete antithesis within their first hemistichs; these and 10:18 are not truly exceptions. In 11:6,25,30 the text is widely regarded as being faulty; and there is support from the versions for a recognizable antithesis in each case. This leaves 13:14; 14:7 and 14:19 as genuine exceptions, for whatever reason. With 14:26, however, we find a break in this usage; of the 43 verses between it and 15:33, a total of 11 lack this feature (14:26-27; 15:3,10-12,23-24,30-31,33). The only mention of the king in chs. 10 to 15 occurs in 14:28 and 14:35. Both 14:26 and 14:27 treat of the "fear of the Lord"—14:27 apparently as a deliberate variant on 13:14. This introduction of the Lord (Hebrew, *Yahweh*) in two successive verses marks the first point in these chapters at which this divine name occurs repeatedly in close context; in the preceding 141 proverbs, there are nine occurrences, each separated from the others, while, beginning with 14:26-27, there are 11 in 43 verses to the end of ch. 15 (cf. 15:3,8-9, 11,16,25-26,29,33).[9]

---

[8] See also below, note 9.

[9] Within chapters 10-14 it is primarily toward the beginning, in chs. 10-11, that a systematic grouping of proverbs by topic or key words is discernible (the same situation obtains in the beginning of the "Hezekiah" collection, in chs. 25-26). Reflection will show that the argument given above is not essentially weakened, but rather broadened in scope, if we accept the hypothesis that Prov 10:27,29;11:1, which speak of Yahweh, once stood together as a group distinct from Prov 10:28,30-32, which deal with the *ṣaddiq*, or "just man." (Cf. J. M. McGlinchey, *The Teaching of Amenemope and the Book of Proverbs*, Catholic University dissertation, 1938, archival copy—not the published part—p. 58, note 2. It is to the archival copy of this work that page references

These points become increasingly significant when we examine the principle on which the sayings are joined together at the end of ch. 15 and the beginning of ch. 16. Proverbs 15:29-32 all contain a word for "hearing" (*yišmaʿ, šᵉmûʿâ, šômaʿat, šômēaʿ*) ; of the four, the first and last proverbs have antithetic parallelism, the two in the middle have not. Prov 15:32 is the point at which antithetic parallelism finally ceases to be a notable feature of the text. The four sayings on "hearing" in 15:29-32 bring the number of proverbs from 10:1 up to 184. At this point, therefore, the editor has added eight successive sayings (15:33-16:7) which deal with the Lord, to bring his collection beyond the halfway mark: a type of procedure which is best accounted for by supposing that here he was working to join together two collections of approximately equal length, in view of the definite number (375) which he had set himself as his goal. In ch. 16, it has often been noted that 16:10,12-15 all treat of the king, who has thereby the same kind of prominence at the beginning of this second half of the collection that he has at the beginning of the Hezekiah collection, in 25:2ff.

There are still other features that deserve notice within the section 14:26-16:15, which we may now take as the portion of text in which the editor is to be seen at work.[10] First of all, the most striking parallel in chs. 10-15 to the *Teaching* of Amenemope (to be discussed again with Prov 22:17ff.) occurs in 15:16-17, in connection with which should be taken 16:8 (this last the only verse between 15:33 and 16:15 which mentions neither the Lord nor the king!).[11] Then too, a goodly part of the duplication of sayings which occurs within the whole collection 10:1-22:16 occurs as between 14:26-16:15 and what precedes or follows. The relation of 15:20 to 10:1 and of 14:27 to 13:14 has already been mentioned. Most striking in the same respect is 21:2, which is used in 16:2 in the series of "Yahweh" sayings at the midpoint of the collection. To these may be added the close similarities between: 14:31 and 17:5; 15:8 and 21:27; 15:13-14 and 18:14-15; 15:22 and 11:14; 15:33 and 18:12, cf. also 16:18; 16:5 and 11:20-21; 16:11 and 11:1. This does not, of course, exhaust the duplications and similarities among the 375 proverbs (cf. notably 14:12 and 16:25), but it suggests a plausible explanation for well over half of them, in that the doublets were not the fruit of leisurely reflection and oral transmission, but were produced *ad hoc*, to round out this particular written work.

It could perhaps be objected to the allegation that 14:26-16:15 show clear

will apply in the following notes.) The beginning of the collection will then be more clearly seen to follow the same technique as is indicated above for the middle part.

[10] Prov 16:16 is the basis for Prov 3:14 in the introductory section.

[11] A detailed comparison in respect of 15:16-17; 16:8 (and 17:1) with *Amenemope* viii, 19-20; ix, 5-8; xvi, 11-14 is contained in the dissertation by J. M. McGlinchey (note 9, above), 93-95, 103-104.

evidence of a systematic editor, that in precisely this section the Septuagint text has a divergent arrangement (between 15:27 and 16:10). However, while it may be conceded that LXX lacked 15:31; 16:1-3 from the beginning, as it still does, and that it seemingly gave 15:27; 16:6; 15:28; 16:7; 15:29; 16:8-9; 15:30,32,33; 16:4,5,10 in that order, this still leaves the verses about the king intact (16:10,12-15). Therefore, it is not plausible that the verses 15:29,30,32, which have to do with "hearing," and the "Yahweh" verses 16:6,7,9; 15:33; 16:4,5 should have appeared in the original intermingled as the Greek gives them; the same two concepts are still identifiable in what LXX preserves for us, and the Hebrew, which groups them topically, must be substantially the original arrangement.

We may, therefore, sum up this investigation of the section 10:1-22:16 by saying that there are fairly clear traces of a systematic editor who has given the collection an artificial external structure based on the number 375, who was interested in disposing his matter to link up with the introductory chapters he had written for it, whose own topically arranged contributions deal mainly with the Lord, the king, and the just, who reworked certain earlier proverbs in order to attain his desired number, and who has recognizable contact with the Wisdom of Amenemope.

3. Proverbs 22:17-24:34

From a textual point of view, this section is quite difficult; it is certainly damaged, as any commentary on it will illustrate. The first matter that calls for justification is the assumption that all this material between the "Solomonic" collection and the "Hezekiah" collection should be treated as originally a unit. The comparison with the Wisdom of Amenemope seems to end with 23:11, and many have seen fit to make a major division at that verse. Also, the presence of "my son" in 23:15ff., though not in what precedes, is taken by many as the sign of a new collection. Again, Prov 24:23-34 has a heading of its own, and is therefore normally regarded as a distinct item.

Nevertheless, it seems that we have adequate indications for treating all the portions referred to as a unit. For this the number 30 will hardly help us *a priori*, since the individual sayings are of unequal length. What may be predicated of the entire section, however, is that it assumes a single speaker, who sometimes appears in the first person; a single listener or pupil, who is addressed in the second person singular masculine throughout; and a single preceptive manner whereby the teacher sets out to give his pupil points of guidance, described at 22:20 as *mô'eṣôt*, for his individual life. Only in very limited areas, 24:3-9 and 24:23-26, do the second person forms disappear. There is no reason to question the heading, "Words of wise men" over this section, to correspond to the headings of the Solomonic and the Hezekian collections. But its sense must be so understood, that once again a single editor gives the fruit of his gleanings from earlier sources. The introduction (22:17-21) makes this quite plain; and the actual assortment of precepts that follows could not cover the area that it does, without duplication of thought, were the selection not one man's work.[12] Nor does the present writer propose to deny that 24:21-22 gives every evidence of being the concluding couplet of this section. In maintaining that 24:23-34 belong to this same collection, he is prepared also to maintain that it is an appendix, and that the heading it now has helps prove this. That heading should not be rendered "These also are of the wise men," but rather "These also belong to the [collection of 'Sayings of] wise men.'" In form 24:23-26 is very like 24:10-12; 24:27, like 22:29 or the opening lines of 23:4-5 and 24:13-14. Then 24:28-29, in thought and in form, approach 24:15-18, and 24:30-34 is a composition of the type of 23:29-35. Also we should note that a link between Prov 24:28 and Amenemope xvi, 1 seems plausible.[13] As for the mention of "My son" in 23:15ff., it admits of a rather direct explanation. The teacher, who has been drawing on scattered material for his lessons (as illustrated by Amenemope)[14] introduces the question of paternal discipline for the first time in Prov 23:13-14 and very naturally falls at once into the habit of addressing his pupil as "son." This would be understandable even if we did not postulate the same writer at work in 22:17ff. as in chs. 1-9; with that postulate, it becomes obvious and inevitable.

Another point that needs no emphasizing for the student of Prov 1-9 is the similarity of subject matter which is to be found as between those chapters and the sayings of Prov 22:17-24:34. Since resemblances in form between the two sections have frequently been pointed out, it should not be necessary to do that again here.[15] As to the topical agreement, it should be remarked that it becomes pronounced at the very point where the relationship to Amenemope peters out! In the "Words of wise men" collection, the editor we have been discussing allows himself a comparatively free hand, as

[12] Prov 22:28 and 23:10 are partial, but only partial, duplicates.

[13] This and other comparisons are to be found in the dissertation by J. M. McGlinchey 122, 129.

[14] From what has been said, it will be seen that the hypothesis of unique editorship for all parts of Prov leads the writer to assume that the Amenemope material is in some sense a source for this section, as Isaiah, Jeremiah, and Deuteronomy were for Prov 1-9; this interpretation, though in conformity with the whole drift of the evidence as the writer sees it, is by no means the source of, or the prime element in, the general hypothesis we are reviewing.

[15] A careful statement of the relationship between these sections is contained in J. M. McGlinchey's dissertation, 105-106.

his thoroughly personal treatment of the topics he shares with Amenemope indicates; and he shows the same tendencies, interests, and techniques as the writer of Prov 1-9.

4. Proverbs 25-29

This Hezekian collection requires less discussion, and has fewer striking features.[16] By appealing to the LXX, further material might possibly be gathered for this collection. In this respect, the writer can profess only diffidence. In 25:9-10 LXX there is only one added hemistich which cannot be accounted for on the basis of the Hebrew we know (ἀλλ ἔσται σοι ἴση θανάτῳ); and this is not very promising, considering the context. The extra verse after 25:20 is an attempt at the Hebrew of 25:19b or 20a plus 25:20b. After 26:11 the Greek gives Sir 4:21. In 27:20-21 two extra verses are contained in LXX which many take for authentic; neither seems plausible to the writer—one has no parallelism, the other is too obvious. After 28:10, an inner-Greek garbling[17] has filled out the extra Hebrew hemistich into a complete, but spurious, saying. After 28:17 come garbled copies of 29:17-18a; after 29:7, a like treatment of the second half of that verse. The doublet after 29:25 is possibly from Symmachus. By appealing to LXX 24:22, where eleven extra hemistichs are found, something might be gained; but there again, the fact that the last such unit is a garbled handling of Prov 30:17d (LXX 24:52c) inspires renewed diffidence.

The most systematic part of the Hezekian collection is, of course, 25-27. The procedure involved in its construction is quite similar to that described for the middle of the Solomonic collection, where we saw an editor at work whom we are tempted to identify with the author of 1-9. Here again, as in 1-9 and in 14:26-22:16, we normally find synonymous, rather than antithetic, parallelism. A good case can be made out for knowledge of the Amenemope material having entered into the composition of these chapters: at 26:24-25,26 cf. Amenemope xii, 13-14; xiii, 11-16; at 25:21-23, cf. Amenemope v, 1, 5-6ff.; and at 27:1, cf. Amenemope xix, 11-13.[18] For the two final chapters (28-29) of this section, there is little to remark. Though their form is for the most part antithetic, their spirit is in accord with what one would expect from the author of 1-9, and a conscious effort to round out this part of the book in the same vein as ch. 3 seems discernible. The references here to the tôrâ (28:4,7,9; 29:18) and the estimate given of rulers (môšēl, šār, nāgîd: only twice, the "king") seem to the present writer to reflect the actuality of post-exilic times more clearly than any other part of

---

[16] The crucial fact is that it is 140 lines long; see n. 7 above.

[17] Cf. P. de Lagarde, *Anmerkungen zur griechischen Übersetzung der Proverbien* (Leipzig, 1863) 88.

[18] Texts and discussion in J. M. McGlinchey's dissertation, 86-90; 100-101.

the entire book. One artificial feature is worth mention: the *tôʿăbat*, thus a word beginning and ending with *tau*, at the head of each hemistich in 29:27, the final verse, is undoubtedly a signature that this verse is indeed the end of the collection.[19]

5. General Conclusions

Some general implications of the analysis on which we have been engaged for the understanding of the whole book grow directly out of chs. 25-29. First of all, if the name Hezekiah has been chosen not primarily for a historical attestation, but as a sort of signpost to indicate the extent of the collection, its use for dating the whole Book of Proverbs, or any of its parts, becomes a far less promising starting point than most, even recent, commentators would lead us to believe. We know that the author of Prov 1-9 was post-exilic. We know, too, that the collector of Prov 25ff. (as of 10ff.) lived close enough to the times of the monarchy to preserve the ideal of, and the appreciation for, an Israelite king who is not viewed as remote, or as attainable only with the advent of the Messiah, but as the normal foundation of everyday human society. If, however, these two personages are one and the same, then the name of Hezekiah is to be interpreted historically in the sense which is regularly accepted for the similar use of the name Solomon: it indicates a fountainhead of tradition, but it is not a fixed point for dating.

The attempt to date Prov 25-27 as the earliest portion of the Book of Proverbs because of their allegedly "secular" character is almost laughable on *a priori* grounds. To ascribe a primitively "secular" character to the origins of any phase of human life in ancient times, in or out of Israel, is to go against all that we really know of ancient man.[20] If now these chapters are viewed as part of a complex, all of whose elements were put together within one lifetime, who can say that the materials of 25-27 in particular antedate the final editor by 300 years, or by 100, or by 50? The "secular" basis for the supposition is altogether gratuitous in afflicting some unidentifiable group of ancient sages with the misfortunes of the modern agnostic; and there is no other valid ground known to the writer for a more accurate dating of these materials—*except* what he takes to be a dependence on Amenemope, which leads in another direction altogether. Similar considera-

---

[19] Compare *tāwi* at the end of Job's speeches, Jb 31:35. One wonders whether the double *taḥat* in Jb 31:40 may not account for the fals͏   ͏tion of Jb 31:38-40 after the real conclusion of this part?

[20] The actual historical background of the sages ir   period of the Hebrew monarchy, to the considerable extent that the histories a͏ᴜ͏ ͏he prophetical books permit us to know it, has been ably set forth by H. Duesberg, *Les Scribes Inspirés: Le livre des Proverbes* (Paris, 1937).

tions apply to most of the points heretofore adduced with regard to a precise date for some, or all, portions of the "Solomon" and the "Hezekiah" collections. There is very little evidence that is at all pertinent for purposes of dating: we have a *terminus ad quem*, but the origins can best be described as *mē'ôlām*.

The point has been made that all three of the main blocks of text after ch. 9 can be interpreted as dependent on Amenemope. The evidences respecting the first block, chs. 1-9, especially when we exclude 6:1-19, are perhaps less convincing,[21] though the parallels to Prov 3:23-24 and 3:25-34 in the Egyptian book are at least thought-provoking. In this more highly personal part of his teaching, the Hebrew sage very naturally draws more directly on the religious tradition of his forebears, and on the native "Wisdom" tradition of the earlier sages whose work he compressed into chs. 10ff. and 25ff. Then he speaks in the language of Isaiah, Jeremiah and Deuteronomy so much that there is little room left for a more remote source.[22]

A word is perhaps in order about the "evolution" of Hebrew gnomic literature. The above analysis, plus the book of Job, tends to show that such an evolution is not demonstrable to any serious degree within our biblical materials; and the writer is prepared to deny as a wholly gratuitous and improbable assumption that any literary period existed in Israel when the sages were producing exclusively one-line proverbs or, at most, couplets. Given the circumstances of the ancient Near East, the supposition is psychologically and historically quite as absurd as many of the worst nineteenth-century vagaries about the evolution of religious institutions within that same society. In the Wisdom books of the Old Testament particularly, the fact that we have preserved for us under divine Providence the best and fullest, and the inspired, products of the ancient Hebrew sages, does not at all mean that we are free to discuss origins as though nothing else had ever been written in that society, and as though we had at hand all the materials, from the crudest and most "primitive" to the latest and most refined, for a full history of the development of the forms. We have not; the principal Author of our biblical text had other ends in view.

One final point. As indicated toward the beginning of this discussion, we have thus far left out of account, in our treatment of the main portions of the Book of Proverbs, the following sections: 6:1-19, most of ch. 30, and all of ch. 31. To find a pattern which includes these sections according to some systematic plan is beyond the discernment of the present writer; as

[21] They are gathered in J. M. McGlinchey's dissertation, 54-77 (published form, Washington, 1938, pp. 9-32).

[22] Cf. A. Robert, "Les attaches littéraires bibliques de Prov. I-IX," in *RB* 43 (1934) 42-68, 172-204, 374-84; 44 (1935) 344-65, 502-25.

has already been said of chapters 1, 8 and 9, it seems very likely that such a pattern existed, though it is now lost to us. No one has questioned that chs. 1, 8 and 9 belong to the author of 2-7. If now we assume it as at least possible that the same author is responsible for assembling the materials in chs. 6, 30 and 31, we might expect to find in his general heading for the Book (1:1-6) some token of an over-all unity in which these portions would be included. As the writer sees it, such a sign of unity, other than the rather tenuous one in the word *ḥîdôṭ* of Prov 1:6, does exist in the proper names of 1:1.

To examine how it works out, let us total the number of individual lines in the entire book, in its four main sections, with the last two chapters, and 6:1-19, as a sort of appendix. Following the analysis already given, the result will be:

Part I:	Chapters 1-9	235 lines
	Ch. 1: 33 lines	
	Chs. 2-5; 6:20-7:27: 154 lines	
	Chs. 8; 9:1-6,10,13-18: 48 lines	
Part II:	Solomonic collection, 10:1-22:16:	375 lines
Part III:	Sayings of wise men, 22:17-24:34:	97 lines
	(with various additions, adjustments, etc., from part IV [ch. 30])	
Part IV:	Hezekiah collection, 25-29:	139 lines
	(a few lines transposed from part III)	
Appended material:		86 lines
6:1-19: 20 lines		
Ch. 30: 36 lines		
(excluding 30:10.17.32-33, counted with part III)		
Ch. 31: 30 lines		

Total, 932 lines[23]

With this result compare the numerical value of the letters in the Hebrew proper names in Prov 1:1, as follows:

The proverbs of SOLOMON (שלמה)	375
son of DAVID (דוד)	14
king of ISRAEL (ישראל)	541
	930

[23] It should be emphasized that though the writer suspects possible glosses, this count excludes no line in the actual present content of the Book of Proverbs except the following: 1:16 (cf. *CBQ* 9 [1947] 195, n. 8, reproduced above p. 12, n. 7); 8:11 (cf. *ibid.*, 197 reproduced above p. 14); 22:28 (cf. above, n. 12); and the titles in 10:1; 25:1; 30:1; 31:1. [These calculations are refined, and the juggling of elements from Parts III, IV and ch. 30 given up, in the 1967 article, "Wisdom's House," reproduced below.]

If this calculation has any value, we have an internal witness in the text of the book itself that it is integral according to the scope planned for it by one sole editor, within two lines of its original length.[24] Whatever may be said of the instances of transposition envisaged in the present article, the correct place of any line has no bearing on the calculation just given.

---

[24] This is subject to the same type of qualification, only, as is represented by note 5, above.

THE MEANING OF THE BOOK OF JOB*

MATITIAHU TSEVAT

Hebrew Union College - Jewish Institute of Religion, Cincinnati

T HE opening of the Book of Job is a case of the rule that a great author can be recognized by the way he fashions the opening of his work.[1] As the prologue (chaps. 1 f.) tells the events on earth and in heaven, it provides the reader with the factual background of what is to come and introduces him with equal clarity to the problem of the book.[2] The poetic part (3:1–42:6) may appear to modern

* My friend Professor H. C. Brichto read the manuscript with painstaking care and made untold invaluable suggestions. I am deeply grateful to him.

[1] Special abbreviations used in this paper are: Kuhl 1953 and Kuhl 1954 = C. Kuhl, *ThR*, N. F. 21 (1953), pp. 163-205, 257-317; and *ThR*, N. F. 22 (1954), 261–316, respectively. Rowley = H. H. Rowley, *From Moses to Qumran* (1963), pp. 141–83. "Com." following the name of an author refers to his commentary; when it follows Tur Sinai, his 1954 Hebrew commentary is intended.

Views widely held and readily available in the scholarly literature are not identified or specifically referred to, nor are the arguments adduced for them. A balanced view, supported by detailed exegesis and a discussion of differing opinions is found in G. Fohrer, *Das Buch Hiob* (1963), 565 pages. The reader who prefers an English book is referred to S. R. Driver and G. B. Gray, *The Book of Job* (1921, and reprints), LXXVIII+376+360 pages. (The commentary of M. Pope did not reach me in time to make use of in this paper.) A detailed and excellent survey on Job research between *cd.* 1921 and 1953 is given by Kuhl 1953 and Kuhl 1954. It is supplemented by the more recent article of Rowley, first published in *BJRL* 41 (1958 f.), pp. 167-207; re-edited and brought up-to-date in his *From Moses to Qumran*. Reference to these articles is primarily to the literature which Kuhl and Rowley survey and only infrequently to their own opinions.

[2] There are three critical views as regards the relation of the prose frame, comprising the prologue (chaps. 1 f.) and the epilogue (42:7-17), to the poetic colloquy it encloses. (1) The author of the poetic part (i. e., the author of the book, since there are almost forty chapters of poetry to two-and-a-half of prose; the reduction of the number of forty to about thirty for critical reasons, such as the excision of the Elihu section [chaps. 32–37; cf. n. 17], does not affect the point I wish to make) used and possibly adapted an older prose story, enclosing in it his own larger work. (2) The author wrote the prose as well as the poetry. (3) A later editor provided the narrative frame for the poet. Cf. Kuhl 1953, pp. 185-205; Rowley, pp. 151-56, 159. I hold with the great majority of students in favoring the first or the second view. A choice between them is of little consequence for the issue at hand, the question of the author's having composed the frame or appropriated an existing one being one of literary prehistory; in either case the resulting book is his creation, and the object of our concern is this book.

readers overly long and, in places, wordy and confused (responsibility for which may be assigned, on the one hand, to an abundance of additions by later hands, textual confusion, and an exceptionally difficult language and, on the other, perhaps to the intention of the author to show by the growing repetitiveness of the *dramatis personae* that they have exhausted their arguments); the 35 verses of the narrative introduction are concise and pithy and yet contain everything the reader has to know.

There is Job, the pious man, on whom God's blessing rests. But this idyl of piety and prosperity is introduced only to be immediately menaced by the accuser, Satan, as he presents himself at the heavenly council and demands: "Is it for nought that Job is pious?" (1:9). He questions not Job's deeds but his motivation. Nor is this an act of viciousness on his part; God Himself has provoked him to probe and shake the foundations of the beautiful edifice of righteousness, serenity, and happiness and finally wreck it completely. For God has asked him: "Have you considered my servant Job, that there is no one on earth as blameless and upright as he?" (1:8). Job is the pious man, if there is one. The problem is: is there one? Which is secondary to the main problem: is there piety? Which is, as the accuser insists: is there disinterested piety? He claims that Job behaves according to standards of religion only as long as he finds it useful, whereas piety begins where usefulness ends. God accepts the challenge as proposed by the accuser and on his terms, and this acceptance determines the meaning of piety for the rest of the book. From now on, he who performs an action in expectation of material reward is not to be credited with religious or moral behavior. Different and less pure concepts of piety which find their way into the speeches of the friends later on (8:5-7, 20-22; 11:13-19; 22:21-28) are thus invalid and implicitly rejected *a limine*.

We now know what piety is; this is a question *quid iuris* in Kant's terminology. What we do not know is the answer to the first question: is there piety? This is a question *quid facti*. While we do not learn the answer at this early stage of the book, we have a preliminary indication that it is likely to be in the affirmative, that there is piety in the world, for it is God Who is the proponent of this view (2:3).

Amplifying what was touched upon before, the narrative content of the prologue and its thought content are not dissociated, but rather the two, plot and ideas, are intimately wedded, and this union now constitutes more than merely the sum of its two components. The prologue informs the reader of the cause of Job's suffering, information which Job himself cannot and must not have. We know more than the hero. But the hero, precisely because of his ignorance, will experience problems and gain insights before which our superior knowledge pales. It is not the spectator's knowledge of the drama but rather Job's problem that matters. The prologue *qua* prologue is a work of genius.

At the beginning of the poetic part we find ourselves in a different world, not only as regards the plot -- if we may so refer to the regular change of speakers and their ever-increasing animosity — but also as regards the ideas. The latter, while not unrelated to the ideas of the prologue, assume very different forms, and it is only towards the end of the book that we recognize them in their earlier formulation. In our treatment the three friends and their philosophies will not be differentiated from one another but be seen as one group with one position, over against which will stand Job's philosophy.

One of the friends speaks up in response to Job's initial lament (of chap. 3). His purport, in which the others join him later: Job should behave himself, live up to the very convictions which he formerly preached to others, and rely on God because afflictions are God's chastisements (chaps. 4 f.). As Job finds this counsel cold comfort, the friends become ever more adamant and finally quite aggressive as they develop their theology. Their view, they claim, is based on both tradition and observed reality. A web of causality is spun over the world. Man's fate is in his hand; what he gets depends on what he does. The just man is rewarded, the sinner punished. This cause-and-effect relation, widely accepted in the ancient Near East, they reverse: distress and tribulation are punishment meted out for sin. The inescapable conclusion is that Job, distressed and afflicted, is a sinner. His sins may be unknown to him, but they are no less real. Causality in the realm of morality is guaranteed by God; this is the meaning of the sentence "God is just." As for Job, let him search out his sins and repent, and the happiness of his former status will be restored to him.

The friends came to comfort (2:11), but their philosophy will afford a grievously harrowed man no consolation. Yet the literary device that spurs the action and aggravates the situation is the ever-increasing vehemence of the friends, their self-righteousness and unqualified condemnation of their disputant, all of which not only fails to console or at least convince Job but increasingly makes a true conversation impossible. There is no meeting of minds. Repeatedly Job says: "If you only would listen to my words" (13:5 f.; 21:2 f.). But they launch a massive assault, attacking him from all sides with such force and viciousness that one might expect his backbone to be broken and his personality, the pivot of the drama, extinguished. We must remind ourselves how hard it was for an ancient Israelite, grounded himself in tradition, to withstand the logic of the friends.

Job's backbone is not broken. Up to the last verses of the book he not only stands upright but actually grows in strength, and as the disputation continues we see the development and integration of his personality. He undertakes to demolish some of the friends' arguments and to reject others. Reality, he contends, does not accord with their theory. The world is not governed by the principle of measure for measure. Almost everywhere the wicked prosper. Against these incontrovertible facts, tradition and authority, to which the friends appeal, are without validity; wisdom is not necessarily found with the elders (12:12)[3] — a shocking pronouncement in those days. So clear is the discrepancy between theory and reality that the theory can only be saved by distortion of observation and misrepresentation of reality, in short by a lie. "You whitewash with lies [the dark side of life]," is the accusation Job hurls at the friends (13:4). A few verses later he demands: "Will you speak falsely for God, speak deceitfully for Him?" (13:7-11). This is probably the first time in history that pious fraud is clearly recognized and denounced for what it is: a contradiction in terms. Fraud is never pious, it is always impious.

But Job does not stop with presenting his own, very different view of the world. Decisive is his rejection of the principle which underlies the argument of the friends: the inference from observed reality to the causation of that reality, and this rejection is independent of the accuracy or inaccuracy of the observation. His misery is no evidence for sin on his part because he did not sin. Neither logic nor clever dispositions of commonly held opinions nor glib talk can produce what does not exist: his iniquity. To be precise, Job does not deny absolutely that he has sinned. He grants the possibility of minor transgressions. (7:21; 13:26). But what he denies categorically is sins of such weight as to warrant their being related to his lot as cause to effect. The friends' argument rests on a doctrine; his argument is grounded in his life, his experience, his person. And since he knows himself, and since the course of his life lies open before everyone, he is compelled to affirm that the cause of the terrible atrocities that God has unleashed against him lies not in him but in God. God wants to torment him, torment him without reason, because God is cruel.

---

[3] The verse presents a rhetorical question the answer to which is no. Cf. Tur Sinai, com.

From the lack of rational reason in a person's behavior we take a clue to his character. God's outstanding characteristic appears therefore to be a demoniac ruthlessness. In ever-repeated and diverse ways Job accuses God of wanton cruelty. God's eyes are on man (and on Job as the representative of mankind) not, as the Bible frequently asserts and as the friends faithfully echo, to guard and protect him but to watch and destroy him. Would that He leave man alone to finish out his days in quiet; but no, He searches him out for horror and doom. The friends speak of God's might and wisdom. Surely, says Job, He is mighty and wise, but might is brute force, and wisdom is craftiness seeing that they serve God's caprice and outrage justice. No wonder that omnipotence and omniscience, ordinarily epithets of praise of God, turn in Job's mouth to expressions of blame.

But Job does not limit himself to such statements of facts, as he sees the divine facts. He describes them so keenly because they concern his own person. He is the target. Thus description becomes accusation. Job, the accuser, wants to bring God, the defendant, to court. Nor is this all. Job craving judgment, objective, rational judgment, knows that there is no judge but God. It is in the rational milieu of the tribunal that God will shed his demoniac features, and Job's troubles will be over. Again and again he wants the encounter, longs to see God. For it is his innermost and strongest hope, implicit for the most part but sometimes pronounced, that God also longs for him, His creature, the work of His hands. This hope upholds Job in the hours of his greatest despair. Beside this all else pales. Progressively his dispute with the friends loses in importance as his address to God — accusation, challenge, prayer, and prediction — gains in importance. In his final long speech (chs. 26 f.; 29–31) the presence of the friends gradually becomes dim, in its last three chapters they are not mentioned at all. The only protagonists on the stage at the end are Job and the Deity, the best man and his God.

The concluding chapter of Job's speech, (ch. 31) has a particular function in the economy of the book. Job is not satisfied with accusing, begging, and hoping; he takes more efficacious action compelling God to leave His uncommitted, whimsical transcendence and to take a stand, to relate Himself to his problems. Ancient man, as he conceptualized his world, had a means of challenging God: the oath. Man swears to a fact or a promise; if he perjures himself, God, Who is evoked in the oath, is bound to punish him; if it is a terrible oath, punishment will be terrible. (It is hardly necessary to remark that ordinarily an oath was not sworn in order to challenge God but to affirm a statement or a promise.) It is otherwise with Job. Ch. 31,

40 verses long, is his oath.⁴ It is the most terrible oath in the Bible, for this reason: A full oath has the following form: "If I did or shall do this, or if I did not or shall not do this, then may God punish me." Ordinarily, however, the apodosis ("then may God punish me") is omitted. The very likely reason for this ellipsis is that one shied away from conjuring up punishment in the unlikely event of an un-intentional factual inaccuracy of the material content of the oath. Although uttered in good faith, such an inaccuracy may set in motion the mechanism of punishment for perjury that the oath envisages. Caution truncated the oath in biblical and post-biblical Israel and among her neighbors.⁵ Job throws caution to the winds. Over and over he explicitly calls upon himself every conceivable punishment if what he says is not true.

He talks long but says in effect only one thing: that he has led an essentially good life, that he has not sinned. For all that he is not verbose. It is worth the reader's notice that the sins which he abjures are not, for the most part, monstrous crimes but minute deviations from the loftiest standards of ethics and piety. Here are a few examples: "If I have disdained the cause of my manservant or maidservant when they brought a complaint against me . . ." (vs. 13). "If I have withheld anything that the poor desired or have caused the eyes of the widow to fail . . ." (vs. 16). "If I have 'rejoiced'⁶ at the ruin of my foe or exulted when evil overtook him . . ." (vs. 29). "If I have concealed my transgression as people (are wont to do) by hiding my iniquity in my bosom because I stood in great fear of the multitude . . . and kept silence . . ." (vss. 33 f.). "If my land has cried out against me . . . if I have eaten its yield without payment and brought low the spirit of its owners"⁷ (vss. 38 f.).

---

⁴ Vss. 35-37, probably to be placed after vs. 40, are not part of the oath but draw the sum total of Job's pleadings from ch. 3 through ch. 31. For the form of this oath, cf. S. H. Blank, *JJS* 2 (1951), pp. 105-107.

⁵ The custom in Jewish Palestine of the first few centuries A. D. is described by S. Lieberman, *Greek in Jewish Palestine* (1942), ch. 5, especially pp. 121-24. It is as interesting as it is not surprising that the simple people were even more cautious than the rabbis in the formulation of the oath.

⁶ Read וְהִתְרָעַעְתִּי with the Targum (ויבהית), commentaries; MT וְהִתְעָרַרְתִּי.

⁷ The meaning of "my land" in conjunction with "its owners" is that Job had distrained real estate of defaulting debtors and, himself consuming its yield, had brought the impoverished original owners to the verge of despair. Had Job behaved in such a manner, he would have been fully within his legal rights, yet by virtue of his own highly developed conscience guilty of a cruel and antisocial act. M. Dahood, taking his cue from Ugaritic, has repeatedly insisted (most recently in *Biblica* 46 [1965], pp. 320 f.) that בְּעָלֶיהָ is dialectical for פעליה (=פֹּעֲלֶיהָ). This is possible but gratuitous. In general, we would observe that resort to dialectical features, non-

The challenge to God is overt and clear. God is bound to act. If Job has perjured himself, God is to punish him even more than he is already punished, if that is yet possible. If not, he is pure; the oath proves it. Then he should be restored *in integrum*, for so judicial procedure requires. If neither of these immediate and plain alternatives result, God is challenged personally to respond to the oath. (Indeed, what Job desires above all else is the personal encounter with God, divine revelation.) Would that He produced counter-accusation; Job will make a crown and an ornament out of it — so certain is he of his case. He will stand up before God like a prince, he will not blink an eye (vss. 35-37). Job has grown to Promethean stature. The miracle is that it is not growth at the expense of piety. This is the most striking case in the Bible of a man so strongly asserting himself against God while yet remaining so loyal to Him.

From this vantage point, looking back over the disputation of Job and the friends and forward to the answer of God, we have no difficulty identifying the problem of the book in a preliminary way. It is the suffering of the innocent. There is broad agreement about this,[8] although the issue is sometimes blurred by the omission of the qualifier "of the innocent." The omission reduces the problem to suffering alone, but this is surely unintentional because the suffering of the non-innocent is deserved suffering, i. e., punishment. The friends indeed attempt repeatedly to construe Job's suffering as punishment. But no one has yet seen in this argument more than a straw man.

The problem of the suffering of the innocent is everywhere in the book. Where is the answer? It is a priori probable that it is found at the end. An answer comes after a question and not in the middle while the questioning is going on. This is a truism, to be sure, but its evocation is forced upon us by proposals that the answer lies in the middle of the book, e. g., in chaps. 19[9] or 28[10] or even in the speeches of Elihu.[11] As to the end, the prose epilogue presents no serious can-

---

standard sound shifts, or the like should not be had except with caution and primarily for the purpose of avoiding forced exegesis or unsupported emendations.

[8] For a different opinion, cf. *infra*, p. 23.

[9] For some of the champions of this proposal, notably those who hold that 19:25-27 refer to Job's resurrection or redemption, cf. Fohrer, com., pp. 318 f. Further recent attempts to detect the solution in ch. 19 are mentioned by Kuhl 1953, p. 304. Add K. Fullerton, *ZAW* 42 (1924), pp. 116-36.

[10] The opinions are cited and discussed by Kuhl 1953, p. 282; Rowley, pp 166 f. Add Tur Sinai, com., pp. 238, 388. It should be remarked, however, that a number of scholars who accept this view place the chapter at the end of the divine address.

[11] K. Budde, com. (1913), pp. XLV-XLVIII; others are listed by Kuhl 1953, pp. 261 f.; Kuhl 1954, pp. 312 f.

didature. It contains little more than the story of Job's restoration to his former state of happiness and the pronouncement of his vindication. Thus by elimination we are directed to the final chapters of the poetry (hereinafter "final chapters"), 38:1–42:6, God's long speech and Job's short response. We assume that the answer is found in either or both of their components, and it will be our task to demonstrate that this assumption is correct, that here indeed lies the answer of the book. As the business of the demonstration begins immediately and extends to the end of the article, this assumption is henceforth our working hypothesis, one we hope will be vindicated in the course of this discussion.

Some critics, however, say that the final chapters are not part of the original book. Their argument runs as follows: The logic of literary structure as well as other considerations require that these chapters contain the answer of the book; this is their *raison d'être*. But they do not contain it (by which the critics mean: we have not detected in them an acceptable answer). Ergo, the chapters have no justification for existence; they were added later. Ergo, the book has no answer to its problem.[12] This is lazy man's logic. The sentence "I have not detected the meaning" should signify to the philologist "I have not yet detected it," and this should spur him to further search in place of recourse to the easy alternative of denying the authenticity of the passage.

Yet since most of those who deny that the answer of the book is contained in its final chapters say that the book has no answer at all,[13] we have first to address ourselves to the question: does the book have an answer? This question we answer in the affirmative for the following reasons.[14]

First, were the book to contain no answer, we should be faced with a literary work posing a problem of the greatest moment without offering or even attempting a solution. The reader would be cut loose from his moorings of tradition and faith and left adrift. The Book of Job without an answer to its problem would constitute a literary torso, an anthology of verbalized doubts; it would betray an utter lack of appreciation of the controlling conceptions which are everywhere in evidence in the work to allow this judgment to stand.

A second reason for postulating an answer to the problem of the suffering of the innocent in Job is the plain and obvious design of the

[12] The latter conclusion is, of course, not shared by the comparatively small group of interpreters who are referred to in nn. 9–11.

[13] Cf. n. 12.

[14] Cf. also R. A. F. MacKenzie, *Biblica* 40 (1959). pp. 437–41.

book. It converges forcefully on the final chapters. Job's long concluding speech (chs. 29–31) containing his oath sums up his position but is not an absolute end. This speech is a transition, an expression of expectation; it culminates in his challenge to God as he subjects himself to the penalties enumerated in the oath; it is the strongest expression of his longing for confrontation. The final chapters bring the fulfillment; the desire to meet God, for a revelation, for an answer is granted there. To declare these chapters unauthentic is to reject the expected when it occurs.

A further support for·the thesis that the problem of the book is answered is to be found in the beginning of the epilogue. It reads: "After having spoken these words to Job, the Lord said to Eliphaz, the Temanite: 'My wrath is kindled against you and your two friends; for you have not spoken of Me what is right, as has My servant Job'" (42:7). As several scholars have observed, this verse refers to a revelation which God has just granted to Job. Job's wish has been fulfilled, his incessant questions have received a reply. Which means that explicit reference to an actual revelation is made in a different part of the book. God's answer to suffering Job is or contains His answer to the suffering of Job, i. e., it constitutes the solution to the problem of the book.[15] The answer of the book is anchored in its ground plan.

Some scholars, however, for whom we may take C. Kuhl as a spokesman, share the extreme skepticism of the critics mentioned before. Overwhelmed by the difficulty of understanding God's reply, by the seeming unrelatedness of its content to Job's words, they say that God's answer is His theophany, the mere fact that He appeared to the man who deemed himself cast out from the presence of God. The theophany itself is genuine, but its verbal content, the long divine address, is a later addition.[16] At first glance, this opinion has much to recommend itself. The theophany rehabilitates Job. Job has suffered, but his suffering is no sign of his rejection. True, he as well as the friends have so interpreted it, but their interpretation is now corrected. Moreover, theophany, personal contact with God has been his greatest desire; now it is realized. Furthermore, revelation is the supreme good in biblical religion. Of Moses, Deuteronomy says (34:10): "There has not risen a prophet in Israel like Moses, whom the Lord

---

[15] Neither this nor the preceding arguments prove the genuineness of the present answer, 38:1–40:14 (for its extent, cf. n. 26); they admit of the highly improbable hypothesis that the original answer of the poem was replaced by the present one. (Whether an originally independent prose story had a different disputation followed by a different speech of God [Fohrer, com., pp. 37, 538] need not detain us.)

[16] Kuhl 1953, pp. 270 f.

knew face to face." Yet Job has come close to this. In general it may be said that all doubts, anguishes, and antagonisms to which a man may be prey, disappear in the presence of a vision. Job himself says as much in his last response: "I had heard of You from hearsay, but now my eye sees You. Therefore . . ." (42:5 f.). The vision has transferred him into a new state. It is the fullest answer.

The importance of the revelation in the Book of Job is immense. It can be overemphasized in only one way: if it is made exclusive, if it is interpreted to be the whole answer. This, however, is a misinterpretation and must be rejected for the following reasons:

(1) The event of a revelation. distinct from its specific, articulate content, is personal, untransmissible, and unrepeatable. A report of a revelatory event as such is pure autobiography. Had the author of the book restricted himself to autobiography at this critical juncture, he would have proclaimed that his own problems were solved, but to his readers he would say implicitly: "If you are grievously afflicted, wait for a personal revelation; there is no salvation outside of revelation." Such an answer would be altogether incongruous.

(2) The design and the construction of the book do not lend themselves to Kuhl's interpretation. The book in its first thirty-one chapters[17] is the result of a supreme conceptual, literary, and poetical effort. Is it conceivable that the author invested this stupendous intellectual energy in the question only to seek, receive, and transmit the whole solution on a nonintellectual level?

The reasoning and the conclusions of the preceding paragraphs are essentially formal, as this summary shows: the Book of Job presents a problem (it is the problem of the suffering of the innocent); the problem has an answer; the answer is contained in the final chapters; and the final chapters are authentic. The conclusions being formal, they must now be put to the test of substantiation through the interpretation of the final chapters that, according to our postulation, contain the answer.

"The Lord answered Job out of the storm" (38:1). Job is granted his request; God answers him. The answer comes from the storm, and since, in the Bible, a storm often precedes or accompanies a theophany, we are prepared for a theophany to occur with the answer. The occurrence is affirmed in Job's response: "Now my eye sees You" (42:5).

---

[17] I accept the prevailing critical opinion that the Elihu pericope (chaps. 32–37) is secondary and therefore do not consider these chapters.

The divine speech has two introductory verses.

> Just who darkens the plan by words without knowledge? ³Gird up your loins like a man; I will question you, and you shall declare to Me (38:2 f.).

We shall learn soon which plan (עֵצָה) Job darkens. But irrespective of which and whose, his approach, possibly his very position, is rejected at the outset; he speaks "without knowledge." In vs. 3b, God formally accepts the challenge. Earlier Job offered God two alternatives: "Call, and I will answer; or let me speak, and You reply to me" (13:22). Now God chooses the first alternative. In contrast with the continuation of the verse, its beginning, "Gird up your loins," is figurative, possibly referring to an ancient custom, which C. H. Gordon calls "belt-wrestling."[18]

Now comes the substance of the speech. We know from vs. 3 that it will be presented in the form of a question, a question which breaks down into a series of detailed questions. The first group, vss. 4–11, concerns creation; within it, the first subgroup, vss. 4–7, contains questions about the creation of the earth, which means in the cosmology and language of the time, the dry land;

> Where were you when I laid the foundation of the earth? Tell me if you have understanding. ⁵Who determined its measurements — if you know that, or who stretched the line on it? ⁶In what were its bases sunk, or who laid its cornerstone, ⁷when the morning stars sang in unison and all the divine beings shouted for joy? (38:4–7).

"You, Job, were not present at the creation of the earth and, consequently, you know nothing about its nature." Take the problem of measurement. How can the infinitely large earth be measured? With which measuring line? After the measuring, the laying of foundations. This is even less comprehensible. On what basis is this immense earth set? On the watery sea, as the Psalmist says (24:2)? Or maybe even on no basis at all, as the Book of Job itself has it ("He hangs the earth upon nothing," 26:7)? All this is a complete mystery. What makes it even more mysterious to man is that other beings, divine or celestial, are presumably able to answer these questions for they were present and involved when these things happened, they celebrated the great event — only human beings were not there and hence do not share the knowledge.

---

[18] Cf. *HUCA* XXIII:1 (1950 f.), pp. 131–36.

'Who'[19] shut in the sea with doors when it burst forth from the womb, [9]when I made clouds its garment and dense fog its swaddling band, [10]making breakers[20] 'its'[21] limit,[22] fixing bars and doors, [11]and said: "Thus far shall you come and no farther; here shall your 'proud'[23] waves 'be stayed' "[23] (38:8–11).

The author of Job was a well-educated man, familiar with the Jewish and non-Jewish literature of his time. His book abounds in allusions to the myths of the ancient Orient. One of the most prominent of them is the story of the fight of the supreme God, the leader of the present pantheon, with the sea which appears in the image of a gigantic dragon; the god is victorious and, according to one version, fashions the sky (and the earth) out of the body of the dead monster.[24] This myth is alluded to in other parts of the book (3:8; 7:12; 9:13; 26:12 f.).[25] Yet nothing of it is present in this passage. The sea is not God's adversary; it is a giant baby, just born, that had to be confined at the moment of birth (vs. 8), when a baby must be wrapped in swaddling clothes. The stripes of fog on the surface of the sea are its swaddle (vs. 9). All this is subsumed under the question of vs. 4: "Where were you then?"

The text now turns from the creation of the world to its survey and management (38:12–39:30).[26] The form of the questions is maintained throughout. We are first shown the inanimate world (38:12–38). At the beginning there is the daily rise of the morning.

Have you ever in your life commanded the morning, have you directed[27] the dawn to its place [13]to take hold of the skirts of the earth so that the wicked are shaken out of it — [14]it changes like clay under the seal and 'it is dyed'[28] like a garment — [15]so that light is withheld from the wicked, and their uplifted arm is broken? (38:12–15).

[19] Read 'מִי סָךְ', commentaries; so also the Vulgate (quis conclusit); MT וַיָּסֶךְ.
[20] וָאֶשְׁבֹּר, denominative from מִשְׁבָּרִים "breakers, surf at the reefs of the shore."
[21] Read 'חֻקִּי', commentaries; MT חֻקִּי.
[22] Cf. 14:5.
[23] Read 'יִשָּׁבֵת גְּאוֹן', commentaries; MT יָשִׁית בִּגְאוֹן.
[24] Cf. the Assyro-Babylonian epic Enuma Elish IV:93 ff.
[25] Cf., e. g., Fohrer, com., pp. 502 f., who offers an inclusive treatment of this and other mythological imagery.
[26] I incline to the critical opinion that 40:15–41:26 are not authentic; cf. the references in Rowley, p. 166, n. 1; also Fohrer, com., p. 39. But the point this article is trying to make is not affected by one's critical position regarding this section; cf. also Rowley's view, p. 166. Other insertions in the final chapters will be critically recognized in their proper places.
[27] Cf. the same meaning of a probably related form of this verb in I Sam. 21:3.
[28] Read 'וְתִצְטַבַּע' or 'וְתִצָּבַע', commentaries; MT וְיִתְיַצְּבוּ.

Has Job ever performed such a routine thing as bringing on a new day? Following up the broad question by special attention to one corner of the tableau, which is nothing but a manifestation of His interest in the world as it is, God describes the dawn by what it does to the earth. The latter looks like a broad piece of cloth, of indistinct color first, but the color changes soon and keeps changing with the brightening of the day. As the sun rises, the contours of the earth are beginning to stand out clearly like the impression of a seal on soft clay.

Next comes a paragraph which may be called "The dimensions of the universe."

> Have you reached the springs of the sea[29] or walked in the recesses of the deep? [17]Have the gates of death been laid bare to your sight, and have you seen the gates to murk? [18]Have you examined well (the universe) as far as the farthest (ends) of the netherworld? Speak, if you know any of this! [19]Where is the way to the abode of the light, and where is the place of darkness, [20]that you may lead either one[30] back to its realm or discern the paths to its home? [21]You surely know all this[31] for you were already born then, and the number of your days is great indeed (38:16-21).

"The first questions, all left unanswered, showed clearly enough," God continues, "that you were not present at the creation of the world. Have you at least seen its full expanse?" The question, like all the

---

[29] The nouns in vss. 16-18 may refer to names of gods or demons in various ancient Oriental mythologies and accordingly be rendered as "Sea," "Deep" (or "Primeval Flood"), "Death," "Murk," and "Netherworld"; or "Yamm," *"Tiham," "Mot," "Ṣalmut," and *"Arṣ." (*Tiham, and *Arṣ may be hypothesized by their appearance [in feminine forms] in the cognate literature. Tiamtu, etc., is well known from the Assyro-Babylonian civilization. Remarkably, ארצית [=Erṣitu] appears in Jewish folklore [M. Gaster, ספר מעשיות, here after S. Krauss, HUCA IV (1927), p. 352; Krauss, however, misinterprets the word].) I cannot decide whether the author, oscillating between the semantic foreground ("sea") and background ("Sea," "Yamm"), intends either of these pairs of meanings ("sea" or "Sea" [or "Yamm," respectively] and in like manner all the others) or both of them. The language of classical Hebrew poetry admits of both, and it is often beyond our means to settle on a single meaning ("sea" or "Sea/Yamm") or the double meaning ("sea-Sea/Yamm"). (A comparable problem is presented in Sumero-Akkadian cuneiform, where, for example, ᵈŠamaš, for all the presence of the divine determinative, in many contexts conveys to the modern reader nothing more than "sun.") The problem of the significance of Near Eastern mythology in Job will be discussed further on, pp. 15, 30.

[30] "Either one" is an attempt to render the distributive function of the Hebrew personal suffixes; this function is present, e. g., in חַרְבוֹ and קַשְׁתוֹ (Isa. 41:2).

[31] The force of כָּלָה after תֵּדַע of vs. 18 extends to תֵּדַע of this verse. The word is not repeated, perhaps in order to avoid crowding the stich.

others, is rhetorical and has an ironical ring; the expected answer is no.
Job knows only a small section of the world. The sarcasm of vs. 21,
however, momentarily disregards the conclusion of vss. 4 ff.: "You
know all this because at the time of their creation you must have been
alive — or so you behave."

The theme of the dimensions of the universe is continued in the
next paragraph, dealing with precipitations and winds.

> Have you reached the storehouses of the snow and have you
> seen the storehouses of the hail, [23]which I have reserved for
> times of trouble, for the day of battle and war? [24]By what route
> does the west wind[32] escape[33] or the east wind fan out over the
> earth? [25]Who has cleft a channel for the rain flood and a way for
> the thunder cloud [26]to cause rain on land where no man is, on
> a desert where no people live [27]to satiate waste and desolate
> terrain and to sprout fresh grass?[34] [28]Has the rain a father, and
> (is there one) who sired the drops[35] of the dew? [29]From whose
> womb does the ice come forth, and who gives birth to the rime
> of heaven, [30]when the water 'becomes solid'[36] like stone, and
> the surface of the waters is 'hidden'?[36] (38:22–30).

Vss. 28–30 raise a new point. God asks Job: "How do rain, ice, and
frost come into being? Give a realistic answer. Do not give Me myths
for facts." Mythological fragments or just allusions to myths are one
of the secondary features of Job, probably more prominent in it than
in any other biblical book.[37] But what was only an inkling in the

---

[32] Vocalize 'אוּר' (?) <Aram. אוריה <Akkad. *amurrū* (Tur Sinai, com.).

[33] Akkad. *ḥalāqu* means both "to flee, escape, slip away" and "to perish." M.
Dahood considers the second meaning for some biblical passages (*Biblica* 45 [1964],
p. 408). The first, however, provides the basis for interpreting Jer. 37:12 (already
Redaq, Rosenmüller, and Gesenius [*Thesaurus*] from the context, as well as Geller and
Tur Sinai based on the Akkadian); Lam. 4:16 (following verbs of motion and naming
the ultimate agent of it: "the face of the Lord chased them away" [cf. Num. 10:35]);
I Sam. 23:28 (an etiological connection of the story with the "Rock of Escape").
There is no basis for judging the masoretic vocalization of the verb here and in the
Jeremiah passage.

[34] מֹצָא, literally "plants" or "growth"; ܨܡܚܐ "plant." Cf. Gen. 1:12.

[35] The meaning of אֶגְלֵי is conjectural. (A. Guillaume's etymology, *Abr-Nahrain*
I [1959 f.], p. 6, had justly been questioned by [Driver and] Gray, com., four decades
before it was proposed.)

[36] Very uncertain. The translation of this verse follows a number of commentaries
in (1) emending the text by exchanging the order of the verbs and (2) assuming for
יִתְלַכָּדוּ the meaning "hold together" (41:9 ‖ יְדֻבָּקוּ), hence "pack, solidify," metaphorical for "freeze." Moreover, "waters" as the rendition of תְּהוֹם has no better
support than Ezek. 31:4 and Ps. 42:6. (It cannot mean here "primeval flood," or
"sea," "rivers," since neither the one nor the others — in and around Palestine —
ever freeze.)

[37] Cf. *supra*, p. 12.

passage about the sea (vss. 8–11), here becomes explicit. Myths in Job, as in general in the other (poetic) books of the Bible, are literary devices, a stylistic feature betraying the broad education of the author, but hardly constitutive elements of his belief. "Has the rain a father?" The myth says yes; explicitly or implicitly, rain is the semen of the weather god. The Book of Job says no. This no, which is clad in the by now familiar form of a rhetorical question, destroys a world of fancy and coherence which everybody understands and in which he can orient himself,[38] without explicitly substituting another one of comparable serviceability.[39]

Vss. 31–38, not reproduced here, contain final questions about the inanimate world, in particular about various celestial phenomena. Beginning with vs. 39 to the end of the descriptive interrogation (39:30)[40] we find ourselves on the road through the kingdom of animals. Several of its members, from the lion down, pass before our eyes. Each member or group of members represents one side of animal life, and God questions Job about it. First providing food for wild animals; this is demonstrated at the lion.

> Can you hunt the prey for the lion or satisfy the appetite of the lions[41] [40]when they crouch in their dens or lie in wait in the thicket? [41]Who provides his prey 'in the evening'[42] when his whelps roving without food cry to God? (38:39–41).

Man is not wont to give much thought to the food supply of wild animals, but it is a problem all the same. Would Job assume the responsibility of providing food for one of their kind who normally has no difficulty in getting what he needs?

Next comes procreation; the texts speak about mountain goats and deer.

> Do you know when the mountain goats give birth, or do you observe the calving of the hinds? [2]Can you number the months that they fulfil and know the time when they give birth, [3]when they crouch to bring forth their offspring and cast their young? [4]Their kids become strong, grow up in the open, and go forth never to return (39:1–4).

---

[38] Cf. infra, p. 30.

[39] But note that vss. 34 and 37 suggest (different) explanations of the origin of rain.

[40] Cf. n. 26 about 40:15–41:26.

[41] כְּפִירים, another of the several Hebrew words for lion.

[42] The vocalization 'לָעֶרֶב' (cf. 4:10 f.; Ps. 104:20 f.) is preferable to masoretic לָעֹרֵב, commentaries; the raven is quite out of place before 39:26 or rather 39:30. Also, יִתְעוּ is more appropriate as applied to young lions than young ravens, so much so, that many who retain לָעֹרֵב find it necessary to emend the end of the verse.

Here it is not the question of responsibility and care but something less. It is only knowledge, obtained through observation of some phases of animal life. But alas, the animals are too swift for observation, or the phases are too long.

The next paragraph, speaking about the zebra(?),[43] the onager, and the wild ox, concerns the freedom and taming of wild beasts.

> Who has let the zebra go free and who has loosened the onager's bonds [6]to whom I have given the steppe for his home and the salt land for his habitat? [7]He scorns the tumult of the city; he does not hear the driver's shouts. [8]He 'ranges'[44] the mountains as his pasture and searches after every bit of green. [9]Is the wild ox willing to serve you? Will he spend the night at your manger? [10]Does a rope[45] bind the wild ox to the furrow? Will he at your heels plow up the valleys?[46] [11]Can you depend on him for the greatness of his strength and shunt your work upon him? [12]Can you rely on him to return,[47] 'to'[48] your threshing floor[48] bring home your grain? (39:5–12).

"Zebra and onager owe you nothing," says God, "not even their freedom. They are far beyond your ken and completely beyond your reach." Speaking of the wild ox, God continues the line of this argument but gives it a practical turn: "The wild ox could be quite a useful beast with his strength, but you are unable to domesticate him. You know little about the world and can do less about it. You are unable to effect so small a change in the order of the created world as would be the transferral of a wild beast to the category of the tame. It is your will against the will of the beast, yet it is his which prevails."

---

[43] The identification is not certain.

[44] Vocalize 'יְתוּר', commentaries; MT יְתוּר.

[45] Literally "his rope," i. e., the rope which would bind him. But the text of the stich is suspect. רִים, not in the LXX, is perhaps a vertical dittography from vs. 9. If so, the translation is: "Can you bind 'I' his rope (as he plows, or: in order that he plow) in the furrow?" Cf. Tur Sinai, com.

[46] The passage would be consistent with the use of a two-handle plow which requires two plowmen, one handling the plow, the other leading the ox; or, since it is highly unlikely that such plows were used in biblical Palestine (cf. J. Feliks, ההקלאות בארץ ישראל בתקופת המשנה והתלמוד [1963], p. 29), it might have reference to the custom of drawing border furrows which require two plowmen irrespective of the type of plow (cf. Fohrer, com., after Guthe); or to a special plowing, before or after the main plowing, similarly requiring two men, which may be the intention of יְשַׂדֵּד (cf. Isa. 28:24; and see the comment of Feliks, supported by rabbinic passages, ibid., pp. 37 f.; "to harrow" is wrong).

[47] The ketiv ישוב is adopted; the qere is יָשִׁיב.

[48] Read 'וְזַרְעֲךָ נָרְנְךָ', commentaries ('and' is not expressed in the translation); MT וְזַרְעֲךָ וְנָרְנְךָ. The word זָרַע assumes the extended meaning "(seed grain >) grain = harvest."

The rest of the road through the animal kingdom (39:13–30), passing in succession the ostrich (vss. 13–18), the horse (vss. 19–25), and the hawk and the vulture[49] (vss. 26–30), need not be traversed here. The form of a string of (rhetorical) questions is preserved throughout. At the end of the journey God looks back as He draws the sum of His questioning. The beginning of the concluding section of His speech (40:2, 8–14)[50] is transitional in form in that it continues, in vss. 2, 8 f., the rhetorical questions of chaps. 38 f.; but they are no longer questions about the world.

> Will the reprover enter suit against Shaddai? Let him who admonishes God give answer. [8]Will you really nullify My judgment, put Me in the wrong so that you may be vindicated? [9]Or is it that you have an arm like God and like Him can thunderously roar? [10]Deck yourself with majesty and dignity, clothe yourself in state and glory. [11]Give free scope to your raging anger. Seeing anyone haughty, bring him low; [12]seeing anyone haughty, abase him and tread down the wicked in their tracks. [13]Conceal them alike in the earth, wrap their faces in concealment. [14]Then I, too, will acknowledge that your right hand is all-prevailing (40:2, 8–14).

"Will the reprover enter suit?" The reprover, of course, is Job, and reproof is exactly what he administered to the Deity throughout the disputation. These words of reproof were the overflow of an embittered soul; but is he really prepared to enter into litigation with Him? "Let him who admonishes God give answer. Yes or no? Do you now, having failed to answer even one of My questions about the world, yet desire to contend with Me? (40:2). Would you nullify My judgment so that you may be vindicated? Is this an issue which concerns your person alone? Are you so wrapped up in yourself as to be closed to all else? Or would you now perhaps admit the possible existence and validity of standards of which you had not dreamed or the possible nonexistence or invalidity of standards in which you have believed or

---

[49] The identification of נֶשֶׁר, "vulture" or/and "eagle," is not settled; cf. G. R. Driver, *PEQ* 86 f. (1955), pp. 9 f.; 90 (1958), pp. 56 f.; M. Dor, לשוננו 27 f. (1963 f.), pp. 290–92; Z. Ben Hayim, *ibid.*, pp. 293 f.; (חשכ'נ השכ'ר) העברית ללשון האקדמיה זיכרונות, 1965, pp. 222–30.

[50] The critical omission of a number of verses and the rearrangement of the remaining ones, which also affects Job's answer, represent the opinion of the scholars named by Kuhl 1953, p. 269; it is convincingly argued by Fohrer, com., pp. 37–39. But again (cf. n. 26), the meaning of this part of Job and thereby of the whole book does not depend on the critical surgery performed on the text here. The transmitted text as well as a number of different critical rearrangements are all compatible with the interpretation offered here.

which you have taken for granted? (40:8). Have you any of the divine
attributes required to govern the world? (40:9. At this juncture it is
might, not knowledge, which Job would have to possess for the task
but does not.) If you have, don the robes of office, take up the scepter
(40:10). Then, having dressed for the part, begin your rule: put the
wicked in their place! (40:13). Do that, and I will recognize your
potency" (40:14). The issue is now clearly drawn. Does Job have the
power? Will he pick up the gauntlet?

It is precisely at this point, no earlier, no later, that Job must
respond. This structural requirement is one of the reasons for the
critical rearrangement of the text. Job's answer, however, is more
than an indispensable element of the literary structure. It is the
outgrowth of the peculiar form that the problem of the suffering of
the innocent takes on in the book: the narration of the experience of a
particular person.[51] The reader of this narration who has seen Job as
more than a spokesman for a philosophical viewpoint, who has involved himself in the person of Job throughout the long, heart-rending
disputation, must ask at its end: "Has the revelation of God in and
of itself had any effect on Job? And if so, what? How does Job see
himself and his problem now that God Himself has spoken? In other
biblical revelations nothing is the same after the event; God calls and
man responds. Is Job a biblical book in this dialogical sense of God's
call and man's response? Is Job after the revelation a wiser, better
man?" The answer to these questions lies in Job's last words, in the
fact that he spoke at all, and in what it was he said.

> Then Job answered the Lord:[52] 4I am indeed of small account;
> what shall I answer You? I lay my hand on my mouth. 5I have
> spoken once but will not 'do so again,'[53] twice indeed, but will
> say no more. 42:2I know that You can do everything, that nothing
> You purpose is impossible for You. 3bVerily,[54] I made pronounce-
> ments but understood not, about things too wondrous for me,
> beyond my ken. 5From hearsay I had heard of You, but now

---

[51] There is a view recorded in the Talmud (not, however, unopposed) that Job
was not a historical personage (Bava Bathra 14b and parallels). My own opinion
is that the understanding of the book as fiction should not be accepted except in the
narrow sense that events did not happen exactly as told. The book is too close to
human experience to be taken as a total invention. In any case, the intensity of direct
involvement shines through the haze rising out of the questions of historical
literalness.

[52] On the arrangement of the text, cf. n. 50.

[53] Read 'אֶשְׁנֶה', commentaries, literal translation " 'do it twice' "; MT אֶעֱנֶה.

[54] לָכֵן as in Gen. 4:15; 30:15; I Sam. 28:2. F. J. Goldbaum, JNES 23 (1964),
pp. 132–34, sweepingly generalizes a special application of the word, viz., the introduction of a vow.

my eye sees You. ⁶Therefore I retract[55] and repent in dust and ashes (40:3–5; 42:2, 3b, 5, 6).

The talk is coming to its end. Toward the conclusion of His address (40:2) God has called upon Job to answer. But this Job declines to do: "I cannot. I can no longer carry on. I am too light" (קַלֹּתִי; RSV: "I am of small account," which is a paraphrase). The root קלל is antonymous to כבד which yields the noun כָּבוֹד "weight, value, substance, essence of personality."[56] Biblical man's כָּבוֹד was most precious to him; take away his כָּבוֹד and you deprive him of his better part. Job concerned himself with כָּבוֹד on two separate occasions in the earlier parts of the book (19:9; 29:20). But when God now asks him about the world and invites him to perform certain acts, Job who has no answer and is unable to meet the challenge disclaims all כָּבוֹד and says קַלֹּתִי. His position has crumbled, he cannot stand up and gird his loins like a man, he brings the disputation to a halt, he "will say no more" (40:4 f.). But if he does not know the answers to God's specific questions about the world, he has gained knowledge about God and thus indirectly about the world in general. God began His speech with the rhetorical question intending Job: "Just who darkens the plan by words without knowledge?" (38:2). God made and is upholding the world according to His plan, but Job misinterpreted it in his words, i. e., according to the light of his own conceptions. Now Job has become wiser. He sees that nothing God purposes is impossible — either of conception or of execution (42:2). Repudiation of his former position is now for Job both a necessary logical and existential consequence (42:3b).

Job's misinterpretation of God and the world was due to his conceptions which were by and large those of Israelite tradition. His argument with the friends rested on this ground common to all of them, and their disagreement was about secondary features and particularly had regard to the application of the philosophy of tradition to his fate. Tradition, the text calls it שֵׁמַע אֹזֶן,[57] was immensely important in ancient Israel. When it was tradition of religious doctrines,

---

⁵⁵ Cf. L. J. Kuyper, VT 9 (1959), pp. 91–94.

⁵⁶ כָּבוֹד as a social concept is "honor." "Die Ehre ist, objektiv, die Meinung Anderer von unserm Wert, und subjektiv, unsere Furcht vor dieser Meinung" (A. Schopenhauer, Parerga und Paralipomena, "Aphorismen zur Lebensweisheit," ch. 4. [Sämtliche Werke, vol. 4, Leipzig, Inselverlag, Grossherzog Wilhelm Ernst Ausgabe, no date, p. 426]).

⁵⁷ Words for hearing, asking, telling, remembering, and the like express the concept of tradition in biblical Hebrew; e. g., II Sam. 7:22; Ps. 44:2; 78:3 f.; Deut. 4:32; 32:7; Job 8:8, 10; Exod. 13:8, 14; Judg. 6:13; Ps. 77:6 f.

and when these doctrines were combined into a comparatively consistent whole, we speak of traditional theology. There is no part in
the Old Testament which represents the most common variety of
traditional theology better than the talk of Job and the friends. But
let us remember that insofar as Israelite tradition was biblical it was
given to eruptions, notably at the appearance of God. Job's experience
of divine revelation has raised him above the hearsay of tradition; he
has "seen" God. This "seeing" is not, to be sure, mere sensory perception by the eye but a personal meeting. And this meeting means for
man that he has achieved the closest contact with the Deity and is
now among His most faithful and intimate ones. Job had desired confrontation with God; he has received much more: communion. Be it
clear, however, that this communion is not mystical oneness of man
and God; "Gott bleibt Gott, Mensch bleibt Mensch."[58] It is the
closest possible meeting of two personalities which remain distinct.

The communion of Job with God resembles the communion of the
prophets with the Divine. As such it has important consequences for
the understanding of the book, consequences in regard to which I find
myself in disagreement with Fohrer despite the fact that he, too,
recognizes the similarity of the experience of Job and that of the
prophets.[59] The prophets are taken into God's counsel. "God does
nothing without revealing His counsel to His servants the prophets,"
says Amos (3:7). God deliberates with Amos (7:1–9; 8:3), with Isaiah
(6:8–13), and others as He deliberated aforetime with Abraham
(Gen. 18:17–21, 23–33) and Moses (Exod. 32–34). Not only is the
intellectual element characteristically present in their communion
with God, the communion involves: usually the understanding of,
often the approval of, sometimes an active sharing in His plan. Job's
communion with God is not bought with an intellectual sacrifice, at
the cost of renouncing his wish to understand the constitution of the
world. True, of its creation, its expanse, its details — of animal life
and of all the other things — he has no more knowledge now than he
had before. But he now has gained an insight into its constitution,
even as the prophets were granted new understanding in the communion with God (42:5).

"Therefore I retract and repent in dust and ashes." These are
Job's final words. Outwardly nothing has changed for him. He is
still sitting in the dirt: "He took a potsherd with which to scrape
himself and sat in the ashes" (2:8). The ashes are the same, but it is
a changed man who is sitting in them.

[58] Fohrer, com., p. 535, n. 6.
[59] Fohrer, com., p. 53

What has changed him? The revelation — by which we mean two things: the fact of the revelation itself and its content; and it is this content that is the answer to the problem of the work, the meaning of the Book of Job. The question is, however, just what is the answer, what is God's reply?

A review of a few interpretations is in order before I offer my own interpretation. The criteria governing the selection are durability, newness, or the importance of the interpretations.

The interpretation that probably enjoys the greatest popularity is the one that might be labelled "education through overwhelming." Job is shown the immensity, complexity, and mystery of the universe; these greatly exceed his comprehension. For all this he can and does relate himself to this stupendous world by recognizing in it its creator, ruler, and sustainer. God is not only infinitely mightier but also wiser than he. God's is that inscrutable business, the government of the world. While man thinks only of his own needs and problems, God sustains a whole world, providing for all His creatures. As Job is made aware of the world's material and spiritual dimensions — dimensions forever beyond his grasp — he is reduced to submission. The long catalog of the complexities and wonders of the universe, culminating in the evidence of the providential care for the animals, seems to bear out this interpretation; but its faults are so fatal — and glaring at that — that the fact of its wide acceptance must in itself be regarded as a problem in the history of the interpretation of the book. Job has never doubted God's power or wisdom. He has, in fact, repeatedly spoken of them, albeit mostly with bitterness because of God's capricious misuse of His superior might and wisdom to thwart justice (see, for instance, chaps. 9 and 12). Although the complexities of the governance of the world have not been Job's concern, we are given no reason to doubt his readiness to recognize them. They are not, however, the issue, nor is God's ability to keep things going. The issue is: Why do I suffer? Why do the righteous suffer?[60]

Distantly related to this interpretation is the one given by M. Buber,[61] with which can loosely be associated that of G. von Rad.[62] Buber does not fail to see that the problem is not the dimensions and

---

[60] It would be altogether consistent with the interpretation under scrutiny to make God answer this question with the counterquestion: "Are things not complicated enough the way they are now? Why do you want to make them more difficult with your question?"

[61] *The Prophetic Faith* (1949), pp. 194 f.; in the German original, *Werke*, vol. 2 (1964), pp. 441 f.

[62] *Theologie des A. T.*, vol. 1 (1957), pp. 414 f.

mysteries of the universe and that parading its complexities will not provide the answer. He sees that the problem is justice. But when it comes to the answer, Buber would have us believe that the answer is as follows: God teaches Job that divine justice, to be exact, the justice of God which is manifest in creation, is greater than human justice; that it is not retributory and egalitarian but allotting, spending, freely flowing; that God gives each creature that which is appropriate, *suum cuique*. But this is no answer at all. For Job's question remains: Is it "appropriate" for the innocent to suffer and for the wicked to prosper? God's allotment of fates is not the issue; this Job has never doubted. What the issue does concern is the fate of the individual, its why and wherefore. What is the reason for God's not shaping this fate in accordance with the standards that He himself has set? In other words, not the *cuique* is the question but the *suum*. But what is particularly disturbing in Buber's interpretation is the very application of the term justice to God's generosity (a generosity which would here consist of a liberal allotment of suffering to the righteous). Nothing is gained by such assignment of private meanings to terms which in ordinary and universal usage — the Book of Job not excepted — denote the opposite.

Robert Gordis has another interpretation, whose essence may be stated in his own words. "Nature is . . . a cosmos, a thing of beauty . . . Just as there is order and harmony in the natural world . . . so there is order and meaning in the moral sphere . . . When man steeps himself in the beauty of the world his troubles . . . dissolve within the larger plan . . . The beauty of the world becomes an anodyne to man's suffering — and the key to truth . . . and it is before this truth that he [Job] yields."[63] The operative words in the above argument are ". . . beauty becomes an anodyne to man's suffering — and the key to truth." If the question is justice, would anyone propose that the demands of justice are met by the administering of an anesthesia to the victim of an unjust sentence? And if the question is pain and torture, the beauty surrounding the tortured may in its contrast intensify the pain. It was just Bialik's sensitivity to the beauty in nature that indeed led him to write in בעיר ההרגה, a poem about the pogrom of Kishinev in 1903:

כִּי קָרָא אֲדֹנָי לָאָבִיב וְלַטֶּבַח גַּם־יָחַד:
הַשֶּׁמֶשׁ זָרְחָה, הַשִּׁטָּה פָּרְחָה, וְהַשּׁוֹחֵט שָׁחַט.[64]

---

[63] In *Great Moral Dilemmas in Literature* . . ., R. M. MacIver ed. (1956), pp. 177 f.; *Judaism* 13 (1964), pp. 48–63. The quotation is from *Judaism*, pp. 62 f.

[64]   "The Lord called forth spring and killing at once:
             The sun shone, the locust bloomed, and the butcher
             butchered" (lines 21 f.)

Moreover, one cannot fail to observe that Gordis does not distinguish between the reality and an artistic description of it. Thus the reader of chs. 38 f. admires the beauty of the description of the world, not the beauty of the world itself. The sea pictured as a baby just breaking forth from the womb and instantly wrapped in swaddling clothes, the fogs which lie on the surface of the waters, as in the words of 38:8–11, is art. The imagery is unquestionably beautiful, but is the sea beautiful? One may be impressed by the creation of the poet, yet not by the sea, which one may never even have seen. If the distinction is made between reality and literature, Gordis's interpretation becomes untenable.[65]

The last interpretation to be examined, that of G. Fohrer, actually attacks the question of the problem itself.[66] The problem of the book, says Fohrer, is not: Why does the righteous man suffer? but: What is the proper conduct of man in suffering? It does not concern theodicy but man's life and his conduct. The question of theodicy is not even raised, for it is one which cannot be answered. From this it follows that the answer of the Book of Job cannot be found in the address of God but only in the final reply of Job. "In der vorbehaltlosen Hingabe an Gott und in der persönlichen Gemeinschaft mit ihm trägt und erträgt Hiob sein Geschick . . . Hiob wird in das grosse Leben und Leiden der Welt eingegliedert, zugleich aber durch die Gemeinschaft mit dem göttlichen Urgrund der Welt herausgehoben. Das ist das rechte Verstehen des Leides und das rechte Verhalten des Menschen in ihm: demütiges und hingebungsvolles Schweigen aus dem Ruhen in Gott . . ."[67]

---

[65] The counterargument may be raised that both Job and the sea of ch. 38 are creations of the author -- poetic, philosophical, and mythological — which exist only in the realm of ideas, and that it is, therefore, erroneous to raise the objection of the confusion of reality and literature. This argument, however, assumes that the intention of the author is to describe the sea as a thing of beauty and to impress Job by this beauty; in so doing it arranges Job, the sea, and the beauty of the sea on the same plane. This is surprising. Not the beauty of the world but its greatness, incomprehensibility, and the like are what readers have so far seen as the intention of the author's description. That the intention is primarily to the beauty of the world, and that this beauty is the essential element in the description is something which Gordis assumes but does not demonstrate.

[66] *ThZ* 18 (1962), pp. 1–24; com., pp. 532, 536, 557–59; cf. the opinions referred to on pp. 557 f., n. 21.

[67] Fohrer, com., p. 558. S. Terrien denies with Fohrer that the main theme of the book is the suffering of the innocent, the problem of theodicy; cf. his contribution to *The Interpreter's Bible*, vol. 3 (1954), pp. 877–1198, particularly pp. 897, 902; and his *Job* (*Commentaire de l'A. T.* 13; 1963), particularly pp. 35 f., 45–49. Terrien differs from Fohrer in that he refuses to deconceptualize the essence of the book as

My earlier remarks indicate how far I am able to go along with
Fohrer.[68] Job's reply and the way he replies are essential to the book.
The book is more than the exposition of a concept; it is the life story
of a man,[69] written with his life blood. The end of the story, his reply
to the divine questioning, is indispensable for without it the beginning
and the middle are without justification. It completes the confrontation and complements the revelation. The fault of Fohrer's interpretation, as I see it, lies in its exclusiveness, i. e., in refusing to see in the
Book of Job a theoretical treatise. It is my view that while it is not
only a theoretical treatise, it is certainly that, and basically that. My
criticism of those scholars who, disregarding the content of God's
speech, restrict the answer of the book to the fact of the revelation,[70]
also applies, in some measure, to Fohrer. Indeed, man's conduct in
suffering may not exist even as a secondary theme.[71] But be that as
it may, the primary theme is the suffering of the innocent. For the
overwhelming majority of readers and commentators this is, and
always has been, the problem of the book.[72]

---

radically and systematically as does Fohrer. But this difference seems, at times, to
be only one of degree. In a context which only slightly mitigates the boldness of his
statement he says: Man "transgresse les limites de son humanité chaque fois qu'il
prononce un jugement sur le caractère de la divinité" (*Job*, p. 45). Cf. also Rowley,
pp. 176, 183.

[68] Cf. *supra*, pp. 18 f.

[69] Cf. *supra*, p. 18.

[70] Cf. *supra*, pp. 9 f.

[71] It would be wrong to posit that in presenting Job's communion with God and
his retraction the book sees a normative model for man's conduct in suffering.

[72] At this juncture it may be remarked that the epilogue, which could be expected
to be relevant to the answer of the book, fails notably to offer confirmation of any
of the foregoing interpretations or any other interpretation known to me. The epilogue
vindicates Job in general but also explicitly in relation to the friends: "After having
spoken these words to Job, the Lord said to Eliphaz, the Temanite: 'My wrath is
kindled against you and your two friends, for you have not spoken of Me what is
right as has My servant Job' " (vs. 7). It is in this verse and in some of the following
that the author takes the occasion, the only time in the entire work, to state explicitly
his opinion of the friends and their philosophy and to sum up his evaluation of Job
and his philosophy and conduct. But he does not even begin to explain why that
which Job has spoken of God — as compared with that which the friends have —
is right. (דִּבֶּר אֶל with the rare meaning "to speak of, concerning" [cf. I Sam. 3:12]
is a case of the otherwise frequent interchange of אֶל and עַל; the standard phrase
with this meaning is דִּבֶּר עַל.) Of even greater moment is the fact that he does not in
any way relate the epilogue's vindication of Job to what must be regarded as absolutely true, namely, the divine answer. This may be accounted for in terms of the
literary prehistory of the book (if the hypothesis is accepted that the author used an
existing prose frame and adapted it imperfectly) or of the genre and purpose of the
prose epilogue (i. e., the narrative hurries to the eventful end and seeks to avoid

In a text of such demonstrated difficulty as is the speech of God (witness the numerous contradictory interpretations) the meaning often eludes a verse-to-verse approach. We shall, therefore, have recourse to another approach: first, we shall derive the answer to the problem of the book from its total conceptual content; second, seek the verification of the answer in the text of the divine address; third, apply two controls to the answer, one external to the address, the other to the book.

Job and his friends, worlds apart in many respects, share one belief; the acrimoniousness of their disputation and its minute details are due to this shared premise: the world is founded on justice, i. e., *quid pro quo*, reward and punishment, which will hereinafter be referred to as the principle of retribution. This principle pervades the world. Job and the friends hold fast to this belief because they have been raised in it; because everybody has it; because man has an intense need to abide by it. The need is so great that he goes to the remotest extremes to uphold it. When reality does not agree with the principle of retribution, whose function is to structure and interpret reality, so much the worse for reality. Man distorts his experience of reality, disregards facts, imagines figments, fashions *ad hoc* theories, and erects superstructures, all so as not to give up or substantially change the principle. A parade example of this phenomenon is the discussion of Job and the friends. What accounts for this phenomenon? The fact that this principle of retribution is the touchstone of man's life and his conduct within his society. Whether in the rearing of children or

---

retarding complications). Whatever the reason, the reader may regret that the author is not more helpful in his last verses.

A characteristically modern approach deplores the very existence of the epilogue coming, as it does, after the heights of the poetry achieved in the final chapters. Admitting the literary requirement of a complete narrative frame, beginning and end, and even the desirability of the idyllic tones of the finale, a number of readers yet regard this finale as anticlimatic (cf. Kuhl 1953, pp. 204 f.; Rowley, pp. 159 f.). This approach elicits two comments. One, it cannot be assumed as a matter of course that the ancient Israelite would have been disturbed by this anticlimax in the same manner as the contemporary Westerner reared on the canons of Greek literary style and theory. The Israelite may indeed have welcomed it with relief. Secondly, the epilogue provides the needed resolution of the plot. Job was afflicted with physical ailments and social ostracism and suffered spiritual torments. He was freed of the last of these afflictions in the final chapters of the poetry; the physical and social penalties remain. The problem of the book, which is spiritual, is solved, and Job is vindicated -- as will be shown -- before the epilogue. But he remains in his physical pain and in social disgrace. His pain was a necessary device in the drama of ideas. This drama now over and pain having played out its role, that pain should be removed. The epilogue does just this.

the administration of justice, it is this principle which guides him. From it flow some of his noblest deeds. And so it is natural that God is conceived as guaranteeing it in the governance of the world.

But give up the principle, reject causality in the physical-ethical world, and the problem of Job, the man and the book, disappears. Where justice is possible, injustice is, too. Where it is not, where the principle of retribution has no validity, there can be no injustice. In the absence of this principle, for Job to expect a lot corresponding morally with his deed is absurd. Where there is no ground for expecting anything, it is pointless for him to complain of his disappointment: that though he has been pious and upright his lot is bitter. Nor is there any point to the inference drawn by the friends from Job's lot to his conduct. To repeat: only the awareness that the world of ideas, unlike the world of matter, is not governed by the category of cause and effect, i. e., only the elimination of the principle of retribution, can solve the problem of the book.

This is the inescapable conclusion from the conceptual content of the book and an analysis of its problem. Its verification must be sought in God's address. God says to Job: "You were not present when the universe was created. You do not know its blueprint or the stuff that went into its making." No less than three times God refers to the "foundation," "the basis," and "the cornerstone" of the inhabited world, the earth (38:4, 6). "What, then, makes you assume that it is justice which is its foundation?" "Moreover," God continues, "you do not know the mundane phenomena of the natural world." And He draws progressively tighter circles around Job, proceeding in order of diminishing expanse from the realm of heaven and the underworld to that of those wild beasts which Job, for all his desire, cannot domesticate. Arriving at what is most familiar to Job, He finally asks: "Perhaps, at least, you know your own homestead?" No answer. "If, then, you know nothing and can do nothing, why ever should you assume that retribution, justice (צֶדֶק) is a constituent element in the plan (עֵצָה [38:2], מְזִמָּה [42:2]) of the world?" (38:2). Thus God leads Job through the macrocosm and microcosm, but nowhere does Job see justice. From the linguistic approach, it is striking that √צדק and other roots which express the idea of justice, viz. √ישר and √תמם, while moderately frequent in chs. 1–31,[73] are not found at all in the story of Job's journey through the world.[74]

---

[73] The Elihu chapters (32–37) are disregarded; cf. n. 17.

[74] √צדק occurs 19 times, √ישר 7 times, √תמם 16 times. √צדק, with the legal meaning "to be vindicated," occurs in 40:8 after the journey through the world;

And, let us note, the centrality of the idea of justice in the book and the broadness of the canvas on which the universe is painted preclude the deprecation of this observation as an argument from silence.

But we are not left with negative argumentation alone. The divine address contains some passages that have not, it seems to me, received due attention in the commentaries. It is striking that the description of the inanimate world, comprising almost all of chapter 38, is interrupted by an evaluative and teleological proposition centering on man: "Have you ever in your life commanded the morning, have you directed the dawn to its place ¹³to take hold of the skirts of the earth so that the wicked are shaken out of it, ¹⁵so that light is withheld from the wicked, and their uplifted arm is broken?" (38:12 f., 15). This can mean one thing only: there is no provision for retribution, nor any manifestation of it in the order of the world. The dawn of every day provides an occasion to punish the wicked, but this possibility is not in practice realized and is therefore not in the plan of the world. "Consider this fundamental fact," Job is told: "The sun rises over the righteous and the sinners alike. Can you change that?"

The end of God's speech is similar in meaning. Here is an excerpt: "Will the reprover enter suit against Shaddai? ⁸Will you put Me in the wrong so that you may be vindicated? ⁹Or is it that you have an arm like God? ¹²Seeing anyone haughty, abase him and tread down the wicked in their tracks. ¹⁴Then I, too, will acknowledge that your right hand is all-prevailing" (40:2, 8–14). Everything is rhetorical or hypothetical. God and Job know that he cannot possibly do these things: it is not in the plan, not in the plan for the wicked to be punished. If Job were able to perform these things, his criticism of God would be justified, not only by the demonstration of his own prowess but, more important, by the demonstration that retribution is at least potentially operative in the world and need only be actualized. Failing a demonstration of this ability, the assumption of punishment of the wicked and reward of the righteous is without ground, and Job has no right to blame God.

The third passage I shall cite is the least conspicuous but the most interesting: "Who has cleft a channel for the rain flood and a way for the thunder cloud ²⁶to cause rain on land where no man is, on a desert where no people live ²⁷to satiate waste and desolate terrain and to sprout fresh grass?" (38:25–27). As God describes the meteorological phenomena, he is implying: "Consider this, Job: precious rain, that

---

the occurrence is therefore not counted. √חםם in 31:40 means "to finish," and this passage is also not counted.

would be so beneficial to human beings, is wasted on land uninhabited and uninhabitable. In the natural world, where the category of cause and effect is operative, man is not as central as you fancy." This is, in effect, God's polemic with Job. It is, by the same token, the author's polemic with the point of view found in the rest of the Bible, for Job represents the general biblical point of view. Rain, in the Bible, figures prominently as a vehicle of reward and punishment. It is given for good deeds and withheld for evil ones. Here, however, the phenomenon is shown not to be a vehicle of morality at all — the moral purpose ascribed to it just does not exist. (Be it noted that the text does not state that the rain falls partly on the desert and partly on the sown. The point is that it falls on the desert where it has no relevance for man.)

God says: "No retribution is provided for in the blueprint of the world, nor does it exist anywhere in it. None is planned for the non-human world and none for the human world. Divine justice is not an element of reality. It is a figment existing only in the misguided philosophy with which you have been inculcated. The world in which you and the friends are spun is a dream. Wake up, Job!" And wake up is what Job does at the end.

Let us now adduce controls for our thesis. One control, whose substance is acknowledged by all, yet whose significance in the total picture is commonly ignored, is the knowledge that we, the readers of the prologue, possess — we know that Job did not suffer in retribution for what he had done. We know that his presuppositions were wrong in part and those of the friends in toto; that their discussion, earnest though it was, was largely out of touch with reality. The Book of Job is, from the first chapter, the classical statement that a man's lot is not the consequence of his deeds. The prologue, for one thing, shows that in the one exemplary case with which it is concerned, divine justice, retribution, does not enter into the heavenly considerations. Against this reading of the whole book in the light of its prologue it may be argued that, our earlier remark notwithstanding,[75] allowance should be made for a narrative feature which exists purely for the sake of the plot and is probably not intended to have a bearing on the ideas of the book. The argument, however, while legitimate in principle, "makes allowance," i. e., it reckons with a literary flaw in a work so artistic as to make such allowance gratuitous. Be that as it may, the innocence of Job is a feature not confined to the narrative of the prologue but one providing the basis of the entire work; without it there is no problem of Job, indeed there is no Book of Job.

[75] Cf. *supra*, pp. 1–3.

The other control is historical and circumstantial. It is stronger than the previous control for being external to the book and weaker because, resting on its date, it is prey to the uncertainties of literary history. Yet for all the difficulty of dating, the overwhelming majority of scholars, for a variety of reasons, dates the Book of Job between the sixth and the fourth centuries B. C. Now that is the very period in which the earlier doctrine of collective retribution (represented, for instance, in the Pentateuch) had lost its sway without yet being replaced by the doctrine of individual retribution in the world-to-come. (From time to time there was attempted an application of the earlier doctrine of retributory justice to the individual rather than to the group. These attempts, notably in wisdom texts *sensu proprio*, remained ephemeral, the doctrine foundering on the rock of reality: the wicked flourish, and the righteous perish.) Now the earlier and the later doctrines have an effective answer to the problem of the suffering of the innocent. The former, the collective answer, operates with a social unit large in the number of its components, the individual Israelites, and extended in time, the people of Israel through the generations. When dealing with a group as large and long-lived as a nation it is possible to work out solutions in accordance with the principle of collective retribution. The latter, the belief of retribution in the other world, admits by definition no difficulties: retribution, deferred to a future life, cannot be contradicted by experience.[76]

Thus it would seem clear that the sixth through the third centuries represented that one period in the history of biblical religion which is not covered, or, at best, very scantily covered, by one or the other form of this idea of divine justice. It is in this period that the problem of the suffering of the innocent is most likely to have been answered in a way other than, hence opposed to, that of divine justice = retribution. And this is the very period to which the Book of Job is commonly dated. It is through the combination of our view, viz., that the solution which the book offers to the problem is the radical denial of the principle of retribution, and the accepted determination of the date of the book that the gap in the history of thought on this problem

---

[76] In the later history of Judaism and in Christianity these religions continued to experiment with various combinations of the forms of retribution — individual, collective, and otherworldly. Enjoying the shelter of flexible retributory creeds, they have not been troubled by the problem central to the book in a measure at all commensurable with the concern of modern readers who find themselves unable to accept the theological shelter which ideological versatility makes possible for these religions. Hence it is that in modern times, when nontraditional religiosity has come to the fore, the Book of Job figures so much more prominently than was the case hitherto either in the thinking or the liturgy of Judaism and Christianity.

is neatly filled. At some time during the sixth through the third centuries a book was written which said to man: Neither hope for reward for good deeds nor fear punishment for evil deeds; moralists cannot shake the wicked from the surface of the earth and God will not. The laws of the natural order and those of the moral order are not of a piece. If you decide to do what is good, do it because it is good.

Let us now, laying aside our concern for checking conclusions, extend our consideration of the adventure of ideas beyond the biblical period. The Book of Job continues the intellectual and religious enterprise, begun in the earlier books of the Bible, of emptying the world of much that had been put into it during the preceding millennia by human fantasy operating to satisfy human concerns. These books demythologized the world.[77] The Book of Job, in this respect, does not lag behind any of them. It features, as has been observed before, an abundance of images from the then current myths but does not fail to provide its own understanding of them:[78] the world is not as the myths would have it. If, therefore, the myths do not describe reality, their appearance or allusions to them in the book is a matter of literary style and artistic convention somewhat in the manner of the tropes and mythological figures in the libretti of Metastasio.

But the Book of Job does more than demythologize the world; it also "de-moralizes" it, which is to say, makes it amoral. It completes the process whose first phase is known to the reader of the Bible from the opening pages of Genesis: the removal from the conceptual world of an order of superhuman beings independent of the Deity. And it extends it by the denial of the realization of moral values — values deriving from the Deity, to be sure — other than realization effected by man. This new world is as harsh as it is simple, for in it man is deprived of the protection he enjoyed in a world saturated with myth and morality and populated with powers to which he might turn with a view to rendering them favorable to his well-being, foremost by his leading of a meritorious life.

The number of alternative explanations offered for the meaning of the Book of Job confronts each interpreter with the question: If what you say is right, why does the book not say so in so many words? An easy answer is that the dramatic and poetic nature of such a work, containing layer upon layer of depth and hinting at yet others, precludes a plain and direct proposition. The interpretation offered here

[77] "Myth" and its derivatives are used here in the narrow sense, referring to identifiable myths of the ancient Near East, their cognates, and their possible reflexes in Israel.

[78] Cf. the remarks to 38:8–11, 28 f., *supra*, pp. 12, 15.

suggests an additional answer, which might be adduced in support of the interpretation: the very radicalism of the book's answer, shattering a central biblical doctrine and a belief cherished in ancient Israel, would itself demand the protection of a veil. The book is, to be sure, uniquely daring in many other respects and according to any interpretation: the pronouncements of Job against God, agonized and agonizing, must have evoked a shudder in the biblical audience. Yet these outbursts do not constitute a new and radical doctrine; they can be passed off as cries of a man in pain. But the answer of God, presenting a doctrine as radical as it is new, a doctrine in diametrical opposition to the teaching of tradition, may never have been tolerated or preserved for us but for the protection of its form, its eschewal of the direct, categorical pronouncement.

If we look once more at the structure of the work, the unity of frame and colloquy, whether primary or secondary,[79] now appears in a brighter light. Two questions were posed in the prologue; one, What is piety? the other, Is there piety?[80] We had some reason to answer the second question in the affirmative. The final chapters strengthen the affirmation: it is to Job, the man who, above all other men, exemplifies piety (1:8), that God reveals Himself. In this context, revelation connotes more than relativity and rank ("there is none as pious as he") denote; it constitutes, in effect, the affirmation by God that Job is pious. Our main interest, however, is in the first question, the essential feature of whose answer was put forward in the prologue without equivocation: piety, whatever its other attributes, must be disinterested. Egoistically motivated connection between the religio-moral and the natural worlds, common since the beginning of the history of the human kind and evident in many parts of the Bible, is forever precluded by this unequivocal answer of the prologue; for to make this connection is to deprive attitude, behavior, or action of the dignity of piety. God's answer, however, goes a step further. It severs any causal connection, hitherto assumed in the world at large and prominent everywhere in the Bible, between these two worlds; a person's fate is dissociated from, and unrelated to, his religio-moral attitude or actions. The prologue says that one ought not to, the divine address says that one cannot, expect anything for one's behavior.[81] Job behaved piously throughout, but his behavior had, in the

---

[79] Cf. n. 2.   [80] Cf. *supra*, p. 2.

[81] This generalization has two aspects. (1) The prologue, to be sure, deals only with reward, the expected result of pious behavior, and not with punishment; only the discourse extends the doctrine to include punishment (4:7-11; and elsewhere). (2) Strictly speaking, the prologue does not say that man ought to expect nothing

narrated time[82] of 1:13–31:40, no consequences compatible with the accepted idea of reward and punishment; yet he most ardently hoped for these consequences and was utterly shaken when his hopes were not realized. God tells him in chaps. 38–40 that these consequences nowhere and never follow, and that it is, therefore, futile to hope for them. In his final reply (40:3–5; 42:2 f., 5 f.) Job acknowledges this fact and thus, free of misconception, is now prepared for a pious and moral life uncluttered by false hopes and unfounded claims. To resort to a simile: the unity of the book may be likened to a switchback traversing rugged territory yet ever maintaining the general direction toward the goal; on a lower bend, the answer of the prologue — on an upper bend, the divine answer.

The Book of Job, a supreme expression of religious faith, presents the purest moral theory in the Bible. Now it would be a grave error to interpret its denial of divine retribution as constituting a legitimate excuse for man from his obligations to establish justice on earth. Justice is not woven into the stuff of the universe nor is God occupied with its administration but it is an ideal to be realized by society and in it. As to God Himself, while the book does not say so explicitly, it does not exclude the possibility of God's obligating Himself to abide by human standards in regard to specific occasions and contexts. Thus God, while often the author of the standards for human conduct, is Himself bound by them only in exceptional cases.

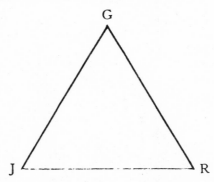

Let us imagine an equilateral triangle, at the three vertexes of which we have *G* standing for God Who turns His face to man and is

---

for his behavior; it says only that his behavior ought to be independent of the fulfillment or nonfulfillment of his expectations. The generalization is nonetheless, in my opinion, unobjectionable. The prologue is a narrative which singles out parts which characterize the whole and does not constitute a discursive, comprehensive treatment of the whole.

[82] Cf. M. Weiss, *Biblica* 46 (1965), p. 182.

accessible to him, *J* for Job, the upright man, and *R* for the philosophy of retribution or justice in the world. The Book of Job, then, tells of an attempt to maintain these ideas simultaneously — an attempt which ends in failure. It is the purpose of the book to demonstrate the impossibility of the coexistence of these three ideas and the consequent logical necessity to give up one of them. The friends cancel *J*, maintaining *G* and *R*. God eliminates *R*, maintaining *G* and *J*. Job all but gives up *G*, as he maintains *J* and *R*. Now it is the limiting phrase "all but" that makes a religious book of what would otherwise have been merely a theological treatise. It epitomizes Job's struggle with himself and with God. He knew in his bones that he was just. At the same time he shared the concept of his age that it is the business of God to maintain the category of cause and effect in the moral as well as in the natural world. Unable to compromise the fact of his innocence or to divest himself of the concept of his age, he distorted perforce the image of God. But this distortion accomplished nothing; he yet felt that he was wrong, he hoped and, for moments, even held the conviction that God had His face turned toward him, if not with favor then at least with interest, that God would one day "long for" him (14:15). He wanted therefore to "come" to God (23:3), to "see" Him, i. e., His true image (19:26 f.). In his unflagging but futile attempt to interpret the vicious triangle he became ever more enmeshed in contradictions. He maintained *J* and *R* and despaired of, yet did not surrender, *G*. At times observation of reality led him nonetheless to the conclusion that *R* was wrong, i. e., that the world is not governed by justice. At these moments he came close to one aspect of God's position. Yet only close: he could only conceive of the dichotomy justice/injustice, until God showed him that this dichotomy is not adequate for the structuring of reality, for it lacks the third required element: nonjustice. These three elements should indeed be grouped in a dichotomy, but in the form: justice-injustice/nonjustice. The left side of the dichotomy, justice-injustice, is societal, the right one, nonjustice, is extrasocietal. The error of Job and the friends lay in this that they permitted the societal aspect of the dichotomy to encroach on the extrasocietal one. This is the error of *R*. But once the error is recognized, *R* is eliminated, *G* and *J* remain — this is God's answer. Job accepts the answer. Unencumbered now by the old doctrine of justice and retribution, he receives confirmation of his former hope that God does turn His face to man, that He is accessible to him — confirmation provided by the theophany. To put it differently: He Who speaks to man in the Book of Job is neither a just nor an unjust god but God.

Of Job, enmeshed in his contradictions, who at the end recanted everything he had said, God says to the friends: "You have not spoken of Me what is right as has My servant Job" (42:7). The error that Job upheld and was compelled to renounce was yet closer to the truth than the arguments of the friends for all the support of many authorities that these arguments enjoyed. This is the judgment of the book. From the contradictions of Job there is a way to truth, from the consistencies of the friends, none.

Deeper and more beautiful yet are the words of the Midrash (*Pesiqta Rabbati*, ed. M. Friedmann, 190b): אלו לא קרא תגר כשם שאומרים עכשו בתפילה אלהי אברהם אלהי יצחק ואלהי יעקב כך היו אומרים ואלהי איוב. "Had he [Job] not clamored so — as it is now the practice to say in prayer 'God of Abraham, God of Isaac, and God of Jacob,' so one would say 'and God of Job'."

What Does It Profit A Man?: The Wisdom of Koheleth

JAMES G. WILLIAMS

WHAT DOES IT PROFIT A MAN TO EXIST, TO STRIVE, to seek, to achieve? This is a recurring question of Koheleth, and to this question the answer comes through clearly, even to a superficial reader of the Jewish sage: There is *no* profit. Let me state my thesis at the outset: According to Koheleth, there is no profit for man in his existence, but there is, nevertheless, a "portion" (*ḥeleq*), a "share" in the world which cannot be preserved, but simply enjoyed at the right time, as God gives the right time in an inscrutable way.

I

Especially characteristic of Koheleth is his use of traditional wisdom, which he "quotes" (in a broad sense) and employs for his own purposes, sometimes simply to support an argument, sometimes as a text for his own commenatry, sometimes to contrast proverbs as a way of negating accepted doctrines.[1] Also, the question before or after a series of assertions is a rhetorical feature of Koheleth's speech that stamps his style. The question usually calls for a negative answer: no profit, no good, no reward can be expected. All is *hebel.*[2]

These two features of Koheleth's style, his use of traditional wisdom and his rhetorical questions, are among the factors indicating that he was a teacher, probably in Jerusalem in the early Hellenistic period.[3] His orientation is pessimistic-skeptical and his speaking expresses an overwhelming sense of irony concerning the discrepancy between the human appetite to become wise, and the insurpassable limits of human wisdom.

But as Zimmerli has pointed out, most characteristic of Koheleth's speech forms is his preference for speaking in the first person, a "confession style" (*Bekenntnisstil*). Here Koheleth exhibits his departure from the security and self-certainty of the wise.[4] This recourse to personal experience and seeking, the desire to "see," to know for oneself, is the outcome of the life of a man who cannot participate in the whole of things, who is closed off to satisfaction or the full life.

---

1. Robert Gordis, *Koheleth: the Man and His World*, 3d ed. (New York, 1968), pp. 95–108.
2. W. Zimmerli, *Die Weisheit des Predigers Salomo* (Berlin, 1936), p. 24.
3. Cf. Gordis, *op. cit.*, pp. 63–68, 75–86; Elias Bickerman, *Four Strange Books of the Bible* (New York, 1967), pp. 141ff.
4. Zimmerli, *op. cit.*, pp. 26ff.

JAMES G. WILLIAMS *is Assistant Professor in Religion at Syracuse University.*

This "confession style" is, undoubtedly, a symptom of the crisis of wisdom in ancient Israel, and for Koheleth, at least, the loosing of the self from its community and world—which leaves the self and world "empty," or only enigmatically meaningful and connected. The deed-consequence is broken for Koheleth. No longer can he establish the world and find his place in it. If older wisdom, Israelite and ancient Near Eastern, presupposed and communicated man's "place to be" in the cosmos—if, in fact, the human actualization of wisdom constituted the world order⁵—Koheleth can no longer participate in this wisdom tradition, and is thrown back on his "I"—I know, I see, I have explored, as indicated in his forms of speech.

Now let us carry these statements further and explore them by examining three key words of Koheleth: *hebel* (as contrasted with "the everlasting," *'ōlām*), "profit," and "portion."

II

"Vapors of vapors, says Koheleth, all is vapor" (1:2). Here I have rendered the Hebrew *hebel* in a neutral way; its translation is commonly known to English readers as "vanity," which Gordis uses in his translation. It has also been translated as "zero,"⁶ and "eitel/Eitelkeit" in German,⁷ although Schmid argues that this is a misunderstanding of the word and renders it as "nichtig/Nichtigkeit."⁸

At any rate, the positing of "vapor" sets the theme of the collection of Koheleth's sayings at the very beginning: *the all (hakkōl) is vapor*. Everything that comes and goes, the round of the seasons and natural phenomena, whatever happens by men or to men—all is vapor (1:2, 14). In this unceasing round,

> All words/things (*hadd⁰barim*) are tiring,
> One cannot bring it to word (*l⁰dabber*, 1:8).
> There is no remembrance of former things,
> Even the later things to come
> Will not have remembrance by a later generation (1:11).

Here, in another way, Koheleth states his theme: of what value am I, are we, if we are not remembered, if we are not "recognized?" Koheleth is expressing *the* problem of human existence: of what value is man in his total environment?

We can observe already in 1:2–11 how far Koheleth is from the prophetic understanding of existence and the traditional faith of the psalmist and wise man. He states,

---

5. H. H. Schmid, *Wesen und Geschichte der Weisheit*. BZAW 101, ed. G. Fohrer (Berlin, 1966), pp. 22ff., 188.
6. H. L. Ginsberg, *Studies in Koheleth* (New York, 1950), p. 1.
7. Luther's translation; see Zimmerli, *op. cit.*, pp. 13–14 and Galling, *Prediger Salomo*. HZAT, ed. O. Eissfeldt, vol. 18 (Tübingen, 1940), pp. 52, *passim*.
8. Schmid, *op. cit.*, p. 187, n. 221.

A generation comes, a generation goes,
But the earth stands forever (*le'ōlām 'ōmedet*, 1:4).

For Deutero-Isaiah it is all things of the "earth" that perish, whereas the word of God stands forever (Isa. 40:8). For the psalmist—and this would apply to the sage also—it is the fear of YHWH that endures forever (*'ōmedet lā 'ad*, Ps. 19:10). Koheleth finds no hope in the word of God or the fear of YHWH. The "earth" and the "everlasting" may, however, be closely connected for Koheleth (see note 46).

In the section 1:12–2:26, everything Koheleth tries out, "experiments" with, is *hebel:* searching out and exploring in wisdom; pleasure (*hattôb*); toil (*'āmāl*)—all are vapor. God favors some men by giving them wisdom and joy, but on the "sinner" (*hōtē'*)[9] he imposes work whose fruits go to the one pleasing to God. But this is all a deep mystery; and all we can know is "vapor and a herding of the wind" (2:26). How is it that God favors some men and not others? There is no answer, unless it be in chapter 3: the man to whom gifts from God come is the man who accepts everything in its "right time."

There is a time and a season for everything (3:1–8). But what gain (*yitrôn*) has the worker from his toil (3:9)? None. Then what does it mean to speak of the right time? Everything is "beautiful" or "proper" in its "time." But how does one know the right time? Koheleth does not answer this question.

Koheleth probably draws upon common ancient Near Eastern wisdom which Israelites borrowed and assumed within or outside of Yahwist faith. There is a right time for rain and for fruit, for going to war, for persecution and deliverance (see Deut. 11:14, Jer. 5:24; Ps. 1:3; II Sam. 11:1; Ps. 31:16). Koheleth simply assumes the content of traditional wisdom: anyone will know the right time for a certain action or a certain decision, for enjoyment, or whatever. "Right times" are simply given and knowable. But our teacher departs from traditional wisdom in concluding that it is impossible to take anything out, any "surplus," from this time. It must be enjoyed or suffered as it comes.

It is in recognition of this that H. Gese sees Koheleth presenting an "answer" to man's predicament. If man gives up alienation from his world-context in the fear of God, open-being will replace alien-being.[10] This is open-being for the *'ēt* ("appropriate time"), the *kairos:* Man will thankfully receive the good *kairos;* in the bad time he will recognize that this time is also purposed by God and that it is only his inability to understand the *'ōlām* that brings him to his existential impasse.[11] Meanwhile, he can accept certain things as gifts of God.

---

9. Gordis, *op. cit.*, note pp 227–28.
10. H. Gese, "Die Krise der Weisheit bei Koheleth," *Les Sagesses des Proche-Orient Ancien* (Paris, 1963), p. 150.
11. *Ibid.*, p. 151.

But it is doubtful whether Koheleth comes to such a recognition, to a bridging of the abyss between alien-being and open-being. As Schmid cogently observes, if Koheleth arrives at a "fear of God" it differs from the traditional wisdom understanding.[12] Only in occasional "appropriate times," can one find joy, and what brings these times is inscrutable —it is certainly not the *ṣᵉdāqāh*, the righteousness of man. Gese states that *ṣᵉdāqāh*, resulting in health and wholeness, is, for Koheleth, directly a gift of God to man.[13] But that does not solve the problem. The gift is arbitrarily, not graciously given. And it remains to be seen whether *ṣᵉdāqāh* means anything to Koheleth.

We can see the reason for the unhealable alienation of man from his world in chapter 3: God has put the *'ōlām* in the heart of man, but "man cannot discover the work of God from beginning to end" (3:11). *'ōlām* is usually a temporal word for world; it is world in the sense of age (thus translated *aion* in LXX). Galling translates "Zeitablauf."[14] Gordis takes *'ōlām* as a circumlocution for "love of the world,"[15] as does Rabbi bar R. Levi in the Midrash Rabbah on Koheleth. O. Rankin repoints the vowels to *hā-'elem*, the hidden, the forgotten,[16] which is an attractive suggestion. Likewise attractive is Scott's translation of *'ōlām* as "enigma."[17]

However the word *'ōlām* may be translated, more important is it that it is whatever lies at the core of existence. Perhaps the "earth," love of the world, true wisdom, everlasting life. It appears to be that which moves man, that which makes him distinctive as a creature. It moves him toward God, yet he cannot fathom God's works. Koheleth says, "I know that whatever God does remains forever" (*yihyeh lᵉ'ōlām*, 3:14). Men cannot add or subtract from it, "and God has acted so that men should fear him" (3:15).

Section 3:1–15, indeed, is all about the *'ōlām*, and it is one of the few series of sayings in Koheleth that does not express the vapor of existence in the world. This is, I believe, because it is the *'ōlām*, the hidden mystery of the whole, the "foundation" of the earth's remaining, the deepest source of human striving—it is the *'ōlām* which is the opposite of *hebel*, of breath, vanity. *And perhaps God does not want man to attain this 'ōlām.* Scott appropriately refers[18] to the statement in the "Babylonian Theodicy":

12. Schmid, *op. cit.*, p. 193.   13. Gese, *op. cit.*

14. Galling, *op. cit.*, p. 62. "... Die ausgedehnte Zeit, auch bei Koheleth, wenn er 1.3 [*sic!*] sagt, die Erde steht dauernd, oder wenn er von dem endlichen Vergessenwerden in den langen Zeiten (der Zukunft) spricht (2:16)" (p. 61).

15. Gordis, *op. cit.*, pp. 56, 231ff.

16. *Interpreter's Bible*, ed. G. Buttrick, *et al.* vol. V (New York and Nashville, 1954), pp. 46ff.

17. R. B. Y. Scott, *Proverbs and Ecclesiastes.* Anchor Bible, vol. 18 (Garden City, N.Y., 1965), pp. 220–21.

18. *Ibid.*, p. 221.

> The mind of the god, like the center of heavens,
>   is remote;
> His knowledge is difficult, men cannot
>   understand it.[19]

It is ancient wisdom—the divine mind is remote. Indeed, there are stories indicating that the divine mind wishes to stay remote. Man must not go too far; the gift of immortality is withheld from him. This occurs, for example, in the Adapa myth, in which Adapa refuses the food and water of life because his father Ea has previously counseled him that they bring death.[20] And Ea is the god of wisdom!

This is an ancient motif—man is kept from *life,* life itself, the divine life, the hidden spring of things, the very depth of being. One might interpret Ea's deception of Adapa as an expression of wisdom on man's behalf—man can never be other than human, limited, finite. But in such stories there is often the theme of divine jealousy in guarding the wisdom of life, which is creativity and control of the world. We see this in Greek myths, and a primitive residue thereof in the Biblical Garden of Eden story.[21] Man cannot be allowed to reach too far, he has become "like one of us," the *'elōhīm* (Gen. 3:22). The one further step must be prevented: eating from the tree of life, so that Adam would "live forever" (*wāḥay lᵉōlām*).

If man could live "to the *'ōlām*" he could know it. Then all would not be vapor. The perishing of what he explores by thought could be seen in its fullness; pleasure lost could be regained eventually; his toil, or the results of his toil, might pass but he would have ever new opportunities. A man would not have to ask himself for whom am I laboring—but he could enjoy his success if he lived to the *'ōlām;* he, at least, could remember it. Also, if a man could live to the *'ōlām*, he need have no fear of divine anger at breaches of religious etiquette (4:17–5:16).

Would the immortal be greedy (5:9ff.)? Perhaps it is thinkable. On the other hand, perhaps the vapor of seeking wealth is a symptom of man's awareness of his perishing. He tries to build or store up something lasting. For an immortal, greed would be unnecessary. Even the human sage can be perverted by a bribe (7:7), but one who could look out at the *'ōlām* would have no need of bribes. At any rate, as it stands, this, also, is vapor: the "righteous" (*ṣāddīq*) and the "wicked" (*rāšā'*) are not rewarded according to their respective deeds (7:15; cf. 8:14; 9:2). The deed-consequence connection is broken; *ṣāddīq, sedeq,* and *sᵉdāqāh* are no longer clues to reality. And this means that language and reality no longer correspond.

Reflection on "righteousness" in Koheleth brings us back to chapter

---

19. J. Pritchard, ed., *Ancient Near Eastern Texts Relating to the OT,* 2d ed. (Princeton, 1955), p. 440a.
20. A. Heidel, *The Babylonian Genesis,* 2d ed. (Chicago, 1951), pp. 122ff., 147ff.
21. Gordis, *op. cit.,* p. 233 for comment and bibliography.

3, specifically 3:16–4:3. Will God finally judge every deed, set everything right? No—the "fate" (the "meeting," *miqreh*) of man and beast is the same; man has no superiority over the beast, all is breath (3:19). All go to one place, all come from the dust, all return to the dust (3:20; cf. Gen. 3:19).

So things cannot be set right or justified; acts of oppression are ubiquitous, with none to comfort the oppressed (4:1–3). Faith in a hidden, transcendent God can be adequately symbolized and maintained only if the world order coheres in a myth that "makes sense." If the two become severed, then a new mythos must emerge, perhaps one which expresses the ultimate worth of human existence in the symbols of some kind of afterlife. But Koheleth rejects this possibility, or at most says, Who knows? (3:21).

Our reflection to this point confirms, in my estimation, that '*ōlām* is the opposite of vapor and is at the root of vain human striving. God puts the '*ōlām* in men's hearts, he wills that they fear him—and they could not fear God if they were unaware of the '*ōlām*, which is the "divine dimension." Yet justice and righteousness cannot be observed in the world, and oppression cannot be rectified by a final judgment or a release of the spirit to a heavenly realm.

Now we are in a position to reaffirm Schmid's position, *contra* Gese: the "break-through" of Koheleth to a "fear of God" comes through the two-fold experience of an '*ōlām* sealed off from man and the dissolution of a world order that operates according to righteousness. One must, therefore, accept the rough times as they come. Koheleth's fear of God is prudent; it is "religious" (grounded in ultimate concern) only insofar as he, by his own obvious sighing over the vapor of everything, longs for knowledge of the '*ōlām*, the total course of things,[22] which would be found trustworthy and allow one to become truly wise. As it is, the wise man and the fool are in the same boat.

Koheleth thus arrives at a pessimism and a skepticism that is far from the usual affirmations of wisdom and the law and the prophets. But there are themes of ancient Israelite faith that have left their deposit in Koheleth's thinking, and have become enlarged in their negative aspects:

1. In his own way Koheleth, like the great prophets, is iconoclastic. "A crashing destruction of idols, of easy answers to the question of life's meaning—including religious answers—sounds throughout this book."[23]

---

22. My understanding of '*ōlām* is thus very close to Galling's: the totality of the temporal world-course. But I would add that for Koheleth this '*ōlām*, if attained, would be the opposite of "Vergessenwerden." It would be "becoming remembered," and the being in which one "becomes remembered" is truly divine being. It is participation in God, "the remembering one."

23. W. Harrelson, *Interpreting the Old Testament* (New York, 1964), p. 443.

2. A recognition of vapor is a recognition of life's irony. "The whole of life . . . is a tissue of incongruity."[24] Irony is integral to the Bible; it arises out of the experience of discrepancy between the real and the appearing, or an extreme tension between the present state of things and a transcendent reality that stands over against it.[25] Koheleth knows vapor because he has a deep awareness of its opposite, the 'ōlām, what God does from beginning to end.

III

The experience of vapor as the human condition leads Koheleth to his recurring question, "What does anything profit a man? The nouns signifying "profit" are from the root ytr: yiṭrōn, yōṭēr, and mōṭār.[26] They denote "advantage gained, surplus, what is left over," and their frequency in Koheleth probably points to a commercial environment in which trade has opened up and become a preoccupation of the sage's life-situation.[27]

The question concerning man's profit in existence and the question concerning his "portion" are interrelated.[28] I would maintain, however, that "portion" and "profit" are not usually identical for Koheleth.

We can already see from our study of hebel why Koheleth can find no profit: everything perishes, nothing can be grasped, held as an advantage or surplus. Who can hold on to breath, vapor, or the wind? What profit is there? Everything goes in a wearisome cycle, and nothing is remembered (1:2–11). How can there be "something left over" to value if there is no remembrance of former events, previous achievements? This question lays the foundation of all of Koheleth's further observations about profit.

Do the results of toil last? No. Is there profit to wisdom (2:13)? Perhaps, but one "fate" occurs to both wise men and fools (2:14). "I have become wise"—so how is this an advantage over the fool? We both die. There is no remembrance forever (zikrōn . . . lᵉʿōlām) for either wise man or fool (2:16; cf. 6:8, 11).

There is a proper time, an appointed time, for everything (3:1–8). So what does the worker profit from his achievements (3:9), which depend, after all, upon struggling in another dimension from the "times" given in the deep mystery of things. The toiler, Dasein, is history-being, working against death; he does not usually plan to pluck up when the enigmatic time is right. He cannot stand losing—or laughing

---

24. E. Good, *Irony in the Old Testament* (Philadelphia, 1965), p. 182.
25. J. G. Williams, " 'You have Not Spoken Truth of Me': Mystery and Irony in Job," forthcoming in *Zeitschrift für die Altestamentliche Wissenschaft*.
26. *Yitrôn*, a *qitlan* type noun: 1:3; 2:11, 13; 3:9; 5:8, 15; 7:12; 10:10, 11; *yôtēr*: 2:15; 6:8, 11; 7:11, 16; 12:9, 12; *môtār*: 3:19.
27. M. J. Dahood, S. J., *Canaanite-Phoenician Influence in Qoheleth* (Rome, 1952), pp. 52–53.
28. Schmid, *Weisheit, op. cit.*, p. 187, who identifies the two with each other.

or mourning, or whatever, if it interferes with his business. His clock or hour-glass is set against eternity. It is a vain business to be busy for profit.

Man, indeed, has no advantage over the beasts (3:19) —and who thinks of the non-human animals as seeking profit? For man, as for them, the *'ōlām* is sealed off; for man, as for them, there is only "being forgotten," not "being remembered." As a man comes, even if he amasses wealth, so he goes: "and what profit to him who toiled for the wind?" (5:15).

In the script of the human condition there is thus written: no profit. In this condition Koheleth at times seems to advocate a golden mean, as for example in 7:15–16. Here is a righteous man who perishes in his "rightness," and an evil man who lives long in his evil. So—

Be not a *saddiq* (righteous) too much,
and be not wise to excess *(yôtēr)*.
Why destroy yourself? (7:16)

But a golden mean philosophy is usually based on the conviction of a cosmic order that is just. The matter is different for Koheleth. The received tradition concerning right, righteousness, and the righteous man simply does not hold up for him; it cannot make sense of what he experiences and observes. So why waste oneself on a state of being, *saddiq*hood, which is of no profit? And here Koheleth thinks not of monetary profit, but the advantage of *life* and a full human existence.

Before continuing we should note that some passages where the root *y-t-r* occurs have not been considered. And I would say quite honestly that not all of Koheleth's sayings can be placed within this sketch. If his thinking expresses *themes*, it is still not systematic. We should remember, too, the collecting feature of wisdom literature, which Gese indicates,[29] the *ad hominem* character of many sayings in a teaching situation, and recognize also the editorial addition(s) of later disciples of redactors (12:9–14).[30]

"Profit" or "advantage" in 12:9, 12; 5:8; 10:10–11 appears to fall outside of our concern here and does not affect this discussion. But 7:11–12 seems to offer a crux:

Wisdom is better *(tôbāh)* with an inheritance, an advantage *(yôtēr)* to those who see the sun. For with the protection of wisdom one is with the protection of money, and the advantage *(yitrôn)* of knowledge is that it preserves the life of its possessor.

---

29. Gese, *op. cit.*, p. 139.
30. *Yôtēr* in 12:9, 12 means simply "in addition to." *Yitrôn* in 5:8 is part of a saying concerning the injustice wrought by hierarchies, although 5:8 is admittedly difficult to translate. Gordis' comment, *op. cit.*, p. 250, is in keeping with his position that Koheleth anticipates a Sadducaic perspective. The occurrences of *yitrôn* in 10:10, 11 are usages of conventional wisdom speech, and do not pertain to the main theme of Koheleth's understanding of *yitrôn/yôtēr/môtār.*

Here wisdom appears to be profitable. It even preserves its possessor's life. I admit the difficulty of "making it fit," yet would offer two comments. First, I understand the tenor of the verses as ironic: wisdom is good, yes—with an inheritance (*nᵃḥālāh*)! The protection of wisdom is *with* the protection of money. When a man is wise *and* wealthy, it is good (v. 11); the advantage of knowledge in this case, when one has an inheritance, is that it preserves the wise man's life. The "profit" of the wise man is the wealth he has fortuitously inherited. But Koheleth's recurrent refrain is that trying to procure or preserve wealth is vapor.

Second, 7:11–12 should be taken in its immediate context, and here I refer especially to 7:13 (cf. 7:14–18):

See the work of God:
Who can fix what he has made crooked?

In other words, there is no advantage to so-called wisdom in the final scheme of things. There may be some practical value in wisdom and knowledge—if one also has an inheritance!

So nothing profits a man. And the seeking of profit in toil results in rivalry (or "jealousy") with one's fellows (4:4). This is vapor and herding the wind. Then there is no "good," no value in human existence? No, not if the good is identified with profit.

Is this to say, then, that one must give up on existence? Koheleth does not, as we shall see in our study of *ḥeleq*, portion. Furthermore, his denial of profit is in its own way iconoclastic, and in a negative way he teaches that nothing profits a man except his own life, even if it is vapor. The realization of this could take a skeptical or cynical direction, and admittedly Koheleth never moves decisively beyond skepticism (though he is not cynical). But the same realization could take another direction. As Jesus taught:

For what will it profit a man if he gains the whole world and forfeits his life? (Matt. 16:26; cf. Mark 8:36).

In this New Testament context the vaporous quality of existence is recognized within the call to discipleship and hope in the Son of Man and the Kingdom of God.

Or the saying attributed to Akabya ben Mahalaleel sounds as though it could come from Koheleth: a man comes from a putrid drop; returns to the place of dust, worm, and maggot; and must give account to the Holy One (Pirkê Abôt, 3:1).[31] Here the vaporous quality of existence is recognized within the way of Torah.

Integral to later Judaism and Christianity is the conviction that man's condition is vapor. Both Judaism and Christianity found a way,

---

31. T. *Berākôt* 5b (it is appropriate to weep over beauty that withers) and T. *Berākôt* 17a (a man's form of work matters little, if he only direct his heart to Heaven).

a way to bridge the gap between "vapor *(hebel)* and the "world-course" *('ōlām).* In order to *live,* to exist meaningfully in a sense of being valued or accepted—"saved"—there must be an adequate myth or story, with potent symbols and figures. To bridge the gap between the awareness of finitude and the mysterious "goal" that man feels deep within him: to find the good, the whole, the complete, or to be declared ultimately valuable or accepted. It is this bridge, this mediation or myth which Koheleth lacks.

IV

H. H. Schmid, following Zimmerli, cogently clarifies the basic question of Koheleth: what is the "portion" of man in the totality of the world?[32] One's "portion" *(heleq)* signified originally the portion of land that fell to a bride or an individual by the casting of lots.[33] This idea of "portion" could sometimes become spiritualized (see Ps. 16:5f.; Num. 18:20).[34]

This basic question of Koheleth is a way of stating one of the basic questions of ancient Near Eastern wisdom: "Where is the place of the living acting man in this world?"[35] And if Koheleth departs from ancient wisdom in not finding a portion of place, or a sacred place, or YHWH as the believer's "portion," he nevertheless indicates a *heleq* in human existence.

"Portion," *heleq,* occurs eight times in Koheleth.[36] He finds no profit in his toil (2:11)—nothing is left over to retain, yet his heart or mind did rejoice in all his work (2:10). For Koheleth this is one of the primary aspects of findings one's portion and, thus, some joy in life. It is a portion, thus a joy, that is found "immediately"[37] in the activity itself, for who can store it up or can see what will happen later?

> And I saw that there is no good except a
> man enjoy his work, for that is his
> portion. For who can bring him to see
> what will be after him? (3:22).

The place of justice, the place of right; immortality; *'ōlām,* the totality of God's doing—these are all cut off from man though he might be aware of their possibility or their necessity. Yet there is a portion—to

---

32. Schmid, *op. cit.,* pp. 187–88. As I have previously stated, however, when Schmid identifies the two, profit and portion, I believe he misreads Koheleth.

33. *Ibid.,* p. 188, no. 227. We can discern details of how land apportionments were made in cultic ritual; see Josh. 18:1–10; Micah 2:1–5.

34. G. von Rad, "'Gerechtigkeit' und 'Leben' in den Psalmen," *Gesammelte Studien zum Alten Testament* (München, 1961), pp. 241ff.

35. Schmid, *op. cit.,* my translation.

36. 2:10, 21; 3:22; 5:17, 18; 9:6, 9; 11:2.

37. I am not using "immediately" in a strict epistemological sense, but simply to mean "in the midst of, in the very process," not preoccupied with consequences or rewards.

enjoy what one puts one's hand to do (cf. 5:17, 18). In this enjoyment the *remembering* of one's vaporous course will be diminished (5:19).

It is better to be alive than dead (9:4; contradicted by the aphorisms in 4:2–3). The living, at least, know *something*, that they will die, and in spite of the grief of knowing, it is still better for Koheleth than not knowing. But "not knowing" takes its final form in forgetting and being forgotten: the memory of the dead is forgotten (9:5).

Existence is composed of opposites, it is full of strife and conflict, yet *in* all of this one may find a share, some portion:

Their [the dead ones'] love, their hate, their
    envy—already perished;
they have no more portion (*heleq*) forever
in all that is done under the sun (9:6).

If one can speak of a gift of God it is *life,* for much of life may be miserable but in it one may find a portion. What most basically constitutes living, not righteousness but the rudiments of human existence is a gift of God if it is enjoyed (3:13). Life (*hayyim*) has not profit, but to see good in it is a gift, even if Elohim is forever sealed off. Real life is finding one's portion in partaking of, and partaking in, the good things: what is pleasant or responsive to consciousness or human being. *But,* one cannot profit from them; one can only enjoy them. This enjoyment is enhanced by recognizing life's ingredient of sorrow (11:7ff.).[38]

It is the man who enjoys "immediately" whom God "has already approved" (9:7).

Go, eat with joy your bread,
drink with merry heart your wine,
for God has already approved your actions.
At every proper time let your garments be white,
Lack not for oil on your head.
"Enjoy" life with the woman whom you love
all the days of your vain life—
which he has give you under the sun
all the days of your vain life (*y^emê heblekā,* 9:7–9).

"All the days of your vain (vaporous) life!" One could take this phrase and conclude that Koheleth is a thorough pessimist. Skeptic, yes. Thorough pessimist, no. For this is not Koheleth's complete thought. Going into Koheleth's intention as presented in the Biblical text, we must read the full thought: "Enjoy your portion all the days of your vain life." The realization of vapor may lead to despair (the end of the sentence is absolutized). But it may point one back to the beauty of the portion that can be found in "immediate" experience. One's

---

38. Good, *op. cit.,* p. 193. Cf. pp. 190–94.

work, his eating and drinking, his wife—these may be a portion, and in the midst of vapor they say no to perishing, to the final darkness.

Koheleth must have internalized a breakdown of Israelite traditions and ancient Near Eastern wisdom that we can now scarcely discern in the Hellenistic period. The human condition is vapor. There is no profit in existence. Yet there is a *heleq*, there is a portion which brings joy, and in which one is no longer an "outsider" in the cosmos—even if the cosmos and its "deep, deep eternity" are veiled from man.

There is an occurrence of *heleq* not yet considered. Sometimes a man wise, skillful and knowledgeable leaves his portion to one who did not toil for it (2:21). Here *heleq* and profit sound much alike, though of course one can keep neither. At this point I must simply refer to the total context of Koheleth's reflections. My own conclusion is that Koheleth speaks of a profit-portion (2:21 and 11:2) and a joy-portion. The profit-portion falls within the range of traditional wisdom.

As a rule, profit and portion are not identical for Koheleth. One can feel the cool soothing breeze on his face, though one cannot capture the breeze. But, then, is Koheleth the skeptic also Koheleth the hedonist? The answer must be no, for to be a hedonist implies seeking pleasure (physical, emotional, intellectual,) which one gains. And that would be profit! There is no profit. A man finds his joy, his portion, in the process of "doing his thing."[39] If "hedonist," however, signifies a positive evaluation of the "flesh," of eating, drinking, copulation, then Koheleth is indeed a hedonist, but, then, so are most of the Biblical writers and tradents.

Rather than trying to classify Koheleth, perhaps it would be best to close with a meditation on his wisdom.

V

In this study I have concluded that Koheleth has experienced a loosing of his self from the world, as indicated in his style of presentation. For Koheleth the human condition is vapor, as over against the *'ōlām*, and there is no profit in the breath-like quality of everything. But one can find a "portion," which cannot be carried over into profit.

Koheleth agonizes over the human condition, over man's inability to move from his vaporous existence to a full or satisfying knowledge

---

39. Koheleth does not consider how the severely oppressed might enjoy their toil, eating and drinking, and human relationships, when they are obviously in a state of extreme deprivation (he does take account of the oppressed, 4:1ff). This may reflect an upper class background and conservative orientation (Gordis). Not only is he convinced that nothing in the total scheme of things can be changed, he prefers things (socially and economically) the way they are. I do not think, however, that the matter is so simple, and shall make comments related to this point in section V of the essay.

of the everlasting, the total world course. This conflict he feels to such a degree that he must, if consistent, either withdraw from life or love life with an intensity even greater precisely because of his agony over non-being, the final "becoming forgotten" of man and his world.

Existence is vapor, without profit, yet there is a portion in the "light"—light is sweet:

> And the light is sweet,
> And good for the eyes to see the sun.
> For it a man lives many years,
> Let him rejoice in them all,
> But remember the days of darkness, that they are many—
> All that comes is vapor (11:7–8) .

Remember!—Remember the days of darkness. Hopeless, no—not hopeless to remember non-being; to remember it *may* lead to turning back to the light. Sweet is the light!

How did Koheleth get into the canon? Perhaps the addition of the orthodox conclusion to the book, 12:13–14, is not a sufficient explanation.[40] With all his unorthodoxy, both in the ancient Israelite wisdom tradition and from the perspective of later Judaism, Koheleth is, nonetheless, Jewish through and through. Kingdoms come and go. Bondage —exile—diaspora—persecution. Gloomy, unhealthy preoccupation with vapor? Perhaps—but never Israel's last word and not Koheleth's conclusion. Miskotte has said it well:

> . . . Through the centuries it is Israel that says this: Onward! . . . As no other people Israel clings to life. . . . This life, which is now so incomprehensible, has me in its grip. This is not paganism (though sometimes it is deceptively like it) only because the 'grip of life' is really the way in which YHWH holds his own in expectation; for He, too, in His way, holds on to this earthly life with an intensity that shows he has something great and wonderful in store for it.[41]

YHWH, the Name, has disappeared for Koheleth. Only Elohim remains; but, perhaps, when one enjoys life and light, the Name, the Presence, will reappear. There is, at any rate, opportunity—*heleq* might be paraphrased for our time as opportunity. In the simple things of existence there is a portion: "For what is offered to us hour by hour and breath by breath is the 'one opportunity.' "[42]

For some, this counsel of Koheleth will sound banal and boring.

---

40. Schmid, *op. cit.*, p. 196. At any rate, the Rabbis were able to interpret other parts of Koheleth in light of the Torah myth. For example, Koheleth Rabbah on 11:7 interprets "the light is sweet" to mean "sweet is the light of Torah." This is not to deny that the addition of 12:13–14 was *one* of the factors in the book's reception as Scripture.

41. K. H. Miskotte, *When the Gods are Silent*, tr. and intro. by J. W. Doberstein (New York, 1967), p. 453; meditation on Ecclesiastes, pp. 450–60.

42. *Ibid.*, p. 454.

Enjoy the light; take one's portion as it is given: work, eating, drinking, marital relationship. But is not *enjoying* this portion the meaning of spiritual life?

> The answer is that precisely when this meagre portion is spiritually lived, Ecclesiastes with his wisdom commends to us a life which is an anticipation of the time to come when every man shall 'sit under his vine and under his fig tree' (Micah 4:4) and invite his neighbor to sit there with him.[43]

Yes, very boring, unless one likes a place to sit, a tree, some figs, a friend or neighbor to talk with. But does not all our talk of utopia, a new age, or the "great society" come out here, where Koheleth sees into what is good? Is this not harmony and communion, the "other world," the sweetness of light and life in the world here and now, right under our noses?

I understand Koheleth as a sage who has had an experience and dim vision of authentic human existence, but who has not adequate symbols to express this and pull men toward human community—symbols and images found, for example, in the prophetic speaking.[44] He is caught up in the impasse of his personal history and the broken symbols of his time. But is the "word of God" absent from Koheleth? I think not. To enjoy one's cup and one's woman and to remember that "the all" in which man participates is vapor: this, too, is the divine word. Koheleth is not here non-Israelite or non-Biblical. "All flesh is grass," says Second Isaiah (Isa. 40:6). Everything begins *tōhû wābōhû*, in darkness, says the priestly author in Genesis (1:2). Man is made from the dust and returns to the dust according to the Yahwist (Gen. 2:7, 3:19). If Koheleth cannot promise creation and liberation, he *can* remind us of vapor—what does anything profit a man? He can point us to a portion, an opportunity, here and now. That is his wisdom.

Koheleth is not radical like Job. He does not go the root and wrestle with God and his own soul until he gets some kind of divine response. But he points to the possibility of portion, and to the sweetness of the light. And the light *(hā'ōr)* in 11:7 must mean more than the particles of energy in the wavelength that man can see, or the warmth of the sun that man feels, though that, indeed, is pleasant and beneficial to man and earth. Light in 11:7 must be a symbol of life itself, of creating, of enjoying, of remembering what is valuable. There is no portion in the sun *per se*. The sun travels wearily toward its place (1:5), and everything that occurs "under the sun" is vapor (1:14, *passim*). It is good for the eyes to behold the sun, but Koheleth is not speaking of the sun, as such. He is rather articulating the sweetness of

---

43. *Ibid.*
44. Thus, reforming or transforming the status quo is not considered by Koheleth.

life: *light,* the first of God's creations; and it is very good (Gen. 1:3–4). "Let the sunshine in" while you can!

All is vapor, man and beast perish, nothing and no one is remembered—so Koheleth. "In the depth of the anxiety of having to die is the anxiety of being eternally forgotten."[45] But there is still portion in the light!

Is Koheleth Jewish? Again we ask the question. And again the answer is yes. At the great festival of Sukkot, the appointed time of thanksgiving for harvest and shelter, the scroll of Koheleth is read. Like the booths, Koheleth is a reminder of *galut,* of exile, of dispersion, of God's hiddenness. Koheleth is a representation of both the human condition and the fear of God (12:13f.). Koheleth is a reminder that all is not well. And it is the wisdom of Israel to read Koheleth at Sukkot. Israel and Israel's son, Christianity, must hear these words: winter and darkness are near. But the light is sweet.

The words of Koheleth are often iconoclastic words. Taken seriously they shatter fixation on, or worship of, anything that man builds; they deny final profit in anything that man achieves. Nothing we see or hear or touch or smell or taste is the final reality although the *'ōlām* may be hidden within everything. Koheleth's wisdom might be understood as a muted or darkened parablic word not brought to full expression i.e., the word expressing human existence as the divine actuality, the worldliness of God's reality.[46]

What is forgotten by man is remembered by God. God has the world "in mind." "Nothing real is absolutely lost and forgotten. We are together with everything real in the divine life."[47]

Koheleth does not attain this recognition. But he must be taken as he is and for what he says. Even if he concludes that all is vapor, he is still concerned to share his reflction on his experience and to point to the light, which is sweet. I am inclined to agree with Koheleth's disciple:

> Koheleth tried to find attractive words,
> And to write honestly words of truth (12:10).

45. P. Tillich, *The Eternal Now* (New York, 1963), p. 33.
46. Cf. G. Vahanian, *No Other God* (New York, 1966), esp. pp. 37–84, and S. M. Ogden, *The Reality of God* (New York, 1966), esp. pp. 57–70, 221–30. The Convoker says the earth remains forever, to the *'ōlām* (Koh. 1:4); so if all is vapor, Ha-Elohim must be especially concerned with the earth, since it is God who makes everything (11:5). Thus *'ōlām* and what pertains to *'ōlām* must be the basic meaning of "the earth" *(hā-'āreṣ);* the *'ōlām* in 3:11 is not the opposite of earthly being, but its fullness.
47. Tillich, *op. cit.,* p. 35.

PROVERBS VIII 22-31 AND ITS SUPPOSED PROTOTYPES

BY

R. N. WHYBRAY
Tokyo

B. Gemser in his commentary on Proverbs remarks that viii 22-31 is reminiscent of the style of a creation hymn, and that especially vv. 24-26, in which wisdom asserts in a series of negative clauses that she was born before the depths, mountains and fields had been created, have their prototype [1]) in Egyptian and Babylonian creation poems and in Gen. i 2; ii 5 [2]). H. Ringgren expressed a similar opinion: these verses (24-31) are expressed "in words which remind one of Egyptian and Babylonian texts of creation" [3]). It is our purpose here to test the correctness of these statements by comparing the texts to which Gemser and Ringgren refer with one another and with Prov. viii 22-31 with regard to their form, content and purpose [4]).

Gemser and Ringgren between them mention 5 texts: the Egyptian *Book of the Apophis* (*ANET*, p. 6 [5])); *Enuma Eliš* Tab I, lines 1-8 (9) (translations in *ANET*, p. 60 f.; A. Heidel, *The Babylonian Genesis*, Chicago, 1951, p. 18); a bilingual account of the creation of the world by Marduk (Heidel, *op. cit.*, p. 62 f.; *AOT* [6]), p. 130 f.) [7]); and the two biblical passages Gen. i 1-3; ii 4b-7. There are others which could have been included in the list; but these will suffice for our present purpose. The relevant passages are as follow:

---

[1]) „Vorbild".

[2]) B. Gemser, *Sprüche Salomos, HAT*[1], 1937, p. 38 f.; [2] 1963, p. 47 f.

[3]) H. Ringgren, *Word and Wisdom: Studies in the Hypostatization of Divine Qualities and Functions in the Ancient Near East*, Uppsala, 1947, p. 102. Cf. also H. Ringgren, *Sprüche, ATD*, Göttingen, 1962, p. 40.

[4]) The other numerous problems of viii 22-31 will not be considered here except in so far as they are relevant to this question. For my views on the passage as a whole and in particular on the concept of wisdom here see my book, *Wisdom in Proverbs (SBT)*, London, 1965, p.p. 99 ff.

[5]) J. B. Pritchard, *Ancient Near Eastern Texts relating to the Old Testament*, Princeton, 1951. The reference is to the first paragraph on p. 6.

[6]) H. Gressmann, *Altorientalische Texte zum alten Testament*, Berlin and Leipzig, 1926. The relevant passage is lines 1-17.

[7]) For editions of these texts and bibliography see Heidel and *ANET, ad loc.*

390

Book of the Apophis

The All-Lord said, after he had come into being: I am he who came into being as Khepri. When I had come into being, being (itself) came into being, and all beings came into being after I came into being. Many were the beings which came forth from my mouth, before heaven came into being, before earth came into being, before the ground and creeping things had been created in this place. I put together (some) of them in Nun as weary ones, before I could find a place in which I might stand. It (seemed) advantageous to me in my heart; I planned with my face; and I made (in concept) every form when I was alone, before I had spat out what was Shu, before I had sputtered out what was Tefnut, and before (any) other had come into being who could act with me.

Enuma Eliš [1])

1 When on high the heaven had not been named,
2 Firm ground below had not been called by name,
3 Naught but primordial Apsu, their begetter,
4 (And) Mummu-Tiamat, she who bore them all,
5 Their waters commingling as a single body;
6 No reed hut had been matted, no marsh land had appeared,
7 When no gods whatever had been brought into being,
8 Uncalled by name, their destinies undetermined—
9 Then it was that the gods were formed within them.

The Creation of the World by Marduk [2])

1 A holy house, a house of the gods in a holy place, had not been made;
2 A reed had not come forth, a tree had not been created;
3 A brick had not been laid, a brick mold had not been built;
4 A house had not been made, a city had not been built;
5 A city had not been made, a living creature had not been placed (therein);
. . . .
9 A holy house, a house of the gods, its dwelling, had not been made;
10 All the lands were sea;
11 The spring which is in the sea was a water pipe;
12 Then Eridu was made, Esagila was built—
13 Esagila whose foundations Lugaldukuga laid within the *Apsû*—
14 Babylon was made, Esagila was completed;
15 The gods the Anunnaki he created equal.
. . . .
17 Marduk constructed a reed frame on the face of the waters . . .

---

[1]) E. A. Speiser's translation in *ANET*.
[2]) Heidel's translation. Lines omitted (for the sake of space) are merely repetitive or otherwise not significant for a study of the form or content of the text. The text continues with a detailed description of Marduk's creation of the world: mankind, wild animals, Tigris and Euphrates, vegetation, domestic animals, cities, with some repetition and lack of logical arrangement.

GEN. i 1-3

Either [1])

In the beginning God created the heavens and the earth. The earth was without form and void, and darkness was upon the face of the deep; and the Spirit of God was moving over the face of the waters. And God said...

Or 2)

When God began to create heaven and earth — the earth being without form and void, with darkness upon the face of the deep and the Spirit of God moving over the face of the waters — God said...

GEN. ii 4b-7

In the day that the Lord God made the earth and the heavens, when no plant of the field was yet in the earth and no herb of the field had yet sprung up—for the Lord God had not caused it to rain upon the earth, and there was no man to till the ground; but a mist went up from the earth and watered the whole face of the ground—then the Lord God formed man of dust from the ground...

PROV. viii 22-31 [3])

22 The Lord created me at the beginning of his work,
   The first of his acts of old.
23 Ages ago I was set up,
   At the first, before the beginning of the earth.
24 When there were no depths I was brought forth,
   When there were no springs abounding with water.
25 Before the mountains had been shaped,
   Before the hills, I was brought forth;
26 Before he had made the earth with its fields,
   Or the first of the dust of the world.
27 When he established the heavens, I was there,
   When he drew a circle on the face of the deep,
28 When he made firm the skies above,
   When he established the fountains of the deep
29 When he assigned to the sea its limit,
   So that the waters might not transgress his command,
   When he marked out the foundations of the earth,
30 Then I was beside him...

---

[1]) Here and in Gen. ii 4b-7 *RSV* is followed.
[2]) For another alternative rendering see p. 510 *infra*.
[3]) *RSV* is used also here for convenience. The differences of opinion concerning the meaning of individual words in this passage are not relevant to the present argument.

All these passages (with the possible exception of Gen. i 1-3) have one obvious common characteristic: they all refer to the creation of the world negatively in a series of temporal clauses ("when not...", "before...", etc.) which indicate that some other event or state occurred or existed previously. In spite of this common characteristic, however, it may at once be observed that these clauses in Prov. viii 22-31 differ markedly from the others in that they alone give an orderly and detailed—though brief and perhaps fragmentary—presentation of the events of creation. In the corresponding passages in the *Book of the Apophis* and *Enuma Eliš* the main parts of creation are merely mentioned briefly with no attempt at completeness or logical order. *Apophis* is content with the simplest list of things created— heaven, earth, ground, creeping things. The lines in *Enuma Eliš* are—as was pointed out by G. CASTELLINO—an example of the stately opening to a major work which was "une des lois stylistiques de l'ancien Orient sémitique" [1]), rather than a systematic description of the actual process of creation. Both these texts give fuller accounts of creation at a later stage, but this is done in a positive manner, without the use of the kind of negative temporal clause which is the subject of the present comparison. The corresponding lines in the *Creation of the World by Marduk* are equally sketchy, though more repetitive, and its author clearly concentrated on features in which he was especially interested. In all of these three texts the details given in the temporal clauses are not of primary interest. This is equally true of Gen. ii 4b-7, which appears to take for granted a more detailed knowledge of the process of creation and merely sketches briefly the state of created things before the creation of man, which is the event with which the author is mainly concerned [2]). In Gen. i 1-3 also the negative clauses merely describe briefly the chaos which existed before the first act of creation, and can in no sense be said to give an account of the creation itself, these verses being only *preparatory* to the creation story. It is only in Prov. viii 22-31 that the temporal clauses, in spite of their subordinate syntactical position,

---

[1]) G. CASTELLINO, ,,Les origines de la civilisation selon les textes bibliques et les textes cunéiformes", *VT Suppl.* IV, 1957, p. 127.

[2]) CASTELLINO's distinction (p. 128), made with reference to Sumerian myths, between "myths of organisation", in which the description of the creative acts is only secondary, and "myths of action", where it is the main theme, may perhaps also be applied to these three texts.

constitute an ordered statement of the actual creative process [1]).
Moreover, as GEMSER himself hinted, it is really only vv. 24-26
which can be compared, even in form, with the other texts. Vv. 27 ff.
are *positive* temporal clauses. It is only the "when not" and "before" of
vv. 24-26 which could be regarded as reminiscences of a stylistic
tradition represented by the other texts quoted [2]).

A closer comparative examination of the form of these passages
and of the functions of the temporal clauses in each provides additional evidence that the resemblances are not as striking as they may
at first appear to be.

Prov. viii 22-31 begins with a positive statement—"The Lord
created me"—and only then proceeds to the "when not" and "before"
clauses; these are then followed by positive "when" clauses. The
temporal clauses do not form a single series, but are broken up,
in accordance with the special purpose of the passage, by a series
of apodoses each having roughly the same meaning: "I was brought
forth", "I was there", "I was beside him". The structure of the
passage thus has several distinctive features, of which the most
significant—and the most characteristically biblical—is the fact
that the positive reference to God's creative activity occurs in a main

---

[1]) The account apparently breaks off with v. 29 when the temporal clauses
come to an end. V. 31 mentions a further creature —man— but 30 f. cannot properly
be taken as a continuation of the account of creation begun in vv. 24-29, which
therefore must be regarded either as deliberately incomplete or as a fragment
of a longer account which has been utilized by the author for his own particular
purpose. The fact remains, however, that as far as it goes vv. 24-29 has more of
the characteristics of a genuine creation story (a "myth of action") than any of the
other texts. On the question of the unity of vv. 22-31, which cannot be discussed
here, see *inter alia* C. H. TOY, *Proverbs, ICC*, 1899, p. 172 ff. and W. SCHENCKE,
Die Chokma (Sophia) in der jüdischen Hypostasenspekulation, Kristiania, 1913, pp. 20 ff.

[2]) It may be noted that the temporal clauses in vv. 27-29 (apart from a superficial resemblance to Gen. ii 4 ff.; v 1 and possibly Gen. i 1) most closely resemble
Job xxviii 25-27, not only in their grammatical construction but also in their
relating the creation of the world to the antiquity of wisdom. A number of other
Babylonian creation texts also begin with positive temporal clauses: "When
the gods in their assembly had created..." (HEIDEL, *op. cit.*, p. 64); "When Anu
had created the heavens..." (*ibid.*, p. 65); "When heaven had been separated
from earth..." (*ibid.*, p. 68); "After Anu had created the heaven..." (*ibid.*,
p. 72); "When Anu, Enlil and Enki... had established the great decrees of heaven
and earth..." (*ibid.*, p. 73). (See also CASTELLINO's article for further examples).
But the similarity with Prov. viii 27-29 is only superficial, since in the cuneiform
examples the sense of the "when" clauses is pluperfect (i.e. "after") and looks
forward to further events in the process of creation, while the "when" in the
former (*be*, 6 times) can only mean "at the time when", expressing contemporaneity
with the following clauses.

clause *before* the temporal clauses. In this it is similar to the traditional interpretation of Gen. i 1. None of the other texts under discussion has this feature. The function of the temporal clauses is simply to expand the words "at the beginning of his work" and "the first of his acts" in v. 22, asserting the priority of wisdom over all creatures. That Yahweh himself existed before all things is taken for granted. The temporal clauses do not refer to the *Creator's* priority over other gods or over matter; they refer to the *relative* priority of one of his creatures, wisdom, over the others.

In the *Book of the Apophis*, which is a magical text composed for the purpose of securing the victory of Re over the demon Apophis which threatens the cosmos, the function of the temporal clauses is to assert the pre-existence of Re himself. The text therefore begins with a statement by Re, not about the creation of the world but about his own coming into existence before all other things. There is thus nothing but a purely grammatical similarity (positive statement followed by temporal clauses) with Prov. viii 22 ff.

The two texts from Mesopotamia resemble one another in various ways, possibly reflecting a common tradition [1]). Only here do we have a series of negative temporal clauses placed at the *beginning*, leading up to a positive statement about creation. In the case of *Enuma Eliš* the elaborate series of temporal clauses almost certainly has a literary and artistic motive. The main purpose of this poem is similar to that of the *Book of the Apophis*: to glorify the creator-god (here Marduk) and to ensure the victory of the cosmic order over chaos [2]); but the temporal clauses are not in this case closely connected with this purpose, since the glory of Marduk consists not in his pre-existence (he is a comparatively young god, the son of Ea the son of Anshar) but in his valour and strength which are greater than those of the other gods [3]). The function of the initial temporal clauses is thus quite secondary, creating for the reader a picture of the infinitely remote time before the world was created, as part of the introduction to the main narrative and in a suitably elevated style.

In the other cuneiform text, the *Creation of the World by Marduk* [4]), which is also part of a magical text [5]), the purpose is again the glori-

---

[1]) On the possibility of Sumerian influence, see HEIDEL, *op. cit.*, p. 12. For other forms of introductions to Sumerian and Babylonian creation stories see CASTELLINO, *op. cit.*, p. 128 f.

[2]) HEIDEL, *op. cit.*, p. 10 f.   [4]) HEIDEL, *op cit.*, p. 62 f.

[3]) Tab. II, lines 90 ff. *et al.*   [5]) *Ibid.*, p. 61.

fication of Marduk as creator [1]). The text begins, like *Enuma Eliš*, with a long series of negative temporal clauses, which in this case lead straight to a positive account of creation [2]). The purpose of these clauses was to add to Marduk's glory by emphasizing that there was nothing which was not created by Marduk except the primeval Ocean ("all the lands were sea", line 10).

Thus none of these non-biblical texts resembles Prov. viii 22-31 either in form or purpose. None begins with a positive statement about the creation: the Egyptian text begins with a statement about how Re himself had come into existence; the Mesopotamian ones begin with the negative clauses referring to the state of affairs before the world was created, and have no prior positive statement about creation. All three texts have as their purpose the glorification of the creator-god, but they all differ in their use of the temporal clauses: *Apophis* uses them to assert the pre-existence of the creator, *Enuma Eliš* merely as an introduction to a mythological narrative, and the other Marduk-text to emphasize the completeness of Marduk's creative act.

Of the two *biblical texts* under discussion, Gen. i 1-3 has, as is well known, been translated in several different ways [3]), the main problem being whether the first clause is to be taken as a simple statement ("In the beginning God created...") or as a temporal clause ("When God began to create..."). In the latter case the succeeding clauses may either be translated as a parenthesis ("the earth being without form and void, with darkness upon the face of the deep and the Spirit of God hovering over the waters") followed by "(then) God said..." as the first positive statement, or the second clause may be treated as the main clause ("the earth was without form and void"). Leaving aside the question of the relative probabilities of these various renderings and taking them separately, we may say that the form of the first, beginning with a positive statement that God created the world in the beginning and then continuing with a more detailed

---

[1]) *Ibid.*

[2]) If "he" in line 15 refers to Lugaldukuga (HEIDEL, p. 62 n. 11) and Lugal-dukuga here refers to Marduk (*AOT*, p. 131, *n.* b), Marduk created the Anunnaki-gods as well as the world. But *AOT* translates line 15 differently: "The Anunnaki-gods together created (the city)". This does not, however, affect the point.

[3]) For recent studies of this question see W. EICHRODT, "In the Beginning" (*Israel's Prophetic Heritage: Essays in Honor of James Muilenburg*, London, 1962, pp. 1 ff.), and a reply by P. HUMBERT, "Encore le premier mot de la Bible", *ZAW* 76, 1964, pp. 121 ff.

description of the process, is quite different from the non-biblical supposed parallels. The first clause (a main clause with the deity as subject of a verb meaning 'to create') is grammatically similar to that of Prov. viii 22, but there the resemblance ends, since Prov. viii 22, far from making the fact of the creation of the world its main point, takes it for granted as a fact already known to the reader, and uses it as a basis for the main assertion about the priority of wisdom over the other creatures. (The fact that more detailed creation material then follows in vv. 24 ff. does not affect this point, since this material also is given not for its own sake but to reinforce the point about wisdom).

The other translations of Gen. i 1-3 also differ fundamentally from all the other passages, both biblical and non-biblical, for while the thought-sequence—a general statement about the act of creation preceding the temporal clauses—remains different from that of the Mesopotamian and Egyptian texts, the first statement itself now has the form of a temporal clause ("When God began"), and this is different from Prov. viii 22. Its only close parallel is now the other biblical text, Gen. ii 4b-7[1]).

At first sight it is Gen. ii 4b-7 which most closely resembles Prov. viii 22-31. The negative temporal clauses, especially the words $w^e k\bar{o}l$... $terem$ (twice), '$ayin$ and $ki\ l\bar{o}$' in v. 5 are reminiscent of the temporal particles of Prov. viii 22-31 (b^e'$\bar{e}n$, twice, v. 24; $b^e terem$, v. 25; '$ad\ l\bar{o}$', v. 26) and are also similar to the opening words of the Mesopotamian texts; but there the similarity ends. The opening phrase "In the day that the Lord God made the heavens" once again distinguishes it both from the non-biblical texts by its taking the act of creation for granted, and from Prov. viii 22-31 by its placing this statement in a subordinate clause. The actual function of the temporal clauses is also unlike that of Prov. viii 24 ff. The purpose of the passage as a whole is not to describe the entire process of the creation of the world but only that of man; and even this motive is subordinate to the purpose of chs. 2 & 3 as a whole. The theme is that of the fall of man due to his overstepping his true allotted function. The first part of ch. 2 is thus an introduction intended to

---

[1]) Gen. v 1 ("When God created man, he made him in the likeness of God") is also not comparable with it, as the purpose of this clause is simply to recapitulate briefly what was already stated in ch. 1. The Babylonian texts referred to on p. 508, n. 2, *supra* are also not comparable, since there the function of the temporal clauses is to summarize the first stages of creation and to introduce a further stage.

define what that function was by means of an account of man's creation. In the first stage of creation there was no vegetation on the earth and no man to control such vegetation if it were created. These temporal clauses thus prepare for the two initial acts of the second stage of creation in vv. 7-9, which reveal man's true function and relation to the rest of creation: God created man, and then created the sphere of man's activity, the garden in Eden, into which he put him. This primary function of man is made quite explicit in v. 15— man was placed in the garden "to till it and keep it". The temporal clauses have thus nothing to do with establishing God's antiquity (as in *Apophis*) or his glory (as in the Mesopotamian texts). These things are all taken for granted in the very first words of the text, "*In the day that* the Lord God made...". But also they have nothing to do with either the purpose of Prov. viii 22-31 as we have it now (the proving of wisdom's antiquity) or with what we may suppose to have been the purpose of the original material used by the author of that passage in his temporal clauses— a systematic description of the creative process. Their purpose is merely to give a brief *résumé* of the already familiar creation story, laying stress on certain aspects which are relevant to the main theme— the creation and fall of man. The material in these verses may be based on that older material, but if so the summary is so brief that we cannot say what it was like.

The foregoing examination of Prov. viii 22-31 and the other texts which have been compared with it leads to the conclusion that these texts are of various kinds and hardly comparable one with another except for the simple facts that they all refer to the creation of the world and that in doing this they (in most cases at least) employ similar grammatical constructions: negative temporal clauses. Neither in their general purpose nor in the function of these temporal clauses can any strong similarities be found. This raises the question whether we can speak here of a common tradition or prototype at all. Prov. viii 24-29 certainly describes the creation of the world—as far as it goes—in terms which belong to a cosmological tradition which Israel shared with the Babylonians [1]), and may well be closely modelled on an older text which was concerned, not with the antiquity of wisdom but simply with describing the creation of the world; but we do not at present possess any text, biblical or non-biblical, which

---

[1]) See, e.g., W. EICHRODT, *Theologie des alten Testaments*, Teil 2-3, Stuttgart, 1961, pp. 57 ff.

bears a close literary relationship to it, although several phrases (especially *hoṭbāʿū*, used of the 'sinking' of the mountains on their bases, cf. Job xxxviii 6) and concepts (e.g. the prescribing of limits to the sea, cf. Job xxxviii 8-11) point to a common Israelite stock of ideas and vocabulary. It is possible that the author took over the negative clauses in vv. 24-26 as part of the tradition which he was following, but in view of the widely differing uses to which this grammatical construction is put in the texts which we have examined, it is also possible that his choice of this construction may be merely fortuitous. If ALBRIGHT's theory about the provenance of Prov. viii 22-31 [1]) is correct, its source, if non-Israelite, would be more likely to be Canaanite-Phoenician than Babylonian; but so far no comparable text has come to light from that quarter.

In comparing texts for which we have no external evidence either of direct borrowing or of the use of a common literary source we must constantly pay due attention to the possibility of coincidence. Any account of the creation of the world is likely, in view of the nature of the subject, to have some points of resemblance with others -e.g. one would expect references to heaven, earth, plants, living creatures, man etc. That a number of different creation stories or stories in which the creation of the world is mentioned should use negative temporal clauses of the kind which we have investigated in order to indicate the absolute priority of the Creator, or the relative order of the various acts of creation, or for some similar purpose, is so natural that there is no need, in the absence of other evidence, to postulate the existence of a common tradition. We may illustrate this point by some further examples from sources where contact with ancient Near Eastern sources can hardly be postulated. In the Brahmin *Rigveda* there occurs the following passage:

Then there was nothing that is, neither anything that is not, neither the air, nor the heavens beyond it... Then there was neither death, nor immortality, neither day nor night. Solitary and alone brooded the One, by himself alone, unmoved by any wind; beside him there was no other. Darkness was there, covered with darkness was this All in the beginning of infinite Water. The Power shrouded in empty Space was brought forth by the might of the brooding Contemplation [2]).

---

[1]) W. F. ALBRIGHT, "Some Canaanite-Phoenician Sources of Hebrew Wisdom", *VT. Suppl.* III, 1955, esp. p. 7 f. On this theory see further my comments in *Wisdom in Proverbs*, pp. 83 ff.

[2]) Translation in A. JEREMIAS, *The Old Testament in the Light of the Ancient East*, vol. I, London, 1911, p. 165.

And the Japanese *Nihongi*, where Japanese mythology is described in terms influenced by Chinese ideas, begins thus;

.   Of old, Heaven and Earth were not yet separated, and the In and Yô not yet divided. They formed a chaotic mass like an egg... The purer and clearer part was thinly drawn out, and formed Heaven, while the heavier and grosser element settled down and became Earth [1]).

The cosmogonies expressed in these texts are of course quite different from those of the Near Eastern texts. Yet they also use the device of the negative temporal phrase ("then there was nothing"; "not yet") to describe the original state of things before the first act of 'creation. This should warn us that more cogent evidence is required before we can speak of a prototype or a common tradition.

---

[1]) Translation in W. G. Aston, *Nihongi*, London, 1924, p. 1 f. There are even more striking parallels in the northern mythologies, in the *Edda* and the Teutonic *Wessobrunner Prayer* (translations in Jeremias, *op. cit.*, pp. 170-173), but there influence from biblical sources is probable on other grounds.

CONSERVATIVE AND PROGRESSIVE THEOLOGY: SIRACH AND WISDOM

ALEXANDER A. DI LELLA, O.F.M.

The two centuries before the birth of Christ can be accurately described as a period of turmoil, confusion and crisis for Judaism, both in Palestine and in the Diaspora. Hellenistic science and humanism had views about God, man and the world which all too often were diametrically opposed to the beliefs of traditional Judaism. Unable to resist the enchanting beauty of Greek painting, sculpture and architecture, and the positive attraction of Greek customs and culture, many Jews gave up the faith of their fathers for a casual syncretism in religion and ethics which demanded little, but promised much. Others tried to remain faithful, but found themselves doubting Israel's inspired books or disparaging the sacred traditions. The deadly spirit of accommodation and compromise was rampant.

In the Deuterocanonical books of the OT we find two basic approaches to the crisis of Hellenism. One is conservative, the other progressive. The first approach is best exemplified by the Book of Sirach which was written c. 180 B.C.; the second, by the Wisdom of Solomon (or the Book of Wisdom), composed shortly before or after the beginning of the first century B.C. Since the adjectives "conservative" and "progressive" have a wide range of meanings, I think it wise for me to define the sense in which I use these terms. By *conservative* I mean "characterized by a tendency to preserve or keep unchanged the truths and answers of the past because only these are adequate as solutions for present problems." By *progressive* I mean "characterized by a tendency to reexamine, rephrase, or adapt the truths and answers of the past in order to make them relevant to present problems."

The chief issues about which one may rightly speak of a conservative or a progressive theology, are these: (1) attitude toward Hellenistic learning and philosophy; (2) anthropology, or the nature of man; (3) the problem of earthly retribution and retribution in the afterlife.

I. The Book of Sirach

Sirach's full name was *Yēšûaʿ ben ʾElʿāzār ben Sírāʾ*, "Jesus, son of Eleazar, son of Sirach," as we read in 50,27 of the emended Hebrew text from the Cairo Geniza.[1] In the prologue to the Greek translation made by

---

[1] Unless otherwise indicated, I have used the CCD version for all references to and citations from Sir because it is based on the Hebrew text discovered in the Geniza of the Qaraite Synagogue in Old Cairo. Since, however, the CCD verse numbering does not always correspond to the Greek, I have given in brackets the Greek numbering in those cases where there is a discrepancy.

the author's grandson some time after 132 B.C., we learn that Sirach "had devoted himself for a long time to the diligent study of the Law, the Prophets and the rest of the books" of his ancestors, and "had developed a thorough familiarity with them." Sirach was a professional scribe or wise man who composed his book for "every seeker after wisdom" (33,18; 50,27). He lived in Jerusalem (50,27: Greek text) but traveled widely, gaining much experience (34,11). He imparted wisdom to young men of the leisure class.

To call Sirach a Sadducee would be anachronistic.[2] But Albright is certainly correct in considering Sirach "as the prototype of the Sadducees,"[3] for many of the doctrines later espoused by the Sadducees can be found in Sir. Like the Sadducees, Sirach was a conservative with respect to the Law, the Prophets and the Writings. He was disinclined to go beyond the traditions contained in those books as regards the nature of man, rewards and punishments in the present life, and the fate of man after death.

A. Sirach's Reaction to Hellenism

The Hellenization of Judaism reached a critical stage when Jason, brother of Onias III, the legitimate high priest, obtained the high priesthood through the intervention of Antiochus IV. A devout Jew, Onias was head of the party that tried to keep the people true to the faith of their fathers. Jason, however, was leader of the Hellenizing party.[4] Since Antiochus viewed Hellenization as a means of achieving some measure of political stability through religious and cultural unity, he was more than happy to depose Onias and to install Jason as high priest. Antiochus was even happier to accept Jason's generous bribe of 360 silver talents, the equivalent of almost $360,000. As high priest, Jason did his utmost to paganize his countrymen. He erected a gymnasium (Greek sports arena and pertinent buildings) in Jerusalem itself and introduced the people to Greek games, dress, and other customs that were considered abominations by pious Jews. Holy Zion was even recognized as a Greek *polis*. The dismal story of those troublous times is told in 2 Mc 4.

Now even though Jason was high priest from 174-171 B.C.—some ten years after Sir was written—the Jerusalem sage was keenly aware of the threat that Hellenism posed for orthodox Judaism.[5] Indeed, it is not un-

---

[2] Cf. H. Duesberg-P. Auvray, *Le livre de l'Ecclésiastique* (*SBJ*; Paris, ²1958) 18.

[3] *From the Stone Age to Christianity* (2d ed., Anchor Books; New York, 1957) 354.

[4] The Hellenizers either took Greek names or Grecized their Jewish names. Josephus (*Antiquities*, xii, 5, 1) mentions that Jason's original name was Jesus (Joshua in Hebrew).

[5] Cf. R. Smend, *Die Weisheit des Jesus Sirach erklärt* (Berlin, 1906) xx-xxi.

likely that Sirach knew Jason, for Jason's father was Simon II, the high priest whom Sirach praises so highly in ch. 50. In his travels, Sirach undoubtedly saw many of the baneful effects of Hellenization. He must have met many Jews whose faith was shaken by the questions and doubts that Greek philosophy and religion had raised. These Jews had a gnawing, unexpressed fear that the religion of their fathers was inadequate to cope with the needs of a vastly changed social and political structure.

To bolster the faith and confidence of his fellow Jews, Sirach published his book. His purpose was not so much to engage in a systematic polemic against Hellenism, but rather to convince Jews and even well-disposed Gentiles that true wisdom is to be found in Jerusalem, not in Athens; in the inspired books of Israel, not in the clever writings of Hellenistic humanism.

As a genuine conservative in the best sense of the word, Sirach urges his readers to look to the past for answers to the present crisis. He writes:

> Study the generations long past and understand;
> has anyone hoped in the Lord and been disappointed?
> Has anyone persevered in his fear and been forsaken?
> has anyone called upon him and been rebuffed? (2,10)

Sirach feels compelled to issue a stern warning to Jews who were captivated by the allurements of Greek ways and were tempted to work out a convenient compromise with Hellenism:

> Woe to craven hearts and drooping hands,
> to the sinner who treads a double path! (2,12)

The double path is Judaism and Hellenism. Sirach addresses stronger words to renegades:

> Woe to you, O sinful men,
> who forsake the law of the Most High. (41,8)

Sirach also contrasts the foolish apostate with the faithful Jew:

> He who hates the Law is without wisdom,
> and is tossed about like a boat in a storm.
> The prudent man trusts in the word of the Lord,
> and the Law is dependable for him as a divine oracle. (33,2-3)

Greek thinkers offered carefully reasoned opinions on almost every conceivable subject, from the most high God to the lowliest atom. Sirach perceived the danger as well as the enticement of such learning. For man wants to know all he can about himself and the world he lives in. To remind his fellow Jews that true wisdom resides only in Israel, Sirach devotes the first 43 chapters of his lengthy book to an explanation of that wisdom and to its application in day-to-day living. *Sophia,* "wisdom," was one of the most cherished words in the Hellenistic world. So Sirach writes:

> If you desire wisdom, keep the commandments,
>   and the Lord will bestow her upon you;
> For fear of the Lord is wisdom and culture;
>   loyal humility is his delight. (1,23-24 [26-27])

True wisdom comes forth from the mouth of God (24,3) and finds its dwelling in Israel (24,8). Sirach identifies wisdom with the Torah of Moses (24,22 [23]). Utilizing the inspired literature of his predecessors and building upon it, Sirach offers his readers rules of conduct and doctrinal directives in the form of gnomic poetry. He has something to say on almost every aspect of life.[6]

In this soundly conservative approach no attempt is made to employ the methods and techniques of Greek learning, for Sirach was convinced that only a careful study of Israel's glorious heritage could provide sufficient answers to man's basic questions about himself and his ultimate destiny. Thus, the Jerusalem sage cautions his readers about the futility of Greek speculation into the nature of reality:

> What is too sublime for you, seek not,
>   into things beyond your strength search not.
> What is committed to you, attend to;
>   for what is hidden is not your concern.
> With what is too much for you meddle not,
>   when shown things beyond human understanding.
> Their own opinion has misled many,
>   and false reasoning unbalanced their judgment. (3,20-23 [21-24])

In the section entitled "Praise of the Fathers" (44,1—50,21), Sirach pulls out all the stops to celebrate the glories of Israel's past. He gives a rapid review of salvation history from Adam to Simon II, the high priest whom Sirach himself saw officiating in the Temple "vested in his magnificent robes, and wearing his garments of splendor" (50,11). Hellenistic humanism had its Homer, Socrates, Plato, Aristotle, Epicurus, Zeno, and Cleanthes. But who are these when compared with such mighty heroes as Abraham, "father of many peoples" (44,19); or Moses, "whose memory is held in benediction" (45,1); or Aaron, who was chosen "from all mankind to offer holocausts and choice offerings" (45,16); or Joshua, the "valiant leader" (46,1); or Samuel, who "anointed princes to rule the people" (46,13); or David, whose strength Yahweh exalted forever (47,11); or Solomon, whose "fame reached distant coasts" (47,16)?

---

6 Cf. the topical outline I have given in my article on Sirach in the *New Catholic Encyclopedia* to be published this year.

B. Sirach's View of Man

With respect to the nature of man, conservative Sirach uses the same vocabulary and thought categories that one finds in the other parts of the Hebrew OT. He made absolutely no attempt to accommodate his outlook to the more enlightened anthropological views of the Greeks. Thus, terms like *bāśār*, *nᵉšāmâ*, *nepeš*, *rûaḥ*, and *lēb/lēbāb* generally have the same range of meanings in Sir as in the Hebrew Canon.[7]

What needs to be emphasized here is that Sirach does not subscribe to the body-soul dualism that was taught in Greek philosophy. Rather, he views man as a vital unity. Man is *bāśār*, "flesh" or "body" (44,20), but *bāśār* can also mean "human being" (14,17). When man has *nᵉšāmâ*, "breath," he is alive (33,21 [30,29]).[8] Sirach also uses *nᵉšāmâ* as a synonym for "life" (9,13), *zōē* in the grandson's Greek. In addition to *bāśār* and *nᵉšāmâ*, man has *nepeš*, which is often inaccurately translated as "soul." Now *nepeš* has a wide variety of meanings. It can mean "life" (51,3.6) or "spirit" (40,29c), but it also denotes those things that make a man alive: for example, in 6,2.4 and 19,3, *nepeš* means "desire" or "passion."[9] In the Hebrew view of man, *nepeš* or "life" resides in the *dām*, "blood,"[10] which of course is found in the *bāśār*, "flesh." Hence, in 14,18 Sirach uses the expression *bāśār wᵉdām*, "flesh and blood,"[11] to designate man. But man also has *rûaḥ*, "spirit" or "vigor" (48,12.24). Finally, man possesses *lēb/lēbāb*, "heart," which is the seat of intelligence (4,17; 37,12) as well as the source of sentiment and desire (9,9).

C. Sirach's Ideas about Retribution

The normative doctrine of retribution in Sirach's time was simply this: observance of the Law brought material prosperity and long life to nation

---

[7] On biblical anthropology in general, cf. J. Pedersen, *Israel: Its Life and Culture* 1-2 (London-Copenhagen, 1926) 99-181; G. von Rad, *Old Testament Theology* (tr. D. M. G. Stalker; Edinburgh-London, 1962) I, 152-153; and M. Baily, "Biblical Man and Some Formulae of Christian Teaching," *IrTQ* 27 (1960) 173-200.

[8] Cf. Gn 2,7; 1 Kgs 17,17; Is 2,22; 45,5; Jb 27,3.

[9] In Sir, as in biblical Hebrew, *nepeš* is used also as a reflexive and intensive pronoun; cf. 7,20.21; 9,6; 10,27.28 [28.29]; 14,16; 30,21; 32 [35],23; 37,8.19.21 [22]; 50,25.

[10] Gn 9,4; Lv 17,11.14; Dt 12,23.

[11] This expression is not found in the Hebrew canon nor in the non-biblical Qumrân literature published prior to 1960; the phrase is not found in K. G. Kuhn (ed.), *Konkordanz zu den Qumrantexten* (Göttingen, 1960). Interestingly enough, however, the Greek expression *sarx kai haima* occurs in Mt 16,17; 1 Cor 15,50; and Gal 1,16; and *haima kai sarx* in Eph 6,12 and Heb 2,14. The Hebrew phrase *bāśār wᵉdām* is found very frequently in the rabbinic literature; cf. M. Jastrow, *A Dictionary of the Targumim, the Talmud Babli and Yerushalmi, and the Midrashic Literature* (London-New York, 1903) I, 199.

and to individual; sin brought adversity and early death.[12] Rewards and punishments after death were not even considered. This doctrine can be called the Deuteronomic theology of retribution[13] because it was applied as an interpretative principle by the Deuteronomic redactors of Israel's historical records, and is set forth clearly in Dt 28. This doctrine admitted that adversity can serve as a test of fidelity (cf. Jgs 2,22—3,6). But later the doctrine developed into a rigid, almost mathematical equation—prosperity equals virtue practiced; suffering equals sin committed.[14] Because after death all men—saints and sinners—went to Sheol, and because the dead will not rise again (Jb 14,12), Sheol cannot be considered as a place of retribution. In Sheol the dead shared alike a dark, listless, dismal existence separated from God.

Now the well-travelled and well-read Sirach probably knew that the doctrine of the resurrection of the dead was gaining currency at least in some Jewish circles, for the Book of Daniel (ch. 12), composed some 15 years after Sir, speaks of the doctrine as if it were not something new. But since the resurrection was not normative Jewish theology in the earlier part of the second century B.C., conservative Sirach reflects the old Deuteronomic doctrine of retribution: reward for virtue and punishment for sin take place only here on earth. Hence, he gives this advice to his students:

> Do no evil, and evil will not overtake you;
>> avoid wickedness, and it will turn aside from you. (7,1-2)
> Rejoice not at a proud man's success;
>> remember he will not reach death unpunished. (9,12)

Since "death does not tarry" (14,12), Sirach writes:

> Give, take, and treat yourself well,
>> for in the nether world there are no joys to seek.
> All flesh grows old, like a garment;
>> the age-old law is: All must die. (14,16-17)

Thus, man must seek his complete fulfillment only during his earthly life.

Since there is no return from Sheol, Sirach urges moderation in mourning for the dead lest "heartache destroy one's health" (38,19 [18]). The advice sounds offensive:

[12] Cf. von Rad, *op. cit.* 384-386, for an excellent discussion of Israel's theology of sin and virtue.

[13] A fine treatment of this doctrine can be found in O. S. Rankin, *Israel's Wisdom Literature: Its Bearing on Theology and the History of Religion* (Edinburgh, 1936 [reprinted 1954]) 77-80.

[14] Compare 2 Kgs 15,1-5 (by the Deuteronomist) with 2 Chr 26,16-23 (by the Chronicler). Rankin, *op. cit.* 79-80, gives other examples too.

> Recall him not, for there is no hope of his return;
> it will not help him, but will do you harm. (38,21)

We should not be harsh with the Jerusalem sage, because after all he was merely applying the traditional teaching on retribution to everyday life. Sirach dispels all doubts regarding the nature of the dismal, dark, gloomy existence man endured in Sheol:

> Who in the nether world can glorify the Most High
> in place of the living who offer their praise?
> No more can the dead give praise than those who have never lived;
> they glorify the Lord who are alive and well. (17,22-23 [27-28])

For the devout Israelite, life without the worship and praise of God was meaningless.[15]

In Sir one finds the flexible Deuteronomic doctrine that made allowance for probationary suffering:

> My son, when you come to serve the Lord,
> prepare yourself for trials.
> Be sincere of heart and steadfast,
> undisturbed in time of adversity.
> For in fire gold is tested,
> and worthy men in the crucible of humiliation. (2,1-2.5)

The point of this admonition is that the virtuous should not be dismayed by ill-fortune, for eventually they will be rewarded with the usual material blessings: long life, good health, numerous children, etc. As a keen observer of the disconcerting facts of experience, Sirach was painfully conscious of the anomaly that the wicked often prosper right up to the time of their death. But, we are assured, disaster indeed awaits the sinner, even though it may be delayed to the last hours of life:

> For it is easy with the Lord on the day of death
> to repay man according to his deeds.
> A moment's affliction brings forgetfulness of past delights;
> when a man dies, his life is revealed. (11,26-27)

After death, the only way man lives on is in his children and in his good, or bad, name (30,4-5; 41,5-13). Even the possibility of rewards or punishments in some sort of afterlife receives no mention in the original Hebrew text of our book.[16] But the Greek translation does make definite allusions

---

[15] Von Rad writes (*op. cit.* 369-370): "Praise is man's most characteristic mode of existence: praising and not praising stand over against one another like life and death." Hence, existence in Sheol was a living death.

[16] Cf. E. F. Sutcliffe, *The Old Testament and the Future Life* (Westminster, ²1947) 30-36. G. H. Box-W. O. E. Oesterley, "Sirach" in *The Apocrypha and Pseudepigrapha of the Old Testament*, ed. by R. H. Charles (Oxford, 1913) I, 314, see in texts like

to retribution in the world to come.[17] This should cause no surprise, for Sirach's grandson made the translation in Alexandria shortly before the author of the Wisdom of Solomon spelt out the truth of a blessed immortality for the righteous and a miserable fate for the wicked.

II. The Wisdom of Solomon

The author of the book entitled the Wisdom of Solomon is unknown. Though Solomon is not actually mentioned in the book, he is obviously the speaker who addresses kings in chs. 6 to 9, for in 9,7-8 he says that it was he who built the Temple in Jerusalem. Solomon, of course, could not have written the book. Unlike Sirach who provides so much biographical information in his book, the author of Wis—usually called Pseudo-Solomon—tells us very little about himself. It is generally agreed, however, that Pseudo-Solomon was a pious Alexandrian Jew who had a good command of the Greek language and must have had more than a nodding acquaintance with the works of Hellenistic humanism.

As in most matters dealing with the Bible, there is no unanimity of scholarly opinion with respect to the unity of the book, its date, or its original language. I am assuming: (1) a single author composed all 19 chapters of the book; (2) the book was written about the beginning of the first century B.C.; (3) the original language of the entire book was Greek; and (4) the author used Greek as a first language.[18]

A. Pseudo-Solomon's Reaction to Hellenism

We have already seen that the process of Hellenization in Palestine reached a high point during the reign of Antiochus IV who received enthusiastic support from the high priest Jason (174-171 B.C.). But thanks to the Maccabean revolt, which began in 167 B.C., the religious situation had improved considerably. However, in the Egyptian Diaspora, especially in Alexandria, Hellenism continued to make penetrating inroads into the

---

22,10 [11], in which the dead man is said to be at rest, "the adumbration of a belief in something more than a mere shadowy existence beyond the grave." These scholars can hardly be correct, for in texts like 14,16, which is cited above, there is an unambiguous affirmation that Sheol is nothing to look forward to. The "rest" that Sirach speaks of in 22,10 [11] is nothing more than the sluggish existence akin to sleep or unconsciousness that we would not call life, but rather mere survival—such was the lot of the inhabitants of Sheol.

[17] Cf. M. Fang Che-Yong, *Quaestiones theologicae selectae libri Sira ex comparatione textus graeci et hebraici ortae* (Rome, 1964) 37-54.

[18] Cf. R. H. Pfeiffer, *History of New Testament Times with an Introduction to the Apocrypha* (New York, 1949) 319-328, for a survey of scholarly views regarding these critical problems.

minds and hearts of the Jews. Uprooted from the land of their forefathers and far removed from the religious center of their faith, Alexandrian Jews were more prone to give in to the blandishments of Hellenism. Many gave up their faith altogether; others attempted to combine Hellenism and Judaism—the double path that was deplored by Sirach almost a century earlier (Sir 2,12). To make the situation even worse, Hellenizers and renegade Jews often harassed faithful Jews by attempting to convert them to the new way of life that Hellenism offered.[19]

Pseudo-Solomon played a key role during this critical period. A well-educated Jew, he utilized all his intellectual resources to encourage his demoralized and weak-willed coreligionists to remain steadfast in their faith. Though he employed some of the language and techniques of the Greek philosophers, Pseudo-Solomon's purpose was not to reconcile Judaism with Hellenism—a task that Philo attempted[20] a few years later—but rather to prevent the Hellenization of Judaism. In all of this, Pseudo-Solomon stressed the enduring realities of the Jewish religion which had no apologies to make to Hellenism. Thus, his purpose was similar to, though much broader than, Sirach's: viz., (1) to strengthen the pious Jews by demonstrating that the prosperity of the wicked was only apparent and quite transitory; (2) to warn those who wavered in their faith by showing that the very Hellenistic philosophy and culture that had been the source of so many troublesome doubts can actually lend support to their faith; (3) to bring back the many apostates who had renounced their faith because they felt it inferior to the Greek way of life; and (4) to convert the pagans by showing them the folly of their idolatrous practices and by proving to them that the Jews were not barbarians or enemies of the human race.[21]

But unlike conservative Sirach, Pseudo-Solomon was a genuine progressive who felt the urgent need to restudy the inspired books and to present a new synthesis in a language that the new age would understand. Since language and civilization are inseparable, one should not be surprised to find the Greek speaking Pseudo-Solomon employing some Greek thought categories, even though these are quite different from the more primitive and less adaptable Hebrew categories.[22] Thus, one finds in Wis terms and

---

[19] J. Reider, *The Book of Wisdom* (New York, 1957) 11.

[20] Cf. E. Schürer, *A History of the Jewish People in the Time of Jesus Christ,* 2d division, vol. 3, tr. by S. Taylor and P. Christie (Edinburgh, 1896) 364-365.

[21] Cf. W. O. E. Oesterley, *An Introduction to the Books of the Apocrypha* (London, 1935 [reprinted 1953]) 212-214; E. Osty, *Le livre de la Sagesse* (*SBJ*; Paris, ²1957) 14-15; M. Hadas, "Wisdom of Solomon," *Interpreter's Dictionary of the Bible* 4 (New York-Nashville, 1962) 863.

[22] Cf. Osty, *op. cit.* 22-23.

dialectical methods that had been used previously by Greek philosophers, but Pseudo-Solomon's message remains nonetheless thoroughly Jewish. The richness of Greek vocabulary, the precision of Greek grammar and syntax, and the insights of Greek philosophy and science, Pseudo-Solomon put to good use for the purpose of demonstrating the relevance of Jewish theology to a sophisticated age. For example, he writes:[23]

> ... Wisdom is mobile beyond all motion,
>   and she penetrates and pervades all things by reason of her purity. (7,24)

The verbs "penetrates" and "pervades"—*diēkei* and *chōrei*—must have been familiar to his readers because those terms are used by Stoic philosophers to describe the diffusion of the world-soul.[24] But Pseudo-Solomon insists that what "penetrates" and "pervades" all things is not the world-soul of the Stoics, but wisdom which finds its source in the God of the Jews.

Pseudo-Solomon had a high regard for the scientific advances made by the Greeks, for he was convinced that there could be no conflict between true religious faith and science. Truth is one because God is óne. And wisdom, which comes from God, both teaches man the truths of faith and leads man to a knowledge of science. Thus, in 7,15-22a we read what may be an autobiographical note about Pseudo-Solomon's education:

> Now God grant [that] I speak suitably
>   and value these endowments at their worth!
> For he is the guide of Wisdom
>   and the director of the wise.
> For both we and our words are in his hand,
>   as well as all prudence and knowledge of crafts.
> For he gave me sound knowledge of existing things [metaphysics],
>   that I might know the organization of the
>   universe and the force of its elements [cosmology],
> The beginning and the end and the midpoint of times [chronology],
>   the changes in the sun's course and the variations of the seasons,
> Cycles of years, positions of the stars [astronomy],
>   natures of animals, tempers of beasts [zoology],
> Powers of the winds and thoughts of men [psychology],
>   uses of plants and virtues of roots [medicine]—
> Such things as are secret I learned, and such as are plain;
>   for Wisdom, the artificer of all, taught me.

Although Pseudo-Solomon had a sympathetic understanding of Greek philosophy and science, he by no means glorified knowledge for the sake of

[23] All citations are from the CCD version. But for the words "just" and "justice" I have substituted the more exact terms "righteous" and "righteousness."

[24] Cf. Reider, *op. cit.* 115. The four cardinal virtues listed in 8,7 are found also in the writings of Plato and the Stoics; cf. S. Holmes, "The Wisdom of Solomon" in *The Apocrypha and Pseudepigrapha of the Old Testament* 1, 548.

knowledge. On the contrary, knowledge must be coupled with the faithful observance of the Law; there is no other way to achieve true wisdom, the precondition of righteousness which leads to immortality. Pseudo-Solomon employs a *sorites,* or chain syllogism—a type of argument often used by Stoic philosophers—to drive home this truth:

> For the first step toward discipline is a very earnest desire for her;
> then, care for discipline is love of her;
> Love means the keeping of her laws;
> to observe her laws is the basis for incorruptibility;
> And incorruptibility makes one close to God;
> thus the desire for Wisdom leads up to a kingdom. (6,17-20)

Texts such as these prove that Pseudo-Solomon was a conscientious and convinced Jew who in no way compromised his religious beliefs when utilizing the resources of Greek humanism to convey his message.[25]

B. *Pseudo-Solomon's View of Man*

Pseudo-Solomon's statements on the nature of man lack semantic consistency. This is not surprising for two reasons: (1) in order to emphasize the enduring relevance of Israel's inspired books, Pseudo-Solomon couched his message in the language of the more primitive anthropological categories found in those books which he knew so well;[26] and (2) as a well-educated progressive who felt compelled to rethink and adapt the teachings of the past for a generation of Jews who were thinking in categories different from the ones contained in the older Scriptures, Pseudo-Solomon employed some of the terms and thought patterns of Greek philosophical speculation regarding the nature of man. Because of this twofold intent, one occasionally finds a certain ambiguity in Pseudo-Solomon's use of such anthropological terms as *psychē* ("soul, life"), *pneuma* ("spirit"), *nous* ("mind"), *sōma* ("body"), *sarx* ("flesh"), and *kardia* ("heart"). Hence, it would be a mistake to assume that these terms invariably have the meaning which Greek philosophy attached to them. For example, *kardia*, which occurs six times in Wis, has a strictly Greek meaning only once: "Reason is a spark at the beating of our

---

[25] M.-J. Lagrange, "Le livre de la Sagesse: sa doctrine des fins dernières," *RB* n.s. 4 (1907) 88, notes that when Pseudo-Solomon writes that God created the world *ex amorphou hylēs,* "out of formless matter" (11,17), we should not assume that he agreed with Plato's doctrine regarding the eternity of matter; rather, Pseudo-Solomon attempted to restate Gn 1,1-2 in language understandable to his contemporaries. Cf. also S. Lange, "The Wisdom of Solomon and Plato," *JBL* 55 (1936) 293-302.

[26] P. W. Skehan, "Isaias and the Teaching of the Book of Wisdom," *CBQ* 2 (1940) 290, writes: "It may be said that the nineteen chapters of Wisdom contain not many lines, and extremely few connected passages that have not been derived in large part from fruitful meditation on the earlier sacred books."

hearts" (2,2). This statement, which Pseudo-Solomon places in the mouth
of the wicked, reflects the teaching of some Greek philosophers who assumed
that the beating of the heart produced thought in the form of sparks from
the fire-substance of the soul.[27] In the five other occurrences, however,
kardia has essentially the same signification as Hebrew *lēb*, of which we
spoke earlier.

In 1,6 we find the word *nephroi*, "kidneys," used in exactly the same
sense as Hebrew *kᵉlāyôt*, viz., as the source of man's most secret feelings and
desires.[28] Such a meaning of *nephroi* is apparently unknown in Classical or
Hellenistic literature.[29] The word *psychē* Pseudo-Solomon uses 25 times,
often with the same meaning as Hebrew *nepeš* (12,6; 14,5; 16,9). *Pneuma*,
which occurs 20 times, is sometimes used, like Hebrew *rûah*, in such expressions as "the *spirit* of Wisdom" (7,7) and "wisdom is a kindly *spirit*" (1,6).
When applied to man, *pneuma* has the same meaning as *psychē* (15,11.16;
16,14).[30] In fact, the three terms *psychē*, *pneuma*, and *nous* refer alike to a
single reality, viz., the "soul" which is one of the two constitutive elements
of man, the other being *sōma*, "body" (1,4; 8,19-20; 9,15; 15,8.11.16;
16,14).[31] From texts like these, especially 9,15—"For the corruptible *body*
burdens the *soul* and the *earthen shelter* weighs down the *mind* that has
many concerns"—we may rightly conclude that Pseudo-Solomon assented
to the body-soul dualism which was characteristic of Greek anthropological
theory.[32]

C. Pseudo-Solomon's Ideas about Retribution

The pious Israelite must have experienced intense anguish over the Deuteronomic theory of earthly retribution. In fact, the Book of Job is concerned precisely with the dilemmas which this doctrine posed. Qoheleth who
knew from bitter experience that the doctrine did not apply in all cases,
simply rejected it (Eccl 8,14; 9,2-3). But a few years later, conservative

[27] Osty, *op. cit.* 35; Reider, *op. cit.* 61.

[28] Cf. Ps 73,21; Jer 11,20; 12,2; 17,10; 20,12.

[29] Cf. *ThWNT* 4, 912f.; H. G. Liddell-R. Scott-H. S. Jones-R. McKenzie, *A Greek-
English Lexicon* (Oxford, 1953) 1172.

[30] Cf. Holmes, *op. cit.* 560.

[31] As regards the equivalence of *psychē* and *nous*, cf. R. Schütz, *Les idées eschato-
logiques du livre de la Sagesse* (Strasbourg, 1935) 24-25.

[32] But, unlike Plato and Philo, Pseudo-Solomon does not view man as a trichotomy
of *sōma, psychē,* and *nous*; cf. P. Heinisch, *Das Buch der Weisheit* (Münster i.W.,
1912) 186-188. There is considerable dispute as to whether or not in 8,19-20 Pseudo-
Solomon reflects the Platonic doctrine of the pre-existence of the soul; cf. Pfeiffer,
op. cit. 328, for pertinent literature. In 7,1-2 and 15,11, both of which texts speak of the
creation of man, there is no mention of pre-existence; in fact, pre-existence seems to
be explicitly excluded in 15,11.

Sirach endorsed wholeheartedly the old Deuteronomic teaching of rewards and punishments on this side of the grave.

Of the OT wise men only the progressive Pseudo-Solomon provides an adequate and satisfying solution to the vexing problem of retribution, viz., by the doctrine of sanctions in the afterlife.[33] It is a central teaching of Wis that the older theories on death, Sheol (as the abode of *all* the dead), and earthly rewards and punishments, are false. In fact, many of the statements made by the wicked in 2,1-9 are tenets of the older theology of death and retribution. For example, compare the following statements of the wicked with certain texts from Job:

Brief and troublous is our lifetime; neither is there any remedy for man's dying, nor is anyone known to have come back from the nether world (Wis 2,1).	Man, born of woman, is short-lived and full of trouble (Jb 14,1).
	He who goes down to the nether world shall come up no more (7,9b).
	Our days on earth are but a shadow (8,9b).
Our lifetime is the passing of a shadow; and our dying cannot be deferred because it is fixed with a seal; and no one returns (2,5).	I go whence I shall not return, to the land of darkness and of gloom (10, 21).[34]

In answer to the words of the wicked, Pseudo-Solomon writes:

> These were their thoughts, but they erred;
> for their wickedness blinded them,
> And they knew not the hidden counsels of God;
> neither did they count on a recompense of holiness
> nor discern the innocent souls' reward.
> For God formed man to be imperishable. (2,21-23a)

OT man finally learned the consoling truth of blessed immortality as the ultimate answer to the problem of retribution.

Progressive Pseudo-Solomon also says comforting things to those who had been considered, in the older theology, as objects of reproach or of punishment. "Better is childlessness with virtue; for immortal is its memory"

[33] The Wisdom of Solomon was written after Dn and 2 Mc, both of which teach the doctrine of the resurrection of the dead. But in Dn (12,2-3.13), there is doubt whether or not all the righteous, or just the martyrs, will rise from the dead; and in 2 Mc (7,7-22; 12,38-46; 14,45-46), resurrection does not apply to the wicked. Cf. L. F. Hartman-J. T. Nelis, "Resurrection of the Dead," *Encyclopedic Dictionary of the Bible* (New York, 1963) 2027; F.-M. Abel—J. Starcky, *Les livres des Maccabées* (*SBJ;* Paris, ⁸1961) 21. In Wis, however, retribution in the hereafter applies to both the righteous and the wicked.

[34] P. W. Skehan, *The Literary Relationship between the Book of Wisdom and the Protocanonical Wisdom Books of the Old Testament* (Washington, 1938) 3-5, gives a rather complete list of similarities between Wis 2,1-9 and Jb.

(4,1).[35] And an early death is not a curse, for "the righteous man, though he die early, shall be at rest" (4,7). Even the faithful eunuch, who could not be admitted into "the community of the LORD" (Dt 23,2), will receive "fidelity's choice reward and a more gratifying heritage in the Lord's temple" (Wis 3,14).

Because the righteous have as their lot *athanasia*, "immortality" (3,4; 4,1; 8,13.17; 15,3), and *aphtharsia*, "incorruption" or "(blessed) immortality"[36] (2,23; 6,18.19), scholars[37] have often assumed that Pseudo-Solomon adopted the Platonic notion of the soul's native immortality.[38] But this assumption appears quite unlikely, for Pseudo-Solomon regarded immortality not as a philosophical conclusion, but rather as a pure gift of God which is accorded to those who live virtuously (6,17-20).[39] True, Pseudo-Solomon borrowed some vocabulary from Greek philosophy, but his thoughts are authentically Jewish. In the very first chapter of his book he places his teaching on blessed immortality completely within the framework of Jewish religious categories when he states "Love righteousness" (1,1) and then explains the reason: "For righteousness is immortal" (1,15). And his description of the happy destiny of the virtuous and the miserable fate of the impious could have been written only by a Jew.

"The souls of the righteous are in the hand of God, and no torment shall touch them" (3,1). They are not really dead (3,2); rather "they are in peace" (3,3) and "at rest" (4,7). The upright man is "accounted among the sons of God [i.e., among the angels[40]]," and "his lot is with the saints" (5,5). "The righteous live forever, and in the Lord is their recompense" (5,15). "Therefore shall they receive the splendid crown, the beauteous diadem, from the hand of the Lord" (5,16) and "shall judge nations and rule over peoples, and the Lord shall be their King forever" (3,8). They shall be resplendent (3,7), "shall understand truth," and "shall abide with (the Lord) in love" (3,9). Pseudo-Solomon is less clear about the final destiny

---

[35] Cf. also 3,13. In the OT barrenness had been considered a disgrace (Gn 30,23; 1 Sm 1,5-8), or a punishment (2 Sm 6,23; Hos 9,11). Even Elizabeth praises the Lord for removing her "reproach" (Lk 1,25).

[36] Cf. J. P. Weisengoff, "Death and Immortality in the Book of Wisdom," *CBQ* 3 (1941) 129.

[37] The most recent is R. B. Y. Scott, *Proverbs. Ecclesiastes* (*Anchor Bible*; New York, 1965) xxiii.

[38] Cf. F. Copleston, *A History of Philosophy*, 1 (new rev. ed.; Westminster, Md., 1950) 211-215, for a good summary of Plato's arguments for the immortality of the soul.

[39] Cf. M. Delcor, "L'immortalité de l'âme dans le livre de la Sagesse et dans les documents de Qumrân," *NRT* 77 (1955) 615.

[40] Cf. P. W. Skehan, *CBQ* 21 (1959) 526-527.

of the wicked. He does not state explicitly that their punishment will be eternal. But he does say that they are in the possession of the devil, through whom "death entered the world" (2,24). "They shall . . . become dishonored corpses and an unceasing mockery among the dead. . . . They shall be utterly laid waste and shall be in grief and their memory shall perish" (4,19). In the final confrontation with the righteous, the wicked shall groan "through anguish of spirit" (5,3), conscious of the bitter fact that they were fools (5,4). Pseudo-Solomon does not say what happens to the wicked after the final confrontation. It remained for NT revelation to make explicit the doctrine of eternal punishment for unrepentant sinners.

In none of the above quotations, or elsewhere in the book, is the soul represented as having of its very nature a sufficient reason for its continued existence after death. Nor do we find anywhere in Wis Plato's theory of ideas. In his *Phaedo,* Plato "declares that the belief in the immortality of the soul stands or falls with this theory."[41]

What, then, is the nature of the immortality which Pseudo-Solomon obviously teaches? Is his anthropological view on the body-soul dualism relevant to his teaching? Does God's gift of blessed immortality pertain only to the soul? or is the resurrection of the dead the immortality spoken of? or are both kinds of immortality to be understood? These are knotty questions. And scholars have given a variety of answers.[42]

My own answers are these:

1. Pseudo-Solomon's view that man is a body-soul composite is relevant to his teaching on immortality. For it seems impossible even to discuss immortality without at least some clear notions regarding the nature of man.

2. Except in 3,1 where souls are spoken of, Pseudo-Solomon describes the happy state which righteous *persons* will enjoy (3,2-9 and the other texts given above). It seems, therefore, that blessed immortality is a gift granted primarily to the person.

3. Although Pseudo-Solomon does not make clear the manner in which virtuous persons will be immortal, he does state in 3,1 that "the *souls* of the righteous are in the hand of God." Moreover, he implies that the reward of the upright will take place immediately after death (3, 2-3; 4,7; 5,5.15). Hence, he seems to imply, but does not actually state, that blessed immortality is granted to the soul of the person right after his death.

4. Since resurrection is not explicitly excluded and since emphasis is

---

[41] W. Jaeger, "The Greek Ideas of Immortality" in *Immortality and Resurrection,* ed. by K. Stendahl (New York, 1965) 103.

[42] In addition to the commentaries already referred to, cf. Skehan, *CBQ* 21 (1959) 526-527; and R. E. Murphy, *Seven Books of Wisdom* (Milwaukee, 1960) 137-142.

placed on the happy state of the *whole person,* it seems likely that the final retribution of the righteous will include resurrection of the body.[43]

ALEXANDER A. DI LELLA, O.F.M.
Holy Name College
Washington, D. C.

[43] The doctrine of the resurrection seems to be definitely implied in the third part of Wis (chs. 10—19), so that those Jews who already believed it would see it reflected there. Perhaps because the resurrection repelled his Hellenized fellow citizens (cf. Acts 17,32), Pseudo-Solomon spoke only of the blessed immortality of the person or soul. Cf. A. Lefèvre, "La Sagesse" in A. Robert-A. Feuillet, *Introduction à la Bible* (Tournai, ²1959) 1, 769-770. P. Beauchamp, "Le salut corporel des justes et la conclusion du livre de la Sagesse," *Bib* 45 (1964) 491-526, provides a fine discussion of this whole problem and gives some interesting conclusions.

≪≪ ≪≪

Folk Proverbs of the Ancient Near East

R. B. Y. SCOTT, F.R.S.C.

ARCHBISHOP Trench opens his comparison of the proverbs of different nations with a quotation from Francis Bacon, "The genius, wit and spirit of a nation are discovered in its proverbs," and he proceeds to discuss these national characteristics and also the appearance of essentially the same proverb in many languages, ancient and modern.[1] Even when the verbal parallel is not close,[2] there seems to be a psychological common denominator to the folk wisdom of different peoples. The same or similar attitudes, interests, and judgments are represented. With due allowance for distinctions in language structure, similar thought patterns and verbal formulations recur. Some of these undoubtedly must be attributed to the migration and adaptation of popular sayings and literary epigrams as the result of intercommunication between contemporary cultures. Some of the similarity is due to literary dependence, because Babylonian culture drew from the Sumerian, and Western European has drawn many of its proverbs from the classical world, the Hebrew Bible, and the New Testament. Biblical proverbs and proverbial metaphors have made themselves at home in literary and colloquial English. If they are less used today (and, if used, go unrecognized), this is due partly to a decline in the art of conversation, partly to decreasing familiarity with the Bible, and partly, perhaps, to a lesser emphasis on the moral instruction of children in the home. The moralizing tone of the Biblical "Proverbs of Solomon" is certainly less congenial to us than it was to our fathers.

Not all Biblical proverbs, however, are moralistic. A distinction must be made between the picturesque adages of folk wisdom and the pointed sayings of prophets and wise men on the one hand, and, on the other hand, the deliberately didactic materials of the Book of Proverbs. The preface to that book, 1:1–7, explains that its various materials and several collections had been assembled as a kind of source-book for training in moral and religious wisdom. Two of its major elements[3] are collections of what are designated as "Proverbs of Solomon," a term denoting a literary form—the bilinear couplet in poetic parallelism—rather than ascribing authorship to the traditional patron of wisdom. In any case, the basic regularity of the Solomonic

[1] R. C. Trench, *Proverbs and their Lessons*, ed. A. S. Palmer (London, 1905), pp. 46–68.

[2] As it is in examples cited by Trench, *ibid.*, p. 64: the English "coals to Newcastle," the Greek "owls to Athens," the Latin "logs to the wood," etc.

[3] Chapters 10–22:16; 25–29.

couplet,[4] its air of ponderous authority, its generally complacent and unreflective moralizing, mark it as originating with the schoolmaster rather than with the orator or the village wit.

When one undertakes to read consecutively through these sections of the Book of Proverbs, one is struck by the almost complete lack of continuity, which points to their growth by gradual accumulation rather than by continuous composition. Moreover, here and there the prevalent monotony is relieved by the occurrence of striking and picturesque sayings which have all the marks of folk wisdom, in contrast to academic moralizing: "Like vinegar to the teeth or smoke in the eyes is a laggard to one who sends him on an errand" (10:26); "Like a gold nose-ring in a wild pig's snout is a pretty woman who lacks good manners" (11:22); and "A slack hunter takes no game (but a keen one gets plenty of it)" (11:27).[5]

When such sayings are compared with the folk sayings scattered through other parts of the Old Testament,[6] it seems evident that here the instructor in the school for youth makes use of popular proverbs which serve his purpose of moral instruction. These can be recognized usually from their formal characteristics, as well as through their divergence from the predominantly catechetical tone of their context. They are short, pithy, and complete in themselves. They show the fondness for alliteration and assonance which mark colloquial sayings in many languages:[7] *bā' zādōn, bā' qālōn,* "Comes insolence, comes disgrace" (Prov. 11:2); *shōmēr miswāh, shōmēr nafshō,* "He who observes a commandment, preserves himself" (Prov. 19:16). The prophet Amos either quotes or coins a similar epigram with assonance, this time with a chiastic structure, *'aryeh shā'ag mī lō' yīrā',* "Who does not tremble when a lion roars?" (Am. 3:8).

There are a good many examples of popular proverbs which are quoted incidentally in the prophetic and narrative books of the Old Testament, in addition to those collected in Proverbs and Ecclesiastes. They are concise, picturesque, thought-provoking, and sometimes witty and amusing. They include generalized comments on common experience, on social relationships, on particular types of persons and behaviour, and on recurrent situations of a special kind. Not infrequently the comment made is scornful or sarcastic. It may express a warning admonition, or suggest a maxim based on common unfortunate experiences. Such folk sayings have their own note of authority, but it is the social authority of general consent or of the obvious truism, rather than the personal authority of the learned religious teacher, as in the "Solomonic" proverb. Basic to all proverbs, both the colloquial

[4]Not all the proverbs in chapters 25–29 are bilinear, but this is still the predominant form and the typical one.

[5]In this example the first line is complete in itself and represents the popular saying; the second line adds nothing but a formal contrast to bring it into line with the bilinear form.

[6]Gen. 10:9; Judg. 8:21; 15:16; I Sam. 10:12; 24:14; I Kings 20:11; Jer. 17:11; 13:12, 23; 23:28; 31:29; Ezek. 16:44; etc.

[7]Cf. "Where there's a will there's a way"; "Never buy a pig in a poke"; "Qui porte épée, porte paix"; "Morgenstunde hat Gold im Munde"; "præmonitus, præmunitus."

and the didactic, is the *idea of order*, of norms, rules, right values, and due proportions. They speak in terms of identity and non-identity, of cause, and consequence, of the reality beneath the appearance, of common factors and characteristics, and of what is contrary to order and reality—the irregular, the absurd, the paradoxical, and the impossible.

It is instructive to compare these Israelite adages and aphorisms with their counterparts from ancient Mesopotamia and Egypt. Many of these have been available in English translation in Pritchard's standard collection,[8] which has been supplemented recently by two important new publications of Mesopotamian material.[9] The comparison suggests, among other things, that certain idea patterns—what might be called "proverb idioms"—are characteristic of folk wisdom in the ancient Near East, in the classical world, and even in Europe in recent times. These "idea patterns" provide a kind of instinctive classification of the experiences of life, which may be of interest to the philosopher and the psychologist.

In the first place, many proverbs turn on the idea of *identity, equivalence,* or *invariable association*: "This is really (or, always) that"; "Where (or, when) this is, that is"; "Without this, there is no that." Familiar examples in English are: "Business is business" (where the tautology is apparent only); "A friend in need is a friend indeed"; "A penny saved is a penny earned"; "Easy come, easy go"; "Where there's life, there's hope"; "No gains without pains."[10]

With these may be compared Aesop's maxim from the fable of the Ass and the Grasshopper: "One man's meat is another man's poison," and the Latin maxim *prior tempore, prior jure,* "First in time, first by right," or, "First come, first served." Among Biblical proverbs of this type may be cited: "As the man, so his strength" (Judg. 8:21); "In all toil there is profit" (Prov. 14:23); "To observe a commandment is to preserve yourself" (Prov. 19:16); "Where there are no oxen, there will be no grain" (Prov. 14:4); "Without a people, a prince is nothing" (Prov. 14:28); "What a man sows is what he will reap" (Gal. 6:7).

Two examples of this idiom of identity from Gordon's collections of Sumerian proverbs are: "Bread was given (or, dropped) unawares, water was spilt, the earth drank it up; in all the barren places of the nether-world, being drink and food, it will be called a libation" (i.e., what seems a loss, may be a gain) (Gordon, *Sumerian Proverbs*, 1:38, pp. 58–9); "Barley-flour in the field is animal-fat" (i.e., on a journey or a campaign plain food is as welcome as rich food at home) (*Ibid.,* 1:48, pp. 65, 501).

From Lambert's bilingual tablets (Sumerian, with Akkadian translation)

---

[8]J. B. Pritchard (ed.), *Ancient Near Eastern Texts Related to the Old Testament* (2nd ed.; Princeton, 1955).

[9]E. I. Gordon, *Sumerian Proverbs* (Philadelphia, 1959), and W. G. Lambert, *Babylonian Wisdom Literature* (Oxford, 1960).

[10]Variants of the last are "No sweet without sweat" and the German "Ohne Fleiss, kein Preis," in which we have examples of the typical fondness for alliteration and for internal and external rhyme.

come the following: "Flesh is flesh, blood is blood, alien is alien, foreigner is indeed foreigner" (i.e., what is identical must be recognized as such) (Lambert, *Babylonian Wisdom Literature,* p. 271); "You have gone. So what? You have stayed. So what? You have stood. So what? You have returned. So what?" (i.e. "Plus ça change, plus c'est la même chose") (Lambert, p. 278).

The second of these intercultural proverb idioms is *contrast, non-identity, paradox*: "This is not really that," "Not every this is that," "This, yet paradoxically that," "This, and its opposite, that." Examples are: "All is not gold that glisters"; "Not all are hunters, who blow horns"; "Much noise, few eggs"; "A cobbler's wife is always ill-shod"; "Good fences make good neighbours."

Of this type are the Greek proverb, *"megalē polis megalē erēmia,* "Great city, great solitude"; Sophocles' epigram *echthrōn adōra dōra,* "The gifts of enemies are not gifts" (Ajax, 665); and Aesop's maxim, "Those who cry loudest are not always the most hurt." Biblical examples are: "What has straw in common with wheat?" (Jer. 23:28); "He who is girding himself [i.e., for battle] should not boast as if he were ungirding himself" (I Kings 20:11); "A soft tongue can break a bone" (Prov. 25:15), cf. "Soft is the tongue [of a king], but it breaks a dragon's ribs" (Egyptian), and "The tongue is not steel, but it cuts" (English); "What is bitter tastes sweet to a hungry man" (Prov. 27:7), cf. the Akkadian aphorism in the (Aramaic) Sayings of Ahiqar (xii, 188), "Hunger makes bitterness sweet." "A prophet will always be held in honour, except in his home town" (Matt. 13:57); "Can anything good come from Nazareth?"[11] (John 1:46).

The last two examples may or may not have been proverbs in common use; it is not always possible to distinguish these from epigrams coined for the occasion by a speaker or writer. "To err is human, to forgive divine" was coined by Pope in his "Essay on Criticism" (l. 525), by adding the second line to a Latin saying of St. Jerome,[12] and the longer form has become proverbial.

Several instances of the idiom of non-identity occur in Egyptian literary works. "That great one who is covetous is not really great" is from *The Protests of the Eloquent Peasant,* as is the sarcastic paradox "Thou art a butler whose delight is butchering." The common Biblical contrast of the wise man and the fool appears in the *Instruction of Ptah-hotep,* "The wise man rises early in the morning to establish himself, the fool rises early in the morning [only] to . . . himself." From the *Instruction of Amen-em-ope,* "One thing are the words men say, another is that which the god does,"[13]

---

[11]Probably an example of *blason populaire,* the sarcastic characterization of a neighbouring place or people, like "Cretans are always liars" (Titus 1:12); "Wise as a man of Gotham."

[12]*Errasse humanum est,* Epist. 57:12. Cicero has a similar saying, *cujusvis hominis est errare,* Phil. 12:2.

[13]Pritchard, *Ancient Near Eastern Texts Related to the Old Testament,* pp. 409a, 409b, 414b, 423b.

with which we may compare Prov. 16:9, "A man's mind plans his way, but the Lord determines where he goes" (lit., "his step").

Sumerian proverbs of this type are: "In a city without dogs, the fox is overseer" (Gordon, *Sumerian Proverbs*, 1:65, pp. 72, 502); "A shepherd should not [try to] be a farmer" (*Ibid.*, 1:100, p. 92); "For his pleasure— married; on thinking it over—divorced" (*Ibid.*, 2:124, p. 265); "Hand added to hand—the house of a man is built up! Stomach added to stomach —the house of a man is destroyed!" (*Ibid.*, 2:138, p. 271); "Marrying several wives is of men; having many children is of the gods" (*Ibid.*, 1:160, p. 126); "Wealth is distant; poverty is close by" (*Ibid.*, 1:15); "What the weather· might consume, the beasts have spared; What the beasts might consume, the weather has spared" (*Ibid.*, 1:20).[14]

A similar note of mournful reflection on the vicissitudes of existence, which seems to be characteristic of these Sumerian sayings, appears in "When a poor man has died, do not try to revive him; when he has salt, he has no bread; when he has bread, he has no salt; when he has meat, he has no condiment, when he has condiment, he has no meat" (Gordon, *Sumerian Proverbs*, 1:55, pp. 68-9, 459).

From Lambert's bilinguals, the following are apposite: "The wise man is girded with a loin-cloth; the fool is clad in a scarlet cloak"; "Winter is evil; summer has sense"; "If I put things in store, I shall be robbed; if I squander, who will give it to me"; "The strong man lives off what is paid for his strength, and the weak man off what is paid for his children"; "A foreigner's ox eats plants; one's own ox lies down in green pastures."[15] "Giving pertains to a king, doing good to a cup-bearer." An alternative form of this saying reads in the second line, "showing favour, to a steward." Such variants of the same proverb are found also in the Book of Proverbs.[16] "Perform the wish of the one present; slander the one not present."[17] Lambert draws attention to the remarkable fact that Babylonian proverbs (as distinguished from Sumerian proverbs translated in the bilingual tablets) have left hardly a trace. He attributes this to the fact that "the codifiers of traditional litera- ture during the Cassite period were very academic scholars, who may well have frowned on proverbs which were passed around among the unedu- cated."[18] One Babylonian proverb, however, is quoted by an Assyrian king, probably Esarhaddon, in a letter, "When the potter's dog enters the kiln, it will bark at the potter."[19]

The third "proverb idiom" to be noted is that of *similarity, analogy, typology*: "This is (or, acts) like that"; "As this, so that"; "This is (meta-

[14]Gordon. *Sumerian Proverbs*, pp. 72, 502, 92, 265, 271, 126, 496-7, 51.

[15]That is, presumably, the strange ox which invades the pasture makes the most of his opportunities, while one's own ox is too lazy to do so. Lambert, *Babylonian Wisdom Literature*, pp. 232, 247, 248, 258.

[16]*Ibid.*, p. 259. Cf. 13:9 and 24:20; 15:18 and 29:22; 17:3 and 27:21, etc.

[17]Lambert, *Babylonian Wisdom Literature*, p. 269.

[18]*Ibid.*, pp. 275-6.

[19]That is, the paradox of impertinence. Cf. *ibid.*, p. 281, where variants of this proverb from the Syriac and Arabic versions of Ahiqar are given.

phorically) that"; "Like so-and-so, who. . . ." Well-known examples are: "A chip off the old block"; "Time and tide wait for no man"; "He who keeps company with a wolf learns to howl"; "Like master, like man."[20] The last corresponds exactly to two Biblical proverbs, "Like people, like priest" (Hos. 4:9), "Like mother, like daughter" (Ezek. 16:44;), cf. Gen. 18:25.

The typological comparison appears in such sayings as: "Like Nimrod, a mighty hunter before the Lord" (Gen. 10:9); "Like Rachel and Leah, both of whom built up the house of Israel" (Ruth 4:11); "No prophet like Moses" (Deut. 34:10). Striking similes are common, for example: "Like arrows in the hands of a warrior are the sons of one's youth" (Ps. 127:4); "He who amasses wealth through injustice is like the partridge which hatches eggs she has not laid" (Jer. 17:11); "Like the coolness of snow in the heat of harvest time is a reliable messenger to the one who sends him" (Prov. 25:13); "To rely on a deceiver in a time of trouble is like having a loose tooth or a trembling foot" (Prov. 25:19); "To sing gay songs to one whose heart is heavy is like disrobing a man on a cold day, or adding sour wine to soda" (Prov. 25:20); "Good news from a distant land is like a drink of cold water to a weary man" (Prov. 25:25).

The saying "Sleep is the brother of death" is found both in the Iliad (14:231) and in the Aeneid (6:278). Cicero (*de Senectute* 3) quotes as an ancient proverb, "Like associates most easily with like." The saying of the Egyptian *Instruction of Amen-em-ope* (chapter vii) that "riches have made themselves wings like geese and are flown away to the heavens" closely resembles its Hebrew counterpart in Prov. 23:4–5, "Riches . . . will have grown wings, and like an eagle will have flown away into the heavens." A Sumerian adage makes a different point with the same metaphor, "Possessions are sparrows in flight which can find no place to alight" (Gordon, *Sumerian Proverbs* 1:18, p. 50). Lambert gives several examples: "A people without a king are sheep without a shepherd"; "A people without a foreman are water without a canal inspector"; "A house without an owner is a woman without a husband" (p. 232); "A wound without a doctor is hunger without food" (p. 249); "[As] man is the shadow of a god, [so] a slave is the shadow of a man" (p. 282).

The fourth proverb idiom focuses on what is *contrary to order, futile, absurd*. It makes use of the mocking description, for instance, "A whistling woman and a crowing hen are liked neither by God nor men"; the rhetorical question, for example, "What's the use of running when you're on the wrong road?"; and the maxim, as in "Don't count your chickens before they are hatched!"

The Hebrews were fond of the mocking description or taunt. When Jeremiah said "Every wine-jar shall be filled with wine" (Jer. 13:12), he was talking not about ceramic jars but about men. "Like a door turning on its hinges, is a lazy man on his bed" (Prov. 26:14). "And who is their

[20]After Petronius, *Qualis dominus, talis et servus*.

father?" was the way in which Saul's contemporaries cast a reflection on the ancestry of the dervish prophets. In the same breath they expressed themselves on the impropriety of Saul's association with such people, "Is [even] Saul among the [dervish] prophets?" (I Sam. 10:12). "Do horses run on a[perpendicular]cliff? Do you plow the sea with an ox?" cried Amos in derision (Am. 6:12). Jeremiah's challenge is more familiar, "Can an Ethiopian change [the colour of] his skin, or a leopard his spots?" (Jer. 13:23).[21] In Prov. 17:16 a teacher of privileged youth reflected ruefully, "Why ever should a fool come with money in hand to buy wisdom, when he has no mind?" In the same way that proverbs, and especially legal maxims, are often used to clinch an argument, the instructor in Prov. 1:17 points out to his class that "It's no use setting a net where the birds can see it plainly."

Rhetorical questions are found among the Sumerian sayings : "Who will listen to the interpretations which you express?" "Do you strike the face of a moving ox with a (strap)?" "Would you place a lump of clay in the hand of him who throws?" "Has she become pregnant without intercourse? Has she become fat without eating?" "Do you pay out money for a pig's squeak?" "Can strong warriors resist a flood, and mighty men quieten the fire-god?"[22] One Babylonian question of this kind is recorded, "He who has not king and queen, who is his lord?"[23] In affirmative form we find, "Like a fool . . . you perform your ablutions, after sacrifice; like . . . you put in a drain pipe after it has rained."[24]

The fifth idiom is that of proverbs which classify and characterize persons, actions or situations, as: "Children and fools speak the truth"; "You can't spoil a rotten egg"; "A rolling stone gathers no moss"; "He that steals an egg will steal an ox"; "Three things drive a man out of the house—smoke, rain, and a scolding wife"; "Flies, dogs, and jesters come first to meals" (mediaeval Latin).

A special form of the numerical proverb which groups three or more things as similar, is the "x, x + 1" opening derived from the parallelistic structure of Semitic verse. Of several examples in Prov. 30:15–31 the most famous is: "Three things astonish me, there are four I cannot fathom— how an eagle soars in the sky; how a snake glides across a rock; how a ship moves over the sea; and how a man wins his way with a girl." From the Aramaic "Words of Ahiqar" comes, "Two things are meet, and the third is pleasing to Shamash—one who drinks wine and gives it to drink; one who guards wisdom; and one who hears a word and does not tell." Another

---

21Cf. the English saying, "You can't wash a blackamoor white."

22Gordon, *Sumerian Proverbs*, 1:36, p. 57; Lambert, *Babylonian Wisdom Literature*, p. 248, 235, 247, 250, 266.

23Lambert, *Babylonian Wisdom Literature*, p. 277. This recalls the saying from the Wat Tyler insurrection of 1381, "When Adam dolve and Eve span, who then was the gentleman?"

24*Ibid.*, p. 282.

example from *Ahiqar* omits the "x, x + 1" feature, "I have tasted even the bitter medlar, and [I have eaten] endives; but there is naught which is more bitter than poverty."[25] A similar climactic classification is found in Prov. 27:3, "A stone may be heavy, or a load of sand, but a provoking fool is harder to bear than both together."

Many proverbs characterize, complainingly or contemptuously, a type of person or situation. From Egyptian come two sayings illuminating what it meant to be poor:"The name of the poor man is pronounced [only] for his master's sake"; "The poor man asks for an afternoon meal, [but] his wife says to him, 'It's for supper.'"

In a Sumerian saying, the grumbler is told, "Of what you have found you do not speak; [only] of what you have lost do you speak." The desperation of hunger is pictured in, "A hungry man breaks into a building of kiln-fired bricks."[26] This idiom is very common in the Book of Proverbs, picturing the fool, the scoffer, the sluggard, and the shrewish wife, for. instance: "A simpleton believes everything he hears"; "A scoffer will not listen to rebuke"; "The sluggard puts his hand into the pan, but he is too tired to lift it to his mouth"; "A wife's grumbling is a continual dripping."[27]

The sixth identifiable idiom is that of *value, lack of value, relative value, proportion* or *degree*: "This is worth that," "Better this than that," "The more [or, less] this, the more [or, less] that." "First this, then that," "If this, how much more that!" Familiar examples come to mind; "A bird in the hand is worth two in the bush"; "Better late than never"; "The nearer the bone, the sweeter the meat"; "Out of the frying pan into the fire"; "Cut your coat according to the cloth." From many ancient examples the following may be noted: "A camel, even though mangy, bears the burden of many asses," which is preserved in Greek, but doubtless originated among the Semites. A Latin example is *Praestat amicitia propinquitati*, "Friendship is better than relationship." This is a common Biblical type: "A good name is more desirable than great riches"; "A poor man is better than a liar"; "Better the end of a thing than its beginning"; "The more words, the greater the vanity"; "A sacrifice offered by wicked men is an abomination, all the more so if their purpose is shameful"; "Better a serving of vegetables where love is, than prime beef garnished with hate."[28] The last has a close Egyptian parallel, "Better is bread when the heart is happy, than riches with sorrow." The Biblical sayings about the shrewish wife are recalled by the Sumero-Babylonian, "A spendthrift woman in the house is worse than all devils." The Hebrew prophetic dictum "To obey [God] is better than [to offer] sacrifice" echoes the *Instruction for King Meri-ka-re,*

[25]Cf. Pritchard, *Ancient Near Eastern Texts Related to the Old Testament*, pp. 428b, 429a.
[26]That is, into the well-built house of the wealthy. See *ibid.*, pp. 408a, 406a; Gordon, *Sumerian Proverbs*, 1:11, p. 47; Lambert, *Babylonian Wisdom Literature*, p. 235.
[27]Prov. 14:15; 13:1; 26:15; 19:13.
[28]Prov. 22:1; 19:22; Eccles. 7:8; 6:11; Prov. 21:27; 15:17.

"More acceptable is the character of one upright in heart, than the ox of the evildoer."[29]

A statement of comparative value which is perhaps too philosophic to be classed as a proverb, comes from *Ptah-hotep*, "Though fraud gain riches, the strength of justice is that it lasts." The Sumerian "The boat has gone too deep into the water; it has caused the crates to be swept overboard," seems to mean that overdoing a thing defeats its purpose, as with our "More haste, less speed." Comparative and superlative are expressed in the Sumerian, "A sick person is [relatively] well; a woman in childbirth is ill; a sick woman in childbirth is the worst of all." The rhetorical question, "Seeing you have done evil to your friend, what will you do to your enemy?" recalls the New Testament saying, "If these things are done when the wood is green, what will happen when it is dry?"[30]

The last of the proverb idioms to be treated here is that of *cause and consequence*.[31] This is obviously appropriate for folk proverbs with their frequent taunts, cynicism, humour, and pathos, and is adaptable to the admonitions of the elder and the teacher. It is one of the predominant Biblical forms, for example: "The fathers eat sour grapes, the sons' teeth are set on edge" (Jer. 31:29); "They sow the wind, they shall reap the whirlwind" (Hos. 8:7); "He who digs a pit will fall into it" (Prov. 26:27); "A happy heart lights up the face" (Prov. 15:13).

From the older wisdom of Mesopotamia come such sayings as these: "By marrying an unseemly wife, by begetting an unseemly child, I satisfied and [then] established for myself a discontented heart"; "He went fowling without a bird trap; [naturally] he caught nothing"; "Tell a lie, [then] tell the truth [and] it will be considered a lie"; "Last year I ate garlic; this year my inside burns"; "Long life begets for you a sense of satisfaction; concealing a thing—sleepless worry; wealth—respect."[32]A special type of this idiom found frequently in the Book of Proverbs is a statement of the reward or punishment by God, consequent on a man's deeds, for instance, "The Lord is a stronghold to him whose way is upright, but destruction to evildoers." This is most unusual in the Sumerian proverbs, but one example at least is at hand, "A boat bent on fraudulent pursuits sailed downstream with the wind; he [Utu, the sun god] will wreck [?] it on the beaches." Another special type of the cause-and-consequence idiom uses the metaphor

---

[29]Cf. Pritchard, *Ancient Near Eastern Texts Related to the Old Testament*, pp. 422b, 417b; Lambert, *op. cit.*, p. 267.

[30]Cf. *ibid.*, p. 412b; Gordon, *Sumerian Proverbs*, pp. 87, 516; Lambert, *Babylonian Wisdom Literature*, p. 232; Luke 23:31.

[31]By no means all ancient Near Eastern proverbs examined can be classified as expressions of one or other of the seven proverb idioms noted here. But if the phenomena of transcultural similarities have been observed and interpreted with any degree of validity, this may provide an additional clue for the exploration of the vast field of the comparative study of folk proverbs and literary epigrams.

[32]Gordon, *Sumerian Proverbs*, 1:151, pp. 119, 468, 511; 2:71, p. 229; Lambert, *Babylonian Wisdom Literature*, pp. 230, 249, 253.

of parenthood, as in "The thought is father of the deed," and "Necessity is the mother of invention." This appears in the sententious maxim of a wise man of Babylonia, "The scribal art is the mother of orators and the father of scholars."[33]

The same pride in the profession of wisdom shows itself again nearly two thousand years later in the words of the son of Sirach, "He who devotes himself to the study of the Law of the Most High will seek out the wisdom of all the ancients . . . he will preserve the discourse of notable men . . . he will seek out the hidden meaning of proverbs . . . he will travel through the lands of foreign nations, for he tests the good and evil among men" (Ecclesiasticus 39:1–4). Thus, the wisdom of Israel was consciously heir to, and part of, the ancient cosmopolitan wisdom of the Near East.

[33]Prov. 10:29; Gordon, *Sumerian Proverbs*, 1:87, p. 84; Lambert, *Babylonian Wisdom Literature*, p. 259.

V.

THE "WISDOM CORPUS" AND THE REST OF THE HEBREW SCRIPTURES

ISAIAH AMONG THE WISE*

By JOHANNES FICHTNER

In the spiritual history of Israel, there are few so completely antithetical phenomena as prophecy and ḥokmah (wisdom). Two worlds stand in total opposition: the proclaimer and admonisher who is seized by God and laid completely under claim and who carries out his lofty and dangerous mission to his people without any personal considerations, and the clever and prudent worldly-wise sage who goes his peaceable way cautiously looking right and left and who instructs his proteges in the same wise style of mastering life. To appreciate this vast difference, one has only to read a few sentences from the Book of Amos and then a few proverbs from Prov 10 or 27!

Thus, the title of this inquiry, "Isaiah among the Wise," may seem strange to the reader, and he might well ask—if he is less conversant with more recent research into the wisdom literature—what the eighth-century prophet should be doing among the wise of the post-exilic period. Hence, it should certainly be stated that the extensive work on the ancient Near East and Israelite wisdom literature of the last two-and-a-half decades has taught us that wisdom in Israel is of an earlier date and that a considerable portion of Proverbs should best be assigned to pre-exilic times.[1] Today it is quite possible to ask how the pre-exilic prophets reacted to Israel's wise and the wisdom they represented, whether they were acquainted with them and entered into debate with them, learned from them or rejected them.

Without question, there are various points at which the views of the pre-exilic prophets seem to be directly compatible with those of the wise

*Originally published as "Jesaja unter den Weisen," *ThLZ* LXXIV (1949), pp. 75-80. It is dedicated by Fichtner to Prof. Carl Steuernagel, Dr. D., on his eightieth birthday. Translated by Brian W. Kovacs, Associate Professor of Sociology, Centenary College of Louisiana, Shreveport.

men of the Book of Proverbs. Further areas of ethical admonition were cultivated by both groups. I need only mention here their active championing of righteousness and charity toward the *personae miserabiles*[2] and in addition refer to the range of commonalities I pointed out in my work on ancient Near Eastern wisdom in its Israelite-Jewish configuration[3]: assimilation of foreign materials, displacing boundaries, use of false weights and measures, partisanship and corruption, disrespect for elders, etc. Moreover, both pre-exilic prophecy and ḥokmah took a critical stance toward the cult (Am 5:25ff.; Hos 6:7; 12:9; Isa 1:10ff.; Jer 7:22ff.; and Prov 15:8, 29; 20:25; 21:3, 27; 28:9; 30:12). On that basis, one might arrive at the opinion that they may exhibit some sort of affinity in the graphic vividness of their style of expression. In seems, however, that there can be no talk of literary dependency in all of these relationships. The stuff of ethical admonition which wisdom appropriates in its instruction is common property of the Israelite—and generally the ancient Near-eastern!—spiritual world (more, the connections between law and wisdom should be noted[4]). The critical attitude toward the cult which crops up openly here and there from various roots is also encountered first in the Egyptian wisdom literature and second even among other circles in Israel (cf. Ps 40; 50; 51!). In addition, the prophet speaks in large measure on the basis of the authority conferred with his commission and tells his hearers "God's word"; while the wise man—especially in the earlier period!—gives advice and instruction from tradition and his own insight without explicit or implicitly-assumed divine authorization.[5]

A more detailed study demonstrates that the writings of the eighth-century prophets Amos, Hosea and Micah—insofar as they are to be attributed to them—show no ḥokmatic influence, either in style and diction or in their literary forms, and also that the wise as a class obviously did not fall within the purview of the prophets. Among other things, it would be consistent with this evidence if these men came from the rural countryside and therefore had no direct contact with the circles of the "wise" who went about their profession in the court or in close proximity to the great of the court.

A few phrases in the Books of Amos, Hosea and Micah which sound genuinely ḥokmatic are now almost universally taken to be additions from a later hand. Thus, the words laken hammaskîl baᶜet hahî' yiddom[6] ("therefore the prudent man will keep silence in this time; because it is an evil time") of Am 5:13 are generally deleted as an addition; Sellin interprets them with a different significance—maskîl as hymn—and places them between 5:26 and 27. Without any question, in Hos 14:10, we read words with an authentic ḥokmatic stamp (the last verse of the Book!): mî ḥakam wᵉyaben 'ellæ/nabôn wᵉyedaᶜem kî yᵉšarîm darkê yhwh wᵉṣaddiqîm yelᵉkû bam ûpošᵉᶜîm yikkašᵉlû bam ("Who is so wise that he comprehends this and so intelligent that he understands it? Truly the ways of Yahweh are straight; the righteous travel upon them, but the godless stumble on them"). One may compare for example Prov 11:5 or 15:9. On the basis of location and content, these words are also generally recognized as an addition (even by Sellin), and therefore not to be attributed to the prophet Hosea. The expression ben lo' ḥakam (13:13) which is used in the same book, makes use of the word "wise" in an entirely general, rather than a technical, sense. Further, Robinson emends this so that ḥakam is omitted.[7] Finally, mention should be made of Mic 6:9 as well, and the phrase wᵉtûšiyya yiræ' sᵉmæka within the verse. Outside the wisdom literature, the term tûšiyya appears only here and in Isa 28:29, and indeed alongside ḥakma, ᶜoz and ᶜeṣa. Here, its significance as well as the reading and translation of the three terms mentioned is completely obscure. If one reads with the MT and translates "and well-being, who sees your name," then one looks in vain for any meaning to these words: if one emends yir'æ to yir'a or yir'at, then one can certainly translate it "and it is wisdom to fear your name" which leaves the distinct impression, however, that we have a marginal gloss before us.

Among the classes Amos, Hosea and Micah expressly address or mention in passing, there appear mælæk (king), šopet (judge), nabî' (prophet), and sar (high official), even yôᶜᵃṣîm (counsellor) once, but nowhere else any typically ḥokmatic class terminology.

In the period *after* Proto-Isaiah, matters are different. In general, here too there is admittedly no observable relationship of the prophetic writings to wisdom; thus, e.g., for Nahum, Zeph, Hag, Zech I and III, Mal, Joel and the little book of Jonah. In various "oracles to the nations" of the post-Isaianic era, the wisdom of the peoples they deal with or of their rulers is stressed and its overthrow by Yahweh proclaimed. Thus Ob 7 and 8 with a view toward Edom; Zech 9:2 Tyre and Sidon; Ez 28 Tyre; Jer 49:7ff. Edom; chs. 50f. Babylon. At best, one can speak of a harmony with the world of wisdom in Habbakuk and Jeremiah. With justification, Horst speaks of an "intrusion of proverbial wisdom into prophetic speech recognizeable in Habbakuk and Jeremiah."[8] Compare Hab 1:4b, 14; 2:4, 12, 13b, 17; and alongside the well-known verses in Jeremiah 17:5ff. (parallel to Ps 1!) and 9:22f. the frequent appearance of ḥokmatic terms,

and over and above that the prophet's obvious familiarity with the class
of the wise: lo' to'bad tôra mikkohen w^ec^eṣa meḥakam w^edabar minnabî'
("[There will be] no lack of direction to the priest, advice to the wise and
[God's] word to the prophet") Jer 18:18. Even Deutero-Isaiah uses here
and there terminology that is typical of ḥokmah (40:13f., 21; 41:20;
44:18f., 25), while Ezekiel—apart from ch. 28!—is rather free of it unless
one wishes to attribute the constant recurrence of yada^c (mostly in the
expression "that they may know that I am Yahweh") to the influence of
wisdom, which would seem however to be rather difficult to defend. Still,
one cannot evaluate the relationships of these two prophets, or any others,
with wisdom solely on the basis of the appearance of ḥokmatic terminology
in their writings. More thorough-going studies would be necessary, which
would for example investigate particularly the origins of Ezekiel's teaching
on retribution and its relations to the ḥokmatic belief in retribution. Still,
it is significant that Ezekiel attributes ^ceṣa (counsel) not to the wise, but
to the elders, in the statement at 7:26 which runs parallel to Jer 18:18 by
subordinating ḥazôn (vision) to the prophet and tôra (direction) to the
priest. Have the "wise," who were so influential and diplomatically important in the preexilic period, played out and left the field to the elders?

When we turn now to *Isaiah,* in my opinion we observe in him a completely unique relationship to wisdom that—if it should prove itself to be
justified!—would essentially alter our view of the great prophet of the
eighth century. First (I), Isaiah clearly turns against human wisdom, which
overrates itself and disassociates itself from God, and assails the wise of
his own people and of other nations who go their own shrewd political
ways without (and therefore against) God. On the other hand (II), unlike
the rest of the prophets of his century, Isaiah himself clearly stands in the
tradition of the wisdom-perspectives, exhibits various relationships (perhaps even literary dependency!) to the wisdom literature and its forms,
and even formulates his image of the future hokmatically. I should like to
propose that both these observations—apparently so antithetical—can be
brought into complete harmony with one another and thereby produce a
vital picture of the prophet's origins and the particular stamp of his consciousness of prophetic commission.

I

In the woe-oracles concerning Judah's ruling classes (5:8-14), Isaiah
raises his voice as well against those "who are wise (ḥ^akamîm) in their
own eyes and shrewd (n^ebonîm) in their own sight" (5:21), and in a

later statement (29:14) he proclaims to the wise the end of their wisdom: Yahwe will deal wondrously with the people "that the wisdom of their wise (ḥakmat ḥᵉkamâw) will perish and the shrewdness of their shrewd men (bînot nᵉbonâw) must hide itself." Thus, he is obviously thinking of the wise as a group of self-secure politicians whose deportation he announces in 3:1-3. Further, one can also read, alongside the judge and the prophet, elder and soothsayer, etc., in this same place (3:1ff.) "counsellor and wise man" (yôᶜeṣ wᵉḥakam), if the next word (ḥᵃrasîm) is deleted as a gloss.[9] According to Isaiah, these wise men rely on their own intuition and on their wise comrades-in-arms the Egyptians. By means of their position at court, they cultivate their foreign contacts, by that learn something about Egyptian wisdom, and lead king and nation into an erroneous politics of alliance (cf. especially 30:1ff.; 31:1ff.). But Yahweh through his purpose will bring their wisdom to ruin and prove before all eyes that the Egyptians, with all their wisdom, are only men, not God; in just the same way, he will strike down to earth the king of Assyria who overstepped his punitive mission against Judah, acting despotically and triumphantly: "through the might of my hand will I do it and through my wisdom (bᵉḥakmatî); for I am cunning (kî nᵉbunôtî 10:13)." Over and above that, if one may—e.g. with Procksch, *Jesaja*, I, pp. 244ff.—consider a part of ch. 19 Isaianic, viz. verses 1-4 and 11-15,[10] then in this oracle to the nation one would have direct testimony to Isaiah's struggle against the—for Judah's politics of alliance, so dangerous—"wise counsellors of pharaoh." I shall cite the most important phrases here:

Utter fools are the princes of Zoan (cf. 30:4!),
the wisest of pharaoh's counsellors, a foolish counsel!
How could you say to pharaoh:
    I am a wise man,[11] a descendant of the ancient rulers?
Then where are your wise men,
    that they might proclaim and make known,[12]
    what Yahwe Ṣabaoth plans for Egypt?

One might also be able to categorize Isaiah's struggle against the foreign officials at the royal court of Shebna in this context (cf. 22:15ff.). More specific associations with "wisdom" can in any case not be demonstrated for Shebna. Oesterley finds it possible that Prov 25:5 ("Take the wicked away from the king, then his throne will be fixed in righteousness") might allude to Shebna, who was sôper (scribe) at the court of Hezekiah according to 2 Kings 18:18; 19:2. This particular proverb is found within that very collection of proverbs attributed to the "men of Hezekiah"; cf. also 26:1.

In any case, it is already evident from the indisputably authentic words of Isaiah that the prophet hàs turned against the wise who have misused their "wisdom" politically and self-confidently elaborated their plans, and has announced to them that Yahweh will make their wisdom perish and will root them out.

II

On the other hand, in my opinion one can contend that—unlike the rest of the eighth century prophets—Isaiah himself draws from the tradition of ḥokmah. He not only shows a particular preference for extended metaphors (5:1ff.; 28:23ff.) and a special preference for word-play[13]— that alone would hardly serve to justify this hypothesis!—but also makes use to some extent of the terminology of ḥokmah which occurs never or only quite sporadically in Amos, Hosea and Micah (hakam and ḥakma, bîn and bîna, yaᶜas and ᶜeṣà, yadaᶜ and deᶜa tûšiyya, among others). Also, Isaiah coins "proverbs" which formally resemble the ḥokmatic "proverbs" (1:3; 2:22; 3:10ff.; 5:6ff.; 10:15).

Above all, however, it seems to me to be significant in two ways: [first,] it serves to confirm a more than coincidental affinity between the Isaiah-sayings and Proverbs, and indeed it is a question in the first place of proverbs from the collection which is supposed to have been put together by the "men of Hezekiah," thus in Isaiah's own time (Prov 25-29).

The expression "wise in his own eyes (ḥakam bᵉᶜênâw) in Isa 5:21 occurs elsewhere only in Proverbs (26:5, 12, 16; 28:11; and 3:7). In his oracle of judgment against Jerusalem 1:21-26, the prophet says "your silver has become slag" (kaspek haya lᵉsîgîm) and declares that therefore God will "refine out the slag" (wᵉᵉæṣrop sîgayik). That is strongly reminiscent of Prov 25:4 "remove the slag from the silver (sîgîm mikkæsæp), thus does the smith produce his vessel"; cf. also Prov 26:23! The word sîg (lead-polish, silverdross, slag) is rare in the OT and elsewhere occurs only in Ez 22:18f. in a possible imitation of the Isaiah oracle and in the late law-psalm which is heavily influenced by ḥokmah, Ps 119, in v. 119. The odd image of the fool who (like a dog) returns to his vomit (qeʾô Prov 26:11) Isaiah may have picked up in 19:14 when he proclaims to the wise who become fools that, as Yahweh's punishment, they will bring Egypt to the point of staggering "like a drunk staggers about in his vomit (bᵉqîʾô)."

Even qy' (vomit) is a rare root; we find qî' (vomit, puke) otherwise only at Isa 28:8 (!) and Jer 48:26. In Isa 29:13, "... this people honors[14] me with its *lips,* but keeps its *heart* far from me" sounds something like Prov 26:23, where we read, "silver-slag encrusted pottery fragments, that is smooth[15] *lips* and an evil *heart*"—particularly if one notes in what context the Isaianic statement appears (29:14 Yahweh will "bring the wisdom of the wise to ruin") and that the word sîg just mentioned occurs in Prov 26:23a! In Isa 3:9, the prophet uses the hiphil-abstract hakkarat panîm for "partisanship"; in Prov 28:21 (= 24:23) we read for that, hakker panîm, which is found otherwise first in Deuteronomy (1:17, 16:19) and then in Şir 38:10. Other words were readily available for the same vice frequently attacked both in Prov and elsewhere in the OT. Closely related to the "king who judges the poor in truth" (mælæk šôpet bæ'ᵉmæt dallîm Prov 29:14) is the Lord of the Future, of whom it is said in Isa 11:4 that he "will judge the poor in righteousness" (wᵉšapat bᵉşædæq dallîm); moreover, the proverb continues "his throne will always remain firm" (kis'ô laᶜad yikkôn) which recalls the "Eternal Father" ('ᵃbî ᶜad) of Isa 9:5 and also clearly seems to echo Isa 9:6 (lᵉhakîn related to the throne of David and his dominion). On the other hand, this verse also suggests a connection to Prov 16:12 "through righteousness is the throne established (bişdaqa yikkôn kisse'). And finally, to mention a last example from the royal proverbs, the formula "to *sustain* (saᶜad) the throne (and the dominion) through righteousness" occurs only in Prov 20:28 and Isa 9:6.

These last observations (set in fine print)[16] have now led us to the subject I want to refer to second. It is Isaiah's image of the future. Here, the strange phenomenon confronts us that the prophet who so clearly turned against the "wise leaders" of his time thoroughly endows his portrait of the expected lord with hokmatic features. In that connection, I am thinking of the passages 9:1-6 and 11:1ff.—generally not disputed as to their authenticity any more—whose derivation for Isaiah I already covered in the previous section of the inquiry concerning the literary relationships of the Book of Isaiah to Proverbs. According to 9:5, the Lord of the Future is "a wonder of a counsellor" (pælæ' yôᶜeş[17]); according to 11:2, the perfect wise man, endowed with the spirit of wisdom (hakma) and insight (bîna), of counsel (ᶜeşa), of understanding and fear of the Lord (daᶜat wᵉyir'at yhwh). If one combines the various terminological harmonies between Isaiah and the royal aphorisms in Proverbs, then one can justifiably say that here he can grasp the influence of hokmah in his hands. This, however, is the proclamation of the prophet: The king of Assyria

believes that he has accomplished it with "his own wisdom" (10:12f.)
and is overthrown by Yahweh; the same results for the wise counsellors
of pharaoh (Isa 19:11ff.; 31:3) and Judah (29:14; 31:3). But, the
looked-for Lord of the people of God will reign in *divine wisdom* endowed
with Yahweh's spirit.

III

How is this remarkable dual-orientation of Isaiah to be explained—as
opponent of wisdom and disciple of wisdom? It seems to me to follow
from that that Isaiah belonged to the class of the "wise" [18] before his commission as a prophet and had lived in the world of ḥokmah as it appears
to us in the proverbs of the men of Hezekiah (Prov 25-29) and perhaps
in chs. 10-22 of the Book of Proverbs. In his call—which thereby would
gain a very special poignancy if it had summoned Isaiah as a wise man!—
it becomes clear to him that he would have to separate himself from the
to-a-certain-degree non-binding wisdom and its advice and must allow
himself to be sent as the emissary of God with the unique mission, so to
speak, that people in all their (human!) wisdom should not grasp his
message, though they be aware of it.

> Say to this people:
>
> > Hear but more and more and do not comprehend ('al tabînû),
> > See but more and more and do not understand ('al tedaᶜû) . . .
> That (the people) with its eyes may see
> > and may hear with its ears
> > but not comprehend with its heart (yabîn)! (Is 6:9f.)

To this, Isaiah's frightening confession may also relate:

> Woe to me, I am lost;
> > for I am of unclean lips
> > and live among a people of unclean lips! (Isa 6:4)

The contention that Isaiah originally belonged to the wise is confirmed
through various other observations. It should not go unmentioned, but
also be taken account of, that he can write (8:1; 30:8) and obviously
also has a tablet at hand (8:1 gillayôn[19] and 30:8 lûan[20]) as well as a
book (30:8). And, that his disciples are called limmudîm, that is "students"
(8:16), also is not simply a coincidence. More significant, however, is

what we learn from Isaiah's dispute with the priests and prophets which he reports in 28:7ff. Because: they publicly ridicule him with his former occupation which is well-known to them, as they jeer, "Then whom does understanding want to teach?" (28:8.) Does he believe perhaps that he could impart to us—like his one-time students!—rudimentary understanding?[21] They sense that this former wisdom teacher is grasped by a spirit which is superior to them and which therefore they would like to dispose of with scorn and derision. Now perhaps he may have an audition (or something of the kind) over and above his "cognition," they suggest scornfully. Isaiah ensnares them in their own stammering utterances and declares their ruin to them.

Thus, the portrait is rounded out and delineated for us in the following way: Isaiah originally belongs to the guild of the wise in Jerusalem. But, the longer he did, the more he must have come to realize that the wisdom of these wise men isolated them in their self-confidence from the rightful divine wisdom (5:21) so that Israel "does not understand and God's people does not comprehend" (1:3). Their representatives—who, because of their profession—have close contact with the great people at court and foreign diplomats—direct the nation into a politics of alliance that is contrary to God; they forge their own plans (29:15; 30:1), rely on the wisdom of Egypt (30:1ff.; 31:1ff.; 19:11-15), do not want to recognize Yahweh's plan (5:19), and dispute his wisdom (29:16). In his commission, Isaiah learns that he is on the wrong track in his wisdom and has polluted his lips (6:4), and thus is so commissioned to speak to the people that they will not understand him in all wisdom and will continue to confirm themselves in self-assurance and remoteness from God. The prophet understands: Yahweh alone is wise (31:2 wᵉgam hu' ḥakam[22] and 28:29 higdîl tûšîyya) and brings the wisdom of the conventional sages to ruin in Israel (5:21; 29:14), Egypt (31:3; 19:15) and Assyria (10:12f.); after the judgment, he will give his people a counsellor again as in former times (1:26) and promises them a king who shall govern in righteousness as a wonder of a counsellor (9:5) endowed with divine wisdom and intuition (11:2). This ideal of the future lord is consonant with the portrait which Proverbs draws of the righteous king, and thus it is clear that Isaiah does not renounce his affiliation with ḥokmah here—as in some other points as well—but simply resists its representatives because they have disassociated themselves from their most basic foundation and become corrupt in false self-confidence and godlessness.

NOTES

[1] O. Eissfeldt, *Introduction to the OT* ([German ed.] 1934), pp. 524ff.; B. Gemser, *Sprüche Salomos* (1937), pp. 3f.

[2] Am 5:7; Hos 5:11; Isa 1:21ff.; Mic 2:2; Jer 22:17 *et passim;* and Prov 3:27; 14:21, 31; 22:9; 28:27; 29:14; *et passim.*

[3] *BZAW* LXII (1933), pp. 24ff.

[4] On this, see *BZAW* LXII (1933), pp. 25ff.

[5] Cf. W. Zimmerli, "Zur Struktur der alttestamentlichen Weisheit," *ZAW* (1933), p. 181. [The beginning of Section II in the ET of this article which appears elsewhere in this volume.] Baumgartner is certainly correct when he maintains that "wise man and prophet as well as wise man and priest are to be considered as quite clearly distinct . . . circles" (*Israelitische und altorientalische Weisheit* (1933), p. 6).

[6] Cf. Prov 10:19 wᵉhosek sᵉpatâw maskîl ("and whoever restrains his lips is intelligent") and Sir 20:7.

[7] Th. H. Robinson and F. Horst, *Die Kleinen Propheten* (1938), p. 50.

[8] *Ibid.,* p. 171.

[9] Cf. BH.

[10] On the basis of the historical situation and the usages of speech presupposed here, few serious considerations could be raised against it.

[11] Cf. to this expression baen ḥᵃkamîm the other one baen nᵉbî'îm!

[12] Read the hiphil (LXX).

[13] sarayik sôrᵉrîm (your leaders are rebels) 1:23; kî taḥat yopî (brand instead of beauty) 3:24; mišpaṭ (justice), mispaḥ (lawbook), sᵉdaqa (righteousness), seᶜaqā (call for help) 5:7; 'im lo' ta'ᵃmînû kî lo' te'amenû (if you do not have faith, you will not endure).

[14] According to BH.

[15] According to LXX.

[16] I.e., in the last paragraph.

[17] In the early period of his work, Isaiah expected that Yahweh would make Jerusalem's "counsellors" (yoᶜᵃṣîm) as at the beginning, 1:26.

[18] As an additional thought, I would contend that this opinion had already been expressed by Sellin in his *Introduction* (7th. [German] ed. [1935], p. 81): "by occupation, perhaps a teacher of law or wisdom 8:16; 28:9, 23ff."

[19] In this meaning, only here in the OT.

[20] Generally designates the stone tablets of the law and a few times boards; as tablets upon which to write, elsewhere only in Hab 2:2.

[21] Cf. on this Procksch, *Jesaja* I, p. 354.

[22] The formula "he too is wise" is meant ironically!

CHAPTER XV

THE JOSEPH NARRATIVE AND ANCIENT WISDOM
1953

GERHARD von RAD

The Joseph story is in every respect distinct from the patri-archal narratives which it follows. Whereas almost all the stories of Abraham and of Jacob are limited in length to twenty or thirty verses, the four hundred or so verses of the Joseph narrative patently show it to be a document of quite a different literary form. Quite evidently it is not a "cycle" of sagas, that is, a catena of what were originally self-contained narrative units.[1] If we go on to compare the internal charac-teristics of the two, the differences become still more marked.

The stories about Abraham, Isaac, and Jacob consist of local, cultic saga-material, brought together by the Yahwist or an even earlier writer under the heading of promises made to the forefathers of Israel with regard to the land and to their progeny. The Joseph narrative is a novel through and through, and the material is in no way associated at any point with genuine local traditions.[2] From the point of view of literary technique the Joseph story displays resources far beyond those of the ancient sagas—in the depiction of involved psychological situations, for example, or in the use of telling phrases in the course of action. In this respect it has affinities with the Court History of David (*II Sam.* vi to *I Kings* ii), and for this reason it may be taken for granted that it cannot have been written before the early part of the monarchic period.

1. This despite Gunkel, who leaned far too heavily on the assumption that the Jospeh story was in origin a saga in making his analysis of it.

2. The writer was able to establish only a quite marginal contact between the Joseph narrative and the promise made to the Patriarchs, i.e. at *Gen.* L.24. So far as the history of the tradition itself is concerned (although not from a literary point of view) this is a quite secondary reference, unknown to the original, independent Joseph narrative.

There are, however, many factors which link the Joseph narrative even more closely with the spiritual outlook of this period. Gunkel himself remarked upon the delight in all things foreign which characterises the Joseph story,[3] the enlightened interest in the customs and social structure of a distant nation, the magnificence of Pharaoh's court, the installation of the vizier, the storage of cereal crops, the mummification of dead bodies, and so on. The early monarchic period saw the abandonment of many patriarchal traditions, but it also saw a wholly new departure in spirituality, a kind of "enlightenment", an awakening of spiritual self-consciousness. Men became aware of their own spiritual and rational powers, and whole new dimensions of experience opened up before their eyes, inwardly as well as outwardly. They were dimensions of which the faith of their forefathers had taken no account.[4]

One of these new dimensions with which we have become familiar in the literature of the period is what might be called the anthropological factor, a concentration upon the phenomenon of man in the broadest sense, his potentialities and his limitations, his psychological complexity and profundity. A further step immediately dependent upon this one was the recognition of the fact that this human factor can and must be developed and educated. This was the underlying purpose of the earliest wisdom literature.[5] Such education, however, is impossible unless there exists some guiding pattern of humanity, even though it may not offer a final and definitive ideal of development. Ancient Israelite wisdom had such a pattern, and applied it in no uncertain manner. We shall try to point out some of its characteristics, for it is the purpose of this study to show that the Joseph narrative is closely related to the earlier wisdom writings as a manifestation of this educational ideal.

None would dispute the fact that this early wisdom literature belongs within the context of the royal court, and that its principal aim was to build up a competent body of future

3. H. Gunkel, *Genesis*, p. 397.
4. There is also a newly awakened interest in scientific natural history at this time: A. Alt, *Die Weisheit Salomos*, *ThLZ*, 1951, pp. 139ff. (*Kl. Schr.*, II, pp. 90ff.).
5. To this early wisdom literature we assign the collections of proverbs, dating from the monarchic period: *Prov.* x.1-xxII.16; xxII.17-xxIV.22, 25-29.

administrators. Joseph himself is an administrator, who became one by demonstrating to Pharaoh that he possessed the twin virtues of outspokenness and good counsel—precisely the qualities upon which the wisdom-teachers continually insist. To speak well at the decisive moment, to give sound advice in any and every contingency of state affairs, and so if possible to take his place among the king's entourage—such was the main aim of the education of the scribe.

> Do you see a man skilful in his work?
> He will stand before kings.
>
> (*Prov.* XXII.29)

As Ben Sira was later to say,

> Neglect not the discourse of the wise . . .
> For of them thou shalt learn instruction
> And how to minister to great men.
>
> (Ben Sira VIII.8)

It could equally well have been said in the days of Solomon. Let us cite but one out of the multitude of examples available in Egyptian literature:

"If you are a tried counsellor who sits in the hall of his lord, gather your wits together right well. When you are silent, it will be better than tef-tef flowers. When you speak, you must know how to bring the matter to a conclusion. The one who gives counsel is an accomplished man; to speak is harder than any labour."[6]

It would certainly be a mistake to see in these and many similar exhortations no more than a desire to impart a superficial gloss which would enable a young man to climb rapidly in his profession. If it were so, we could not properly speak of an educational ideal here. Yet the wise men present us with a very imposing and well-found pattern for human living, which in some respects has striking points of contact with the humanistic idea of antiquity.[7] They depict a man who by his upbringing, his modesty, his learning, his courtesy and his self-discipline has acquired true nobility of character. He is, let us

6. Ptahhotep, 24, from the translation by H. Kees.
7. H. Kees, *Aegypten, Handbuch der Altertumswissenschaft*, Series III, Pt. I, Vol. III, *Kulturgeschichte des alten Orients*, Munich 1933, pp. 268, 283.

say it at once, the image of Joseph! Joseph, as the writer of the narrative draws him, is the very picture of just such a young man at his best, well-bred and finely educated, steadfast in faith and versed in the ways of the world. The foundation on which such a character is built, as Joseph himself recognises, is "godly fear"; and the fear of Yahweh is quite simply obedience to the divine law (*Prov.* I.7; xv.33; *Gen.* xLII.18).[8]

Theologically speaking this foundation is the most important factor in the whole educational programme, for wisdom is not directed *towards* the cultus and *towards* divine revelation, but works outwards from them. Because it knows nothing of man's yearning for salvation, the programme has a certain undogmatic flexibility of approach, and shows pronounced realism in its concern for that which is practicable. Concern for the absolute standards of divine law emerges with particular clarity in the story of Joseph's temptation by Potiphar's wife (*Gen.* xxxix), which brings to mind a vast area of wisdom-teaching on the subject of "strange women" (נָכְרִיּת).[9]

The narrative of *Gen.* xxxix reads as if it had been devised expressly to illustrate the warnings of the wisdom writers.[10] Another person concerning whom the wise men give a warning is the "hot tempered man". the uncontrolled, passionate man whose exact opposite is to be seen in the "cool spirited", patient man (קַר רוּחַ).[11]

> He who is slow to anger has great understanding, but he who has a hasty temper exacts folly.
>
> (*Prov.* xIV.29)

In his relationship with his brothers, Joseph is the very pattern of the man who can "keep silence", as described in Egyptian wisdom-lore. He is the "prudent man who conceals his knowledge" (*Prov.* xII.23), and who "restrains his lips" (*Prov.* x.19). Above all, the "patient man" does not give way

8. L. Köhler, *Old Testament Theology*, p. 110.
9. G. Boström, *Proverbiastudien*, Lund 1935, pp. 15ff.
10. *Prov.* xxII.14; xxIII.27f. Cf. The Wisdom of Ani: "A woman who is far from her husband says to you every day, 'I am beautiful', when there is no one to see." Erman, *The Literature of the Ancient Egyptians*, p. 240.
11. *Prov.* xVII.27; xv.18; xVI.32. On the ideal of the taciturn man, see H. O. Lange, *Die Weisheit des Amen em ope*, Copenhagen 1925.

to his passions, and the writer intends us to be amazed at the extraordinary control which Joseph is able to exercise over his emotions.[12] It must not be forgotten that this prohibition of any display of emotion[13] ran counter to the whole instinct of the ancient Hebrew. Israelite wisdom-writers refer to a self-controlled man as מֹשֵׁל בְּרוּחוֹ, and a "tranquil mind" such as he has (*Prov.* xiv.30) is a constructive force for good in the life of the community: "He who is slow to anger quietens contention" (*Prov.* xv.18). Of whom is this more true than of Joseph? We may go yet further: even Joseph's magnanimity and his general forbearance from any kind of revenge find striking parallels in proverbial wisdom:

> Do not say, "I will do to him as he has done to me; I will pay the man back for what he has done."
>
> (*Prov.* xxiv.29)

> Love covers all offences.
>
> (*Prov.* x.12)

To build up the whole man in this way is not the work of a night; such discipline is learnt only in the hard school of humility, עֲנָוָה. That "humility comes before honour" and that "the reward of humility is riches and honour"—these are the lessons so richly illustrated in the first part of the Joseph story.

So much, then, for the educational ideal and the pattern of human living exemplified in the Joseph narrative, as compared with the teaching of early wisdom-literature. Let us now turn to the underlying theological presuppositions. Our case could not be regarded as proven if there were divergence between the Joseph story and the wisdom writings on this fundamental issue.

Early wisdom literature is notoriously sparing of strictly theological pronouncements, but so, too, is the Joseph narrative. There are only two passages which explicitly refer to the purposes of God. The first occurs in the recognition scene, when Joseph makes himself known and ascribes the past events to the guidance of God, who has brought all the vicissitudes they have suffered to a happy conclusion (*Gen.* xlv.5ff.). The

12. *Gen.* xlii.24; xliii.30f.; xlv.1.   13. H. Kees, *Aegypten*, p. 284.

same thought is still more pointedly expressed in the words, "You meant evil against me, but God meant it for good" (*Gen.* L.20). Here the problem of the relationship between human intentions and the divine control of events is still more keenly felt: God has all the threads firmly in his hands even when men are least aware of it. But this is a bare statement of fact, and the way in which God's will is related to human purposes remains a mystery. Thus the statements of what "you meant" and what "God meant" are in the last analysis irreconcilable.

Let us, however, compare Joseph's comments, both here and in *Gen.* XLV.8, with the dictum of *Proverbs* that "A man's mind plans his way, but Yahweh directs his steps" (*Prov.* XVI.9). Here, too, we have a statement that Yahweh controls all things, and also a sharply-drawn contrast between human plans and the divine direction of affairs. The similarity of thought is most striking, and that it is not fortuitous is shown by the aphorism of *Prov.* XIX.21: "Many are the plans in the mind of a man, but it is Yahweh's purpose that will be stablished."

Just as in Joseph's dictum, the purposes of God and man are set over against each other, and the purposes of God prevail. As a final demonstration that this opposition between the divine economy and human intentions is a central issue in the theology of wisdom-writing, I quote the Egyptian Amenemope: "That which men propose is one thing; what God does is another" (Amenemope XIX.16).[14] In each case the human purpose is expressed in the first sentence, the divine activity in the second, and in view of this similarity of form and content between the proverb of Amenemope and the comment made by Joseph it may well be asked whether the latter is not in fact a wisdom-saying which has been adapted to the purpose of the story: "You meant evil against me, but God meant it for good."

There is a further saying in the *Book of Proverbs* which is very closely related to this dictum from the Joseph story: "A man's steps are ordered by Yahweh, how then can man understand his way?" (*Prov.* XX.24). The writer's bewilderment here contains an element of resignation which should not be overlooked. There is evidently another side to the wisdom-writers' impres-

14. From the translation by H. Kees, *Lesebuch* (*Aegypten*), Tübingen 1928, p. 46; cf. K. Sethe, "*Der Mensch denkt, Gott lenkt*" *bei den alten Aegyptern, Nachrichten der Gesellschaft der Wissenschaft*, Göttingen 1925, pp. 141ff.

sive faith in the overriding providence of God, a side which manifests itself as a frank scepticism with regard to all human activity and purpose. The topic is too wide for discussion at this point. It cannot be denied, however, that even in the Joseph narrative a deep cleavage threatens to arise between divine and human purposes, and that human activity is so heavily fettered by the all-embracing divine control of events that it comes dangerously near to losing all significance whatever.

> No wisdom, no understanding, no counsel, can avail against Yahweh. The horse is made ready for the day of battle, but the victory belongs to Yahweh.
>
> (*Prov.* xxi.30ff.)

In this remarkable passage, the whole doctrine is made explicit: Yahweh is wholly free to dispose of the issue as he will. What then remains for men to do? They can, and indeed must, make decisions and preparations, only to find that all their plans meet with an insuperable obstacle, and that all their wisdom comes to nothing against the will of Yahweh.

According to this doctrine, all earthly events are subject to a law which is wholly beyond the grasp of the human mind. "God's life is achievement, but man's is a denial", says Amenemope (xix.14), expressing an attitude which is common both to the wisdom-sayings quoted above and also to the Joseph story; all of them regard the purposes of God as altogether hidden, incomprehensible and unfathomable. So long as there was present a divinely inspired interpreter, there was no danger in this. When, however, man is left alone with this uncompromising doctrine, we at once discern an undertone of despair in his questioning, "How can a man understand what his purpose is?" This is what has happened in Qoheleth (iii.11; vii.24; viii.17), whose scepticism has its roots deep in the past.[15]

What place, then, ought we to assign to the Joseph story, both spiritually and with regard to the ancient traditions? It

15. This intrusive scepticism is easily illustrated from the work of Amenemope. The faith which "puts itself into God's arms" (xxii.7) is close akin to an embittered resignation: there is no success to be found at God's hands, and yet there is no opposing him. The man who strives to succeed is brought to nothing the very next moment (xix.22-xx.2).

displays no historico-political interests, nor any cultic, aetio-
logical motive. It is equally devoid of any specifically theological interest in redemptive history. We can only say that the
Joseph story, with its strong didactic motive, belongs to the
category of early wisdom writing. Several consequences follow,
which can only be lightly touched upon here.

First, with regard to wisdom writing as a whole, seen not
simply as collections of proverbs but as a literary phenomenon,
which from the beginning had an extremely wide spiritual
scope: If the influence of wisdom was so significant over so wide
a field of literature in ancient Egypt,[16] it would be very surprising if a similar state of affairs had not also prevailed in
Israel. In that case, however, we must be prepared to reassess
the Joseph story in the light of the possibility that it is closely
related to contemporary Egyptian literature. There is, of
course, no question of its being an Egyptian story, at all events
in anything like its present form: it is far too clearly stamped as
a story about a non-Egyptian, written for non-Egyptians. On
the other hand it must certainly be presumed that Egyptian
literary influences and models, even specific literary sources, all
played their part in the formation of the Joseph narrative. It
cannot be accidental that the Wisdom of Amenemope speaks
of that same control of events by "God",[17] with a similar
emphasis on the fact that it is incomprehensible to man, which
characterises the history of Joseph.

The educational ideal of Amenemope, too, is one of discretion, modesty, self-control and deliberation,[18] the very qualities displayed by Joseph. If, further, we look for a close parallel
to the narrative technique of the Joseph story, we shall find it
pre-eminently in Egyptian stories such as the Peasant's Lament,[19] whose psychological realism is of a very similar type.

Finally, the whole question of the mythological background
of the Joseph story calls for re-examination if we are to postulate the presence of Egyptian influence,[20] for we cannot exclude

16. H. Brunner, *Aegyptologie, Handbuch der Orientalistik*, p. 109.
17. H. Brunner, *Aegyptologie,* pp. 107f.
18. H. O. Lange, *Die Weisheit des Amen em ope*, p. 21.
19. J. Spiegel, *Aegyptologie*, pp. 117, 131.
20. B. Reicke, *Analogier mellan Josefsberättelsen i Genesis och Ras Shamra-
Texterna, Svensk Exegetic Årsbok*, Vol. x, 1945, pp. 5ff.

the possibility of such a background in the very early stages of the development of the narrative as we have it. It is a remarkable coincidence that the Tale of the Two Brothers, which has often been compared with the Joseph story, has recently been convincingly explained as deriving from mythological sources.[21]

In short, then, we may say that the Joseph narrative is a didactic wisdom-story which leans heavily upon influences emanating from Egypt, not only with regard to its conception of an educational ideal, but also in its fundamental theological ideas.

21. Jacobsohn, *Die dogmatische Stellung des Königs in der Theologie der alten Aegypter, Aegyptologische Forschungen*, Vol. VIII, pp. 13ff.

VII

Amos and Wisdom

SAMUEL TERRIEN

Parallels between the Book of Amos and the wisdom literature of the Old Testament have been observed for a long time, but usually they have been explained as a result of a unilateral influence exercised by the eighth-century prophet on the post-Exilic sages. Fifty years ago, for instance, William R. Harper could write:

> The external relation of the book of Amos to the wisdom literature is not indicated by anything that has come down to us. That its influence was felt can scarcely be doubted, since in it we have the first definite formulation of Yahweh's relation to the outside world, the idea which lay at the basis of all Hebrew wisdom, the assignment of Israel to a place upon a level with other nations (cf. the absence of any reference to Israel in the book of Proverbs); an example of Oriental learning in history, geography, social customs; the very essence of wisdom, in the emphasis placed upon honesty, purity, etc.; together with an almost total absence of the religious sentiment. . . .[1]

For the past decades, both the prophetic literature and the wisdom literature of Israel have appeared in a new light. Scholars have pointed out especially that the sapiential books, although edited in their present form at a relatively late date, have preserved many substantial sources of the pre-Exilic period and

[1] William R. Harper, *A Critical and Exegetical Commentary on Amos and Hosea*, ICC (1910), p. cxxxvii.

belong indeed to the literary movement of international wisdom[2] which seems to have begun in the third millennium B.C.[3] Proper emphasis on the early date of an oral tradition among the wise may reopen the question of the influences which the prophets have received. The investigation of possible contacts between Amos and the *hokmic* language, style, and ideas assumes therefore a hitherto unsuspected importance.

Among the many words and expressions of Amos which may reflect an acquaintance with the language and speech habits of the wisemen, only a few will be selected for discussion here.

1. Consecutive numerals are used in pairs. "On account of three transgressions of Damascus, yea, even four . . ." (Am. 1:3; cf. vss. 6, 9, 11, 13; 2:1, 4, 6). There can be little doubt that this formula is a device which is typical of the wisdom style. "In one way, yea, even in two" (Job 33:14); "I have spoken once, and I

[2] A. Causse, "Introduction à l'étude de la sagesse juive," RHPR, I (1921), pp. 45-60; "Les origines étrangères et la tendance humaniste de la sagesse juive," *Congrès d'Histoire des Religions*, II (1923), pp. 45-54; "Sagesse égyptienne et sagesse juive," RHPR, IX (1929), pp. 154 ff.; H. Gressmann, *Israels Spruchweisheit im Zusammenhang der Weltliteratur* (1925); W. O. E. Oesterley, *The Wisdom of Egypt and the Old Testament* (1927); P. Humbert, *Recherches sur les sources égyptiennes de la littérature sapientiale d'Israël* (1929); T. E. Peet, *A Comparative Study of the Literatures of Egypt, Palestine, and Mesopotamia* (1929); W. Baumgartner, *Israelitische und altorientalische Weisheit* (1933); W. Baumgartner, "The Wisdom Literature," in *The Old Testament and Modern Study*, H. H. Rowley, ed. (1951), pp. 210-237; J. Fichtner, *Die altorientalische Weisheit in ihrer israelitisch-jüdischen Ausprägung* (1933); W. Zimmerli, "Zur Struktur der alttestamentlichen Weisheit," ZAW, 51 (1933), pp. 177 ff.; O. S. Rankin, *Israel's Wisdom Literature* (1936); A. Drubbel, *Les livres sapientiaux d'Israël dans leurs sources préexiliques* (1936); "Le conflit entre la sagesse profane et la sagesse religieuse," *Biblica*, XVII (1936), pp. 45-70, 407-428; J. Schmidt, *Studien zur Stilistik der alttestamentlichen Spruchliteratur* (1936); H. Duesberg, *Les scribes inspirés*, 2 vols. (1938-39); A. Dubarle, *Les sages d'Israël* (1946); J. C. Rylaarsdam, *Revelation in Jewish Wisdom Literature* (1946); A. Bentzen, *Introduction to the Old Testament* (1948), I, pp. 167-183; II, pp. 171-179, 188-191; B. Couroyer, "Idéal sapientiel en Egypte et en Israël," RB, LVII (1950), pp. 174-179; W. F. Albright, "Some Canaanite-Phoenician Sources of Hebrew Wisdom," in *Wisdom in Israel and in the Ancient Near East*, M. Noth and D. Winton Thomas, eds. (Suppl. VT, III [1955], pp. 1-15; R. B. Y. Scott, "Solomon and the Beginning of Wisdom in Israel," in *ibid.*, pp. 262-279; G. von Rad, *Theologie des Alten Testaments*, I (1957), pp. 381-457.

[3] J. J. A. vanDijk, *La sagesse suméro-accadienne* (1953); S. N. Kramer, " 'Man and His God': A Sumerian Variation on the 'Job' Motif," Suppl. VT, III (1955), pp. 170-182; *From the Tablets of Sumer* (1956), pp. 71-168.

will not answer; twice, but I will proceed no further" (Job 40:5; cf. Ps. 62:12). Other examples with higher numerals are all found in the wisdom literature: "Two times and three times" (Sirach 23:16; 26:28; 50:25; cf. Ahiqar vi, Aramaic); "three times and four times" as in Amos (Pr. 30:15, 18, 21, 29; Sirach 36:5); "four times and five times" (Pr. 6:16; Job 5:19); "seven times and eight times" (Ec. 11:2); "nine times and ten times" (Sirach 25:7). It will be observed that such a phrase is employed by Amos but not by any of the other prophets. The expression "seven shepherds and eight princes of men" (Mic. 5:5), whatever its precise meaning may be, does not appear to belong to the same form of numerical gradation with an implication of indefiniteness. Likewise, the words "three columns and four" (Jer. 36:23) must be taken literally, and therefore do not constitute a parallel. There is evidence that the numerical pattern was already common in the second millennium B.C.[4] We are thus justified in asking the question, Why is it that in the Old Testament only Amos and the wisdom literature show an acquaintance with this form of speaking? Many exegetes recognize that this formula originated among the wise.[5]

2. In Am. 9:2 Yahweh describes through the mouth of his prophet the completeness of eschatological retribution. "If they dig into Sheol, from there shall my hand seize them!" For the Old Testament in general Sheol remains outside of Yahweh's realm of activity or jurisdiction. It is a place of horror because in it the dead are estranged from the Deity (Isa. 38:18; Ps. 88:11; etc.). Either Yahweh has no possibility of access to the grave or, more probably, he does not concern himself with it.[6] Outside of Amos, only the wisdom literature (Pr. 15:11; Job

---

[4] In the Ugaritic poem of Keret, the device of numerical gradation appears under several forms. "One-third, one-fourth, one-fifth, one-sixth, one-seventh" (col. i, 16-20); "a fifth and a sixth" (col. ii, 83); "in thousands, in myriads; after two, after three" (col. ii, 92-95); "a fifth and a sixth" (col. iv, 174-175); "a day, a second, on a third" (col iv, 194-195).

[5] See J. Lindblom, "Wisdom in the Old Testament Prophets," Suppl. VT, III (1955), p. 203.

[6] See J. Pedersen, *Israel, Its Life and Culture*, I-II (1926), pp. 453-470; Ch. Barth, *Die Errettung vom Tode in den individuellen Klage- und Dankliedern des Alten Testaments* (1947); von Rad, *op. cit.*, pp. 385-386; E. Jacob, *Theology of the Old Testament* (1958), pp. 303-304.

26:6; cf. 7:21?) and a hymnic meditation (Ps. 139:7) of the sapiential type[7] dare to conceive poetically the imagery of a rapport between Yahweh and the sojourn of the dead. It seems hardly possible that Amos influenced the wisdom poets. The prophet referred to Sheol incidentally. His purpose was to show that there was no escape from the reach of divine wrath; it was not to affirm that Yahweh had access to the underworld. He took this idea for granted. On the contrary, the *ḥokmic* passages mentioned above state a general truth according to which no limit or restriction is opposed to God's omnipotence, omniscience, and omnipresence. The tone of Amos is one of urgency and violence. That of the wise is one of awe in serenity. While the tenor of Ps. 139 is much more somber than is generally recognized, since the psalmist attempts to flee from the presence of Yahweh, no one will seriously maintain that in this psalm as in Am. 9 Yahweh is said to go to Sheol in order to exercise his retributive justice. Quite clearly, the wise held cosmological beliefs which were different from those generally followed by the prophets and the priests or the reciters of cultic traditions.[8] Amos alone appears to agree with the wise in accepting the view that the underworld was completely within the sphere of Yahweh's influence.

3. In the poetic sequence on prophetic authority (Am. 3:3-8), the prophet uses the didactic method of appealing to common sense by running through a series of cause-and-effect relation-

---

[7] It is difficult to escape the conclusion that Ps. 139 has come from a milieu strongly influenced by the Joban poetic school (cf. Ps. 139:3 with Job 22:21; Ps. 139:5 with Job 9:33; Ps. 139:6 with Job 11:6; Ps. 139:8 with Job 17:13; Ps. 139:13 with Job 10-11; etc.).

[8] The enigmatic reference of Amos to Yahweh's trial of the great abyss by fire (7:4) may constitute another evidence of contact with the sapiential beliefs. The precise meaning of the expression *tᵉhôm rabbâ*, however, is open to question. If *tᵉhôm* in this passage designates the primeval waters (as in Gen. 1:2; Job 38:16, 30; Ps. 104:6; cf. Ps. 33:7; 36:6; 78:15), the prophet displays a belief in Yahweh's unopposed sway over the universe in its totality, including the watery deep. While Amos does not explicitly state that Yahweh has created the *tᵉhôm*, his reference implies that there is no room in his cosmogonic scheme for the theme of the dualistic fight or for a belief in the non-created or pre-existent character of the abyss. If this interpretation is correct, Amos may show once again a close affinity with the sapiential idea of the creation of the deep (Pr. 8:24, 27-28).

451

ships in the form of rhetorical questions (cf. also 5:25; 6:2, 12; 9:7). The use of the interrogative maxim is so widespread in the Old Testament in general that it cannot be presented as an argument tending to show points of contact between the wise and Amos. Nevertheless, the fact that the prophet expects to stimulate audience approval in a matter of logical thinking involving assent to the principle of empirically observed causation is strongly reminiscent of the teaching method of the wise.[9]

4. In the climax of the same poetic sequence on prophetic authority, Amos declares, "Surely, Adonay Yahweh will do nothing without revealing his secret to his servants the prophets" (3:7). The use of the word *sôd*, "secret," is not restricted to Amos. The word occurs quite frequently with several different meanings in pericopes of various literary types (Gen. 49:6; Jer. 23:18, 22; Ezek. 13:9; Pss. 25:14; 55:15; 64:3; 83:4; 89:8; 111:1). In the sense of "intimate secret," however, the word appears to be typical of the wisdom literature (Job 15:8, 17; 19:19; 29:4; Pr. 3:32; 11:13; 15:22; 20:19; 25:9; Sirach 8:17; 9:4, 14; 42:12). We may say that the word *sôd* is par excellence a sapiential term, conveying the idea of confidential and intimate exchange in an atmosphere of friendship and mutual trust.[10]

5. Amos accuses Israel of not knowing "how to do what is right" (*nᵉkôḥâ;* 3:10). For a pre-Exilic prophet, this is a most unusual way of speaking. Isaiah alone (30:10) besides Amos in the monarchic period employs the same word (in the plural), but only when he quotes his adversaries, who probably include the party of the royal wise (see Isa. 5:21; 29:14). The other occurrences of the word are confined almost exclusively to the Exilic and post-Exilic passages of the Isaianic school (Isa. 57:2; 59:14; 26:10). Undoubtedly it is a favorite term of wisdom (Pr. 8:9; 24:26; 26:28; Sirach 11:21), and the fact that it was used by Absalom (II Sam. 15:3) is perhaps an indication of its origin in courtly circles. In any case, Amos did not select a term

---

[9] See Pr. 6:27; 17:16; 30:4; Job 8:11; etc. Cf. J. Hempel, *Die althebräische Literatur* (1930), pp. 49-50; Schmidt, *op. cit.*, pp. 56-57.

[10] Even when the sapiential poet speaks of the *sôd* of God, he places the word in parallelism with *ḥokmâ* (Job 15:8). Amos associates the secret of God with the prophetic word, and this idea is taken up by Jeremiah (23:19). See A. Neher, *Amos* (1950), p. 16; cf. A. Weiser, *Die Profetie des Amos* (1929), pp. 127-128.

typical of the covenant traditions or of the legal literature, with which he shows otherwise a close acquaintance.[11]

6. In the indictment of Edom Amos says, "And his anger did tear as a prey continually" (1:11). While a number of exegetes wish to correct the difficult verb *wayyiṭrōp*, "and he tore," on the basis of the Syriac and Vulgate, the MT appears to be supported here by the fact that in Job 16:9, "his anger has found a prey," the same verb occurs with the same subject, *'ap*, "anger," and in Job 18:4, "in his anger he tears himself as a prey," the same verb occurs with the same noun as an indirect object. The double occurrence of the two words together in Job suggests the existence of a sapiential idiom which was familiar to Amos. It will be observed that nowhere else in the Old Testament are the verb and the noun found together.

7. While the prophets never spoke of the nation under the appellation of "Isaac," Amos did so twice (7:9 and 7:16). Such a peculiarity needs to be treated with another, which follows.

8. Only Amos among the prophets referred to Beer-sheba, and he did so in two different passages (5:5 and 8:14). The connection between Isaac and Beer-sheba is well known (see Gen. 21:31-33; 26:15-25). The ethnic group which is related to the patronym "Isaac" included the Israelites and the Edomites (Gen. 25:29, 30), and the two peoples were described as "brothers" (Num. 20:14; Dt. 23:8). The historical affinities which united Judah and Edom, and eventually made their mutual hatred especially virulent, are repeatedly displayed in the Judah traditions. Caleb and Othniel, who played a part in the conquest of what later on became Judah territory (Jos. 15:16, 17; Jg. 1:13-21), were related to Kenaz, an Edomite (Gen. 36:11, 40, 42; cf. Num. 32:12; Jos. 14:6, 14). The Jerahmeelites, who were descendants of a brother of Caleb and Othniel (I Chr. 2:34, 42), came to the tribal territory of Judah from the general vicinity of Edom (I Sam. 27:10; 30:29). The geographical proximity of Teqoa to Beer-sheba on the one hand and to Edom on the other

---

[11] A point which is to be held side by side with the opinion that Amos is acquainted with international customs in law and morality. See Neher, "The Noahidic Berith," *op. cit.*, pp. 49-81; R. Bach, "Gottesrecht und weltliches Recht in der Verkündigung des Propheten Amos," *Festschrift für Günther Dehn* (1957), pp. 23-34.

offers at least the possibility of cultural exchanges between the
milieu to which tradition had connected Amos (Am. 1:1; cf.
7:12) and the Edomites themselves. The reputation of Edom for
wisdom[12] offers support to the hypothesis that the prophet may
have received from the seminomads who lived in the south and
the southeast of the Dead Sea an outlook on man and a world
view which were generally those of the international wisdom
movement.[13]

The above remarks, which deal chiefly with matters of terminology and style, tend to show that peculiar affinities existed
between Amos and the wise. A conjecture may therefore be
elaborated, according to which the prophet received from the
sapiential circles some of his ideas. Like the wise, Amos was
uncommonly well versed in Oriental learning, especially in
astronomy. He was acquainted with the geography, the history,
and the social customs of nations outside of Israel. He thought
of the Deity as the ruler of all peoples and he was aware of
standards of ethical behavior which were common to all men,
independently of a revealed legislation. He was not concerned
with the problems of idolatry (in spite of 5:26), and the importance of ritual was subsumed by him under the questions of
morality. Unlike the wise, Amos was an eschatologist whose
thinking moved within the framework of an interpretation of
history which was dominated by the reality of election and cove-

[12] See I Kg. 4:30-31; Jer. 49:7; Baruch 3:22-23. The location of the action in the
folk tale of Job should be sought in Edom rather than in Hauran (cf. Job 1:1
and Jer. 25:19 ff.; Lam. 4:21; P. Dhorme, *Le livre de Job* [1926], pp. xix-xxii;
R. H. Pfeiffer, "Edomitic Wisdom," ZAW, 44 [1926], pp. 13-25); A. Musil, *Arabia
Petraea* (1908), vol. II, pp. 337 and 339, note d: *The Northern Heǧāz* (1926),
pp. 249-52; J. Simons, *The Geographical and Topographical Texts of the Old
Testament* (1959), p. 25 and map III c.

[13] This hypothesis, however, should not include another, according to which
Amos himself might have been an Edomite through the clan of Zerah (Gen.
36:13; see G. Hölscher, *Die Profeten* [1914], pp. 189-190, who refers to the discussion of E. Meyer on Teqoa: *Die Israeliten und ihre Nachbarstämme* [1906],
p. 435). In any case, one should not affirm too confidently that Amos was a native
of Teqoa. The editorial note states that he "was among shepherds from Teqoa"
(1:1). The use of the preposition "among" suggests that he was not one of them.
The fact that nothing is told about his family, that he has no genealogy, that
even the name of his father is unknown, further indicates the obscure origins of
the prophet.

nant. He was not a humanistic moralist. He was moved by a
sense of prophetic compulsion. Nevertheless, there is in his message the seed of a moralistic conception of salvation. He made
repentance a condition of forgiveness rather than considering
repentance itself as a fruit of creative grace. His soteriological
implications are not far distant from those of the ancient wise
of the Babylonian and Egyptian literatures, the poets of the
canonical proverbs, and the friends of Job. His utter pessimism
concerning the ability of man to repent led him to predict the
doom of Israel. Even if the saying, "Perhaps Yahweh God of
Hosts will have mercy for the remnant of Joseph" (5:15) is considered authentic, one may remark that this mercy is hypothetical and that it is moreover conditioned by the fulfillment of
morality: hate evil, love good, and establish justice at the gate.
In other words, like the wise, Amos makes ethical behavior the
prerequisite of divine favor.

Such a hypothesis should not be construed as meaning that
the prophet was not primarily steeped in the covenant theology
of Israel.[14] It rather tends to prevent the overstressing of the
separation of classes among the leaders of the eighth century
B.C. That various groups, such as priests, prophets, and wisemen,
existed should not be denied. At the same time, such groups
were not alien one from the others, and they lived in a common
and mutually interacting environment.[15]

---

[14] See E. Würthwein, "Amos-Studien," ZAW, 62 (1950), pp. 10-52, pp. 49 ff.;
von Rad, *op. cit.*, II (1960), pp. 141-149.
[15] See A. Robert, "Le Yahwisme de Prov. x, 1-xii, 16; xxv-xxix," *Mémorial
Lagrange* (1940), p. 165.

A CONSIDERATION OF THE CLASSIFICATION, 'WISDOM PSALMS'

BY

ROLAND E. MURPHY

Washington

The pioneer work of Hermann GUNKEL in literary analysis of the Psalms has been rightly acknowledged as fundamental for understanding them [1]). Since his time there has also been some refinement of his methods. H. SCHMIDT [2]) offered a more detailed study of the complaints, and the studies of C. WESTERMANN [3]) have also centred upon this category, as well as upon the distinction between hymn and thanksgiving psalm. G. CASTELLINO [4]) added a new classification, *liturgia della fedeltà Jahwistica*, independently of A. WEISER [5]), whose feast of covenant renewal provided another frame of reference for psalm interpretation. S. MOWINCKEL [6]) is in a class by himself, dependent upon GUNKEL as he himself affirms, but going beyond him in many aspects (cultic emphasis) of the classification and life-setting of the Pss. Despite this progress it may be said that perhaps not enough attention has been paid to refining the methods of form-analysis in the case of individual types of Pss [7]).

In one area, that of the so-called Wisdom Psalms, this is particularly true, because no two authors will agree in listing these Pss [8]).

---

[1]) H. GUNKEL-J. BEGRICH, *Einleitung in die Psalmen* (Göttingen, 1933).

[2]) H. SCHMIDT, *Das Gebet der Angeklagten im Alten Testament* (*BZAW*, 49; Berlin, 1928).

[3]) C. WESTERMANN, *Das Loben Gottes in den Psalmen*[2] (Göttingen, 1961); see *CBQ* 21 (1959) 83-87.

[4]) G. CASTELLINO, *Libro dei Salmi* (La Sacra Bibbia; Roma, 1954).

[5]) A. WEISER, *Die Psalmen*[4] (*ATD* 14/15; Göttingen, 1955).

[6]) S. MOWINCKEL, *Psalmenstudien* (Oslo, 1921-24; Amsterdam, 1961).

[7]) Only a few studies have appeared: C. WESTERMANN, "Struktur und Geschichte der Klage im Alten Testament", *ZAW* 66 (1954) 44-80; F. MAND, "Die Eigenständigkeit der Danklieder des Psalters als Bekenntnislieder", *ZAW* 70 (1958) 185 199; J. W. WEVERS, "A Study in the Form Criticism of Individual Complaint Psalms", *VT* 6 (1956) 80-96.

[8]) See note 4, p. 161 for more details. But we may note here the treatment by O. EISSFELDT, *Einleitung in das Alte Testament*[2] (Tübingen, 1956) 147 ff., who admits: "Wie überall die Grenzen zwischen den Gattungen, denen die innerhalb und ausserhalb des Psalters stehenden Lieder angehören fliessend sind, so lässt sich

GUNKEL himself did not classify them in the same way he did the others [1]). He entitled his study, "Weisheitsdichtung in den Psalmen", since there did not seem to be any clear characteristics that could be pointed out for these, as had been done for other psalm types. He spoke of *Weisheitsgedichten* and numbered among them 49, 1, 91, 112, 128, 37, 73; and perhaps not all would agree that these seven poems are the list GUNKEL intended, since he is not explicit [2]). He spoke of *eine ganz umfassende Gattung*, that embraced both saying and poems. The vagueness of his characterisation has not been eliminated by studies since his time.

Recently, there has been a tendency to recognize a *milieu sapientiel* to which many Pss besides those generally recognized as sapiential, are ascribed. This view is found among those scholars who are particularly alert to the *style anthologique* found in postexilic Hebrew literature, A. ROBERT, A. DEISSLER, R. TOURNAY [3]).

This sapiential milieu has been concretely described in the most recent treatment of the problem of wisdom and Pss by S. MOWIN-CKEL [4]). Characteristically, he approaches the problem from the point

---

für die Aussonderung der Weisheitslieder aus ihnen auch nur eine bedingte Gültigkeit in Anspruch nehmen". He recognizes in the group: 1, 37, 49, 73, 78, 91, 128 and 133; hesitantly, he would include 139 and 91. A. BENTZEN, *Introduction to the Old Testament* [3] (Copenhagen, 1957) I, 161, writes: "Taken de rigueur the pure type of Wisdom literature is only found in the Psalter in Ps. 1 and 112 and 127 ... The theory of 'didactic poems' in the Psalter has—as Mowinckel has pointed out—often been exaggerated". Finally, it would appear that ENGNELL rejects altogether the notion of Wisdom Psalms, according to SVEND HOLM-NIELSEN, "The Importance of Late Jewish Psalmody for the Understanding of Old Testament Psalmodic Tradition", *Studia Theologica* 14 (1960) 1-53; see p. 45, n. 90.

[1]) *Op. cit.*, section 10 is entitled "Weisheitsdichtung in den Psalmen".

[2]) For a different understanding of GUNKEL's enumeration, see A. DESCAMPS, "Pour un classement littéraire des psaumes", *Mélanges Bibliques André Robert* (Paris, 1957) 187-196.

[3]) Among ROBERT's writings, see especially "L'exégèse des psaumes selon les méthodes de la 'Formgeschichteschule'", *Miscellanea Biblica B. Ubach* (Montserrat, 1953) 211-225; R. TOURNAY, "En marge d'une traduction des psaumes", *RB* 63 (1956) 503, 511-512; A. DEISSLER, *Psalm* 119 (118) *und seine Theologie* (München, 1955); in a study of Ps. 19, DEISSLER writes: "als Mutterboden das nachexilische Milieu der 'theologischen Weisheit'" in "Zur Datierung und Situierung der 'kosmischen Hymnen' Pss. 8 19 29," *Lex Tua Veritas* Festschrift für Hubert Junker (Trier, 1961) 47-59, esp. p. 51; see also A. DEISSLER, "Der anthologische Charakter des Psalmes 33 (32)," *Mélanges Bibliques André Robert* (Paris, 1957) 225-233.

[4]) S. MOWINCKEL, "Psalms and Wisdom", *Wisdom in Israel and in the Ancient Near East* (ROWLEY *Festschrift*; *VTS*, III, Brill, Leiden, 1955) 205-224. See already *Psalmenstudien* VI, 65 ff., and "Traditionalism and Personality in the Psalms", *HUCA* 23/1 (1950-51) 205-231.

of view of cult; the so-called wisdom psalms pose a problem for him since their non-cultic character has to be explained. He considers them to be the product of a "learned psalmography" of a private nature, which had for its purpose praise (and thanksgiving), and the teaching of this art to young people. They are characterized by a dissolution of style, and mixture of motifs, as exemplified in the alphabetic psalms; and the poetry of the wisdom books directly influenced the style and content of these prayers. The psalms concerned are "perhaps": 1, 34, 37, 49, 78, 105, 106, 111, 112, 127.

MOWINCKEL agrees substantially with the studies of M. LUDIN JANSEN and P. A. MUNCH, which were both published in 1937 [1]). According to them, this poetry arose as a pious practice among the sages, who found it useful for edification and for instruction of their students. MUNCH is very definite in speaking about "Schulandachtspsalmen" that were used in devotions at school and in the synagogue (e.g., Pss 19B, 25, 119), and "Unterrichtspsalmen" (e.g., 32, 34, Pss of Solomon) that were used for instruction in the wisdom schools. LUDIN JANSEN is not quite as specific, but he acknowledges that this poetry was used for edification and instruction in teaching, and that it served for purposes of prayer at home or in the Temple without being associated with official worship. By way of evidence, these men compare the wisdom psalms with the poems preserved in Sirach (51 : 1-12; 42 : 15—43 : 33; 33 : 1-13a; 33 : 16b-22, etc.) and in the Pss of Solomon. There are real similarities, and the conclusion that all these poems took their origin among the sages seems reasonable. Thus, a somewhat elaborate, detailed, reconstruction of the life-setting psalms is offered by the Scandinavian scholars [2]).

---

[1]) P. A. MUNCH, "Die jüdischen 'Weisheitspsalmen' und ihr Platz im Leben", *Acta Orientalia* 15 (1937) 112-140; H. LUDIN JANSEN, *Die spätjüdische Psalmendichtung. Ihr Entstehungskreis und ihr „Sitz im Leben"* (Oslo, 1937). In line with these studies one should also mention the valuable analysis of S. HOLM-NIELSEN, cited in note 8, p. 156/7.

[2]) MOWINCKEL writes concerning the wisdom psalms, "We do not know much about the way this calling upon God and thanksgiving were performed. As we have seen, it is just possible that the person who brought a thank-offering would even on some occasions recite his private thanksgiving psalm in the circle of relations and friends at the thank-offering feast. And from Sirach's book of wisdom we may at any rate infer that such poems were recited before the students of the schools of wisdom, in the circle gathered around the teacher. And this brings us to the second object: that of teaching young people the art of calling upon and praising the Lord in inspired songs of wisdom'. But then this is the true religious element: the poet wants to share his religious experiences with the young people, bear witness to them, and through this personal example

This summary of opinion would seem to indicate that the *Gattung* of wisdom psalms is subject to no clear-cut characterization, such as has been worked out for the other types of psalms. In this paper we hope to offer acceptable criteria for a more accurate determination of this type of psalm.

The Characteristics of Wisdom Psalms

At the outset we must ask ourselves what we mean by the term, "wisdom psalm." The very idea is as broad as the wisdom literature (Prv, Job, Eccles, Sirach, Wisdom) itself [1]). Is this the wisdom proper to a royal courtier, or the more distinctly Yahwistic teaching of Proverbs 1-9 ("fear of the Lord") or the wisdom which Sirach identifies with the Torah? Are we to look for the "saying" or a more continuous narrative? The long development of the various styles and themes in the wisdom literature suggests that these are all legitimate areas in which a psalm can be composed. And then there is the cultic problem: what relation, if any, do these psalms bear to the cult, particularly in view of the relative absence of cultic references in the corpus of the Old Testament wisdom literature? Despite these difficult questions, it would appear that the principles of GUNKEL's form criticism can still be utilized, but one must avoid the danger of judging and applying these criteria too rigidly. We may look for a certain uniformity of style (GUNKEL's *Formensprache*), structure and recurrence of motifs (content), as well as the life-setting.

As regards style, one should expect to find the typical stylistic peculiarities that are to be found in the Old Testament wisdom literature, such as *'ashrê* formulas [2]), numerical sayings, "better" sayings,

---

admonish them to walk in the right way". Cf. "Psalms and Wisdom", *VTS* III (1955) 212-213.

[1]) R. E. MURPHY, "The Concept of Old Testament Wisdom Literature", *The Bible in Current Catholic Thought* (New York, 1962) 46-54; G. COUTURIER, "Sagesse babylonienne et Sagesse israélite", *Sciences Ecclésiastiques* 14 (1962) 293-309.

[2]) Cf. H. SCHMIDT, „Grüsse und Gluckwünsche im Psalter", *ThStKr* 103 (1931) 141-150, who understands Pss. 128 and 133 as expressing the typical oriental blessing; Ps 127 would have been uttered on the occasion of the birth of a child; A. GEORGES, "La 'Forme' des béatitudes jusqu'à Jésus", *Mélanges Bibliques André Robert* (Paris, 1957) 398-403, aptly remarks that the OT beatitudes "sont une forme classique de l'exhortation morale et religieuse" (p. 400); C. KELLER, "Les 'Béatitudes' de l'Ancien Testament", *Hommage à Wilhelm Vischer* (Montpellier, 1960), claims that *'ashrê* is a blessing—therefore a cultic formula—which has been adopted into the wisdom style.

an address of a teacher to a "son", alphabetic structure [1]), simple comparisons, and the admonition. Content often goes hand in hand with style, as is apparent in the accepted classification of "Royal Psalms" which can be in fact thanksgiving (Ps 21) or even a plea (Ps 20). Content is reckoned as a determining factor in sub-types, such as the "Songs of Sion" among the hymns, or the "Songs of Trust" (BIRKELAND's *Schutzpsalmen*) wich develop a theme from the Individual Lament. Similarly, if there is a true wisdom psalm, we may expect that it reflects the themes of Old Testament wisdom literature: the contrast between the *rasha'* and the *ṣaddíq*, the two ways, preoccupation with the problem of retribution, practical advice as regards conduct (diligence, responsibility, avoiding evil women, etc.), fear of the Lord (which is eventually identified with the observance of Torah).

The life-setting of these psalms is a much more difficult question. As this term (*Sitz im Leben*) is understood with regard to the other types of psalms, it means the occasion which prompted the prayer, the occasion upon which it was recited. Ps 45 is on the occasion of the marriage of the king; 74 is a community lamentation centred upon the desecration of the Jerusalem temple by enemies; 138 is a prayer offered in the temple in thanksgiving for deliverance. The life-setting is clearly defined. But to what situation would one relate Ps 1 or Ps 49, for example? Their character as wisdom psalms tells us nothing about their concrete life-setting, as one usually understands it, and applies it to the rest of the psalter. There is no gainsaying the informative and helpful reconstruction of the *Sitz* or *Platz im Leben* by LUDIN JANSEN and MUNCH. But their demonstration has shown only that these poems are the product of the sages, that they spring from the *milieu sapientiel*; it has not captured the precise life-setting of the alleged wisdom psalms.

The comparison of the canonical psalms with the poems in Sirach is somewhat deceptive. One may indeed ask, how do the Pss in Sirach differ from the corresponding classifications in the Psalter? The fact that a psalm was composed by Sirach and incorporated into his book does not make it a wisdom psalm. From a sapiential milieu he

---

[1]) For alphabetic patterns in the wisdom literature, cf. P. W. SKEHAN, "The Seven Columns of Wisdom's House in Proverbs 1-9", *CBQ* 9 (1947) 190-98; "Strophic Patterns in the Book of Job", *CBQ* 23 (1961) 125-142. S. HOLM-NIELSEN gives an analysis of all the alphabetic psalms in the article cited above (n. 8, p. 156/7).

writes hymns (42 : 15—43 : 33; 39 : 12-35); a thanksgiving psalm (51 : 1-12); a lamentation (36 : 1-22). There is a typical wisdom influence and a certain looseness of structure in these compositions, but they are still properly classified as hymns, etc.,—not as wisdom psalms [1]). The *Hodayot* of Qumran, as late as they are, still show an attempt to express praise in the traditional psalm forms. The influences in the Qumran community are not very different from the piety and Torah emphases cultivated in the wisdom schools, and yet among them the psalm forms still live [2]). This fact may be brought forward to support the point of view that in a sapiential milieu the distinction between hymns, etc., and the specifically "wisdom" psalm was retained.

The determination of the life-setting is further complicated by the assumption that these psalms are not cultic; hence, it is argued, their *Sitz im Leben* is to be sought in the wisdom schools. But is there any good reason to rule out cultic use and cultic life-setting? As S. HOLM-NIELSEN points out, one cannot operate with a univocal concept of cult; the pre-exilic pattern is merely different from the postexilic [3]). And it is not apparent why the wisdom psalms should be excluded from the cult. One argument in favor of their cultic use is their relationship to the testimony or *Bekenntnis* of the Thanksgiving Pss. As the testimony took on more and more a didactic character, the role of wisdom within the cult would have been secured, and with it the independence of the wisdom psalm form. All things considered, however, it must be admitted that the precise life-setting of these poems eludes us.

The Wisdom Psalms

If we apply the standards of style and content described above, and allow for the fact that not all characteristics are to be expected in any one poem, we would assign the following to this category: 1, 32, 34, 37, 49, 112, 128 [4]).

---

[1]) For the forms in Sirach, see W. BAUMGARTNER, "Die literarischen Gattungen in der Weisheit des Jesus Sirach", *ZAW* 34 (1914) 161-198.

[2]) A markedly sapiential style appears in 1QH 1, 35 ff; cf. also 1Q26.

[3]) *Art. cit.*, 9 ff; see also his *Hodayot Psalms from Qumran* (Aarhus, 1960) 333 ff.

[4]) As indicated in note 8 on p. 156/7, there is a wide variation in enumerating the wisdom psalms. We have already drawn attention to MOWINCKEL's list. In his commentary (n. 4, p. 156) CASTELLINO has a very large number: 1, 15, 52, 112, 119, 127, 128 (these derived from the covenant); 9-10, 12, 14, 94 (appeal for a solution to the problem of retribution); 36, 91, 139 (deny problem of retribution);

Psalm 1 is perhaps the most successful example; it begins with the *'ashrê* formula, and it is an implicit admonition. Its content has to do with the *rasha'/ṣaddîq* contrast and the retribution that awaits each (conveyed by the comparisons of tree and chaff). Moreover, Ps 1 acquires added status as a wisdom piece if we accept the usual contention that it serves as a deliberate introduction to the Psalter. Then its intention is to present the psalter as a study-book, as a work to be learned from, in much the same way as the book of Hosea is held up by the sapiential tag that concludes it (14 : 10). The psalter describes, therefore, the way of the wicked, as opposed to the way of the just. In view of the total incidence of wisdom themes in Pss 1-41 (cf. Pss 31, 32, 34, 37, 39, 40, 41), it is very tempting to see here evidence that this first book (1-41) was put together under particular influence of wisdom writers, from beginning to end. Both Pss 1 and 41 are *'ashrê* psalms.

Psalm 32 is generally classified as a Thanksgiving psalm, marked by didactic influence [1]. The problem is to determine which is the preponderant element, or the determining spirit. The introduction and the ending can help us here. The *'ashrê* formula in vv. 1-2 is a flash-back, a conclusion (similar to Prv 28 : 13) which the following verses (3-5) support. The sapiential themes stand out clearly in the ending, vv. 8-11: offering of instruction and counsel (8), admonition (9), saying (10), and invitation (11). Thus, the structure of the psalm is sapiential; the wisdom elements (1-2; 8-11) serve as a wrapper for a thanksgiving testimony (vv. 3-7) in which the psalmist addresses God directly. Here is the example which the psalmist teaches; *'al zo't yitpallel kōl ḥasîd* (v. 6). The testimony exists only for the lesson which the writer wants to communicate; the psalm as a whole is not addressed to Yahweh, merely the exemplary part of it. Hence it deserves to be classified as a wisdom psalm.

Psalm 34 is alphabetic in structure and contains the address of a

---

37, 49, 73, 17 (solve problem of retribution). The recent commentary of KRAUS does not give an explicit list, but it may be concluded that he recognizes the following: 34 (at least, influenced by wisdom), 78 (history), 1, 119 (Torah psalms), 37, 73 (retribution), 127, 133 (*Spruch*), 112, 128 (*Sentenzen*); cf. H. -J. KRAUS, *Psalmen* (*BK* 15/1-2; Neukirchen, 1960) lv. A. WEISER, *op. cit.*, 60, points to 127, 133, 49, 1, 112, 128 as wisdom psalms; 37, 49, 73 are termed *Lehrgedicht*.

[1]) So, for example, KRAUS, *op. cit.*, 254: ,,Ps 32 gehört zur Gattung der individuellen Danklieder . . . Didaktische Sentenzen in 6-7 und 10, aber auch die Glückwünsche in 1-2, machen es wahrscheinlich, dass Elemente der Weisheitsdichtung bei der Konzipierung des Liedes mitbestimmend waren".

sage to "children" (v. 12). It is filled with typical maxims in favor of the *ṣaddîq* as against the *rashaʿ* (vv. 13-22). The *lamed* verse (12, in which *ᵃlammedᵉkem* occurs) clearly begins a wisdom portion. But the concluding three lines of the first half are also in the wisdom style; so this is not a *Mischung*. The wisdom intent becomes evident even in the introduction, where the psalmist urges the *ᶜanawîm* to rejoice, and invites his audience to join with him in extolling the name of the Lord (vv. 3-4). Here is the testimony of the Thanksgiving Song [1]), and only in vv. 5-7 is found the story of the distress from which Yahweh saved the author. These verses would seem to justify the classification of Ps 34 as a Thanksgiving Song [2]). But these few lines are not enough to *classify* the poem; the author shows hardly any interest in the story of his deliverance—v. 5 is the only clear reference to it. He generalizes on this experience in v. 7 and immediately goes into the instruction. This is in sharp contrast to a true Thanksgiving Psalm. It is admitted by all that the *Bekenntnis* in such a psalm tends to become "preachy." But here almost everything is didactic; the event itself is glossed over and merely serves as a springboard into wisdom teaching. Thus, the wisdom character of this psalm is much more explicit than that of Ps 32, in which so much emphasis is placed on the description of the psalmist's sorry situation.

Psalm 37 is alphabetic in structure and suggests the air of an old, experienced, teacher (37 : 25) who is intent upon admonishing his pupil. The content is the problem of retribution, and there is frequent allusion to the *rashaʿ/ṣaddîq* contrast; wisdom and the Law are associated (vv. 30 f.) in a manner reminiscent of Sirach [3]).

Psalm 49 has the vivid beginning in the style of Dame Wisdom preaching in the streets (Prv 6), and the author proclaims *ḥokmah* (v. 4). Like the introduction to Proverbs (1 : 6), *mashal* and *ḥîdah* are put in parallelism (v. 5). The problem is that of retribution.

Psalm 112 is characterized by the *'ashrê* formula, the *rashaʿ/ṣaddîq*

---

[1]) Cf. the article by F. MAND, cited in note 7 p. 156.

[2]) So, for example, GUNKEL, *Die Psalmen* (Göttingen, 1926) 142; KRAUS, *op. cit.*, 267 ("tendiert jedoch stark zur Form des Lehrgedichtes").

[3]) Cf. the remarks of S. HOLM-NIELSEN, *art. cit.*, 45: "It is difficult for me to rid myself of the view that Ps. xxxvii makes it justifiable to talk about wisdom psalms in the O.T. Indeed, it is no doubt correct to seek their origin in the instruction which in oracular form belonged in the cultic situation of certain psalms; but the wisdom psalms indicate how this instruction is made independent, either by being detached from the cult or perhaps rather by having been made an independent part of the cult at a late period".

contrast, and its description of the rewards offered to the just make it an implicit admonition.

Psalm 128 also begins with an *'ashrê* formula and it describes the prosperity of the man who "fears the Lord".

The rest of the Pss that are frequently alleged to be wisdom Pss fail to qualify as such on the basis of style and content characteristics. The most obvious absence from our list is perhaps 73 [1]). While its content is a wisdom theme, retribution, this is not enough. Preoccupation with the problem of retribution does not define a wisdom psalm, and in literary style this poem resembles more a thanksgiving song; it begins with a conclusion that is the reason for the poet's grateful prayer ("How good God is to the upright"). Pss 78, 105, 106 should be classified as historical psalms, even if an introduction in the wisdom style is prefixed to 78 [2]). These had a didactic purpose, but this does not constitute them wisdom psalms.

Psalm 111, although written in the alphabetic form and marked by *style anthologique*, is composed in hymn style. The content certainly shows the emphases of wisdom teaching—as the final verse reminds us: "The fear of the Lord is the beginning of wisdom." But again, content alone should not determine the classification. There seems no doubt that Pss 111, 112 are a pair that are intended to match. If 112 is wisdom, then 111 is a sage's hymn of praise—this is teaching by example. Nevertheless, the form of this psalm is that of a hymn, even if there is wisdom influence [3]).

There are two Pss that show definite wisdom influences, but which defy conventional classification: Ps 127 consists of two sayings that reflect preoccupations of the sages (vanity, gift of sons); Ps 119 is a collection of sayings that reflect Torah piety [4]).

---

[1]) In the *HUCA* article cited above Mowinckel classifies Ps 73 as a thanksgiving psalm (p. 229); he also remarks that "a 'didactic psalm' is a contradictio in adjecto" (p. 226).

[2]) A. Lauha, *Die Geschichtsmotive in den alttestamentlichen Psalmen* (Helsinki, 1945).

[3]) However, cf. S. Holm-Nielsen, *art. cit.*, 37 for a contrary view: "The whole is held together by the final verse, which as a typical wisdom apophthegm perhaps here occupies the position generally held by the admonition and request in the hymns. Considering further the concentrated, proverbial style, I find it reasonable to include the psalm in the *mashal* literature known as a special kind of literature in post-Exilic times".

[4]) *Ibid.*, 32-37.

Wisdom Elements in the Psalms

If there is only a small number of wisdom psalms in the technical sense, the influences of the sages has nevertheless been very strong. We have already indicated this in the case of several poems just mentioned above. There are many others that incorporate typical wisdom sayings or that develop a topic in the wisdom style. The accompanying schema, while not exhaustive, enables one to see at a glance the significant examples, and should help in recognizing that objective criteria must be required for classifying the wisdom elements.

Psalm	Literary	Motif	Form	Content
25 : 8-10	Ind. Complaint	induce Yahweh to intervene	maxims	divine guidance; the way
25 : 12-14	Ind. Complaint	induce Yahweh to intervene	"who" question in acrostic poem	fear of Lord; retribution
31 : 24-25	Ind. Complaint	testimony	command	encouragement and retribution
39 : 5-7	Ind. Complaint	induce Yahweh to intervene	maxims	short and vain life
40A : 5-6 (cp. 41 : 2-4)	Ind. Thanksgiving	testimony	*'ashrê* formula	trust because of Yahweh's deeds
62 : 9-11	Trust	testimony	admonition	man and human devices unreliable
92 : 7-9	Ind. Thanksgiving	testimony?	statement	*rasha'* / *ṣaddiq* contrast and retribution
94 : 8-15	Complaint	*Trostgedanke* (vv. 12-15)	admonition and *'ashrê* formula	man's folly and vanity; Yahweh teaches and exercises retribution

Psalm 25. Verses 8-10 are not as clearly sapiential as vv. 12-14, but they form a "teaching" that enables the psalmist to ask the Lord's forgiveness in v. 11. The cachet of wisdom in vv. 12-14 is introduced by a question reminiscent of the *Torliturgie* (Ps 24 : 3), and the thought is centred upon the reward to be given to one who fears Yahweh: prosperity, inheritance for descendants, friendship with God. All this is good wisdom doctrine. The key idea of this alphabetic psalm is the *way*, a common theme in Prv 2 : 20; 3 : 6; 11 : 20, etc., along with the corresponding rewards (Prv 2 : 21; 3 : 9, etc.). The interruptive presence of the wisdom elements is indicated by the absence of direct address to the Lord, which generally characterizes the complaint (vv. 1-7, 11, 16 ff).

Psalm 31. Although this poem is generally classified as a complaint, it has the mood of thanksgiving in the final verses (20-25). The sapiential style of vv. 24 f is problematical, but we have included it here anyway. This is really a testimony, but there is no indication of specifically wisdom influence; the command to love God (which is not found elsewhere in the Pss) is Deuteronomic (Dt 6 : 5; cf. 10 : 12), and the statement of retribution is general doctrine.

Psalm 39. The complaint is somewhat reminiscent of Job and Ecclesiastes in the choice of motifs (Jb 7 : 6 ff; 14 : 1 ff; Eccles 2 : 16 ff; 4 : 8).

Psalm 40. The only real influence is the adoption of the *'ashrê* formula and the recommendation to trust (cf. 2 : 12; 31 : 25, etc.).

Psalm 62. Verses 10 and 11 have the appearance of wisdom sayings.

Psalm 92. The preoccupation of this poem is moral retribution, which is perhaps reason enough to include it here, as well as the comparison of the prosperity of a just man to the growth of a tree (Ps 1 : 3; 37 : 25; Jer 17 : 8).

Psalm 94. While this poem is basically a complaint, the sapiential influence is manifest; in vv. 8-11 the admonition is directed to fools and there is a rare description of Yahweh as teacher.

The most impressive statistic in these Pss is the motif: a teaching alleged as an inducement for Yahweh to intervene or as a testimony. This observation is not new; GUNKEL pointed out this aspect of the testimony and others have agreed [1]. The poet not only gives his own acknowledgement of Yahweh, but includes in it all those who

---

[1] Cf. *Einleitung* . . . 277, 387; S. MOWINCKEL, "Psalms . . ." 213 f. Some of the classifications in the accompanying schema are contrary to those of GUNKEL.

are somehow present. The occasion, doubtless rooted in the liturgy, became an opportunity for "teaching"—presenting a practical conclusion based on experience, that should be an encouragement and fruitful lesson for the faithful [1]). Similarly, the wisdom theme may occur as a *Trostgedanke*, which is an implicit appeal to Yahweh to intervene. While there is a wide variation in the actual form, the *'ashrê* formula is most frequent [2]). It is clear that the psalmists found wisdom themes useful and that they exploited the wisdom style as an apt mode of expression.

We may conclude that it is still feasible to speak of "wisdom psalms" as a literary form parallel to the other psalm types. They merit separate classification: 1, 32, 34, 37, 49, 112, 128. Other types of Psalms incorporate wisdom elements but remain formally hymns, or thankgivings, etc. If the *milieu sapientiel* is the appropriate background (but not precisely the "life-setting") from which the wisdom psalms proceed, there is no reason to postulate such a *milieu* for the others which show wisdom influence. The psalmists could incorporate wisdom elements freely, and it was the testimony in the Thanksgiving Psalms that offered an opportunity for teaching.

---

[1]) Cf. F. MAND, *art. cit.*, 193: "Aus dem Beter ist ein Lehrer geworden".

[2]) Cf. note 2, p. 159. The formula occurs also in the ending of Ps 2; the LXX translator betrayed his wisdom preoccupations (*draksasthe paideias*) in Ps 2: 10,12 which itself shows wisdom influence.

Sapiential and Covenant Themes in Genesis 2–3*

LUIS ALONSO-SCHÖKEL, S.J.

Father Alonso-Schökel, professor of Biblical Theology at the Pontifical Biblical Institute, has specialized in the application of modern theories of literary criticism to biblical texts. Here is an example of the technique of literary analysis and the study of literary form. He has also applied his expertise in this area brilliantly in his book, The Inspired Word, the standard study of the theological import of the word.

In an article of *Lexikon für Theologie und Kirche*, Karl Rahner offers a theory concerning the origin of the knowledge of original sin. Presupposing the dogmatic fact of original sin, he speculates on the mental process and the literary datum of Gn 2–3. With terminology all his own he distinguishes etiological narratives of fiction and etiological narratives of fact. Etiology explains an actual human state through a return to an original cause. This cause can be either an event that really occurred, or a creation of the imagination on the basis of a reality which is not historical but may be profoundly psychological and ontological. This path of ascending explanation is readily accepted in other cases — e.g., the unity of the human race, or the equality of the sexes — and could be admitted in the case of original sin. When a sacred writer follows this path, (a) the general light of revelation and the specific inspiration can guarantee the discovery of the fact; (b) the narrative does not reflect the appearance of the original phenomenon, but rather the literary or historical world of the author's experience; and (c) the narrative reflects the actual situation of man.

---

* "Motivos sapienciales y de alianza en Gn 2–3," *Biblica* 43 (1962) 295–315.

Rahner's speculation invites the exegete to examine the problem by way of literary analysis. In the exegetical field Rahner was anticipated by A.-M. Dubarle's *Sages of Israel*. Its first chapter is devoted to the Genesis creation-narratives, whose author is virtually thus equated with the sapientials. Dubarle shows that the ingrained pattern of tracing a tribe back to its antecedents leads ultimately back to antecedents of the whole human race. In another volume, on original sin, Dubarle shows how Genesis must first trace "the human condition" as the framework in which the fall has its setting. Something of a sage himself, Dubarle retraces the path from the universal fact to the original fact. Compared with the minimalizing of some exegetes, the method of Dubarle offers solid and rich results. Faithful to the mentality which he is explaining, he shows more concern for the downward movement of *that which* is transmitted from father to son, than for the upward movement of *how to retrace* it by inference from effect to cause.

The narratives are expressed largely in mythic terms, but these are incidental rather than a cause of the author's ideas. Nor will Dubarle allow that the narratives are due to a faithfully transmitted primal revelation. Rather, by a process similar to that by which other peoples have created myths, Israel has creatively recaptured history. The original fact has been reconstructed by reasoning and imagination, guided by faith in Yahweh. Thus Dubarle as exegete got to the same explanation of the thought-procedures of the author of Gn 2–3 which would be later attained by Rahner from the dogmatic theology approach.

Almost simultaneous with Dubarle's work are the insights of H. Renckens, using a more strictly exegetical process and not focusing precisely on the theme of original sin. Israel's historical experience of Yahweh have given her definite convictions. The sacred writer offers us a synthesis of the Yahwist conception, though he also uses literary motifs from a wide tradition. He arrives at the original fact, not by copying a primal tradition transmitted intact, nor by receiving a new and explicit revelation, but by a reflection illumined by faith in various ways.

Renckens notes the broad mental context of the author of Gn 2–3 as parallel with the sapiential and especially with the prophetic literature.

While acknowledging in these three authors a richness which I have only touched upon here, I hope to advance a step upon Rahner exegetically and upon Dubarle and Renckens epistemologically. *Humani Generis* proposed two points: that Gn 2–3 is true history in the sense that it narrates facts that really happened, and that exegetes must find out more fully what type of history it is. We must for clarity's sake keep in mind the basic distinction between revelation and inspiration. What we know from Gn 2–3 or anywhere else in Scripture is God's revelation to us; but the charisma of inspiration by which God conveys his message to us need not have been accompanied by a revelation to the inspired writer.

To determine further the specific type of history with which we are dealing, we must use literary analysis. This is not merely statistics of vocabulary, but embraces structures and mentality as well. We will examine the alleged mythic material, the sapiential mentality, the experience of salvation-history. That history itself is structured proximately by the covenant, but more amply by the sequence: covenant-sin-punishment-reconciliation. As a final contribution, we will characterize the mental pattern of getting back to origins as an "ascent by triangulation."

The effort to explain Gn 2–3 as myth is not dead, as an article of J. Dus most recently shows. Vocabulary, style, and themes are pressed to confirm the probability of mythical influences from Canaanite mythology. The text, moreover, reveals a series of breaks which are better explained if the text is an elaboration of previous matter rather than an original creation. Dus bases much of his interpretation upon the precarious process of conjectural reconstruction. The literary text is explained by comparison with a model, which in turn had been extracted conjecturally from the text. Since there is no really parallel text outside the Bible, we end up with nothing more than a circular proof of what we had constructed.

Thus far the most significant parallel is Ezek 28:12–19, an elegy for the prince of Tyre involving such mythical motifs as the garden of God, rich garments, divine mountain, sons of God, sin and expulsion. John McKenzie considers this parallel as a variant form of the story of the first man. It is more mythical in character, though both are original pieces of Hebrew tradition. Motif gives greater assurance than mere structure in literary analysis. The text, whether of Genesis or of Ezekiel, is not a myth and does not elaborate one or other previous myths; rather it incorporates in its history mythical motifs.

In contrast with other biblical settings, such as the historical traditions of the monarchy, the exploits of the Judges, or the epic of the conquest, Gn 2–3 carries us to a marvelous world in a primordial time and a fairyland space, with magic trees, a talking serpent, and a God who forms clay and breathes into it, then extracts a woman from a slumbering mate. This poetic tonality raises the question: If we had discovered the story in the literature of Babylonia, Egypt, or Canaan, would we not just call it "myth" without further ado? Really we are dealing with a series of questions regarding "origins," concretely concerning the major themes of earth, life, fertility, and death. Alongside them are ranged subordinate queries such as clothes and work. To cope with these inquiries, there seems to have been fashioned a narrative that takes place outside of normal time and place, with God as one of the cast — all of which might indicate that the story is a myth. However, such a conclusion would be based on false initial reasoning. It would be reading the text out of context, and in a mental context not only distinct from but opposite to its view of history.

Any explanation of Gn 2–3 as a mere recasting of a previous myth or two, is a postulate rather than an explanation. The undeniable presence of mythical motifs and the quasi-mythical tonality partially account for some intriguing incidentals while leaving many essentials unexplained.

In the beginning his array of the sages of Israel with the

author of Gn 2–3, Dubarle declares that this author is not a prophet appealing to a revelation for the content of his oracle; nor is he a historian with access to court archives. He is a sage, who examines the good and evil of men and employs human reflection as the instrument of his intellectual progress. Coppens finds this sapientialism as explained by Dubarle exaggerated, but it is supported and even strengthened by statistical studies of Humbert and Renckens.

"Knowledge of good and evil" is a sapiential motif. Jesus ben Sirach described the sage as one "knowing the good and evil of men" (Sir 39:4). This discernment is not lacking in other professions; the priests could well distinguish between "good and evil" offerings (Lv 27). Moses proposes to the people "the life and the good, the death and the evil" (Dt 30:15) — good and evil as specified terms of the covenant. This agrees with Israel's specific definition of "wisdom and understanding," which is living with God and the precepts of the covenant (Dt 4:6–8). But this sapiential quest is for knowledge of good and evil taken in their generic meaning. This search can lead to the extreme experience of good exemplified by Qoheleth, but also to the extreme experience of evil as suffered by Job. In Gn 2–3, it is true, the characteristic word for wisdom (hokmah) is not present, and thus Adam's knowledge before the sin seems to be the knowledge of good only, though after the sin his knowledge is of good and evil. Another interpretation is possible: The author assumes a tone of challenge as if to say, "Your knowledge consists in living with God and observing his command" (Dt 4:6–8), or "If they do not value the word of Yahweh, where is their wisdom?" (Jer 8:9). At any rate one of the central points of Gn 2–3 — the knowledge of good and evil — is of sapiential origin.

A second motif: The serpent was "shrewd." The editor of Proverbs explains in his prologue the diverse qualities and virtues into which hokmah is divided, and the typical literary genres. The snake possesses "slyness," a sapiential quality which is either perverse shrewdness or tactful cleverness. The context could mean that the serpent was shrewd; the rest of the animals were not. In fact it appears as different from them, as a mind reader and siren.

Third motif (perhaps): the sage. Though the narrative does not call Adam a sage, the tradition attested by Ezek 28 and Job 15:6–7 would suggest this interpretation. Adam is presented as an authentic sage, because he was the first to make up lists or classifications of reality, such as were prized in Egypt and Babylon and in Solomon's case (1 Kg 5). The sage's art of coining maxims or proverbs is not far from the dexterity Adam showed in naming his wife (ishâ from îsh Gn 2:23). Snaky slyness traps only the woman; but the wise Adam, like Solomon, can be felled by love.

A fourth sapiential motif: the detailed discussion of the four rivers. In general, the transcending of the closed horizon of the people to meditate on the whole of humanity has much of the sapiential attitude, and partially coincides with the illuminism noted in the time of Solomon and his Near East neighbors. Along with the world-view is the attention given to the ordinary world of the family, clothing, food and work. Preoccupation with the simple life of the domestic hearth is one of the favorite sapiential themes, as many refrains of proverbs and many chapters of Sirach show. The alphabetic poem at the end of the book of Proverbs leads one to suspect that the author has Gn 2–3 open before him and is alluding to it, not altogether in agreement. Eve really behaves as naïvely as those who "believe anybody" (Pr 14:15) do not know how to defend themselves from danger (22:3) and end up in real trouble (1:32).

The stylistic dexterity of Gn 2–3, its play upon words, psychological penetration, and reserve are characteristic of almost all biblical authors. But only in the wisdom-corpus do we find explicit commendation of the literary knack (Pr 1, Ec 12, 1 Kg 5, Sir 39). Finally, note how often Gn 2–3 — virtually ignored by the prophets — has been pondered and commented on by the wisdom authors. They found a congenial theme in the enigma of evil and of universal sin.

It would be wrong to imagine either that all wisdom themes

are present in Gn 2–3, or that the ones which are explain all its problems. After all, the creation account is a narrative, not a collection of maxims. The insight of Adam and Eve is not called wisdom, and is more of a snare than a blessing. Nevertheless we find in the wisdom motifs a guidepost to further inquiry.

In bare skeleton the narrative of the two chapters is: God creates Adam, brings him to a garden, presents him with animals, a wife, and some trees; then lays upon him a command under sanction. Adam and his wife rebel. After a brief trial, God condemns them, but does not break with them totally. More concisely: God gives benefits and imposes a precept; man rebels; God punishes, then reconciles. What is the source of this narrative pattern? Derivation from myths has failed. The narrative of Gn 2–3 is simply the classical outline of salvation history. There is a minor pattern, that of the covenant. The benefits of God appear in historical prologue; then come the requirements in the apodictic form of blessings and curses. This minor pattern turns out to serve as the first of three or four acts in a drama: covenant, sin, punishment, reconciliation. In Gn 2–3 we have a perfect example of that larger pattern; the covenant sub-pattern is present only partially.

The divine initiative first confers benefits. Man is created in a neutral terrain; then God plants a garden and brings man in. "He picked him up and put him" reflects the twofold movement with which the Israelite expressed redemption. He took them from Egypt and brought them to the promised land. Moreover, Palestine as the land of God is a kind of paradise.

The tasks imposed upon Adam in the second half of Gn 2:15, nowhere earlier identified, are to cultivate and keep the land. These tasks seem out of place in this divine garden, but are understandable as terms of the covenant and sacred history. These verbs are technical terms used frequently for the service of God and observance of the commandments. They express responsibility, the burden of man faced with the divine initiative. The vocabulary of this verse is thus of great theological weight. God's gifts and his demand reflect the minor or covenant pattern.

The next verse makes the covenant theme more explicit by giving an apodictic precept with a threat, after the gift of the garden and all the trees. In later verses the animals are created and brought to Adam; then God takes a rib from Adam and fashions woman and brings her to Adam. The result is that man abandons his parents and clings to his wife. Here the gift is not followed by a command. The description of future love (two verses removed from the appearance of the serpent), applied to Adam who had no parents to leave, has a resonance of premonition which is nonetheless familiar from the parenetic terminology of Dt — a weak resonance, but a key to what follows. For with the appearance of the third force, the gifts of companionship and love become a mortal danger — symbolic of the temptations of the promised land.

The serpent makes a subtle attack upon the divine command. You shall eat of all the trees (gift) — you shall not eat of the tree of knowledge (apodictic command) — you will die (threat or curse). By suppressing mention of the gift, the serpent makes the command appear arbitrary. Eve corrects the insinuation and softens the command from apodictic to parenetic. Then the serpent, by denying the threat outright, reduces the command to an invidious monopoly. To this attack Eve does not know how to respond. She doubts and begins to look at the tree in another light. This watering down of an apodictic command of God recurs throughout the history of the people. But there is not a perfect parallel with other instances: Gn 2–3 does not merely describe a psychological process, but introduces a third force exterior to man. Before the first sin there was no inclination to evil; it is the enemy who introduces the suggestion.

Man's fall is rapid, without resistance, debate, or recrimination. The terrible experience of Baal Peor at the threshold of nationhood, then of Solomon near the origins of the dynasty, and of Ahab with Jezebel, and the insistent preaching of the Deuteronomist all echo the phrase, "She held it out to the man, and he took a bite."

The divine inquiry is paralleled by Moses' questioning Aaron after the sin of Sinai, by Joshua's questioning Achan, by Nathan's questioning David. The verbs, *heard* and *feared*, belong to the religious tradition of Israel and especially to the language of Dt. Dubarle explained the theological meaning of this new human attitude toward God. I merely wish to emphasize its relevance to the vocabulary used for faithfulness to the covenant. The divine verdict too employs the style of the covenant, but all is not finished with punishment and curse. Punishment remains along with hope. Punishment is mitigated, and the blessings continue in a minor key. Thus it happened at Sinai and in the sin of David. The struggle with the serpent brings the hope of victory; Adam and Eve do not die then and there, but are blessed with fertility, clothing, the fruitfulness of the earth fecundated now by their own labor.

If I take a straight, horizontal line and raise from the extremities two converging lines, I form a triangle which is suspended from a single point. By an analogous process I can explain an actual human situation by returning in ascent to the single original fact which effected it. For example, a group of individuals with the same surname is reducible to a common ancestor. Modern historians do not proceed by the simplicity of the triangular argumentation characteristic of the Hebrews, ·who often argued from a common horizon to a common point of origin. Dubarle has shown that according to the Israelite mentality sin has consequences for posterity — a descending dynamism, the *thing which* is transmitted. For the *human ascertaining* of this transmission, mounting upward in the reverse direction, Scripture gives only hints, such as tracing the Calebites to Caleb and the Semites to Sem. I am going to complete his exposition by setting forth the cognitive remounting to the fact of original sin.

Hosea is a specialist in the mentality of triangular ascent. In chiding the people he returns "as in the days of Gibeah" (9:9) and then summarizes the origins of Israel. If the horizon is Samaria, the sin is the "calf of Bethaven" (10:5); the sins of Israel date from the time of Gibeah (10:9). If the horizon is the whole of the chosen people, the prophet returns to Jacob who supplanted his brother from the womb (12:3).

Psalm 51 has an individual as horizon; his life of sin is explained by returning to an initial deed: "I have been conceived in sin" (cf. Ps 58:4). Psalm 106 is a public confession of sins: in the introduction the penitents return to the "original" sin of the people: "We have sinned as our fathers" (v. 6); then there follows an enumeration of the great sins of their history.

The horizon of Dan 9:11 is the universal sin of Israel which goes back to the fathers by a stylized history (9:6, 8). The confession in Ezra 9:7 runs: "From the days of our fathers up to today we have sinned." The sin of Jeroboam weighs down the whole history of Israel (1 Kg 12:30, 13:24, 14:16, 15:26 ff; 2 Kg 10:29–31, 17:21 ff).

The ascent to a sin, original in respect to the concrete horizon, is an Israelite habit. Similarly in the structuring of the historical narratives we discover a conscious concern to underline a deadly sin at the initial moment. Thus the first action of the people of God after the Sinaitic covenant — which made them a people — was a sin against the most "positive" of the commandments. At the beginning of Dt the Israelites have only to enter into the promised land that the Lord had delivered to them; at this moment a sin is committed against a positive commandment (1:26, 32). The kingship of Saul begins with a sin and the northern kingdom with a sin. David scarcely receives the kingdom for himself and his dynasty when he sins.

Let us now suppose a thinker who extends the horizon to all of humanity and repeats to himself the words: "For there is no man who does not sin" (1 Kg 8:46). In pondering this situation and in searching for an explanation, the natural thing is to apply the triangular ascent to the origin of all humanity. In this mental process he does not project a subsequent event back into the past, nor does he project back in allegory the experience of all men. He really returns to the original event. If history describes the narration of an event that really occurred, then the narrator is writing history, even though in his method of investigation and in his exposition he may not be writing the technical history of the nineteenth and twentieth centuries. He arrives by reflection illumined by the historical revelation of Israel at a fact — not in all its details or even in its precise pattern. To analyze and explain the original fact, the sacred writer is aided by his experience of the history of God's mercies and the sins of his people. He sees the original sin as a rebellion against a command of God who had taken the initiative in giving. And history does not end with total punishment. He knows by experience that the mercy of God is without end. In the narrative development the hagiographer gives us the true meaning of the original event, guaranteed by his inspiration.

Thus the pursuit of Dubarle's exegetical method confirms his position. But does the literary analysis confirm the theory of Rahner? We answer point by point: (a) Literary analysis confirms that the writer arrived at the discovery of the fact by reflection upon the actual situation and upon salvation history. (b) The exactness of the fact asserted is guaranteed by inspiration. Though literary analysis cannot, of course, arrive at inspiration as an operative element, it can take over the dogmatic fact and apply it to a literary cadre, in accord with St. Thomas and recent encyclicals. The biblical writer's preliminary inquiries are directed by faith and by the particular gifts of the author; the basic insight occurs "under the light of divine truth"; the entire subsequent literary process is elevated by inspiration. (c) Literary analysis confirms that the point of departure for reflection is not the abstract nature of man, but the concrete experience of man in salvation history. (d) The theory can explain why the paradise narrative appears in terms corresponding to the epoch in which it was written; literary analysis confirms and renders more precise this observation by revealing the traces of salvation history in the general pattern of the narrative. (e) The sapiential tonality ("nothing human is alien to me") of universal man explains why "the man of all time" is what we encounter in the story.

However venturesome it may be to try to enter into the mind of a writer, especially of a writer who lived thirty centuries ago, I propose to reconstruct hypothetically the creative process of the author. Since he has left no other clues, literary analysis is our only path.

An author familiar with the sapiential milieu asks himself: Where does evil come from? He answers: from sin. And where does everybody's sin come from? To answer this, he reflects upon the religious experience of the chosen people, as it appears in sacred traditions, oral or written, cultic or non-cultic. This religious world drives him with an ascending force back toward the origin; and he answers: the sin of all men comes from the sin at their origin, from the original pair. That inspired answer he then translates into narrative. For this he employs the classical pattern of salvation-history, with its profound explanation of sin. The sequence is: God's initiative in giving, categorical precept, rebellion, punishment, mercy, and then the continuation of history. The author chose this pattern under the light of inspiration. He cannot content himself with just another history of his own people in the background of its familiar neighbors. He transfers the pattern to an elemental and universally human world of food and dress, of family and labor — a world that is also transformed into the marvelous by the removal of all evil and by the use of mystic motifs. The verb, to eat, and the theme of food runs through the whole narrative. For geography the author uses the basic theme of a fenced-in area belonging to God, again with mythical and sapiental motifs. Along with all this he exploits his own literary genius; and from the first intuition to the full realization, the author works under the charism of inspiration.

Where does he find out that the woman played so prominent a role in the original sin? Israelite tradition offers sufficient data in Dt 7:1–4 and Pr 2 and 5 and 7. But where does the author get what he tells about the third force, the serpent? That is less easily traceable. Perhaps we find a hint in the words akin to "listen" and "serpent" in the prohibition of divination (Dt 18:10). But perhaps we are rather to conclude that it was simply his own reflection which led the author to realize that there must have been such a third force in the drama: with only the human protagonists, he could not account for what took place. We cannot exclude what he may have known about demons and evil spirits (2 Sam 16:14, 25; 18:10; 19:9) and seducers (1 Kg 22:20–23), though the Genesis concept is much more precise and difficult to situate within the Old Testament demonological data.

A general difficulty is the dating. According to the common opinion, Gn 2–3 is the work of the ninth-century Yahwist. I propose that the literary enigma and silence of other books is better explained by accepting a later composition.

Following Rahner's suggestion and the studies of Dubarle and Renckens, I have attempted to determine the intellectual and literary milieu by means of literary analysis. The theological consequences are clear. For the narrator the history of the first sin pertains strictly to the history of salvation. Man by his creation pertains to the earth; by the divine initiative he is translated to a sacred land. Sin is the rebellion against a positive command; the command is founded on the person of God and rests upon his previous benefits. Sin brings on the threatened punishment, but in the punishment the mercy of God is not entirely broken off. After the sin there begins the long path of salvation-history. Sin is social; the woman brings sin to her husband. In sin a third force intervenes, a satan opposed to God who actually sets in motion the concrete plan of God, the history of revelation, as we know it; this original sin explains the sinful condition of all humanity.

METHOD IN DETERMINING WISDOM INFLUENCE UPON "HISTORICAL" LITERATURE

J. L. CRENSHAW

MERCER UNIVERSITY

THE influence of wisdom upon nonhagiographic literature is increasingly emphasized. Such kinship is claimed for Gen 1–11, 37, 39–50, Exod 34 6 f., Deut, II Sam 9–20, I Kings 1–2, Amos, Habakkuk, Isaiah, and Jonah.[1] Impetus for the new tendency was furnished by von Rad's provocative study of the Joseph narrative, an article that has been almost directly responsible for similar claims of wisdom influence upon Esther and the "succession document."[2] But the publication of new wisdom texts from Mesopotamia and Ugarit and fresh comparison with Egyptian wisdom have spurred the trend to unprecedented heights.[3] The excitement of new directions in scholarship has led to exaggerated claims supported by dubious arguments and assumptions, so that a study of methodology in determining wisdom influence is imperative at this

[1] For Gen 1–11, R. H. Pfeiffer, "Wisdom and Vision in the Old Testament," *ZAW*, 52 (1934), pp. 93–101, particularly 97 f.; and J. L. McKenzie, "Reflections on Wisdom," *JBL*, 86 (1967), pp. 1–9; L. Alonso-Schökel, "Motivos sapienciales y de alianza en Gen. 2–3," *Bib*, 43 (1962), pp. 295–316. For Gen 37, 39–50, G. von Rad, "The Joseph Narrative and Ancient Wisdom," *The Problem of the Hexateuch and other Essays*, 1966, pp. 292–300, originally published in *SVT*, 1, 1953. For Exod 34 6 f., R. C. Dentan, "The Literary Affinities of Exod. XXXIV 6 f.," *VT*, 13 (1963), pp. 34–51. For Deut, M. Weinfeld, "The Origin of Humanism in Deuteronomy," *JBL*, 80 (1961), pp. 241–47, and "Deuteronomy — The Present State of Inquiry," *JBL*, 86 (1967), pp. 249–62, J. Malfroy, "Sagesse et Loi dans le Deutéronome," *VT*, 15 (1965), pp. 49–65; J. R. Boston, "The Wisdom Influence upon the Song of Moses," *JBL*, 88 (1968), pp. 196–202. For II Sam 9–20 and I Kings 1–2, R. N. Whybray, *The Succession Narrative* (*SBT*, 2nd ser., 9), 1968. For Amos, S. Terrien, "Amos and Wisdom," *Israel's Prophetic Heritage*, ed. by B. W. Anderson and W. Harrelson, 1962, pp. 108–15; H. W. Wolff, *Amos' geistige Heimat*, 1964, and *Dodekapropheton, Amos*, 1967–, and for a critique of the position, J. L. Crenshaw, "The Influence of the Wise upon Amos," *ZAW*, 79 (1967), pp. 42–52. For Hab, D. E. Gowan, "Habakkuk and Wisdom," paper read at the 103rd meeting of SBL, 1967. For Isa, J. Fichtner, "Jesaja unter den Weisen," *ThLZ*, 74, (1949), pp. 76–80, and R. J. Anderson, "Was Isaiah a Scribe?" *JBL*, 79 (1960), pp. 57 f. For prophecy in general, J. Lindblom, "Wisdom in the Old Testament Prophets," *SVT*, 3 (1960), pp. 192–204, and W. McKane, *Prophets and Wise Men* (*SBT*, 44), 1965. For Jonah, P. L. Trible, *Studies in the Book of Jonah*, Diss. Columbia, 1964, and R. Augé, *Profetes Menors*, 1957.

[2] S. Talmon, " 'Wisdom' in the Book of Esther," *VT*, 13 (1963), pp. 419–55, and Whybray, *The Succession Narrative*.

[3] Besides J. B. Pritchard, ed. *ANET*, 1955, and *Wisdom in Israel and in the Ancient Near East*, ed. by M. Noth and D. Winton Thomas, 1960, the following may be mentioned: J. Van Dijk, *La sagesse suméro accadienne*, 1953; W. G. Lambert, *Babylonian Wisdom Literature*, 1960; E. I. Gordon, *Sumerian Proverbs*, 1959, and "A New Look at

juncture. This paper will seek to outline some methodological principles in the study of wisdom influence, and on the basis of these will evaluate the claims about the Joseph narrative, succession document, and Esther.

I. *Statement of the Method*

Crucial to the study of any movement is its definition, which can be neither too broad nor too narrow, but must be both inclusive and exclusive. A distinction between wisdom literature, wisdom tradition, and wisdom thinking is essential, for these terms refer to the literary deposit of a specifically defined movement characterized by a particular approach to reality.[4] It must be recognized that wisdom speech is not *a se* wisdom,[5] and that several kinds of wisdom are discernible: (1) juridical, (2) nature, (3) practical, and (4) theological — each with a distinct *Sitz im Leben*.[6] Accordingly, one must distinguish between family/clan wisdom, the goal of which is the mastering of life, the stance hortatory and style proverbial;[7] court wisdom, with the goal of education for a select group, the stance secular, and method didactic;[8] and scribal wisdom, the goal being education for all, the stance dogmatico-religious, and the method dialogico-admonitory.[9] Moreover, the wisdom movement is self-critical, Job and Qoheleth emphasizing the disparity between wisdom's claims and reality itself.

---

the Wisdom of Sumer and Akkad," *BiblOr*, 17 (1960), pp. 122–52; *Les sagesse du proche-orient ancien*, 1963 (which contains excellent articles on wisdom's history and ideology, as well as extensive bibliography, especially on Egyptian wisdom); H. Gese, *Lehre und Wirklichkeit in der alten Weisheit*, 1958; and H. H. Schmid, *Wesen und Geschichte der Weisheit* (Beih., *ZAW*, 101), 1966.

[4] Schmid, *Wesen und Geschichte der Weisheit*, p. 7. It would be less confusing to speak in terms of wisdom literature, *paideia*, and *hokmah*. The first would refer to Prov, Qoh, Job, Sir, Wisd of Sol, and Wisdom Pss; *paideia* would suggest the wisdom movement itself, its educational curriculum and pedagogy; *hokmah* would indicate a particular stance, an approach to reality.

[5] *Ibid.*, p. 120. Schmid's point is that Sumerian lists (originally an attempt at ordering the world) are taken over by the Babylonians for their philological value.

[6] R. E. Murphy, "Assumptions and Problems in Old Testament Wisdom Research," *CBQ*, 29 (1967), p. 104. It is in this context that Murphy observes that "wisdom language does not constitute wisdom," and rejects both the method of "anthological composition" and "*topoi*" for determining wisdom influence.

[7] E. Gerstenberger, *Wesen und Herkunft des 'Apodiktischen Rechts'* (*WMANT*, 20) 1965, and J. P. Audet, "Origines comparées de la double tradition de la loi et de la sagesse dans la proche-orient ancien," *International Congress of Orientalists* (Moscow, 1960), I, pp. 352–57.

[8] H. Duesberg, *Les scribes inspirés*³, has given a helpful analysis of the courtly background of wisdom.

[9] W. Richter, *Recht und Ethos* (*StANT*, 15), 1966, stresses the school as the locus of wisdom. A. Barucq, *Le Livre des Proverbes*, 1964, pp. 12–15, thinks the prophets attacked the scribe (court official) rather than the sage.

The multiplicity of wisdom's representatives and answers[10] must not force one into a definition that is so comprehensive that it becomes unusable. This is the weakness of von Rad's definition of wisdom, taken over by McKenzie. If one views wisdom as "practical knowledge of the laws of life and of the world, based on experience" and thinks that "wisdom had to do with the whole of life, and had to be occupied with all of its departments,"[11] or that wisdom is an "approach to reality," "a firm belief in the validity of experience,"[12] it is little surprise to discover wisdom everywhere, for what literature does not grow out of and reflect experience?

On the other hand, it is likewise true that the understanding of wisdom as eudemonistic, humanistic, international, and nonhistorical is inadequate, for it is both too narrow and false. As Schmid has emphasized, the religious basis of wisdom rests on the assumption that the Creator has established the world so that accord with its governing principle (*Maat, Me, Mišpat*) does pay off, but this is not exactly eudemonism.[13] The deep religious cast of wisdom from its earliest stages demands that the claim of humanism be rejected, even though emphasis is placed on man and his behavior. Even the position that wisdom is international is erroneous for Sirach and Wisdom of Solomon, and may be contested at other points. Nevertheless, there is a measure of truth in R. Pautrel's remark that "De toute façon, le genre sapientiel avait été l'une des fenêtres d'Israël sur le monde."[14] Von Rad has discussed the tension between the universal and particular in the ancient Israelite world view of the sage in brilliant fashion, concluding that man "lives within a created order from which ascends an unending hymn of praise, yet he himself hears nothing of it . . . He must be taught, as if he were blind and deaf, that he lives in a world which could be revealed to him . . . ."[15]

---

[10] Frankfort, *Ancient Egyptian Religion*, 1961 (first published in 1948), p. 4, has characterized ancient thought as a "multiplicity of approaches and answers."

[11] G. von Rad, *Old Testament Theology*, I, pp. 418, 428. This discussion of wisdom is still perhaps the most provocative available.

[12] McKenzie, "Reflections on Wisdom," pp. 2, 4. Similarly, if one with S. Blank views wisdom as "philosophy rooted in the soil of life: truth springs out of the earth" (*IntDB*, 4, pp. 853–61), it follows that a discussion of wisdom in the OT will include Aaron, Moses, Daniel, and others. Again, Lambert (*Babylonian Wisdom Literature*) has even suggested that "a case could be made for including many of the Babylonian epics in the wisdom category, since they deal with cosmological problems" (p. 1).

[13] *Wesen und Geschichte der Weisheit*, pp. 3, 20–22, 115–17, 159–61; see also A. Volten, "Der Begriff der Maat in den Ägyptischen Weisheitstexten," *Les sagesses du proche-orient ancien*, pp. 73–101, and Gese, *Lehre und Wirklichkeit in der alten Weisheit*, pp. 11–21 (and pp. 45–50, where Yahweh's freedom over against this "order" is recognized as an Israelite theme).

[14] *L'Ecclésiaste*, p. 8.

[15] "Some Aspects of the Old Testament World View," *The Problem of the Hexateuch and other Essays*, p. 164 (originally published in *EvTh*, 11, 1964).

As for the view that wisdom is nonhistorical, Schmid has shown convincingly that there is a structural history of wisdom, one that has its changing *Sitzen im Leben*, and that wisdom is itself aware of this history.[16]

It has also been claimed that wisdom is individualistic as opposed to the corporate emphasis of prophecy and priesthood, but even this judgment must be corrected by the recognition that courtly wisdom is social in orientation, especially in its juridical concern.[17] The same may be said of the wisdom of the clan, for there is growing acceptance of the close association of law and wisdom championed by Gerstenberger.[18]

Wisdom, then, may be defined as the quest for self-understanding in terms of relationships with things, people, and the Creator. This search for meaning moves on three levels: (1) nature wisdom which is an attempt to master things for human survival and well-being, and which includes the drawing up of onomastica and study of natural phenomena as they relate to man and the universe;[19] (2) juridical and *Erfahrungsweisheit* (practical wisdom), with the focus upon human relationships in an ordered society or state; and (3) theological wisdom, which moves in the realm of theodicy,[20] and in so doing affirms God as ultimate meaning (even when denying any purpose in life as does Qoheleth, for the pathos of this masterpiece grows out of the fact that the true source of meaning is theological rather than anthropological).[21]

First, then, is the question of definition. A second observation is that wisdom influence can only be proved by a stylistic or ideological peculiarity found primarily in wisdom literature. This implies the exclusion of a common cultural stock, much of which is environmental or derives from the period of the family/clan before the separation into distinct compartments of prophet, priest, and sage. Accordingly, the appeal to Deuter-

---

[16] *Wesen und Geschichte der Weisheit, passim.* Furthermore sacred history plays an important rôle in Sirach and Wisdom of Solomon. The classic discussion is J. Fichtner, "Zum Problem Glaube und Geschichte in der israelitisch-jüdischen Weisheitsliteratur," *ThLZ*, 76 (1951), pp. 145–50, reprinted in *Gottes Weisheit*, pp. 9–17.

[17] Schmid, *Wesen und Geschichte der Weisheit*, pp. 110–14. Conversely, there is growing recognition that individual responsibility was basic to legal procedure from the earliest times (B. Lindars, "Ezekiel and Individual Responsibility," *VT*, 15 [1965], pp. 452–67, particularly 454).

[18] "Covenant and Commandment," *JBL*, 84 (1965), pp. 38–51, particularly 50 f.

[19] See especially von Rad, "Job XXXVIII and Ancient Egpytian Wisdom," *The Problem of the Hexateuch and other Essays*, pp. 281–91 (originally in *SVT*, 3, 1960), and W. Zimmerli, "The Place and Limit of the Wisdom in the Framework of the Old Testament Theology," *SJT*, 18 (1964), pp. 146–58, originally in *Les sagesses du proche-orient ancien*.

[20] R. J. Williams, "Theodicy in the Ancient Near East," *CJT*, 2 (1956), pp. 14–26. A. Bentzen (*Introduction to the Old Testament*, I, p. 173) quotes an observation by Hylmö that wisdom literature became little by little a literature written by scholars for other scholars. This would be especially pertinent to reflective or theological wisdom.

[21] Gese ("Die Krisis der Weisheit bei Koheleth," *Les sagesses du proche-orient ancien*, pp. 139–51) rightly perceives the deep religious stance of Qoheleth.

onomy's use of such common words as "hear, know, take, keep, law, teach, etc." by Weinfeld and Malfroy carries little cogency.[22] The use of word tabulation is also particularly vulnerable in this regard, unless employed with extreme caution.[23] When one recognizes that wisdom is rooted in experience, it should be no surprise to discover a common vocabulary among sage, prophet, and priest. Moreover, it needs to be pointed out that to call one wise is not to identify him as a sage (cf. Judg 5 29).

This leads to a third observation: differences in nuance must be explained. Whenever a wisdom phrase or motif is found outside wisdom literature the scholar must determine whether or not the meaning has been changed. This can be illustrated by the motif of silence in Egypt and Israel, and by the literary genre of "disputation" in wisdom and prophetic literature.

Egyptian wisdom literature distinguishes between the passionate and the silent man, the latter of whom is like a fertile tree (cf. Ps 1) and is acceptable to the gods who dwell in the land of silence. In the later period the wise man describes himself as the truly silent one (Amenemope; Merikare), and excessive talkativeness (ecstasy and gossip) are viewed as sin. This is in strong contrast to the premium placed on fine speech in the Old Kingdom, at first viewed as a possession of the king or sage, but later recognized even among maid servants at the grindstones (Ptahhotep — ANET, p. 412). But this freedom of speech and high esteem in which it was held posed a political threat, so that both anthropological (contrast between silent man and passionate one) and theological (God of silence favors diplomatic silence) arguments were employed to combat the danger (Ani; Amenemope).[24]

Silence is a prominent theme in Israelite wisdom, but never does it serve as an epithet of the sage. Rather this emphasis is a means of combatting slander and gossip, and depicts the proper reverence before the Holy One (Job 4 12–21, 40 4 f., Hab 2 20, Qoh 5 2; cf. ANET, p. 408) and in the presence of death (Amos 6 10, 8 3, 5 13, Judg 3 19, Zeph 1 7,

---

[22] Weinfeld, "The Origin of Humanism in Deuteronomy," and Malfroy, "Sagesse et Loi dans le Deutéronome." Into this category also falls the attempt by B. Couroyer to find literary dependence between Ps 34 13 and Egyptian wisdom ("Idéal sapiential en Égypte et en Israel," RB, 57, 1950, pp. 174–79). It may be observed that Weinfeld's thesis that Deuteronomy is the composition of scribes associated with the courts of Hezekiah and Josiah who "achieved a religio-national ideology which was inspired by the sapiential-didactic school" ("Deuteronomy — The Present State of Inquiry," p. 262) is more ideologically based than philological.

[23] A good example of a judicious use of this method is the recent article by Boston, "The Wisdom Influence upon the Song of Moses."

[24] G. Lanczkowski, "Reden und Schweigen im ägyptischen Verständnis, vornehmlich des Mittleren Reiches," Ägyptologische Studien, 29 (1955), pp. 186–96. For the importance of silence see ANET, pp. 414 (silence is better than teftef-plants), 418, 420–24, 438.

Zech 2 13, Esther 4 14; cf. *ANET*, pp. 9, 18, 27, 49, 51, 55, 91, 408, 419 [n. 17]). Accordingly it is important to priest and prophet. Not without justification has Y. Kaufmann called the priestly temple the "kingdom of silence."[25] The prophetic emphasis on silence occurs in Amos, where wisdom language may be used, but with nonwisdom nuance. This is true both of 6 9–10, where a severe epidemic has decimated the city and the prophet urges silence lest the customary benediction remind the destructive deity that survivors have been left, and of 5 13, which suggests that the prudent man will keep silent in such an evil time. If from Amos, this latter statement is full of irony, the wisdom theme being used in a totally new sense, for the last thing Amos would do is keep quiet in the midst of human oppression. In sum, the mere use of wisdom phraseology by a prophet does not make him a sage,[26] for his meaning may be completely alien to wisdom thinking.

A comparison of the "disputation" in wisdom literature and in prophetic traditions (particularly Malachi) indicates that differences in nuance must not be ignored.[27] Whereas the prophetic dispute grows out of and vividly reflects a real confrontation between a prophet and his opponent, and announces the divine decision of judgment and basis for it, the wisdom disputation may be purely literary, often concerns the relative value of things or professions, and resembles the fable in many instances.

Fourth, the negative attitude to wisdom in much of the OT must be kept in mind, especially in looking for changes in nuance. It is certainly striking that wisdom frequently leads to destruction in the historical and prophetic literature. This is true of the wise men of Egypt (Exod 7 8–13), the scheming plan of Jonadab to satisfy Amnon's passion for Tamar (II Sam 13 3–5), the clever ruse instigated by Joab and articulated by the wise woman of Tekoa (II Sam 14 1–21), the traitorous behavior of the wise woman of Abel (II Sam 20), the bloody actions of Solomon upon succeeding David (I Kings 1–2), the successful deceitful counsel of Hushai (II Sam 16 23–17 23), the clever serpent (Gen 3), and the foolish advisers of Pharaoh (Isa 19 11 ff., 30 1 ff., 31 1 ff.).[28] Furthermore, the hesitancy to attribute wisdom to Yahweh until quite late indicates an

---

[25] *The Religion of Israel*, p. 303.

[26] H. Schmid, "Hauptprobleme der neueren Prophetenforschung," *STU*, 25 (1965), p. 142, has asked if a wisdom word in the mouth of a prophet means the same as that word spoken by a teacher. Similarly, in *Wesen und Geschichte der Weisheit*, Schmid recognizes that even etiology can argue from wisdom categories (p. 101), and that wisdom thinking often appears in nonwisdom forms, such as hymns, laws, and omens (pp. 110–14, 142).

[27] E. Pfeiffer, "Die Disputationsworte im Buche Maleachi," *EvTh*, 12 (1959), pp. 546–68.

[28] H. Cazelles, "Les débuts de la Sagesse en Israël," *Les sagesses du proche-orient ancien*, pp. 34–36.

early negative attitude to wisdom,[29] as does the opposition to the building of the Solomonic temple, the achievement of human wisdom (cf. Baal and Anat).

Fifth, wisdom's history must be taken into consideration, insofar as it is possible to determine its structural development, geographic spread, and ideological formulation. The most striking observation here is the change in wisdom reflected in the apocryphal works, specifically the inclusion of priestly and *heilsgeschichtliche* concerns. Especially important is the recognition of the crisis in wisdom and ensuing dogmatizing and democratizing of wisdom stressed so provocatively by Schmid, a phenomenon common to the wisdom of Egypt, Mesopotamia, and Israel. Moreover, the difference between courtly and clan wisdom, with urban and rural settings respectively, must be recognized, and the literature of each identified. This means that the difficult question of Solomon's rôle in wisdom must be evaluated, as well as that of Hezekiah.[30] Special attention must be given to the pronounced nationalism of the reforms of Hezekiah and Josiah. Those who claim that these are times of great wisdom influence must show how coexistence with a strongly particularistic governmental policy was possible.

II. *Application of the Methodological Observations*

A. THE JOSEPH NARRATIVE. Von Rad has described the Joseph narrative as an ideal portrait of the courtly wise man, written during the Solomonic enlightenment characterized by anthropological interests. This claim is based on an analysis of the educational ideal and theological ideas permeating Gen 37, 39–50. The fear of the Lord as the point of departure, and the goal of humility, tact, patience, and avoidance of the snares of evil women and hot-temperedness are said to be the educational ideals of Egyptian and Israelite wisdom. The absence of cultic etiology, *Heilsgeschichte*, and revelation, together with the presence of a thoroughly religious stance that stresses the hidden providence of God and frustration of man's plans by the Creator (a kind of skepticism that reaches its apex in Qoheleth!) demand for von Rad the conclusion that the *Sitz im Leben* of the narratives is wisdom of the court. Von Rad thinks the parallels with Egyptian wisdom at all these points confirm this hypothesis of a wisdom setting.[31]

---

[29] M. Noth, "Die Bewährung von Salomos 'Göttlicher Weisheit,' " *Wisdom in Israel and in the Ancient Near East*, pp. 225–37. McKane, *Prophets and Wise Men*, has dealt with the conflict between prophecy and wisdom, particularly in regard to statecraft.

[30] R. B. Y. Scott, "Solomon and the Beginnings of Wisdom in Israel," *Wisdom in Israel and in the Ancient Near East*, pp. 262–79; and A. Alt, "Die Weisheit Salomos," *ThLZ*, 76 (1951), pp. 139–44.

[31] "The Joseph Narrative and Ancient Wisdom," *pass.*

Despite the general acceptance of this ingenious hypothesis, a number of questions must be raised, because the case for von Rad's view cannot be said to have been closed. The difficulty in this instance is not so much with definition or failure to consider the history of wisdom, for on both these issues von Rad has much to say in this article, even if the assumption of a Solomonic sponsorship of wisdom is questioned by some. But in view of the other three principles discussed above, von Rad's hypothesis cannot be sustained.

First, wisdom influence can only be proved by stylistic and ideological peculiarities. The argument from psychological interest in the phenomenon of man in its broadest sense overlooks the fact that this is a concern common to much of the ancient literature. Von Rad himself recognizes its presence in the "succession document";[32] one must ask whether there is a qualitative difference between these two literary complexes and Gen 3, 22, Exod 32, and I Kings 13. Moreover, the claim that the Joseph narrative is anthropological in tone overlooks the decisive episode of Joseph's refusing the advances of Potiphar's wife. Here the reason for rejecting her favors is not that Joseph wishes to deal justly with his fellow man, but rather the high point of the reasoning is, "How then can I do this great wickedness, and sin against *God*?" (39 9). Again it must be pointed out that the theme of evil women is a common one, far too ubiquitous to demand wisdom influence.

The third methodological observation that differences in nuance must be explained requires the following correction of von Rad's thesis. In spite of the use of a theme popular in wisdom circles, this story introduces a nuance alien to wisdom. The emphasis on the providence of God, indeed the hidden action of God despite human intentions, is in one particular quite distant from the skepticism of Qoheleth: here the will of God is hidden from evil men, and the wicked schemes are thwarted, while the secrets of God are revealed to Joseph, the favorite of God. There is no place in the Egyptian wisdom literature cited or in Israelite wisdom for this pattern; rather the point of the skeptical emphasis is that there is no one who knows the ways of God, and even the plans of the righteous man may be frustrated by the mysterious God. Still another caveat at this point must be given: the stress on providence is not peculiar to wisdom, but pervades the literature of the OT.[33]

More devastating, however, is the presence in the Joseph narrative of nonwisdom themes. At the outset it may be observed that a man whose story begins and ends in defeat provides a very poor model for the wise men of the court; the story opens with the account of Joseph's frustration in fraternal relations, and ends with the paternal negation of

---

[32] "The Beginnings of Historical Writing in Ancient Israel," *The Problem of the Hexateuch and other Essays* (originally published in *AfK*, 22, 1944), pp. 175–204.

[33] Von Rad has taught us, more provocatively than any other, of the significance of this theme in the Hexateuch.

his heart's desire for his sons (48 17–20). Moreover, it is a strange model of education that has as its hero one who has not been trained at a school, and a peculiar propaganda for courtly wisdom that has the ruler choose a man as his counselor on the basis of his "spiritualistic" qualifications. Again, the failure of Joseph to control his emotions must not be over-looked (45 2, 14 f., 50 1, 17), as well as his lack of tact in telling his dreams to his brothers and his harsh treatment of them at a later time (even if the latter is mitigated somewhat by understanding it as a sort of test to ascertain whether the brothers had truly changed).

The nonwisdom themes are numerous, in part growing out of the material itself. These include: (1) the appeal to special revelation and theophanic visions; (2) the emphasis on dreams and divining cup as mediating divine intentions; (3) sacrifice; (4) genealogy (46 8 ff.); (5) kosher food (43 31–34); (6) etiology for taxes (47 20 ff.); and (7) *Heilsgeschichte* (place names, including Hebron, Shechem, Dothan, Luz, Bethlehem, Beer-sheba; patriarchs and their deities, such as "the God of Isaac," El Shaddai, Yahweh,[34] the God of the fathers; the holy war formula, "The Lord was with Joseph" and "I fear God";[35] and the narrative as a prologue to the exodus).

In view of the preceding analysis, von Rad's thesis that the Joseph narrative is a manifestation of the wisdom ideal of education and theology cannot be accepted. What, then, of the other two works stimulated by this article?

B. THE SUCCESSION DOCUMENT. R. N. Whybray has recently sub-mitted the "succession document" to detailed analysis, reaching the conclusion that it is neither history, (in intention or fact), a novel, a national epic, or a moral-religious tale; rather "it is a work of political propaganda intended to support the régime (of Solomon) by demon-strating its legitimacy and justifying its policies."[36] A comparison of the narrative with Proverbs in regard to the importance of counsel, the ideas of retribution and the hidden control of human destiny by the Creator, and the attitude toward the cult, together with a study of didactic literature in general (use of simile, comparison and narration, dramatization of proverbial wisdom, the irresistible power of a multitude, wisdom and folly, control of sexual passion, humility, learning from experience, danger of treacherous companions, proper speech, education of children, ideal king, ambition, frustration and fulfillment, friendship, loyalty and treachery, and revenge) prompts Whybray to write that the author of the succession narrative "set out deliberately to illustrate

---

[34] J. L. Crenshaw, "*YHWH Ṣᵉba'ôt Šᵉmô*: A Form-critical Analysis," forthcoming in *ZAW*.

[35] J. L. Crenshaw, "Amos and the Theophanic Tradition," *ZAW*, 80 (1968), pp. 203–15; and K. W. Neubauer, "Erwägungen zu Amos 5:4–15," *ZAW*, 78 (1966), pp. 294–302.

[36] *The Succession Narrative*, p. 55.

specific proverbial teaching for the benefit of the pupils and ex-pupils of the schools."[37] An examination of comparable political novels in Egypt, namely, the Prophecy of Neferty, Kemit, Satire on the Trades, Instruction of Amenemhet, and Story of Sinuhe, all of which were written during the period of Amenemhet and Sesostris, suggests to Whybray that the political novel, sophisticated psychological novel, and narrative based on wisdom themes were known in Egypt long before Solomon, and that the author of the succession narrative probably had such literature among his models.[38]

First, a few words about the general thesis of the book. The conclusion that the succession document is not historical in intention or fact, nor that it is a novel or national epic carries conviction, and is argued with keen insight. However, the rejection of the narrative as a religio-moral tale seems premature, for this view is not negated by the psychological complexity concealing the simple moral. It is difficult to envision a reading of the story without grasping the moral implied about family relations (adultery, sibling rivalry, and sex) and obligations of office and friendship, in spite of (or *because of*) the psychological concerns of the narrative. The hypothesis that the story was written to demonstrate the legitimacy of the Solomonic régime and to justify its policies suffers from the well-known fact that neither David nor Solomon is displayed in a favorable light. Quite the contrary, for David's weaknesses and their effect are elaborated in all their poignancy, whereas Solomon is represented as ascending the throne through the scheming plans of the court prophet and the aged Bathsheba, and his first action is almost unsurpassed in the OT for cruelty. In view of this Achilles' heel to Whybray's thesis, a study of his arguments in terms of the five methodological principles enumerated above will be particularly instructive.

The fundamental error of this work of Whybray is the failure to search for stylistic and ideological peculiarities found primarily in wisdom literature. The book suffers grossly from this standpoint. The various themes from Proverbs said to be consciously illustrated by the story are common ones in legal and prophetic literature. It is difficult to see how any story could fail to "illustrate" themes in Proverbs, for this book covers the whole gamut of human existence.[39] The examples below are but a few of the many falling under this category.

The idea of retribution is not only a wisdom theme, but occurs frequently in legal material, where the punishment is made to suit the offense. The hidden control of God over human affairs despite man's

---

[37] *Ibid.*, p. 95.

[38] *Ibid.*, p. 116.

[39] The prophetic legend in I Kings 13 will illustrate the point rather graphically. Nearly every category listed by Whybray in the discussion of parallels between Proverbs and the succession narrative is appropriate here, too. The polarities of wisdom and folly are illustrated by Jeroboam's refusal to listen to the man of God and by the desire

intentions is a basic assumption of the Yahwist, Elohist, deuteronomist, and prophecy; furthermore, the tenuous nature of human plans is made all the more finite by the stress upon the demonic in Yahweh and freedom of God to override human intentions.[40] The attitude to the cult in Proverbs has parallels in prophetic literature, and the case is not so clear with the succession document, for sacrifice is practiced, and the absence of the oracle grows out of the fact that David does not go to battle against non-Israelites in the succession document, the oracle in the earlier stories of David being the means of determining whether to wage war or not.[41] The concern for ethical conduct, humility, and private prayer is not unique to wisdom, for both prophets and priests shared this interest. Likewise, the ra'îtî and wa'erê formulas[42] are reminiscent of prophetic visions, and use language that every human being employed. Again, it is impossible to converse without using simile and comparison, for the sages did not monopolize metaphorical language. The belief that a multitude is irresistible does not demand wisdom provenance, for Gen 11 uses this idea with special force. Furthermore, the desire to avoid evil women and treacherous companions is a common one (cf. Amos), and the emphasis upon humility and learning from experience is equally as pronounced in Isaiah as in Proverbs.[43] In the same category are the appeal to the use of fine speech and the concern for education. The sages are not sole guardians of either.

Whybray's argument also suffers from a failure to explain nonwisdom emphases in the succession document. Especially damaging to his thesis is the minor rôle played by wisdom's representatives, indeed the questionable function of each. The total effect of counselors, both private and

---

of the aged nabi to provide for his existence in Sheol by requesting burial beside the man of God. The danger of pride can be seen in the arrogant boast of the nabi that he was also a prophet, despite the falsity of the statement. The value of experience is recognized both by Jeroboam and the nabi, and the disaster caused by treacherous companions could not be more dramatically depicted. Of course both prophets recognized the necessity of good speech, and the old nabi had taught his children proper respect and obedience, as can be seen from their actions. The value of an ideal king can be recognized by noting its opposite in Jeroboam, while the ambition of the nabi is seen in his desire to associate with the powerful man of God. The frustration of human plans by the hidden God is poignantly depicted, for the fate of the man of God is outside his own hands. The joys of friendship and loyalty, as well as the woes of treachery and revenge, are also illustrated by the relationship between the man of God and the old nabi. Indeed, the man of God would have fared better had he taken seriously the advice about not eating where love is absent, or heeded Prov 22 13 and 26 13.

[40] P. Volz, Das Dämonische im Jahwe.

[41] This also explains the attitude to the ark, which was associated with battle. There is one "great exception" to Whybray's thesis about special revelation, as he himself admits (p. 69), namely, the oracle of Nathan in II Sam 12.

[42] Whybray, The Succession Narrative, p. 75.

[43] For the view that wisdom literature made use of the prophetic tradition, see A. Robert's series of articles on Prov 1–9 in RB, 43–44 (1934–35) under the title, "Les attaches littéraires bibliques de Proverbs I–IX."

courtly, is ruinous. This is true of the women of Tekoa and Abel, as well as of Ahithophel, while Hushai's advice is pure treachery. It seems likely that, if Whybray's view were true, the scribes would have presented the wisdom representatives in a far more favorable light. It is difficult to conceive of scribes calling attention to the frustration of Ahithophel's counsel by Yahweh, for this would undermine their position immeasurably.

A third methodological weakness can be observed in the work under investigation. The history of wisdom does not appear to have been considered carefully enough. The hypothesis of the book assumes a fully developed wisdom tradition in the early days of Solomon's reign (indeed, during David's rule!),[44] one that taught proverbial lore now found in Proverbs, and that Egyptian literature had already been mastered this early. This assumption is, at the very least, debatable; to build a whole superstructure on such a flimsy foundation is hazardous indeed.

Finally, differences in nuance between the succession document and wisdom are ignored. Much closer to the truth is von Rad's argument that there is a sharp distinction between the theological standpoints of the Joseph narrative and the succession document, the latter of which does not reflect skepticism as to the hidden control of God over human affairs.[45]

If the preceding arguments have any cogency, the hypothesis of Whybray that the succession narrative is a conscious attempt to illustrate Proverbs by scribes who desired to justify Solomon's régime and policies fares no better than von Rad's thesis about the Joseph narrative, and suggests that an examination of Talmon's comparatively recent article on Esther and wisdom is in place.

C. THE BOOK OF ESTHER. Taking his cue from von Rad's study of the Joseph narrative and L. A. Rosenthal's demonstration of Esther's dependence on that account,[46] S. Talmon concludes that the Esther narrative is "a historicized wisdom tale," an "enactment of standard wisdom motifs," "having typical wisdom themes and precepts."[47] He thinks that the "outline of the plot and the presentation of the central characters show the wise men in action,"[48] and that the book is made

---

[44] In agreement with McKenzie, "Reflections on Wisdom."

[45] "The Beginnings of Historical Writing in Ancient Israel," pp. 198 ff. But the skepticism of the Joseph narrative is much farther from Qoheleth than von Rad admits.

[46] "Die Josephgeschichte mit den Büchern Ester und Daniel verglichen," ZAW, 15 (1895), pp. 278–84, and "Nochmals der Vergleich Ester-Joseph-Daniel," ZAW, 17 (1897), pp. 126–28.

[47] " 'Wisdom' in the Book of Esther," p. 426.

[48] Ibid., p. 427.

up of an ancient Near Eastern wisdom nucleus in specific biblical variation together with Persian literary motifs.[49] Talmon rests his case on
similarities in situations and general trends and ideas in Esther and
wisdom, rather than on literary parallels. Accordingly appeal is made to
the absence of specifically Jewish religiosity and history, the "concept of
an unspecified and remote deity devoid of any individual character,"
the presence of an individualistic slant and anthropocentric stance, a
fondness for court life, and typological concepts (the powerful but witless
dupe, the righteous wise, and the conniving schemer).

Talmon has succeeded in forcing biblical scholars to ask a question
that would almost never have occurred to them, for it is difficult to conceive of a book more alien to wisdom literature than Esther. A number
of his arguments must be challenged, however, as misstatements of fact or
erroneous conclusions. First, it is quite a leap from the idea that help
may come to the Jews from another source (מָקוֹם אַחֵר) to the wisdom
notion of a remote deity, for there is no assurance that the reference is
to divine assistance.[50] Again, the argument about typology is singularly
unconvincing, for it must resort to an hypothesis about the splitting up
of the Ahiqar-Nadin typology, and rests on an analogy between a wise
man's adoption of students and the Ugaritic and biblical tales of the loss
of progeny by Keret, Danel, and Job. Furthermore, the emphasis upon
retribution of the measure-for-measure variety overlooks the natural
legal offense, where punishment by human beings is to be expected. As
for the claim that Ahasuerus is a type of witless dupe in power, one must
note that the impression is certainly a subtle one if that is intended.
A more cogent case could be made for the description of Saul in such
terms. Particularly weak is Talmon's reference to wise women in Israel,
use of sex for desired ends, and erotic interest, all of which prove nothing
about the book of Esther and wisdom. In this regard, the claim that the
inclusion of women courtiers is a novel feature in the ancient Near East
overlooks their presence in Canaan (cf. Judg 5), if such they be! Finally,
Talmon himself admits that Mordecai is a very poor type of wise man,
possessing neither the necessary linguistic ability nor proper tact, the
latter illustrated by his refusal to bow before Haman.[51] These observations are reinforced by a study of Talmon's hypothesis from the point of
view of the five methodological principles discussed above.

Perhaps the most striking violation of these principles is the failure
to reckon with nonwisdom elements. The most glaring of these is the
pronounced nationalistic fervor permeating the book of Esther, a spirit

---

[49] *Ibid.*, p. 453.

[50] For opposing views, see A. Spanier, "Die Gottesbezeichnungen המקום und
הקדוש ברוך הוא in der frühtalmudischen Literatur," *MGWJ*, 1922, pp. 309–14; and H.
Bardtke, *Das Buch Esther (KAT, 17)*, p. 333.

[51] " 'Wisdom' in the Book of Esther," pp. 448, 440 f.

that has been an offense to Christian and Jew alike.[52] Any hypothesis that Esther derives from wisdom must explain the presence of narrow nationalism. To ignore this factor is to leave the case hanging in mid-air.

The history of wisdom is not given proper treatment in this study either, for a kinship between the supposed wisdom of Esther and that of Sirach and Wisdom of Solomon would be expected, since the date of Esther is nearer these works than to older traditions of Proverbs. Therefore, *Heilsgeschichte* and the identification of Torah and wisdom should be present in Esther, while just the reverse is the case (the only link with Israel's sacred history being the Amalekite and Davidic ancestries given Haman and Mordecai, and the mention of the exile of Jeconiah in 2 6).

Lastly, the author consciously limited his study to broad themes and ideas, falling prey to the appeal to ideas common to literature other than wisdom. Despite the mention of individualism as proof of wisdom influence, Talmon admits that both Mordecai and Esther sacrifice private interests for communal weal, and writes that the "glossing over of strictly individual traits enhances the general applicability of the moral illustrated and is perfectly in tune with wisdom literature."[53] To this category of common themes also belong the argument that a description of court life proves wisdom influence, and the contention that Nehemiah's knowledge of linguistics proves something about courtiers and wisdom.

In conclusion, a study of the arguments for wisdom influence as the exclusive background for the Joseph narrative, succession document, and book of Esther suggests that a negative answer must be given in every case, and demands that modern enthusiasts who rush to find conscious and direct wisdom influence hither and yon would do well to think twice before venturing in that direction.[54]

[52] *Ibid.*, p. 428. G. Fohrer (*Introduction to the Old Testament*, p. 177) writes that Deuteronomy parts company with the sages at precisely this point. The failure of McKenzie ("Reflections on Wisdom") to consider whether sages asked the question of *national identity* is particularly damaging to an otherwise helpful article. R. B. Y. Scott (*Proverbs and Ecclesiastes* [*AB*, 18], p. xvi) sums up the view of most scholars that the sages spoke to individuals, whereas prophets and priests thought of Israel as chosen for a unique mission. There is, it may be admitted, a famous saying that ridicules three peoples, the Edomites, Philistines, and Samaritans in Sir 50 25 f., but this, like so much else in Sirach, is not the normal path of wisdom, and is mild in comparison with Esther. Appeal may also be made to von Rad's contention that wisdom works outwards from the covenant ("The Joseph Narrative and Ancient Wisdom," p. 295), Murphy's observation that wisdom has its concrete setting in the daily life of a people who believed in God as Savior and Creator ("Assumptions and Problems in Old Testament Wisdom Research," pp. 108 f.), and Zimmerli's discussion of the place of creation theology in Israelite faith ("The Place and Limit of the Wisdom in the Framework of the Old Testament Theology"), all necessary correctives. But this in no way negates the argument that intense nationalism is alien to wisdom.

[53] " 'Wisdom' in the Book of Esther," pp. 437, 447.

[54] The positive contribution of these works under consideration is the reminder that we have compartmentalized Israelite society far too rigidly, seen already by O. S. Rankin, *Israel's Wisdom Literature*, p. 14.